Employment Discrimination Law

Fifth Edition

2014 Supplement

For Frayda
and George,
Love
Barbara

Bloomberg BNA Books Authored by the ABA Section of Labor and Employment Law

Age Discrimination in Employment Law

Covenants Not to Compete: A State-by-State Survey

The Developing Labor Law

Discipline and Discharge in Arbitration

Elkouri & Elkouri: How Arbitration Works

Employee Benefits Law

Employee Duty of Loyalty: A State-by-State Survey

Employment at Will: A State-by-State Survey

Employment Discrimination Law

The Fair Labor Standards Act

The Family and Medical Leave Act

How ADR Works

How to Take a Case Before the NLRB

International Labor and Employment Laws

Labor Arbitration: A Practical Guide for Advocates

Labor Arbitration: Cases and Materials for Advocates

Labor Arbitrator Development: A Handbook

Labor Union Law and Regulation

Occupational Safety and Health Law

The Railway Labor Act

Restrictive Covenants and Trade Secrets in Employment Law: An International Survey

Tortious Interference in the Employment Context: A State-by-State Survey

Trade Secrets: A State-by-State Survey

The Uniformed Services Employment and Reemployment Rights Act

Wage and Hour Laws: A State-by-State Survey

Workplace Data: Law and Litigation

Employment Discrimination Law

Fifth Edition

2014 Supplement

Barbara T. Lindemann
Seyfarth Shaw LLP
Los Angeles, CA

Paul Grossman
Paul Hastings LLP
Los Angeles, CA

C. Geoffrey Weirich
Paul Hastings LLP
Atlanta, GA

Executive Editors

Debra A. Millenson
The Millenson Law Firm
Washington, DC

Richard J. Gonzalez
Chicago-Kent College of Law
Chicago, IL

Laurie E. Leader
Chicago-Kent College of Law
Chicago, IL

Associate Editors

Carlos F. Bermudez
Kevin Brodar
Julia Campins
Jillian M. Cutler
Leonard Court
Eric S. Dreiband
Philip C. Eschels
Christie J. Fix
Kenneth W. Gage
Erika Leonard
Dana Lossia
Nora L. Macey
Paul W. Mollica
Roberta Steele
Carolyn Witherspoon

Bloomberg BNA, Arlington, VA

Library of Congress Cataloging-in-Publication Data

Lindemann, Barbara, 1935-
Employment discrimination law / Barbara T. Lindemann, Attorney at Law, Los Angeles, CA, Paul Grossman, Paul Hastings LLP, Los Angeles, CA, C. Geoffrey Weirich, Paul Hastings LLP, Atlanta, GA. -- Fifth Edition.
pages cm
Includes bibliographical references and index.
ISBN 978-1-61746-015-9 (set : alk. paper) -- ISBN 978-1-61746-013-5 (volume 1 : alk. paper) -- ISBN 978-1-61746-014-2 (volume 2 : alk. paper) 1. Discrimination in employment--Law and legislation--United States. I. Grossman, Paul, 1939- II. Weirich, C. Geoffrey. III. Title.
KF3464.L56 2012
344.7301'133--dc23

2012047969

Published by Bloomberg BNA, Arlington Virginia
1801 S. Bell St.
Arlington, VA 22202
bna.com/bnabooks

International Standard Book Number: 978-1-61746-291-7

BOARD OF EDITORS

ASSOCIATE EDITORS, CHAPTER CHAIRS, AND CONTRIBUTORS

Chapter 1 — Overview

Executive Editors

DEBRA A. MILLENSON
The Millenson Law Firm
Washington, DC

RICHARD J. GONZALEZ
Chicago-Kent College of Law
Chicago, IL

LAURIE E. LEADER
Chicago-Kent College of Law
Chicago, IL

Chapter 2 — Disparate Treatment

Associate Editors

LEONARD COURT
Crowe & Dunlevy
Oklahoma City, OK

PAUL W. MOLLICA
Outten & Golden LLP
Chicago, IL

CARLOS F. BERMUDEZ
International Union, UAW
Detroit, MI

Chapter Chair

ERIC S. DREIBAND
Jones Day
Washington, DC

Chapter 4—*Cont'd*

Contributor

PAUL R. BARSNESS
Parker Hudson Rainer & Dobbs LLP
Atlanta, GA

Chapter 5 — Failure to Provide a Reasonable Accommodation

Associate Editors

KENNETH W. GAGE
Paul Hastings LLP
Chicago, IL

JULIA CAMPINS
Campins Benham-Baker LLP
San Francisco, CA

CARLOS F. BERMUDEZ
International Union, UAW
Detroit, MI

Chapter Chair

ALYESHA ASGHAR DOTSON
Spilman Thomas & Battle PLLC
Charleston, WV

Chapter 6 — Race and Color

Associate Editors

ERIKA LEONARD
Paul Hastings LLP
Atlanta, GA

JULIA CAMPINS
Campins Benham-Baker LLP
San Francisco, CA

Chapter Chairs

RICHARD R. BRANN
Baker Botts LLP
Houston, TX

JENNIFER M. TRULOCK
Baker Botts LLP
Dallas, TX

Chapter 8—*Cont'd*

Contributor

NITYA S. LOHITSA
Clark Hill PLC
Detroit, MI

Chapter 9 — Religion

Associate Editors

PHILIP C. ESCHELS
Bingham Greenebaum Doll LLP
Louisville, KY

JILLIAN M. CUTLER
Frank Freed Subit & Thomas LLC
Seattle, WA

Chapter Chair

STEVEN HYMOWITZ
Ogletree, Deakins, Nash, Smoak & Stewart P.C.
New Orleans, LA

Contributors

PAUL BALANON
Ogletree, Deakins, Nash, Smoak & Stewart, P.C.
New Orleans, LA

JENNIFER L. ENGLANDER
Ogletree, Deakins, Nash, Smoak & Stewart, P.C.
New Orleans, LA

SARAH J. MURPHY
Ogletree, Deakins, Nash, Smoak & Stewart, P.C.
New Orleans, LA

Chapter 10 — Sex

Associate Editors

PHILIP C. ESCHELS
Bingham Greenebaum Doll LLP
Louisville, KY

JILLIAN M. CUTLER
Frank Freed Subit & Thomas LLC
Seattle, WA

Chapter 13 — Disability

Associate Editors

CAROLYN WITHERSPOON
Cross, Gunter, Witherspoon & Galchus, P.C.
Little Rock, AR

PAUL W. MOLLICA
Outten & Golden LLP
Chicago, IL

Chapter Chairs

JENNIFER L. SABOURIN
Miller Canfield PLC
Detroit, MI

RACHEL SCHALLER
Taft, Stettinius & Hollister LLP
Chicago, IL

Contributors

LAVON M. AMMORI
Miller Canfield PLC
Detroit, MI

DAVID G. KING
Miller Canfield PLC
Detroit, MI

CHARLES T. OXENDER
Miller Canfield PLC
Detroit, MI

Chapter 14 — Genetic Information

Associate Editors

ERIKA LEONARD
Paul Hastings LLP
Atlanta, GA

CHRISTIE J. FIX
Frank Freed Subit & Thomas LLC
Seattle, WA

Chapter Chair

KAREN M. BUESING
Akerman LLP
Tampa, FL

Chapter 16—*Cont'd*

Chapter Chair

Grace E. Speights
Morgan, Lewis & Bockius LLP
Washington, DC

Contributors

Joyce E. Taber
Morgan, Lewis & Bockius LLP
Washington, DC

Marianne Hogan
Morgan, Lewis & Bockius LLP
Washington, DC

Chapter 17 — Promotion, Advancement, and Reclassification

Associate Editors

Eric S. Dreiband
Jones Day
Washington, DC

Paul W. Mollica
Outten & Golden LLP
Chicago, IL

Carlos F. Bermudez
International Union, UAW
Detroit, MI

Chapter Chair

Michael Delikat
Orrick, Herrington & Sutcliffe LLP
New York, NY

Contributor

David B. Smith
Orrick, Herrington & Sutcliffe LLP
Washington, DC

Chapter 20 — Sexual and Other Forms of Harassment

Associate Editors

PHILIP C. ESCHELS
Bingham Greenebaum Doll LLP
Louisville, KY

JULIA CAMPINS
Campins Benham-Baker LLP
San Francisco, CA

Chapter Chairs

JILL ROSENBERG
Orrick, Herrington & Sutcliffe LLP
New York, NY

BRADFORD LEHEW
Law Offices of Bradford LeHew
Chicago, IL

Contributors

ADAM PRIMM
Littler Mendelson P.C.
Cleveland, OH

LINDSAY NICHOLS
Orrick, Herrington & Sutcliffe LLP
Wheeling, WV

TRACY SCHEIDTMANN
Orrick, Herrington & Sutcliffe LLP
Menlo Park, CA

Chapter 21 — Discharge and Reduction in Force

Associate Editors

KENNETH W. GAGE
Paul Hastings LLP
Chicago, IL

JULIA CAMPINS
Campins Benham-Baker LLP
San Francisco, CA

Chapter Chair

JOHN W. SHEFFIELD
Johnston, Barton, Proctor & Rose, LLP
Birmingham, AL

Chapter 22 — Employers

Chapter 23 — Unions

Chapter 24 — Employment Agencies

Associate Editors

KENNETH W. GAGE
Paul Hastings LLP
Chicago, IL

JULIA CAMPINS
Campins Benham-Baker LLP
San Francisco, CA

Chapter Chair

W.V. BERNIE SIEBERT
Sherman & Howard LLC
Denver, CO

Contributor

HEATHER F. VICKLES
Sherman & Howard
Denver, CO

Chapter 25 — Charging Parties and Plaintiffs

Associate Editors

PHILIP C. ESCHELS
Bingham Greenebaum Doll LLP
Louisville, KY

PAUL W. MOLLICA
Outten & Golden LLP
Chicago, IL

Chapter Chair

CHARLES A. POWELL IV
Littler Mendelson P.C.
Birmingham, AL

Contributors

ANNA C. GUALANO
Littler Mendelson P.C.
Birmingham, AL

KEITH CHAPMAN
Littler Mendelson P.C.
San Francisco, CA

JESSICA ROTHENBERG
Littler Mendelson P.C.
San Francisco, CA

MICHELLE CHRISTIAN
Littler Mendelson P.C.
Sacramento, CA

Chapter 28 — Jurisprudential Bars to Action

Associate Editors

PHILIP C. ESCHELS
Bingham Greenebaum Doll LLP
Louisville, KY

JILLIAN M. CUTLER
Frank Freed Subit & Thomas LLC
Seattle, WA

Chapter Chair

JOHN V. JANSONIUS
Jackson Walker LLP
Dallas, TX

Contributor

DAVID R. SCHLOTTMAN
Jackson Walker LLP
Dallas, TX

Chapter 29 — Title VII Litigation Procedure

Associate Editors

LEONARD COURT
Crowe & Dunlevy
Oklahoma City, OK

ROBERTA STEELE
National Employment Lawyers Association
San Francisco, CA

Chapter Chair

LEONARD COURT
Crowe & Dunlevy
Oklahoma City, OK

Chapter 32 — Federal Employee Litigation

Associate Editors

KENNETH W. GAGE
Paul Hastings LLP
Chicago, IL

ROBERTA STEELE
National Employment Lawyers Association
San Francisco, CA

Chapter Chair

RAYMOND PEELER
Attorney at Law
Washington, D.C.

Chapter 33 — Class Actions

Associate Editors

LEONARD COURT
Crowe & Dunlevy
Oklahoma City, OK

PAUL W. MOLLICA
Outten & Golden LLP
Chicago, IL

Chapter Chair

ALVA L. CROSS
Cross HR Law
Wesley Chapel, FL

Chapter 34 — Discovery

Associate Editors

ERIC S. DREIBAND
Jones Day
Washington, DC

PAUL W. MOLLICA
Outten & Golden LLP
Chicago, IL

Chapter Chair

GREGORY PARKER ROGERS
Taft Stettinius & Hollister LLP
Cincinnati, OH

Chapter 36—*Cont'd*

Contributors

MELISSA K. MORDY
Davis Wright Tremaine LLP
Seattle, WA

AMY M. DE SANTIS
Davis Wright Tremaine LLP
Seattle, WA

ASHLEY L. WATKINS
Davis Wright Tremaine LLP
Seattle, WA

Chapter 37 — The National Labor Relations Act

Associate Editors

CAROLYN WITHERSPOON
Cross, Gunter, Witherspoon & Galchus, P.C.
Little Rock, AR

CHRISTIE J. FIX
Frank Freed Subit & Thomas LLC
Seattle, WA

CARLOS F. BERMUDEZ
International Union, UAW
Detroit, MI

Chapter Chairs

GREGORY V. MURRAY
Vercruysse Murray, PC
Bingham Farms, MI

GARY S. FEALK
Vercruysse Murray, PC
Bingham Farms, MI

Chapter 38 — "Reverse" Discrimination and Affirmative Action

Associate Editors

CAROLYN WITHERSPOON
Cross, Gunter, Witherspoon & Galchus, P.C.
Little Rock, AR

CHRISTIE J. FIX
Frank Freed Subit & Thomas LLC
Seattle, WA

Chapter 40 — Injunctive and Affirmative Relief

Associate Editors

KENNETH W. GAGE
Paul Hastings LLP
Chicago, IL

ROBERTA STEELE
National Employment Lawyers Association
San Francisco, CA

DANA LOSSIA
Levy Ratner, PC
New York, NY

Chapter Chair

THOMAS A. LEMLY
Davis Wright Tremaine LLP
Seattle, WA

Contributor

AMY DE SANTIS
Davis Wright Tremaine LLP
Seattle, WA

Chapter 41 — Monetary Relief

Associate Editors

ERIKA LEONARD
Paul Hastings LLP
Atlanta, GA

ROBERTA STEELE
National Employment Lawyers Association
San Francisco, CA

Chapter Chair

THOMAS H. KIGGANS
Phelps Dunbar LLP
Baton Rouge, LA

Chapter 44 — Settlement

Associate Editors

ERIC S. DREIBAND
Jones Day
Washington, DC

PAUL W. MOLLICA
Outten & Golden LLP
Chicago, IL

CARLOS F. BERMUDEZ
International Union, UAW
Detroit, MI

Chapter Chair

KIMBERLY J. KORANDO
Smith, Anderson, Blount, Dorsett, Mitchell & Jernigan, LLP
Raleigh, NC

Contributor

MEGAN PRIDGEN BLACK
Smith, Anderson, Blount, Dorsett, Mitchell & Jernigan, LLP
Raleigh, NC

FOREWORD

Since 1945 the ABA Section of Labor and Employment Law has expanded its stated purposes in response to the evolution of the field. Currently, they include the following: (a) to study and report upon continuing developments in the field of labor and employment law; (b) to provide a forum for members of the Association interested in the field of labor and employment law to meet and confer; (c) to assist the professional growth and development of practitioners in the field of labor and employment law; (d) to establish and maintain working liaison with state, federal, and, where applicable, multinational agencies having jurisdiction over matters affecting labor and employment law toward achieving procedural reform and administrative due process; (e) to study and report upon proposed and necessary legislation and rule making within the field encompassed by the jurisdiction of this Section; (f) to promote justice, human welfare, industrial peace, and the recognition of the supremacy of law in labor-management relations and the employment relationship; and (g) to establish, moderate, and sponsor seminars, workshops, forums, and other programs promoting the advancement of knowledge and practice in the field of labor and employment law.

Through the publication of books such as *Employment Discrimination Law* and through annual and committee meeting programs designed to provide a forum for the exchange of ideas, the Section has pursued these stated goals. Gradually, the Section has built a library of comprehensive legal works intended for the use of the Section membership as well as the bar generally.

The Section of Labor and Employment Law is pleased to provide this first supplement to the Fifth Edition of its treatise on employment discrimination law as part of its library of books published by Bloomberg BNA. As was the case with the previous editions and their supplements, the combined efforts of many individual authors from the Committee on Equal Employment Opportunity Law of the Section are reflected in this work.

The Section wishes to express its appreciation to the Committee members, and in particular to the Executive Editors, Debra A. Millenson, Richard J. Gonzalez, and Laurie E. Leader, the Collaborating Author, C. Geoffrey Weirich, and the Coordinating Editor, Amy E. Jensen. This group has tried to accomplish two primary objectives: (1) to be equally balanced and nonpartisan in its viewpoints, and (2) to ensure the book is of significant value to the practitioner, student, and sophisticated nonlawyer.

The views expressed herein do not necessarily represent the views of the American Bar Association, or its Section of Labor and Employment Law, or the National Labor Relations Board, United States government, or any other organization, but are simply the collective, but not necessarily the individual, views of the authors. Information on the affiliation of government employees who contributed to this work is for informational purposes only and does not constitute any official endorsement of the information provided herein.

Joel A. D'Alba
Chair

Joyce E. Margulies
Chair-Elect

Section of Labor
and Employment Law
American Bar Association

June 2014

PREFACE

Covers generally the years 2011 and 2012 and decisions issued during the 2012–13 Supreme Court term

As the executive editors of the *Employment Discrimination Law Supplement* we are pleased to provide this first supplement to 2012's Fifth Edition. Employment discrimination continues to be an exceptionally active area of the law. During this period several sets of regulations were issued, additional policy guidance was published, and the two major enforcement agencies—the EEOC and the Office of Federal Contract Compliance Programs of the Department of Labor—each issued revised compliance manuals containing additional statutory interpretations and a description of their administrative processes. Some of the early decisions in cases brought under the Genetic Information Nondiscrimination Act were published and appellate courts began to address the changes brought about by the passage of the Americans with Disabilities Act Amendments Act. All in all a busy time.

As has been true from the beginning, the management of this project is dependent upon the efforts of the Equal Employment Opportunity Law Committee of the American Bar Association's Section of Labor and Employment Law. Volunteers from the management, union, and plaintiff/public membership of the committee provide the basic material from which the supplements are drawn, and still other volunteers review our drafts and offer their comments. Their names are listed in the Board of Editors and we could not proceed without them. The Section leadership—Stewart Manela, Joel D'Alba, Richard Seymour, and Joyce Margulies—and the co-chairs of the both the EEO Law Committee and the Section's Publications Committee have helped smooth our way. Geoff Weirich, the principal author of the Fifth Edition, offered us his comments and expertise and was most generous with his time. His colleague Amy Jensen kept us organized and more or less on schedule, and we are grateful for her hard work as well. Finally, we would not be anywhere without the steady hand of our publisher, Tim Darby of Bloomberg BNA, who keeps us focused on the big picture when we might otherwise be lost in the minutiae, and Senior Book Editor Anne Scott, who has come to know us well and asks the questions everyone else has overlooked.

We are now back to the beginning—gathering the material for the second supplement. We hope that you will find the current volume to be a valuable addition to your EEO library and an asset to you in your practice. The meetings of the EEO Law Committee often include a dinner at which stories are shared and tales told. The hallmark of these dinners is a toast offered by members from all of the committee's component groups: "to equal employment opportunity!" It is equally the credo of this work.

DEBRA A. MILLENSON
RICHARD J. GONZALEZ
LAURIE E. LEADER

June 2014

SUMMARY TABLE OF CONTENTS

PART VII: REMEDIES AND RESOLUTION

DETAILED TABLE OF CONTENTS

Part III: Employment Actions

PART IV: THE PARTIES

PART V: PROCEDURAL ISSUES

PART VI: OTHER SOURCES OF PROTECTION

PART VII: REMEDIES AND RESOLUTION

CHAPTER 1

AN OVERVIEW

This is the first Supplement to the Fifth Edition of *Employment Discrimination Law* (2012). It covers those developments in the courts and the agencies responsible for enforcing the nation's employment discrimination laws during the years 2011 and 2012 that were not covered by the Fifth Edition, as well as U.S. Supreme Court cases through the end of the Court's 2012–2013 term. The forthcoming second Supplement will address developments that occurred in 2013.

The years since the completion of the Fifth Edition have seen a great deal of activity—decisions by the Supreme Court, important appellate decisions, implementation of the Genetic Information Nondiscrimination Act of 2008 (GINA), adoption of new regulations by the Equal Employment Opportunity Commission (EEOC) and the Office of Federal Contract Compliance Programs (OFCCP) in several areas, and issuance by both agencies of new compliance manuals setting out their internal procedures. In discussing these matters, the Supplement tracks the chapter structure of the Fifth Edition. As was true with the Main Volume, this Supplement is the product of the Section of Labor and Employment Law's Committee on Equal Employment Opportunity Law. The Board of Editors presented in the front of this Supplement lists the many members of that committee who contributed to this effort. We thank them all.

The chapter-by-chapter highlights of this Supplement include the following:

Chapter 2 (Disparate Treatment): Discusses the Supreme Court's decision in *Texas Southwestern Medical Center v. Nassar*,[1] in which the Court applied "but for" causation to retaliation cases. The Court previously had applied this standard to age discrimination

[1] 133 S. Ct. 2517, 118 FEP 1504 (2013).

disparate treatment cases in *Gross v. FBL Financial Services, Inc.*[2] As a result, plaintiffs are precluded from proving age discrimination and retaliation under a mixed-motive framework. Lower courts continue to define the proofs necessary to prevail in all other types of disparate treatment cases.[3] Increasingly, they have struggled with the theories to apply in same-sex harassment cases in light of the absence of language in Title VII prohibiting sexual orientation discrimination. Although courts are reluctant to apply a gender stereotyping model to same-sex harassment, at least one court has applied the theory to transgendered individuals alleging discrimination based on gender nonconformity.[4]

Chapter 3 (Adverse Impact) and Chapter 4 (Application of Disparate Impact to Employment Decisions): Describes the issues with which lower courts have struggled since the Supreme Court decision in *Ricci v. DeStefano*.[5] *Ricci*'s holding that an employer can avoid liability for race-conscious employment decisions only if it can show a "strong basis in evidence" to believe that it otherwise would be at risk of disparate impact liability[6] has proved difficult to apply. Among the decisions analyzed in these chapters is the Second Circuit's decision in *Briscoe v. City of New Haven*,[7] discussing the factual converse of *Ricci* and holding that an employer could not defend a disparate impact case by arguing a strong basis in evidence that otherwise its decisions might incur disparate treatment liability.[8]

Chapter 5 (Failure to Provide a Reasonable Accommodation): Discusses the scope of accommodation required and the burden of proof where an employee claims that such accommodation has been denied. Although courts have held that an unreasonable or extended delay in providing an accommodation is tantamount to a refusal to

---

[2]557 U.S. 167, 106 FEP 833 (2009).

[3]*See, e.g.*, Brown v. City of Syracuse, 673 F.3d 141, 150, 114 FEP 992 (2d Cir. 2012) (plaintiff's Title VII and § 1981 claims both analyzed under *McDonnell Douglas* burden-shifting framework); Torgerson v. City of Rochester, 643 F.3d 1031, 1047–49, 112 FEP 613 (8th Cir.) (en banc) (plaintiffs claiming sex and national origin discrimination did not have to prove that they were best-qualified candidates at prima facie stage of their failure-to-rehire case, but comparative analysis of candidates' relative qualifications was relevant to pretext), *cert. denied*, 132 S. Ct. 513 (2011).

[4]Glenn v. Brumby, 663 F.3d 1312, 1316–20, 113 FEP 1543 (11th Cir. 2011).

[5]129 S. Ct. 2658, 106 FEP 929 (2009).

[6]*Id.* at 2677.

[7]654 F.3d 200, 112 FEP 1793 (2d Cir. 2011), *cert. denied*, 132 S. Ct. 2741, 115 FEP 352 (2012).

[8]*Id.* at 209.

accommodate,[9] there is no magic time period that must be met. The courts remain divided concerning the burden of proof where failure to accommodate is claimed. In general, the cases impose the burden on the employee to prove that an accommodation was requested (although the request need not be specific) and that a reasonable accommodation existed. The employer's burden is to explain the reason (e.g., undue cost) that an accommodation was not provided. One court has declined to establish a bright line. In *Beck v. University of Wisconsin Board of Regents*,[10] the Seventh Circuit instructed courts to look at the facts of the interactive process in a particular case, analyze the source of the breakdown in that process, and impose the burden on the party responsible for that breakdown.

Chapter 6 (Race and Color): Examines the proof necessary to show racial harassment.[11] Courts have continued to hold that Title VII prohibits the use of disparate treatment discrimination to achieve racial balancing[12] and to satisfy customer preferences.[13]

Chapter 7 (National Origin and Citizenship): Underscores the national discourse on immigration and citizenship as reflected in cases alleging employment discrimination on the basis of national origin. Courts have struggled with some difficult issues concerning who is protected under the laws. In *Onyiah v. St. Cloud State University*,[14] for example, the Eight Circuit followed an earlier ruling by the Ninth Circuit that "national origin" included African tribal

---

[9]*See, e.g.*, Valle-Arce v. Puerto Rico Ports Auth., 651 F.3d 190, 200–01, 24 AD 1547 (1st Cir. 2011) (employee provided sufficient evidence that her employer's unreasonable delay in providing reasonable accommodation to her disability constituted failure to provide such accommodation that she should have been permitted to proceed to jury).

[10]75 F.3d 1130, 1135–36, 5 AD 304 (7th Cir. 1996).

[11]Bennett v. Nucor Corp., 656 F.3d 802, 810–11, 113 FEP 616 (8th Cir. 2011) (in hostile environment case, evidence of prior acts of discrimination against nonparties can be probative of type of workplace environment to which plaintiffs were subjected and of employer's knowledge and motives); Hernandez v. Valley View Hosp. Ass'n, 684 F.3d 950, 959, 115 FEP 592 (10th Cir. 2012) ("'[E]vidence of a general work atmosphere, including evidence of harassment of other racial minorities may be considered in evaluating a [sex harassment] claim, as long as [the plaintiff] presents evidence that she knew about the offending behavior'") (quoting Tademy v. Union Pac. Corp., 614 F.3d 1132, 1146 (10th Cir. 2008)).

[12]Ondricko v. MGM Grand Detroit, LLC, 689 F.3d 642, 650, 115 FEP 1300 (6th Cir. 2012).

[13]Chaney v. Plainfield Healthcare Ctr., 612 F.3d 908, 912, 109 FEP 1377 (7th Cir. 2010).

[14]684 F.3d 711, 718–19, 115 FEP 582 (8th Cir. 2012), *cert. denied*, 133 S. Ct. 1502 (2013).

affiliation, holding that a Nigerian of Igbo descent who claimed that university officials who were Nigerian of Yoruba descent discriminated against him in his compensation.

Chapter 8 (Native Americans): Reports on the extent to which American Indian Tribes are exempt from coverage under various labor laws. In *Menominee Tribal Enterprises v. Solis*,[15] the Seventh Circuit agreed with an earlier holding by the Tenth Circuit, in *Donovan v. Navajo Forest Products Industries*,[16] a case brought under the Occupational Safety and Health Act (OSHA)[17] that where Congress expressly exempted other entities from coverage but did not mention Indian tribes, the statute applies to those tribes. A "state cannot legislate an exemption from OSHA and neither can a tribe."

Chapter 9 (Religion): Expands the discussion of the intersection of religious beliefs and effective operation of a business (including issues of safety) as well as the important question of intentionality. In *Xodus v. Wackenhut Corp.*,[18] the Seventh Circuit held that a job applicant did not adequately inform the employer of his religious beliefs where he stated only that he would not cut his dreadlocks because it was "against [his] belief," and did not indicate that the belief was religious in nature. In *Dixon v. Hallmark Cos.*,[19] by contrast, the Eleventh Circuit found that it was not essential that the supervisor knew all of the details of the plaintiffs' religious belief as long as she understood that there was a tension between those beliefs and the employer's policies. The question of whether the employee's religious observance creates a threat to safety often arises in the context of religious garb. In *EEOC v. GEO Group, Inc.*,[20] the employer was a private contractor operating a state prison that maintained a policy limiting the type of head covering that its employees could wear. The EEOC challenged the policy as a failure to accommodate the religious requirements of those Muslim women who wished to wear a full scarf (a "khimar"), rather than the less-concealing head covering that the employer permitted. The Third Circuit agreed with the employer that its concerns about the threat to safety posed by the khimar were legitimate and constituted an undue burden, notwithstanding

---

[15]601 F.3d 669, 673 (7th Cir. 2010).
[16]692 F.2d 709 (10th Cir. 1982).
[17]29 U.S.C. § 651 et seq.
[18]619 F.3d 683, 686–87, 110 FEP 1 (7th Cir. 2010).
[19]627 F.3d 849, 856, 110 FEP 1675 (11th Cir. 2010).
[20]616 F.3d 265, 271, 273, 109 FEP 1633 (3d Cir. 2010).

the more general focus on cost as the relevant issue in religious accommodation cases.

Chapter 10 (Sex): Updates and summarizes the cases, primarily those involving prisons, in which an employer asserts that sex-conscious assignment in the placement of certain personnel is warranted by either privacy considerations or concerns about employee safety. In *Breiner v. Nevada Department of Corrections*,[21] for example, sex-based assignment of prison personnel was found to be unwarranted. The Ninth Circuit distinguished the situation in the Nevada case from those in earlier cases where there was evidence of a history of violence and sexual abuse. The chapter also discusses new cases addressing several issues raised by pregnant employees. The most significant of these questions is the availability of light-duty assignments where they are requested as an accommodation by pregnant employees, particularly those whose physicians have prescribed weight-lifting restrictions during their pregnancy. Other recent cases add to the discussion of adverse actions taken against pregnant employees and the considerations involved in determining whether these actions are a pretext for pregnancy discrimination.

Chapter 11 (Sexual Orientation and Gender Identity): Explores more fully issues touched on in Chapter 10 related to discrimination on the basis of gender orientation. The chapter details a growing number of cases distinguishing between sexual stereotyping, discrimination against men or women because they do not present an appearance or behavior that meets the employer's notion of how a person of their gender should appear or act, which is covered by Title VII, and discrimination based upon an individual's gender orientation or gender identity, which most courts have held is not covered. The chapter also reports on alternative paths through which individuals aggrieved by discrimination because of their gender identity or gender orientation may seek relief. It updates information on states that have adopted laws prohibiting such discrimination and discusses as well situations in which public employees may proceed under § 1983. Finally, the chapter reports on developments in the law relating to the entitlement of same-sex spouses and partners in light of the Supreme Court's decision in *United States v. Windsor*,[22] which held that the exclusion of same-sex partners from

---

[21]610 F.3d 1202, 109 FEP 1153 (9th Cir. 2010).
[22]133 S. Ct. 2675, 118 FEP 1417 (2013).

the definition of "spouse" in the Defense of Marriage Act[23] violated the Fifth Amendment.

Chapter 12 (Age): Reports the continuing development of the law following the Supreme Court's decision in *Gross v. FBL Financial Services, Inc.*,[24] establishing that "a plaintiff must prove that age was the 'but for' cause of the employer's adverse decision" in order to prevail under the Age Discrimination in Employment Act (ADEA).[25]

Chapter 13 (Disability): Covers new cases that continue to focus on the definition of "disability" and the meaning of "substantially limited in a major life activity" as matters filed before the 2009 effective date of the Americans with Disabilities Act Amendments Act (ADAAA) still percolate through the courts. The chapter reports on these cases but highlights as well the changes in analysis that reflect the amendments contained in the ADAAA. New regulations have been issued by both the EEOC and the OFCCP, but have not yet been the subject of significant judicial review.[26] The most substantial cases address the need to harmonize considerations of confidentiality under the ADAAA and GINA, limits on employer inquiries concerning applicants' disabilities, and the programs and procedures established by the Affordable Care Act. For example, in *Seff v. Broward County, Florida*,[27] the Eleventh Circuit upheld a wellness program adopted by the county for its employees that included a questionnaire used to construct optional health management programs for employees with certain impairments. The court found that the program was part of a bona fide benefit plan—group health—and fell within the "safe harbor" provision of the Americans with Disabilities Act (ADA),[28] which protects the terms of a bona fide benefit plan that is based on underwriting risks, classifying risks, or administering such risks.

The decriminalization of marijuana use by a number of states, whether generally or when used for medical reasons, presents interesting questions under the ADA. In *Casias v. Wal-Mart Stores, Inc.*,[29] an employee who had sinus cancer and an inoperable brain

[23]28 U.S.C. § 1738C.
[24]557 U.S. 167 (2009).
[25]*Id.* at 170.
[26]29 C.F.R. pt. 1630 (2011); 41 C.F.R. pt. 60-741 (2013).
[27]691 F.3d 1221, 1223–24, 29 AD 1153 (11th Cir. 2012).
[28]42 U.S.C. § 12201(c)(2).
[29]695 F.3d 428, 27 AD 18 (6th Cir. 2012), *reh'g en banc denied*, 2012 U.S. App. LEXIS 23969 (Oct. 26, 2012).

tumor was discharged because he failed a drug test. The employee brought a wrongful discharge action claiming that his marijuana use was not illegal because he was a certified user under the Michigan Medical Marijuana Act.[30] The Sixth Circuit, citing state court decisions on the issue from several states, decided that the law provides only a "defense to criminal charges or other adverse state action," and that applying it to claims against private employers would be unduly broad.[31]

Chapter 14 (Genetic Information): Discusses the regulations promulgated by the EEOC to implement the provisions of GINA that relate to employment.[32] It highlights one of the first decisions involving an employment discrimination claim under GINA, *Poore v. Peterbilt of Bristol, LLC*.[33] One interesting aspect of GINA is that it is silent on the issue of associational discrimination. In *Poore*, a discharged employee challenged his discharge, claiming that it was motivated by his disclosure on the employer's "health questionnaire" that his wife suffered from multiple sclerosis. The district court dismissed the case, holding that the wife's genetic information was not protected because it did not disclose any information about the employee himself.

Chapter 15 (Retaliation): Addresses how proof of retaliation was affected by the Supreme Court's decision in *Texas Southwestern Medical Center v. Nassar*,[34] which extended to Title VII retaliation actions the "but for" causation standard articulated by the Court under the ADEA in *Gross v. FBL Financial Services, Inc.*[35]

Chapter 16 (Hiring): Includes a review of the lower courts' explorations of the unique difficulties of determining what constitutes proof of pretext within the hiring context, in which the plaintiff lacks evidence of a level of substantive performance within the particular position at issue.

Chapter 17 (Promotion, Advancement, and Reclassification): Updates and expands the case law defining the comparative evidence needed to prove discrimination at the prima facie and pretext stages

---

[30]MICH. COMP. LAWS § 333.26421 et seq.

[31]*Casias*, 695 F.3d at 435–36.

[32]The provisions of GINA relating to employment appear at 42 U.S.C. §§ 2000ff–2000ff (11) (2010); the regulations appear at 29 C.F.R. pt. 1635 (2013).

[33]852 F. Supp. 2d 727, 729, 26 AD 174 (W.D. Va. 2012).

[34]133 S. Ct. 2517, 118 FEP 1504 (2013).

[35]557 U.S. 167 (2009).

of a promotion case,[36] and the use of statistical evidence in promotion cases.[37]

Chapter 18 (Seniority): Discusses the Second Circuit decision in *United States v. Brennan*,[38] which defined the limitations on the extent to which employers may lawfully modify seniority systems through voluntary settlements.

Chapter 19 (Compensation): Continues the discussion over the standard for analyzing compensation under Title VII, and the meaning of "equal work" under the Equal Pay Act. In *Randall v. Rolls-Royce Corp.*,[39] the plaintiff, a "director of operations," unsuccessfully challenged a disparity between her salary and that of men holding the same position. The Seventh Circuit held that a job title itself did not establish equality of work where many people held the same title but performed different functions. Courts have also ruled that pay disparities did not establish unlawful discrimination where the employer had a policy of "red-circling" a new employee's wage at the level of his or her previous job, and where the lower-paid employee was only temporarily promoted and the comparator held the same position on a permanent basis.

Chapter 20 (Sexual and Other Forms of Harassment): Includes a comprehensive review of appellate court decisions on troublesome issues such as the level of conduct sufficient to establish a hostile environment, as well as an analysis of the Supreme Court's 2013 decision in *Vance v. Ball State University*,[40] which held that

---

[36]*Compare* Provenzano v. LCI Holdings, Inc., 663 F.3d 806, 814, 114 FEP 90 (6th Cir. 2011) (at prima facie stage, plaintiff must show that she possessed "similar qualifications" to selectee, rather than identical qualifications), *and* Torgerson v. City of Rochester, 643 F.3d 1031, 1047, 112 FEP 613 (8th Cir.) (rejecting proposition that plaintiff must prove her relative qualifications at prima facie stage), *cert. denied*, 132 S. Ct. 513, 113 FEP 1152 (2011), *with* Ford v. Mabus, 629 F.3d 198, 203, 110 FEP 165 (D.C. Cir. 2010) (plaintiff proves pretext by showing that he or she was "significantly better qualified" than selectee).

[37]*See* Bennett v. Nucor Corp., 656 F.3d 802, 818, 113 FEP 616 (8th Cir. 2011) (rejecting plaintiffs' statistical evidence as inadequate to create genuine issue on summary judgment where plaintiffs' expert failed to identify specific employment practices responsible for alleged disparate impact in promotions or to show that their statistical "applicant pools" contained only individuals who were at least minimally qualified for promotions in question); Tyler v. University of Ark. Bd. of Trs., 628 F.3d 980, 990, 111 FEP 161 (8th Cir. 2011) (inference of discriminatory intent not supported where top two contenders for position happened to be female but sample consisted of only six applicants).

[38]650 F.3d 65 (2d Cir. 2009).

[39]637 F.3d 818, 823, 111 FEP 1565 (7th Cir. 2011).

[40]133 S. Ct. 2434, 118 FEP 1481 (2013).

a "negligence" standard applies to employer liability for sexual harassment by a co-worker who lacks supervisory status, and provides guidance on the factors that distinguish a supervisor from a co-worker.[41]

Chapter 21 (Discharge and Reduction in Force): Reports that of the approximately 100,000 charges that the EEOC received during fiscal year 2012 under all of the statutes that it enforces, nearly 78,000 listed discharge as at least one of the issues as to which the charging party was alleging discrimination.[42] A primary focus in the current cases is whether similarly situated employees were discharged for similar misconduct. Even where such disparate treatment is shown, a discharge may be upheld where it appears that there were good grounds for the termination and nothing to suggest that the employer's actions were suspect.[43]

Chapter 22 (Employers): Addresses the circumstances that determine when a volunteer is treated as an employee entitled to protection against employment discrimination. The issue arises, among other situations, in communities that rely on volunteer fire departments to supplement (or in lieu of) their usual workers. Another important issue is whether a particular individual is a supervisor who acts as an agent of the employer. The Supreme Court addressed this question in *Vance v. Ball State University*,[44] in which the Court distinguished between true supervisors and those who were merely co-workers serving as "straw bosses," "leadmen," or working foremen; supervisor status is limited to those with the power to cause direct economic harm by taking a tangible employment action.

Chapter 23 (Unions): Updates how, since the Supreme Court decision in *14 Penn Plaza LLC v. Pyett*,[45] courts continue to clarify the circumstances under which collective bargaining agreements mandate the arbitration of statutory discrimination claims. Where a collective bargaining agreement mandates arbitration, there is a clear waiver of the judicial forum;[46] by contrast, there is no claim preclusion or waiver of judicial forum where the arbitration clause

[41]*Id.* at 2454, 2451.

[42]*See* http://www.eeoc.gov/eeoc/statistics/enforcement/statutes_by_issue.cfm.

[43]Good v. University of Chi. Med. Ctr., 673 F.3d 670, 679, 114 FEP 903 (7th Cir. 2012).

[44]133 S. Ct. 2434, 118 FEP 1481 (2013).

[45]556 U.S. 247, 105 FEP 1441 (2009).

[46]Thompson v. Air Transp. Int'l Ltd. Liab. Co., 664 F.3d 723, 726–27, 192 LRRM 2454 (8th Cir. 2011).

of a collective bargaining agreement does not clearly mandate the arbitration of statutory discrimination claims.[47]

Chapter 24 (Employment Agencies): Discusses continuing efforts by courts to define the sometimes complicated relationship between employment and staffing agencies, the individuals they refer for employment, and the companies to whom those individuals are referred. The Fifth Circuit in *Johnson v. Manpower Professional Services*[48] emphasized the right to control the conditions of the individual's employment in determining that the company to whom the person was referred was the employer, rather than the agency. The client company decided which of the individuals referred by Manpower to hire and assigned and supervised their work. In contrast, the Fourth Circuit in *EEOC v. Randstad*[49] upheld enforcement of an EEOC investigative subpoena where the underlying charge presumed that the agency was the aggrieved individual's employer and challenged its English literacy requirement, which was a prerequisite to referral.

Chapter 25 (Charging Parties and Plaintiffs): Adds noteworthy appellate court decisions that help clarify common issues, including Title VII coverage of independent contractors, volunteers, and former employees, and issues related to standing.

Chapter 26 (EEOC Administrative Process): Reports that a number of cases have addressed the permissible scope of an EEOC investigative subpoena, and that most have given the agency wide latitude in the range of documents that it seeks. Relevance in this context warrants giving EEOC access to any material "that might cast light on the allegations against the employer."[50] The Tenth Circuit in *EEOC v. Burlington Northern Santa Fe Railroad*,[51] however, cautioned that the relevance requirement should not be read so broadly that it is rendered a nullity.

Chapter 27 (Timeliness): Contains analysis of a significant number of appellate court decisions on timeliness issues, including such issues as the point in time at which employment decisions become actionable, continuing violation issues interpreting *National*

---

[47]*See* Coleman v. Donahoe, 667 F.3d 835, 854, 114 FEP 160 (7th Cir. 2012).

[48]442 F. App'x 977, 982, 113 FEP 809 (5th Cir. 2011).

[49]685 F.3d 433, 439, 452, 115 FEP 801 (4th Cir. 2012).

[50]EEOC v. Kronos, Inc., 620 F.3d 287, 296, 23 AD 1105 (3d Cir. 2010) (*Kronos I*) (quoting EEOC v. Shell Oil Co., 466 U.S. 54, 68–69 (1984)).

[51]669 F.3d 1154, 1156–57, 25 AD 1572 (10th Cir. 2012).

Railroad Passenger Corp. v. Morgan,[52] and the special problems unique to causes of action based upon compensation issues following the Lilly Ledbetter Fair Pay Act.

Chapter 28 (Jurisprudential Bars to Action): Reviews appellate case law regarding such issues as preclusion due to prior arbitration decisions or prior federal agency determinations, as well as developments related to judicial estoppel, and adds a new section on the topic of forum-selection clauses within employment contracts.

Chapter 29 (Title VII Litigation Procedure): Includes cases in which courts continue to define the extent to which the EEOC charge limits the scope of a subsequent Title VII lawsuit,[53] as well as the pleading and proof requirements for such lawsuits.[54]

Chapter 30 (EEOC Litigation): Discusses recent cases generally affirming broad interpretations of the EEOC's subpoena authority during its investigation (even where the employer argues that the charge being investigated is invalid because it was not timely filed),[55] but points out that the Commission's ability to subpoena information is not without limits. In *EEOC v. Burlington Northern Santa Fe Railroad*,[56] the Tenth Circuit held that the Commission could not subpoena companywide information where the investigation was based on two charges that did not contain allegations of systemic

---

[52]536 U.S. 101, 88 FEP 1601 (2002).

[53]*See, e.g.*, Velazquez-Ortiz v. Vilsack, 657 F.3d 64, 71, 113 FEP 627 (1st Cir. 2011) (allegations in charge must "bear some close relation" to claims in subsequent judicial complaint); Rios-Colón v. Toledo-Dávila, 641 F.3d 1, 4, 111 FEP 1571 (1st Cir. 2011) (dismissal of complaint that named supervisory officers in their official capacities instead of police department was error where officers were acting as agents of department and department had knowledge of EEOC charge underlying action).

[54]*See, e.g.*, Khalik v. United Air Lines, 671 F.3d 1188, 1193, 114 FEP 500 (10th Cir. 2012) (conclusory complaint allegations not entitled to assumption of truth at pleading stage; "*Twombly/Iqbal* standard recognizes plaintiff should have at least some relevant information to make the claims plausible on their face"); Romans v. Michigan Dep't of Human Servs., 668 F.3d 826, 839, 114 FEP 1404 (6th Cir. 2012) (employer's well-founded belief plaintiff was harassing co-employee sufficient to rebut plaintiff's pretext claim); Lefevers v. GAF Fiberglass Corp., 667 F.3d 721, 725–26, 114 FEP 385 (6th Cir. 2012) (where employer proffered evidence of plaintiff's poor work performance and retained employees near or above plaintiff's age, plaintiff cannot prove justification for termination was pretext for age discrimination); Adams v. Trustees of Univ. of N.C.-Wilmington, 640 F.3d 550, 559–60, 111 FEP 1665 (4th Cir. 2011) (plaintiff cannot rely on own assertions of discrimination to prove pretext when there is substantial evidence of legitimate, nondiscriminatory reasons for adverse employment action).

[55]EEOC v. Schwan's Home Serv., 644 F.3d 742, 746–47, 112 FEP 1227 (8th Cir. 2011).

[56]669 F.3d 1154, 1157–59, 25 AD 1572 (10th Cir. 2012).

discrimination and the EEOC had provided no basis for expanding its investigation. Similarly, in *EEOC v. Kronos, Inc.*,[57] the Third Circuit denied enforcement of an EEOC subpoena seeking information relating to possible race discrimination where the underlying charge was limited to an allegation of disability discrimination.

Chapter 31 (Justice Department Litigation): Addresses the circumstances under which the Department of Justice becomes involved in Title VII litigation.[58]

Chapter 32 (Federal Employee Litigation): Discusses EEOC regulations issued in 2012 and the impact of these regulations on litigation brought by federal employees.

Chapter 33 (Class Actions): Presents cases decided after *Wal-Mart Stores, Inc. v. Dukes*,[59] in which the Supreme Court held that certification is improper under Rule 23(b)(2) where monetary relief is claimed that is not merely incidental to the equitable remedies sought.[60] In *Comcast Corp. v. Behrend*,[61] the Court held that certification is improper where the injuries arising out of the challenged conduct are not capable of proof common to the class, so that damages could not be calculated through a common methodology. Although several post-*Dukes* decisions have found class treatment to be inappropriate in disparate impact cases,[62] the Seventh Circuit certified a class challenge to companywide policies in *McReynolds v. Merrill Lynch, Pierce, Fenner & Smith, Inc.*[63] As the Supreme Court explained in *Amgen, Inc. v. Connecticut Retirement Plans & Trust*

---

[57]620 F.3d 287, 298–99, 300–02, 110 FEP 392 (3d Cir. 2010).

[58]42 U.S.C. §§ 2000e-5(f)(1), 2000e-6(a).

[59]131 S. Ct. 2541, 112 FEP 769 (2011).

[60]*Id.* at 2557.

[61]133 S. Ct. 1426 (2013).

[62]Bolden v. Walsh Constr. Co., 688 F.3d 893, 898, 115 FEP 1153 (7th Cir. 2012) (reversing class certification of multi-site classes in reliance on *Dukes*; "when multiple managers exercise independent discretion, conditions at different stores (or sites) do not present a common question"—"*Wal-Mart* tells us that local discretion cannot support a company-wide class no matter how cleverly lawyers may try to repackage local variability as uniformity"); Ellis v. Costco Wholesale Corp., 657 F.3d 970, 981, 113 FEP 496 (9th Cir. 2011) (remanding question of nationwide class certification where district court failed to conduct "rigorous analysis" required by *Dukes* with respect to commonality); Bennett v. Nucor Corp., 656 F.3d 802, 813–16, 113 FEP 616 (8th Cir. 2011) (affirming denial of class certification in disparate treatment and impact case based on finding that plaintiffs failed to establish commonality, because defendant's "departments varied widely in their employment practices, working environments, and functions"), *cert. denied*, 132 S. Ct. 1861, 114 FEP 1088 (2012).

[63]672 F.3d 482, 490–91, 114 FEP 710 (7th Cir.), *cert. denied*, 133 S. Ct. 338, 116 FEP 288 (2012).

Funds,[64] a plaintiff need not prove that each element of a claim can be established by classwide proof; what Rule 23(a) requires is that "common questions '*predominate* over any questions affecting only individual [class] members.'"[65]

Chapter 34 (Discovery): Examines the scope of discovery permissible in discrimination cases,[66] the circumstances under which a duty to preserve evidence is triggered,[67] and whether particular actions constitute spoliation, so that sanctions are warranted.[68]

Chapter 35 (Statistical and Other Expert Proof): Analyzes the circumstances under which expert testimony and statistical proof are appropriate in discrimination cases, as well as the statistical models and sources of statistics recognized by the courts in such cases. The Supreme Court decision in *Comcast Corp. v. Behrend*[69] held that courts must examine the merits and related expert testimony at the class certification stage, to the extent necessary to determine whether class certification is proper; however, the *Comcast* Court declined to define the standard for analyzing expert evidence at the time that certification is considered.[70]

Chapter 36 (The Civil Rights Acts of 1866 and 1871): Covers court decisions that have focused on the scope of qualified immunity available to governmental actors under § 1983, as well as the

---

[64] 133 S. Ct. 1184 (2013).

[65] *Id.* at 1195–96 (quoting FED. R. CIV. P. 23(b)(3) (emphasis by Court)).

[66] *See* EEOC v. Burlington N. Santa Fe R.R., 669 F.3d 1154, 1157, 25 AD 1572 (10th Cir. 2012) (EEOC not entitled to nationwide database where information was not "relevant" to charge).

[67] Everett v. Cook Cnty., 655 F.3d 723, 727, 113 FEP 9 (7th Cir. 2011) (defendant's destruction of documents does not create inference of spoliation in Title VII action absent showing that documents were intentionally destroyed in bad faith); Scalera v. Electrograph Sys., Inc., 262 F.R.D. 162, 171 (E.D.N.Y. 2009) (EEOC charge triggered duty to preserve evidence related to charge); Goodman v. Praxair Servs., Inc., 632 F. Supp. 2d 494, 511 (D. Md. 2009) ("litigation hold" letters trigger duty to preserve).

[68] Port Auth. Police Asian Jade Soc'y of N.Y. & N.J., Inc. v. Port Auth. of N.Y. & N.J., 601 F. Supp. 2d 566, 570–71 (S.D.N.Y. 2009) (failure to preserve documents and to issue "litigation hold" did not warrant adverse inference instruction as sanction where failure to preserve was partly attributable to 9/11/01 attack on Port Authority offices and where plaintiffs had other information and documents in their possession to support their allegations at trial), *aff'd sub nom.* Chin v. Port Auth. of N.Y. & N.J., 685 F.3d 135, 115 FEP 720 (2d Cir. 2012); Talavera v. Shah, 638 F.3d 303, 311–13, 111 FEP 1574 (D.C. Cir. 2011) (presumption that destroyed documents contained information favorable to opposing party is sanction most commonly imposed for such destruction; more drastic measure such as entry of default judgment is warranted only when lesser sanction would be futile).

[69] 133 S. Ct. 1426 (2013).

[70] *Id.* at 1432–34.

bases of discrimination prohibited by that statute. Whether the immunity defense is available depends on whether the alleged constitutional violation was clearly established at the time of the violation.[71] Courts have considered sexual orientation discrimination claims and claims based on gender nonconformity under § 1983 and the Equal Protection Clause.[72]

Chapter 37 (The National Labor Relations Act): Highlights judicial interpretations of the scope and preclusive effect of collectively bargained arbitration clauses under both the National Labor Relations Act and the Railway Labor Act.

Chapter 38 ("Reverse" Discrimination and Affirmative Action): Addresses the Supreme Court's decision in *Fisher v. University of Texas at Austin*,[73] which clarified the proof that is sufficient to show that a race-conscious university admissions plan is sufficiently narrowly tailored to withstand constitutional scrutiny, as well as the 2014 Supreme Court decision in *Schuette v. Coalition to Defend Affirmative Action, Integration, Immigration Rights and Fight for Equality by Any Means Necessary*,[74] which held that amendments to state constitutions outlawing race-conscious admissions policies are not to be set aside by the judiciary.

Chapter 39 (Federal Contractor Affirmative Action Compliance): Focuses on final rulings of the Department of Labor's Administrative Review Board (ARB) that apply Executive Order 11246, § 503 of the Rehabilitation Act of 1978, and the nondiscrimination provisions of the Jobs for Veterans Act. In *OFCCP v. O'Melveny & Meyers, LLP*,[75] the ARB vacated the recommended decision of an administrative law judge (ALJ) that a law firm that provided legal advice to

---

[71]Levin v. Madigan, 692 F.3d 607, 622, 115 FEP 1281 (7th Cir. 2012).

[72]*See* Ayala-Sepúlveda v. Municipality of San Germán, 671 F.3d 24, 30–33, 114 FEP 234 (1st Cir. 2012) (examining claims of hostile work environment, retaliatory transfer, and improper classification based on sexual orientation under Equal Protection Clause; summary judgment affirmed because no evidence of disparate treatment); *see also* Flaherty v. Massapequa Pub. Schs., 462 F. App'x 38, 39 (2d Cir. 2012) (expressing no opinion "[w]hether a person perceived as a homosexual is in a protected class for equal protection purposes"); Glenn v. Brumby, 663 F.3d 1312, 1329, 113 FEP 1542 (11th Cir. 2011) ("government agent violates the Equal Protection Clause's prohibition of sex-based discrimination when he or she fires a transgender or transsexual employee because of his or her gender non-conformity").

[73]133 S. Ct. 2411, 118 FEP 1459 (2013).

[74]134 S. Ct. 1623, 1637–38 (2014).

[75]Case No. 2011-OFC-00007, 2011 WL 5668757, at *6 (U.S. Dep't of Labor) (Aug. 31, 2011).

the Department of Energy was a covered contractor required to comply with the obligations imposed by the OFCCP programs. The ARB held that coverage of contracts to provide such services must be considered in light of two factors: (1) whether agency personnel were or could be performing the same services; and (2) the nature and degree of agency supervision of the law firm's personnel. In another important area relating to OFCCP coverage, the ARB decided in *OFCCP v. Florida Hospital of Orlando*[76] that § 715 of the National Defense Authorization Act exempted from OFCCP coverage contracts relating to TRICARE (the Department of Defense's health care program for active and retired members of the military and their families). Thereafter, the OFCCP announced a moratorium on compliance reviews based on the provision of TRICARE services.

Chapter 40 (Injunctive and Affirmative Relief): Discusses the effect of *Southwestern University Medical Center v. Nassar*[77] on the availability of injunctive relief, as well as appellate decisions focusing on such issues as the sets of facts that can defeat the presumptive right to reinstatement or an award of front pay.

Chapter 41 (Monetary Relief): Further clarifies the circumstances under which front pay, back pay, and compensatory, liquidated, and punitive damages are awarded in discrimination cases.

Chapter 42 (Attorney's Fees): Adds to the Main Volume's guidance on issues such as the degree of success that a plaintiff need attain in order to be treated as a prevailing party for purposes of a fee award and fee awards for interim or injunctive success.

Chapter 43 (Alternative Dispute Resolution): Discusses the role of the parties' written agreement to arbitrate in defining the scope of any arbitration held and the status of such an agreement trumps state law.[78] The Supreme Court has held that class arbitration is a matter of consent.[79]

---

[76]Case No. 2009-OFC-00002, Recommended Decision of the ALJ, at *1 (Oct. 18, 2010).

[77]133 S. Ct. 2517, 118 FEP 1504 (2013).

[78]Nitro-Lift Techs., LLC v. Howard, 133 S. Ct. 500, 503 (2012) (reversing Oklahoma Supreme Court decision that invalidated on state-law grounds noncompetition agreement without addressing enforceability of pre-dispute arbitration agreement); Marmet Health Care Ctr., Inc. v. Brown, 132 S. Ct. 1201 (2012) (West Virginia's prohibition against pre-dispute arbitration agreements for personal-injury or wrongful-death claims against nursing homes is categorical rule prohibiting arbitration of particular type of claim, which is preempted by Federal Arbitration Act).

[79]Oxford Health Plans, LLC v. Sutter, 133 S. Ct. 2064, 2069 (2013); American Express Co. v. Italian Colors Rest., 133 S. Ct. 2304 (2013).

Chapter 44 (Settlement): Includes a discussion of the relevant evidence and burdens of proof where the employer breaches an agreement with the EEOC to provide specific relief to third-party individuals. The cases address the proper forum for enforcement of such an agreement depending upon the stage at which settlement occurred. One court has held that a Title VII settlement agreement can be interpreted as mandating payment of money damages for breach by the federal government and therefore may fall under the Tucker Act jurisdiction of the Court of Federal Claims.[80] The Ninth Circuit held that the Tucker Act provides the exclusive basis for enforcement of such a breach and that enforcement requires the aggrieved party to satisfy the separate prerequisites of that act before proceeding with litigation.[81]

---

[80]Holmes v. United States, 657 F.3d 1303, 1307, 113 FEP 395 (Fed. Cir. 2011).
[81]Munoz v. Mabus, 630 F.3d 856, 861, 864, 111 FEP 40 (9th Cir. 2010).

CHAPTER 2

DISPARATE TREATMENT

II. Proof of Disparate Treatment in the Individual Case

A. The *McDonnell Douglas-Burdine-Hicks-Reeves* Analysis: Proof of Disparate Treatment Through Circumstantial Evidence

1. Evolution of the Allocation and Order of Proof

[18][On page 2-4 of the Main Volume, in footnote 18, add the following after "*See, e.g.*,".]

St. Martin v. City of St. Paul, 680 F.3d 1027, 1033, 26 AD 516 (8th Cir. 2012) (direct evidence may be used in lieu of *McDonnell Douglas*); Holland v. Gee, 677 F.3d 1047, 1055, 114 FEP 1449 (11th Cir. 2012) (*McDonnell Douglas* applies to cases involving circumstantial evidence); Spees v. James Marine, Inc., 617 F.3d 380, 390, 109 FEP 1748 (6th Cir. 2010) (*McDonnell Douglas* framework does not apply to mixed-motive claims in which employee produces evidence that protected characteristic was motivating factor in adverse employment decision); Hawn v. Executive Jet Mgmt., Inc., 615 F.3d 1151, 1156–57, 109 FEP 1824 (9th Cir. 2010) ("A plaintiff may show 'an inference of discrimination in whatever manner is appropriate in the particular circumstances'.");

[18]**[On page 2-4 of the Main Volume, in footnote 18, add the following at the end of the footnote.]**

But see Ford v. Mabus, 629 F.3d 198, 207, 110 FEP 1665 (D.C. Cir. 2010) (*Gross* does not apply to age discrimination claims of federal employees who may obtain declaratory or possibly injunctive relief, but not instatement and back pay, "by showing that age was a factor in the challenged employment action").

[20]**[On page 2-5 of the Main Volume, in footnote 20, add the following at the beginning of the footnote.]**

Amini v. City of Minneapolis, 643 F.3d 1068, 1075–77, 112 FEP 1089 (8th Cir. 2011) (Afghanistan-born job applicant alleging race, color, and national origin discrimination did not meet his burden of showing that employer's proffered justification for failure to hire him was pretextual), *cert. denied*, 132 S. Ct. 1144, 114 FEP 288 (2012); Torgerson v. City of Rochester, 643 F.3d 1031, 1052, 112 FEP 613 (8th Cir. 2011) (en banc) (employer was entitled to summary judgment in failure-to-hire case where plaintiffs alleging sex and national origin discrimination did not "identify evidence from which a reasonable trier of fact could conclude that the City's reason for not hiring them was pretextual"); Ahern v. Shinseki, 629 F.3d 49, 55, 110 FEP 1785 (1st Cir. 2010) (female employees could not make out prima facie case of discriminatory hiring when none of them applied for an open position); Chhim v. Spring Branch Indep. Sch. Dist., 2010 U.S. App. LEXIS 19694, at *3–4, 110 FEP 629 (5th Cir. 2010) (refusal to hire individual of Cambodian descent for custodial supervisor position based on preference for capability in both Spanish and English does not constitute discrimination based on national origin);

[21]**[On page 2-5 of the Main Volume, in footnote 21, add the following after "*See*".]**

Romans v. Michigan Dep't of Human Servs., 668 F.3d 826, 838, 114 FEP 1404 (6th Cir. 2012) (plaintiff failed to establish prima facie case of discriminatory discharge where he could not demonstrate that he was treated differently than similarly situated non-white employee); Lefevers v. GAF Fiberglass Corp., 667 F.3d 721, 725, 114 FEP 385 (6th Cir. 2012) (employee alleging termination in violation of Age Discrimination in Employment Act (ADEA) failed to demonstrate that employer's proffered explanation was pretextual); Coleman v. Donahoe, 667 F.3d 835, 841–42, 114 FEP 160 (7th Cir. 2012) (evidence that employees were similarly situated relevant to both prima facie case and pretext in *McDonnell Douglas* analysis of discriminatory discharge);

[22]**[On page 2-5 of the Main Volume, in footnote 22, add the following after "*See, e.g.,*".]**

Turner v. Kansas City S. Ry., 675 F.3d 887, 892–93, 114 FEP 1044 (5th Cir. 2012) ("in work-rule violation cases . . . a Title VII plaintiff may establish a prima facie case by showing either [1] that he did not violate the rule, or [2] that, if he did, white employees who engaged in similar acts were not punished similarly");

[23]**[On page 2-6 of the Main Volume, in footnote 23, add the following after "*See*".]**

Gilbert v. Napolitano, 670 F.3d 258, 262, 114 FEP 923 (D.C. Cir. 2012) (reasonable jury could find that Mexican-American's national origin was deciding factor in nonpromotion decision where his qualifications "dwarfed" those of non-Hispanic employee promoted to position); Bennett v. Nucor Corp., 656 F.3d 802, 820, 113 FEP 616 (8th Cir. 2011) (plaintiffs could not rely on "conclusory assertions that they possessed the qualifications necessary for promotion" to rebut employer's nondiscriminatory explanation for failing to promote them);

[26]**[On page 2-7 of the Main Volume, in footnote 26, add the following at the beginning of the footnote.]**

Geleta v. Gray, 645 F.3d 408, 411–13, 112 FEP 981 (D.C. Cir. 2011) (transfer from position overseeing mental health project with supervisory responsibilities to nonsupervisory desk job clearing bureaucratic backlog was materially adverse action for purposes of prima facie case of retaliation); Tyler v. University of Ark. Bd. of Trs., 628 F.3d 980, 985–88, 111 FEP 161 (8th Cir. 2011) (plaintiff failed to establish prima facie case of retaliation because he failed to establish causal nexus between decision not to hire him as Director of Recruitment for Diversity in 2007 and his 2004 complaint of discrimination);

[27]**[On page 2-7 of the Main Volume, in footnote 27, add the following after "*E.g.*,".]**

Silverman v. Board of Educ. of Chi., 637 F.3d 729, 736–40, 111 FEP 1461 (7th Cir. 2011) (nonrenewal of contract);

[28]**[On page 2-7 of the Main Volume, in footnote 28, add the following before "King v. Hardesty".]**

Brown v. City of Syracuse, 673 F.3d 141, 150, 114 FEP 992 (2d Cir. 2012) (plaintiff's Title VII and § 1981 claims both analyzed under *McDonnell Douglas* burden-shifting framework); Wesley v. General Drivers, Warehousemen & Helpers Local 745, 660 F.3d 211, 213–14, 113 FEP 705 (5th Cir. 2011) (*McDonnell Douglas* framework reworked in context of § 1981 complaint against union based on race discrimination in grievance process); Twigg v. Hawker Beechcraft Corp., 659 F.3d 987, 998–1000, 113 FEP 938 (10th Cir. 2011) (plaintiff may establish § 1981 retaliation claim by direct/mixed-motive approach or indirect approach established in *McDonnell Douglas*);

[29]**[On page 2-8 of the Main Volume, in footnote 29, add the following after "*See, e.g.*,".]**

Lefevers v. GAF Fiberglass Corp., 667 F.3d 721, 725, 114 FEP 385 (6th Cir. 2012) (employee alleging termination in violation of ADEA failed to demonstrate that employer's proffered explanation was pretextual); Shelley v. Geren, 666 F.3d 599, 606–08, 114 FEP 303 (9th Cir. 2012) (*Gross v. FBL Fin. Servs., Inc.* does not preclude application of *McDonnell Douglas* framework in ADEA cases); Tusing v. Des Moines Indep. Cnty. Sch. Dist., 639 F.3d 507, 514–17, 111 FEP 1761 (8th Cir. 2011) (ADEA plaintiff failed to rebut employer's assertion that she was not hired for counseling job because she lacked counseling license);

[On page 2-8 of the Main Volume, after footnote 30, add the following.]

the Family and Medical Leave Act (FMLA),[1]

[31]**[On page 2-9 of the Main Volume, in footnote 31, add the following after "*E.g.*,".]**

Papelino v. Albany Coll. of Pharmacy of Union Univ., 633 F.3d 81, 89 (2d Cir. 2011) ("a Title IX sex discrimination claim requires the same kind of proof required in a Title VII sex discrimination claim");

[34]**[On page 2-9 of the Main Volume, in footnote 34, add the following before "Timmons v. GMC" .]**

Carter v. Pathfinder Energy Servs., Inc., 662 F.3d 1134, 1142, 25 AD 679 (10th Cir. 2011) ("[w]e apply the burden-shifting framework set forth in *McDonnell Douglas Corp. v. Green* to ADA discrimination claims"); Ramos-Echevarria v. Pichis, Inc., 659 F.3d 182, 186–87, 25 AD 545 (1st Cir. 2011) (plaintiff did not establish prima facie case because he did not show that he had disability as defined by ADA); Stansberry v. Air Wis. Airlines Corp., 651 F.3d 482, 487–88, 24 AD 1544 (6th Cir. 2011) (applying *McDonnell Douglas* burden-shifting framework to "disability by association" claim); Whitfield v. Tennessee, 639 F.3d 253, 258–59, 24 AD 641 (6th Cir. 2011) ("to make out a prima facie case of employment discrimination through indirect evidence under [the ADA], a plaintiff must show that (1) he or she is disabled; (2) otherwise qualified for the position, with or without reasonable accommodation; (3) suffered an adverse employment decision; (4) the employer knew or had reason to know the plaintiff's disability; and (5) the position remained open while the employer sought other applicants or the disabled individual was replaced") (internal quotations omitted);

---

[1]Romans v. Michigan Dep't of Human Servs., 668 F.3d 826, 842, 114 FEP 1404 (6th Cir. 2012) (applying *McDonnell Douglas* burden-shifting framework to FMLA retaliation claims); Wierman v. Casey Gen. Stores, Inc., 638 F.3d 984, 999, 111 FEP 1547 (8th Cir. 2011) (same). *But see* Sanders v. City of Newport, 657 F.3d 772, 778, 17 WH Cases 2d 588 (9th Cir. 2011) (declining to apply *McDonnell Douglas* to FMLA interference claims and noting circuit conflict on point).

2. *Elements of the Prima Facie Case*

[47]**[On page 2-11 of the Main Volume, in footnote 47, add the following after "*See, e.g.,*".]**

Martinez-Burgos v. Guayama Corp., 656 F.3d 7, 12–13, 113 FEP 253 (1st Cir. 2011) (plaintiff failed to establish prima facie case of pregnancy discrimination in connection with nonrenewal of her temporary services contract where "record amply demonstrate[d] that [she] was not qualified for the position" that she sought);

[47]**[On page 2-11 of the Main Volume, in footnote 47, add the following after "*See* Section II.C.4, *infra.*".]**

See also Torgerson v. City of Rochester, 643 F.3d 1031, 1047–49, 112 FEP 613 (8th Cir.) (en banc) (plaintiffs claiming sex and national origin discrimination did not have to prove that they were best-qualified candidates at prima facie stage of their failure-to-hire case, but comparative analysis of candidates' relative qualifications is relevant to pretext), *cert. denied*, 132 S. Ct. 513 (2011); Norman-Nunnery v. Madison Area Tech. Coll., 625 F.3d 422, 432–34, 110 FEP 1121 (7th Cir. 2010) (plaintiff satisfied her prima facie burden by showing that she met minimum qualifications for job but could not rebut employer's explanation that it did not hire her because she scored lower on selection criteria than other candidates interviewed where selection criteria were equally applied); Moss v. BMC Software, Inc., 610 F.3d 917, 923, 109 FEP 1173 (5th Cir. 2010) (to rebut employer's "legitimate nondiscriminatory reason," plaintiff must show that he was "clearly better qualified" than candidate hired).

[55]**[On page 2-14 of the Main Volume, in footnote 55, add the following after "*See, e.g.,*".]**

Bonds v. Leavitt, 629 F.3d 369, 386, 111 FEP 171 (4th Cir.) (outlining requirements of prima facie case of discriminatory discharge), *cert. denied*, 132 S. Ct. 398 (2011);

[56]**[On page 2-14 of the Main Volume, in footnote 56, add the following at the end of the footnote.]**

Cf. Blizzard v. Marion Tech. Coll., 698 F.3d 275, 284, 116 FEP 392 (6th Cir. 2012) (courts may, in their discretion, find that substantial age difference gives rise to inference of discrimination in cases "involving replacement by a person who is between six and ten years younger than the plaintiff"), *cert. denied*, 2013 U.S. LEXIS 3626 (May 13, 2013).

[57][On page 2-14 of the Main Volume, in footnote 57, add the following after "*See*".]

Wierman v. Casey's Gen. Stores, Inc., 638 F.3d 984, 994, 1001, 111 FEP 1547 (8th Cir. 2011) (plaintiff established prima facie case by inference simply because of "suspicious timing" of her discharge "just days" after she took time off for pregnancy-related reasons);

[60][On page 2-16 of the Main Volume, in footnote 60, add the following after "*See*".]

Harper v. C.R. England, Inc., 687 F.3d 297, 309–11, 115 FEP 290 (7th Cir. 2012) (plaintiff failed to establish prima facie case where he failed to demonstrate either that he was performing his job adequately at time of his termination or that he was treated less favorably than others who were similarly situated); Burnell v. Gates Rubber Co., 647 F.3d 704, 709, 112 FEP 1441 (7th Cir. 2011) (granting summary judgment on discriminatory discharge claim where plaintiff provided no evidence that his job performance met expectations and that similarly situated persons outside protected class received better treatment);

[66][On page 2-18 of the Main Volume, in footnote 66, add the following after "*See, e.g.,*".]

Dass v. Chicago Bd. of Educ., 675 F.3d 1060, 1069, 114 FEP 1288 (7th Cir. 2012) (teacher's reassignment from third grade class to seventh grade class not materially adverse);

[66][On page 2-19 of the Main Volume, in the carryover of footnote 66, add the following after "*But see*".]

Youssef v. FBI, 687 F.3d 397, 402, 115 FEP 974 (D.C. Cir. 2012) (post-9/11 transfer of Egyptian counterintelligence officer from supervisory position on detail to nonsupervisory position in office of Central Intelligence Agency to analyzing documents constituted adverse action, even though it did not involve change in pay or grade, based on removal of supervisory duties and fact that work assignments were far less complex than warranted by individual's qualifications and prior work history with agency); Holland v. Gee, 677 F.3d 1047, 1058, 114 FEP 1449 (11th Cir. 2012) (transfer from on-site technician job to help desk job requiring less technical and more administrative work could constitute adverse employment action);

[71]**[On page 2-21 of the Main Volume, in footnote 71, add the following at the beginning of the footnote.]**

See Brown v. City of Syracuse, 673 F.3d 141, 150, 114 FEP 992 (2d Cir. 2012) (paid suspension pending investigation could be adverse employment action "if the employer takes action beyond an employee's normal exposure to disciplinary policies," so that terms and conditions of employment changed; by contrast, suspension within application of reasonable disciplinary policies will not qualify as adverse action); Lore v. City of Syracuse, 670 F.3d 127, 170–71, 114 FEP 466 (2d Cir. 2012) (genuine dispute of material fact whether removal as spokesperson for police department was materially adverse employment action where transfer was objectively from elite position to one of less prestige with less opportunity for advancement);

[71]**[On page 2-21 of the Main Volume, in footnote 71, add the following after "Benuzzi v. Board of Educ.".]**

Fercello v. County of Ramsey, 612 F.3d 1069, 1079, 109 FEP 1516 (8th Cir. 2010) ("exclusion from workplace meetings and management email lists could be materially adverse employment action, particularly when those meetings or emails could contribute to an employee's professional advancement");

[71]**[On page 2-21 of the Main Volume, in footnote 71, add the following after "*cf.*".]**

Youssef, 687 F.3d at 402 (transfer of Egyptian-born counterintelligence officer with long history of outstanding work at supervisory level to nonsupervisory position analyzing documents, where he was supervised by lower-grade employees, was adverse action even though it involved no change in pay or grade); *Lore*, 670 F.3d 127, 171, 114 FEP 466 (retaliation) ("even though [plaintiff's] rank and salary were not reduced, a reasonable police officer could easily view the change from the position of public information officer in the office of the chief of police, to that of general factotum in that office and thence to equipment, patrol, and uniformed positions, as materially adverse changes"); Geleta v. Gray, 645 F.3d 408, 411, 112 FEP 981 (D.C. Cir. 2011) (retaliation) (lateral transfer involving no diminution in pay or benefits may qualify as adverse employment action if it "result[s] in materially adverse consequences affecting the terms, conditions, or privileges of the plaintiff's employment") (quotations omitted);

[73]**[On page 2-22 of the Main Volume, in footnote 73, add the following at the end of the footnote.]**

Cf. Khalik v. United Air Lines, 671 F.3d 1188, 1192, 114 FEP 500 (10th Cir. 2012) ("While the 12(b)(6) standard does not require that Plaintiff establish a prima facie case in her complaint, the elements of each alleged cause of action help to determine whether Plaintiff has set forth a plausible claim.").

[On page 2-22 of the Main Volume, replace the sentence that ends with footnote 76 with the following.]

Courts have read this language narrowly to extend the period of limitations only for unequal pay claims. Claims alleging discriminatory demotion or failure to promote—even if styled as pay discrimination claims—have not been afforded the extended limitations period.[2]

[77]**[On page 2-22 of the Main Volume, in footnote 77, add the following after "*See*".]**

Bone v. G4S Youth Serv., LLC, 686 F.3d 948, 955–56, 115 FEP 1077 (8th Cir. 2012) (summary judgment affirmed where white special education supervisor discharged for misconduct; young black alleged comparators who received progressive discipline not similar to plaintiff "in all relevant respects" where they had different immediate supervisors and did not engage in same conduct), *cert. denied*, 133 S. Ct. 1252 (2013); Barber v. C1 Truck Driver Training, LLC, 656 F.3d 782, 796–97, 113 FEP 507 (8th Cir. 2011) (plaintiff's

---

[2]*See* Almond v. Unified Sch. Dist. No. 501, 665 F.3d 1174, 1175, 113 FEP 1473 (10th Cir. 2011) (Lilly Ledbetter Fair Pay Act does not apply to discriminatory demotion claim), *cert. denied*, 133 S. Ct. 317, 116 FEP 224 (2012); Noel v. Boeing Co., 622 F.3d 266, 272–75, 110 FEP 609 (3d Cir. 2010) (Lilly Ledbetter Fair Pay Act does not apply to failure-to-promote claim). *But see* Groesch v. City of Springfield, 635 F.3d 1020, 1026–29, 111 FEP 1441 (7th Cir. 2011); (Lilly Ledbetter Fair Pay Act allows courts to apply paycheck accrual rule to § 1983 pay discrimination claims). For a discussion of the Lilly Ledbetter Fair Pay Act and its application, *see generally* Chapter 27 (Timeliness).

proposed comparators not "similarly situated in all relevant respects" where, among other things, they were accused of different types of misconduct);

[77]**[On page 2-22 of the Main Volume, in footnote 77, add the following after "*see also*".]**

Johnson v. Holder, 700 F.3d 979, 982, 116 FEP 821 (7th Cir. 2012) (summary judgment affirmed in race, sex, and age case; comparators not similarly situated because they did not share "a similar record of misconduct, performance, qualifications or disciplining supervisors such that their different treatment reflects a discriminatory intent on the part of the [employer]"); Harper v. C.R. England, Inc., 687 F.3d 297, 309–10, 115 FEP 290 (7th Cir. 2012) (affirming summary judgment in discharge case because comparators not similarly situated where they were not on probation for excessive absenteeism; similarly situated individuals need not be identical, but they must have dealt with same supervisor, been subjected to same standards, and engaged in similar conduct);

[78]**[On page 2-23 of the Main Volume, in footnote 78, add the following after "*See, e.g.,*".]**

Turner v. Kansas City S. Ry., 675 F.3d 887, 893, 114 FEP 1044 (5th Cir. 2012) (in work-rule violation case, plaintiff establishes prima facie case by showing that employees outside of plaintiff's protected class were treated differently under "nearly identical" circumstances; "nearly identical is not synonymous with identical"); Good v. University of Chi. Med. Ctr., 673 F.3d 670, 676–77, 114 FEP 903 (7th Cir. 2012) (white plaintiff discharged for misconduct similar to that for which three non-white employees were merely demoted; although three were comparable in all material respects, difference in treatment for comparators must lead "*directly* to the conclusion that an employer was illegally motivated, without reliance on speculation"; otherwise inference of reverse discrimination will not arise without some evidence of anti-white bias); Vaughn v. Woodforest Bank, 665 F.3d 632, 637, 114 FEP 118 (5th Cir. 2011) ("disparate treatment occurs where an employer treats one employee more harshly than other 'similarly situated' employees for nearly identical conduct");

[79]**[On page 2-23 of the Main Volume, in footnote 79, add the following after "*See, e.g.*,".]**

Coleman v. Donahoe, 667 F.3d 835, 846–47, 114 FEP 160 (7th Cir. 2012) ("so long as the distinctions between the plaintiff and the proposed comparators are not so significant that they render the comparison effectively useless, the similarly situated requirement is satisfied") (internal quotations omitted); Bobo v. United Parcel Serv., Inc., 665 F.3d 741, 751–53, 114 FEP 254 (6th Cir. 2012) ("similarly situated" standard does not require "exact correlation"; plaintiff had to show that he and his proposed comparators were similar in all relevant respects, that they engaged in acts of comparable seriousness but that comparators were treated more favorably); Rodgers v. White, 657 F.3d 511, 518, 520, 113 FEP 241 (7th Cir. 2011) (although employees of differing ranks usually make poor comparators because they commonly have different job duties or performance standards, supervisor may be similarly situated when he was disciplined by same superior as plaintiff and "except for missing a meeting, [the supervisor] engaged in the same alleged misconduct and committed the same purported recordkeeping mistakes and yet received only a demotion"); Pye v. Nu Aire, Inc., 641 F.3d 1011, 1019, 112 FEP 865 (8th Cir. 2011) (observing that Eighth Circuit "has two lines of cases" on similarly situated standard at prima facie stage, one setting "low threshold" and requiring only that employees are "involved in or accused of the same or similar conduct and are disciplined in different ways," and the other "more rigorously requir[ing] that the employees be similarly situated in all respects") (internal quotations omitted);

[80]**[On page 2-24 of the Main Volume, in footnote 80, add the following at the beginning of the footnote.]**

Luster v. Illinois Dep't of Corr., 652 F.3d 726, 730, 112 FEP 1321 (7th Cir. 2011) (courts "should apply a flexible and factual, commonsense approach" to similarly situated analysis, asking "whether the other employees' situations were similar enough to the plaintiff's that it is reasonable to infer . . . that the different treatment was a result of race or some other unlawful basis");

3. *Pleading Requirements*

[91]**[On page 2-26 of the Main Volume, in footnote 91, add the following at the end of the footnote.]**

See, e.g., Keys v. Humana, Inc., 684 F.3d 605, 609–10, 115 FEP 588 (6th Cir.) (affirming continued viability of *Swierkiewicz* after *Iqbal* and *Twombly*), *aff'd on other grounds*, 132 S. Ct. 1327, 18 WH Cases 2d 1537 (2012); Khalik v. United Air Lines, 671 F.3d 1188, 1191, 114 FEP 500 (10th Cir. 2012) (*Iqbal* and *Twombly* did not signal return to more stringent pre–Rule 8 pleading requirements). *But see* Starr v. Baca, 652 F.3d 1202, 1215 (9th Cir. 2011) (observing that *Iqbal* and *Twombly* appear to apply higher pleading standard than *Swierkiewicz*).

[93]**[On page 2-26 of the Main Volume, in footnote 93, add the following after "*see also*".]**

Morales-Cruz v. University of P.R., 676 F.3d 220, 225, 114 FEP 1185 (1st Cir. 2012) ("[t]o say that women, but not men, are expected to be forthcoming about the sexual foibles of others is sheer speculation—and speculation, unaccompanied by any factual predicate, is not sufficient to confer plausibility" under *Iqbal*); *Khalik*, 671 F.3d at 1193 (plaintiff's "general assertions of discrimination and retaliation, without any details whatsoever of events leading up to her termination, are insufficient to survive a motion to dismiss") (applying *Twombly/Iqbal*); Coleman v. Maryland Ct. of Appeals, 626 F.3d 187, 190–91, 110 FEP 1217 (4th Cir. 2010) (plaintiff failed to state Title VII claim where "complaint conclusorily allege[d] that [he] was terminated based on his race [but did] not assert facts establishing the plausibility of that allegation");

[94]**[On page 2-27 of the Main Volume, in footnote 94, add the following at the end of the footnote.]**

See, e.g., *Keys*, 684 F.3d at 610 (race discrimination complaint "allege[d] facts that easily state a plausible claim" where systemic race discrimination as well as several specific events were alleged and key supervisors were identified).

4. *Special Formulations*

a. *"Reverse Discrimination"*

[102]**[On page 2-28 of the Main Volume, in footnote 102, add the following after "*See*".]**

Romans v. Michigan Dep't of Human Servs., 668 F.3d 826, 837, 114 FEP 1404 (6th Cir. 2012) (in case involving majority plaintiff, plaintiff "must establish the first prong of a prima facie case by showing background circumstances to support the suspicion that the defendant is the unusual employer who discriminates against the majority"); Good v. University of Chi. Med. Ctr., 673 F.3d 670, 679, 114 FEP 903 (7th Cir. 2012) (plaintiff failed to present sufficient evidence of "fishy background circumstances" from which reasonable fact finder could conclude that her employer was motivated by race when it terminated [the] plaintiff instead of demoting her); Everett v. Cook Cnty., 655 F.3d 723, 730, 113 FEP 9 (7th Cir. 2011) (plaintiff failed to establish prima facie case of reverse discrimination because "she [did] not explain what evidence show[ed] background circumstances of discriminatory conduct");

[104]**[On page 2-29 of the Main Volume, in footnote 104, add the following after "*see also*".]**

Good, 673 F.3d at 679 ("Good has failed to present sufficient evidence of the first prong for this reverse race discrimination case: evidence of 'background circumstances' demonstrating that UCMC has 'reason or inclination to discriminate invidiously against whites,' or evidence that there is something 'fishy' about her termination") (internal citations omitted); *Romans*, 668 F.3d at 837 ("Plaintiff may show the necessary 'background circumstances' using 'evidence of [defendants'] unlawful consideration of race as a factor in hiring in the past [, which] justifies a suspicion that incidents of capricious discrimination against whites because of their race may be likely'") (internal citations omitted);

b. *Reductions in Force*

[107]**[On page 2-29 of the Main Volume, in footnote 107, add the following at the beginning of the footnote.]**

Griffin v. Finkbeiner, 689 F.3d 584, 590, 115 FEP 1422 (6th Cir. 2012) (although African-American employee was terminated ostensibly because of RIF, white employee assumed his former duties six to eight months later);

[108]**[On page 2-30 of the Main Volume, in footnote 108, add the following at the beginning of the footnote.]**

Schechner v. KPIX-TV, 686 F.3d 1018, 1025, 115 FEP 307 (9th Cir. 2012) (statistical analyses "showing stark age disparities between the on-air talent who were retained and those who were laid off" was "sufficient to carry [plaintiffs'] minimal burden at step one of the *McDonnell Douglas* framework"); Gerner v. County of Chesterfield, 674 F.3d 264, 267–69, 114 FEP 976 (4th Cir. 2012) (former female human resources manager stated claim of disparate treatment where she received severance package less favorable than that offered to males in similar positions);

[109]**[On page 2-30 of the Main Volume, in footnote 109, add the following at the beginning of the footnote.]**

Lefevers v. GAF Fiberglass Corp., 667 F.3d 721, 724–25, 114 FEP 385 (6th Cir. 2012) (plaintiff terminated as part of RIF did not present direct evidence of discrimination when he identified general statements about age and retirement by non–decision makers and failed to present evidence that decision maker considered age in terminating him);

[On page 2-30 of the Main Volume, in the sentence that ends with footnote 110, delete the period after "age discrimination" and add the following.]

or discrimination on another prohibited basis.

d. Gender Stereotyping

[113]**[On page 2-32 of the Main Volume, in the carryover of footnote 113, add the following at the end of the footnote.]**

But cf. Morales-Cruz v. University of P.R., 676 F.3d 220, 225, 114 FEP 1185 (1st Cir. 2012) (plaintiff failed to establish that she was unfairly terminated because her employer expected her, "as a woman," to report illicit student–teacher relationship based on "the supposed stereotype of which the plaintiff complain[ed] not one that, by common knowledge or widely shared perception, is understood to be attributable to women").

[On page 2-32 of the Main Volume, after the sentence that ends with footnote 116, add the following new paragraph.]

Although courts have been reluctant to apply the theory of gender stereotyping to same-sex harassment,[3] at least one court applied the theory to transgendered individuals alleging discrimination based on gender nonconformity.[4]

B. The Employer's Burden of Producing Evidence of a Legitimate, Nondiscriminatory Reason

[137]**[On page 2-38 of the Main Volume, in footnote 137, add the following after "*E.g.*,".]**

Turner v. Kansas City S. Ry., 675 F.3d 887, 902–04, 114 FEP 1044 (5th Cir. 2012) (defendant employer failed to meet its burden of producing legitimate, nondiscriminatory reason for dismissals at issue, because its evidence was not sufficiently detailed or specific and because articulated reason was not made at "moment" by decision maker);

[144]**[On page 2-39 of the Main Volume, in footnote 144, add the following after "*See, e.g.*,".]**

Tucker v. Fulton Cnty., 470 F. A'ppx 832, 835 (11th Cir. 2012) (employer's honest but mistaken belief that employee's pay raise request was based on his qualifications rather than on his expanded job duties was legitimate, nondiscriminatory reason for denying pay raise request);

[158]**[On page 2-43 of the Main Volume, in footnote 158, add the following after "*See, e.g.*,".]**

Lucas v. Attorney Gen., 467 F. App'x 854, 858–59 (11th Cir. 2012) (subjective promotion criteria was not evidence of discrimination

---

[3]*See, e.g.*, Dawson v. Entek Int'l, 630 F.3d 928, 937–38, 111 FEP 306 (9th Cir. 2011) (dismissing harassment claim where homosexual male "presented no evidence that he failed to conform to a gender stereotype"). *But see* EEOC v. Boh Bros. Constr. Co., LLC, 731 F.3d 444, 456, 120 FEP 15 (5th Cir. 2013) (evidence warranted assertion that sex-stereotyping demonstrated that same-sex discrimination occurred "because of sex" in violation of Title VII).

[4]*See* Glenn v. Brumby, 663 F.3d 1312, 1316–20, 113 FEP 1543 (11th Cir. 2011) ("all persons, whether transgender or not, are protected from discrimination on the basis of gender stereotype") (internal citations omitted).

because employer used reasonably specific factual basis for its subjective opinions);

[162]**[On page 2-45 of the Main Volume, in footnote 162, add the following after "*See, e.g.*,".]**

Wilcher v. Postmaster Gen., 441 F. App'x 879, 881 (3d Cir. 2011) (internal investigation revealed that plaintiff committed time and attendance fraud);

[164]**[On page 2-46 of the Main Volume, in footnote 164, add the following after "*See, e.g.*,".]**

Duffy v. Belk, Inc., 477 F. App'x 91, 95 (4th Cir. 2012) (consolidation of plaintiff's position as part of companywide RIF resulted in his termination; employee retained was better suited for consolidated position because of her experience with marketing strategies that would enhance company's direct-mail marketing);

[168]**[On page 2-48 of the Main Volume, in footnote 168, add the following at the beginning of the footnote.]**

Whitby v. Secretary for Dep't of Homeland Security, 480 F. App'x 960, 964 (11th Cir. 2012) (plaintiff failed each section of structured interview assessment given to candidates eligible for promotion to Bomb Appraisal Officer position; plaintiff produced no evidence that his failing scores "were contrived in an effort to deny him the position or that other candidates did not have to go through the same interview process");

[169]**[On page 2-48 of the Main Volume, in footnote 169, add the following after "*See, e.g.*,".]**

Martinez v. W.W. Grainger, Inc., 664 F.3d 225, 230, 114 FEP 98 (8th Cir. 2011) (plaintiff discharged because of problematic managerial style);

[172]**[On page 2-49 of the Main Volume, in footnote 172, add the following after "*See, e.g.*,".]**

Tusing v. Des Moines Indep. Cmty. Sch. Dist., 639 F.3d 507, 515–16, 111 FEP 1761 (8th Cir. 2011) (plaintiff not hired for school counselor position because she was not licensed as counselor, either permanently or conditionally);

[172]**[On page 2-50 of the Main Volume, in carryover of footnote 172, add the following at the end of the footnote.]**

Cf. Zeinali v. Raytheon Co., 636 F.3d 544, 554–55, 111 FEP 1681 (9th Cir. 2011) (Iranian-born plaintiff discharged from engineering position for revocation of his security clearance established triable issue of pretext under California law where he showed retention of two non-Iranian engineers whose security clearances were denied and where company's articulated distinction between revocation and denial of clearance was unpersuasive).

C. Evidence Concerning Pretext

1. Pretext in General

[179]**[On page 2-51 of the Main Volume, in footnote 179, add the following after "*see also*".]**

Coleman v. Donahoe, 667 F.3d 835, 858, 114 FEP 160 (7th Cir. 2012) ("where the plaintiff argues that an employer's discipline is meted out in an uneven manner, the similarly-situated inquiry dovetails with the pretext question"; evidence that the employer selectively enforced a policy goes to both damages and liability);

[203]**[On page 2-60 of the Main Volume, in footnote 203, add the following after "*See*".]**

Benuzzi v. Board of Educ. of Chi., 647 F.3d 652, 663, 112 FEP 1444 (7th Cir. 2011) (to show pretext, plaintiff must show not only that employer's stated reasons for suspending her were dishonest or phony, but also that true reason was based on prohibited discriminatory animus); Loudermilk v. Best Pallet Co., 636 F.3d 312, 315, 111 FEP 865 (7th Cir. 2011) ("an evaluation of context is essential to determine whether an employer's explanation is fishy enough to support an inference that the real reason must be discriminatory");

[210]**[On page 2-62 of the Main Volume, in footnote 210, add the following after "*See*".]**

Hamilton v. Southland Christian Sch., Inc., 680 F.3d 1316, 1320, 114 FEP 1633 (11th Cir. 2012) (summary judgment for employer reversed; material issues of fact existed as to whether teacher was fired because of her pregnancy or because she had premarital sex; after plaintiff told principal of her pregnancy, he expressed concerns about plaintiff's request for maternity leave and told her of need to go on leave for the year, because finding replacement during school year was "hard to do"); Brooks v. Davey Tree Expert Co., 478 F. App'x 934, 943–44 (6th Cir. 2012) (multiple age-based remarks made by manager, such as calling plaintiff "old fart" and telling plaintiff that he was "too old to do his work anymore," was evidence of pretext and supported reversal of summary judgment); Colbert v. Tapella, 649 F.3d 756, 760, 112 FEP 884 (D.C. Cir. 2011) (summary judgment reversed where employer lied about plaintiff's nonselection and had apparent lack of knowledge about his qualifications, and where there was evidence that employer's hiring and promotion practices favored nonminorities);

[211]**[On page 2-63 of the Main Volume, in footnote 211, add the following after "*See, e.g.*,".]**

Ross v. Jefferson Cnty. Dep't of Health, 701 F.3d 655, 661, 27 AD 1 (11th Cir. 2012) (summary judgment properly granted in race discrimination action where plaintiff admitted in deposition that her race was not factor in her termination); Johnson v. Holder, 700 F.3d 979, 982, 116 FEP 821 (7th Cir. 2012) (summary judgment affirmed in race, sex, and age case where comparators did not share "a similar record of misconduct, performance, qualifications or disciplining supervisors such that their different treatment reflects a discriminatory intent on the part of the [employer]"); Pulczinski v. Trinity Structural Towers, Inc., 691 F.3d 996, 1002–03, 26 AD 1293 (8th Cir. 2012) (summary judgment affirmed where employer reasonably believed that plaintiff was organizing his crew to refuse to work overtime; distinction exists between "mistaken" reason and "false" one; scope of employer's investigation held to be valid business judgment not subject to review); Silverman v. Board of Educ. of Chi., 637 F.3d 729, 737–38, 111 FEP 1461 (7th Cir. 2011) (summary judgment affirmed; one probationary teacher had to be dismissed and plaintiff was selected for dismissal based on principal's negative evaluations of her teaching skills; plaintiff's disagreement with those evaluations did not create material issue of fact regarding honesty of evaluations or principal's reliance on them); Vatel v. Alliance of Auto. Mfrs., 627 F.3d 1245, 1247–48, 111 FEP 389 (D.C. Cir. 2011) (summary judgment affirmed against African-American female fired for her working style; "evidence overwhelmingly show[ed] that [the decision maker] honestly and reasonably believed that their working styles were incompatible");

2. *Biased Comments—Evidence of Pretext or "Stray Remarks"*

[218]**[On page 2-65 of the Main Volume, in footnote 218, add the following before "Rothman v. Emory Univ.".]**

Chattman v. TohoTenax Am., Inc., 686 F.3d 339, 347, 115 FEP 845 (6th Cir. 2012) (repeated racist comments by human resources director alone constituted direct evidence of discriminatory intent; "The statements are particularly troubling because they include both racist language and the threat or suggestion of violence or death based on race.");

[219]**[On page 2-65 of the Main Volume, in footnote 219, add the following before "Diaz v. Kraft Foods Global, Inc.".]**

Ondricko v. MGM Grand Detroit, LLC, 689 F.3d 642, 650, 115 FEP 1300 (6th Cir. 2012) (white female floor supervisor discharged allegedly for work rule violation; decision maker stated that because African-American female floor supervisor discharged for comparable violation had complained of race discrimination he had no choice but to fire white female; "[d]o you think I wanted to fire [the plaintiff], I didn't want to fire [her, but] how could I keep the White girl?");

[222]**[On page 2-69 of the Main Volume, in footnote 222, add the following after "*See, e.g.,*".]**

Griffin v. Finkbeiner, 689 F.3d 584, 596, 115 FEP 1422 (6th Cir. 2012) ("In certain circumstances, even statements by a non-decisionmaker can be probative of discrimination, such as when the speaker holds a management position, the statements are commonplace or made in a relevant context (such as a meeting in which personnel decisions are made) or where other evidence of animus exist.");

[227]**[On page 2-71 of the Main Volume, in footnote 227, add the following after "*See, e.g.,*".]**

Hampton v. Vilsack, 685 F.3d 1096, 1102, 115 FEP 854 (D.C. Cir. 2012) (plaintiff terminated for expense fraud; although racially biased supervisor initiated investigation into plaintiff's expenses, plaintiff's termination resulted "for reasons unrelated to the supervisor's original biased action"); Romans v. Michigan Dep't of Human Servs., 668 F.3d 826, 836, 114 FEP 1404 (6th Cir. 2012) (terminated white employee failed to establish race discrimination claim through direct evidence because, even if investigator's report falsely accusing him of racially motivated harassment directly evinced racial animus, plaintiff did not show that investigator's intent to discriminate could be imputed to ultimate decision maker in plaintiff's termination under "cat's paw" theory);

[236]**[On page 2-75 of the Main Volume, in footnote 236, add the following after "*see also*".]**

Chattman v. Toho Tenax Am., Inc., 686 F.3d 339, 351–53, 115 FEP 845 (6th Cir. 2012) (under *Staub*, plaintiff established requisites for imputing racially biased motive by human resources manager to decision makers in recommending discharge of African-American employee for horseplay via "cat's paw" theory; further investigation by upper management did not necessarily dispel liability); Hicks v. Forest Preserve Dist., 677 F.3d 781, 789–90, 114 FEP 1281 (7th Cir. 2012) (employee established "cat's paw" liability through testimony that lower-level supervisor who recommended terminations said that plaintiffs needed to be fired because they had filed charges of discrimination against him, and upper-level decision makers relied on supervisor's reports);

[239]**[On page 2-75 of the Main Volume, in footnote 239, add the following after "*See, e.g.*,".]**

Alvarez v. Royal Atl. Developers, Inc., 610 F.3d 1253, 1268, 109 FEP 1162 (11th Cir. 2010) (isolated remark that "Cubans are dumb," not made by one of decision makers, was insufficient to establish genuine issue of material fact regarding pretext); Wagoner v. Pfizer, Inc., 391 F. App'x 701, 707–08 (10th Cir. 2010) (in age discrimination action, stray remarks and "isolated or ambiguous comments" are too abstract to support finding of discrimination; manager's comments regarding plaintiff's "adult learning style" and preference to "hire his own reps" held to be too abstract to establish pretext);

[240]**[On page 2-76 of the Main Volume, in footnote 240, add the following after "*See, e.g.*,".]**

Worthy v. Michigan Bell Tel. Co., 472 F. App'x 342, 346–49 (6th Cir. 2012) (three-year difference between comment referring to plaintiff as "boy" and adverse employment decision made comment insufficient to show pretext in race discrimination case);

4. *Comparative Evidence*

[255][On page 2-81 of the Main Volume, in footnote 255, add the following after "*E.g.*,".]

Turner v. Kansas City S. Ry., 675 F.3d 887, 895–99, 114 FEP 1044 (5th Cir. 2012) (genuine issue of material fact created by disparity in discipline given to white and African-American employees for nearly identical infractions); Coleman v. Donahoe, 667 F.3d 835, 847–49, 114 FEP 160 (7th Cir. 2012) (plaintiff similarly situated to two non–protected-class co-workers who were disciplined by same decision maker, subjected to same standards of conduct, and violated same rule; plaintiff alone was terminated, in contrast to non–protected-class employees who were suspended);

[255][On page 2-81 of the Main Volume, in footnote 255, add the following before "Gorzynski v. JetBlue Airways Corp.".]

Hawn v. Executive Jet Mgmt., Inc., 615 F.3d 1151, 1160–61, 109 FEP 1824 (9th Cir. 2010);

[257][On page 2-83 of the Main Volume, in footnote 257, add the following after "*See, e.g.*,".]

Torgerson v. City of Rochester, 643 F.3d 1031, 1051, 112 FEP 613 (8th Cir.) (en banc) (plaintiffs have "burden to prove that they and [comparators] were similarly situated in all relevant respects—a rigorous standard at the pretext stage") (internal quotation marks omitted), *cert. denied*, 132 S. Ct. 513, 113 FEP 1152 (2011);

[258][On page 2-83 of the Main Volume, in footnote 258, add the following after "*See, e.g.*,".]

Turner, 675 F.3d at 893 (comparator's situation need be only "nearly identical," not "identical," to plaintiff's); Smith v. Lockheed-Martin Corp., 644 F.3d 1321, 1326 n.17, 12 FEP 1119 (11th Cir. 2011) ("[t]o be an adequate comparator, the preferentially treated individual from outside the plaintiff's protected class has to be similarly situated to the plaintiff in all relevant respects"); *Coleman*, 667 F.3d at 846 ("[s]o long as the distinctions between the plaintiff and the proposed comparators are not so significant that they render the comparison effectively useless, the similarly-situated requirement is satisfied") (internal quotation marks omitted); Silverman v. Board of Educ. of Chi., 637 F.3d 729, 742, 11 FEP 1461 (7th Cir. 2011) (although similarly situated inquiry is flexible one, "the comparators must be similar enough that any differences in their treatment cannot be attributed to other variables," such as positions, performance, or supervisors);

[259]**[On page 2-84 of the Main Volume, in footnote 259, add the following after "*See*".]**

Davis v. Jefferson Hosp. Ass'n, 685 F.3d 675, 681–82, 115 FEP 705 (8th Cir. 2012) (black cardiologist who had hospital privileges revoked because of staff abuse, poor patient care, and failure to maintain proper medical records not similarly situated to white comparators who also behaved inappropriately toward staff, absent evidence that they also provided poor patient care or kept insufficient medical records); Harris v. Warrick Cnty. Sheriff's Dep't, 666 F.3d 444, 449, 114 FEP 266 (7th Cir. 2012) (deputy fired for insubordination and lack of job commitment not similarly situated to deputies who made errors but did not disobey direct orders or manifest cavalier attitude toward job); Amini v. City of Minneapolis, 643 F.3d 1068, 1076, 112 FEP 1089 (8th Cir. 2011) (plaintiff not similarly situated to other candidates for peace-officer job where background interview revealed that plaintiff alone was argumentative and defensive and there was no evidence that City overlooked temperaments of other candidates), *cert. denied*, 132 S. Ct. 1144 (2012); *Silverman*, 637 F.3d at 742–43 (plaintiff rated "satisfactory" in performance review not similarly situated to putative comparator rated "superior," absent evidence that evaluations were biased); *Hawn*, 615 F.3d at 1160 (pilots terminated for engaging in unwelcome conduct toward flight attendants not similarly situated to those flight attendants where pilots' conduct gave rise to complaint of sexual harassment and conduct of putative comparators did not result in complaint and was not subject to comment until pilots were terminated);

[262]**[On page 2-85 of the Main Volume, in footnote 262, add the following after "*See, e.g.*,".]**

Bobo v. United Parcel Serv., Inc., 665 F.3d 741, 751, 114 FEP 254 (6th Cir. 2012) (plaintiff need show "only that he and his proposed comparators were similar in all relevant respects and that he and his proposed comparators engaged in acts of comparable seriousness") (citation omitted); Coleman v. Donahoe, 667 F.3d 835, 841, 114 FEP 160 (7th Cir. 2012) ("the proposed comparator must be similar enough to permit a reasonable juror to infer, in light of all the circumstances, that an impermissible animus motivated the employer's decision"); Barber v. C1 Truck Driver Training, LLC, 656 F.3d 782, 797, 113 FEP 507 (8th Cir. 2011) ("[t]o allow an inference of discrimination, the misconduct must be of comparable seriousness and the employees must be similarly situated in all relevant respects"); *Amini*, 643 F.3d at 1076 (plaintiff must "show that he and the other candidates are similarly situated in all relevant respects") (internal quotation marks omitted); Hawn v. Executive Jet Mgmt., Inc., 615 F.3d 1151, 1157, 109 FEP 1824 (9th Cir. 2010) ("whether employees are similarly situated—i.e., whether they are similar in all material respects—is a fact-intensive inquiry, and what facts are material will vary depending on the case") (citation and internal quotation marks omitted);

[267]**[On page 2-87 of the Main Volume, in footnote 267, add the following before "Porter v. Shah".]**

Hamilton v. Geithner, 666 F.3d 1344, 1352–55, 114 FEP 239 (D.C. Cir. 2012) (employee presented genuine dispute of material fact regarding pretext in 2003 promotion decision, including evidence that: employee possessed superior qualifications for Safety Manager position to those of successful candidate; plaintiff had MA in public health, with specialty in occupational health and 19 years of experience as industrial hygienist, in contrast to successful candidate, who had no college degree and 8 years of experience; and plaintiff had wide-ranging experience in developing safety policies as opposed to "thin" actual experience of successful candidate in developing and implementing programs);

5. *Statistics*

[271]**[On page 2-88 of the Main Volume, in footnote 271, add the following after "*see, e.g.,*".]**

Acevedo-Parrilla v. Novartis Ex-Lax, Inc., 696 F.3d 128, 146, 116 FEP 289 (1st Cir. 2012) ("[A]fter 2003—the year in which [the decision maker] became Site Leader—the company hired approximately 140 employees, 114 of whom were less than forty years of age. In the same period, Ex-Lax only fired 17 employees, 15 of whom were older than forty.");

[272]**[On page 2-88 of the Main Volume, in footnote 272, add the following after "*See, e.g.*,".]**

Norman-Nunnery v. Madison Area Tech. Coll., 625 F.3d 422, 432, 110 FEP 1121 (7th Cir. 2010) ("statistical data, although relevant, cannot alone meet the 'more likely than not' standard for a specific hiring decision about an individual");

[276]**[On page 2-91 of the Main Volume, in footnote 276, add the following after "*See*".]**

Schechner v. KPIX-TV, 686 F.3d 1018, 1023, 115 FEP 307 (9th Cir. 2012) ("a plaintiff's statistical evidence need not necessarily account for an employer's proffered non-discriminatory reason for the adverse employment action to make a prima facie case of discrimination");

6. Strength of the Employer's Explanation

[279]**[On page 2-92 of the Main Volume, in footnote 279, add the following after "*See, e.g.*,".]**

Kragor v. Takeda Pharms. Am., Inc., 702 F.3d 1304, 1311, 116 FEP 1483 (11th Cir. 2012) ("When the employer's actual decisionmaker, after terminating an employee for misconduct (or the appearance of misconduct), says without qualification that the employee is exceptional, did nothing wrong, did everything right, and should not have been fired, that contradiction—when combined with a prima facie case—is enough to create a jury question on the ultimate issue of discrimination.");

[280]**[On page 2-93 of the Main Volume, in footnote 280, add the following after "*See, e.g.*,".]**

Carter v. Pathfinder Energy Servs., Inc., 662 F.3d 1134, 1149, 114 FEP 927 (8th Cir.) (reasonable jury could find that written reprimands did not undermine employee's argument that he was fired because of his employer's desire to no longer provide him with reasonable accommodations), *cert. denied*, 2012 U.S. LEXIS 6289 (Oct. 1, 2012);

[280]**[On page 2-93 of the Main Volume, in footnote 280, add the following before "Forrester v. Rauland-Borg Corp.".]**

Silverman v. Board of Educ. of Chi., 637 F.3d 729, 739, 111 FEP 1461 (7th Cir. 2011) (negative evaluation could not have demonstrated antipregnancy bias because supervisor did not know of plaintiff's pregnancy at time of evaluation);

b. Multiple Explanations by the Employer

[287]**[On page 2-95 of the Main Volume, in footnote 287, add the following after "*See, e.g.*,".]**

Twigg v. Hawker Beechcraft Corp., 659 F.3d 987, 1002, 113 FEP 938 (10th Cir. 2011) ("inconsistency in evidence [of pretext] is only helpful to a plaintiff if the employer has changed its explanation under circumstances that suggest dishonesty or bad faith") (internal quotations omitted); Wierman v. Casey's Gen. Stores, Inc., 638 F.3d 984, 996, 111 FEP 1547 (8th Cir. 2011) (discrepancy in documented reasons for plaintiff's termination immaterial where underlying reason remains consistent);

c. Role of Employer's "Honest Belief"

[295]**[On page 2-98 of the Main Volume, in footnote 295, add the following at the end of the footnote.]**

But see Coleman v. Donahoe, 667 F.3d 835, 855, 114 FEP 160 (7th Cir. 2012) (employer terminated African-American female plaintiff after 32 years for telling her psychiatrist that she had thoughts of killing her supervisor; as to pretext, court doubted that statements made to plaintiff's psychiatrist in private therapy constituted true threat and evidence showed that plaintiff's manager did not enforce company rule against threats evenhandedly; within week of plaintiff's termination, same manager only suspended two white male employees who threatened another employee at knife-point).

[296]**[On page 2-98 of the Main Volume, in footnote 296, add the following after "*See, e.g.*,".]**

Pulczinski v. Trinity Structural Towers, Inc., 691 F.3d 996, 1002–03, 19 WH Cases 2d 1017 (8th Cir. 2012) (honest belief that plaintiff was organizing his crew to refuse overtime did not constitute pretext even if belief was mistaken or based on incomplete investigation); Silverman v. Board of Educ. of Chi., 637 F.3d 729, 744, 111 FEP

1461 (7th Cir. 2011) (no pretext exists when employer honestly believes proffered reason);

7. *Other Evidence*

[302][On page 2-100 of the Main Volume, in footnote 302, add the following after "*See, e.g.*,".]

Hamilton v. Geithner, 666 F.3d 1344, 1355–57, 114 FEP 239 (D.C. Cir. 2012) (employee presented genuine dispute of material fact regarding pretext in 2003 promotion decision, including: record that agency used highly subjective and unsubstantiated basis to support decision not to promote employee; absence of contemporaneous documentation of Secretary's proffered explanation for decision; and other procedural irregularities in selection process, e.g., page missing from notes of panelist who reviewed candidates); Jajeh v. County of Cook, 678 F.3d 560, 572–73, 114 FEP 1441 (7th Cir. 2012) (failure to follow established seniority procedures in determining layoffs not probative of discriminatory intent toward individual employee when 200 other employees were laid off under same irregular procedure); Twigg v. Hawker Beechcraft Corp., 659 F.3d 987, 1002–03, 113 FEP 938 (10th Cir. 2011) ("Although [t]his court recognizes that disturbing procedural irregularities, including deviations from normal company procedure, provide support for a plaintiff's assertion of pretext, such irregularities do not directly demonstrate an employer's retaliatory motive. Deviation evidence can do no more than permit[ ] a reasonable inference that [the employer] acted with an ulterior motive and . . . engineered and manufactured the reasons [it] proffered for terminating [the employee's] employment, thereby suggesting retaliation only indirectly.") (citations and internal quotation marks omitted; brackets in original);

[304][On page 2-101 of the Main Volume, in footnote 304, add the following after "*See, e.g.*,".]

Acevedo-Parrilla v. Novartis Ex-Lax, Inc., 696 F.3d 128, 141–42, 116 FEP 289 (1st Cir. 2012) (evidence of pretext included record that employee: had 21-year positive history with company; had already addressed alleged 2004 performance issues raised by his 2005 Performance Improvement Plan (PIP), which could not be used in support of his termination because he successfully completed PIP; and received "Fully Met Expectations" performance ratings in 2005 for which he was awarded performance bonus by same supervisor who fired him in 2006);

D. The Order of Proof

[306][On page 2-102 of the Main Volume, in footnote 306, add the following at the beginning of the footnote.]

Sisk v. Picture People, Inc., 669 F.3d 896, 900, 18 WH Cases 2d 1313 (8th Cir. 2012) ("The district court should not have stated that the prima facie case is not relevant once an FMLA retaliation case goes to trial. The evidence produced—not the stage of proceeding—determines the burden on the plaintiff. Because Picture People did not offer a non-discriminatory reason for its alleged act, the proper inquiry for the district court—even at trial—was whether Sisk's evidence was sufficient to establish a prima facie case."); Holland v. Gee, 677 F.3d 1047, 1056, 114 FEP 1449 (11th Cir. 2012) ("[a]fter a trial on the merits, [we] should not revisit whether the plaintiff established a prima facie case") (brackets in original); Henry v. Wyeth Pharm., Inc., 616 F.3d 134, 154, 109 FEP 1618 (2d Cir. 2010) (courts should not uncritically import burden-shifting framework into jury instructions, because framework is "at best irrelevant, and at worst misleading to a jury"), *cert. denied*, 131 S. Ct. 1602, 111 FEP 1184 (2011);

E. Instructing the Jury

[317][On page 2-105 of the Main Volume, in footnote 317, add the following at the beginning of the footnote.]

Henry v. Wyeth Pharm., Inc., 616 F.3d 134, 154, 109 FEP 1618 (2d Cir. 2010) (courts should not "uncritically import" burden-shifting framework into jury instructions, because framework was developed for use by judges and is "at best irrelevant, and at worst misleading to a jury"), *cert. denied*, 131 S. Ct. 1602, 111 FEP 1184 (2011);

[323][On page 2-105 of the Main Volume, in footnote 323, add the following after "*see also*".]

Rapold v. Baxter Int'l, Inc., 718 F.3d 602, 611–12, 117 FEP 129 (7th Cir.) (district court properly denied requested mixed-motive instruction where each party asserted single motive for challenged action), *cert. denied,* 2013 U.S. LEXIS 7852 (Nov. 4, 2013); Ponce

v. Billington, 679 F.3d 840, 846–47, 115 FEP 1 (D.C. Cir. 2012) (district court did not err in failing to give mixed-motive instruction where plaintiff argued only "but for" causation; jury was improperly instructed that plaintiff must prove that discrimination "was the sole reason" for adverse action but because "sole reason" was defined in "but for" terms, any error was harmless);

[On page 2-106 of the Main Volume, add the following after the sentence that ends with footnote 327.]

In *Nassar v. University of Texas Southwestern Medical Center*,[5] the Supreme Court applied the reasoning of *Gross* to Title VII retaliation claims, holding that "traditional principles of but-for causation" apply to such claims.[6] "This requires proof that the unlawful retaliation would not have occurred in the absence of the alleged wrongful action or actions of the employer."[7] Mixed-motive analysis thus has no place in retaliation cases since *Nassar*.

F. Proof of Disparate Treatment Through Direct Evidence

[330]**[On page 2-107 of the Main Volume, in footnote 330, add the following after "*See*".]**

Holland v. Gee, 677 F.3d 1047, 1059, 114 FEP 1449 (11th Cir. 2012) (supervisor's decision to give female employee lighter assignment because of her pregnancy is direct evidence of intent; fact that it was benignly intended is "beside the point");

[331]**[On page 2-108 of the Main Volume, in footnote 331, add the following after "*See, e.g.*,".]**

Acevedo-Parrilla v. Novartis Ex-Lax, Inc., 696 F.3d 128, 146, 116 FEP 289 (1st Cir. 2012) (manager testified that, when site leader arrived in unit in 2003, he declared that he wanted to develop plan to get rid of employees near retirement age); Dixon v. Hallmark Cos., 627 F.3d 849, 853, 110 FEP 1675 (11th Cir. 2010) (supervisor's comments to employee on termination—"You're fired, too. You're too religious."—constituted direct evidence of discrimination precluding summary judgment);

---

[5]133 S. Ct. 2517, 118 FEP 1504 (2013).
[6]*Id.* at 2527–30, 2533.
[7]*Id.* at 2533.

G. Proof of Disparate Treatment in Mixed-Motive Cases

[344][On page 2-112 of the Main Volume, in footnote 344, add the following at the beginning of the footnote.]

See, e.g., Ponce v. Billington, 679 F.3d 840, 846, 115 FEP 1 (D.C. Cir. 2012) (plaintiff may prevail in mixed-motive case without showing that unlawful discrimination was sole or "but for" motive for employment action;" "a motivating factor test" (applicable in mixed-motive cases) is "less significant than either a sole or but-for cause");

[On page 2-112 of the Main Volume, after the last sentence in the carryover paragraph, add the following.]

Nor do plaintiffs in retaliation cases have the option of proving their cases under the mixed-motive framework.[8]

III. DISPARATE TREATMENT CLASS ACTIONS AND PATTERN-OR-PRACTICE CASES

[365][On page 2-115 of the Main Volume, in footnote 365, add the following after "*with*".]

Chin v. Port Auth. of N.Y. & N.J., 685 F.3d 135, 149, 115 FEP 720 (2d Cir. 2012) (pattern-or-practice theory inapplicable in individual disparate treatment case),

[370][On page 2-116 of the Main Volume, in footnote 370, add the following before "Morgan v. United Parcel Serv., Inc.".]

Artis v. Bernanke, 630 F.3d 1031, 1035, 111 FEP 300 (D.C. Cir. 2011) ("[u]nlike an allegation of overt harassment or a specific instance of retaliation against an individual employee, class-wide claims of systemically depressed salaries, performance ratings, advancement opportunities, and the like can often be proven only by a statistical comparison of the employer's treatment of the class to its treatment of non-minority employees");

---

[8] *See* Nassar v. University of Tex. Sw. Med. Ctr., 133 S. Ct. 2517, 2527–30, 2533, 118 FEP 1504 (2013).

[371]**[On page 2-116 of the Main Volume, in footnote 371, add the following after "*see also*".]**

Aliotta v. Bair, 614 F.3d 556, 562, 109 FEP 1701 (D.C. Cir. 2010) ("[s]tatistical evidence may suffice to establish a prima facie case if the disparities in treatment are significant");

[374]**[On page 2-117 of the Main Volume, in footnote 374, add the following before "*Robinson*".]**

Aliotta, 614 F.3d at 565 ("FDIC's alternative statistical analysis demonstrated class members' statistics could not support an inference of discrimination");

[375]**[On page 2-117 of the Main Volume, in footnote 375, add the following at the end of the footnote.]**

See also Aliotta, 614 F.3d at 564–65 (employer presented evidence of business necessity of RIF, making it less likely that RIF was motivated by ageism).

CHAPTER 3

DISPARATE IMPACT

I. The Theory

[4]**[On page 3-2 of the Main Volume, in footnote 4, replace the citation following "*see, e.g.*," with the following.]**

Local 189, United Papermakers & Paperworkers v. United States, 416 F.2d 980, 1 FEP 875 (5th Cir. 1969)

[7]**[On page 3-3 of the Main Volume, in footnote 7, add the following after "*See, e.g.*,".]**

Watson v. Fort Worth Bank & Trust, 487 U.S. 977, 47 FEP 102 (1988) (discussing disparate impact theory in context of individual case of race discrimination);

[15]**[On page 3-4 of the Main Volume, in footnote 15, add the following after "*See, e.g.*,".]**

Wood v. City of San Diego, 678 F.3d 1075, 1082, 114 FEP 1552 (9th Cir. 2012) (although recognizing that plaintiff can pursue claim under both disparate impact and disparate treatment theories, affirming district court's dismissal without leave to amend where plaintiff failed to properly state either disparate impact or disparate treatment claim);

[On page 3-8 of the Main Volume, replace the first sentence of the first full paragraph with the following.]

The Supreme Court held that an employer may not be in violation of Title VII if it engages in disparate treatment against one group in order to avoid or remedy disparate impact against another group, but only if the employer has a strong basis in evidence to believe that it will be subject to liability if it fails to engage in such race-conscious decision making.[1]

[30]**[On page 3-8 of the Main Volume, in footnote 30, add the following at the end of the footnote.]**

See also United States v. Brennan, 650 F.3d 65, 124–25, 112 FEP 193 (2d Cir. 2011) (school board liable for "reverse" discrimination

---

[1]*Id.* at 585 ("before an employer can engage in intentional discrimination for the asserted purpose of avoiding or remedying an unintentional disparate impact, the employer must have a strong basis in evidence to believe it will be subject to disparate-impact liability if it fails to take the race-conscious, discriminatory action").

where it failed to prove it had strong basis in evidence that it would be subject to disparate impact liability under Title VII before it provided retroactive seniority to Hispanic, African-American, Asian, and female custodial employees in order to remedy past discrimination in its testing and recruiting practices).

[On page 3-8 of the Main Volume, after the sentence that ends with footnote 30, add the following new paragraphs.]

The Second Circuit considered the implications of the Supreme Court's *Ricci* holding in *Briscoe v. City of New Haven*,[2] in which an African-American firefighter alleged that the weighting of factors in the promotional examinations administered pursuant to the collective bargaining agreement had a significant disparate impact on minorities. He claimed that this disparate impact violated Title VII because the examination was neither job-related nor justified by business necessity. The City attempted to defend based on the converse of the *Ricci* holding, maintaining that an employer may defeat a disparate impact claim if it has a strong basis in evidence that it otherwise would have been subject to disparate treatment liability.[3]

The Second Circuit rejected the City's argument, reasoning that it directly contradicted both *Ricci*'s limiting language and the longstanding, fundamental principles of Title VII law.[4] Expressing sympathy for the plight of employers caught between potential disparate impact liability and potential disparate treatment liability, the court outlined procedural mechanisms that could prevent employers from facing burdensome litigation on multiple fronts.[5]

---

[2]654 F.3d 200, 112 FEP 1793 (2d Cir. 2011) (citing dicta in *Ricci*), *cert. denied*, 132 S. Ct. 2741, 115 FEP 352 (2012).

[3]*Id.* at 205–06.

[4]*Id.*

[5]*Id.* at 209; *accord* N.A.A.C.P. v. North Hudson Reg'l Fire & Rescue, 665 F.3d 464, 479, 113 FEP 1633 (3d Cir. 2011) (municipality's residency requirement for firefighter positions caused disparate impact by excluding well-qualified African Americans who would otherwise be eligible; disparate impact was not justified by any business necessity, and municipality had no basis for believing that it would be liable to Hispanic resident candidates under disparate-treatment theory if it eliminated residency requirement), *cert. denied*, 132 S. Ct. 2749, 115 FEP 352 (2012).

II. Historical Development and Statutory Authority

A. Title VII

[On page 3-11 of the Main Volume, in the first paragraph, move the sentence following footnote 46 to the beginning of the second paragraph.]

[On page 3-11 of the Main Volume, in the second paragraph, replace the previously first sentence but now the second sentence of the paragraph with the following.]

The 1991 Act confirmed the general rule announced in *Ward's Cove*—that plaintiffs' causation burden generally requires plaintiffs to identify the specific policy or practice resulting in the disparity.

B. The Age Discrimination in Employment Act

[On page 3-14 of the Main Volume, in the last line on the page, delete "ADA" and replace it with "ADEA".]

[70]**[On page 3-15 of the Main Volume, in footnote 70, add the following before "*see also*".]**

Bondurant v. Air Line Pilots Ass'n, Int'l, 679 F.3d 386, 396, 114 FEP 1645 (6th Cir. 2012) (cutoff date adopted by union in which to distribute claim shares was based on RFOAs, precluding disparate impact ADEA claims);

III. Order and Burdens of Proof in Title VII Disparate Impact Cases

A. The Plaintiff's Prima Facie Case

[80]**[On page 3-17 of the Main Volume, in footnote 80, add the following after "*See*".]**

Apsley v. Boeing Co., 691 F.3d 1184, 1199 (10th Cir. 2012) (statistical evidence that employer's predecessor discriminated against older employees in deciding whom to retain and whom to terminate, although statistically significant, was insufficient where, because of sample size, disparities lacked practical significance);

[80]**[On page 3-17 of the Main Volume, in footnote 80, add the following before "*See generally*".]**

See also Young v. Covington & Burling, LLP, 846 F. Supp. 2d 141, 159–60, 114 FEP 876 (D.D.C. 2012) (non-probative statistical evidence comparing law firm's African-American staff attorneys to its associate attorneys failed to support allegation that policy of refusing to promote staff attorneys to associate positions had adverse impact; candidates for associate positions were hired on criteria not applicable to staff attorneys, including legal research and writing abilities, and other statistical evidence also failed to establish causal connection between promotion policy and disparity between percentage of African-American and white lawyers employed as partners, counsel, or associates).

[81]**[On page 3-17 of the Main Volume, in footnote 81, add the following after "*But see*".]**

Aliotta v. Bair, 614 F.3d 556, 566, 109 FEP 1701 (D.C. Cir. 2010) (statistics related to group of employees who had voluntarily accepted buyout and suffered no adverse employment action did not constitute relevant evidence of discrimination in ADEA class action absent evidence that employer's buyout was motivated by desire to rid company of older employees);

[83]**[On page 3-18 of the Main Volume, replace footnote 83 with the following.]**

[83]*See, e.g.*, Adams v. City of Chi., 469 F.3d 609, 611, 99 FEP 327 (7th Cir. 2006) (plaintiffs unable to meet their burden of showing that there was alternative method of evaluation that was valid and that employer had opportunity to adopt it); Gulino v. New York State Educ. Dep't, 460 F.3d 361, 383, 103 FEP 1381 (2d Cir. 2006) (employer had shown that its tests were job-related); Electrical Workers (IBEW) Local 605 v. Mississippi Power & Light Co., 442 F.3d 313, 319, 97 FEP 1501 (5th Cir. 2006) (employer did not have burden of demonstrating alternative business practice evidence).

[84]**[On page 3-18 of the Main Volume, in footnote 84, delete the first citation after "*See*" and add the following.]**

Bennett v. Nucor Corp., 656 F.3d 802, 820, 113 FEP 616 (8th Cir. 2011) (African-American employees' statistical evidence was inadequate to demonstrate that employer's promotion practices had disparate impact on them; employees' expert failed to identify any specific employment practices responsible for alleged disparate impact, and statistical evidence assumed that all applicants were qualified for promotion to each available position, rather than including only individuals who were at least minimally qualified for promotions in question); Carpenter v. Boeing, Inc., 456 F.3d 1183, 1194, 98 FEP 1763 (10th Cir. 2006) (to make out prima facie case, plaintiffs needed to compare statistics of promotions of qualified males to those of qualified females, rather than merely comparing promotional rates between males and females in general);

[114]**[On page 3-25 of the Main Volume, in footnote 114, add the following at the end of the footnote.]**

See also Apsley v. Boeing Co., 691 F.3d 1184, 1199 (10th Cir. 2012) (statistical evidence that employer's predecessor discriminated against older employees in deciding whom to retain and whom to let go, although statistically significant, was insufficient where, because of sample size, disparities lacked practical significance).

[116]**[On page 3-25 of the Main Volume, in footnote 116, replace the citation for "Apsley v. Boeing Co." with the following.]**

Apsley, 691 F.3d at 1199.

2. The Appropriate Method of Comparison

a. The Relevant Labor Market

[122]**[On page 3-27 of the Main Volume, in footnote 122, add the following after "*accord*".]**

Meditz v. City of Newark, 658 F.3d 364, 374, 113 FEP 727 (3d Cir. 2011) (statistical analysis is required to include calculation of standard deviation between qualified minorities employed by City and number of qualified minorities in relevant labor market, rather than subjective view of relative percentages);

B. Business Necessity and Job-Relatedness

[173][On page 3-39 of the Main Volume, in footnote 173, add the following at the end of the footnote.]

See also Meditz v. City of Newark, 658 F.3d 364, 374, 113 FEP 727 (3d Cir. 2011) (correct standard for business necessity defense is whether hiring criteria effectively measured minimum qualifications for successful job performance; district court applied wrong standard by focusing on only whether business justifications had any connection to disputed hiring policy, without taking into consideration plaintiff's ability to perform job in question).

CHAPTER 4

APPLICATION OF DISPARATE IMPACT TO EMPLOYMENT DECISIONS

I. SCORED TESTS

A. Overview

[On page 4-6 of the Main Volume, replace the sentence that ends with footnote 11 with the following, retaining the footnote 11.]

Plaintiffs retain the burden of proving sufficient disparate impact and, where business necessity has been proved, most courts have held that plaintiffs have the burden of demonstrating the existence of a valid and effective alternative that is less adverse.[11]

C. ADA Coverage

[33][On page 4-11 of the Main Volume, in footnote 33, add the following at the end of the footnote.]

and 29 C.F.R. § 1630.10 (2012).

D. The Uniform Guidelines on Employee Selection Procedures

2. Basic Provisions of the Uniform Guidelines

[58][On page 4-15 of the Main Volume, in footnote 58, add the following after "*See*".]

M.O.C.H.A. Soc'y, Inc. v. City of Buffalo, 689 F.3d 263, 281, 115 FEP 929 (2d Cir. 2012) (employees' challenge to test's construct validity was not fatal to employer's defense, where district court had found test to be content valid; "content validation does not require [a] predictive validation study");

3. The Weight to Be Accorded the Uniform Guidelines

[84][On page 4-20 of the Main Volume, in footnote 84, add the following after "*See, e.g.*,".]

M.O.C.H.A. Soc'y, Inc. v. City of Buffalo, 689 F.3d 263, 274, 115 FEP 929 (2d Cir. 2012) (district court properly deferred to Uniform Guidelines' "80-percent rule" in finding that plaintiff met prima facie burden);

E. Allocation of Proof in Scored Test Cases

3. Validation Methodologies

c. Content Validation

[178][On page 4-38 of the Main Volume, in footnote 178, add the following at the end of the footnote.]

Id.; *see also* M.O.C.H.A. Soc'y, Inc. v. City of Buffalo, 689 F.3d 263, 281, 115 FEP 929 (2d Cir. 2012) (employees' challenge to test's construct validity was not fatal to employer's defense, where district court had found test to be content valid; "content validation does not require [a] predictive validation study").

4. *Differential, Single-Group, and Situational Validity*

[239]**[On page 4-49 of the Main Volume, in footnote 239, add the following at the end of the footnote.]**

See also M.O.C.H.A. Soc'y, Inc. v. City of Buffalo, 689 F.3d 263, 267, 115 FEP 929 (2d Cir. 2012) (district court found sufficient evidence that fire lieutenants across state and nation performed similar critical tasks and required same critical skills, and therefore that defendant established that its fire lieutenant selection methods were consistent with business necessity).

5. *Validity Problems in the Application of Scored Tests*

a. *Rank-Ordering*

[260]**[On page 4-53 of the Main Volume, in footnote 260, add the following at the end of the footnote.]**

In *Briscoe v. City of New Haven*, 654 F.3d 200, 205, 112 FEP 1793 (2d Cir. 2011), the Second Circuit dealt with the aftermath of the *Ricci* decision. After the lower court entered judgment for the City, an African-American firefighter filed suit challenging the subsequent decision by the City to utilize the promotional lists created by using the exam scores. The district court dismissed the plaintiff's claims, citing the following language from the Supreme Court in *Ricci*: "If, after it certifies the test results, the City faces a disparate-impact suit, then in light of our holding today it should be clear that the City would avoid disparate-impact liability based on the strong basis in evidence that, had it not certified the results, it would have been subject to disparate-treatment liability." 654 F.3d at 205 (quoting *Ricci*, 129 S. Ct. at 2681). The Second Circuit rejected the view of some commentators that this language may constitute a new affirmative defense, under which the employer could presumably certify and utilize the test results, notwithstanding the disparate impact, because failing to do so would subject it to liability. "[W]e see no way to reconcile the dicta, on which the city's argument relies, with either the Court's actual holding in *Ricci* or long-standing, fundamental principles of Title VII law." *Briscoe*, 654 F.3d at 206.

[On page 4-53 of the Main Volume, after the sentence that ends with footnote 260, add the following new paragraph.]

In two consolidated "reverse" discrimination cases, incumbent New York City Department of Education employees challenged a settlement agreement regarding the use of civil service examinations.[1] The Second Circuit, concluding that part of the settlement agreement violated Title VII, provided insight on what constitutes a "strong basis in evidence" under *Ricci*. The court concluded that the standard is objective, not subjective, focusing on the strength of the evidence of liability rather than the fear of litigation, and the evidence's strength is evaluated at the time the employer made the challenged decision.[2] Further, there needs to be a "strong basis in evidence" that either: (1) the employer's procedures are not job related, or (2) the employer refused to adopt a known less-adverse alternative.[3] Even after an employer has a "strong basis in evidence" that it faces disparate impact liability, it does not have "carte blanche to take whatever race- or gender-conscious actions it pleases."[4]

II. NON-SCORED OBJECTIVE CRITERIA

E. Other Objective Criteria

3. *Residency Requirements*

[415][On page 4-82 of the Main Volume, in footnote 415, add the following at the end of the footnote.]

See also NAACP v. North Hudson Reg'l Fire & Rescue, 665 F.3d 464, 479–80, 113 FEP 1633 (3d Cir. 2011) (entire state deemed appropriate relevant labor market, based on average commute times and fact that individuals in protective service positions tend to seek positions statewide); Meditz v. City of Newark, 658 F.3d 364, 373 & n.16, 113 FEP 727 (3d Cir. 2011) (fact that nearly 10% of the non-uniformed workforce, through various exemptions, resided outside city limits "strongly suggests that the relevant labor market is not limited to the City of Newark"; district court instructed to consider

---

[1]United States v. Brennan, 650 F.3d 65, 112 FEP 193 (2d Cir. 2011).
[2]*Id.* at 110–11.
[3]*Id.* at 112.
[4]*Id.* at 113–14.

relevant factors such as geographic location, availability of transportation facilities, locations from which employers draw their workforces, and commuting patterns).

[416]**[On page 4-82 of the Main Volume, in footnote 416, add the following at the end of the footnote.]**

See also North Hudson Reg'l Fire & Rescue, 665 F.3d at 477 (rejecting argument that municipal residency requirement was needed to improve response times or facilitate bilingual force; because hired firefighters not required to remain in area, less than 40% of force could meet residency requirements, and there was no objective evidence that requirement increased level of Spanish-speaking firefighters).

III. SUBJECTIVE CRITERIA

A. The Theory

[On page 4-85 of the Main Volume, at the end of the carryover paragraph, add new footnote 427a.]

[427a]*Id. But see* McReynolds v. Merrill Lynch, Pierce, Fenner & Smith, Inc., 672 F.3d 482, 489–91, 114 FEP 710 (7th Cir. 2012) (granting class certification in disparate impact case challenging companywide policies granting brokers broad discretion to form partnership teams and to distribute accounts based on past success).

CHAPTER 5

FAILURE TO PROVIDE A REASONABLE ACCOMODATION

II. ACCOMMODATING RELIGION

[6]**[On page 5-2 of the Main Volume, in footnote 6, add the following after "*see also*".]**

Harrell v. Donahue, 638 F.3d 975, 978–90, 111 FEP 1559 (8th Cir. 2011) (post office was not required to accommodate religious beliefs of postal carrier who was Seventh-day Adventist by permitting him to have every Saturday off to observe Sabbath, where granting him leave or adjusting his schedule would have required employer to violate collective bargaining agreement and effectively violate office's longstanding seniority system);

[8]**[On page 5-3 of the Main Volume, in footnote 8, add the following at the end of the footnote.]**

See also Sánchez-Rodríguez v. AT&T Mobility P.R., Inc., 673 F.3d 1, 12, 114 FEP 912 (1st Cir. 2012) (employer does not have to accept employee's choice of religious accommodation, but employer must participate in interactive discussion with employee to determine reasonable accommodation); Walden v. Centers for Disease Control & Prevention, 669 F.3d 1277, 1294, 114 FEP 454 (11th Cir.

2012) (emphasizing employee's obligation to make good faith effort to participate in interactive accommodation process).

[On page 5-3 of the Main Volume, in the first full paragraph after the fourth sentence ending with "the uniform policy.", add new footnote 10a.]

[10a]*See also* EEOC v. GEO Grp., Inc., 616 F.3d 265, 273–75, 109 FEP 1653 (3d Cir. 2010) (prison warden did not violate duty to reasonably accommodate employees' religious beliefs when he refused to exempt them from prison's dress policy, which precluded wearing head coverings (such as Muslim khimar) at work, where khimar posed security risk because it could be used to smuggle contraband into prison, obscured employee's face, could possibly be used as weapon, and impeded prison's ability to monitor personnel by security camera movement about facility) (citing *Webb*).

III. ACCOMMODATING DISABILITY

[On page 5-5 of the Main Volume, at the end of the first sentence in the first full paragraph, add new footnote 20a after "... Title VII.".]

[20a]*See, e.g.*, Valle-Arce v. Puerto Rico Ports Auth., 651 F.3d 190, 200–01, 24 AD 1547 (1st Cir. 2011) (employee provided sufficient evidence that her employer's unreasonable delay in reasonably accommodating her disability constituted failure to provide such accommodations and that she should have been permitted to proceed to jury).

[On page 5-5 of the Main Volume, after the sentence that ends with footnote 21, add the following new paragraph.]

Courts have disagreed on whether an employer must restructure an individual's work schedule to accommodate his or her disability.[1] The EEOC's position is that allowing an employee to work

[1]*Compare* Regan v. Faurecia Auto. Seating, Inc., 679 F.3d 475, 480, 114 FEP 1651 (6th Cir. 2012) (ADA does not require employer to accommodate employee's request for schedule adjustment so that she may have less difficult, non-rush hour commute), *with* Colwell v. Rite Aid Corp., 602 F.3d 495, 506, 22 AD 1857 (3d Cir. 2010) (ADA contemplates that employers may need to make reasonable shift changes in order to accommodate disabled employee's disability-related difficulties in getting to work), Miller v. Illinois Dep't of Transp., 643 F.3d 190, 199, 24 AD 1025 (7th Cir. 2011)

a modified schedule is a reasonable accommodation in the absence of undue hardship.[2]

[24][On page 5-6 of the Main Volume, in footnote 24, add the following after "*cf.*".]

Jones v. Walgreen Co., 679 F.3d 9, 20, 26 AD 261 (1st Cir. 2012) (employee asserting ADA claim has burden of proffering accommodations that are reasonable under circumstances);

[30][On page 5-7 of the Main Volume, in footnote 30, add the following at the end of the footnote.]

See, e.g., Jones v. Walgreen Co., 679 F.3d 9, 20, 26 AD 261 (1st Cir. 2012) (employee asserting ADA claim has burden to proffer accommodations that are reasonable under circumstances); EEOC v. Sears, Roebuck & Co., 417 F.3d 789, 803–04, 16 AD 1761 (7th Cir. 2005) (initial notice need not be detailed or specific: "[w]here notice is ambiguous as to the precise nature of the disability or the desired accommodation, it is sufficient to notify the employer that the employee may have a disability that requires accommodation, ... the employer must ask for clarification"); Gile v. United Airlines, Inc., 213 F.3d 365, 373, 10 AD 968 (7th Cir. 2000) (employer's duty extends to affirmative obligation to seek out employee and work with him or her to craft reasonable accommodation); Bultemeyer v. Fort Wayne Cmty. Sch., 100 F.3d 1281, 1285, 6 AD 67 (7th Cir. 1996) (employee need not use word "accommodation" or any other "magic words" when making request); Beck v. University of Wis. Bd. of Regents,

---

(term "reasonable accommodation" may include job restructuring; part-time or modified work schedules; reassignment to vacant position; acquisition or modification of equipment or devices; appropriate adjustment or modifications of examinations, training materials, or policies; provision of qualified readers or interpreters; and other similar accommodations for individuals with disabilities), *and* Carter v. Pathfinder Energy Servs., Inc., 662 F.3d 1134, 1145–47, 25 AD 679 (10th Cir. 2011) (permitting employee to work part-time may be reasonable accommodation where full-time attendance is not essential element of job and employee is able to perform those functions that are essential while working part-time).

[2]*See* EEOC, *Enforcement Guidance: Reasonable Accommodation and Undue Hardship Under the Americans with Disabilities Act*, No. 915.002 (Oct. 17, 2002), *available at* http://www.eeoc.gov/policy/docs/accommodation.html ("A modified schedule may involve adjusting arrival or departure times, providing periodic breaks, altering when certain functions are performed, allowing an employee to use accrued paid leave, or providing additional unpaid leave. An employer must provide a modified or part-time schedule when required as a reasonable accommodation, absent undue hardship, even if it does not provide such schedules for other employees.").

75 F.3d 1130, 1135–36, 5 AD 304 (7th Cir. 1996) (court should attempt to isolate cause of breakdown in interactive process and then assign responsibility accordingly). *But see* Zivkovic v. Southern Cal. Edison Co., 302 F.3d 1080, 1089, 13 AD 882 (9th Cir. 2002) ("employee bears the burden of proving the existence of specific reasonable accommodations that the employer failed to provide").

[31]**[On page 5-7 of the Main Volume, in footnote 31, add the following after "*see also*".]**

Griffin v. United Parcel Serv., Inc., 661 F.3d 216, 224, 25 AD 551 (5th Cir. 2011) ("an employer cannot be found to have violated the ADA when responsibility for the breakdown of the 'informal, interactive process' is traceable to the employee and not the employer"; Act "provides a right to a reasonable accommodation, not to the employee's preferred accommodation") (citations omitted);

CHAPTER 6

RACE AND COLOR

I. DISCRIMINATION BASED ON COLOR

[On pages 6-1 to 6-2 of the Main Volume, delete the carryover sentence that ends with footnote 4 and also delete footnote 4.]

[On page 6-2 of the Main Volume, before the first full paragraph, add the following new paragraph.]

The EEOC and the courts often conflate race and color discrimination,[1] but the two concepts are distinct.[2] Color discrimination can be intra-racial as well as across racial lines.[3] For example, color discrimination claims have been asserted by Hispanic

---

[1]*See, e.g.*, Hansborough v. City of Elkhart Parks & Recreation Dep't, 802 F. Supp. 199, 207 (N.D. Ind. 1992) ("[Title VII] only addresses discrimination on the basis of race, sex, religion, and national origin. . . ."). A number of commentators have advocated (from varying perspectives) that the distinctions between race and color discrimination need to be made clear, because the two address different types of discrimination and color discrimination is increasing and largely unaddressed in the workplace. *See, e.g.*, T. McCray, *Coloring Inside the Lines: Finding a Solution for Workplace Colorism Claims*, 30 LAW & INEQ. 149 (Winter 2012); E. Schaerer, *Intragroup Discrimination in the Workplace: The Case for "Race Plus,"* 45 HARV. C.R.-C.L. L. REV. 57 (Winter 2010); C.E. Nance, *Colorable Claims: The Continuing Significance of Color Under Title VII Forty Years After its Passage*, 26 BERKELEY J. EMP. & LAB. L. 435, 453 (2005); D.W. Greene, *Title VII: What's Hair (and Other Race-Based Characteristics) Got to Do With It?*, 79 COLO. L. REV. 1355 (2008). For an example of a court ignoring such distinctions, see *Hill v. Mississippi State Emp't Serv.*, 91 F.2d 1233, 1240–41, 54 FEP 997 (5th Cir. 1990) (rejecting district court's reasoning that "blacks never discriminate against other blacks").

[2]Over time, plaintiffs have increasingly asserted claims of color discrimination based on the light or dark tone of their skin. *See* Press Release, Equal Employment Opportunity Commission, EEOC Settles Color Harassment Lawsuit with Applebee's Neighborhood Bar and Grill (Aug. 7, 2003), 2003 WL 23823560 ("Color bias filings have increased by over 200% since the mid-1990s from 413 in Fiscal Year 1994 to 1,382 in FY 2002.").

[3]*See* Williams v. Wendler, 530 F.3d 584, 587 (7th Cir. 2008) (noting that "[l]ight-skinned blacks sometimes discriminate against dark-skinned blacks, and vice versa, and either form of discrimination is literally color discrimination," but finding no suggestion of such discrimination in that case); Santiago v. Stryker Corp., 10 F. Supp. 2d 93, 96 (D.P.R. 1998) (finding that plaintiff established prima facie case of color discrimination where he was harassed by lighter-skinned Puerto Rican supervisor and also replaced by someone with lighter skin; "[c]olor may be a rare claim, because color is usually mixed with or subordinated to claims of race discrimination, but considering the mixture of races and ancestral national origins in Puerto Rico, color may be the most practical claim to present"). Commentators also have noted intra-racial discrimination among segments of the Mexican and Asian communities. *See* Nance, 26 BERKELEY J. EMP. & LAB. L. at 453, 456 (describing color as markers of social distinction or acceptance in some Asian cultures); McCray, 30 LAW & INEQ. at 154–55 (noting "[f]or those of Mexican descent, color stratification is as much a part of their existence as it is for Blacks," and highlighting history of color discrimination in certain segments of Asian

employees separate and distinct from any claims of national origin discrimination.[4]

[5][On page 6-2 of the Main Volume, in footnote 5, add the following at the beginning of the footnote.]

713 F. Supp. 403, 408, 55 FEP 1859 (N.D. Ga. 1989) (light-colored black plaintiff who had been terminated by her dark-skinned supervisor stated Title VII claim for color discrimination sufficient to survive summary judgment); *see also* Carmona Rios v. Aramark Corp., 139 F. Supp. 2d 210, 224 (D.P.R. 2001) (citing *Walker* for proposition that Title VII authorizes intra-racial color discrimination claims); Franchesci v. Hyatt Corp., 782 F. Supp. 712, 723 (D.P.R. 1992) (same). The plaintiff in *Walker* ultimately lost her case at trial, where the court held that she was terminated because of a personality conflict rather than color discrimination. *See*

[On page 6-2 of the Main Volume, delete the sentence that ends with footnote 6 and also delete footnote 6.]

III. Discrimination Based on Race-Linked Characteristics

[On page 6-5 of the Main Volume, replace the period at the end of the second full paragraph with a comma; after footnote 26, add the following.]

or to engage in disparate treatment in order to achieve racial balancing.[5]

---

community). There is a dearth of reported decisions on point and the few reported decisions are generally at the district court level.

[4]*See, e.g.*, *Santiago*, 10 F. Supp. 2d at 96 (color discrimination claim of darker-skinned Puerto Rican related to alleged harassment by his lighter-skinned Puerto Rican supervisor).

[5]*See* Ondricko v. MGM Grand Detroit, LLC, 689 F.3d 642, 650, 115 FEP 1300 (6th Cir. 2012) (Caucasian plaintiff was unlawfully terminated as means of racial balancing after African-American casino employee alleged that she was victim of disparate treatment when she was terminated for "bad shuffle" at blackjack table and plaintiff was not; supervisor's comment "How can I keep the white girl!" was based on allegations of disparate treatment, suggesting that plaintiff's termination was motivated by employer's "desire to be racially balanced in its terminations for conduct related to shuffling").

IV. DISCRIMINATION BASED ON GROOMING AND CULTURAL IDENTIFICATION

[On page 6-5 of the Main Volume, at the end of the last sentence in the first full paragraph, add new footnote 27a.]

[27a]Courts have held that Title VII's prohibitions refer to immutable characteristics, such as skin color, as opposed to mutable characteristics that may be associated with a particular race, national origin, or color. *See, e.g.*, Eastman v. United Parcel Serv., 194 F. Supp. 2d 256, 262, 268 (S.D.N.Y. 2000) (African-American employee with dreadlocks brought Title VII action against former employer alleging race and religious discrimination in connection with employer's appearance policy, which required all of its drivers with "unconventional hairstyles" to wear hats; policy was not discriminatory on either basis where plaintiff's decision to wear dreadlocks was personal choice rather than religious mandate); Rogers v. American Airlines, Inc., 527 F. Supp. 2d 229, 232 (S.D.N.Y. 1981) ("An all-braided hair style is an 'easily changed characteristic,' and even if socioculturally associated with a particular race or nationality, is not an impermissible basis for distinctions in the application of employment policies by an employer.").

[On page 6-5 of the Main Volume, delete the sentence that ends with footnote 28 and also delete footnote 28.]

V. ASSOCIATION DISCRIMINATION

[On page 6-8 of the Main Volume, after the carryover sentence that ends with footnote 44, add the following.]

The showing required to establish retaliation is identical under § 1981 and Title VII.[6]

---

[6]*See* Twigg v. Hawker Beechcraft Corp., 659 F.3d 987, 998, 113 FEP 938 (10th Cir. 2011) (noting that nature of retaliation proofs under Title VII and § 1981 is the same, but finding that plaintiff failed to establish retaliation under "mixed motives framework" despite some indirect evidence of retaliation). *See generally* Chapter 15 (Retaliation), § VI.B.2. Subsequent to *Twigg*, the U.S. Supreme Court determined in *University of Tex. S.W. Med. Ctr. v. Nassar*, 133 S. Ct. 2517 (2013), that the mixed-motive framework does not apply to Title VII retaliation claims. Rather, such claims must be proven "according to traditional principles of but-for causation." *Id.* at 2533.

VI. Segregated Employment and Employment Facilities

[On page 6-9 of the Main Volume, delete the period after footnote 51 and add the following.]

or assigning caregivers to nursing home residents based on the residents' racial preferences.[7]

VII. Racial Harassment

[53]**[On page 6-9 of the Main Volume, in footnote 53, delete the period at the end of the footnote and add the following.]**

(discussing evidentiary requirements for Title VII sexual harassment hostile environment claims and noting that lower courts in sexual harassment cases "have properly drawn on standards developed in cases involving racial harassment").

[54]**[On page 6-9 of the Main Volume, in footnote 54, add the following after "*Sufficiently Severe or Pervasive: See*".]**

Chaney, 612 F.3d at 912 (over 3-month period, co-workers called plaintiff "black bitch" and "nigger" on multiple occasions, engaged in more subtle racial slights and comments after management was notified of harassment, and "[m]ost importantly, [plaintiff's employer] acted to foster or engender a racially-charged environment through its assignment sheet that unambiguously, and daily, reminded Chaney and her co-workers that certain residents preferred no black CNAs," and, based on such preferences, restricted plaintiff's access to those rooms and limited residents to whom she could provide care);

[54]**[On page 6-11 of the Main Volume, in the carryover for footnote 54, add the following after "*Not Sufficiently Severe or Pervasive: See*".]**

Ellis v. CCA of Tenn., LLC, 650 F.3d 640, 647–48, 112 FEP 791 (7th Cir. 2011) (offensive comments related to skin color, confederate

---

[7]Chaney v. Plainfield Healthcare Ctr., 612 F.3d 908, 912, 109 FEP 1377 (7th Cir. 2010) (unlawful to refuse to assign and to restrict room access of African-American certified nursing assistant (CNA) to meet preferences of residents who preferred "no black CNAs").

flag garb in workplace, and disparate discipline held not sufficiently severe or pervasive to support racial harassment claim);

[On page 6-13 of the Main Volume, in the sentence that ends with footnote 56, delete the comma after "redneck" and add the following]

or "monkey," or displays of confederate flags or garb in the workplace,

[56]**[On page 6-13 of the Main Volume, in footnote 56, add the following at the end of the footnote.]**

See also Jones v. UPS Ground Freight, 683 F.3d 1283, 1303–04, 115 FEP 278 (11th Cir. 2012) (calling plaintiff "monkey" or leaving banana peels on his car, and implied threats from co-workers who donned shirts or caps bearing confederate flags, could support claim of racial harassment). *But see Ellis*, 650 F.3d at 647–48 (finding employer's use of management book called "The One Minute Manager Meets the Monkey" not objectively offensive although plaintiffs subjectively found it to be so; two incidents of employee wearing confederate flag garb and calling person named Cole either "black ass coal" or "black as coal" were not sufficiently severe or pervasive to support racial harassment claim).

[On page 6-13 of the Main Volume, after the sentence that ends with footnote 59, add the following.]

Evidence of harassment or discrimination against non-party co-workers may be relevant to hostile environment claims, depending on the circumstances.[8]

---

[8]Bennett v. Nucor Corp., 656 F.3d 802, 810–11, 113 FEP 616 (8th Cir. 2011) (in hostile environment case, evidence of prior acts of discrimination against non-parties can be probative of type of workplace environment to which plaintiffs were subjected and of employer's knowledge and motives); Hernandez v. Valley View Hosp. Ass'n, 684 F.3d 950, 959, 115 FEP 592 (10th Cir. 2012) ("evidence of a general work atmosphere, including evidence of harassment of other racial minorities, may be considered in evaluating a [sex harassment] claim, as long as [the plaintiff] presents evidence that she knew about the offending behavior") (quoting Harris v. Forklift Sys., Inc., 510 U.S. 17, 23, 63 FEP 225 (1993)).

[65]**[On page 6-14 of the Main Volume, in footnote 65, add the following at the end of the footnote.]**

The U.S. Supreme Court defined who qualifies as a "supervisor" for purposes of a Title VII harassment claim in *Vance v. Ball State University*, 133 S. Ct. 2434, 2443–44, 118 FEP 1481 (2013).

CHAPTER 7

NATIONAL ORIGIN AND CITIZENSHIP

I. INTRODUCTION

[7][On page 7-5 of the Main Volume, in footnote 7, add the following after "*See*".]

Grigsby v. LaHood, 628 F.3d 354, 358–60, 110 FEP 1681 (7th Cir. 2010) (Native American development controller for Federal Aviation Administration (FAA) who was laid off at one facility and unsuccessfully sought positions at other facilities did not establish that he was denied those positions because of his national origin where those hired had certifications and experience that he did not); Chhim v. Spring Branch Indep. Sch. Dist., 396 F. App'x 73, 74, 110 FEP 629 (5th Cir. 2010) (refusal to hire individual of Cambodian descent for custodial supervisor position based on preference for capability in both Spanish and English did not constitute discrimination based on national origin);

[11][On page 7-6 of the Main Volume, in footnote 11, add the following after "*Compare*".]

Othman v. City of Country Club Hills, 671 F.3d 672, 675–77, 114 FEP 804 (8th Cir. 2012) (derogatory remarks of police department "background checker" did not establish that part-time police officer of Jordanian ancestry who was rejected by Police Chief for two full-time positions did not establish that his rejection was discriminatory because: (1) the allegedly biased Police Captain was not decision maker; (2) discriminatory animus not proximate cause of decision not to hire; and (3) plaintiff could not establish pretext as other candidates were similarly qualified, not less qualified),

[11]**[On page 7-6 of the Main Volume, in footnote 11, add the following after "*with*".]**

Gilbert v. Napolitano, 670 F.3d 258, 262, 114 FEP 923 (D.C. Cir. 2012) (reasonable jury could easily conclude that Mexican-American employee denied promotion was unlawfully discriminated against based on supervisor's testimony that plaintiff's qualification and experience "dwarfed" those of non-Hispanic person promoted to position),

[15]**[On page 7-7 of the Main Volume, in footnote 15, add the following after "*Compare*".]**

Dass v. Chicago Bd. of Educ., 675 F.3d 1060, 1071–72, 114 FEP 1288 (7th Cir. 2012) (nonrenewed teacher of Indian descent who presented circumstantial evidence that her nonrenewal was motivated by "mosaic" of discrimination, including remark by principal that she should look for job on the side of town where most Indian kids go, did not rebut undisputed evidence of her inability to control her classroom where evidence failed to "point directly to a discriminatory reason for the employer's action"), Guimaraes v. SuperValu, Inc., 674 F.3d 962, 973–74, 114 FEP 1032 (8th Cir. 2012) (green card is matter of citizenship or immigration status and is "facially neutral" as to national origin; thus, supervisor's comment to co-worker that she was trying to get plaintiff, individual of Brazilian nationality, fired and to stop her green card process did not establish that she was discharged from employment because of her Brazilian national origin), Naik v. Boehringer, 627 F.3d 596, 110 FEP 1443 (7th Cir. 2010) (individual of Indian origin who claimed that his termination was discriminatory did not establish prima facie case notwithstanding manager's questions about his experience as call representative in India where individual was terminated for falsifying his call logs), Alvarado-Santos v. Department of Health of Commonwealth of P.R., 619 F.3d 126, 132–33, 110 FEP 385 (1st Cir. 2010) (nonrenewal of Puerto Rican physician was not discriminatory, despite isolated comment made by plaintiff's Dominican manager that "Dominican doctors were better" than Puerto Rican doctors; comment failed to establish national origin discrimination where person who received position in lieu of plaintiff was also Puerto Rican), *cert. denied*, 132 S. Ct. 121 (2011), Alvarez v. Royal

Atl. Developers, Inc., 610 F.3d 1253, 1267–68, 109 FEP 1162 (11th Cir. 2010) (terminated Cuban-American failed to establish national origin discrimination based on non–decision maker's stray remark that "Cubans are dumb" and plaintiff's conclusory observation that Cubans were terminated at higher rate than other nationalities where employer's evidence demonstrated that plaintiff's supervisor found his performance substandard and that manager discharged employees equally regardless of their national origin),

[15][On page 7-8 of the Main Volume, in the carryover of footnote 15, add the following after "*with*".]

Zeinali v. Raytheon Co., 636 F.3d 544, 553, 111 FEP 1681 (9th Cir. 2011) (individual whose security clearance was not renewed raised triable issue of whether security clearance was bona fide job requirement for engineers where company retained number of non-Iranian engineers after their security clearances were revoked),

[16][On page 7-8 of the Main Volume, in footnote 16, add the following after "*Compare*".]

Hernandez v. Valley View Hosp. Ass'n, 684 F.3d 950, 958, 115 FEP 592 (10th Cir. 2012) (Mexican-American hospital employee presented sufficient evidence for jury to conclude that her workplace was permeated with severe and pervasive discriminatory intimidation, ridicule, and insult, including numerous racially insensitive and offensive comments, derogatory jokes about her Mexican heritage, and accusation that family member was murderer based solely on same surname),

[16][On page 7-9 of the Main Volume, in the carryover of footnote 16, add the following after "*with*".]

Hernandez v. Yellow Transp., 670 F.3d 644, 653–54, 114 FEP 545 (5th Cir. 2011) (evidence of harassment and cross-category discrimination toward African-American employees can support claims of hostile environment toward Hispanic employees in appropriate cases where there is sufficient correlation but not where, as here, evidence did not show frequent, severe, and pervasive hostility toward employees of different racial group, much less toward employees of plaintiff's race),

II. SOURCES OF PROTECTION

A. Title VII

1. Defining "National Origin"

[22]**[On page 7-11 of the Main Volume, in footnote 22, add the following after "*But cf.*".]**

Onyiah v. St. Cloud State Univ., 684 F.3d 711, 718–19, 115 FEP 582 (8th Cir. 2012) (court did not determine whether Title VII "national origin" included African tribal affiliation, but noted that Ninth Circuit has found that it does; Nigerian of Igbo descent claimed that university officials who were Nigerian of Yoruba descent discriminated against him in his compensation), *cert. denied*, 133 S. Ct. 1502 (2013); Cortezano v. Salin Bank & Trust Co., 680 F.3d 936, 939–40, 115 FEP 77 (7th Cir. 2012) (noting that, although Second, Sixth, and Eleventh Circuits have held that claim of race or national origin discrimination under Title VII based on race or ethnicity of individual's spouse is cognizable, Seventh Circuit has not decided issue; however, question was immaterial where employee was discharged because bank learned that she had joint bank account with her husband, who was undocumented alien, which is not protected status under Title VII);

[On page 7-12 of the Main Volume, in the first sentence of the first full paragraph, add new footnote 26a after "... recognized 'nation,' ...".]

[26a]*See, e.g.*, Vitalis v. Sun Constructors, Inc., 481 F. App'x 718, 721–22 (3d Cir. 2012) (unpublished) ("local Virgin Islanders" and "locals" did not constitute protected class based on their national origin where no evidence demonstrated that they shared "unique historical, political and/or social circumstance").

2. National Origin Versus Citizenship

a. Title VII's Coverage of Noncitizens

[On page 7-15 of the Main Volume, at the end of the third sentence in the second full paragraph, add new footnote 44a after "... on the basis of national origin.".]

[44a]*Cf.* Cortezano v. Salin Bank & Trust Co., 680 F.3d 936, 939–40, 115 FEP 77 (7th Cir. 2012) ("national origin discrimination as defined in Title VII encompasses discrimination based on one's ancestry, but not discrimination based on citizenship or immigration status").

B. The Fourteenth Amendment and the 1871 Civil Rights Act

[72][On page 7-21 of the Main Volume, in footnote 72, add the following at the end of the footnote.]

See also Van Staden v. St. Martin, 664 F.3d 56, 60–61 (5th Cir. 2011) (applying rational basis review and holding that rule of Louisiana State Board of Practical Nurse Examiners that allowed only "permanent residents" or "citizens" to obtain nursing license did not violate Equal Protection Clause of U.S. Constitution), *cert. denied*, 133 S. Ct. 110 (2012).

C. Section 1981 of the 1866 Civil Rights Act

[86][On page 7-23 of the Main Volume, in footnote 86, add the following at the end of the footnote.]

Cf. Udoewa v. Plus4 Credit Union, 457 F. App'x 391, 392 (5th Cir. 2012) (individual's national origin discrimination claim based solely on fact that he was born in Nigeria was not cognizable under § 1981).

[89][On page 7-24 of the Main Volume, in footnote 89, add the following after "*See*".]

Martinez v. W.W. Grainger, Inc., 664 F.3d 225, 230–31, 114 FEP 98 (8th Cir. 2011) (former employee established prima facie case under § 1981 by showing "that he is Hispanic and Cuban born," but ultimately could not demonstrate pretext for his termination);

[92][On page 7-24 of the Main Volume, in footnote 92, add the following after "*See, e.g.*,".]

Torgerson v. City of Rochester, 643 F.3d 1031, 1052, 112 FEP 613 (8th Cir. 2011) (en banc) (action under § 1981 based upon "Native American status" could have proceeded as race discrimination claim had that been alleged, but could not go forward as national origin claim because such claims are not cognizable under § 1981);

D. The Immigration Reform and Control Act of 1986

1. The IRCA's Antidiscrimination Provisions

[101][On page 7-26 of the Main Volume, in footnote 101, add the following at the end of the footnote.]

Cf. Zhang v. Office of Chief Admin. Hearing Officer, 441 F. App'x 524 (9th Cir. 2011) (dismissal of claim for national origin discrimination under IRCA affirmed where employer had sufficient number of employees to be covered by Title VII).

III. LANGUAGE AND ACCENT

A. Fluency Requirements

[137][On page 7-31 of the Main Volume, in footnote 137, replace "*E.g.*," with "*See*", and then insert the following.]

Chhim v. Spring Branch Indep. Sch. Dist., 396 F. App'x 73, 74, 110 FEP 629 (5th Cir. 2010) (unpublished) (refusal to hire applicant of Cambodian descent for custodial supervisor position does not constitute discrimination based on race or national origin where decision was based upon preference for capability in both Spanish and English);

C. Accents

[163][On page 7-37 of the Main Volume, in footnote 163, add the following after "*E.g.*,".]

Albert-Aluya v. Burlington Coat Factory Warehouse Corp., 470 F. App'x 847, 851 (11th Cir. 2012) (unpublished) (derogatory statements by individual's supervisor about her Nigerian ethnicity, her "thick African accent," "being too brash" and failing "to speak more like an American" were sufficient to demonstrate that employer's explanation for her termination was pretext);

[164][On page 7-37 of the Main Volume, in footnote 164, add the following after "*E.g.*,".]

Guimaraes v. SuperValu, Inc., 674 F.3d 962, 974, 114 FEP 1032 (8th Cir. 2012) (supervisor's practice of pretending not to understand employee from Brazil, constantly asking her to repeat herself, and requiring her to repeat directions verbatim did not mean, without more, that supervisor was mocking her accent and national origin because supervisor never referenced her accent, derisively or otherwise, and employee did not identify any other person who witnessed supervisor's behavior and believed that supervisor was mocking plaintiff's accent);

Chapter 8

NATIVE AMERICANS

I. Antidiscrimination Protection of Native Americans

[4]**[On page 8-2 of the Main Volume, in footnote 4, add the following at the end of the footnote.]**

But cf. Salt River Project Agric. & Power Dist. v. Lee, 672 F.3d 1176, 1180, 114 FEP 1068 (9th Cir. 2012) (Navajo Nation enjoys sovereign immunity but it is not party necessary to action for prospective injunctive relief prohibiting tribal officials from applying Navajo Labor Relations Act to employer who was not Native American and was doing business on reservation; tribal officials, who are not immune from suit, can adequately represent tribal interests and complete relief is available to employers).

III. LIABILITY OF INDIAN TRIBES

B. Exemption From Other Antidiscrimination Statutes

[66][On page 8-11 of the Main Volume, in footnote 66, add the following at the end of the footnote.]

See also Donovan v. Navajo Forest Prods. Indus., 692 F.2d 709 (10th Cir. 1982) (where Congress exempted other entities but did not mention Indian tribes, Occupational Safety and Health Act (OSHA), 29 U.S.C. § 651 et seq., is applicable to tribes; "a state cannot legislate an exemption from OSHA and neither can a tribe"). The holding in *Donovan* was also adopted in *Menominee Tribal Enterprises v. Solis*, 601 F.3d 669, 673 (7th Cir. 2010).

[77][On page 8-12 of the Main Volume, in footnote 77, add the following at the end of the footnote.]

See also Salt River Project Agric. & Power Dist. v. Lee, 672 F.3d 1176, 1180, 114 FEP 1068 (9th Cir. 2012) (Navajo Nation enjoys sovereign immunity but it is not party necessary to action for prospective injunctive relief prohibiting tribal officials from applying Navajo Labor Relations Act to employer who was not Native American and was doing business on reservation; tribal officials, who are not immune from suit, can adequately represent tribal interests and complete relief is available to employers).

[79][On page 8-13 of the Main Volume, in footnote 79, add the following at the end of the footnote.]

But see Becker v. Kikiktagruk Inupiat Corp., 488 F. App'x 227, 228–29, 115 FEP 772 (9th Cir. 2012) (individual who alleged that he was terminated in retaliation for his opposition to tribe's preference for hiring Alaskan natives may maintain action under § 1981 where he had good faith belief that practice was unlawful).

CHAPTER 9

RELIGION

II. What Is Protected as Religion?

A. Sincerely Held Religious Beliefs

[23][On page 9-5 of the Main Volume, in footnote 23, add the following at the end of the footnote.]

Cf. Walden v. Centers for Disease Control & Prevention, 669 F.3d 1277, 1286, 114 FEP 454 (11th Cir. 2012) (termination of counselor in agency's employee assistance program who asserted that her religious beliefs precluded her from advising homosexual employees did not constitute unlawful religious discrimination, where counselor was not removed from her position for failing to offer assistance to client who was in same-sex relationship, and sincerity of her beliefs was never questioned; rather, she was terminated because of her hostility and demeaning attitude while referring homosexual client to another counselor).

B. The Religious Freedom Restoration Act

[41][On page 9-8 of the Main Volume, in footnote 41, add the following after "*with*".]

Harrell v. Donahue, 638 F.3d 975, 979, 111 FEP 1559 (8th Cir. 2011) (federal employee discharged because of his objecting to working on Saturdays could not proceed with action under RFRA; Title VII provides exclusive remedy for federal employee claims of religious discrimination), *and*

III. THE EMPLOYER'S DUTY TO ACCOMMODATE

A. The Source of the Duty to Accommodate

[On page 9-9 of the Main Volume, at the end of the first sentence of the only paragraph in the section, delete the period and add the following after "to reasonably accommodate".]

an employee's "religious observance and practice, as well as belief, unless an employer demonstrates that he is unable to reasonably accommodate to an employee's or prospective employee's religious observance or practice without undue hardship on the conduct of the employer's business."

C. The Extent of the Duty to Accommodate

1. The Elements of Proof

[On page 9-11 of the Main Volume, after the sentence that ends with footnote 58, add the following.]

The Eleventh Circuit has taken a similar position.[1]

[59]**[On page 9-12 of the Main Volume, in footnote 59, add the following after "*See*".]**

Xodus v. Wackenhut Corp., 619 F.3d 683, 686–87, 110 FEP 1 (7th Cir. 2010) (job applicant did not adequately inform employer of his religious beliefs even though he told employer he would not cut his dreadlocks because it was "against [his] belief"; "employer is not charged with detailed knowledge of the beliefs and observances associated with particular sects") (quoting Reed v. Great Lakes Co., 330 F.3d 931, 936 (7th Cir. 2003));

---

[1]*See* Dixon v. Hallmark Cos., 627 F.3d 849, 855–56, 110 FEP 1675 (11th Cir. 2010) (jury could find that plaintiffs satisfied second element of their religious discrimination claim (i.e., that employer was aware of their religious beliefs) based on plaintiffs' previous opposition to company policy prohibiting displays of religious art and supervisor's awareness of tension between order to take down religious artwork and plaintiffs' religious beliefs and previous opposition to policy).

[59]**[On page 9-12 of the Main Volume, in footnote 59, add the following at the end of the footnote.]**

See also Dixon, 627 F.3d at 856 (not essential that supervisor knew all details of plaintiffs' religious beliefs so long as she understood that there was tension between those beliefs and employer's policy prohibiting display of religious art).

[60]**[On page 9-12 of the Main Volume, in footnote 60, add the following at the beginning of the footnote.]**

See Xodus, 619 F.3d at 686–87 (statement by job applicant that cutting dreadlocks was contrary to "his beliefs" was insufficient to inform his employer that applicant wore dreadlocks for religious reasons);

[62]**[On page 9-12 of the Main Volume, in footnote 62, add the following after "*See*".]**

Leifer v. New York State Div. of Parole, 391 F. App'x 32, 34, 110 FEP 23 (2d Cir. 2010) (employee who was allowed to miss work on Jewish holidays failed to satisfy third element of prima facie case where he presented no evidence to demonstrate that his absence from mandatory meetings scheduled on Jewish holidays resulted in materially adverse change in terms and conditions of his employment, or that his failure to receive training on new drug-testing machine, which he missed while observing Jewish holiday, significantly altered his supervisory duties) (citing Joseph v. Leavitt, 465 F.3d 87, 90 (2d Cir. 2006); Terry v. Ashcroft, 336 F.3d 128, 138 (2d Cir. 2003));

[64]**[On page 9-13 of the Main Volume, in footnote 64, add the following after "*See*".]**

Sánchez-Rodríguez v. AT&T Mobility P.R., Inc., 673 F.3d 1, 12–13, 114 FEP 912 (1st Cir. 2012) (where employer offers multiple accommodations, they must be viewed together to determine whether employer's efforts constitute reasonable accommodation); EEOC v. GEO Grp., Inc., 616 F.3d 265, 271, 109 FEP 1633 (3d Cir. 2010) ("A religious accommodation that creates a genuine security or safety risk can undoubtedly constitute an undue hardship for an employer-prison.");

2. *The Scope of the Duty to Accommodate*

a. *A Framework of Analysis*

[67][On page 9-14 of the Main Volume, in footnote 67, add the following at the end of the footnote.]

See also Sánchez-Rodríguez, 673 F.3d at 12–13 (summary judgment properly granted to cellular phone company on failure-to-accommodate claim of Seventh-Day Adventist employee whose religion directed that he not work on Saturdays, where employer did not grant his proposed accommodation but did offer several reasonable alternatives including: proposing that employee transfer to positions that did not require Saturday work, allowing employee to swap shifts with co-workers, and electing not to discipline him for Saturday absences until after it gave him fair warning); Walden v. Centers for Disease Control & Prevention, 669 F.3d 1277, 1294, 114 FEP 454 (11th Cir. 2012) ("CDC was only obligated to offer [plaintiff] some reasonable accommodation. It was not required to provide Ms. Walden with her preferred accommodation.").

[On page 9-14 of the Main Volume, after the sentence that ends with footnote 67, add the following.]

One court has determined that where an employer offers multiple accommodations, the accommodations must be viewed together to determine whether the employer's efforts were reasonable.[2]

[68][On page 9-14 of the Main Volume, in footnote 68, add the following at the end of the footnote.]

See also Sánchez-Rodríguez, 673 F.3d at 12 (employer's offer of transfer to lower-paying position, when combined with other accommodations, constituted reasonable religious accommodation).

---

[2]*See Sánchez-Rodríguez*, 673 F.3d at 12 (employer's offer of multiple accommodations, including transfer to lower-paying positions, allowing employee to arrange voluntary shift swaps with other employees, and refraining from disciplining employee for his absences from work for eight months, together constituted reasonable accommodation).

[72]**[On page 9-15 of the Main Volume, in footnote 72, add the following after "*See*".]**

Walden, 669 F.3d at 1294 (employer has duty to reasonably accommodate religious practices of its employees, but similarly, employee has duty to make good faith attempt to accommodate her religious needs through means offered by employer); Tomasino v. St. John's Univ., 476 F. App'x 923, 925 (2d Cir. 2012) (employer offered employee reasonable accommodation in form of early lunch break to allow employee to act as lector at weekday Mass; employee's objection to early lunch hour did not render accommodation unreasonable);

b. The Extent of Accommodation Required

[74]**[On page 9-15 of the Main Volume, in footnote 74, add the following after "*See, e.g.,*".]**

Walden v. Centers for Disease Control & Prevention, 669 F.3d 1277, 1293–94, 114 FEP 454 (11th Cir. 2012) (CDC reasonably accommodated Walden "when it encouraged her to obtain new employment with the company and offered her assistance in obtaining a new position" so as to retain her tenure; plaintiff chose not to apply);

[75]**[On page 9-16 of the Main Volume, in footnote 75, add the following at the end of the footnote.]**

See also EEOC v. GEO Grp., Inc., 616 F.3d 265, 271, 273, 109 FEP 1633 (3d Cir. 2010) (whether particular accommodation is reasonable or poses undue hardship is question of fact; there is no "per se" rule that determines how particular religious belief or practice may be reasonably accommodated).

[On page 9-16 of the Main Volume, after the carryover sentence that ends with footnote 75, add the following new paragraph.]

Although the focus in determining whether a particular accommodation constitutes an "undue hardship" is on cost, courts have held that "both economic and non-economic costs can pose an undue hardship upon employers."[3] In deciding whether undue hardship

---

[3]*GEO Grp., Inc.*, 616 F.3d at 271, 273 (quoting Webb v. City of Phila., 562 F.3d 256, 260, 105 FEP 1665 (3d Cir. 2009)) (it would "undoubtedly constitute an undue hardship" for Muslim employees to be completely excepted from no-headwear policy, because it would compromise prison-employer's interest in safety and security).

exists, the "focus [must be] on the specific context of each case, looking to both the facts as well as the magnitude of the alleged undue hardship."[4] For example, in *EEOC v. GEO Group, Inc.*,[5] the Third Circuit held that it would be an undue hardship for Muslim employees to be completely excepted from a non-headgear policy, because it would compromise the prison-employer's interest in safety and security. According to the majority, a religious accommodation that creates a genuine safety or security risk "can undoubtedly constitute an undue hardship for an employer-prison."[6] However, the court rejected the employer's argument that, because one female Muslim employee had accepted the prison's offer to allow her to wear a hairpiece in lieu of a "khimar," the offer of the hairpiece was a reasonable accommodation sufficient to permit all Muslim women to meet their religious obligation to cover their hair.[7]

[77][On page 9-16 of the Main Volume, in footnote 77, add the following at the end of the footnote.]

But see GEO Grp., 616 F.3d at 274 (accommodation of female prison employees of Muslim faith whose religious belief required them to wear head covering—a "khimar"—was not possible where khimars could be used to smuggle contraband into prison, could be used against employee in attack, and could result in identification problems; foreseeable security and safety risk constituted undue hardship even though there were no reports of these incidents occurring at facility).

3. *Specific Accommodations*

a. *Work Scheduling*

[82][On page 9-17 of the Main Volume, in footnote 82, add the following after "*see also*".]

Harrell v. Donahue, 638 F.3d 975, 980–82, 111 FEP 1559 (8th Cir. 2011) (undue hardship excuses U.S. Postal Service from having to accommodate Seventh-Day Adventist letter carrier's request

---

[4]*GEO Grp. Inc.*, 616 F.3d at 271, 273 (citing Protos v. Volkswagen of Am., Inc., 797 F.2d 129, 134 (3d Cir. 1986)).

[5]616 F.3d at 273.

[6]*Id.*

[7]*Id.* at 271.

to have every Saturday as scheduled day off, or as annual leave or leave without pay, where accommodation would violate collective bargaining agreement and deprive co-workers of their rights under seniority system);

[84][On page 9-18 of the Main Volume, in footnote 84, add the following after "*See*".]

Sánchez-Rodríguez v. AT&T Mobility P.R., Inc., 673 F.3d 1, 12–13, 114 FEP 912 (1st Cir. 2012) (allowing employee to find volunteers to swap shifts with him so that he did not have to work on Sabbath constituted reasonable accommodation, even though employer rejected plaintiff's requested accommodation that he not be assigned rotating Saturday shifts); Porter v. City of Chi., 700 F.3d 944, 951–52, 116 FEP 705 (7th Cir. 2012) (Christian employee of police department, who requested time off so that she could attend church services on Sunday mornings, was reasonably accommodated where supervisor suggested that she change to second shift, which would have eliminated conflict between her work schedule and religious practice, with no evidence change would have impacted pay or benefits; that she did not want to work later shift did not make proposed accommodation unreasonable); *Harrell*, 638 F.3d at 980–82 (employee's request that U.S. Postal Service give him off every Saturday by approving annual leave and leave without pay to accommodate his religious beliefs as member of Seventh-Day Adventist Church would have imposed undue hardship on Postal Service; requested accommodation would have substantially impacted co-workers by depriving them of their right to shift preferences under collective bargaining agreement);

VI. HARASSMENT

[135][On page 9-26 of the Main Volume, in footnote 135, add the following after "*See*".]

May v. Chrysler Grp., LLC, 716 F.3d 963, 971–72, 118 FEP 447 (7th Cir. 2012) (severe harassment of Cuban-Jewish employee violated Title VII where employer failed to promptly and adequately respond to employee's complaint of multiple racist and anti-Semitic death threats by co-worker, did not interview anyone on employee's list of suspected perpetrators, or install surveillance camera, as employee had requested);

VII. Permissible Religious Discrimination—Special Exemptions

B. Religious Corporations

[On page 9-29 of the Main Volume, after the sentence that ends with footnote 152, add the following.]

However, Section 702 is interpreted broadly to exempt all personnel decisions related to a religious corporation furthering its religious purposes.[8]

D. Ministerial Exception

[On page 9-35 of the Main Volume, after the sentence that ends with footnote 184, add the following new paragraph.]

In *Cannata v. Catholic Diocese of Austin*,[9] the Fifth Circuit relied on *Hosanna-Tabor* to extend the ministerial exemption and bar a suit by a church music director alleging that he was terminated in violation of the ADEA and ADA. Based on testimony from priests that "music in the liturgy is sacred and has ritual and spiritual dimensions,"[10] the court held that the exemption applied despite the fact that the plaintiff was neither ordained nor trained as a spiritual leader.

---

[8]*See* Kennedy v. St. Joseph's Ministries, Inc., 657 F.3d 189, 192, 113 FEP 374 (4th Cir. 2011) (Catholic nursing home terminated nursing assistant who continued to wear modest garb, long dresses, and hair coverings required of her religious sect despite nursing home's request that she not do so because it made residents and their families uncomfortable; termination was exempt within the meaning of Section 702, which covers all employment decisions and not merely those related to hiring).

[9]700 F.3d 169, 116 FEP 513 (5th Cir. 2012).

[10]*Id.* at 177 & n.5. (liturgy is integral part of Mass in furthering church's missions by "allow[ing] the congregation to act together in celebration by singing praises and hymns to the Lord").

CHAPTER 10

SEX

I. OVERVIEW

[On page 10-4 of the Main Volume, after the first full paragraph, add the following new paragraph.]

With the exception of the availability of the bona fide occupational qualification (BFOQ) defense, sex discrimination cases follow the same basic model established in discrimination cases founded on other bases. This chapter focuses on issues that are specific to allegations of sex discrimination and related claims.[1]

II. BONA FIDE OCCUPATIONAL QUALIFICATION (BFOQ)

B. Elements of the BFOQ Defense

1. Direct Relationship Between Sex and the Ability to Perform the Job

[37]**[On page 10-11 of the Main Volume, in footnote 37, add the following after "*See, e.g.*,".]**

Breiner v. Nevada Dep't of Corr., 610 F.3d 1202, 1213–16, 109 FEP 1153 (9th Cir. 2010) (state's policy limiting correctional lieutenant positions at women's prison to female officers because of perceived risk of sexual abuse of inmates did not constitute BFOQ under Title VII, where there was no evidence that male lieutenants would condone or engage in such abuse, and theory that female lieutenants have "instinct and innate ability" to deal with female inmates relies on invidious stereotype);

[1]Part III (Employment Actions) (Chapters 16–21) discusses in greater detail the various employment decisions that may be the subject of claims of sex discrimination.

2. *Essence of the Business*

[On page 10-14 of the Main Volume, after the sentence that ends with footnote 56, add the following new paragraph.]

In *Breiner v. Nevada Department of Corrections*,[2] the Ninth Circuit distinguished the evidence produced by Nevada's Department of Corrections from the situations in *Dothard* and *Everson* because in those cases there was evidence of a history of violence, a history of sexual abuse, or a specific population of offenders that created a particularly high risk to prison security.[3] The *Breiner* court noted that *Dothard* involved a maximum security facility where violent sex offenders were housed with others in the general population. In *Everson*, an extensive prior history of sexual violence perpetrated by male staff against female inmates had been the subject of a civil rights action by the Department of Justice. The transition to an all-female staff was part of the settlement of that litigation. The *Breiner* court instead followed the reasoning in *Gunther v. Iowa State Men's Reformatory*,[4] which held that absent a specific reason at a particular facility, limiting prison officers on the basis of gender does not meet the requirements of a BFOQ. The Nevada Department of Corrections failed to introduce evidence in *Breiner* demonstrating "a basis in fact" for its conclusion that male correctional lieutenants would abuse female inmates themselves or tolerate such abuse by male subordinates, or that female lieutenants inherently could perform better in the supervisory position.[5]

3. *No Reasonable Alternative*

[66]**[On page 10-17 of the Main Volume, in footnote 66, add the following after "*E.g.*,".]**

Healey v. Southwest Psychiatric Hosp., 78 F.3d 128, 70 FEP 439 (3d Cir. 1996) (hospital established specific therapeutic and privacy

---

[2] 610 F.3d 1202, 109 FEP 1153 (9th Cir. 2010).

[3] *Id.* at 1213–14. The *Breiner* court likewise distinguished *Robino v. Iranon*, 145 F.3d 1109 (9th Cir. 1998), which involved a maximum security prison and a study prepared in the context of an EEOC settlement. *Breiner*, 610 F.3d at 1215–16.

[4] 612 F.2d 1079, 21 FEP 1031 (8th Cir. 1980) (prison system failed to show that sex was BFOQ warranting refusal to promote female Correctional Officer I at men's reformatory to Correctional Officer II status, where there existed at least as many level II functions as level I functions that could be performed without invading inmate privacy).

[5] *Breiner*, 610 F.3d at 1216.

concerns associated with treating mentally ill children of both sexes, including children who had been victims of sexual abuse, and demonstrated that specific emotional illnesses it was treating made it essential that therapists of both genders be available on every shift);

C. The Theories of BFOQ

1. *Safety*

[74][On page 10-18 of the Main Volume, in footnote 74, add the following at the end of the footnote.]

See also Spees v. James Marine, Inc., 617 F.3d 380, 391–94,109 FEP 1748 (6th Cir. 2010) (employer was not entitled to summary judgment where it failed to undertake objective evaluation to determine whether employee could perform her welding job while pregnant and instead subjectively viewed pregnancy as rendering employee unable to weld and transferred her to unskilled tool room position based on only its "concern for her pregnancy and the well-being of her unborn child"); Breiner v. Nevada Dep't of Corr., 610 F.3d 1202, 1212–13 n.5, 109 FEP 1153 (9th Cir. 2010) (employer failed to substantiate that permitting male officers to serve in positions of authority in correctional facility for women threatened inmates' safety because of possibility that they would be sexually assaulted by male officers).

2. *Privacy*

[81][On page 10-19 of the Main Volume, in footnote 81, add the following at the end of the footnote.]

But see Robino v. Iranon, 145 F.3d 1109, 1111, 76 FEP 1793 (9th Cir. 1998) (per curiam) (prison facility for women did not violate Title VII by assigning only female guards to posts from which inmates could be observed showering or using toilet; interest in preserving privacy of inmates was legitimate and because male and female guards had same position descriptions, pay, and promotional opportunities, assignment to different duties within scope of position did not constitute adverse action).

IV. SEX DISCRIMINATION IN EXECUTIVE AND PROFESSIONAL EMPLOYMENT

B. Sex Stereotyping

[173][On page 10-40 of the Main Volume, in footnote 173, add the following at the end of the footnote.]

But see Hill v. City of Pine Bluff, Ark., 696 F.3d 709, 116 FEP 407 (8th Cir. 2012) (female employee failed to establish that city violated Equal Protection Clause when mayor selected man who had not applied for particular position instead of promoting plaintiff, who had been unanimously recommended by hiring committee, where evidence established that man was more qualified and there was no evidence that city had policy of hiring only those who apply for position).

[On page 10-41 of the Main Volume, after the sentence that ends with footnote 176, add the following.]

Women have also alleged that they have been required to meet standards of conduct different from those expected of men because of stereotyped beliefs about gender differences in attitudes.[6]

[180][On page 10-41 of the Main Volume, in footnote 180, add the following at the end of the footnote.]

Id.; *see also* Lewis v. Heartland Inns of Am., LLC, 591 F.3d 1033, 1041–42, 108 FEP 449 (8th Cir. 2010) (hotel employee challenging termination made out prima facie case and presented sufficient evidence of pretext to defeat summary judgment where employer had de facto policy that female front-desk employees conform to gender stereotypes by being "pretty" and having "Midwestern girl look," and practice applied to only women). *But see* McBride v. Peak Wellness Ctr., Inc., 688 F.3d 698, 711–12, 115 FEP 1185 (10th Cir. 2012)

---

[6]*See* Morales-Cruz v. University of P.R., 676 F.3d 220, 225–26, 114 FEP 1185 (1st Cir. 2012) (female law professor, who claimed that her termination for failing to report that male professor impregnated student was discriminatory under gender stereotyping theory, and that women were held to higher standard of responsibility for reporting such situations, failed to make out prima facie case where she alleged no facts that would show that she was held to different standard or that defendant acted on basis of gender).

(female accountant discharged for poor performance and morale issues did not state claim for discrimination based on sex stereotyping; although she alleged that her supervisor required her to comply with "submissive stereotype," tolerating financial irregularities had nothing to do with conforming to stereotypical gender norms); EEOC v. Boh Bros. Constr. Co., 689 F.3d 458, 462–63, 115 FEP 946 (5th Cir. 2012) (male employee who was subjected to homophobic epithets and lewd gestures by male co-worker, including being called "faggot" and "princess," failed to establish same-sex harassment claim based on sex stereotyping theory, even assuming claim was viable under this theory, where except for his use of "Wet Ones" there was no evidence that he did not conform to male stereotypes or that co-worker's treatment was based on gender), *revised*, 712 F.3d 883 (5th Cir. 2013); Dawson v. Entek Int'l, 630 F.3d 928, 937–38, 111 FEP 306 (9th Cir. 2011) (male homosexual employee failed to establish hostile work environment claim under Title VII where he alleged that he was harassed because he appeared effeminate but presented no evidence that he failed to conform to gender stereotypes).

C. Second-Guessing the Employer

[On page 10-43 of the Main Volume, after the first sentence of the last paragraph on the bottom of the page, add the following.]

"[A]lthough the legal standard is the same whether the plaintiff in an employment discrimination case is a salesman or a scientist, practical considerations make a challenge to the denial of tenure at the college or university level an uphill fight—notably the absence of fixed, objective criteria for tenure at that level."[7]

---

[7]Blasdel v. Northwestern Univ., 687 F.3d 813, 815, 115 FEP 837 (7th Cir. 2012) (citing Vanasco v. National-Louis Univ., 137 F.3d 962, 968, 76 FEP 629 (7th Cir. 1998)).

VII. PREGNANCY, CHILDBIRTH, AND PARENTING

A. Discrimination on the Basis of Pregnancy

3. The Pregnancy Discrimination Act (PDA)

a. Passage of the PDA

[294]**[On page 10-63 of the Main Volume, in footnote 294, add the following after "*See, e.g.*,".]**

Wierman v. Casey's Gen. Stores, 638 F.3d 984, 994–98, 111 FEP 1547 (8th Cir. 2011) (employee's pregnancy discrimination claim failed where she did not present sufficient evidence that employer's proffered legitimate reasons for termination, including theft, chronic lateness, and violation of company policy, were pretext for discrimination);

[299]**[On page 10-64 of the Main Volume, in footnote 299, replace "; *cf.*" with ". *Compare*" and replace parenthetical after "Spees v. James Marine, Inc." with the following.]**

(former employee established that employer failed to undertake objective evaluation to determine whether she could perform her welding job while pregnant and instead subjectively viewed pregnancy as rendering employee unable to weld and transferred her to unskilled position based on only its "concern for her pregnancy and the well-being of her unborn child" and not on whether she was able to perform her job as welder), *with Wierman*, 638 F.3d at 994–98 (discharged store manager placed her own limitations on her ability to perform certain of her assigned duties and was not discriminated against because of her pregnancy where she failed to respond to employer's repeated requests that she provide letter from her doctor to establish that her frequent absences and chronic lateness could be treated as Family and Medical Leave Act (FMLA) leave rather than violation of company attendance policy).

[301]**[On page 10-64 of the Main Volume, in footnote 301, add the following at the end of the footnote.]**

See also Martinez-Burgos v. Guayama Corp., 656 F.3d 7, 14–15, 113 FEP 253 (1st Cir. 2011) (affirming summary judgment; employer that did not rehire plaintiff as temporary employee after her pregnancy did not discriminate against her where it documented her noncompliance with company policies and rules, she was not qualified for full-time position, and employer had made decision not to hire temporary employees who were not qualified for full-time employment); Serednyj v. Beverly Healthcare, LLC, 656 F.3d 540, 548–49, 113 FEP 104 (7th Cir. 2011) (female employee, who alleged that she was discriminatorily discharged from position as activity director of nursing home when employer refused changes in her usual workload based on physician's note proscribing heavy lifting or strenuous activity in light of her pregnancy, failed to establish direct case of discrimination where employer treated pregnant and non-pregnant employees identically in that it did not provide light-duty work for non–work-related injuries).

d. Employment Decisions Based on Employee Conduct Permissible Even if Related to Pregnancy

[On page 10-68 of the Main Volume, after the sentence that ends with footnote 316, add the following.]

An employer's deviation from established policy, however, may constitute evidence of a PDA violation.[8]

[322]**[On page 10-69 of the Main Volume, in footnote 322, add the following at the end of the footnote.]**

But see Hamilton v. Southland Christian Sch. Inc., 680 F.3d 1316, 1320–21, 114 FEP 1633 (11th Cir. 2012) (pregnant, unmarried teacher at Christian school created genuine issue of material fact regarding whether she was terminated due to pregnancy, rather than for having had premarital sex, even though she could not show that non-pregnant comparator was treated more favorably, where she presented evidence that school was more concerned about her pregnancy and request to take maternity leave than about her admission

[8]Chapter 7 Tr. v. Gate Gourmet, Inc., 683 F.3d 1249, 1256–57, 115 FEP 391 (11th Cir. 2012) (catering truck driver adduced sufficient evidence for reasonable jury to conclude that she was discharged due to her pregnancy, even though she did not identify non-pregnant employee who was treated differently, where supervisor told her that she would be unable to handle her duties and that there were no light-duty jobs available, terminated her after reading note from her doctor that listed her medical restrictions, made no effort to determine whether there were light-duty jobs available, and employer had policy that it would provide employees with medical conditions with light-duty work when such jobs were available).

that she had premarital sex; although administrator testified that plaintiff would not have been fired if she had apologized for her sin, she testified that she did apologize and was fired anyway).

e. Failure to Provide Light Duty

[327]**[On page 10-71 of the Main Volume, in the carryover of footnote 327, add the following after "*see also*".]**

Arizanovska v. Wal-Mart Stores, Inc., 682 F.3d 698, 703, 115 FEP 270 (7th Cir. 2012) (pregnant employee with temporary 10-pound lifting restriction failed to establish prima facie case that store discriminated against her when it refused her request for light duty and placed her on unpaid leave, where policy provided no light-duty position for any employee); Serednyj v. Beverly Healthcare, LLC, 656 F.3d 540, 548–49, 113 FEP 104 (7th Cir. 2011) (female employee, who alleged that she was discriminatorily discharged from position as activity director of nursing home when employer refused changes in her usual workload based on physician's note proscribing heavy lifting or strenuous activity in light of her pregnancy, failed to present direct case of discrimination, despite employer's application of disabilities accommodation policy, because employer treated pregnant and non-pregnant employees identically in denying light-duty work for non–work-related injuries);

[329]**[On page 10-71 of the Main Volume, in footnote 329, add the following after "*see also*".]**

Chapter 7 Tr. v. Gate Gourmet, Inc., 683 F.3d 1249, 1256–57, 115 FEP 391 (11th Cir. 2012) (catering truck driver adduced sufficient evidence for reasonable jury to conclude that she was discharged due to her pregnancy, even though she did not identify non-pregnant employee who was treated differently, where supervisor told her that she would be unable to handle her duties and that there were no light-duty jobs available, terminated her after reading note from her doctor that listed her medical restrictions, made no effort to determine whether there were light-duty jobs available, and employer had policy that it would provide employees with medical conditions with light-duty work when such jobs were available);

f. Elimination of Position or Demotion During Pregnancy or Maternity Leave

[331]**[On page 10-71 of the Main Volume, in footnote 331, add the following after "*See, e.g.*,".]**

Silverman v. Board of Educ. of Chi., 637 F.3d 729, 737–40, 111 FEP 1461 (7th Cir. 2011) (pregnant teacher whose position was eliminated during her pregnancy did not establish that action was connected to her pregnancy where employer showed that, in selecting her position for elimination, it had relied on performance evaluations conducted by school's principal before he was aware of her pregnancy, and teacher failed to establish that similarly situated employees were treated more favorably); LaFary v. Rogers Grp., Inc., 591 F.3d 903, 908–09, 108 FEP 97 (7th Cir. 2010) (employee created no genuine issue of fact that she was terminated due to pregnancy for requesting leave to deal with complications with her pregnancy, where she was terminated under policy requiring automatic discharge of any employee who did not return to work after 180 days of leave; she was not similarly situated to male employee who was rehired after exceeding 180-day period, inasmuch as he was rehired during time of financial success and employer needed his expertise);

[331]**[On page 10-72 of the Main Volume, in the carryover of footnote 331, add the following at the end of the footnote.]**

But see Makowski v. SmithAmundsen, LLC, 662 F.3d 818, 824, 113 FEP 1351 (7th Cir. 2011) (employee whose position was eliminated while she was pregnant and on maternity leave created a triable issue on her claim for discriminatory discharge where director of human resources stated that: (1) employee was terminated because she was pregnant; (2) director believed employer was discriminating against people because they were pregnant or took medical leave; (3) it might be good idea for employee to speak with lawyer; and (4) employer's outside counsel had suggested to director that employee's termination and that of certain other employee be labeled as part of reduction in force, providing direct evidence that employee's pregnancy was motivating factor in her discharge).

k. Actual Knowledge of Pregnancy or Attempted Pregnancy

[349]**[On page 10-75 of the Main Volume, in footnote 349, add the following after "*See*".]**

Silverman v. Board of Educ. of Chi., 637 F.3d 729, 737–40, 111 FEP 1461 (7th Cir. 2011) ("negative evaluation could not possibly have been affected by any supposed bias against pregnancy" where it occurred prior to time employer learned of teacher's pregnancy); LaFary v. Rogers Grp., Inc., 591 F.3d 903, 108 FEP 97 (7th Cir. 2010) (employee failed to establish prima facie case that she was transferred due to pregnancy, where she failed to show that employer knew of her condition when it decided to transfer her);

[353]**[On page 10-76 of the Main Volume, in footnote 353, add the following at the end of the footnote.]**

See also Silverman, 637 F.3d at 737–40 ("negative evaluation could not possibly have been affected by any supposed bias against pregnancy" where it occurred prior to time employer learned of teacher's pregnancy); LaFary v. Rogers Grp., Inc., 591 F.3d 903, 908, 108 FEP 97 (7th Cir. 2010) (employee failed to establish genuine issue of material fact as to whether she was transferred due to pregnancy, where she failed to show that employer knew of her condition when it decided to transfer her).

IX. TRANSSEXUALITY

[521]**[On page 10-106 of the Main Volume, in footnote 521, add the following at the end of the footnote.]**

But cf. Glenn v. Brumby, 663 F.3d 1312, 1319–20, 113 FEP 1543 (11th Cir. 2011) (transsexual individual seeking declaratory and injunctive relief under 42 U.S.C. § 1983 established that she was fired from her position as editor in Georgia General Assembly's Office of Legislative Counsel due to sex discrimination in violation of Equal Protection Clause; discrimination on basis of "perceived gender-nonconformity" is form of sex-based discrimination that is to be reviewed under heightened-scrutiny standard of Equal Protection

Clause, and discharge because of gender nonconformity by government agency violates that clause unless the employer can establish important governmental interest for discrimination).

[531][On page 10-108 of the Main Volume, in footnote 531, add the following at the end of the footnote.]

But see Hunter v. United Parcel Serv., Inc., 697 F.3d 697, 704–05, 116 FEP 1 (8th Cir. 2012) (biological female who identified as male failed to establish prima facie case that employer discriminated by refusing to hire him because of his nonconformity to gender stereotypes or being perceived as transgendered, where he failed to show that interviewer knew he was transgendered or perceived him so and employer's articulated reason for not hiring him—poor references and questionable job history—were pretextual).

XI. TITLE IX OF THE EDUCATION AMENDMENTS ACT OF 1972

C. Application of Title IX to Employers

[On pages 10-122 to 10-123 of the Main Volume, replace the carryover paragraph with the following.]

The Supreme Court has held in a nonemployment context that Title IX does not preclude claims of unconstitutional gender discrimination under § 1983. In *Fitzgerald v. Barnstable School Committee*,[9] the parents of a grade school student alleged that the school system violated Title IX and § 1983 by failing to adequately investigate their complaints that their daughter was being sexually harassed by another student on the school bus and in school. The district court dismissed the § 1983 claim, holding that it was precluded by Title IX, and the court of appeals affirmed.[10] The Supreme Court reversed.

Writing for a unanimous court, Justice Alito concluded that the remedies available under Title IX—withdrawal of federal funds and an implied cause of action—were not comprehensive enough to preclude suit under § 1983. The Court noted that it has "never held that an implied right of action had the effect of precluding suit under

[9]555 U.S. 246, 105 FEP 358 (2009).

[10]504 F.3d 165 (1st Cir. 2007), *aff'g* 456 F. Supp. 2d 255 (D. Mass. 2006).

§ 1983."[11] "In light of the divergent coverage of Title IX and the Equal Protection Clause, as well as the absence of a comprehensive remedial scheme ... we conclude that Title IX was not meant to be an exclusive mechanism for addressing gender discrimination in schools, or a substitute for § 1983 suits as a means of enforcing constitutional rights."[12] Accordingly, the Court held that "§ 1983 suits based on the Equal Protection Clause remain available to plaintiffs alleging unconstitutional gender discrimination in schools."[13]

The Court pointed out that Title IX had been modeled on Title VI of the Civil Rights Act and that in 1972 Congress was aware that "Title VI was routinely interpreted to allow for parallel and concurrent § 1983 claims." For that reason, the plaintiff's § 1983 claim was reinstated.

---

[11] 555 U.S. at 256.
[12] *Id.* at 258.
[13] *Id.*

Chapter 11

SEXUAL ORIENTATION AND GENDER IDENTITY*

**Authors' Note:* The law addressing issues of gender identity and sexual orientation is developing rapidly. As it does, the vocabulary used to describe various aspects of this topic is changing as well. This Supplement retains the terminology reflected in the Fifth Edition of *Employment Discrimination Law*, which is consistent with that used in most court decisions and statutes. Appendix 1 of this chapter presents an excerpt from the forthcoming book, Gender Identity and Sexual Orientation Discrimination in the Workplace: A Practical Guide (Christine Michelle Duffy ed., Bloomberg BNA forthcoming 2014), discussing the evolving lexicon in this area. The authors appreciate Ms. Duffy's assistance and her permission to reproduce this excerpt, which is included in order to further inform the reader regarding the issue, rather than to express any opinion as to the terminology that should be used. Appendix 2 of this chapter, from the same book, presents a table of state fair employment practices statutes that prohibit employment discrimination on the basis of gender identity or expression, or sexual orientation.

I. TITLE VII

[**Editors' Note:** On June 16, 2014, the White House announced President Obama's intention to sign an executive order prohibiting discrimination by federal contractors on the basis of sexual orientation or gender identity. The statement indicated that the order "would build upon existing protections, which generally prohibit federal contractors and subcontractors from discriminating in employment decisions on the basis of race, color, religion, sex, or national origin." *White House to Issue Executive Order Banning LGBT Bias by Federal Contractors*, 115 DAILY LAB. REP. A-1 (June 16, 2014)]

A. Sexual Orientation

[1]**[On page 11-2 of the Main Volume, in footnote 1, after the fifth sentence ("Over the years…enacted.") delete "*See*" and insert the following.]**

The Employment Non-Discrimination Act of 2013 (ENDA), S.815, 113th Congress (2013), passed the Senate on November 12, 2013, and was referred to the House.

[2]**[On page 11-2 of the Main Volume, in footnote 2, add the following after "*See, e.g.,*".]**

Gilbert v. Country Music Ass'n, Inc., 432 F. App'x 516, 519–20, 112 FEP 1711 (6th Cir. 2011) (discrimination on basis of union member's homosexual orientation not cognizable under Title VII); Dawson v. Entek Int'l, 630 F.3d 928, 938, 111 FEP 306 (9th Cir. 2011) (former employee could not maintain hostile work environment claim under Title VII based on derogatory comments about his sexuality, where he "was not being verbally harassed for appearing non-masculine or for otherwise not fitting the male stereotype");

B. Same-Sex Sexual Harassment

[12]**[On page 11-5 of the Main Volume, in footnote 12, add the following after "*see also*".]**

McBride v. Peak Wellness Ctr., Inc., 688 F.3d 698, 712, 115 FEP 1185 (10th Cir 2012) (female former employee asserting that harassment by other female employees created hostile environment cannot prevail on Title VII claim where she did not establish that vulgar e-mails about her that were circulated by those co-workers were motivated by sexual desire, hostility to presence of women in workplace, or that harassers treated men and women differently); Wasek v. Arrow Energy Servs., Inc., 682 F.3d 463, 468, 115 FEP 384 (6th Cir. 2012) (male oil rig worker failed to establish that conduct of male co-worker—making sexually offensive remarks, grabbing his buttocks, and poking his rear with hammer handle simulating sodomy—was "because of" his sex, where claimant's speculative statement that co-worker was "possibly bisexual" fell short of establishing that alleged harasser was homosexual); Kalich v. AT&T Mobility, LLC, 679 F.3d 464, 469–71, 114 FEP 1560 (6th Cir. 2012) (male employee did not establish that male manager's conduct toward him—which included graphically sexual gestures and vulgar comments—was "because of" his gender, where there was no evidence that manager had general hostility toward men or treated women more favorably; he was rude to all employees and particularly "teased" employee because he suspected that he was homosexual); Cherry v. Shaw Coastal, Inc., 668 F.3d 182, 188, 114 FEP 320 (5th Cir. 2012) (male employee proved violation of Title VII based on same-sex supervisor's sexual harassment, where supervisor repeatedly touched employee in sexual manner and sent him sexual text messages);

[15]**[On page 11-7 of the Main Volume, in footnote 15, add the following at the beginning of the footnote.]**

See Wasek, 682 F.3d at 468 (male oil rig worker failed to establish that male co-worker's conduct—making sexually offensive remarks, grabbing his buttocks, and poking his rear with hammer handle simulating sodomy—was "because of" his sex, where claimant's speculative statement that co-worker was "possibly bisexual" fell short of establishing that alleged harasser was homosexual); *Kalich*, 679 F.3d at 469–71 (male employee did not establish that male manager's conduct toward him—which included graphically sexual gestures and vulgar comments—was "because of" his gender, where there was no evidence that manager had general hostility toward men or treated women more favorably; he was rude to all employees and particularly "teased" employee because he suspected that he was homosexual); *Cherry*, 668 F.3d at 188 (male employee proved violation of Title VII based on same-sex supervisor's sexual harassment, where supervisor repeatedly touched employee in sexual manner and sent him sexual text messages); *see also* EEOC v. Boh Bros. Constr. Co., 731 F.3d 444, 456, 459, 468, 120 FEP 15 (5th Cir. 2013) (en banc) (affirming jury verdict for Equal Employment Opportunity Commission (EEOC) suing on behalf of male employee where evidence established that he was subject to "almost daily" homophobic epithets, including "faggot" and "princess," and lewd gestures by male crew superintendent demonstrating that he was viewed as "insufficiently masculine," which was sufficient to prove same-sex harassment claim based on sex stereotyping theory; vacating punitive damages award because legal application sufficiently novel that failure to train not malicious or recklessly indifferent);

C. Gender Stereotyping

[27]**[On page 11-9 of the Main Volume, in footnote 27, add the following after "*See, e.g.,*".]**

EEOC v. Boh Bros. Constr. Co., 731 F.3d 444, 456, 459, 468, 120 FEP 15 (5th Cir. 2013) (en banc) ((affirming jury verdict for EEOC suing on behalf of male employee where evidence established that he was subject to "almost daily" homophobic epithets, including "faggot" and "princess," and lewd gestures by male crew superintendent demonstrating that he was viewed as "insufficiently masculine," which was sufficient to prove same-sex harassment claim based on sex stereotyping theory; vacating punitive damages award because legal application sufficiently novel that failure to train not malicious or recklessly indifferent); Lewis v. Heartland Inns of Am., LLC, 591 F.3d 1033, 1040–42, 108 FEP 449 (8th Cir. 2010) (reversing summary judgment for employer; hotel employee made out prima facie case that employer had de facto policy requiring female employees to conform to gender stereotypes by being "pretty" and having "Midwestern girl look" in order to work certain front-desk shift, even though she provided no evidence that she was treated differently than similarly situated men, where practice applied only to women, primary decision maker indicated that female front-desk workers needed to be "pretty" and criticized her lack of "Midwestern girl look," and she had history of good performance);

[27]**[On page 11-10 of the Main Volume, in the carryover of footnote 27, add the following after "*But see*".]**

McBride v. Peak Wellness Ctr., Inc., 688 F.3d 698, 712, 115 FEP 1185 (10th Cir. 2012) (female business manager, who was discharged for poor performance and morale issues, did not state claim for discrimination based on sex stereotyping against nonprofit drug rehabilitation center, where allegation that her supervisor required her to comply with "submissive stereotype" by tolerating financial irregularities had nothing to do with conforming to stereotypical gender norms); Dawson v. Entek Int'l, 630 F.3d 928, 938, 111 FEP 306 (9th Cir. 2011) (male homosexual employee failed to establish that hostile work environment he experienced was because of his failing to conform to male stereotype inasmuch as claimant's own testimony established that he did not exhibit effeminate traits);

D. Transgender Discrimination

[40]**[On page 11-12 of the Main Volume, in footnote 40, add parallel citation to "Barnes v. City of Cincinnati".]**

, 95 FEP 994

[40]**[On page 11-13 of the Main Volume, in the carryover of footnote 40, add the following before "*But see*".]**

See also Hunter v. United Parcel Serv., Inc., 697 F.3d 697, 116 FEP 1 (8th Cir. 2012) (biological female who identified as male failed to establish prima facie case that employer discriminatorily refused to hire him because of nonconformity to gender stereotypes or being perceived as transgendered, where he failed to show that interviewer knew that he was transgendered or perceived him so); Glenn v. Brumby, 663 F.3d 1312, 1314, 1320–21, 113 FEP 1543 (11th Cir. 2011) (transgender employee, who was born biological male, stated claim under § 1983 for Fourteenth Amendment equal protection violation against supervisor and officials in Georgia legislature's Office of Legal Counsel who terminated her on basis of her nonconformity with female stereotype; employer's justification that other female employees might be uncomfortable with and object to plaintiff's transgendered appearance was not sufficiently important governmental interest under Fourteenth Amendment to justify discharge).

[43][On page 11-13 of the Main Volume, in footnote 43, add the following at the end of the footnote.]

Cf. County of Onondaga v. Mayock, 78 A.D.3d 1632, 910 N.Y.S.2d 628 (N.Y. App. Div. 2010) (county probation officer who had supervised probationers for 20 years established by preponderance of evidence that he was discriminated against on basis of sexual orientation in violation of New York Human Rights Law where he was transferred from those duties when employer learned of his sexual orientation and employer refused his requests to return to former position).

II. STATE STATUTES AND INITIATIVES

A. State Statutes, Executive Orders, and Local Ordinances

1. Sexual Orientation

[51][On page 11-15 of the Main Volume, in footnote 51, add the following before the second sentence ("An employee may be a member…").]

See also Castillo v. Roche Labs., 467 F. App'x 859, 861–62 (11th Cir. 2012) (per curiam) (although Miami-Dade Code, MDC § 11A-26(1)(a), (4), prohibits discrimination on basis of sexual orientation, homosexual county employee who was terminated for falsifying vouchers failed to show that he was treated differently than heterosexual employees who committed same violations); Kalich v. AT&T

Mobility, LLC, 679 F.3d 464, 469–71, 114 FEP 1560 (6th Cir. 2012) (former employee asserting under Michigan Elliott-Larsen Civil Rights Act, MICH. COMP. LAWS § 37.2102, that he was harassed because of his sexual orientation failed to establish that his supervisor's teasing and name-calling was "because of" his gender, where supervisor exhibited rude, aggressive, and unapproachable behavior toward all employees and created unpleasant working environment for all employees under his chain of command).

[51]**[On page 11-15 of the Main Volume, in footnote 51, add the following at the end of the footnote.]**

Cf. Yontay v. Mincolla, 97 A.D.3d 141, 142, 144–45, 945 N.Y.S.2d 774 (N.Y. App. Div. 2012) (because N.Y. Human Rights Law expressly prohibits discrimination based on sexual orientation in employment, and given attitude of community as reflected by state legislature's passage of Marriage Equality Act granting same-sex couples right to marry, third-party's statements—republished by defendant—that plaintiff was gay or bisexual did not have defamatory connotation and were not slanderous per se); Albunio v. City of N.Y., 947 N.E.2d 135, 137–38, 111 FEP 1797 (N.Y. 2011) (two police officers—captain and lieutenant—were subjected to unlawful retaliation under New York City Human Rights Law, N.Y.C. ADMIN. CODE § 8-107(7), when they were coerced into transferring to less-desirable positions based on their opposition to nonselection for transfer into their unit of third police officer because of his perceived sexual orientation); Kelley v. Conco Cos., 196 Cal. App. 4th 191, 126 Cal. Rptr. 3d 651, 664, 671, 112 FEP 1301 (2011) (affirming summary judgment against ironworker alleging harassment and hostile environment because of his sexual orientation under California Fair Employment and Housing Act (FEHA), where graphic and vulgar same-sex verbal taunts from supervisor, including references to homosexual sex and rape, were "commonplace" and not "intended to be taken literally"; although tinged with sexual connotations, there was no evidence from which trier of fact could reasonably infer actual sexual desire; however, employee may pursue state-law claims of retaliation and tortious discharge).

[52][On page 11-16 of the Main Volume, in footnote 52, add the following after "*See, e.g.*,".]

Kalich, 679 F.3d at 471 (setting out five-prong proof formulation required of plaintiff under Michigan Elliott-Larsen Civil Rights Act, Mich. Comp. Laws § 37.2102); Dawson v. Entek Int'l, 630 F.3d 928, 934, 111 FEP 306 (9th Cir. 2011) (homosexual former employee established under *McDonnell Douglas* allocation of proof required by Or. Rev. Stat. § 659A.030 that he was discharged in retaliation for filing complaint of discrimination on basis of sexual orientation with company's human resources office); Wasek v. Arrow Energy Servs., Inc., 682 F.3d 463, 115 FEP 384 (6th Cir. 2012) (applying Title VII analysis to hold that homosexual oil rig worker had not established under proof standards required by Michigan Elliott-Larsen Civil Rights Act, Mich. Comp. Laws § 37.2202(1)(a), § 37.2701(a), that his employer permitted hostile work environment to exist or retaliated against him because of his sexual orientation or complaints of harassment); Putnam v. Westchester Cnty. Human Rights Comm'n, 81 A.D.3d 733, 735, 917 N.Y.S.2d 635, 111 FEP 889 (N.Y. App. Div. 2011) (heterosexual employee did not establish that county's policy of providing benefits to same-sex partners but not to unmarried heterosexual partners violated Westchester County Human Rights Law, §§ 700.02(10), 700.03(a)(1), which prohibits employers from discriminating against employees on basis of sexual orientation; employer articulated legitimate, nondiscriminatory reason for policy under which same-sex couples could not obtain benefits by marrying but heterosexual couples could);

2. *Gender Identity*

[On pages 11-17–11-18 of the Main Volume, delete first two sentences of the paragraph.]

[On page 11-18, at the end of the carryover paragraph, add the following new paragraph.]

Appendix 2 presents a table of state fair employment practices statutes relating to employment discrimination based on gender identity or expression, or sexual orientation. On pages 11-16–11-17 of the Main Volume, footnotes 55 and 56 contain examples of the more than 250 state executive orders and local ordinances that prohibit discrimination.

C. State Common Law and Other Statutory Claims

[83][On page 11-21 of the Main Volume, in footnote 83, add the following after "*See, e.g.*,".]

Kalich v. AT&T Mobility, LLC, 679 F.3d 464, 469–71, 114 FEP 1560 (6th Cir. 2012) (Michigan Elliott-Larsen Civil Rights Act, MICH. COMP. LAWS § 37.2102, prohibits discrimination in employment based on sexual orientation); Yontay v. Mincolla, 97 A.D.3d 141, 142, 144–45, 945 N.Y.S.2d 774 (N.Y. App. Div. 2012) (N.Y. Human Rights Law expressly prohibits discrimination based on sexual orientation in employment); Castillo v. Roche Labs., 467 F. App'x 859, 862–64, 2012 U.S. App. LEXIS 9554 (11th Cir. 2012) (per curiam) (Miami-Dade County ordinance creates cause of action for retaliation against transgender individuals); Putnam v. Westchester Cnty. Human Rights Comm'n, 81 A.D.3d 733, 735, 917 N.Y.S.2d 635, 111 FEP 889 (N.Y. App. Div. 2011) (WESTCHESTER COUNTY HUMAN RIGHTS LAW, §§ 700.02(10), 700.03(a)(1), prohibits employers from discriminating against employees on basis of sexual orientation; however, employer articulated legitimate, nondiscriminatory reason for policy of permitting unmarried employees to obtain benefits for same-sex partner but not for partner of opposite sex where same-sex couples could not obtain benefits by marrying but heterosexual couples could);

[On page 11-22 of the Main Volume, add the following after footnote 88.]

breach of the duty of fair representation,[1]

D. Different Treatment in Benefits

[On page 11-23 of the Main Volume, after the sentence that ends with footnote 96, add the following.]

In *Diaz v. Brewer*,[2] the Ninth Circuit concluded that an Arizona law eliminating health insurance benefits for same-sex domestic partners of state employees by limiting eligibility to the employee's "spouse" contravened established Fourteenth Amendment equal-protection

---

[1]*See* Gilbert v. Country Music Ass'n, Inc., 432 F. App'x 516, 112 FEP 1711 (6th Cir. 2011).

[2]656 F.3d 1008, 113 FEP 248 (9th Cir. 2011), *cert. denied*, 133 S. Ct. 2884 (2013).

jurisprudence, holding that some objectives, such as the desire to harm an unpopular group, are not legitimate state interests.

In *Putnam v. Westchester County Human Rights Commission*,[3] an unmarried heterosexual employee who was not permitted to obtain benefits for her opposite-sex partner asserted that the policy violated the Westchester County Human Rights Law,[4] which prohibits employers from discriminating on the basis of sexual orientation in the distribution of benefits. The court held that the plaintiff made out a prima facie case of discrimination, but concluded that the employer had articulated a legitimate, nondiscriminatory reason for its policy because at the time of the decision same-sex couples could not obtain benefits by marrying but heterosexual couples could.

In two decisions,[5] the Ninth Circuit ruled that under its Employment Disputes Resolution Plan, the judicial branch of the federal government has the authority to determine the eligibility of its own employees for federal health and other benefits. Chief Judge Kozinski, acting pursuant to that Plan, ordered the federal Office of Personnel Management to process the applications of two court employees for same-sex health benefits, given that the applications had been approved by the Administrative Office of the Courts.

[On page 11-25 of the Main Volume, after the sentence that ends with footnote 103, add the following new paragraphs.]

The Supreme Court provided greater clarity on the question of access to benefits in its decision in *United States v. Windsor*,[6] in which it held that Section 3 of the Defense of Marriage Act (DOMA),[7] which excludes a same-sex partner from the definition of "spouse" as that term is used in federal statutes,[8] is an unconstitutional deprivation of the liberty of those individuals protected by the Fifth Amendment of the Constitution. The Court stated that the "principal purpose and the necessary effect of this law are to demean those persons who are in a lawful same-sex marriage,"[9] and that, "while the Fifth Amendment itself withdraws from Government the

---

[3]917 N.Y.S.2d 635, 81 A.D.3d 733, 735, 111 FEP 889 (N.Y. App. Div. 2011).

[4]§§ 700.02(10), 700.03(a)(1).

[5]*In re* Golinski, 587 F.3d 956, 108 FEP 341 (9th Cir. 2009); *In re* Levenson, 587 F.3d 925, 108 FEP 331 (9th Cir. 2009).

[6]133 S. Ct. 2675, 118 FEP 1417 (2013).

[7]28 U.S.C. § 1738C.

[8]*See* 1 U.S.C. § 7.

[9]*Windsor*, 133 S. Ct. at 2695.

power to degrade or demean in the way this law does, the equal protection guarantee of the Fourteenth Amendment makes that Fifth Amendment right all the more specific and all the better understood and preserved."[10]

Although *Windsor* itself involved a question of estate law, the Court noted that its definition of marriage affected more than one thousand federal laws and orders, including laws affecting access to benefits. Moreover, as more states recognize same-sex marriage, DOMA imposes a disability on same-sex couples "by refusing to acknowledge a status the State finds to be dignified and proper."[11] By departing from the historic norm of deferring to state definitions of marriage, DOMA "operates to deprive same-sex couples of the benefits and responsibilities that come with the federal recognition of their marriages. This is strong evidence of a law having the purpose and effect of disapproval of that class."[12] Indeed, the Court noted that DOMA affirmatively frustrates the intent of those states recognizing same-sex marriage to provide equal rights and benefits for all their citizens.[13]

III. CONSTITUTIONAL ISSUES AND FEDERAL STATUTES APPLICABLE TO PUBLIC EMPLOYMENT

B. Due Process and Equal Protection

[120][On page 11-29 of the Main Volume, in footnote 120, add the following at the end of the footnote.]

See also Ayala-Sepúlveda v. Municipality of San Germán, 671 F.3d 24, 31–32, 114 FEP 234 (1st Cir. 2012) (homosexual municipal

[10]*Id.*

[11]*Id.* at 2696.

[12]*Id.* at 2693.

[13]"Under DOMA, same-sex married couples have their lives burdened, by reason of government decree, in visible and public ways.... It prevents same-sex married couples from obtaining government healthcare benefits they would otherwise receive.... It deprives them of the Bankruptcy Code's special protections for domestic-support obligations.... It forces them to follow a complicated procedure to file their state and federal taxes jointly.... It prohibits them from being buried together in veterans' cemeteries.... It raises the cost of health care for families by taxing health benefits provided by employers to their workers' same-sex spouses.... And it denies or reduces benefits allowed to families upon the loss of a spouse and parent, benefits that are an integral part of family security (benefits available to a surviving spouse caring for the couple's child)." 133 S. Ct. at 2694 (citations omitted).

employee did not establish that he had been victim of retaliation shortly after he filed complaint of harassment based on his sexual orientation, where he failed to show that denial of transfer was adverse employment action or that heterosexual employees were not similarly transferred); Glenn v. Brumby, 663 F.3d 1312, 1316, 113 FEP 1543 (11th Cir. 2011) ("discriminating against someone on the basis of his or her gender non-conformity constitutes sex-based discrimination under the Equal Protection Clause [and thus] . . . is subject to heightened scrutiny under the Equal Protection Clause").

C. The First Amendment

[133]**[On page 11-32 of the Main Volume, in footnote 133, add the following after "*see also*".]**

Walden v. Centers for Disease Control & Prevention, 669 F.3d 1277, 1286–88, 114 FEP 454 (11th Cir. 2012) (discharge of contract employee assistance program (EAP) counselor, who refused to offer counseling services to employee in same-sex relationship because doing so would conflict with her Christian beliefs, did not violate her rights under either First Amendment or Religious Freedom Restoration Act where she was not discharged for refusing to counsel employee, but rather for her harsh approach to him and disapproving manner in which she treated him); Savage v. Gee, 665 F.3d 732, 33 IER Cases 193 (6th Cir. 2012) (university librarian's recommendation of book describing homosexuality as aberrant behavior was not entitled to First Amendment protection because recommedation was made pursuant to his official duties as member of committee formed to choose book for incoming freshmen, and was not related to his classroom duties or academic scholarship; faculty members' criticism of his book suggestion, expression of their discomfort in seeking research assistance from him, and public challenge to his professionalism amounted to no more than hurt feelings and not constructive discharge);

[On page 11-32 of the Main Volume, after the sentence that ends with footnote 134, add the following new paragraph.]

Even where the issue is one of public concern, the expression of personal opinion by an individual in a position that has, or appears to have, policy-making implications may not be protected under the First Amendment. Thus a Christian, African-American, female human rights official at a state university who was terminated for writing an op-ed column in which she took "great umbrage at the notion that those choosing the homosexual lifestyle are 'civil rights victims,'" and who challenged her discharge on First Amendment grounds,[14] failed to establish a First Amendment retaliation claim. Her speech was deemed unprotected by the Sixth Circuit because of the presumption that arises from her position that she was a policymaker at the university who engaged in speech on a policy issue related to her job.[15]

IV. SPECIAL ISSUES REGARDING SERVICE IN THE ARMED FORCES

[On page 11-35 of the Main Volume, after the sentence that ends with footnote 151, add the following new paragraph.]

In addition to the primary question of whether service members who were open about their gender orientation could lawfully be discharged, challenges have arisen to the military's policy of halving the normal severance pay for servicemen discharged under "Don't ask, don't tell." In *Collins v. United States*,[16] the Federal Court of Claims held that a service member who did not challenge his discharge, but alleged that the reduction in his severance pay was impermissible, presented a justiciable question for the court because it was implemented pursuant to regulations that were promulgated by the Department of Defense and subject to judicial review. The court denied the government's motion to dismiss the plaintiff's claim alleging that under the Equal Protection Clause of the Fifth Amendment sexual orientation should be stricken from the regulation identifying appropriate bases for limiting severance pay.[17]

---

[14]Dixon v. University of Toledo, 702 F.3d 269, 116 FEP 1604 (6th Cir. 2012), *cert. denied*, 134 S. Ct. 119, 120 FEP 368 (2013).

[15]*Id.*, 702 F.3d at 277.

[16]101 Fed. Cl. 435, 113 FEP 1089 (Fed. Cl. 2011).

[17]*Id.* at 463.

APPENDIX 1

TERMINOLOGY IN CASES CONCERNING GENDER IDENTITY AND SEXUAL ORIENTATION*

CHAPTER 2

THE TRANSFORMATIVE POWER OF WORDS

I. INTRODUCTION

A. Background

When we began preparing this treatise, one of the more significant issues that we confronted was whether we should strive to use a standard set of terms throughout. The initial thought was that such uniformity [would assist readers.... However,] discussions among the first few volunteers to join this writing project confirmed that there simply is no one set of words that is satisfactory to everyone....[1]

We have confidence that readers will come to see that there is no "right" set of words to use, although we do hope that they will appreciate that there are some "wrong" words that should be avoided, especially in the workplace. And employers will need to decide whether some words should not be used at all even though some employees gravitate toward them....

[T]ribunals (and others) have slowly evolved in their usage of terms, and many now use language that is less pejorative—or not

---

*Adapted from Christine Michelle Duffy, Natalie F. Hrubos, & Susan B. Marine, *The Transformative Power of Words* 2-2 to 2-3, in GENDER IDENTITY AND SEXUAL ORIENTATION IN THE WORKPLACE: A PRACTICAL GUIDE (Christine Michelle Duffy ed., 2014).

[1]In this treatise, we use "LGBT" [lesbian, gay, bisexual, and transgender] because it is widely used and we have not come up with a better short descriptive acronym. It should be noted that some individuals who would fit within the meaning of this acronym do not care to be referred to as being an LGBT individual. Accordingly, employers need to be sensitive to this consideration.

pejorative at all—as demonstrated, for example, by the evolution of phraseology from "sex change operation" to "sex reassignment surgery" to "gender reassignment surgery" to "gender confirming surgery" and "gender affirmation surgery." Similarly, the term "transsexualism" has faded somewhat into "gender identity disorder" (GID), which in turn is being replaced with "gender dysphoria." And the term "hermaphroditic conditions" became "intersex conditions," which is now evolving into the competing terms "disorders of sex development" and "differences in sex development" (DSD). This evolution in language, in and of itself, is very educational. That said, it should be noted that, by reciting the terminology used in opinions and articles, this treatise is neither endorsing the continued use of language that is pejorative or stigmatizing nor suggesting that LGBT (and non-LGBT) individuals are anything other than a normal part of the richness of human diversity.[2] Rather, we are suggesting that employers exercise caution in deciding what terminology they will use in the workplace, including in written policies. . . .

B. Pronouns and Different-Sex Persons

The use of masculine and feminine pronouns can be problematic when it comes to people who do not identify as male or female or who identify as "two spirit." One option to consider is the adoption of gender-neutral pronouns. However, the current proposed pronouns—such as "ey," "ne," "ve," "xe," and "ze"[3]—have not caught

---

[2]*See* FENWAY HEALTH, GLOSSARY OF GENDER AND TRANSGENDER TERMS 2 (rev. Jan. 2010), *available at* www.fenwayhealth.org/site/DocServer/Handout_7-C_Glossary_of_Gender_and_Transgender_Terms__fi.pdf:

> Terminology confusion . . . exists because terms that were widely used just 15 years ago are now passé, or even deemed highly offensive. So when you review the literature, and read about or listen to current events, be cognizant that transgender language is in flux and that some authors innocently use certain words without understanding the nuances involved. . . .
>
> The best advice is to listen to your clients—what terms do they use to describe themselves and their lives, what pronouns do they use, what words do they use to explain their medical needs? If you are not sure what terms to use, be forthright and ask your clients what terms they prefer.

Id. (emphasis omitted); Milton Diamond & Hazel Beh, Letter to the Editor, Variations of Sex Development Instead of Disorders of Sex Development, ARCHIVES DISEASE IN CHILDHOOD (July 27, 2006), *available at* http://adc.bmj.com/content/91/7/554/reply# *and* www.hawaii.edu/PCSS/biblio/articles/2005to2009/2006-variations.html.

[3]*See, e.g.*, *The Need for a Gender-Neutral Pronoun* (Jan. 24, 2010), GENDER NEUTRAL PRONOUN BLOG, http://genderneutralpronoun.wordpress.com ("One of the

on in the mainstream media or in commerce, which makes it very difficult to use them in everyday conversation without people stumbling over the words and losing concentration on what the speaker is actually saying. That said, at least one federal agency has a policy document that provides that "ze" is "[a] gender-neutral pronoun that can be used in place of he or she."[4] ...

Until gender-neutral pronouns catch on, employers should ensure that coworkers use the traditional pronouns that a gender-variant person prefers. If coworkers are willing to adapt and use gender-neutral pronouns in conversations among willing participants, then the employer should not discourage such a positive development.

When in doubt about whether a person is expressing a feminine or masculine gender, politely asking for the person's name (e.g., James) may help resolve the issue. Absent reason to do otherwise, use pronouns that match a person's gender expression and name.

Pronouns can be used as a means to harass and belittle LGBT employees. For example, referring to a gay man with female pronouns or vulgar names cast in female terms was held sufficient to constitute same-sex sexual harassment.[5] Similarly, an employee who is unaccepting of a coworker who has "come out" as a woman might purposely refer to her as "he" or, worse yet, as "he-she" or "it." Another way to purposely offend is to place an employee's name and/or matching pronouns in quotations.[6] As one judge has noted,

---

biggest problems facing the adoption of a new gender-neutral pronoun is the lack of unity and organization among supporters of the idea. People propose new pronouns without knowing about the scores of previous ones, and people interested in using gender-neutral pronouns can't find any they like, or can't figure out why they like or dislike certain forms."); Trans Issues Group, Gender Neutral Pronoun Usage (undated), *available at* http://web.mit.edu/trans/GenderNeutralPronouns.pdf; *Spivak Pronoun*, Wikipedia (June 16, 2013), http://en.wikipedia.org/wiki/Spivak_pronoun.

[4]U.S. Department of the Interior, Transgender and Other Gender Non-Conforming Employee Policy, Personnel Bulletin No. 13-03 (Apr. 10, 2013), *available at* http://elips.doi.gov/ELIPS/0/doc/3815/Electronic.aspx.

[5]Nichols v. Azteca Rest. Enters., 256 F.3d 864, 870, 874–75, 86 FEP 336 (9th Cir. 2001).

[6]See, for example, *Mathis v. Fountain-Fort Carson School District 8*, No. P20130034X, at 11, 13 (Colo. Div. Civ. Rts. June 17, 2013), *available at* www.transgenderlegal.org/media/uploads/doc_529.pdf, in which a school district referred to a gender-affirmed six-year-old girl whose "appearance and mannerisms are wholly female" (see www.transgenderlegal.org/headline_show.php?id=415 for her picture) as "he," and when it did use the female pronoun for her in written documents, it put the

"calling a transsexual or transgendered person a 'he/she' is a deeply insulting and offensive slur, and ... is strongly indicative of a negative animus towards gender nonconforming people."[7] Another judge held that referring to an employee as a "he-she," "cross-dresser," "cross-gender," "transsexual," and "drag queen" can create a hostile environment.[8] Employers will need to be prepared to respond to such offensive behavior.

---

pronoun "her" within quotation marks. The Colorado Division of Civil Rights found that there was probable cause to conclude that barring the girl—who was socially, medically, and legally a girl—from using the girls' bathroom, violated Colorado's prohibition against discrimination based on sex and transgender status.

[7]Myers v. Cuyahoga Cnty., 182 F. App'x 510, 520, 98 FEP 959 (6th Cir.), *cert. denied*, 549 U.S. 965 (2006). Transgender people frequently are subjected to disparaging comments, such as a presidential appointment and an aide to a House member being referred to as "she-males," a term that *The Washington Times* used in a 2010 editorial opposing the proposed Employment Non-Discrimination in Employment Act. *See, e.g.*, Traditional Values Coalition, *Obama Re-Nominates Extremists to High Posts* (undated), *available at* www.traditionalvalues.org/content/action_alerts/30669/Obama%20Re-Nominates%20Extremists%20To%20High%20Posts ("More recently, Obama picked his first she-male for a cushy appointment in the Commerce Department. [A] gender confused man who had his sex organs removed and has had breast enhancements to make him look like a woman."); Autumn Sandeen, *TVC Thinks Nothing of Continuing to Use Anti-Trans Pejoratives*, PAM'S HOUSE BLEND (June 23, 2009), http://pamshouseblend.firedoglake.com/2009/06/23/tvc-thinks-nothing-of-continuing-to-use-antitrans-pejoratives (reprinting a posting by the Traditional Values Coalition that referred to Rep. Barney Frank's legislative aide as a "she-male"); Editorial, *Discrimination Is Necessary*, WASH. TIMES, Apr. 23, 2010, www.washingtontimes.com/news/2010/apr/23/discrimination-is-necessary ("ENDA would make it impossible for a non-church-based charter school, for instance, to remove from the classroom a 'she-male' who insists on exposing her pupils to her unnatural transformation."); *see also* J. Matt Barber, *"Gay" Conquest Spells the ENDA Reason,* CONCERNED WOMEN FOR AMERICA (undated), http://web.archive.org/web/20110708011425/http://www.cwfa.org/articledisplay.asp?id=13852&department=CFI&categoryid=freedom (referring to transgender people as "she-male activists").

[8]Trevino v. Center for Health Care Servs., 2009 WL 2406196, at *3 (W.D. Tex. Aug. 1, 2009); *see also* Tates v. Blanas, 2003 WL 23864868, at *8 (E.D. Cal. Mar. 11, 2003) (in holding that transgender prisoners were disparately treated compared to non-transgender inmates, the court found, among other things, that the former were derided by being called "'he/she,' 'it,' 'faggot,' 'bitch,' 'queer,' and 'homo'").

APPENDIX 2

STATE FAIR EMPLOYMENT PRACTICES STATUTES RELATING TO DISCRIMINATION BASED ON GENDER IDENTITY OR EXPRESSION, GENDER DYSPHORIA, AND/OR SEXUAL ORIENTATION*

State Fair Employment Practices Law**	**Gender Identity or Expression**				**Sexual Orientation**	
	Expressly covered as its own protected characteristic?[1]	**Expressly covered as part of the definition of the protected characteristic "sexual orientation"?[2]**	**Gender dysphoria as a "disability"?[3]**	**Other potentially relevant prohibited bases for discrimination?[4]**	**Expressly covered as its own protected characteristic?[5]**	**Other potentially relevant prohibited bases for discrimination?[6]**
Alabama			No	None		None
Alaska				Sex		Marital status; sex

*Adapted from Denise M. Visconti & D'Arcy Kemnitz, *Survey of State Laws Regarding Gender Identity and Sexual Orientation Discrimination in the Workplace* ex. 20.1, in GENDER IDENTITY AND SEXUAL ORIENTATION IN THE WORKPLACE: A PRACTICAL GUIDE (Christine Michelle Duffy ed., 2014).

**Please note: footnotes to this chart appear at the end of this appendix, on page 11-30.

State Fair Employment Practices Law**	Gender Identity or Expression				Sexual Orientation	
	Expressly covered as its own protected characteristic?[1]	Expressly covered as part of the definition of the protected characteristic "sexual orientation"?[2]	Gender dysphoria as a "disability"?[3]	Other potentially relevant prohibited bases for discrimination?[4]	Expressly covered as its own protected characteristic?[5]	Other potentially relevant prohibited bases for discrimination?[6]
Arizona				Sex		Sex
Arkansas				Gender		Gender
California	Yes			Gender; sex	Yes	Gender; marital status; sex
Colorado		Yes		Off-duty conduct; sex	Yes	Marital status; off-duty conduct; sex
Connecticut	Yes		Yes	Sex	Yes	Marital status; sex
Delaware	Yes			Sex	Yes	Marital status; sex
District of Columbia	Yes			Personal appearance; sex	Yes	Marital status; personal appearance; sex

**Please note: footnotes to this chart appear at the end of this appendix, on page 11-30.

State Fair Employment Practices Law**	Gender Identity or Expression				Sexual Orientation	
	Expressly covered as its own protected characteristic?[1]	Expressly covered as part of the definition of the protected characteristic "sexual orientation"?[2]	Gender dysphoria as a "disability"?[3]	Other potentially relevant prohibited bases for discrimination?[4]	Expressly covered as its own protected characteristic?[5]	Other potentially relevant prohibited bases for discrimination?[6]
Florida			Unclear	Sex		Marital status; sex
Georgia				Sex (public employees only)		Sex (public employees only)
Hawaii	Yes		GIDs not resulting from physical impairments and transsexualism are not disabilities	Sex	Yes	Marital status; sex

State Fair Employment Practices Law**	Gender Identity or Expression				Sexual Orientation	
	Expressly covered as its own protected characteristic?[1]	Expressly covered as part of the definition of the protected characteristic "sexual orientation"?[2]	Gender dysphoria as a "disability"?[3]	Other potentially relevant prohibited bases for discrimination?[4]	Expressly covered as its own protected characteristic?[5]	Other potentially relevant prohibited bases for discrimination?[6]
Idaho			GIDs not resulting from physical impairments and trans-sexualism are not disabilities	Sex		Sex
Illinois		Yes		Sex	Yes	Marital status; sex
Indiana			GIDs not resulting from physical impairments and trans-sexualism are not disabilities	Sex		Sex

**Please note: footnotes to this chart appear at the end of this appendix, on page 11-30.

State Fair Employment Practices Law**	Gender Identity or Expression				Sexual Orientation	
	Expressly covered as its own protected characteristic?[1]	Expressly covered as part of the definition of the protected characteristic "sexual orientation"?[2]	Gender dysphoria as a "disability"?[3]	Other potentially relevant prohibited bases for discrimination?[4]	Expressly covered as its own protected characteristic?[5]	Other potentially relevant prohibited bases for discrimination?[6]
Iowa	Yes		Probably no	Sex	Yes	Sex
Kansas				Sex		Sex
Kentucky			GIDs not resulting from physical impairments and trans-sexualism are not disabilities	Sex		Sex
Louisiana				Sex		Sex
Maine		Yes	Yes	Sex	Yes	Sex
Maryland	Yes		Possibly	Sex	Yes	Marital status; sex
Massachusetts	Yes		Yes	Sex	Yes	Sex

State Fair Employment Practices Law**	Gender Identity or Expression				Sexual Orientation	
	Expressly covered as its own protected characteristic?[1]	Expressly covered as part of the definition of the protected characteristic "sexual orientation"?[2]	Gender dysphoria as a "disability"?[3]	Other potentially relevant prohibited bases for discrimination?[4]	Expressly covered as its own protected characteristic?[5]	Other potentially relevant prohibited bases for discrimination?[6]
Michigan				Sex		Marital status; sex
Minnesota		Yes		Sex	Yes	Marital status; sex
Mississippi				Sex (public state employees only)		Sex (public state employees only)
Missouri				Sex		Sex
Montana				Sex		Marital status; sex
Nebraska			GIDs not resulting from physical impairments and trans-sexualism are not disabilities	Sex		Marital status; sex

**Please note: footnotes to this chart appear at the end of this appendix, on page 11-30.

State Fair Employment Practices Law**	Gender Identity or Expression				Sexual Orientation	
	Expressly covered as its own protected characteristic?[1]	Expressly covered as part of the definition of the protected characteristic "sexual orientation"?[2]	Gender dysphoria as a "disability"?[3]	Other potentially relevant prohibited bases for discrimination?[4]	Expressly covered as its own protected characteristic?[5]	Other potentially relevant prohibited bases for discrimination?[6]
Nevada	Yes			Sex	Yes	Sex
New Hampshire			Yes	Sex	Yes	Marital status; sex
New Jersey	Yes		Yes	Sex	Yes	Civil union, domestic partnership, or marital status; sex
New Mexico	Yes			Sex	Yes	Sex; spousal affiliation
New York			Yes	Sex	Yes	Marital status; sex
North Carolina			Possibly no	Sex		Sex
North Dakota				Off-duty conduct; sex		Marital status; off-duty conduct; sex

State Fair Employment Practices Law**	**Gender Identity or Expression**				**Sexual Orientation**	
	Expressly covered as its own protected characteristic?[1]	**Expressly covered as part of the definition of the protected characteristic "sexual orientation"?[2]**	**Gender dysphoria as a "disability"?[3]**	**Other potentially relevant prohibited bases for discrimination?[4]**	**Expressly covered as its own protected characteristic?[5]**	**Other potentially relevant prohibited bases for discrimination?[6]**
Ohio			GIDs not resulting from physical impairments and trans-sexualism are not disabilities	Sex		Sex
Oklahoma				Sex		Sex
Oregon		Yes	Yes	Sex	Yes	Marital status; sex
Pennsylvania			Unclear	Sex		Sex

**Please note: footnotes to this chart appear at the end of this appendix, on page 11-30.

State Fair Employment Practices Law**	**Gender Identity or Expression**				**Sexual Orientation**	
	Expressly covered as its own protected characteristic?[1]	**Expressly covered as part of the definition of the protected characteristic "sexual orientation"?**[2]	**Gender dysphoria as a "disability"?**[3]	**Other potentially relevant prohibited bases for discrimination?**[4]	**Expressly covered as its own protected characteristic?**[5]	**Other potentially relevant prohibited bases for discrimination?**[6]
Puerto Rico	Yes		Sexual identity disorders not resulting from physical disabilities and transsexualism are not disabilities	Sex	Yes	Marital status; sex
Rhode Island	Yes			Sex	Yes	Sex
South Carolina			GIDs not resulting from physical impairments and transsexualism are not disabilities	Sex		Sex

State Fair Employment Practices Law**	**Gender Identity or Expression**				**Sexual Orientation**	
	Expressly covered as its own protected characteristic?[1]	**Expressly covered as part of the definition of the protected characteristic "sexual orientation"?[2]**	**Gender dysphoria as a "disability"?[3]**	**Other potentially relevant prohibited bases for discrimination?[4]**	**Expressly covered as its own protected characteristic?[5]**	**Other potentially relevant prohibited bases for discrimination?[6]**
South Dakota				Sex		Sex
Tennessee				Sex		Sex
Texas				Sex		Sex
Utah				Sex		Sex
Vermont	Yes			Sex	Yes	Sex
Virginia				Sex		Marital status; sex
Washington		Yes	Yes	Sex	Yes	Marital status; sex

**Please note: footnotes to this chart appear at the end of this appendix, on page 11-30.

State Fair Employment Practices Law**	Gender Identity or Expression				Sexual Orientation	
	Expressly covered as its own protected characteristic?[1]	**Expressly covered as part of the definition of the protected characteristic "sexual orientation"?[2]**	**Gender dysphoria as a "disability"?[3]**	**Other potentially relevant prohibited bases for discrimination?[4]**	**Expressly covered as its own protected characteristic?[5]**	**Other potentially relevant prohibited bases for discrimination?[6]**
West Virginia			GIDs not resulting from physical impairments and trans-sexualism are not disabilities	Sex		Sex
Wisconsin				Sex	Yes (but as part of the definition of "sex")	Marital status; sex
Wyoming				Sex		Sex

[1]If there is no entry in this column for a particular jurisdiction, it means that the jurisdiction does not expressly include gender identity or expression as its own protected characteristic.

[2]This column identifies the jurisdictions with fair employment practices (FEP) laws that expressly prohibit discrimination based on sexual orientation and include gender identity and/or gender expression within the definition of the term "sexual orientation."

[3]"Gender dysphoria" is the term used in the new [Diagnostic and Statistical Manual of Mental Disorders, 5th ed.] DSM-5 (2013) for what had been referred to previously as "gender identity disorder [GID]." Except for Alabama, all listed jurisdictions expressly prohibit discrimination against a qualified individual with disability. If there is no entry in this column for a particular state, it means that there is no statutory, regulatory, or case law guidance on point.

[4]California and New York have statutory provisions outside of their FEP laws that limit an employer's right to regulate the off-duty conduct of employees.

[5]If there is no entry in this column for a particular jurisdiction, it means that the jurisdiction does not expressly include sexual orientation as its own protected characteristic.

[6]California and New York have statutory provisions outside of their FEP laws that limit an employer's right to regulate the off-duty conduct of employees.

Chapter 12

AGE

I. SOURCES OF PROTECTION

A. The Age Discrimination in Employment Act (ADEA)

[On pages 12-4–12-5 of the Main Volume, replace the second, third, and fourth sentences of the carryover paragraph with the following.]

In *O'Connor v. Consolidated Coin Caterers Corp.*,[1] the Court held that a decision adverse to the older of the two may constitute actionable age discrimination. Assuming, as the parties and lower courts had, that the *McDonnell Douglas*[2] evidentiary framework utilized in Title VII cases also applied in cases under the ADEA,[3] the Court held that a discharged plaintiff need not demonstrate that he was replaced by someone who was not within the protected class.[4] The ADEA "does not ban discrimination against employees because they aged 40 or older; it bans discrimination against employees because of their age, but limits the protected class to those who are 40 or older. The fact that one person in the protected class has lost out to another person in the protected class is thus irrelevant, so long as he has lost out *because of his age*."[5] The Court explained further that "the fact that a replacement is substantially younger than the plaintiff is a far more reliable indicator of age discrimination than is the fact that the plaintiff was replaced by someone outside the protected class."[6]

[20][On page 12-6 of the Main Volume, in footnote 20, add the following after "*See*".]

Dediol v. Best Chevrolet, Inc., 655 F.3d 435, 441, 113 FEP 353 (5th Cir. 2011) (hostile work environment claim is cognizable under ADEA where elements of proof are met);

---

[1]517 U.S. 308, 70 FEP 486 (1996).

[2]McDonnell Douglas Corp. v. Green, 411 U.S. 792 (1973).

[3]517 U.S. at 311.

[4]*Id.* at 312.

[5]*Id.* (emphasis in original); *see also* Kralman v. Illinois Dep't of Veterans Affairs, 23 F.3d 150, 156, 64 FEP 1645 (7th Cir. 1994) (fact that person ultimately hired for position was also in class protected by ADEA did not preclude showing of discrimination where plaintiff, at age 71, was of entirely different generation than employee, age 46, who was hired).

[6]*O'Connor*, 517 U.S. at 313.

II. The Theory

[40][On page 12-9 of the Main Volume, in footnote 40, add the following at the end of the footnote.]

But see Jones v. Oklahoma City Pub. Sch., 617 F.3d 1273, 1277–78, 110 FEP 4 (10th Cir. 2010) (although *Gross* "clarified" meaning of "because of" within context of ADEA, Supreme Court did not say that plaintiff must prove that age was sole basis for employer's action).

III. Who Is Protected

A. Individuals Age 40 and Above

[47][On page 12-10 of the Main Volume, in footnote 47, add the following at the end of the footnote.]

In *Rabé v. United Airlines*, 636 F.3d 866, 111 FEP 1094 (7th Cir. 2011), the Seventh Circuit determined that even though the ADEA generally does not extend to aliens who work outside the United States, a foreign flight attendant who worked mostly abroad was covered by the ADEA where her employment agreement included a choice of law provision dictating that her employment would be "governed exclusively by applicable United States law"; this provision extended to the employee the protection of U.S. employment discrimination laws, including the ADEA. *Id.* at 871–72.

B. Exemptions for Certain Military Personnel and Executives

[56][On page 12-12 of the Main Volume, in footnote 56, add the following after the C.F.R. citation.]

Opp v. Office of State's Attorney of Cook Cnty., 630 F.3d 616, 621–22, 111 FEP 1 (7th Cir. 2010) (assistant state's attorney is "policy making official" who may not sue under ADEA; under Illinois law, assistant state's attorneys are "surrogates" for State's Attorney, are appointed by State's Attorney, and have inherent policymaking authority);

C. Exclusion of Independent Contractors and Partners in a Bona Fide Partnership

[67][On page 12-14 of the Main Volume, in footnote 67, add the following after "*See*".]

Ligon v. Lahood, 614 F.3d 150, 157 n.2, 109 FEP 1743 (5th Cir. 2010) (plaintiff's primary challenge to Federal Aviation Administration (FAA) determination not to renew his delegations of authority was not subject to review under ADEA because it was final order of FAA Administrator under Federal Aviation Act, 49 U.S.C. § 46110(a), review of which was not within district court's subject matter jurisdiction; remaining ADEA claims failed because plaintiff was not employee of FAA);

IV. WHO ARE COVERED ENTITIES

A. Private Employers

[99][On page 12-18 of the Main Volume, in footnote 99, add the following at the end of the footnote.]

But see Somerlott v. Cherokee Nation Distribs., Inc., 686 F.3d 1144, 115 FEP 1085 (10th Cir. 2012) (tribal sovereign immunity is coextensive with federal sovereign immunity; where entity is owned by tribe but incorporated under state law, it may be sued under ADEA just as sub-entity of federal government incorporated under state law would be susceptible to suit).

B. The Federal Government

[103][On page 12-19 of the Main Volume, in footnote 103, add the following at the end of the footnote.]

Certain actions of federal agencies fall within specific statutory schemes for review, and are not subject to challenge under the ADEA. *See* Ligon v. Lahood, 614 F.3d 150, 156–57, 109 FEP 1743 (5th Cir. 2010) (Designated Engineering Representative's primary challenge to FAA determination not to renew his delegations of authority was not subject to review under ADEA because it was final order of FAA Administrator under Federal Aviation Act, 49 U.S.C. § 46110(a), review of which was not within district court's subject matter jurisdiction; remaining ADEA claims failed because plaintiff was not employee of FAA).

[104][On page 12-19 of the Main Volume, in footnote 104, add the following after the parenthetical for "Lehman v. Nakshian".]

Cf. Velazquez-Ortiz v. Vilsack, 657 F.3d 64, 74–75, 113 FEP 627 (1st Cir. 2011) (even if "but for" standard under *Gross v. FBL Financial Services, Inc.*, 557 U.S. 167, 106 FEP 833 (2009), does not apply to ADEA action against federal government under 29 U.S.C. § 633(a), plaintiff failed to establish proof of even mixed motive, where memorandum citing need for "new blood" was issued in connection with entirely different employment decision, at different time, and was "profoundly ambiguous," and there was no evidence of pretext in employer's conclusion that other candidate had more relevant experience and performed better in interview) (citing Ford v. Mabus, 629 F.3d 198, 204–06 (D.C. Cir. 2010)).

C. State and Local Governments

[120][On page 12-22 of the Main Volume, in the carryover of footnote 120, add the following at the end of the footnote.]

But see EEOC v. Washington Suburban Sanitary Comm'n, 631 F.3d 174, 184–85, 111 FEP 481 (4th Cir. 2011) (legislative immunity did not preclude EEOC's subpoena for information regarding potential age discrimination; subpoena sought information about alleged discrimination before and after legislative decision making concerning organization's restructuring, rather than information about decision making itself).

[On page 12-23 of the Main Volume, in the fourth sentence of the carryover paragraph, add the following after "Consequently,".]

some

[132][On page 12-23 of the Main Volume, in footnote 132, add the following at the end of the footnote.]

But see Levin v. Madigan, 692 F.3d 607, 618, 115 FEP 1281 (7th Cir. 2012) ("Congress's silence ... tells us nothing about preclusion—we do not know whether Congress even considered alternative constitutional remedies in enacting the ADEA. ... But, as to constitutional claims, ... we have a hard time concluding that Congress's mere creation of a statutory scheme for age discrimination claims was intended to foreclose pre-existing constitutional claims. Congress frequently enacts new legal remedies that are not intended to repeal their predecessors."), *cert. dismissed*, 134 S. Ct. 2 (2013).

[On page 12-24 of the Main Volume, at the end of the carryover paragraph, add new footnote 134a.]

[134a]*Id.* at 1057. However, in *Levin*, 692 F.3d at 618, the Seventh Circuit held that the ADEA is not the exclusive remedy for age discrimination in employment claims and that § 1983 equal protection claims remain available to age discrimination plaintiffs.

VI. Procedural Issues Unique to Age

B. Filing With the EEOC

1. The Charge

[190]**[On page 12-35 of the Main Volume, in footnote 190, add the following after "*with*".]**

Spengler v. Worthington Cylinders, 615 F.3d 481, 490–91, 109 FEP 1526 (6th Cir. 2010) (plaintiff alleged sufficient facts in charge to put EEOC on notice of retaliation claim even though he did not check retaliation box; under "expected scope of investigation test," charge sufficiently asserted retaliation by stating that after complaining to plant manager about age discrimination, supervisor refused to talk to him or make eye contact, and that termination was "all about my last meeting with" supervisor), *and*

3. Determining When Discrimination Has Occurred

[201]**[On page 12-36 of the Main Volume, in footnote 201, add the following after "*E.g.*,".]**

Phillips v. Leggett & Platt, Inc., 658 F.3d 452, 456–59, 113 FEP 490 (5th Cir. 2011) (applying objective standard, 180-day period began when employer gave notice that plaintiff was being laid off when facility closed, notwithstanding post-termination decision to rehire her on temporary basis; no equitable tolling where plaintiff presented no evidence that she was prevented or discouraged from timely filing charge);

VIII. REPRESENTATIVE ACTIONS UNDER THE ADEA

A. Introduction

[On page 12-57 of the Main Volume, after the carryover sentence, add the following new paragraph.]

Whether an arbitration agreement permits class or representative proceedings continues to be a hotly contested issue.[7] In *Jock v. Sterling Jewelers, Inc.*,[8] the arbitration clause in the applicable employment agreement was silent on whether employees could arbitrate their ADEA claims in a representative action, yet the parties presented and argued that issue before the arbitrator.[9] The Second Circuit determined that the authority the parties delegated to the arbitrator empowered her to decide whether the plaintiffs could pursue their ADEA claims in a representative action arbitration, and therefore reversed the district court's order vacating the arbitrator's award.[10]

X. PROOF ISSUES UNIQUE TO AGE CASES

B. Disparate Treatment

1. The Plaintiff's Prima Facie Case

[362]**[On page 12-66 of the Main Volume, in footnote 362, add the following at the beginning of the footnote.]**

See Shelley v. Geren, 666 F.3d 599, 607, 114 FEP 303 (9th Cir. 2012) (*McDonnell Douglas* framework still applies to ADEA claims at summary judgment; shifting burden to defendant to produce but not persuade is not inconsistent with *Gross*); Jones v. Oklahoma City Pub. Sch., 617 F.3d 1273, 1278–79,110 FEP 4 (10th Cir. 2010) (*Gross* does not affect circuit precedent applying the *McDonnell Douglas* framework in disparate treatment cases under ADEA);

---

[7]*See generally* Chapter 43 (Alternative Dispute Resolution).

[8]646 F.3d 113, 112 FEP 1137 (2d Cir. 2011), *cert. denied*, 132 S. Ct. 1742 (2012).

[9]646 F.3d at 124.

[10]*Id.* at 127 ("Regardless whether the arbitrator was right or wrong in her analysis, she had the authority to make the decision, and the parties to the arbitration are bound by it.").

[364]**[On page 12-67 of the Main Volume, in footnote 364, add the following at the end of the footnote.]**

In an ADEA retaliation case, this element of the prima facie case is modified to require demonstration that the plaintiff "engaged in statutorily protected activity." *See* Smith v. Lafayette Bank & Trust Co., 674 F.3d 655, 658, 114 FEP 901 (7th Cir. 2012) (general complaints about pension calculation, 401(k) contributions, and cutbacks to branch staff were not protected activity under ADEA because they stated no specific references or objections to discrimination based on age; filing of discrimination charge after termination is protected activity, but employer must have actual notice of charge before making challenged decision); *see also* Porter v. City of Lake Lotawana, 651 F.3d 894, 899, 113 FEP 136 (8th Cir. 2011) ("causation element of the prima facie case of retaliation requires proof that decision maker was aware of plaintiff's protected activity at time of adverse employment action"; plaintiff therefore failed to prove that age was "but for" cause of termination) (citing Robinson v. Potter, 453 F.3d 990, 994 (8th Cir. 2006)).

[On page 12-67 of the Main Volume, in list item (3), add new footnote 364a after "... affected;".]

[364a]Courts have also adapted the prima facie case requirements to the age harassment context. *See* Dediol v. Best Chevrolet, Inc., 655 F.3d 435, 441–43, 113 FEP 353 (5th Cir. 2011) (establishing that age-based hostile work environment is actionable; "plaintiff advances such a claim by establishing that (1) he was over the age of 40; (2) the employee was subjected to harassment, either through words or actions, based on age; (3) the nature of the harassment was such that it created an objectively intimidating, hostile, or offensive work environment; and (4) there exists some basis for liability on the part of the employer"; summary judgment for employer reversed where material issue of fact created by supervisor's daily profanity, ageist comments, and threats).

[367]**[On page 12-67 of the Main Volume, in footnote 367, add the following at the end of the footnote.]**

See Provenzano v. LCI Holdings, Inc., 663 F.3d 806, 813, 114 FEP 90 (6th Cir. 2011) (evaluation of prima facie case must be conducted independently of company's "proffered nondiscriminatory reason and must not conflate the prima facie and pretext stages of the

McDonnell Douglas test"); Goncalves v. Plymouth Cnty. Sheriff's Dep't, 659 F.3d 101, 107, 113 FEP 805 (1st Cir. 2011) (employee failed to state prima facie case of age discrimination because she was not minimally qualified for promotion she sought; court will not "sit as a super personnel department, assessing the merits—or even the rationality—of employers' nondiscriminatory business decisions").

a. *Plaintiff's Qualifications*

[370]**[On page 12-68 of the Main Volume, in footnote 370, add the following after "*See*".]**

Acevedo-Parrilla v. Novartis Ex-Lax, Inc., 696 F.3d 128, 138, 116 FEP 289 (1st Cir. 2012) (terminated protected-age employee satisfied second prong of prima facie case by establishing his unbroken history of receiving satisfactory performance evaluations; company's assertion that he was terminated for violating quality control standards comes into play only after burden has shifted to employer to articulate legitimate, nondiscriminatory reason for its action); Melendez v. Autogermana, Inc., 622 F.3d 46, 51, 110 FEP 832 (1st Cir. 2010) (discharged salesman established prima facie case that he was meeting employer's legitimate performance expectations despite recent failure to meet sales goals where he presented 10-year history of satisfactory performance appraisals, past awards for outstanding performance, and evidence that present failure to meet goals at least in part reflected downturn in economy and that other salesmen also failed to meet goals);

[370]**[On page 12-69 of the Main Volume, in the carryover of footnote 370, add the following after "*cf.*".]**

Naik v. Boehringer Ingelheims Pharms., 627 F.3d 596, 600–01, 110 FEP 1443 (7th Cir. 2010) (discharged protected-age salesman who falsified his call records failed to establish prima facie case of discriminatory discharge where employer's legitimate expectation was that records would be kept accurately); Webb v. ServiceMaster BSC, LLC, 438 F. App'x 451, 453, 113 FEP 536 (6th Cir. 2011) (unpublished) (discharged protected-age tax manager could not rely on history of satisfactory performance appraisals to establish prima facie case that he was qualified where appraisals were stale and employer's legitimate expectations may have changed over time);

[373]**[On page 12-70 of the Main Volume, in the carryover of footnote 373, add the following at the end of the footnote.]**

Some courts have insisted that this determination must be made prior to any consideration of the employer's proffered legitimate, nondiscriminatory business reason for the action in question. *See Melendez v. Autogermana, Inc.*, 622 F.3d at 51 (refusing to analyze employer's reason at first stage of the *McDonnell Douglas* framework, or to allow it to undermine plaintiff's prima facie case).

b. Selection or Retention of Someone "Younger"

[380]**[On page 12-71 of the Main Volume, in footnote 380, add the following after "*accord*".]**

Earl v. Nielsen Media Research, 658 F.3d 1108, 1116, 113 FEP 609 (9th Cir. 2011) (comparison with younger employee within protected class is permissible; "Rigid insistence that a comparator be a member of the protected class overlooks a key difference between age and other forms of discrimination.");

[382]**[On page 12-72 of the Main Volume, in footnote 382, add the following at the end of the footnote.]**

See also Blizzard v. Marion Tech. Coll., 698 F.3d 275, 284, 116 FEP 392 (6th Cir. 2012) (summary judgment affirmed, in part, because plaintiff's replacement was only 6½ years younger than plaintiff and noting that—under *Grosjean*—in absence of direct evidence that employer considered age to be factor in its decision making, age difference of 6 years or less between employee and replacement is not significant and that difference of 6 to 10 years is to be considered on case-by-case basis in light of rule that age difference of 10 years or more is generally considered to be significant), *cert. denied*, 133 S. Ct. 2359, 118 FEP 884 (2013).

[385]**[On page 12-73 of the Main Volume, in footnote 385, add the following after "*see also*".]**

Chambers v. Travelers Cos., 668 F.3d 559, 566, 114 FEP 539 (8th Cir. 2012) (neither original replacement for 52-year-old plaintiff, who was 51, nor subsequent alleged replacement, who was 44, was "sufficiently younger");

[392]**[On page 12-74 of the Main Volume, in footnote 392, add the following after "*Compare*".]**

Shah v. NXP Semiconductors USA Inc., 507 F. App'x 483, 489, 116 FEP 1167 (6th Cir. 2012) (unpublished) (reassignment of laid-off protected-age employee's duties to younger employee who was retained in RIF insufficient to establish that older employee was "replaced" where retained employee was already performing many of same duties as well as additional duties as manager and technical liaison);

[410]**[On page 12-79 of the Main Volume, in footnote 410, add the following at the beginning of the footnote.]**

See, e.g., Shah v. NXP Semiconductors USA Inc., 507 F. App'x 483, 492, 116 FEP 1167 (6th Cir. 2012) (unpublished) (protected-age employee must do more than show that employer's articulated reason for selecting him for RIF was untrue, he must also demonstrate intent to discriminate in order to prevail on age discrimination claim);

2. *Defendant's Articulation of a Legitimate, Nondiscriminatory Reason*

[426]**[On page 12-82 of the Main Volume, in footnote 426, after parenthetical for "*Id.* at 691–92" replace the ";" with a "."; then add the following before "Senske v. Sybase Inc.,".]**

See also Lefevers v. GAF Fiberglass Corp., 667 F.3d 721, 725–26, 114 FEP 385 (6th Cir. 2012) (no showing that employer's explanation for selecting protected-age shift supervisor for RIF—poor performance—was pretextual; assessment of performance substantiated by performance reviews and other records); Clark v. Matthews Int'l Corp., 628 F.3d 462, 470, 111 FEP 33 (8th Cir. 2010) (protected-age graphic artist failed to refute employer's explanation that he was selected for layoff because of his poor performance, among other reasons);

[427]**[On page 12-83 of the Main Volume, in footnote 427, add the following after "*E.g.*,".]**

Cruz v. Bristol-Myers Squibb Co., 699 F.3d 563, 571, 116 FEP 713 (1st Cir. 2012) (protected-age individual failed to show that employer's explanation that it had selected employees for RIF using ranking system that considered only skill level and seniority was pretext for discrimination);

[437]**[On page 12-85 of the Main Volume, in footnote 437, add the following after "*E.g.*,".]**

Clark v. Matthews Int'l Corp., 628 F.3d 462, 470, 111 FEP 33 (8th Cir. 2010) (protected-age graphic artist failed to refute company's explanation that RIF involving employee's position reflected shift in its production lines from corrugated packaging to "primary "packaging"); *vacated in part,* 639 F.3d 391, 112 FEP 249 (8th Cir. 2011);

[445]**[On page 12-87 of the Main Volume, in footnote 445, add the following after "*See*".]**

Rahlf v. Mo-Tech Corp., 642 F.3d 633, 639–40, 112 FEP 787 (8th Cir. 2011) (protected-age individual failed to show that employer, who relied on both subjective and objective performance criteria in selecting individuals for layoff, impermissibly discriminated on basis of age; employer was not required to rely on only objective standards and performance evaluations);

3. *Plaintiff's Proof of Pretext*

[457]**[On page 12-91 of the Main Volume, in footnote 457, add the following at the end of the footnote.]**

See also Muñoz v. Sociedad Española de Auxilio Mutuo y Beneficiencia de P.R., 671 F.3d 49, 55–57, 114 FEP 412 (1st Cir. 2012) (once matter has been tried to jury, whether plaintiff established prima facie case is not important; "focus then becomes whether a jury reasonably could have inferred, by a preponderance of the evidence, that [plaintiff] was terminated because of his protected conduct"; where employer terminated plaintiff one day after his deposition in his age case, but made decision to terminate him weeks beforehand, without knowledge of his protected activity, proximity to deposition "cannot support an inference of causality"; nevertheless, other circumstantial evidence supported jury verdict for plaintiff); Rahlf v. Mo-Tech. Co., 642 F.3d 633, 639–40, 112 FEP 787 (8th Cir. 2011) (protected-age individual failed to show that employer, who relied on both subjective and objective performance criteria in selecting individuals for layoff, impermissibly discriminated on basis of age; employer was not required to rely on only objective standards and performance evaluations).

[462]**[On page 12-91 of the Main Volume, in footnote 462, add the following after "*E.g.*,".]**

Runyon v. Applied Extrusion Techs., Inc., 619 F.3d 735, 739–41, 110 FEP 147 (7th Cir. 2010) (affirming grant of judgment as matter of law at close of employee's case, at which point *McDonnell Douglas* analysis was irrelevant and only question was whether "plaintiff presented enough evidence to allow a rational jury to rule in his favor"; plaintiff was not similarly situated to younger co-worker who was not discharged following altercation, given plaintiff's other major conflicts with co-workers, and plaintiff therefore did not establish pretext);

[465]**[On page 12-93 of the Main Volume, in footnote 465, add the following after "*E.g.*,".]**

Gibson v. American Greetings Corp., 670 F.3d 844, 854–56, 114 FEP 927 (8th Cir. 2012) (summary judgment granted for employer against spouse co-plaintiffs who failed to introduce "sufficient, specific evidence of disparate treatment"; wife's claim that younger people with less seniority were cross-trained, without specifically identifying similarly situated employee, was unsupported by record, and husband's age claim was meritless where employer presented evidence that he was replaced by older man); Anderson v. Durham D&M, LLC, 606 F.3d 513, 521–24, 109 FEP 561 (8th Cir. 2010) (summary judgment for employer appropriate where plaintiff was terminated because he had three vehicular accidents; plaintiff asserted, without introducing specific evidence, that employer overlooked other employees' accidents);

[466]**[On page 12-94 of the Main Volume, in footnote 466, add the following after "*See*".]**

Gilbert v. Napolitano, 670 F.3d 258, 261–62, 114 FEP 923 (D.C. Cir. 2012) (summary judgment for employer reversed where employer contended that individual promoted had superior qualifications, but plaintiff's supervisor testified that plaintiff's "qualifications and experience" "dwarf[ed]" those of selected individual, and that difference in qualifications was "large enough to slap you in the face");

[468]**[On page 12-95 of the Main Volume, in footnote 468, add the following at the end of the footnote.]**

Notably, the Tenth and Eleventh Circuits have held that the proximate causation standard for "cat's paw" liability set forth in *Staub v. Proctor Hospital*, 131 S. Ct. 1186, 111 FEP 993 (2011), does not apply to ADEA cases. *See* Sims v. MVM, Inc., 704 F.3d 1327, 1335–36, 117 FEP 1 (11th Cir. 2013); Simmons v. Sykes Enters., Inc., 647 F.3d 943, 949–50, 112 FEP 596 (10th Cir. 2011). As the *Sims* court explained, the ADEA's but for causation standard requires "that the proscribed animus have a determinative influence on the employer's adverse decision." 704 F.3d at 1335–36.

[475]**[On page 12-97 of the Main Volume, in footnote 475, add the following after "*See*".]**

Melendez v. Autogermana, Inc., 622 F.3d 46, 51, 110 FEP 832 (1st Cir. 2010) (discharged salesman established prima facie case that he was meeting employer's legitimate performance expectations despite failure to meet recent sales goals, where he presented 10-year history of satisfactory performance appraisals, past awards for outstanding performance, and evidence that present failure to meet goals, at least in part, reflected downturn in economy and that other salesmen also failed to meet goals);

[478]**[On page 12-98 of the Main Volume, in footnote 478, add the following after "*See*".]**

Simmons v. Sykes Enters., Inc., 647 F.3d 943, 948–50, 112 FEP 596 (10th Cir. 2011) (plaintiff's evidence asserting that employer's decision to terminate him should not have been made because employer's perception was wrong was insufficient to prove that employer's legitimate, nondiscriminatory reason was pretext for discrimination; to establish "cat's paw" liability, plaintiff must prove that supervisor with discriminatory animus was "but for" cause of adverse employment action);

[484]**[On page 12-100 of the Main Volume, in footnote 484, add the following after "*See*".]**

Clark v. Matthews Int'l Corp., 628 F.3d 462, 470, 111 FEP 33 (8th Cir. 2010) (protected-age graphic artist failed to refute company's explanation that RIF involving employee's position reflected shift in its production lines from corrugated packaging to "primary "packaging"), *vacated in part on other grounds*, 639 F.3d 391, 112 FEP 249 (8th Cir. 2011); Moss v. BMC Software, Inc., 610 F.3d 917, 925–26, 109 FEP 1173 (5th Cir. 2010) (affirming summary judgment for employer because, although plaintiff had more years of work experience than candidate selected, that did not make him "clearly better qualified," as other candidate had experience with specific types of transactions comprising primary responsibility of position; "[T]he ADEA was not intended to be a vehicle for judicial second-guessing of employment decisions nor was it intended to transform the courts into personnel managers. The ADEA cannot protect older employees from erroneous or even arbitrary personnel decisions, but only from decisions which are unlawfully motivated.");

[486][On page 12-102 of the Main Volume, in footnote 486, add the following after "*See, e.g.,*".]

Gorzynski v. JetBlue Airways Corp., 596 F.3d 93, 108 FEP 769 (2d Cir. 2010) (protected-age manager adequately established that employer's stated reasons for discharging her—customer complaints and poor performance—were pretextual where complaint was minor and investigation of it was inadequate, and appraisal occurred in situation that suggested it was influenced by bias);

[495][On page 12-104 of the Main Volume, in footnote 495, add the following at the end of the footnote.]

See also Rahlf v. Mo-Tech Corp., 642 F.3d 633, 638–40, 112 FEP 787 (8th Cir. 2011) (employer's hiring of new employees within year after RIF did not establish that RIF was pretext for age discrimination; "when a company exercises its business judgment in deciding to reduce its work force, it need not provide evidence of financial distress to make it a legitimate ... RIF"; employer is permitted, in its business judgment, to rely on subjective criteria, to ignore positive performance reviews, and to rely on criteria not stated in employee handbook when determining who to terminate in RIF).

[509][On page 12-112 of the Main Volume, in footnote 509, add the following after "*See*".]

Bondurant v. Air Line Pilots Ass'n, Int'l, 679 F.3d 386, 395, 114 FEP 1645 (6th Cir. 2012) (statements by union decision makers not direct evidence of age discrimination where they were unrelated to plaintiff and indicated union's recognition of applicable law and need to comply with ADEA to avoid age discrimination); Clark v. Matthews Int'l Corp., 628 F.3d 462, 470–71, 111 FEP 33 (8th Cir. 2010) (neither decision maker's "isolated joke" that plaintiff "could always get a job at Wal-Mart as a greeter," made in jest and not in reference to termination decision, nor reasonable and non-excessive inquiry into employee's retirement plans, including sending American Association of Retired Persons (AARP) mailing, sufficed to establish age discrimination; employer had legitimate interest in knowing such plans); Moss v. BMC Software, Inc., 610 F.3d 917, 928–29, 109 FEP 1173 (5th Cir. 2010) (decision maker's remark that she was looking for lawyer who was at "more junior level" than herself was not direct evidence of age discrimination because "more junior level" could refer to someone older than her but with less experience);

[510]**[On page 12-112 of the Main Volume, in footnote 510, add the following after "*See*".]**

Lefevers v. GAF Fiberglass Corp., 667 F.3d 721, 724–25, 114 FEP 385 (6th Cir. 2012) (statements by non–decision makers, and statements by decision makers unrelated to pertinent decision-making process, were not proof of intent to discriminate; statements included "[w]hen are you going to retire?" and "[w]e realize you guys are getting old and would like to know if you are going to retire"); Bonefont-Igaravidez v. International Shipping Corp., 659 F.3d 120, 124, 113 FEP 934 (1st Cir. 2011) (affirming summary judgment for employer; although plaintiff's co-workers had called him "old, sick man," asked him why he had not retired, and "urged him to stay home to watch soap operas and care for his grandchildren," these were "stray comments" by non–decision makers unrelated to termination decision);

4. Mixed-Motive Cases

[557]**[On page 12-125 of the Main Volume, in footnote 557, add the following at the end of the footnote.]**

Notwithstanding the decision in *Gross*, the D.C. Circuit determined in *Ford v. Mabus*, 629 F.3d 198, 110 FEP 1665 (D.C. Cir. 2010), that federal employees may use the mixed-motive framework in an ADEA claim against the federal government because the *Gross* Court was analyzing § 623 of the ADEA, which covers only private employers, whereas § 633 (covering federal government employment) uses "sweeping" language that is more expansive than § 623. 629 F.3d at 206. State-law age claims in some states also may continue to incorporate a mixed-motive framework even after *Gross*. *See* Diaz v. Jiten Hotel Mgmt., Inc., 671 F.3d 78, 82–84, 114 FEP 449 (1st Cir. 2012) (plaintiffs who sue for age discrimination under Massachusetts state law do not have to meet ADEA's "but for" causation standard; mixed-motive jury instruction, "for the time being," is available in federal court for age discrimination cases brought under Massachusetts state law); Newberry v. Burlington Basket Co., 622 F.3d 979, 982, 110 FEP 615 (8th Cir. 2010) (jury instruction stating that if jury found plaintiff's age "played a part" in decision, then age was "determining factor" in plaintiff's termination, was not proper under ADEA after *Gross*, but jury verdict for plaintiff upheld because instruction was permissible under Iowa Civil Rights Act and error therefore was harmless).

[On page 12-125 of the Main Volume, after the block quote that ends with footnote 557, add the following.]

In the period since *Gross* was decided, some courts have interpreted its holding requiring proof of "but for" causation not to require proof that age was the sole motivating factor in the employer's decision.[11]

C. Disparate Impact

1. *The Plaintiff's Prima Facie Case*

b. *Threshold Showing of Disparate Impact*

[575]**[On page 12-129 of the Main Volume, in footnote 575, add the following at the end of the footnote.]**

See also Clark v. Matthews Int'l Corp., 628 F.3d 462, 468–69, 111 FEP 33 (8th Cir. 2010) (plaintiffs challenging RIF had to establish "sufficiently substantial" drop in employment rate of employees 40 years of age or older, which would create inference that employees were terminated because of their age; 4% drop insufficient to infer

[11]*See* Jones v. Oklahoma City Pub. Schs., 617 F.3d 1273, 1277–78, 110 FEP 4 (10th Cir. 2010) ("Instead, an employer may be liable under the ADEA if other factors contributed to its taking an adverse action, as long as 'age was the factor that made a difference.'") (quoting Wilkerson v. Shinseki, 606 F.3d 1256, 1266 (10th Cir. 2010)).

that age was factor), *vacated in part on other grounds*, 639 F.3d 391, 112 FEP 249 (8th Cir. 2011); *cf.* Aliotta v. Bair, 614 F.3d 556, 566, 569, 109 FEP 1701 (D.C. Cir. 2010) (affirming rejection of plaintiffs' statistical analysis of RIF because it included employees who opted for voluntary buyouts/early retirement offers—and thus suffered no adverse employment action—and there was no disparate impact once they were excluded; employers should not be discouraged from proposing such offers, which help mitigate need for RIF).

2. The Employer's Defense

a. Reasonable Factor Other Than Age

[585][On page 12-130 of the Main Volume, in footnote 585, add the following at the end of the footnote.]

See also Bondurant v. Air Line Pilots Ass'n, Int'l, 679 F.3d 386, 396, 114 FEP 1645 (6th Cir. 2012) (plaintiff's disparate impact claim failed where union demonstrated that distribution of funds pursuant to bankruptcy restructuring agreement and its cut-off date was RFOA, even if plan may have effects correlated with age).

XI. OTHER AFFIRMATIVE DEFENSES

B. Reasonable Factor Other Than Age (RFOA)

[606][On page 12-134 of the Main Volume, in footnote 606, add the following after "*see*".]

Bondurant v. Air Line Pilots Ass'n, Int'l, 679 F.3d 386, 396, 114 FEP 1645 (6th Cir. 2012) (plaintiff's disparate impact claim failed where union demonstrated that distribution of funds pursuant to bankruptcy restructuring agreement and its cut-off date was RFOA, even if plan may have effects correlated with age);

C. Bona Fide Occupational Qualification (BFOQ)

[616][On page 12-135 of the Main Volume, in footnote 616, add the following at the end of the footnote.]

Courts have disagreed over whether corporate pilots (pilots of private planes) may be subject to the "age 60" rule applied to commercial carriers. *See, e.g.*, EEOC v. Exxon Mobil Corp., 344 F. App'x

868, 871–72, 107 FEP 66 (5th Cir. 2009) (case remanded to consider continuing validity of FAA "age 60" regulation; regulation is not dispositive unless employer is bound by it).

D. Bona Fide Employee Benefit Plan

1. *Early Retirement Incentives*

[637]**[On page 12-139 of the Main Volume, in footnote 637, add the following after "*See*".]**

EEOC v. Minnesota Dep't of Corr., 648 F.3d 910, 913–15, 113 FEP 6 (8th Cir. 2011) (affirming grant of summary judgment in favor of EEOC; employer's early retirement incentive program facially discriminatory where eligibility for early retirement benefits vanished once employee turned 55, even though employer lawfully could have required firefighters to retire at age 55; safe harbor/affirmative defense in 29 U.S.C. § 623(f)(2)(B)(ii) did not apply because plan was inconsistent with ADEA's purposes);

2. *Pensions*

[678]**[On page 12-147 of the Main Volume, in footnote 678, add the following at the end of the footnote.]**

Cf. Tomlinson v. El Paso Corp., 653 F.3d 1281, 1288, 112 FEP 1687 (10th Cir. 2011) (summary judgment granted to employer; demonstrating age discrimination in cash balance pension plans requires proof of age-discriminatory inputs, e.g., size of cash payments into balance and interest earned, not age-disparate outcomes); Jensen v. Solvay Chems., Inc., 625 F.3d 641, 659–60, 110 FEP 278 (10th Cir. 2010) (affirming grant of summary judgment to employer on ADEA disparate impact claim; retirement plan complied with ADEA's § 4(i) benefits accrual safe harbor, which applies to both disparate treatment and disparate impact claims).

F. Settlement and Release

[701]**[On page 12-152 of the Main Volume, in footnote 701, add the following after "*see*".]**

Ridinger v. Dow Jones & Co., 651 F.3d 309, 313–17, 112 FEP 1221 (2d Cir. 2011) (employer, as party asserting validity of waiver, bore burden of proving that waiver was made knowingly and voluntarily; waiver valid because agreement written in manner calculated to be understood by relevant employee);

XII. REMEDIES

D. Front Pay

[792][On page 12-170 of the Main Volume, in footnote 792, add the following after "*See*".]

Barton v. Zimmer, Inc., 662 F.3d 448, 454, 113 FEP 929 (7th Cir. 2011) (affirming denial of front pay due to lack of such causation; "To recover front pay as an equitable remedy in lieu of reinstatement, plaintiff would have to establish causation—that the discriminatory conduct caused the disability that prevents his reinstatement");

XIII. INTERSECTION OF THE ADEA WITH ERISA

[840][On page 12-180 of the Main Volume, in footnote 840, add the following after "*see also*".]

Northwest Airlines, Inc. v. Phillips, 675 F.3d 1126, 1130–32 & n.12, 114 FEP 1215 (8th Cir. 2012) (affirming grant of summary judgment to defendant under *Hazen Paper* analysis—plaintiff challenging pension calculation methodology under ADEA "must adduce sufficient evidence to show that the differential treatment was 'actually motivated' by age, not pension status"; factors being used here to provide "targeted" benefit—"remaining years of service and final average earnings"—are "analytically distinct from age");

Chapter 13

DISABILITY*

*This chapter references the Equal Employment Opportunity Commission (EEOC) Compliance Manual, which is available at http://www.eeoc.gov/laws/guidance/compliance.cfm (last visited May 7, 2014), and on BBNA's Labor and Employment Law Resource Center.

I. INTRODUCTION

[1][On page 13-6 of the Main Volume, replace footnote 1 with the following.]

[1]As discussed *infra*, the ADA was amended in a number of significant respects by the Americans with Disabilities Act Amendments Act (ADAAA), Pub. L. No. 110-325 (2008). The statute, as amended, appears at 42 U.S.C. §§ 12101 et seq. (2011). The amended Act is referred to throughout this chapter as "the ADA."

[13][On page 13-8 of the Main Volume, replace footnote 13 with the following.]

[13]29 C.F.R. Part 1630 (2012).

[On page 13-9 of the Main Volume, in the last sentence of the carryover paragraph, add the following after "For example, the Amendments clarified that".]

[t]he determination of whether an individual is disabled generally is to be made without reference to the ameliorative effects of mitigating measures, and that"

[On page 13-9 of the Main Volume, at the end of the last sentence of the carryover paragraph, add new footnote 13a.]

[13a]29 C.F.R. §§ 1630.2(j)(1)(vi), 1630.2(o)(4). The statement of purpose contained in the EEOC regulations states that "the ADA, as amended, and these regulations, are intended to provide a clear and comprehensive national mandate for the elimination of discrimination against individuals with disabilities, and to provide clear, strong, consistent, enforceable standards addressing discrimination." 29 C.F.R. § 1630.1 (2012).

II. OVERVIEW OF MAJOR STATUTES

A. The Americans with Disabilities Act

1. General Structure of the ADA

[On page 13-10 of the Main Volume, in footnotes 19–21, all the provisions of the ADA that had been published in supplements to the U.S. Code are now included in the 2012 edition of Titles 42 and 47.]

2. *Title I of the Americans with Disabilities Act*

[On page 13-10 of the Main Volume, in footnote 22, all the provisions of the ADA that had been published in supplements to the U.S. Code are now included in the 2012 edition of Titles 42 and 47.]

[23]**[On page 13-10 of the Main Volume, in footnote 23, replace "§ 794" with the following.]**

§§ 791–794

[24]**[On page 13-11 of the Main Volume, in footnote 24, add the following at the end of the footnote.]**

See Cortés-Rivera v. Department of Corr. & Rehab. of the Commonwealth of P.R., 626 F.3d 21, 26–27, 23 AD 1473 (1st Cir. 2010) (as independent contractor, prison doctor could not challenge his discharge under Title I of ADA, which protects only employees).

[On page 13-11, in the second full paragraph, in the sentences that end with footnotes 30 and 31, replace "§ 504" of the Rehabilitation Act with the following.]

§§ 501–504

[36]**[On page 13-12 of the Main Volume, in footnote 36, add the following after "*cf.*".]**

Field v. Napolitano, 663 F.3d 505, 513–14, 25 AD 673 (1st Cir. 2011) (Aviation Transportation and Security Act preempts application of Rehabilitation Act to field security screeners; collecting cases); Joren v. Napolitano, 633 F.3d 1144, 1146, 111 FEP 612, 24 AD 129 (7th Cir. 2011) (same), *cert. denied*, 132 S. Ct. 290 (2011).

3. *Title II of the Americans with Disabilities Act*

[39]**[On page 13-13 of the Main Volume, in footnote 39, add the following after "*Compare*".]**

Elwell v. Oklahoma *ex rel.* Bd. of Regents of Univ. of Okla., 693 F.3d 1303, 1309–10, 26 AD 1422 (10th Cir. 2012) (Title II's prohibition against bias in providing public services does not extend to employment; Title II is "proper tool for pursuing employment discrimination claims"), *cert. denied*, 133 S. Ct. 1255, 27 AD 928 (2013), *and*

[39][On page 13-13 of the Main Volume, in footnote 39, add the following after "*with*".]

McDonald v. Pennsylvania State Police, 485 F. App'x 612, 27 AD 150 (3d Cir. 2012) (nonprecedential) (reinstating former police chief's ADA Title II action; Title II's prohibition against bias by public entities includes employment discrimination),

5. Americans with Disabilities Act Amendments Act of 2008

[51][On page 13-15 of the Main Volume, in footnote 51, add the following after "*E,g.,*".]

Reynolds v. American Red Cross, 701 F.3d 143, 151–52, 27 AD 263 (4th Cir. 2012) (determination of whether plaintiff's back and neck injury and permanent weight-lifting limitations of 15 pounds substantially limited him in major life activity must be made under standards in effect before ADAAA, where injury occurred in 2008 and ADAAA is not retroactive); Steffen v. Donohoe, 680 F.3d 738, 744–45, 25 AD 1825 (7th Cir. 2012) (claim of postal worker who had back injury and was discharged in 2006 must be decided under pre-ADAAA standards; amendments are not retroactive); Tusing v. Des Moines Indep. Cmty. Sch. Dist., 639 F.3d 507, 518 & n.5, 111 FEP 1761, 24 AD 783 (8th Cir. 2011) (same); Nyrop v. Independent Sch. Dist. No. 11, 616 F.3d 728, 734 n.4, 23 AD 801 (8th Cir. 2010) (collecting cases on proposition that ADAAA is not retroactive but declining to determine issue); Kemp v. Holder, 610 F.3d 231, 235–36, 23 AD 513 (5th Cir. 2010) (determination of whether hearing-impaired former court security officer was substantially limited in major life activity correctly considered his impairment as mitigated by hearing aids where analysis occurred pre-ADAAA and standards of ADAAA are not retroactive);

[54][On page 13-16 of the Main Volume, in footnote 54, add the following at the end of the footnote.]

Notwithstanding its disapproval of the reasoning and implications of *Sutton*, Congress excluded routine visual impairments from its definition of conditions that must be considered without reference to mitigating factors. "The ameliorative effects of the mitigating measures of ordinary eyeglasses or contact lenses shall be considered in determining whether an impairment substantially limits a major life activity." 42 U.S.C. § 12102(4)(E)(ii).

B. The Rehabilitation Act of 1973

1. General Structure of the Rehabilitation Act

[62][On page 13-17 of the Main Volume, in footnote 62, delete the period at the end of the footnote and add the following.]

, as well as the government itself, *id.* §791.

3. Section 503 of the Rehabilitation Act

[On page 13-21 of the Main Volume, add new footnote 84a at the end of the section heading.]

[84a]In August 2012, the Office of Federal Contract Compliance Programs (OFCCP) promulgated regulations that significantly altered the obligations government contractors must meet in order to comply with § 503. Those regulations are found at 41 C.F.R. Part 60-741 (2113).

4. Section 504 of the Rehabilitation Act

a. General Provisions of Section 504

[On page 13-22, after the sentence that ends with footnote 91, add the following.]

Unlike Title VII, there are few exemptions to coverage under the Rehabilitation Act.[1]

---

[1]*See, e.g.*, Doe v. Salvation Army, 685 F.3d 564, 573–74, 26 AD 769 (6th Cir. 2012) (Salvation Army is subject to § 504 of Rehabilitation Act because certain local units receive federal financial assistance and Salvation Army itself is corporation "principally engaged in the business of providing social services"; there is no express exception for activities of religious corporations under § 504).

[92]**[On page 13-22 of the Main Volume, in footnote 92, add the following at the end of the footnote.]**

But see Lee v. City of Columbus, Ohio, 636 F.3d 245, 24 AD 257 (6th Cir. 2011) (unlike ADA, Rehabilitation Act requires proof that discrimination was "sole cause" of adverse employment action).

[93]**[On page 13-22 of the Main Volume, in footnote 93, add the following before "*Compare*".]**

See Cortes-Rivera v. Department of Corr., 626 F.3d 21, 26, 23 AD 1473 (1st Cir. 2010) (circuits are split on whether plaintiffs alleging employment discrimination under § 504 of Rehabilitation Act must meet ADA's definition of employee).

C. The Jobs for Veterans Act of 2002

[On page 13-28 of the Main Volume, add new footnote 124a at the end of the section heading].

[124a]On August 27, 2013, the OFCCP repealed regulations describing the obligations of federal contractors under the pre-amendment Vietnam Era Veterans' Readjustment Assistance Act (formerly at 41 C.F.R. Part 250), and significantly amended the requirements under the Jobs for Veterans' Act at 41 C.F.R. Part 60-300. The new regulations became effective March 14, 2014.

D. State and Local Laws

[150]**[On page 13-32 of the Main Volume, in footnote 150, add the following at the end of the footnote.]**

But see Paul v. Kaiser Found. Health Plan of Ohio, 701 F.3d 514, 523, 27 AD 257 (6th Cir. 2012) (former hospital medical technician's claims under Ohio disability statute were not completely preempted under Labor Management Relations Act (LMRA) § 301, because resolution of those claims was not substantially dependent on, but only tangentially related to, collective bargaining agreement, although potential accommodations would impact scheduling and seniority rights; terms of agreement were invoked only as defense and not as source of relief).

III. CONSTITUTIONAL ISSUES

B. The Eleventh Amendment and Sovereign Immunity

1. Sovereign Immunity and Titles I and II of the ADA

[172][On page 13-35 of the Main Volume, in footnote 172, add the following after "*Compare*".]

Guttman v. Khalsa, 669 F.3d 1101, 1125, 25 AD 1316 (10th Cir. 2012) (state was entitled to sovereign immunity in Title II action brought by physician who challenged revocation of his license as discriminatory, where due process hearing had shown that physician's depression and post-traumatic stress disorder (PTSD) posed imminent threat to health and safety of others if he was allowed to continue to practice),

[On page 13-36 of the Main Volume, in the last sentence of the carryover paragraph, add new footnote 173a after "ADA suits against states for injunctive relief,".]

[173a]*See* Okwu v. McKim, 682 F.3d 841, 845–46, 26 AD 513 (9th Cir. 2012) (state employee could not maintain § 1983 claim predicated on violation of Title I of ADA because Eleventh Amendment immunity was not abrogated by Title I and remedial scheme of ADA is comprehensive enough to foreclose suit under § 1983).

IV. DEFINITION OF DISABILITY

A. Impairment

[198][On page 13-40 of the Main Volume, in footnote 198, add the following after "*See*".]

Spiegel v. Schulmann, 604 F.3d 72, 83, 23 AD 129 (2d Cir. 2010) (obese former karate instructor did not adequately establish that he was disabled under New York state law because he failed to produce evidence that he was medically incapable of losing weight);

[201][On page 13-41 of the Main Volume, in footnote 201, add the following after "*See, e.g.*,".]

Serednyj v. Beverly Healthcare, LLC, 656 F.3d 540, 554, 113 FEP 504 (7th Cir. 2011) (under pre-amendment ADA, even if complications during pregnancy constitute "impairment," these conditions are temporary and of limited duration, and thus are not covered by Act);

B. Major Life Activity

1. ADAAA and the EEOC Implementing Regulations

[On page 13-43 of the Main Volume, in the first sentence of the carryover paragraph, add new footnote 217a after "normal cell growth;".]

[217a]*See* Meinelt v. P.F. Chang's China Bistro, 787 F. Supp. 2d 643, 651, 24 AD 1183 (S.D. Tex. 2011) (individual diagnosed with brain tumor is substantially limited in normal life activity of cell growth).

C. Substantial Limitation

2. Pre-ADAAA

[302]**[On page 13-58 of the Main Volume, in footnote 302, add the following at the end of the footnote.]**

See St. Martin v. City of St. Paul, 680 F.3d 1027, 1032–33, 26 AD 516 (8th Cir. 2012) (fire captain who was denied promotion failed to show that he was actually disabled because he did not establish that his knee injury prevented him from working in broad class of jobs and did not demonstrate that he was limited in other major life activities; fact that he worked as fire arson investigator after surgery and then as fire inspector for city "undermined his contention" that he was substantially limited in working); Kapche v. Holder, 677 F.3d 454, 463–64, 26 AD 1 (D.D.C. 2012) (under Rehabilitation Act, diabetes and treatment regimen substantially limited applicant's major life activity of eating where applicant had to strictly adhere to regimen to avoid "dire and immediate consequences" and where monitoring of his blood sugar and taking insulin was itself substantially limiting); Boitnott v. Corning Inc., 669 F.3d 172, 177, 25 AD 1441 (4th Cir. 2012) (manufacturing plant maintenance engineer, who was medically restricted to eight-hour workday while recovering from cardiac condition and leukemia, was not disabled under ADA, where inability to work overtime was not substantial limitation on major life activity of working, and there was no evidence that this limitation restricted his ability to work broad class of jobs); EEOC v. AutoZone Inc., 630 F.3d 635, 641–43, 23 AD 1841 (7th Cir. 2010) (summary judgment reversed in action alleging failure to accommodate where there were issues of fact as to whether former retail sales manager with back injury was substantially limited in major life activity of self-care—dressing, grooming, bathing, and oral hygiene).

[303]**[On page 13-58 of the Main Volume, in footnote 303, add the following after "*see*".]**

Feldman v. Olin Corp., 692 F.3d 748, 753–54, 26 AD 1305 (7th Cir. 2012) (factual issues existed as to whether laid-off tractor operator with sleep apnea and fibromyalgia suffered sleep problems sufficiently prolonged, severe, and long-term to warrant classification as disability under ADA and whether he was qualified to perform work in certain positions given overtime restrictions where medical records showed substantial limitations on his ability to sleep, effectiveness of his use of constant positive air pressure (CPAP) machine was unclear, and his physician approved of 40-hour work week only if assignment was to straight-time day shift and if he reduced some of his social activities); Carter v. Pathfinder Energy Servs. Inc., 662 F.3d 1134, 1145–46, 25 AD 679 (10th Cir. 2011) (oil well driller with severe long-term diabetes, who also suffered from fibromyalgia and hepatitis C at the time he was fired, established genuine issues of material fact as to whether his physical impairments substantially limited his ability to perform manual tasks, care for himself, or work, where he was able to work full 24-hour shifts with only accommodation of assigning him one, as opposed to usual two, 10- to 12-day tours of duty per month to allow him time for rest and recovery and where he had difficulty with grooming); Faiola v. APCO Graphics, Inc., 629 F.3d 43, 48, 23 AD 1706 (1st Cir. 2010) (inability of sales representative with dysthymia—low-level depression—to travel to conference did not establish that she was substantially limited in major life activity, where her inability to attend meeting did not interfere with performance of essential functions of her job, there were no medical restrictions on her airplane travel, and condition did not preclude her from performing class of jobs);

[304]**[On page 13-58 of the Main Volume, in footnote 304, add the following after "*see, e.g.*,".]**

Sanchez v. Vilsack, 695 F.3d 1174, 1179, 26 AD 1540 (10th Cir. 2012) (secretarial employee, whose brain injury caused vision impairment, raised factual issue under Rehabilitation Act as to whether she was substantially limited in her ability to see as compared to average person where her field of vision was half of what it was before injury; medical experts affirmed that her vision loss was permanent and not correctable; and her abilities to read, drive, and perform household tasks were "difficult, slower, and more dangerous");

[305]**[On page 13-59 of the Main Volume, in footnote 305, add the following before "Aldrich v. Boeing Co.".]**

Powers v. USF Holland, Inc., 667 F.3d 815, 822–23, 25 AD 931 (7th Cir. 2011) (employee with history of back injury, who had been performing successfully as long-haul driver—job that did not require lifting—and who transferred for personal reasons to city driver position that required dock work, and who provided no evidence that his impairment limited his working as a truck driver generally or any aspect of his nonwork activities, was not substantially limited in a major life activity); Griffin v. United Parcel Serv., Inc., 661 F.3d 216, 224, 25 AD 551 (5th Cir. 2011) (under pre-ADAAA standards, diabetes is not disability where it is adequately managed with insulin shots and modest adjustment to diet and lifestyle because, with treatment, there is no substantial limitation on eating); Ramos-Echevarria v. Pichis, Inc., 659 F.3d 182, 189–90, 25 AD 545 (1st Cir. 2011) (no violation of pre-amendment ADA in discharge of kitchen worker who failed to show that his epilepsy, which caused him periodically to experience seizures while at work, substantially limited his ability to work in broad range of jobs where seizures were transitory and of brief duration, and he did not claim that epilepsy interfered with any other major life activity); Serednyj v. Beverly Healthcare, LLC, 656 F.3d 540, 554, 113 FEP 504 (7th Cir. 2011) (physical impairment that threatened to cause employee to miscarry did not substantially limit activities of reproduction and lifting, because pregnancy by its nature is of limited duration and unless pregnancy-related complications are chronic or result of physiological disorders of reproductive system, they cannot be considered substantial limitation); Kirkeberg v. Canadian Pac. Ry., 619 F.3d 898, 905, 23 AD 1000 (8th Cir. 2010) (individual formerly employed as employee assistance plan (EAP) counselor, who lost vision in one eye and suffered from hepatitis C, was not substantially limited in major life activity of seeing, where although he tired more easily and found it more difficult to navigate on foot, he retained much of his depth perception and visual field, could read "fairly normally" despite vision loss, and ability to perform job was unaffected); *Kapche*, 677 F.3d at 463–64 (applying pre-ADAAA standards, diabetes substantially limited applicant's major life activities where applicant had to strictly adhere to regimen or suffer "dire and immediate consequences" and where regimen of monitoring blood sugar and taking insulin was itself substantially limiting);

[306]**[On page 13-59 of the Main Volume, in footnote 306, add the following after "*see, e.g.*,".]**

Serednyj, 656 F.3d at 554, 556 (physical impairment that threatened to cause employee to miscarry did not substantially limit activities of reproduction and lifting because restrictions recommended by her physician were limited to first four months of pregnancy; pregnancy by its nature is of limited duration, unless pregnancy-related complications are chronic or long-term, they cannot be considered substantial limitation);

[306]**[On page 13-60 of the Main Volume, in the carryover of footnote 306, add the following at the end of the footnote.]**

Cf. Gecewicz v. Henry Ford Macomb Hosp. Corp., 683 F.3d 316, 322–23, 26 AD 643 (6th Cir. 2012) (hospital employee, who was discharged for absenteeism pursuant to hospital policy concerning unscheduled absences, failed to establish that she was regarded as disabled by her supervisor; comments made by supervisor over period of years about employee's absences at several points in time because of surgery were remote in time, addressed discrete events, and were made in context of concern over employee's absenteeism rather than based on belief that she suffered from long-term impairment).

[315]**[On page 13-61 of the Main Volume, in footnote 315, add the following after "*See, e.g.*,".]**

Faiola v. APCO Graphics, Inc., 629 F.3d 43, 48, 23 AD 1706 (1st Cir. 2010) (inability to travel to conference did not constitute substantial limitation on major life activity of working where it did not restrict plaintiff's ability to perform class of jobs and plaintiff testified that she was able to perform essential functions of her job); Kirkeberg v. Canadian Pac. Ry., 619 F.3d 898, 905, 23 AD 1000 (8th Cir. 2010) (employee's monocular vision did not substantially limit his major life activities because he adjusted to monocularity so that he was "not substantially limited in any major life activity relative to the average individual");

[317]**[On page 13-62 of the Main Volume, in footnote 317, add the following after "*E.g.*,".]**

Ames v. Home Depot U.S.A., Inc., 629 F.3d 665, 670–71, 24 AD 16 (7th Cir. 2011) (retail store employee, who was discharged for failure to meet employer's legitimate expectations by coming to work under influence of alcohol in violation of store's alcohol use policy, did not establish ADA claims; even though alcoholism may qualify as disability, there was no evidence that plaintiff was substantially limited in major life activity, she alleged that her condition did not interfere with her work performance, and she had been provided reasonable accommodations of leave and counseling through EAP); *Kirkeberg*, 619 F.3d at 905–06 (individual formerly employed as EAP counselor who lost vision in one eye and suffered from hepatitis C was not substantially limited in major life activity where any of the effects of his hepatitis C other than occasional nosebleeds were not apparent at work, he did not self-identify with the hepatitis C until after his discharge, and his doctor testified that he had adjusted to monocularity and compensated so that the remaining eye provided him with "normal vision"); Nyrop v. Independent Sch. Dist. No. 11, 616 F.3d 728, 734–35, 23 AD 801 (8th Cir. 2010) (plaintiff with multiple sclerosis was not substantially limited in major life activities when she admitted that her symptoms were "transient");

D. Record of Disability

[353]**[On page 13-69 of the Main Volume, in footnote 353, add the following at the end of the footnote.]**

See also Reynolds v. American Red Cross, 701 F.3d 143, 153, 27 AD 263 (4th Cir. 2012) (earlier report from physician concerning employee's back injury did not establish record of impairment, particularly where medical report was "at best, inconclusive as to the history and extent of [the employee's] alleged disability" and doctor who wrote report did not consider him disabled); Kotwica v. Rose Packing Co., Inc., 637 F.3d 744, 748–49, 24 AD 513 (7th Cir. 2011) (general laborer in meatpacking plant, who was fired from position due to work restrictions imposed by physician after hip replacement surgery, failed to show that she had record of impairment, despite documentation of her hip problems prior to surgery, where her record also established history of performing "relatively demanding general labor position" without limitation).

E. Regarded as Disabled

2. *Pre-ADAAA*

[371]**[On page 13-74 of the Main Volume, in footnote 371, add the following after "*see also*".]**

Kotwica v. Rose Packing Co., Inc., 637 F.3d 744, 749, 24 AD 513 (7th Cir. 2011) (general laborer in meatpacking plant was not regarded as disabled where employer stated that her restrictions merely precluded her from working as general laborer, while simultaneously noting that her computer and language skills would make it easy for her to find other employment);

[374]**[On page 13-76 of the Main Volume, in footnote 374, add the following after "*See, e.g.*,".]**

Fleishman v. Continental Cas. Co., 698 F.3d 598, 607–08, 116 FEP 400, 26 AD 1775 (7th Cir. 2012) (claim of attorney who suffered brain aneurysm and alleged that he was terminated because, among other things, employer regarded him as disabled was refuted by fact that he continued to work for 18 months and during that period employer transferred him to newly created position to handle higher-value cases); Povey v. City of Jeffersonville, Ind., 697 F.3d 619, 624, 26 AD 1633 (7th Cir. 2012) (employer's remarks about former animal shelter employee's inability to perform her job at shelter after she injured her wrist did not show that she was regarded as disabled where nothing indicated that she was regarded as unable to perform broad range or class of jobs); Gecewicz v. Henry Ford Macomb Hosp. Corp., 683 F.3d 316, 322, 26 AD 643 (6th Cir. 2012) (hospital employee who was discharged for absenteeism pursuant to hospital policy concerning unscheduled absences failed to establish that she was regarded by her supervisor as disabled where supervisor's sporadic comments about her surgery-related absences reflected concern about excessive absenteeism and "not a perceived disability under the ADA"); St. Martin v. City of St. Paul, 680 F.3d 1027, 1035, 26 AD 516 (8th Cir. 2012) (plaintiff did not present sufficient direct evidence that he was perceived as disabled where he alone was required to get medical clearance to interview for position, his supervisor asked him about his knee injury in his promotion interview, and although decision maker told him that he did not believe that he "could physically do the job," he also suggested how plaintiff could improve his chances for promotion); Duello v. Buchanan Cnty. Bd. of Supervisors, 628 F.3d 968, 973, 23 AD 1736 (8th Cir. 2010) (county highway employee who suffered seizure while driving, and was discharged after his additional leave request was denied, did not establish any disputed issues of fact as to whether employer regarded him as disabled; ongoing policy of excusing employees from duties that they could not temporarily perform was irrelevant where employee could not perform essential job functions of commercial driving and operating heavy machinery and where his commercial driver's license had been revoked at time of discharge); Kirkeberg v. Canadian Pac. Ry., 619 F.3d 898, 906, 23 AD 1000 (8th Cir. 2010) (former EAP director with monocular vision and hepatitis C failed to establish that he was regarded as disabled, despite contention that his treatment-related absences and accommodation requests angered his supervisor and that supervisor avoided him after learning of his hepatitis C because of stigma that hepatitis C is often associated with illegal drug use; plaintiff received performance-based bonus and pay raise, and there was no evidence that he was viewed as substantially limited in his ability to work); Nyrop v. Independent Sch. Dist. No. 11, 616 F.3d 728, 737, 23 AD 801 (8th Cir. 2010) (music teacher with multiple sclerosis did not show that she was unlawfully denied administrative positions because she was regarded as disabled where her continued employment as music teacher belied contention that she was regarded as substantially limited in her ability to work and school official who allegedly questioned her stamina was not involved in hiring for administrative position); Kemp v. Holder, 610 F.3d 231, 237–38, 23 AD 513 (5th Cir. 2010) (hearing-impaired federal court security officer, who was medically disqualified for failure to meet U.S. Marshals Service standard for unaided hearing, did not establish that he was regarded as disabled in major life activities of hearing or working, where employer's request for reconsideration of disqualification showed that he was perceived as functionally able to hear, and there was no evidence that he was regarded as unable to perform broad class of jobs);

[374]**[On page 13-77 of the Main Volume, in the carryover of footnote 374, add the following at the end of the footnote.]**

Cf. Stiefel v. Bechtel Corp., 624 F.3d 1240, 1246, 23 AD 1380 (9th Cir. 2010) (individual who had incurred work-related injury and who complained that union did not refer him for reinstatement did not establish claim of refusal to hire under ADA, where he remained at bottom of out-of-work list because of his failure to attend union roll call meetings; his claim that attendance at meetings was futile because of employer's "100% healed policy" failed where he did not give employer opportunity to hire him).

[375]**[On page 13-77 of the Main Volume, in footnote 375, add the following after "*See, e.g.*,".]**

Román-Oliveras v. Puerto Rico Elec. Power Auth., 655 F.3d 43, 49–50, 25 AD 1 (1st Cir. 2011) (claim of former employee of public power company, whose schizophrenia was controlled, should not have been dismissed where he adequately raised issue of whether employer regarded him as disabled; employee alleged that he had history of excellent performance reviews over many years when he was placed on leave and required without explanation to undergo multiple medical evaluations, and then was discharged despite favorable results of those evaluations); Spees v. James Marine, Inc., 617 F.3d 380, 397, 109 FEP 1748, 23 AD 972 (6th Cir. 2010) (pregnant former welder established claim that she was unlawfully transferred to light-duty position because she was regarded as disabled; supervisor's belief that her prior miscarriage increased her health risk showed that she was regarded as having impairment and transfer allowed conclusion that she was viewed as precluded from class of jobs);

[377]**[On page 13-79 of the Main Volume, in footnote 377, add the following at the end of the footnote.]**

See also Powers v. USF Holland, Inc., 667 F.3d 815, 825, 25 AD 931 (7th Cir. 2011) (employer's "100% healed" policy did not establish that it regarded employee with back injury and lifting restrictions as disabled; employer may engage in "risk limiting" behavior in safety-sensitive industry).

[379]**[On page 13-79 of the Main Volume, in footnote 379, add the following at the beginning of the footnote.]**

See Tusing v. Des Moines Indep. Cmty. Sch. Dist., 639 F.3d 507, 518–519, 24 AD 783 (8th Cir. 2011) (employee failed to establish that her supervisors regarded her as disabled, where there was no evidence that they had any knowledge of her depression despite local newspaper article that described her "many difficult life experiences," including abusive childhood, divorce, depression, alcoholism, and periods of homelessness, but failed to identify time period in which she allegedly suffered from depression);

V. QUALIFIED INDIVIDUALS WITH DISABILITIES

[383]**[On page 13-80 of the Main Volume, in footnote 383, add the following after "*see also*".]**

Richardson v. Friendly Ice Cream Corp., 593 F.3d 69, 79, 22 AD 1473 (1st Cir. 2010) (former assistant restaurant manager with permanent shoulder injury failed to raise factual issue as to whether she was qualified to perform essential job functions, where she was required to perform broad range of manual tasks to "assist in kitchen, dining and take-out functions" and could perform only some of those tasks by altering manner in which she performed them, and where she admitted that—even with task modifications—her five-pound lifting restriction and inability to perform repetitive manual tasks rendered her unable to perform substantial number of essential tasks);

[384]**[On page 13-80 of the Main Volume, in footnote 384, add the following at the beginning of the footnote.]**

Kallail v. Allient Energy Corp. Servs., Inc., 691 F.3d 925, 931–32, 26 AD 1281 (8th Cir. 2012) (working rotating shift was essential function of job where it was listed on job description as requirement of Resource Coordinator position and employer supported decision as important to maintaining employee morale in spreading less-desirable shifts and in enhancing training, experience, and coverage in position by allowing all Resource Coordinators to become familiar with all geographic territories in employer's service area; maintenance of morale is legitimate business concern);

[On page 13-81 of the Main Volume, after the carryover sentence that ends with footnote 386, add the following.]

Of course, where a position is subject to federal, state, or other regulation, the employer is entitled to rely upon the requirements set by an outside agency.[2]

[392]**[On page 13-83 of the Main Volume, in footnote 392, add the following at the end of the footnote.]**

See also Duello v. Buchanan Cnty. Bd. of Supervisors, 628 F.3d 968, 972, 23 AD 1736 (8th Cir. 2010) (employee whose commercial driver's license was revoked after he suffered seizure while driving was no longer able to perform essential functions of his job, which required driving trucks and operating heavy equipment).

A. Delineating Essential Job Functions

[404]**[On page 13-87 of the Main Volume, in footnote 404, add the following after "*see*".]**

Richardson v. Friendly Ice Cream Corp., 593 F.3d 69, 75, 22 AD 1473 (1st Cir. 2010) (essential function is "one that is 'fundamental' to a position rather than 'marginal'");

---

[2]Johnson v. Board of Trs. of Boundary Cnty. Sch. Dist. No. 101, 666 F.3d 561, 566–67, 25 AD 944 (9th Cir. 2011) (local school board was not required to provide provisional authorization to teach without certificates as accommodation for bipolar teacher where state law required certification of all persons teaching in elementary or secondary schools and there is no evidence that this requirement had a disparate impact on individuals with disabilities); Wilkerson v. Shinseki, 606 F.3d 1256, 1264–66, 23 AD 321 (10th Cir. 2010) (reassignment of diabetic and obese boiler room operator to lower paying housekeeper position was reasonable accommodation after he had failed annual physical exam required by federal safety guidelines for boiler room position, where there were no available lateral positions, his former position was not vacant, and agency had legitimate concern about danger to the health and safety of others were he placed in a position that required employee to climb ladders); Kinneary v. City of N.Y., 601 F.3d 151, 157, 22 AD 1803 (2d Cir. 2010) (tanker captain who was unable to provide urine sample for drug testing because of his "shy" bladder (paruresis) was unable to perform the essential functions of the position where periodic drug testing was required by federal regulation and employee did not follow employer's instructions on obtaining exception from test).

[404]**[On page 13-87 of the Main Volume, in footnote 404, add the following at the end of the footnote.]**

Compare Kallail v. Allient Energy Corp. Servs., Inc., 691 F.3d 925, 931, 26 AD 1281 (8th Cir. 2012) (giving consideration to employer's inclusion in position description of ability to work rotating shift as essential qualification), *and* Duello v. Buchanan Cnty. Bd. of Supervisors, 628 F.3d 968, 972, 23 AD 1736 (8th Cir. 2010) (rotating shift may be essential function of job), *with* Feldman v. Olin Corp., 692 F.3d 748, 752, 26 AD 1305 (7th Cir. 2012) (tractor operator in manufacturing facility who was unable to work rotating shifts because of his sleep apnea and fibromyalgia and was laid off due to medical restrictions requiring straight-time day shift, raised factual issue as to whether ability to work overtime and rotating shifts were essential job functions; even though job descriptions for truck driver/tractor operator positions listed flextime capability as essential, employee identified available day-shift assignments for which he was qualified to work but that were not offered to him).

1. Whether Employees Are Actually Required to Perform the Function at Issue

[408]**[On page 13-88 of the Main Volume, in footnote 408, add the following after "*See, e.g.*,".]**

Robert v. Board of Cnty. Comm'rs of Brown Cnty., 691 F.3d 1211, 1218–19, 26 AD 1300 (10th Cir. 2012) (county felony offender supervision officer, whose sacroiliac joint dysfunction in her hips and back impaired her mobility, and who was discharged after her medical leave expired, was not qualified individual under ADA, where in-person fieldwork was essential job function as shown by her supervisor's testimony, percentage of time spent for site visits, and strain on office functioning in her absence; previously allowing her to work at home for several months as unrequired accommodation did not render fieldwork nonessential, and her sole possible accommodation of indefinite leave was not reasonable in that she failed to provide definite estimated return date and had already been on leave for six months);

2. *Whether Removing the Function Would Fundamentally Change the Job*

[409]**[On page 13-88 of the Main Volume, in footnote 409, add the following after "*see, e.g.,*".]**

Jones v. Walgreen Co., 679 F.3d 9, 18–19, 26 AD 261 (1st Cir. 2012) (discharge of retail store manager with knee injury, who was discharged after notice that her medical restrictions were permanent, did not violate ADA where job description and supervisor's testimony established that routine physical tasks for store maintenance and merchandising were essential job functions, employer was entitled to rely on physician's post-review opinion that manager was not able to bend, kneel, climb, and walk as required, ability to delegate tasks does not render them non-essential, and there was no duty to engage in interactive process in view of her inability to perform essential job functions); *Robert*, 691 F.3d at 1218–19 (county felony offender supervision officer, whose sacroiliac joint dysfunction in her hips and back impaired her mobility, and who was discharged after her medical leave expired, was not qualified individual under ADA, where in-person fieldwork was essential job function as shown by her supervisor's testimony, percentage of time spent for site visits, and strain on office functioning in her absence);

3. *Other Evidence Relevant to Whether a Particular Function Is Essential*

a. *The Employer's Judgment*

[415]**[On page 13-90 of the Main Volume, in footnote 415, delete the semi-colon after the statutory citation and add the following before "*cf.*".]**

. *See* Kallail v. Allient Energy Corp. Servs., Inc., 691 F.3d 925, 931–32, 26 AD 1281 (8th Cir. 2012) (giving consideration to employer's inclusion in position description of ability to work rotating shift as essential qualification);

[417]**[On page 13-90 of the Main Volume, in footnote 417, add the following after "*See*".]**

Kallail, 691 F.3d at 931–32 (employer legitimately considered impact on employee morale in rejecting diabetic employee's request to be assigned to fixed rather than rotating shift as accommodation);

b. Job Descriptions

[419]**[On page 13-91 of the Main Volume, in footnote 419, add the following at the end of the footnote.]**

See Kallail, 691 F.3d at 932 (giving consideration to employer's inclusion in position description of ability to work rotating shift as essential qualification);

[422]**[On page 13-91 of the Main Volume, in footnote 422, add the following at the beginning of the footnote.]**

See Supinski v. United Parcel Serv., Inc., 413 F. App'x 536, 24 AD 278 (3d Cir. 2011) (nonprecedential) (former package car driver with 70-pound lifting restriction because of shoulder injury raised factual issues that precluded dismissal of his ADA claim, despite contention that he was not qualified individual because lifting requirements exceeded his restrictions, where job descriptions were prepared after he was rejected and did not establish that heavy lifting was essential job function).

c. The Amount of Time Spent on the Job Performing the Function

[424]**[On page 13-91 of the Main Volume, in footnote 424, add the following at the end of the footnote.]**

See Robert v. Board of Cnty. Comm'rs of Brown Cnty., 691 F.3d 1211, 1218–19, 26 AD 1300 (10th Cir. 2012) (county felony offender supervision officer, whose sacroiliac joint dysfunction in her hips and back impaired her mobility, and who was discharged after her medical leave expired, was not qualified individual under ADA, where in-person fieldwork was essential job function as shown by her supervisor's testimony, percentage of time spent for site visits, and strain on office functioning in her absence); EEOC v. Picture People, Inc., 684 F.3d 981, 988–89, 26 AD 776 (10th Cir. 2012) (children's photography studio employee who was deaf and speech impaired could not establish that her termination was discriminatory or that employer could have accommodated her disability where job description showed that verbal communication skills were essential job functions and providing her with sign language interpreters at meetings would not enable her to perform those job functions).

e. The Terms of a Collective Bargaining Agreement

[431]**[On page 13-93 of the Main Volume, in footnote 431, add the following at the end of the footnote.]**

Cf. Watts v. United Parcel Serv., 701 F.3d 188, 192–93, 27 AD 388 (6th Cir. 2012) (LMRA § 301 did not preempt injured package delivery driver's ADA claim alleging that she was refused assignment to light-duty work program after her return from back injury despite contention that claim involved interpretation of collective bargaining contract's light-duty work program provision, because ADA claim is separate federal cause of action independent from contract claim, contract right did not negate statutory right under ADA, and there was no danger of divergent application of contract's provisions by state courts because claim was in federal court).

B. Particular Functions

1. Production Standards

[435]**[On page 13-94 of the Main Volume, in footnote 435, add the following at the end of the footnote.]**

See Jakubowski v. Christ Hosp., Inc., 627 F.3d 195, 201–02, 23 AD 1713 (6th Cir. 2010) ("communicating with professional colleagues and patients in ways that ensure patient safety" was essential function for resident physician in family practice residency program), *cert. denied*, 131 S. Ct. 3071 (2011).

5. Attendance

[450]**[On page 13-97 of the Main Volume, in footnote 450, add the following after "*E.g.*,".]**

Samper v. Providence St. Vincent Med. Ctr., 675 F.3d 1233, 1238–39, 26 AD 11 (9th Cir. 2012) (neonatal intensive care unit nurse with fibromyalgia, who was discharged for absenteeism after her request for attendance policy exemption was denied, may not proceed with unlawful discharge or failure-to-accommodate claims, where regular on-site attendance was essential job function as shown by specialized nature of work and job description, and allowing five unplanned absences per year did not negate hardship posed by unlimited absences);

[459]**[On page 13-100 of the Main Volume, in footnote 459, add the following after "*See*".]**

Carter v. Pathfinder Servs., Inc., 662 F.3d 1134, 1145–46, 25 AD 679 (10th Cir. 2011) (diabetic oil well driller with hepatitis C, who was able to work full required 24-hour shifts with only accommodation of one rather than two 10- to 12-day job assignments per month to allow for rest and recovery, raised contested issue of material fact where he produced evidence that his impairments substantially limited one or more major life activities; substantial limitation must be decided on a case-by-case basis);

C. Impact of Statements Made in Applications for Benefits

[465]**[On page 13-102 of the Main Volume, in footnote 465, add the following after "*see*".]**

Mathews v. Denver Newspaper Agency, 649 F.3d 1199, 1209, 24 AD 1156 (10th Cir. 2011) (employee who had prevailed previously on SSDI claim of total disability was not necessarily estopped from pursuing ADA claim asserting that his demotion from supervisory to nonsupervisory position was discriminatory; however, it was his burden to demonstrate that apparent inconsistency between two claims could be resolved; where employee fails to show that he was qualified to perform supervisory position at time of demotion, ADA claim must fail);

[465]**[On page 13-102 of the Main Volume, in footnote 465, add the following after "*But see*".]**

DeRosa v. National Envelope Corp., 595 F.3d 99, 105, 22 AD 1621 (2d Cir. 2010) (former customer service representative, who alleged in application for SSDI that pain from leg injury prevented him from speaking on phone or working with computer, was not estopped from pursuing ADA action where he had worked at home for two years to accommodate his inability to commute and claimed total disability only after that accommodation was rescinded by employer);

[On page 13-104 of the Main Volume, after the sentence that ends with footnote 472, add the following new paragraphs.]

In *Solomon v. Vilsack*,[3] the D.C. Circuit considered a similar issue with regard to federal employees. In order to receive federal employee retirement system (FERS) disability retirement benefits, employees must represent that they have become "unable, because of disease or injury, to render useful and efficient service in [their] position."[4] Regulations promulgated by OPM state that an employee is eligible for disability benefits under FERS benefits only if accommodating the disability would be "unreasonable."[5] On the other hand, an employee challenging the denial of accommodation of a disability under the Rehabilitation Act[6] must plead that he or she is qualified to perform the essential functions of the job, with or without reasonable accommodation.

The plaintiff in *Vilsack*, a budget analyst at the U.S. Department of Agriculture who suffered from severe chronic depression, demonstrated that she was able to perform her job at a high level with certain accommodations—a flexible schedule, including occasionally working at home, and minor modifications to her office environment to provide her with more privacy and reduce distraction. When these accommodations were withdrawn, she was unable to work and ultimately applied for disability retirement under FERS. She also pursued a failure-to-accommodate claim against the Department of Agriculture. The district court granted judgment in favor of the government under the Rehabilitation Act, citing the inconsistent definitions of disability under FERS and the Act. The court of appeals reversed, noting that the pivotal question on the disability claim was whether the employer had been able to provide reasonable accommodation for the plaintiff's disability, not whether she was able to perform the job if reasonable accommodation was provided. The appellate court held that the two inquiries (under FERS and the Rehabilitation Act) were not inherently inconsistent and that cases had to be resolved on their specific facts. Stated differently, recipients of FERS disability benefits are not presumptively barred from asserting claims under the Rehabilitation Act.[7]

---

[3]628 F.3d 555, 23 AD 1697 (D.C. Cir. 2010).
[4]5 U.S.C. § 8451(a)(1)(A)–(B).
[5]5 C.F.R. § 844.103(a)(4).
[6]29 U.S.C. § 791 et seq.
[7]628 F.3d at 565.

D. Role of Medical Evidence

[473][On page 13-105 of the Main Volume, in footnote 473, add the following after "*cf.*".]

Hanson v. Caterpillar, Inc., 688 F.3d 816, 820, 26 AD 1034 (7th Cir. 2012) (terminated employee's evidence consisting of statements by employer's physician that he believed her to be disabled by her neck injury from jobs requiring heavy lifting was insufficient to prove that company regarded her as disabled, where it was manager and not company physician who made decision to terminate her and where physician's "hyperbole about [the plaintiff's] capabilities was proven untrue when Caterpillar placed her in three different positions"); Sepúlveda-Villarini v. Department of Educ. of P.R., 628 F.3d 25, 30, 23 AD 1709 (1st Cir. 2010) (school teachers who alleged that increase in class size exacerbated their disabilities, and whose assignment to reduced-size classes for at least four years in response to their medically certified requests established that employer was aware of duty to accommodate, adequately stated failure-to-accommodate claim when assignment was discontinued; no medical evidence was required to show causal link between class size and their conditions);

[475][On page 13-105 of the Main Volume, in footnote 475, add the following at the end of the footnote.]

See also Ekstrand v. School Dist. of Somerset, 683 F.3d 826, 828, 26 AD 641 (7th Cir. 2012) (former teacher was allowed to establish through her own testimony and that of her psychologist that she suffered from depression due to seasonal affective disorder; reasonable jury could find that school district was aware that she was qualified individual with disability and failed in its duty to accommodate her disability). *But see* Hoppe v. Lewis Univ., 692 F.3d 833, 841, 26 AD 1286 (7th Cir. 2012) (university that admitted that female professor with adjustment disorder was able to perform essential functions of her position and that continued to employ her did not fail in its duty to accommodate her disability by relocating her office; university did not know of her physician's assessment that her proximity to department chair exacerbated her condition, where physician failed to respond to university's requests for specific information on professor's accommodation needs, and professor rejected university's attempts to engage in interactive process when it offered her three different office locations).

VI. SUBSTANTIVE PROTECTIONS

B. Disparate Treatment Prohibited

[483]**[On page 13-108 of the Main Volume, in footnote 483, add the following after "*see also*".]**

Feldman v. Olin Corp., 692 F.3d 748, 755–56, 26 AD 1305 (7th Cir. 2012) (tractor operator in manufacturing facility, who was unable to work rotating shifts because of his sleep apnea and fibromyalgia, and who was laid off due to medical restrictions requiring straight-time day shift, raised factual issue as to whether ability to work overtime and rotating shifts were essential job functions; even though job descriptions for truck driver/tractor operator positions listed flextime capability as essential, employee's identification of available day-shift assignments established that he was qualified to work but was not offered chance); Carter v. Pathfinder Energy Servs., Inc., 662 F.3d 1134, 1145–46, 25 AD 679 (10th Cir. 2011) (diabetic oil well driller with hepatitis C, who established that his physical impairments substantially limited his ability to care for himself where he had difficulty performing tasks central to daily living and manual tasks, and was able to work full 24-hour shifts with only accommodation of assigning him one 10- to 12-day tour per month (instead of the usual two) to allow for rest and recovery, raised contested issue of material fact where he was totally disabled post-discharge despite medication); Griffin v. United Parcel Serv., Inc., 661 F.3d 216, 224, 25 AD 551 (5th Cir. 2011) (employer did not fail to reasonably accommodate plaintiff with diabetes by refusing to assign him to day shift where note from plaintiff's doctor suggested that daytime shift would be preferable but did not state that working day shift was necessary for management of plaintiff's diabetes);

[483]**[On page 13-108 of the Main Volume, in footnote 483, add the following at the end of the footnote.]**

But see Kallail v. Alliant Energy Corp. Servs., Inc., 691 F.3d 925, 931–33, 26 AD 1281 (8th Cir. 2012) (diabetic former utility company dispatcher's claim that she was unlawfully refused straight-day instead of rotating shift was properly dismissed, even though other facilities used straight shifts and such shifts had been considered for her, where she was unable to perform essential job function of working rotating shifts as listed in job description, facilities' different dispatching practices justified different scheduling decisions, business needs that included possible effect on morale were valid reasons for not offering requested shift, there was no duty to eliminate essential function or promote her, and she rejected alternative jobs that satisfied company's duty to engage in interactive process).

[486]**[On page 13-108 of the Main Volume, in footnote 486, delete case, citation, and parenthetical for "Ekstrand v. School Dist. of Somerset".]**

[486]**[On page 13-108 of the Main Volume, in footnote 486, add the following after "*See, e.g.*,".]**

Feldman, 692 F.3d at 755–56 (tractor operator in manufacturing facility, who was unable to work rotating shifts because of his sleep apnea and fibromyalgia and who was laid off due to medical restrictions requiring straight-time day shift, raised factual issue as to whether ability to work overtime and rotating shifts were essential job functions); Ekstrand v. School Dist. of Somerset, 683 F.3d 826, 828, 26 AD 641 (7th Cir. 2012) (former teacher may establish through her own testimony and that of her psychologist that she suffered from depression due to seasonal affective disorder; reasonable jury could find that school district was aware that she was qualified individual with disability and failed in its duty to accommodate her disability by transferring her to different classroom); *Kallail*, 691 F.3d at 931–33 (diabetic former utility company dispatcher's claim that she was unlawfully refused straight-day instead of rotating shift failed, even though other facilities used straight shifts, where she was unable to perform essential job function of working rotating shifts as listed in job description, facilities' different dispatching practices justified different scheduling decisions, business needs that included possible effect on morale were valid reasons for not offering rescheduled shift, there was no duty to eliminate essential function or promote her, and offer of alternative jobs that she refused satisfied company's duty to engage in interactive process); *Carter*, 662 F.3d at 1145–46 (diabetic oil well driller with hepatitis C who was able to work full 24-hour shifts with accommodation of assigning him one 10- to 12-day tour per month instead of the usual two to allow for rest and recovery raised material issue of whether he could perform essential duties of his position with that accommodation);

[486][On page 13-108 of the Main Volume, in footnote 486, add the following at the end of the footnote.]

Cf. DeLia v. Verizon Commc'ns, Inc., 656 F.3d 1, 6, 25 AD 114 (1st Cir. 2011) (employee of subsidiary corporation cannot pursue claim that parent corporation failed to accommodate her stress-related disability where she failed to establish that parent company was her employer or that it knew of her disability but failed to accommodate it).

D. Requirement to Make Reasonable Accommodation

1. Overview

[503][On page 13-113 of the Main Volume, in footnote 503, add the following after "*See*".]

Stansberry v. Air Wis. Airlines Corp., 651 F.3d 482, 489, 24 AD 1544 (6th Cir. 2011) (employee who was not disabled not entitled to reasonable accommodation because of stress and distraction that he experienced because his wife was disabled);

[510][On page 13-114 of the Main Volume, in footnote 510, add the following after "*see also*".]

Kallail v. Alliant Energy Corp. Servs. Inc., 691 F.3d 925, 933, 26 AD 1281 (8th Cir. 2012) (employer who refused diabetic employee's schedule change from rotating to straight shift satisfied its duty to engage in interactive process with employee by offering her alternative jobs, offer she refused); Hoppe v. Lewis Univ., 692 F.3d 833, 841, 26 AD 1286 (7th Cir. 2012) (university did not fail in its duty to accommodate female professor with adjustment disorder by failing to relocate her office, where university did not know that her physician had advised that her proximity to department chair exacerbated her condition, where physician also failed to respond to university's requests for specific information on professor's accommodation needs, and professor's unwillingness to consider three alternative office locations amounted to a refusal to engage in the interactive process); Jakubowski v. Christ Hosp., Inc., 627 F.3d 195, 202–03, 23 AD 1713 (6th Cir. 2010) ("If an employer takes that [extra] step and offers a reasonable counter accommodation, the employee cannot demand a different accommodation."), *cert. denied*, 131 S. Ct. 3071 (2011);

[526]**[On page 13-119 of the Main Volume, in footnote 526, add the following after "*See*".]**

Department of Fair Emp't & Hous. v. Lucent Techs., Inc., 642 F.3d 728, 743, 24 AD 915 (9th Cir. 2011) (employee's failure to request accommodation for his back injury while in contact with supervisors during his one-year disability leave defeated claim under California law that employer failed to engage in interactive process); Kobus v. College of St. Scholastica, Inc., 604 F.3d 1034, 1038, 23 AD 522 (8th Cir. 2010) (employer did not fail to accommodate disability of employee who requested leave because he was "depressed and stressed" where his impairments were not apparent at work, he did not disclose his diagnosis to employer, and he declined employer's suggestion to pursue Family and Medical Leave Act (FMLA) leave);

2. *Examples of Reasonable Accommodations*

a. *Modifications to Physical Work Environment*

[544]**[On page 13-123 of the Main Volume, in footnote 544, add the following after "*E.g.*,".]**

Valle-Arce v. Puerto Rico Ports Auth., 651 F.3d 190, 200–01, 24 AD 1537 (1st Cir. 2011) (plaintiff was entitled to present to jury question of whether agency failed to reasonably accommodate her chronic fatigue syndrome and fibromyalgia when new supervisor removed her from an office which had been adapted with special lighting and air conditioning to permit her to satisfactorily perform duties of her job without first engaging in any interaction to determine the purpose of these accommodations or whether these accommodations were necessary); Sepúlveda-Villarini v. Department of Educ. of P.R., 628 F.3d 25, 30, 23 AD 1709 (1st Cir. 2010) (public school teachers who alleged that increase in class size exacerbated their disabilities stated failure-to-accommodate claims where their assignments to reduced-size classes for at least four years in response to their medically certified requests established knowledge of duty to accommodate);

[545]**[On page 13-124 of the Main Volume, in footnote 545, add the following at the end of the footnote.]**

Cf. Hoppe v. Lewis Univ., 692 F.3d 833, 841, 26 AD 1286 (7th Cir. 2012) (university did not fail in its duty to accommodate former professor's adjustment disorder by denying her request for office relocation, where university did not know that her physician had advised that her proximity to department chair exacerbated her condition and where professor rejected university's attempts to engage in interactive process offering her three different office locations);

b. Readers, Interpreters, and Other Helpers

[554]**[On page 13-125 of the Main Volume, in footnote 554, add the following after "*see also*".]**

EEOC v. UPS Supply Chain Solutions, 620 F.3d 1103, 1111–13, 23 AD 993 (9th Cir. 2010) (factual issues existed as to whether employer failed to provide reasonable accommodations for deaf employee whose requests for sign language interpreter for one-hour weekly staff meetings, training, and disciplinary sessions were rejected, where notes were not reasonable accommodation in that they provided limited information that may not have enabled deaf employee to enjoy same benefits and privileges in attending and participating in meetings as co-workers, there was question whether employer knew or should have known that such modifications were ineffective, and employer failed to show that cost for limited use of interpreter was unduly burdensome);

c. Transportation-Related Accommodations

[560]**[On page 13-127 of the Main Volume, in footnote 560, add the following immediately after the parenthetical for "Filar v. Board of Educ.".]**

; Colón-Fontánez v. Municipality of San Juan, 660 F.3d 17, 35–36, 25 AD 423 (1st Cir. 2011) (city employee with fibromyalgia was not entitled to accommodation of reserved parking space, despite her excellent performance evaluations, where she had lengthy history of absenteeism even before diagnosis, her evaluations noted her chronic attendance deficiencies, her job description listed physical presence at work as essential job function, and there was no evidence that parking space would have improved her attendance)

d. Exceptions or Modifications to Neutral Policies or Practices

[On page 13-130 of the Main Volume, after the sentence that ends with footnote 572, add the following.]

The employer is not required to put aside the requirements of state, local, or other agency laws and regulations.[8]

e. Leaves of Absence

(ii.) Indefinite leave

[583]**[On page 13-134 of the Main Volume, in footnote 583, add the following after "*See, e.g.*,".]**

EEOC v. C.R. England, Inc., 644 F.3d 1028, 1049–50, 24 AD 897 (10th Cir. 2011) (truck driver who was HIV-positive did not establish failure-to-accommodate claim based on denial of his requests for "home time," where he did not comply with company policy requiring two weeks' notice, did not specify how much leave he was seeking, and did not make it clear to company that his request for leaves was disability related);

---

[8]Johnson v. Board of Trs. of Boundary Cnty. Sch. Dist. No. 101, 666 F.3d 561, 566–67, 25 AD 944 (9th Cir. 2011) (local school board was not required to provide provisional authorization to teach without certificates as accommodation for bipolar teacher where state law required certification of all persons teaching in elementary or secondary schools and there is no evidence that this requirement had a disparate impact on individuals with disabilities); Wilkerson v. Shinseki, 606 F.3d 1256, 1264–66, 23 AD 321 (10th Cir. 2010) (reassignment of diabetic and obese boiler room operator to lower paying housekeeper position was reasonable accommodation after he had failed annual physical exam required by federal safety guidelines for boiler room position, where there were no available lateral positions, his former position was not vacant, and agency had legitimate concern about danger to the health and safety of others were he placed in a position that required employee to climb ladders); Kinneary v. City of N.Y., 601 F.3d 151, 157, 22 AD 1803 (2d Cir. 2010) (tanker captain who was unable to provide urine sample for drug testing because of his "shy" bladder (paruresis) was unable to perform the essential functions of the position where periodic drug testing was required by federal regulation and employee did not follow employer's instructions on obtaining exception from test). *cf.* Budde v. Kane Cnty. Forest Preserve, 597 F.3d 860, 863, 22 AD 1710 (7th Cir. 2010) (alcoholic police chief who was discharged after drunk driving accident was not qualified individual, where he was unable to operate vehicle, essential requirement for his position, due to suspended driver's license).

(iii.) Sporadic absences

[592][On page 13-136 of the Main Volume, in footnote 592, add the following after "*See, e.g.,*".]

Carmona v. Southwest Airlines Co., 604 F.3d 848, 859–60, 23 AD 140 (5th Cir. 2010) (flight attendant with psoriatic arthritis was qualified individual, despite contention that his condition prevented him from working as scheduled, where airline's approval of intermittent medical leave under FMLA permitted him to miss more than half of each working month for seven years and still perform satisfactorily, and leniency of attendance policy called into question whether attendance on specific days was essential element of job);

f. Job Restructuring

(i.) Modified duties, light duty

[611][On page 13-142 of the Main Volume, in footnote 611, add the following after "*see also*".]

Miller v. Illinois Dep't of Transp., 643 F.3d 190, 198–99, 24 AD 1025 (7th Cir. 2011) (former state highway maintenance worker, who was diagnosed with acrophobia after panic attack while working, raised factual issue as to whether trading tasks with co-workers in order to avoid working at heights was reasonable accommodation where crew functioned as team in assigning tasks by individual preferences and ability to rotate into each task was not required);

(iii.) Part-time or modified schedules

[621][On page 13-144 of the Main Volume, in footnote 621, add the following after "*See*".]

Regan v. Faurecia Auto. Seating, Inc., 679 F.3d 475, 480, 26 AD 257 (6th Cir. 2012) (modified work schedule to permit narcoleptic to commute earlier when traffic was lighter was not reasonable accommodation where employee failed to show that modified work schedule had lighter commute, given that she commuted two to four hours each way and testified that she got sleepy in heavy traffic); Griffin v. United Postal Serv., Inc., 661 F.3d 216, 225, 25 AD 551 (5th Cir. 2011) (employer did not fail to reasonably accommodate plaintiff with diabetes by refusing to assign him to day shift where note from his doctor suggested that daytime shift would be preferable but did not report that working day shift was necessary for management of his diabetes); Valle-Arce v. Puerto Rico Ports Auth.,

651 F.3d 190, 200–01, 24 AD 1537 (1st Cir. 2011) (agency failed to reasonably accommodate employee's chronic fatigue syndrome and fibromyalgia by adjusting her schedule when it removed flexible time arrangement that had been implemented informally and under which she had performed successfully for approximately two years; although attendance was essential element of job, she was never reprimanded for poor attendance when given flexible work schedule); Colwell v. Rite Aid Corp., 602 F.3d 495, 506, 22 AD 1857 (3d Cir. 2010) (former clerk, whose partial blindness restricted her ability to drive at night, raised factual issue as to whether rejection of her request for schedule change to day shift so that she could commute independently constituted failure to accommodate where ADA requires reasonable accommodation of disability-related difficulties in getting to work and shift change is workplace condition under employer's control);

(iv.) Working at home

[On page 13-146 of the Main Volume, after the carryover paragraph that ends with footnote 628, add the following new subsection.]

(v.) Training [New Topic]

Although an employer is not required to provide training in order to enable an "otherwise qualified" disabled employee to perform a new job, where the employee has been hired as a "trainee," the employer's duty extends to reasonable accommodations that enable the employee to complete that training.[9] The employer is not required, however, to train its employees to address an individual's disability as an accommodation unless that training relates directly to the individual's inability to perform the essential functions of his job.[10]

---

[9]Rosebrough v. Buckeye Valley High Sch., 690 F.3d 427, 432–33, 26 AD 1025 (6th Cir. 2012) (one-handed school bus driver trainee established prima facie case that she was "otherwise qualified" for her position even though she lacked commercial driver's license required for driver job, where ADA covers bias during job training period, she was qualified to be trainee, and purpose of training was to learn skills needed to obtain commercial license).

[10]Jakubowski v. Christ Hosp., Inc., 627 F.3d 195, 202–03, 23 AD 1713 (6th Cir. 2010) (hospital did not fail in its duty to accommodate family practice medical resident with Asperger's Disorder, where his proposed accommodation of educating staff regarding his condition would not have improved his patient communications skills and

g. Reassignment

(i.) Introduction

[On page 13-147 of the Main Volume, at the end of the last sentence of the carryover paragraph, add new footnote 630a.]

[630a]In some circumstances, accommodation may be required even though it is not related directly to the ability to perform the current job. *See, e.g.*, Sanchez v. Vilsack, 695 F.3d 1174, 1180–82, 26 AD 1540 (10th Cir. 2012) (visually impaired employee's request for job transfer to facilitate medical treatment was not per se unreasonable under Rehabilitation Act, even though she was able to perform essential job functions, where case precedent from other circuits and EEOC regulations require accommodations that enable disabled employee to enjoy same benefits of employment as nondisabled coworkers and to receive treatment for his or her disability).

(iii.) Reassignment is accommodation of last resort

[634]**[On page 13-147 of the Main Volume, in footnote 634, add the following after "*see also*".]**

Gratzl v. Office of Chief Judges of 12th, 18th, 19th & 22d Judicial Circuits, 601 F.3d 674, 680–81, 22 AD 1865 (7th Cir. 2010) (duty to accommodate court reporter, whose incontinence necessitated immediate restroom access, did not include allowing her to resume specialist position that was eliminated in state-level position consolidation and avoid in-court rotation, even though she had been previously assigned exclusively to specialist position; temporary reassignments did not create duty to accommodate with permanent reassignment and she rejected proposed accommodations to enable her to perform in-court reporting);

(iv.) Vacancy required

[639]**[On page 13-149 of the Main Volume, in footnote 639, add the following after "*See, e.g.*,".]**

Otto v. City of Victoria, 685 F.3d 755, 758–59, 26 AD 909 (8th Cir. 2012) (discharged city maintenance employee with back injury was

---

thus would not have rendered him otherwise qualified, and hospital's offer to assist him in obtaining alternative pathology position showed good faith participation in interactive process), *cert. denied*, 131 S. Ct. 3071, 24 AD 1536 (2011).

no longer qualified for that position due to physician-imposed permanent lifting and part-time sedentary work restrictions, and proposed accommodations of part-time position within restrictions or co-worker assistance would unreasonably require creation of new position or removal of essential duties); McFadden v. Ballard Spahr Andrews & Ingersoll LLP, 611 F.3d 1, 5, 23 AD 518 (D.C. Cir. 2010) (legal secretary, who was discharged after expiration of her medical leave for Graves' disease, fibromyalgia, and depression, was not entitled to requested accommodation of reassignment to receptionist position, despite contention that position had been vacated by long-term permanent receptionist whose legally mandated medical leave had expired, where fact that temporary employee filled position while permanent receptionist was on disability leave and law firm did not attempt to hire replacement showed that position was not vacant, and there was no evidence that law firm did not expect permanent receptionist to return as scheduled); Duvall v. Georgia-Pacific Consumer Prods., LP, 607 F.3d 1255, 1262–64, 23 AD 420 (10th Cir. 2010) (duty to reasonably accommodate paper mill employee with cystic fibrosis, who experienced severe breathing difficulty after transfer to operator position, did not include reassigning him to vacant position where desired positions were not available to similarly situated nondisabled co-worker but were staffed by temporary workers during outsourcing transition); *Gratzl*, 601 F.3d at 680–81 (duty to accommodate court reporter, whose incontinence necessitated immediate restroom access, did not include allowing her to resume specialist position that was eliminated in state-level position consolidation and avoid in-court rotation, even though she had been previously assigned exclusively to specialist position; temporary reassignments did not create duty to accommodate with permanent reassignment and she rejected proposed accommodations to enable her to perform in-court reporting);

(v.) Employee must be qualified for new position

[642]**[On page 13-150 of the Main Volume, in footnote 642, add the following before "Cravens v. Blue Cross & Blue Shield".]**

Supinski v. United Parcel Serv., Inc., 413 F. App'x 536, 24 AD 278 (3d Cir. 2011) (nonprecedential) (former package car driver with 70-pound lifting restriction because of shoulder injury raised factual issues that precluded dismissal of his ADA action despite contention that he was not qualified individual because lifting requirements exceeded his restrictions, where job descriptions were prepared after he was rejected and did not establish that heavy lifting was essential job function, and testimony contradicted requirements detailed in descriptions);

(vi.) Competing for a vacant position

[649][On page 13-152 of the Main Volume, in footnote 649, add the following after "(7th Cir. 2000)".]

, *withdrawn and overruled*, EEOC v. United Airlines, Inc., 693 F.3d 760, 26 AD 1431 (7th Cir. 2012), *cert. denied*, 133 S. Ct. 2734 (2013)

[653][On page 13-152 of the Main Volume, in footnote 653, add the following after "*See also*".]

Jackson v. Fuji Photo Film, Inc., 447 F. App'x 515 (4th Cir. 2011) (employer not required to select disabled employee seeking accommodation for vacant position when there was better-qualified applicant), *cert. denied*, 132 S. Ct. 2104 (2012);

[657][On page 13-153 of the Main Volume, in footnote 657, add the following at the end of the footnote.]

The Supreme Court granted certiorari, 552 U.S. 1074 (2007), limited to resolving the split in the circuits on this issue. The petition was subsequently dismissed by stipulation of the parties, however, and no decision was issued. *See* 2008 U.S. LEXIS 1095 (Jan. 14, 2008).

3. Impact of Collective Bargaining Agreements on Reasonable Accommodation

[669][On page 13-156 of the Main Volume, in footnote 669, add the following at the end of the footnote.]

But see EEOC v. United Airlines, Inc., 693 F.3d 760, 764–65, 26 AD 1431 (7th Cir. 2012) (distinguishing between *Barnett*'s holding on seniority systems and its discussion of whether reasonable accommodations may entail preference in selecting disabled employee to fill vacancy), *cert. denied*, 133 S. Ct. 2734 (2013).

4. *Notice to the Employer*

[677][On page 13-158 of the Main Volume, in footnote 677, add the following before "Stewart v. St. Elizabeth's Hosp.".]

Department of Fair Emp't & Hous. v. Lucent Techs., Inc., 642 F.3d 728, 743, 24 AD 915 (9th Cir. 2011) (employer did not violate duty under California law to provide reasonable accommodation to telecommunications installer with lifting restrictions because of back injury, where employee's failure to request accommodation while in contact with supervisors during his one-year disability leave defeated claim that employer failed to engage in interactive process); Schneider v. Giant of Md., LLC, 389 F. App'x 263, 269–70, 23 AD 806 (4th Cir. 2010) (unpublished) (employer did not fail to accommodate diabetic pharmacist, whose driver's license was suspended due to his blackout while driving, where driving was essential element of his job, he did not inform employer that his suggestions concerning alternatives to driving were related to his condition, and employer's awareness of his condition did not create duty to guess that he required accommodation);

5. *Interactive Process*

[687][On page 13-162 of the Main Volume, in footnote 687, add the following at the end of the footnote.]

But see Jones v. Walgreen Co., 679 F.3d 9, 19–20, 26 AD 261 (1st Cir. 2012) (no duty to engage in interactive process where it was apparent that pharmacist who was unable to bend, climb, and walk, as required by her position, could not perform essential duties of her job with or without reasonable accommodation, and reassignment of those duties was not reasonable).

[690][On page 13-164 of the Main Volume, in footnote 690, add the following after "*See, e.g.,*".]

Mogenhan v. Napolitano, 613 F.3d 1162, 1168, 23 AD 705 (D.C. Cir. 2010) (U.S. Secret Service adequately attempted to accommodate analyst's heat-induced migraine headaches, where interactive process began with granting of her preemployment requests for breaks or workers' compensation leave as needed, she was moved to air-conditioned office, and there was no evidence as to when she requested cooling of her workspace); Jakubowski v. Christ Hosp.,

Inc., 627 F.3d 195, 202–03, 23 AD 1713 (6th Cir. 2010) (hospital made adequate efforts to accommodate family practice medical resident with Asperger's Disorder, where his proposed accommodation of staff education regarding his condition would not have improved his patient communications skills and thus would not have rendered him otherwise qualified, and hospital's offer to assist him in obtaining alternative pathology position showed good faith participation in interactive process), *cert. denied*, 131 S. Ct. 3071 (2011);

[692]**[On page 13-164 of the Main Volume, in footnote 692, add the following after "*See, e.g.*,".]**

Jones, 679 F.3d at 19–20 (no duty to engage in interactive process where it was apparent that pharmacist who was unable to bend, climb, and walk as required by her position could not perform essential duties of her job with or without reasonable accommodation and reassignment of those duties was not reasonable);

[On page 13-166 of the Main Volume, at the end of the first sentence of the first paragraph, add new footnote 696a.]

[696a]*See* Department of Fair Emp't & Hous. v. Lucent Techs., Inc., 642 F.3d 728, 742–43, 24 AD 915 (9th Cir. 2011) (discharged telecommunications installer failed in his duty to participate in interactive process where he did not initiate discussion of reasonable accommodation during his one-year disability leave and was discharged only after employer repeatedly assessed whether he could perform essential job function of lifting 30 to 50 pounds and unsuccessfully attempted to locate alternative position).

[700]**[On page 13-167 of the Main Volume, in footnote 700, add the following after "*See, e.g.*,".]**

Griffin v. United Parcel Serv., Inc., 661 F.3d 216, 225, 25 AD 551 (5th Cir. 2011) (employer did not fail to engage adequately in interactive process with diabetic employee where it requested medical information from his doctor that was not supplied in timely manner and where accommodation provided was not that suggested in medical information ultimately provided, but doctor's note did not state that different accommodation was required);

E. Harassment Prohibited

[701][On page 13-168 of the Main Volume, in the carryover of footnote 701, add the following at the end of the footnote.]

Cf. McDonough v. Donahoe, 673 F.3d 41, 49–50, 25 AD 1697 (1st Cir. 2012) (U.S. Postal Service letter carrier with job-related back and neck injuries who failed to establish that she was individual with disabilities protected by Rehabilitation Act could not pursue hostile work environment claim alleging that she was harassed because of her injuries); Farina v. Branford Bd. of Educ., 25 AD 1584 (2d Cir. 2011) (nonprecedential) (rejecting hostile work environment claim by discharged teacher with back injury and cancer-related fatigue and insomnia, where she did not show that she was disabled under ADA or that she was harassed because of alleged disability).

[702][On page 13-168 of the Main Volume, in footnote 702, add the following after "*See, e.g.,*".]

Alvarado v. Donahoe, 687 F.3d 453, 459–61, 26 AD 912 (1st Cir. 2012) (former U.S. Postal Service letter carrier with schizoaffective disorder did not show that alleged harassment, consisting of three discrete verbal exchanges over more than eight months, changed conditions of his employment or that he was subjected to objectively hostile work environment); Ryan v. Capital Contractors, Inc., 679 F.3d 772, 779, 26 AD 385 (8th Cir. 2012) (hostile work environment claim by former employee with intellectual impairment, who alleged that foreman subjected him to derogatory disability-based comments, not established where foreman's lack of supervisory authority barred company's vicarious liability, his conduct, although inappropriate, did not alter conditions of employment and was not objectively offensive given employee's participation in workplace name-calling, and employee failed to complain to management or otherwise show that employer had knowledge of harassment but failed to address it); Colón-Fontánez v. Municipality of San Juan, 660 F.3d 17, 44, 25 AD 423 (1st Cir. 2011) (former city employee with fibromyalgia failed to establish hostile work environment based on her disability where her allegations—that supervisor avoided interacting and socializing with her, yelled at her in front of employees, accused her of faking neck pain, and interfered in her interactions with co-workers—did not rise to level of severity or pervasiveness required to establish hostile or abusive environment);

[704][On page 13-169 of the Main Volume, in footnote 704, add the following at the beginning of the footnote.]

Alvarado, 687 F.3d at 463 (former U.S. Postal Service letter carrier with schizoaffective disorder did not show that alleged harassment consisting of three discrete verbal exchanges over more than eight months changed conditions of his employment or that he was subjected to objectively hostile work environment);

F. Discrimination Through Contractual or Other Relationships Prohibited

[On page 13-169 of the Main Volume, at the end of the first paragraph, add new footnote 707a.]

[707a]*See* EEOC v. Service Temps, Inc., 679 F.3d 323, 26 AD 129 (5th Cir. 2012) (subject matter jurisdiction upheld in ADA action against employment agency that advertised with state employment service a warehouse position that it was seeking to fill for one of its clients, and that refused to permit deaf candidate to apply for that opening).

1. Employer-Provided Health Insurance

[720][On page 13-172 of the Main Volume, in footnote 720, add the following at the end of the footnote.]

Cf. Seff v. Broward Cnty. Fla., 691 F.3d 1221, 1223–24, 29 AD 1153 (11th Cir. 2012) (wellness program adopted by county for its employees, including wellness questionnaire that was used to construct optional health management programs for employees with certain impairments, was part of bona fide benefit plan—group health—and fell within “safe harbor” provision of ADA, 42 U.S.C. § 12201(c)(2), which provides that “Subchapters I through III of this chapter and title IV of this Act shall not be construed to prohibit or restrict— … (2) a person or organization covered by this chapter from establishing, sponsoring, observing or administering the terms of a bona fide benefit plan that are based on underwriting risks, classifying risks, or administering such risks that are based on or not inconsistent with State law”).

G. Accessible Testing Required

[On page 13-174 of the Main Volume, at the end of the first full paragraph, add new footnote 728a.]

[728a]*Cf.* Enyart v. National Conference of Bar Examiners, Inc., 630 F.3d 1153, 1161–63, 24 AD 133 (9th Cir. 2011) (under ADA Title III, legally blind law school graduate was entitled to preliminary injunctions ordering that she be allowed use of laptop computer equipped with JAWS and ZoomText software to take multistate bar examinations; reasonable accommodation standard of ADA Title I employment provision was not incorporated into Title III, and Title III regulations require that professional licensing tests be administered so as to best ensure that results reflect achievement level; alternative accommodations offered caused eye fatigue and nausea, her ophthalmologist certified that requested software was sole means by which graduate could comprehend exams, and her use of alternative accommodations for previous academic tests did not account for progressive nature of her eye condition), *cert. denied*, 132 S. Ct. 366, 25 AD 416 (2011).

H. Discrimination on the Basis of Association Prohibited

[745]**[On page 13-177 of the Main Volume, in footnote 745, add the following after "*See*".]**

Magnus v. St. Mark United Methodist Church, 688 F.3d 331, 26 AD 1029 (7th Cir. 2012) (church receptionist who was discharged for unsatisfactory performance, including her refusal to work weekends because of her responsibility to care for her disabled daughter, was not entitled to accommodation of her schedule; no duty to accommodate needs of nondisabled individuals that arise out of their association with individual who is disabled); Stansberry v. Air Wisconsin Airlines Corp., 651 F.3d 482, 489, 24 AD 1544 (6th Cir. 2011) (employee who was not disabled not entitled to reasonable accommodation because of stress and distraction that he experienced because of his wife's disability);

[749]**[On page 13-178 of the Main Volume, in footnote 749, add the following at the end of the footnote.]**

See Pulczinski v. Trinity Structural Towers, Inc., 691 F.3d 996, 1003–04, 26 AD 1293 (8th Cir. 2012) (painter who alleged that reason for his discharge was his caregiver relationship with his disabled son failed to demonstrate that employer's articulated reason for discharge—its good faith belief that he was discouraging others on his crew from agreeing to work overtime in order to control his own hours—was pretext for discrimination).

I. Limitations on Medical Inquiries and Examinations

2. *Preemployment Medical Examinations and Inquiries*

[759][On page 13-180 of the Main Volume, in footnote 759, add the following at the end of the footnote.]

Cf. Lopez v. Pacific Mar. Ass'n, 657 F.3d 762, 765, 25 AD 443 (9th Cir. 2011) (longshoreman who was recovered drug addict and previously had been rejected because of positive drug test may not challenge as discriminatory employer's reliance on that test seven years later to reject his application for employment where employer's "one-strike" rule was applied equally to all applicants).

4. *Medical Examinations and Inquiries for Existing Employees*

[776][On page 13-183 of the Main Volume, in footnote 776, add the following after "*see, e.g.*,".]

Román-Oliveras v. Puerto Rico Elec. Power Auth., 655 F.3d 43, 49, 25 AD 1 (1st Cir. 2011) (plaintiff stated valid ADA claim based on allegations that public power company violated ADA limits on medical examinations of incumbent employees when it required individual whose schizophrenia was controlled and who had performed satisfactorily for more than 20 years to undergo multiple medical evaluations, and then discharged him despite favorable results of those evaluations);

[776][On page 13-184 of the Main Volume, in the carryover of footnote 776, add the following at the end of the footnote.]

But see Kroll v. White Lake Ambulance Auth., 691 F.3d 809, 819–20, 26 AD 1313 (6th Cir. 2012) (emergency medical technician may pursue discrimination claim challenging her discharge for refusing to undergo psychological counseling where such counseling constitutes medical examination under ADA, her refusal was based on requirement that she pay for counseling, and she had satisfactorily performed her job for more than four years); Lee v. City of Columbus,

Ohio, 636 F.3d 245, 256, 24 AD 257 (6th Cir. 2011) (policy that required each employee returning from sick leave to provide doctor's note regarding nature of employee's injury, which is less specific than "general diagnosis," is not unlawful disability-related inquiry because it is universal policy applicable to all employees, regardless of disability status).

[On page 13-185 of the Main Volume, after the carryover sentence that ends with footnote 781, add the following.]

The employer may also inquire whether an employee who is changing positions is able to perform the essential functions of the new job.[11]

J. Retaliation and Interference Prohibited

[787][On page 13-186 of the Main Volume, in footnote 787, add the following at the end of the footnote.]

Some courts have extended this anti-retaliation provision to cover nonqualified individuals as long as the plaintiff had a good faith belief that a requested accommodation was appropriate. *See, e.g.*, Kirkeberg v. Canadian Pac. Ry., 619 F.3d 898, 907–08, 23 AD 1000 (8th Cir. 2010) (discussing cases).

[788][On page 13-186 of the Main Volume, in footnote 788, add the following at the end of the footnote.]

But see Reynolds v. American Nat'l Red Cross, 701 F.3d 143, 154, 27 AD 263 (4th Cir. 2012) (employee who was discharged several months after his back injury failed to establish ADA retaliation claim; proximity in time alone was insufficient and he failed to show: (1) causal nexus between his request that his employer honor physician-imposed lifting restriction, inquiry into filing for workers' compensation, and his discharge; or (2) that employer's explanation that discharge was based upon lack of adequate funding was pretextual);

---

[11] *See* Denton v. Chicago Transit Auth., 400 F. App'x 90, 92, 23 AD 1478 (7th Cir. 2010) (unpublished) (city transit authority fare collector, whose position was eliminated, was lawfully required to undergo fitness-for-duty examination when he moved into new position in bus operations unit where correspondence showed that he remained under authority's control after his position was eliminated, authority's medical examination policy tracked U.S. Department of Transportation regulations, and testing fitness of bus operations unit employees was business necessity).

Anderson v. Donahoe, 699 F.3d 989, 995–96, 26 AD 1761 (7th Cir. 2012) (asthmatic postal service employee's retaliation claim that he was denied accommodation and threatened with suspension in response to his prior EEO complaints failed both because there was 13-month gap between his protected activity and alleged adverse action, and because he did not provide any evidence suggesting that similarly situated co-workers who did not file complaints were treated differently); Povey v. City of Jeffersonville, Ind., 697 F.3d 619, 624, 26 AD 1633 (7th Cir. 2012) (temporal proximity alone was insufficient to establish causal connection between complaints by animal shelter employee with wrist injury that she was being harassed by co-workers because of her disability, and her discharge three weeks later; stray remark by supervisor and failure of agency to meet with her regarding reasonable accommodation did not alter outcome where she did not establish that injury constituted disability); Feldman v. Olin Corp., 692 F.3d 748, 757, 26 AD 1305 (7th Cir. 2012) (tractor operator's claim that he was refused reinstatement, assigned to physically demanding job, and suspended in retaliation for filing EEOC charge failed where he did not show causal link between employer's actions and charge; delay in rehiring was due to his physician-imposed shift restrictions, there was no evidence that job assignment was punitive, and his suspension for crashing tractor occurred eight months after he filed charge); Palmquist v. Shinseki, 689 F.3d 66, 72–73, 26 AD 1038 (1st Cir. 2012) (former postal service letter carrier with schizoaffective disorder did not establish that he was victim of retaliatory harassment where it was unclear whether supervisors were aware of his EEO charge, alleged harassment consisting of three discrete verbal exchanges over more than eight months, did not change conditions of employment, and there was no evidence that his improper handling of undelivered mail was pretext for 14-day suspension); EEOC v. Picture People, Inc., 684 F.3d 981, 989, 26 AD 776 (10th Cir. 2012) (deaf and speech-impaired former photography studio employee did not show that she was disciplined and removed from work schedule in response to her grievance threat where reduction of hours after holiday was due to reduced business and applicable to all co-workers, she had been counseled previously concerning certain infractions, and there was no evidence to support contention that nondisabled co-workers who engaged in same conduct were not disciplined); Dickerson v. Board of Trs. of Cmty. Coll. Dist. No. 522, 657 F.3d 595, 602–03, 25 AD 193 (7th Cir. 2011) (developmentally disabled part-time janitor who filed EEOC charge did not establish that his discharge was retaliatory even though official made negative comment about that charge, where documented disciplinary warnings and poor performance evaluations showed that he was not meeting employer's legitimate expectations); EEOC v. C.R. England, Inc., 644 F.3d 1028, 1051–52, 24 AD 897 (10th Cir. 2011) (HIV-positive truck driver did not establish that company's referral to collections of claim for debt that he owed on his truck leasing agreement constituted retaliation for filing EEOC charge, where debt was sent to agency more than one year after initial dispute, he did not contest that debt was owed under lease agreement that gave company option to use collection agency, and company notified him that it would use collection agency to collect debt before he filed charge).

[789]**[On page 13-187 of the Main Volume, in footnote 789, add the following after "*See*".]**

Hoppe v. Lewis Univ., 692 F.3d 833, 842–43, 26 AD 1286 (7th Cir. 2012) (dismissal appropriate where alleged unwarranted discipline and reduction in responsibilities were mere snubs without economic injury and did not support professor's claim that she was retaliated against for filing EEOC charge of disability discrimination and for requesting disability accommodation; similarly, professor failed to show that being removed from teaching specific class was retaliatory where it occurred two years after her first protected activity); Colón-Fontánez v. Municipality of San Juan, 660 F.3d 17, 37–38, 25 AD 423 (1st Cir. 2011) (city employee with fibromyalgia did not establish that city retaliated against her after she sought reasonable accommodation for her disability by transferring her assistant to assist entire department and removing certain assistive equipment from her office where there was no evidence of intent, she did not suffer demotion or other materially adverse action, there was no reduction in her salary or reclassification, and employer proffered that it removed equipment for cleaning); Serednyj v. Beverly Healthcare LLC, 656 F.3d 540, 557, 25 AD 103 (7th Cir. 2011) (retaliation claim by former nursing home employee, who alleged that the employer actively sought reasons to discharge her after she requested accommodations for pregnancy complications, did not establish that reason for her discharge—that she was not eligible to work from home under company's modified work policy, had not worked long enough to qualify for FMLA leave, and was not qualified to perform her position at the facility—was not adverse action, and discharge occurred before she requested accommodations); Reinhardt v. Albuquerque Pub. Sch. Bd. of Educ., 595 F.3d 1126, 1134–35, 22 AD 1625 (10th 2010) (speech therapist whose workload and salary were reduced shortly after she spoke publicly seeking additional resources for special needs students established claim of retaliation under § 504 of Rehabilitation Act; speech was protected activity, no credible explanation for reductions was offered, and colleague with comparable experience was not treated same way);

[790][On page 13-187 of the Main Volume, in footnote 790, add the following at the end of the footnote.]

But see Reynolds, 701 F.3d at 154 (filing workers' compensation claim is not protected activity under ADA); Valle-Arce v. Puerto Rico Ports Auth., 651 F.3d 190, 201, 24 AD 1537 (1st Cir. 2011) (employee who suffered from chronic fatigue syndrome and related disorders provided sufficient evidence to support her claim that she was discharged in retaliation for continuing to pursue reasonable accommodations such as flexible work schedule, printer in her office, and office location that minimized her need to walk around during work day, after these and other adjustments that would have accommodated her chronic fatigue syndrome were removed from her by new supervisor, where her satisfactory performance established that she could perform essential functions of position with accommodation, and employer's normal accommodation procedures were not followed).

VII. BURDENS OF PROOF AND DEFENSES

A. Burdens of Proof

3. Proof Relevant to Disparate Treatment

a. In General

[816][On page 13-193 of the Main Volume, in footnote 816, add the following after "*see also*".]

Whitfield v. Tennessee, 639 F.3d 253, 261, 24 AD 641 (6th Cir. 2011) (upholding summary judgment in favor of employer where there was no genuine issue of material fact whether employee was terminated on basis of disability; "overwhelming evidence" showed many of employee's "performance problems were completely unrelated to her disabilities");

[819]**[On page 13-193 of the Main Volume, in footnote 819, add the following after "*See*".]**

Turner v. Saloon Ltd., 595 F.3d 679, 687, 22 AD 1481 (7th Cir. 2010) (waiter who was discharged two months after filing EEOC charge failed in his retaliation claim where seven-week proximity alone was insufficient to establish causal connection between filing and discharge, and there was no evidence that he was performing job satisfactorily or that similarly situated co-worker was treated differently);

b. Burden Shifting

[823]**[On page 13-195 of the Main Volume, in footnote 823, add the following after "*See, e.g.,*".]**

Ryan v. Capital Contractors., Inc., 679 F.3d 772, 777–78, 26 AD 385 (8th Cir. 2012) (although instances of disparate treatment can support claim of pretext, comparators must be similarly situated in all relevant respects; employee with mental disability failed to establish pretext where he was terminated for engaging in physical fight with his supervisor, where employer determined that discharged employee twice acted to escalate incident);

[825]**[On page 13-195 of the Main Volume, in footnote 825, add the following at the beginning of the footnote.]**

Lee v. City of Columbus, Ohio, 636 F.3d 245, 257–258, 24 AD 257 (6th Cir. 2011) (reversing district court's critique of employer's sick leave policy; "The district court has created an artificial distinction where none exists. It is not within the province of the courts to rewrite legislation, superimpose language onto statutes, or 'act as super personnel departments to second guess an employer's facially legitimate business decisions.'") (citing Adams v. Tennessee Dep't of Fin. & Admin., 179 F. App'x 266, 272 (6th Cir. 2006) (unpublished));

[830]**[On page 13-197 of the Main Volume, in footnote 830, add the following after "*E.g.,*".]**

Dickerson v. Board of Trs. of Cmty. Coll. Dist. No. 522, 657 F.3d 595, 602–03, 25 AD 193 (7th Cir. 2011) (developmentally disabled individual, who was fired from his position as part-time janitor, did not make out prima facie case of discrimination because he failed to show that he was meeting his employer's legitimate expectations, where he had received consistently unsatisfactory reviews for years before complaining of disability discrimination);

5. *Failure to Accommodate*

[860][On page 13-203 of the Main Volume, in footnote 860, add the following after "*see also*".]

Jakubowski v. Christ Hosp., Inc., 627 F.3d 195, 202, 23 AD 1713 (6th Cir. 2010) (employee is "saddled with the burden of proposing an accommodation," and proving that it is reasonable and that it will allow him to perform essential functions of job), *cert. denied*, 131 S. Ct. 3071 (2011);

B. Affirmative Defenses

1. *Eligibility Criteria That Are "Job-Related and Consistent With Business Necessity"*

[873][On page 13-205 of the Main Volume, in footnote 873, add the following after "*E.g.*,".]

Wilkerson v. Shinseki, 606 F.3d 1256, 1264–65, 109 FEP 660, 23 AD 321 (10th Cir. 2010) (diabetic boiler room operator, who was transferred to lesser-paying position after failing annual physical examination, was not otherwise qualified to proceed with disability claim where valid and uniformly enforced federal guidelines for operator position exclude those with uncontrolled diabetes and require ability to respond to emergencies; no accommodation would have enabled him to remain in operator position, and employer met duty to engage in interactive process by considering and rejecting his accommodation request and making reasonable accommodation of transfer); Kinneary v. City of N.Y., 601 F.3d 151, 157, 22 AD 1803 (2d Cir. 2010) (discharge of city tanker captain with paruresis (shy bladder syndrome), whose license was revoked for refusal to provide urine sample for federally mandated drug test, did not violate ADA, despite contention that city failed to provide reasonable accommodation of test cancellation based on physician's evaluation, where note from his physician after city allowed him to seek evaluation did not comply with federal requirements for test cancellation; plaintiff was unable to perform essential function of maintaining captain's license);

2. *Undue Hardship*

[881][On page 13-207 of the Main Volume, in footnote 881, add the following before "Colorado Cross Disability Coalition v. Hermanson Family Ltd. P'ship,".]

Jakubowski v. Christ Hosp., Inc., 627 F.3d 195, 202–203, 23 AD 1713 (6th Cir. 2010) ("employer has the burden of showing how the accommodation would cause an undue hardship as that term is defined in the statute and regulations, but the employer is not required to propose a counter accommodation in order to participate in the interactive process in good faith"), *cert. denied*, 131 S. Ct. 3071 (2011);

3. *Direct Threat to Health or Safety*

[913][On page 13-214 of the Main Volume, in footnote 913, add the following after "*E.g.*,".]

Atkins v. Salazar, 677 F.3d 667, 682–83 (5th Cir. 2012) (unpublished) (no violation where diabetic park ranger was demoted under revised medical qualification standards for failing to meet terms of medical waiver; employer showed that revised medical qualification standards were consistent with business necessity because reduced consciousness or concentration attendant with diabetes that was not well managed was threat to public safety);

[913][On page 13-214 of the Main Volume, in footnote 913, add the following at the end of the footnote.]

Cf. Guttman v. Khalsa, 669 F.3d 1101, 1123–25, 25 AD 1316 (10th Cir. 2012) (state was entitled to sovereign immunity in Title II action brought by physician who was challenging as discriminatory revocation of his license to practice, where due process hearing had shown that his depression and PTSD posed imminent threat to health and safety of others if he were permitted to practice).

4. Special Defense Issues

a. HIV and AIDS

[938]**[On page 13-223 of the Main Volume, in footnote 938, add the following at the end of the footnote.]**

See also Roe v. City of Atlanta, 456 F. App'x 820, 822, 25 AD 1313 (11th Cir. 2012) (police department that denied in its answer to rejected applicant's ADA complaint that it considered HIV-positive status as per se disqualifying factor may not rely on HIV status without individual assessment as a basis for rejecting him; at minimum, answer misled plaintiff as to whether he needed to provide evidence that his HIV status did not disqualify him).

c. Drug or Alcohol Impairment

[948]**[On page 13-226 of the Main Volume, in footnote 948, add the following after "*see*".]**

Mauerhan v. Wagner Corp., 649 F.3d 1180, 24 AD 769 (10th Cir. 2011) (employee who was discharged for illegal use of drugs, completed rehabilitation program, and applied for reinstatement could not sustain claim of discrimination where program lasted only 30 days and he sought reemployment immediately after he was discharged; although there is no bright line defining how long known drug abuser must be drug free, one month was insufficient to overcome employer's good faith belief that individual was current user of illegal drugs);

[954]**[On page 13-227 of the Main Volume, in footnote 954, add the following at the end of the footnote.]**

See Ames v. Home Depot U.S.A., Inc., 629 F.3d 665, 670–71, 24 AD 16 (7th Cir. 2011) (alcoholism may be disability under ADA where it significantly affects one or more major life activities; however, retail store employee, who was discharged for coming to work under influence of alcohol in violation of store policy and of her signed EAP agreement, did not establish discrimination claim where there was no evidence that she was substantially limited in major life activity, she denied repeatedly that her condition interfered with her work performance, violation of store's alcohol use policy constituted failure to meet its legitimate expectations, and she had not sought reasonable accommodations of leave and EAP counseling beyond that which had been provided to her previously).

[On page 13-229 of the Main Volume, after the sentence that ends with footnote 965, add the following new paragraph.]

The decriminalization of marijuana use by a number of states, whether generally or when used for medical reasons, presents interesting questions under the ADA. In *Casias v. Wal-Mart Stores, Inc.*,[12] an employee who had sinus cancer and an inoperable brain tumor was discharged because he failed a drug test. The employee brought a wrongful discharge action (which was removed to federal court) claiming that his marijuana use was not illegal because he was a certified user under the Michigan Medical Marijuana Act.[13] Under that law, a certified user may not be subjected to any "penalty of any manner, or denied any right or privilege, including but not limited to civil penalty or disciplinary action by a business."[14] The Sixth Circuit, citing state court decisions on the issue from several states, decided that the law provides only a "defense to criminal charges or other adverse state action," and that applying it to claims against private employers would be unduly broad.[15]

VIII. ENFORCEMENT AND REMEDIES ISSUES UNIQUE TO DISABILITY CLAIMS

A. Under the ADA

1. *Agency Proceedings*

[On page 13-231 of the Main Volume, at the end of the second sentence of the carryover paragraph, add new footnote 973a.]

[973a]*See* EEOC v. Burlington N. Santa Fe R.R., 669 F.3d 1154, 1158, 25 AD 1572 (10th Cir. 2012) (notwithstanding EEOC's broad subpoena authority, court denied Commission's motion to enforce subpoena for nationwide electronic data concerning all Burlington Northern employees from 2006 to the date of the filing of the

---

[12]695 F.3d 428, 27 AD 18 (6th Cir. 2012), *reh'g en banc denied*, 2012 U.S. App. LEXIS 23969 (Oct. 26, 2012).

[13]MICH. COMP. LAWS §§ 333.26421, et seq.

[14]*Id. at* §§ 333.26424(a), (b).

[15]695 F.3d at 435–36.

subpoena as part of its investigation of two individual charges of disability discrimination because it was not relevant to those two charges; individual allegations of disability discrimination are distinguishable from individual charges of race discrimination, which may require disclosure of classwide information in response to EEOC subpoena, because race discrimination is by definition class discrimination).

CHAPTER 14

GENETIC INFORMATION

I. Introduction

[1][On page 14-1 of the Main Volume, in footnote 1, add the following at the end of the footnote.]

The provisions of GINA relating to employment appear at 42 U.S.C. §§ 2000ff–2000ff(11) (2010).

[8][On page 14-2 of the Main Volume, in footnote 8, add the following at the end of the footnote.]

The regulations have been incorporated into 29 U.S.C. pts. 1601 & 1602 (2013).

[10][On page 14-3 of the Main Volume, in footnote 10, add the following at the end of the footnote.]

The regulations have been incorporated into 29 U.S.C. pt. 1635 (2013).

II. Scope of GINA

C. Who Is Protected?

[On page 14-4 of the Main Volume, after the sentence that ends with footnote 22, add the following.]

GINA does not address directly whether associational discrimination is covered under that law as it is under the Americans with Disabilities Act (ADA). Additionally, the EEOC regulations do not mention an employee's spouse in defining the "family" whose genetic information may not be acquired and, if acquired, may not be used to discriminate against that employee.[1]

D. What Is Protected?

[On page 14-5 of the Main Volume, after the sentence that ends with footnote 26, add the following new paragraphs.]

As noted earlier, GINA does not address directly whether associational discrimination is covered. One court has held that there is

---

[1]*See* 29 C.F.R. § 1635.3 (2013). The definition does include the dependents of the employee "as the result of marriage, birth, adoption or placement for adoption."

no associational discrimination claim regarding requests for medical information. In *Poore v. Peterbilt of Bristol, LLC*,[2] the company's new owner requested that all employees complete a "health questionnaire." Poore had worked for the company for several years, and his family (including his wife) was covered by the company's health insurance plan. After stating in his response that his wife had been diagnosed with multiple sclerosis, Poore was questioned about it by a supervisor, and three days later was discharged without explanation. After Poore sued, the district court granted Peterbilt's motion to dismiss his GINA claim, concluding there was no prohibition on associational discrimination and that information concerning Poore's wife was not protected because she was not part of the employee's "genetic family."[3] The court did not discuss either the propriety under GINA of questioning an employee about his family's medical conditions, or whether Poore's termination was unlawfully motivated by a desire to deprive him of the benefits of the health insurance that covered his entire family. *Poore* raises an additional question about the acquisition of genetic information. The statute creates an exemption to the prohibition on collecting such information where the employer is offering health services to its employees (e.g., as part of a wellness program), where the employee voluntarily consents in writing to its collection.[4] Although the EEOC has not yet provided guidance for private employers seeking to collect workforce health data that potentially include genetic information, it has provided guidance to *federal* employers covered by GINA.[5] The guidance includes the following response to a question asking whether an employer may require its workers to provide family medical histories:

> Generally, no. There is one exception: departments and agencies may request family medical history when they are allowed to make disability-related inquiries of post-offer applicants and employees under the Rehabilitation Act. Departments and agencies may only use such family medical history to decide if further medical evaluation is needed to diagnose a *current* disease that could prevent an

---

[2]852 F. Supp. 2d 727, 729, 26 AD 174 (W.D. Va. 2012).

[3]*Id.* at 730–31.

[4]42 U.S.C. § 2000ff-1(b).

[5]*See* Executive Order 13145; Questions and Answers: EEOC Policy Guidance on Executive Order 13145 Prohibiting Discrimination in Federal Employment on the Basis of Genetic Information, *available at* http://www.eeoc.gov/policy/docs/qanda-genetic.html (last visited May 23, 2014).

individual from performing the essential functions of the position held or desired.[6]

III. PROHIBITED EMPLOYMENT PRACTICES

A. Acquisition of Information

[28][On page 14-6 of the Main Volume, in footnote 28, add the following at the end of the footnote.]

The EEOC regulations do not mention an employee's spouse in defining the "family" whose genetic information may not be acquired and, if acquired, may not be used to discriminate against that employee. *See Poore*, 852 F. Supp. 2d at 730–31 (although employee who was discharged three days after he disclosed to physician performing fitness-for-duty exam that his wife had been diagnosed with multiple sclerosis might have made out ADA associational discrimination claim, he had no claim under GINA because wife is not blood relative and her condition is not predictive of employee's likelihood of contracting disease).

IV. ENFORCEMENT

A. Employees Covered by Title VII and the Government Employees Rights Act of 1991

[On page 14-12 of the Main Volume, at the end of the carryover paragraph, add new footnote 62a.]

[62a]*But see* EEOC v. Nestle Prepared Food, 26 AD 825, 2012 WL 1888130, at *3, 2012 U.S. Dist. LEXIS (E.D. Ky. 2012) (EEOC not entitled to enforcement of subpoena seeking medical examination records of all facility employees and applicants in investigating discharged employee's genetic information bias charge, where there was nothing in charge to suggest facilitywide systemic GINA violations and EEOC conceded that there was no other basis for seeking facilitywide data).

---

[6]EEOC COMPL. MAN. § 902:219 (BNA).

CHAPTER 15

RETALIATION

II. THE PARTICIPATION CLAUSE

[36]**[On page 15-9 of the Main Volume, in footnote 36, add the following after "*see also*".]**

Townsend v. Benjamin Enters., Inc., 679 F.3d 41, 48–49, 114 FEP 1537 (2d Cir. 2012) (participation clause of Title VII's antiretaliation provision does not protect participation in internal employer investigation not associated with any formal EEOC charge);

III. THE OPPOSITION CLAUSE

A. Introduction

[54]**[On page 15-12 of the Main Volume, in footnote 54, add the following after "*E.g.*,".]**

Wasek v. Arrow Energy Servs., Inc., 682 F.3d 463, 469, 115 FEP 384 (6th Cir. 2012) (complaining about alleged sexual harassment to company management is "classic opposition activity");

B. The Requirement That the Employment Practice Opposed Be Unlawful Under Title VII

[60]**[On page 15-13 of the Main Volume, in footnote 60, add the following after "*See, e.g.*,".]**

Wasek v. Arrow Energy Servs., Inc., 682 F.3d 463, 470–71, 115 FEP 384 (6th Cir. 2012) (plaintiff, who did not establish as factual matter that he had been subjected to actionable same-sex harassment under Title VII, nevertheless could have had reasonable, good faith belief that he was being sexually harassed; plaintiff failed, however, to establish causal connection between his opposition to harassment and his discharge);

[65]**[On page 15-16 of the Main Volume, in footnote 65, add the following after "*See, e.g.*,".]**

Morales-Cruz v. University of P.R., 676 F.3d 220, 227, 114 FEP 1185 (1st Cir. 2012) (tenured female law professor did not have objectively reasonable belief that gender-neutral comments describing her as "fragile," "immature," and "unable to handle complex and sensitive issues" reflected gender-based discrimination); Bonn v. City of Omaha, 623 F.3d 587, 591, 110 FEP 929 (8th Cir. 2010) (public safety auditor did not harbor reasonable belief that she was opposing Title VII violation in report relating to police department's potentially discriminatory policing tactics; it was not reasonable for her to conclude that those tactics were employment practices that violated Title VII simply because tactics might affect future recruitment of minorities into police force); Dixon v. Hallmark Cos., 627 F.3d 849, 857, 110 FEP 1675 (11th Cir. 2010) (plaintiffs' belief that they were opposing unlawful practice under Title VII was objectively unreasonable where they alleged that they were fired for refusing to follow policy against display of religious artwork in workplace, but were unable to cite any legal authority prohibiting private employer from keeping its workplace free of religious references);

[70][On page 15-18 of the Main Volume, in the carryover of footnote 70, add the following after "*But cf.*".]

Dixon, 627 F.3d at 857 (plaintiffs' beliefs were objectively unreasonable where they alleged that they were fired for refusing to follow policy against display of religious artwork in workplace, but were unable to cite any legal authority affording such protection);

[78][On page 15-19 of the Main Volume, in footnote 78, add the following at the end of the footnote.]

See also Egan v. Freedom Bank, 659 F.3d 639, 642–43, 113 FEP 801 (7th Cir. 2011) (reversing summary judgment for employer where employee presented evidence that bank discharged her in retaliation for reporting board member's sexual remark, despite bank's contention that it eliminated her position because it was losing money; additionally bank hired four new employees, undercutting financial hardship defense).

D. The Manner of Opposition

1. Overview

[106][On page 15-23 of the Main Volume, in footnote 106, add the following after "*accord*".]

Wasek v. Arrow Energy Servs., Inc., 682 F.3d 463, 471, 115 FEP 384 (6th Cir. 2012) (suggesting that leaving worksite in protest could qualify as protected opposition activity if it was reasonable under circumstances, but declining to reach issue because plaintiff did not raise it);

5. *Intra-Office Disruption*

[122]**[On page 15-26 of the Main Volume, in footnote 122, add the following after "*See, e.g.*,".]**

Leitgen v. Franciscan Skemp Healthcare, Inc., 630 F.3d 668, 676, 111 FEP 289 (7th Cir. 2011) (plaintiff failed to show causal connection between discharge and her complaint of discriminatory compensation; temporal proximity between complaint and discharge alone was not enough to show pretext in employer's explanation that she was discharged for hostility to nurses and patients);

IV. PROOF

C. The Adverse Action

[157]**[On page 15-35 of the Main Volume, in footnote 157, add the following at the end of the footnote.]**

See also Millea v. Metro-North R.R., 658 F.3d 154, 164–65, 17 WH Cases 2d 1825 (2d Cir. 2011) (extending *Burlington*'s definition of materially adverse actions to Family and Medical Leave Act (FMLA) retaliation cases and holding that letter of reprimand may qualify as adverse action).

[160]**[On page 15-36 of the Main Volume, in footnote 160, add the following after "*First Circuit*:".]**

Tuli v. Brigham & Women's Hosp., 656 F.3d 33, 42, 113 FEP 116 (1st Cir. 2011) (reasonable jury could conclude that consequences of obligatory counseling required by employer—invasion of privacy, potential stigma, and impact on employment and licensing elsewhere—might dissuade reasonable worker from filing charge); Pérez-Cordero v. Wal-Mart P.R., Inc., 656 F.3d 19, 31–32, 113 FEP 125 (1st Cir. 2011) (summary judgment on claim of retaliation improper where following male employee's rejection of female supervisor's advances she threatened him with negative job evaluations, humiliated him before co-workers, and assigned him to undesirable tasks that kept him from meetings and training opportunities);

[160]**[On page 15-36 of the Main Volume, in footnote 160, add the following after "*Fourth Circuit*:".]**

Hoyle v. Freightliner, LLC, 650 F.3d 321, 337, 111 FEP 1537 (4th Cir. 2011) (mechanic's reassignment to perform janitorial duties was materially adverse);

[160]**[On page 15-36 of the Main Volume, in footnote 160, add the following after "*Sixth Circuit*:".]**

Wasek v. Arrow Energy Servs., Inc., 682 F.3d 463, 470, 115 FEP 384 (6th Cir. 2012) (banning employee from working in particular state was adverse employment action);

[160]**[On page 15-37 of the Main Volume, in the carryover of footnote 160, add the following after "*Seventh Circuit*:".]**

Arizanovska v. Wal-Mart Stores, Inc., 682 F.3d 698, 703–04, 115 FEP 270 (7th Cir. 2012) (employee established materially adverse action in support of her claim that employer retaliated against her by refusing her request for light duty and placing her on unpaid leave; although employer contended that such leave was consistent with its policy for employees with medical conditions and that it did not create light-duty positions for any employees, employer is not shielded from liability simply by complying with its own policy); Hicks v. Forest Preserve Dist. of Cook Cnty., 677 F.3d 781, 787–88, 114 FEP 1281 (7th Cir. 2012) (evidence presented at trial was sufficient for reasonable jury to find that employee's demotion was involuntary and retaliatory and constituted adverse employment action; after plaintiff complained of discriminatory discipline, he was given choice between demotion or further discipline, and he believed that he would be fired if he declined demotion); Benuzzi v. Chicago Bd. of Educ., 647 F.3d 652, 665, 112 FEP 1444 (7th Cir. 2011) (female custodian hired by public school board as building engineer-in-charge raised factual issue as to whether school principal retaliated against her for pursuing sex discrimination claim where she received disciplinary notice and her access to school building was restricted on day following her deposition; although written warnings alone do not generally constitute materially adverse actions, disciplinary notice alleging petty misdeeds that occurred months earlier, coupled with unexplained restrictions on access to building, could deter reasonable employee from filing discrimination complaint, and reasonable jury could infer that claimant's protected activities precipitated these actions);

[160]**[On page 15-37 of the Main Volume, in footnote 160, add the following after "*Eighth Circuit*:".]**

Young-Losee v. Graphic Packaging Int'l, Inc., 631 F.3d 909, 913, 111 FEP 488 (8th Cir. 2011) ("Being fired for making a discrimination complaint—even if firing rescinded after two days—might well dissuade a reasonable employee from making a complaint of harassment.");

[160]**[On page 15-37 of the Main Volume, in footnote 160, add the following after "*Tenth Circuit*:".]**

Bertsch v. Overstock.com, 684 F.3d 1023, 1029, 115 FEP 745 (10th Cir. 2012) (disciplinary action is materially adverse if it is enough to dissuade complainant from making complaint, even if it did not effect significant change in plaintiff's employment status);

[160]**[On page 15-37 of the Main Volume, in footnote 160, add the following after "*Eleventh Circuit*:".]**

Chapter 7 Tr. v. Gate Gourmet, Inc., 683 F.3d 1249, 1260–61, 115 FEP 391 (11th Cir. 2012) (employer's refusal to give pregnant employee light-duty job, to which she was entitled under company policy, unless she dropped EEOC charge, was materially adverse action for purpose of establishing retaliation claim);

[160]**[On page 15-38 of the Main Volume, in the carryover of footnote 160, add the following at the end of the "*Eleventh Circuit*:" paragraph.]**

Cf. Gowski v. Peake, 682 F.3d 1299, 1311–12, 115 FEP 163 (11th Cir. 2012) (in case involving two Department of Veterans Affairs (VA) physicians, court recognizes retaliatory hostile work environment claim under Title VII);

[160]**[On page 15-38 of the Main Volume, in the carryover of footnote 160, add the following after "*D.C. Circuit*:".]**

Solomon v. Vilsack, 628 F.3d 555, 565–68 (D.C. Cir. 2010) (vacating summary judgment; because "recipients of [Federal Employees

Retirement System] FERS disability benefits are not presumptively barred from asserting Rehabilitation Act claims," denial of accommodation could be materially adverse action sufficient to support retaliation claim);

[163]**[On page 15-38 of the Main Volume, in footnote 163, add the following after "*First Circuit*:".]**

Bhatti v. Trustees of Bos. Univ., 659 F.3d 64, 74, 113 FEP 722 (1st Cir. 2011) (reprimands not material because of absence of tangible consequences); Colón-Fontánez v. Municipality of San Juan, 660 F.3d 17, 44, 25 AD 423 (1st Cir. 2011) (city employee's claim that she suffered hostile work environment in retaliation for requesting accommodation for her fibromyalgia failed where incidents in which supervisor allegedly barred employee from her office, yelled at her, monitored her movements, interfered with co-worker's attempts to help her, barred her from attending workshop, and failed to deal with co-workers' derogatory comments were episodic, not severe, and did not affect employee's work performance); Ahern v. Shinseki, 629 F.3d 49, 56–57, 110 FEP 1785 (1st Cir. 2010) (proposing, but not effectuating, change to employees' schedule was not materially adverse, nor were "petty indignities" involving scheduling changes and removal of honorary title without diminution of responsibility or benefits); Vega-Colón v. Wyeth Pharm., 625 F.3d 22, 33, 189 LRRM 2614 (1st Cir. 2010) (name-calling that was not severe or pervasive and that did not escalate after protected activity was not actionable as retaliatory hostile work environment under Uniformed Services Employment and Reemployment Rights Act (USERRA));

[163]**[On page 15-38 of the Main Volume, in footnote 163, add the following after "*Second Circuit*:".]**

Tepperwien v. Entergy Nuclear Operations, Inc., 663 F.3d 556, 568, 113 FEP 1153 (2d Cir. 2011) (institution of three investigations into plaintiff's conduct, counseling, "empty" termination threats, and shift change that plaintiff had requested were not as matter of law materially adverse);

[163]**[On page 15-39 of the Main Volume, in the carryover of footnote 163, add the following after "*Fifth Circuit*:".]**

Hernandez v. Yellow Transp., Inc., 670 F.3d 644, 657–58, 114 FEP 545 (5th Cir. 2012) (co-worker harassment, including name-calling, physical intimidation, false accusations, vandalizing belongings, and verbal threats, not retaliatory and not committed in furtherance of business);

[163]**[On page 15-39 of the Main Volume, in the carryover of footnote 163, add the following after "*Sixth Circuit*:".]**

Wasek v. Arrow Energy Servs., Inc., 682 F.3d 463, 471, 115 FEP 384 (6th Cir. 2012) (one-month delay in reassigning plaintiff to different position was not adverse employment action); Eckerman v. Tennessee Dep't of Pub. Safety, 636 F.3d 202, 207–09, 31 IER Cases 1110 (6th Cir. 2010) (in § 1983 case, written reprimand and changes to assignments were de minimis and therefore not "materially adverse," but could be used at trial to show "pattern of mistreatment" based on plaintiff's protected activities);

[163]**[On page 15-39 of the Main Volume, in the carryover of footnote 163, add the following after "*Seventh Circuit*:".]**

Brown v. Advocate S. Suburban Hosp., 700 F.3d 1101, 1106,116 FEP 1059 (7th Cir. 2012) (being called "cry babies" and "trouble makers" by supervisor did not constitute materially adverse action); Silverman v. Board of Educ. of City of Chi., 637 F.3d 729, 740–41, 111 FEP 1461 (7th Cir. 2011) (following valid termination, rehiring into different, more difficult position was not adverse action); Jones v. Res-Care, Inc., 613 F.3d 665, 671, 109 FEP 1383 (7th Cir. 2010) (corrective action unaccompanied by tangible job consequence, combined with plaintiff's subjective determination of tension in workplace, was not sufficient to constitute adverse employment action);

[163]**[On page 15-39 of the Main Volume, in the carryover of footnote 163, add the following after "*Eighth Circuit*:".]**

Quinn v. St. Louis Cnty., 653 F.3d 745, 751–53, 113 FEP 236 (8th Cir. 2011) (plaintiff failed to state retaliation claim where he did not explain how employer's alleged adverse employment actions—being excluded from meetings, moved, stripped of responsibilities, and yelled at by new supervisor—would have dissuaded reasonable employee from reporting harassment); Chivers v. Wal-Mart Stores, Inc., 641 F.3d 927, 932–33, 112 FEP 673 (8th Cir. 2011) (manager's alleged acts of treating African-American female employee with disrespect, refusing to acknowledge her in common greetings, and demeaning her by offering her piece of candy he had in his mouth, were not adverse employment actions); Tyler v. University of Ark. Bd. of Trs., 628 F.3d 980, 988, 111 FEP 161 (8th Cir. 2011) (transfer of plaintiff into Dean's suite was not materially adverse action); Fanning v. Potter, 614 F.3d 845, 850–51, 109 FEP 1727 (8th Cir. 2010) (occasional delay in receipt of health benefit refund payment amounting to less than 2% of plaintiff's income would not impose sufficient hardship to dissuade objectively reasonable employee from making charge of discrimination);

[163]**[On page 15-40 of the Main Volume, in the carryover of footnote 163, add the following after "*Tenth Circuit*:".]**

Sarkar v. McCallin, 636 F.3d 572, 577, 111 FEP 999 (10th Cir. 2011) (employer contacting prior employers to verify employee's resume information was not materially adverse);

[163]**[On page 15-41 of the Main Volume, in the carryover of footnote 163, add the following after "*D.C. Circuit*:".]**

Gaujacq v. EDF, Inc., 601 F.3d 565, 578, 108 FEP 1601 (D.C. Cir. 2010) (chief operating officer's (COO's) comment to plaintiff that "[y]ou're career is dead" at company if she filed claim not considered materially adverse in light of company's indulgences of employee, including extension of her contract by year, COO's efforts to find way for her to stay in United States, and creation of new position for her);

D. The Causal Connection

1. Overview

[174]**[On page 15-43 of the Main Volume, in footnote 174, add the following after "*see also*".]**

Keeton v. Morningstar, Inc., 667 F.3d 877, 885, 114 FEP 269 (7th Cir. 2012) (permissible for court to skip preliminary steps of prima facie case and articulation of legitimate, nondiscriminatory reason and move directly to pretext analysis);

2. Proving Causation

[181]**[On page 15-44 of the Main Volume, in footnote 181, add the following at the end of the footnote.]**

But see Burnell v. Gates Rubber Co., 647 F.3d 704, 709–10, 112 FEP 1441 (7th Cir. 2011) (despite lack of temporal proximity, terminated

African-American employee established retaliation claim under direct method where he had complained regularly about race discrimination in past, and in response to his complaint about being written up for insubordination—which did not mention race—manager accused him of "playing the race card" and fired him next day); Templeton v. First Tenn. Bank, N.A., 424 F. App'x 249, 112 FEP 123 (4th Cir. 2011) (refusal to rehire woman who had resigned two years earlier because of management failure to address her complaints about sex harassment raised issue of retaliation despite remoteness in time where refusal to rehire was company's first opportunity to retaliate against her).

[182]**[On page 15-44 of the Main Volume, in footnote 182, add the following after "*See, e.g.*,".]**

Seeger v. Cincinnati Bell Tel. Co., LLC, 681 F.3d 274, 284, 18 WH Cases 2d 1831 (6th Cir. 2012) (temporal proximity between plaintiff's return from FMLA leave and his termination, three weeks after reinstatement and fewer than two months after he first notified his employer of his medical leave, was sufficient to meet causation element); Jones v. Walgreen Co., 679 F.3d 9, 21, 26 AD 261 (1st Cir. 2012) (discharge three and one half months after plaintiff filed lawsuit was sufficiently close temporal proximity in light of 20-year tenure); Coleman v. Donahoe, 667 F.3d 835, 861, 114 FEP 160 (7th Cir. 2012) (even if temporal proximity alone is insufficient to show pretext, sequence of events involving protected activity and punitive action may allow reasonable jury to infer retaliation); Bobo v. United Parcel Serv., Inc., 665 F.3d 741, 756, 114 FEP 254 (6th Cir. 2012) (prima facie case of retaliation under USERRA established with sufficient temporal proximity where discharge occurred just two weeks before plaintiff's scheduled military service and fewer than two months after he submitted his military orders); Okoli v. City of Balt., 648 F.3d 216, 223, 112 FEP 1675 (4th Cir. 2011) (deeply suspicious that employee was fired only hours after she made harassment complaint to mayor); Pye v. Nu Aire, Inc., 641 F.3d 1011, 1021–22, 112 FEP 865 (8th Cir. 2011) (causal link established where termination occurred slightly after investigation of employee's internal complaint and there was no evidence of performance issues prior to complaint); Loudermilk v. Best Pallet Co., 636 F.3d 312, 315, 111 FEP 865 (7th Cir. 2011) (one-day gap; "so close on the heels of a protected act that an inference of causation is sensible"); Dawson v. Entek Int'l, 630 F.3d 928, 936–37, 111 FEP 306 (9th Cir. 2011) (employee discharged fewer than 48 hours after complaining to human resources);

[183]**[On page 15-45 of the Main Volume, in footnote 183, add the following after "*E.g.*,".]**

Wasek v. Arrow Energy Servs., Inc., 682 F.3d 463, 472, 115 FEP 384 (6th Cir. 2012) (plaintiff's decision to leave workplace was intervening event between protected activity and adverse action, which dispelled any inference of retaliation based upon temporal proximity); Donald v. Sybra, Inc., 667 F.3d 757, 763, 18 WH Cases 2d 993 (6th Cir. 2012) (termination of plaintiff on same day that she returned from medical leave, standing alone, was insufficient to establish pretext on basis of temporal proximity); *Coleman*, 667 F.3d at 861 (even if sequence of events in plaintiff's claim is not enough to show pretext by itself, sequence of protected activity and punitive action lends support to reasonable juror's inference of retaliation); Twigg v. Hawker Beechcraft Corp., 659 F.3d 987, 1001–02, 113 FEP 938 (10th Cir. 2011) (intervening unreported absences between protected activity and adverse action sufficient to undermine plaintiff's temporal proximity argument);

[184]**[On page 15-46 of the Main Volume, in footnote 184, add the following after "*E.g.*,".]**

Chivers v. Wal-Mart Stores, Inc., 641 F.3d 927, 933, 112 FEP 673 (8th Cir. 2011) (adverse action that occurred between fourth and fifth discrimination reports failed to establish causal connection); Lauck v. Campbell Cnty., 627 F.3d 805, 815–16, 31 IER Cases 1202 (10th Cir. 2010) (employee's § 1983 First Amendment retaliation claim failed where employee was transferred seven months after his attorney sent letter to employer; no inference of causation based on temporal proximity alone where time lapse between protected activity and allegedly retaliatory act exceeded three months);

[185]**[On page 15-47 of the Main Volume, in footnote 185, add the following after "*E.g.*,".]**

Naficy v. Illinois Dep't of Human Servs., 697 F.3d 504, 512–13, 116 FEP 97 (7th Cir. 2012) (failure of causal connection where discrimination complaints were temporally separated from adverse employment action by five years nine months); Calhoun v. Johnson, 632 F.3d 1259, 163 n.2, 111 FEP 499 (D.C. Cir. 2011) (seven-year gap between EEO complaint and alleged retaliation "far too great" lag to suggest causation without additional evidence);

[185]**[On page 15-48 of the Main Volume, in the carryover of footnote 185, add the following at the end of the footnote.]**

But see Muñoz v. Sociedad Española de Auxilio Mutuo, 671 F.3d 49, 58, 114 FEP 412 (1st Cir. 2012) (employee established causal connection in support of his retaliation claim, even though he was terminated more than five years after he filed age discrimination suit, where evidence of his impeccable reputation and other facts "form a mosaic" sufficient to support jury's finding of retaliation); Templeton v. First Tenn. Bank, N.A., 424 F. App'x 249, 250, 112 FEP 123 (4th Cir. 2011) (refusal to rehire woman who had resigned two years earlier because of management failure to address her complaints about sex harassment raised issue of retaliation despite remoteness in time where refusal to rehire was company's first opportunity to retaliate against her).

[188]**[On page 15-50 of the Main Volume, in footnote 188, add the following after "*E.g.*,".]**

Porter v. City of Lake Lotawana, 651 F.3d 894, 898–99, 113 FEP 136 (8th Cir. 2011) (mayor and alderman did not know of complaint letter prior to voting for termination); Rivera-Colon v. Mills, 635 F.3d 9, 12–13, 111 FEP 737 (1st Cir. 2011) (plaintiff who filed anonymous complaint failed to establish that employer knew it was her complaint); Vera v. McHugh, 622 F.3d 17, 34–35, 110 FEP 705 (1st Cir. 2010) (plaintiff could not establish causation where she repeatedly refused to comply with directives issued before supervisor knew of sexual harassment complaint);

[188]**[On page 15-51 of the Main Volume, in the carryover of footnote 188, add the following at the end of the footnote.]**

But see Harrington v. Aggregate Indus. Ne. Region, Inc., 668 F.3d 25, 31, 33 IER Cases 611 (1st Cir. 2012) (in False Claims Act case, plaintiff did not need to show that on-site managers had knowledge of his protected activity, whistleblowing; fact that company executives were aware of plaintiff's whistleblower status several months before his termination was sufficient to fulfill knowledge element of plaintiff's prima facie case); Henry v. Wyeth Pharm., 616 F.3d 134, 148, 109 FEP 1618 (2d Cir. 2010) (plaintiff need show only "general corporate knowledge" of protected activity, rather than knowledge on part of decision maker, because another with knowledge may order or encourage an ignorant decision maker to carry out his retaliatory purpose), *cert. denied*, 131 S. Ct. 1602, 111 FEP 1184 (2011).

[190]**[On page 15-51 of the Main Volume, in footnote 190, add the following after "*See, e.g.,*".]**

Khalik v. United Air Lines, 671 F.3d 1188, 1194, 114 FEP 500 (10th Cir. 2012) (upholding dismissal of Title VII and FMLA retaliation claims because plaintiff did not argue any nexus between person to whom she complained about discrimination (and denial of FMLA leave) and person who terminated her);

[195]**[On page 15-52 of the Main Volume, in footnote 195, add the following after "*E.g.,*".]**

Hill v. Potter, 625 F.3d 998, 1002, 110 FEP 151 (7th Cir. 2010) (postal service supervisor did not create "cat's paw" liability by writing to Department of Labor's Office of Workers' Compensation Programs minimizing plaintiff's injury because latter was independent decision maker and plaintiff failed to show that it considered or rubber stamped supervisor's opinion);

[195]**[On page 15-53 of the Main Volume, in the carryover of footnote 195, add the following at the end of the footnote.]**

But see Tuli v. Brigham & Women's Hosp., 656 F.3d 33, 42, 113 FEP 116 (1st Cir. 2011) (inference of causation reasonably could be supported because biased supervisor recommended negative evaluation for plaintiff; jury could find that causal chain was not broken when second individual re-recommended negative evaluation because second individual, who relied on biased supervisor's information, did not inform evaluation panel of rocky relationship between supervisor and plaintiff); McKenna v. City of Phila., 649 F.3d 171, 178–79, 112 FEP 1799 (3d Cir. 2011) (in light of *Staub*, reasonable jury could find that supervisor's animus played substantial role in ultimate decision by police review board to recommend termination of officer).

[199]**[On page 15-54 of the Main Volume, in footnote 199, add the following after "*E.g.*,".]**

Sabourin v. University of Utah, 676 F.3d 950, 961, 18 WH Cases 2d 1633 (10th Cir. 2012) (in FMLA claim, plaintiff's removal of files and laptop computer from office, which impeded employer's ability to perform plaintiff's job in his absence, justified termination);

[202]**[On page 15-54 of the Main Volume, in footnote 202, add the following after "*E.g.*,".]**

Seeger v. Cincinnati Bell Tel. Co., 681 F.3d 274, 284–85, 18 WH Cases 2d 1831 (6th Cir. 2012) (in FMLA claim, plaintiff's alleged dishonesty in over-reporting his symptoms in order to continue receiving paid leave constituted legitimate, nonretaliatory reason for his discharge); McDonald-Cuba v. Santa Fe Protective Servs., Inc., 644 F.3d 1096, 1102, 112 FEP 327 (10th Cir. 2011) (female accounting director's undisclosed majority ownership interest in company able to compete with employer was considered to be legitimate, nondiscriminatory reason for termination);

[203]**[On page 15-55 of the Main Volume, in footnote 203, add the following after "*E.g.*,".]**

Jajeh v. County of Cook, 678 F.3d 560, 574, 114 FEP 1441 (7th Cir. 2012) (budget cuts and not being "team player" were legitimate reasons to terminate physician and mark him as ineligible for rehire); Leitgen v. Franciscan Skemp Healthcare, Inc., 630 F.3d 668, 676, 111 FEP 289 (7th Cir. 2011) (plaintiff failed to show causal connection between complaints and discharge where she was discharged for hostility to nurses and patients);

[206]**[On page 15-55 of the Main Volume, in footnote 206, add the following after "*E.g.*,".]**

Munoz v. Mabus, 630 F.3d 856, 865, 111 FEP 40 (9th Cir. 2010) (Navy provided legitimate, nonretaliatory reason for denial of training where employee lacked 10 years' experience required in order to be qualified for position);

[208]**[On page 15-56 of the Main Volume, in footnote 208, add the following after "*E.g.*,".]**

Overly v. KeyBank Nat'l Ass'n, 662 F.3d 856, 866, 113 FEP 1345 (7th Cir. 2011) (reassignment of sales territories not considered retaliatory where it was part of national business plan to assign fewer territories to each advisor);

[209]**[On page 15-56 of the Main Volume, in footnote 209, add the following after "*E.g.*,".]**

EEOC v. Picture People, Inc., 684 F.3d 981, 988 (10th Cir. 2012) (reducing employee's hours at end of holiday season, when all employees' hours were reduced, and disciplining her for violating company policy, not pretext for retaliation); *Munoz*, 630 F.3d at 865 (Navy provided legitimate, nonretaliatory reason for denial of training where only available position had already been filled);

[211]**[On page 15-56 of the Main Volume, in footnote 211, add the following after "*E.g.*,".]**

Fanning v. Potter, 614 F.3d 845, 850–51, 109 FEP 1727 (8th Cir. 2010) (agency presented legitimate, nondiscriminatory reason for employee's separation where it had policy for administrative separation of employees who were on leave for more than one year, and where employee had been on unpaid leave for six years and was advised by her physician four times that she would never be able to return to work); Zellner v. Herrick, 639 F.3d 371, 379, 32 IER Cases 279 (7th Cir. 2011) (in First Amendment retaliation case, school district had legitimate, nondiscriminatory reason for termination where teacher had accessed pornography from school computers in violation of school policy, notwithstanding animosity between district and teacher, who previously had been president of teachers' union);

[215]**[On page 15-57 of the Main Volume, in footnote 215, add the following after "*See*".]**

University of Tex. Sw. Med. Ctr. v. Nassar, 133 S. Ct. 2517, 118 FEP 1504 (2013) (plaintiffs in retaliation cases must prove that retaliation for protected activity was "but for" cause of adverse action); Bertsch v. Overstock.com, 684 F.3d 1023, 1029, 115 FEP Cases 745 (10th Cir. 2012) (although employer produced evidence that employee was fired for poor performance, genuine issues of material fact existed where evidence also would permit reasonable jury to find that employee was reassigned and subsequently terminated because she complained of sexually hostile environment in her unit); Egan v. Freedom Bank, 659 F.3d 639, 642–43, 113 FEP 801 (7th Cir. 2011) (female employee established that bank terminated her in retaliation for reporting supervisor's sexual remark, despite contention that bank eliminated her position because it was losing money, where bank hired four new employees); Barber v. C1 Truck Driver Training, LLC, 656 F.3d 782, 798–99, 113 FEP 507 (8th Cir. 2011) (employer's selective investigation of protected-group employee can support claim of discriminatory intent under Title VII, but to show pretext employee must provide evidence that other employees were not subject to same level of investigation for similar conduct);

[217]**[On page 15-57 of the Main Volume, in footnote 217, add the following after "*See, e.g.,*".]**

Coleman v. Donahoe, 667 F.3d 835, 841, 114 FEP 160 (7th Cir. 2012) (even where white male comparators had different supervisors and different positions from plaintiff, evidence that they were disciplined by same decision maker, were subject to same code of conduct, and were disciplined more leniently for violating same rule was sufficient to provide meaningful comparison and permit reasonable jury to infer that plaintiff was retaliated against for her complaints of race and gender discrimination); McDonald-Cuba v. Santa Fe Protective Servs., Inc., 644 F.3d 1096, 1102, 112 FEP 327 (10th Cir. 2011) (where female employee was fired for failing to disclose to employer her majority interest in potential competitor, male comparators were distinguishable from plaintiff; they had fully disclosed their activities in competing businesses before hire, and one employee's interest in his business was not significant one and other employee's business had become inactive); Smith v. Fairview Ridges Hosp., 625 F.3d 1076, 1088, 110 FEP 1025 (8th Cir. 2010) (employee who complained that her co-workers were disciplined less severely for discriminating against her than she was for performance issues did not prove that her employer's reasons for disciplining her amounted to pretext for retaliation because she did not establish that co-workers were "similarly situated in all relevant respects");

[218]**[On page 15-58 of the Main Volume, in footnote 218, add the following after "*See, e.g.,*".]**

Lovland v. Employer Mut. Cas. Co., 674 F.3d 806, 814,18 WH Cases 2d 1552 (8th Cir. 2012) (in FMLA retaliation claim, no genuine issue of fact regarding pretext because plaintiff did not identify any similarly situated employees who were treated differently, and although employer added to its initial rationale for terminating plaintiff, it did not change reason); Overly v. KeyBank Nat'l Ass'n, 662 F.3d 856, 863–64, 113 FEP 1345 (7th Cir. 2011) (reassignment of sales territories not considered retaliatory where it was part of national business plan to assign fewer territories to each advisor);

[221]**[On page 15-60 of the Main Volume, in footnote 221, add the following after "*See, e.g.,*".]**

Harrington v. Aggregate Indus.-Ne. Region, Inc., 668 F.3d 25, 32–34, 33 IER Cases 611 (1st Cir. 2012) (close temporal proximity, doubt regarding whether employer followed company protocol in requiring plaintiff to take drug test, and irregularities in employer's insistence that plaintiff take drug test, created sufficient foundation for reasonable inference that plaintiff was terminated for retaliatory reasons); Shaffer v. American Med. Ass'n, 662 F.3d 439, 444, 18 WH Cases 2d 396 (7th Cir. 2011) (employer's differing explanations for adverse employment action, and timing of decision to terminate plaintiff (after he submitted his leave request), support his claim that his termination was motivated by his FMLA leave); Valle-Arce v. Puerto Rico Ports Auth., 651 F.3d 190, 201–02, 24 AD 1537 (1st Cir. 2011) (flexible work schedule would have accommodated employee's chronic fatigue syndrome, despite finding that her absenteeism showed that she was not qualified because attendance was essential job function; employer's normal accommodation procedures were not followed, and disparate treatment and timing of retaliatory acts supported inference of pretext); Okoli v. City of Balt., 648 F.3d 216, 223, 112 FEP 1675 (4th Cir. 2011) (evidence of director's alteration of date of termination letter, discharge of employee only after learning of complaint, and employee's ability to eliminate legitimate reasons for her discharge raised possibility of pretext); Geleta v. Gray, 645 F.3d 408, 413, 112 FEP 981 (D.C. Cir. 2011) (city employee established that "federal funding mandates" proffered as reason for transferring him were pretext for his transfer in retaliation for supporting African-American co-worker's charge of race discrimination, where city's reasons for transferring him changed over time, city knew about funding conditions for months, and he was told to find new position only one month after he gave statement supporting co-worker's complaint); Miller v. Illinois Dep't of Transp., 643 F.3d 190, 201, 24 AD 1025 (7th Cir. 2011) (where employer claimed that employee was fired for threatening co-worker, combination of ambiguity of asserted threat, tepid response to another employee's violent outburst, hostility toward employee's request for accommodation of disability, and timing provided sufficient evidence to permit reasonable trier of fact to infer pretext and retaliatory intent); Spengler v. Worthington Cylinders, 615 F.3d 481, 494–95, 109 FEP 1526 (6th Cir. 2010) (selective enforcement of policy requiring seasonal employees who failed to be selected for permanent employment to be discharged after 12 months, coupled with supervisor's changed attitude after employee's complaint of age discrimination, could support finding of retaliation under Age Discrimination in Employment Act (ADEA));

[221]**[On page 15-60 of the Main Volume, in footnote 221, add the following at the end of the footnote.]**

But see Smith v. Bray, 681 F.3d 888, 907, 115 FEP 81 (7th Cir. 2012) (refusal by defendant human resources manager to speak to African-American plaintiff about supervisor's refusal to speak to employee showed, at most, concert of action between manager and supervisor, but did not indicate that manager shared supervisor's retaliatory motive); McFadden v. Ballard Spahr Andrews & Ingersoll LLP, 611 F.3d 1, 6, 109 FEP 1057 (D.C. Cir. 2010) (legal secretary, whose impairments prevented her from returning from medical leave to typing position, did not show that she was discharged in retaliation for requesting accommodation by reassignment to receptionist position, despite allegation that law firm officials told her that healthier employees were wanted and that she should "resign and save everybody the trouble," where alleged statements did not concern her exercise of protected rights or suggest retaliatory animus).

[222]**[On page 15-61 of the Main Volume, in footnote 222, add the following before "Scruggs v. Garst Seed Co.".]**

Gibson v. American Greetings Corp., 670 F.3d 844, 856, 114 FEP 927 (8th Cir. 2012) (when timing is sole basis for claim of retaliation, and gradual adverse job actions began well before protected activity, there is no inference of retaliation); EEOC v. C.R. England, Inc., 644 F.3d 1028, 1052, 24 AD 897 (10th Cir. 2011) (company's use of collection agency to collect debt from plaintiff was not retaliation for filing EEOC complaint where company notified him four months before his filing that it would pursue collection through all legal channels, including collection agencies);

[223][On page 15-62 of the Main Volume, in footnote 223, add the following after "*See, e.g.,*".]

Barton v. Zimmer, Inc., 662 F.3d 448, 113 FEP 929 (7th Cir. 2011) (in ADEA claim, unreasonable to infer retaliatory motive from supervisor's earlier actions where supervisor's later actions were favorable to plaintiff); Chapin v. Fort-Rohr Motors, Inc., 621 F.3d 673, 678–79, 110 FEP 129 (7th Cir. 2010) (employer's threat to fire employee unless he withdrew EEOC charge "right away" did not constitute adverse employment action in support of retaliation claim, even though employee refused to withdraw charge and did not return to work, where employer later encouraged him to return to work, and he acknowledged he was still employed);

[223][On page 15-62 of the Main Volume, in footnote 223, add the following after "*see also*".]

Crowe v. ADT Sec. Servs., Inc., 649 F.3d 1189, 1198–99, 112 FEP 1 (10th Cir. 2011) (where African-American employee was terminated allegedly for history of sexual harassment and insubordination, and employer tolerated conduct for many years before he engaged in protected activity, termination was based on his entire personnel file, and prior leniency defeats inference of pretext);

E. "Mixed-Motive" Retaliation Cases

1. "Mixed-Motive" Proof in a Discrimination Case

[232][On page 15-64 of the Main Volume, in footnote 232, add the following at the end of the footnote.]

See also Twigg v. Hawker Beechcraft Corp., 659 F.3d 987, 1004, 113 FEP 938 (10th Cir. 2011) (in light of *Gross*, substantial question exists as to whether mixed-motive analysis applies to FMLA cases).

2. *"Mixed-Motive" Proof in a Retaliation Case*

[On page 15-64 of the Main Volume, after the first paragraph, add the following new paragraphs.]

The Supreme Court extended its holding in *Gross* to Title VII retaliation claims in *Texas Southwestern Medical Center v. Nassar.*[1] In *Nassar*, the Fifth Circuit upheld a jury verdict in favor of a doctor formerly employed by the Center where he had proven that the decision not to offer him a staff position was in retaliation for writing a letter in which he complained of "continuing harassment and discrimination."[2] The court analyzed the retaliation claim applying the "a motivating factor" framework applicable in Title VII discrimination cases. The Supreme Court vacated the ruling and remanded the case, holding that a Title VII plaintiff in a retaliation action must prove that retaliation was a "but for" cause of the adverse employment decision, not merely a motivating factor.[3]

The Court extended the "but for" causation test to retaliation cases because Title VII's retaliation protections arise under "a separate, subsequent section of Title VII, Section 2000e-3(a)," from the prohibitions on discrimination. The Court noted that its 1989 *Price Waterhouse* decision,[4] which applied "a motivating or substantial factor" standard of causation, was based upon analysis of Section 2000e-2(a) of Title VII, which outlawed discrimination based upon race, color, religion, sex, or national origin.[5] The Court reasoned that Title VII's retaliation provisions, which proscribe retaliation against an individual "*because* he has opposed . . . or *because* he has made a charge," are phrased more similarly to the causation language included within the ADEA than to the causation language of Title VII § 2000e-2(a), and that the "but for" test previously applied to ADEA cases under *Gross* is therefore the appropriate causation standard.[6]

In January, 2014, the Supreme Court again addressed the "but for" causation standard applicable to retaliation and age

[1] 133 S. Ct. 2517, 118 FEP 1504 (2013).
[2] *Id.* at 2524.
[3] *Id.* at 2532–33.
[4] Price Waterhouse v. Hopkins, 490 U.S. 228, 49 FEP 954 (1989).
[5] 133 S. Ct. at 2525.
[6] *Id.* at 2529.

discrimination cases in *Burrage v. United States*.[7] Although the question in *Burrage* arose in the context of a criminal case, the Court discussed its holding in *Nassar*, and the "'but for' cause" language in that case, stating that "'but for' causation does not require a showing that an impermissible motive was the sole cause of the challenged action."[8]

[On page 15-64 of the Main Volume, replace the first sentence of the second paragraph with the following.]

Prior to *Nassar*, there had been an open question whether the mixed-motive provisions of the Civil Rights Act of 1991 apply to Title VII retaliation claims.

[On page 15-64 of the Main Volume, replace the first sentence of the carryover paragraph with the following.]

Prior to *Nassar*, the circuits were divided on the applicability of § 703(m) to retaliation cases, and on the standard for determining retaliation liability.

[On page 15-65 of the Main Volume, in the carryover sentence, after footnote 239, delete "and" and add the following after "Eighth".].

, and Eleventh[9]

V. RELIEF IN RETALIATION CASES

A. Reinstatement

[251]**[On page 15-67 of the Main Volume, in footnote 251, add the following after "*see also*".]**

Ameristar Airways, Inc. v. Administrative Review Bd., U.S. Dep't of Labor, 650 F.3d 562, 570, 32 IER Cases 1060 (5th Cir. 2011) (remanding case to determine whether back pay award should be

---

[7]134 S. Ct. 881 (2014).

[8]*Id.* at 888–89.

[9]Gowski v. Peake, 682 F.3d 1299, 1314, 115 FEP 163 (11th Cir. 2012) (mixed-motive theory not available to two VA physicians in retaliation case).

adjusted based upon employer's contention that plaintiff would have been terminated based upon after-acquired evidence of insubordinate e-mail);

VI. ALTERNATIVE CAUSES OF ACTION

B. Private Employers

2. *The Civil Rights Act of 1866*

[286]**[On page 15-73 of the Main Volume, in footnote 286, add the following at the end of the footnote.]**

See also Twigg v. Hawker Beechcraft Corp., 659 F.3d 987, 988, 113 FEP 938 (10th Cir. 2011) (Tenth Circuit also permits application of mixed-motive doctrine to § 1981 retaliation claims).

[On page 15-73 of the Main Volume, in the first sentence of the second full paragraph, replace "The Fifth Circuit has held" with the following.]

The Fifth and Seventh Circuits have held

[287]**[On page 15-73 of the Main Volume, in footnote 287, add the following at the end of the footnote.]**

See also Smith v. Bray, 681 F.3d 888, 889, 115 FEP 81 (7th Cir. 2012) (subordinate employee who intentionally causes decision maker to take adverse action against another employee may be found individually liable under § 1981).

4. *National Labor Relations Act*

[298]**[On page 15-74 of the Main Volume, in footnote 298, add the following after "*See*".]**

Rochelle Waste Disposal, LLC v. NLRB, 673 F.3d 587, 597–98, 192 LRRM 3061 (7th Cir. 2012) (claim of unlawful retaliation established where plaintiff engaged in protected activity five months before his termination, employer was aware of his activity, employer had never before fired any employees, and termination occurred eight days before representation election);

[307]**[On page 15-76 of the Main Volume, in footnote 307, add the following at the end of the footnote.]**

See also Rochelle Waste Disposal, LLC v. NLRB, 673 F.3d 587, 597, 192 LRRM 3061 (7th Cir. 2012) (applying burden-shifting analysis in NLRA retaliation claim where adverse action occurred after protected activity).

[309]**[On page 15-76 of the Main Volume, in footnote 309, add the following after "*See, e.g.*,".]**

Rochelle Waste Disposal, 673 F.3d at 597 (NLRB must make initial showing that antiunion animus was substantial or motivating factor in employer's decision; discerning employer's motivation is question of fact);

5. The Fair Labor Standards Act

[On page 15-77 of the Main Volume, in the fourth sentence of the first paragraph, add the following between "First," and "Fifth,".]

Fourth,

[315]**[On page 15-77 of the Main Volume, in footnote 315, add the following at the beginning of the footnote.]**

See Minor v. Bostwick Lab., Inc., 669 F.3d 428, 430, 439, 18 WH Cases 2d 1248 (4th Cir. 2012) (internal complaint sufficient within context of FLSA claim);

6. Other Federal Avenues

[327]**[On page 15-78 of the Main Volume, in footnote 327, add the following before "McKenzie v. BellSouth Telecomms., Inc,".]**

United States *ex rel.* Schweizer v. Oce N.V., 677 F.3d 1228, 1238–40 (D.C. Cir. 2012) (employee whose job was to investigate fraud demonstrated employer's knowledge of her protected activity where her termination letter stated that she was fired for refusing to follow chain of command in pursuing investigation, and that employer would be referring her allegations to be investigated); Harrington v. Aggregate Indus. Ne. Region, Inc., 668 F.3d 25, 32, 33 IER Cases 611 (1st Cir. 2012) (execution of settlement agreement in FCA action was protected activity because it was conducted in furtherance of FCA action); Mann v. Heckler & Koch Def., Inc., 630 F.3d 338, 344–47, 349–50, 31 IER Cases 1092 (4th Cir. 2010) (where it is clear that employer knew of protected activity, "distinct possibility" standard should be applied using facts known to employee at time of protected conduct; where employer submitted nonconforming bid and disclosed nonconforming elements in its bid, employee's opposition was not protected because there was no fraud; filing of civil action does not per se constitute protected conduct under § 3730(h), nor is it the case that filing retaliation action can never qualify as protected conduct); United States *ex rel.* Owens v. First Kuwaiti Gen. Trading & Contracting Co., 612 F.3d 724, 735, 30 IER Cases 1661 (4th Cir. 2010) (contractor employee's investigation into "construction mistakes" on building project did not amount to investigation of fraud and was therefore not protected activity under FCA);

[330]**[On page 15-80 of the Main Volume, in the carryover of footnote 330, add the following after "*See generally*".]**

Tides v. Boeing Co., 644 F.3d 809, 810–11, 32 IER Cases 129 (9th Cir. 2011) (whistleblower provision of Sarbanes-Oxley Act contained in § 1514A(a)(1) grants protection to disclosures made only to categories of recipients specifically enumerated in statute; leaks to media are not protected);

[333]**[On page 15-80 of the Main Volume, in footnote 333, add the following at the end of the footnote.]**

See also Ameristar Airways, Inc. v. Administrative Review Bd., U.S. Dep't of Labor, 650 F.3d 562, 567, 32 IER Cases 1060 (5th Cir. 2011) (notifying president of company that forcing pilots to work beyond duty-time limits was Federal Aviation Administration (FAA) violation; complaining to company management that maintenance log policy was violation of federal regulations; complaining to head of dispatch that company was using another airline's call signal without FAA approval; and meeting with FAA official about same were all protected activity under Aviation and Investment Reform Act).

C. State and Local Government Employers

2. *First Amendment Right of Free Speech*

[353]**[On page 15-82 of the Main Volume, in footnote 353, add the following after "*see also*".]**

Adams v. Trustees of Univ. of N.C. Wilmington, 640 F.3d 550, 561–64, 111 FEP 1665 (4th Cir. 2011) (whether employee spoke as private citizen is based on facts when speech occurred, regardless of subsequent actions by speaker);

[355]**[On page 15-83 of the Main Volume, in footnote 355, add the following after "*E.g.*,".]**

Savage v. Gee, 665 F.3d 732, 738–39, 33 IER Cases 193 (6th Cir. 2012) (plaintiff, library administrator at university, did not participate in protected speech when commenting on book recommendation as member of committee acting in his official capacity); Bowie v. Maddox, 642 F.3d 1122, 1133–34, 112 FEP 872 (D.C. Cir. 2011) (official who refused to sign employer-drafted affidavit for submission to EEOC in response to subordinate's EEOC charge and drafted his own statement acted pursuant to his official duties and was not protected under First Amendment; he submitted new affidavit to his employer for review and did not submit affidavit directly to EEOC before or after employer rejected the affidavit); Wackett v. City of Beaver Dam, Wis., 642 F.3d 578, 581, 32 IER Cases 743 (7th Cir. 2011) (failure to be promoted to director position was not retaliation against employee for speaking out against board, because he was speaking in official capacity, and board may not have been aware of later speech as private citizen); *Adams*, 640 F.3d at 563–64 (*Garcetti* not applicable where speech addressed issue related to professor's scholarship and teaching and not his employment); Harris v. Pontotoc Cnty. Sch. Dist., 635 F.3d 685, 692 (5th Cir. 2011) (school employee complaining about insufficient due process given in disciplining her child, student at school, and her reassignment to another position did not speak as "public citizen," but as mother and aggrieved employee); Anemone v. Metropolitan Transp. Auth., 629 F.3d 97, 116–20, 31 IER Cases 1167 (2d Cir. 2011) (employee who regularly communicated with district attorney's office as part of his job duties and had initiated discussions with that office as part of investigation did not become "private citizen" when continuing to communicate with that office regarding investigation after being ordered to stop); Lauck v. Campbell Cnty., 627 F.3d 805, 815–16, 31 IER Cases 1202 (10th Cir. 2010) (although incident report challenged police department's actions, it was prepared as part of plaintiff's duties as deputy sheriff, and therefore plaintiff was not entitled to First Amendment protection);

[355]**[On page 15-83 of the Main Volume, in footnote 355, add the following after "*But see*".]**

Rynders v. Williams, 650 F.3d 1188, 1191–92, 1194–95, 32 IER Cases 1169 (8th Cir. 2011) (First Amendment retaliation claim of county employee against public official withstood summary judgment motion because plaintiff presented direct evidence that he was terminated for writing letter in local newspaper asserting that county legislative body refused to raise wages of county employees; although rare, official's single decision to terminate plaintiff can establish county policy if decision was taken by highest official responsible for setting policy at issue);

[On page 15-84 of the Main Volume, after the carryover sentence that ends with footnote 356, add the following.]

Since *Garcetti*, many courts have addressed what constitutes a matter of public concern.[10]

---

[10]*See, e.g.*, Leverington v. City of Colo. Springs, 643 F.3d 719, 725–26, 32 IER Cases 260 (10th Cir. 2011) (public-concern test applied to nurse's statement to police officer during contentious traffic stop that she hoped to never have him as patient because statement pertained to work, but statement was not protected because it concerned private grievance); Pucci v. Nineteenth Dist. Ct., 628 F.3d 752, 768, 110 FEP 1766 (6th Cir. 2010) (complaints regarding propriety and legality of public, in-court judicial conduct warrant First Amendment protection); Dahl v. Rice Cnty., 621 F.3d 740, 744, 31 IER Cases 263 (8th Cir. 2010) (employee's complaints triggered by personal dispute with supervisor were not matter of public concern, even where they concerned low morale for department); Gross v. Town of Cicero, 619 F.3d 697, 705–07, 31 IER Cases 183 (7th Cir. 2010) (employee's vague allusions to matter concerning his daughter, who also worked for employer and was allegedly sexually harassed along with co-workers, were not speech, but expressions of desire to speak; mentioning only his daughter and not co-workers confirmed that any speech was personal grievance, not matter of public concern); LeFande v. District of Columbia, 613 F.3d 1155, 1161, 188 LRRM 3217 (D.C. Cir. 2010) (police department reserve corps volunteer spoke on matter of public concern, not mere intra-office squabbles, when he challenged chief's emergency implementation of rule that would deny reserve corps members right to collectively bargain and would grant chief unchecked power to terminate them because apparent lack of "emergency" suggested constitutional violation and operation of government is matter of public concern); Brownfield v. City of Yakima, 612 F.3d 1140, 1147–48, 16

[374]**[On page 15-87 of the Main Volume, in footnote 374, add the following at the end the of footnote.]**

See also Díaz-Bigio v. Santini, 652 F.3d 45, 53–54, 32 IER Cases 719 (1st Cir. 2011) (finding qualified immunity where employee was terminated for making false and groundless allegations and refusing to comply with investigation into allegations).

[389]**[On page 15-89 of the Main Volume, in footnote 389, add the following after "*Compare*".]**

Navab-Safavi v. Glassman, 637 F.3d 311, 317, 31 IER Cases 1542 (D.C. Cir. 2011) (free-speech interest of translator for Persian News Network, overseen by federal agency, outweighed agency's interest in journalistic integrity because as translator, he did not purport to speak on behalf of board or United States),

[396]**[On page 15-90 of the Main Volume, in footnote 396, add the following after "*See*".]**

Redd v. Nolan, 663 F.3d 287, 295, 33 IER Cases 101 (7th Cir. 2011) (upholding summary judgment because there was no evidence from which reasonable jury could conclude that plaintiff was investigated in retaliation for her "refusal to lie" in criminal investigation);

[397]**[On page 15-91 of the Main Volume, in footnote 397, add the following before "*Baldassare*".]**

Anemone v. Metropolitan Transp. Auth., 629 F.3d 97, 116–20, 31 IER Cases 1167 (2d Cir. 2011) (*Mt. Healthy* defense applied where employee engaged in repeated acts of insubordination and created tension within workplace by going outside chain of command and recklessly or intentionally making false statements to superiors and outside investigators before protected activity occurred);

WH Cases 2d 713 (9th Cir. 2010) (complaints that co-worker was lazy and incompetent, causing employee to complete co-workers' duties, were personal grievances, not matters of public concern); Unger v. City of Mentor, 387 F. App'x 589, 592–93 (6th Cir. 2010) (employee's call for reclassification to allow for union membership, even if applied to all employees allegedly misclassified, was "personal quest" and not matter of public concern).

3. *First Amendment Rights to Petition for Redress of Grievances or Assembly*

[401]**[On page 15-92 of the Main Volume, in footnote 401, add the following at the end of the footnote.]**

But see Eckerman v. Tennessee Dep't of Pub. Safety, 636 F.3d 202, 207–09, 31 IER Cases 1110 (6th Cir. 2010) (plaintiff's filing of lawsuit claiming discrimination due to political affiliation was "clearly protected activity," despite not being matter of public concern).

[403]**[On page 15-92 of the Main Volume, in footnote 403, add the following at the end of the footnote.]**

See also Morris v. Colorado Springs, 666 F.3d 654, 661–662, 114 FEP 225 (10th Cir. 2012) (in right-to-petition claim, public nurse's notice of potential claims against city hospital and surgeon, arising out of her working conditions at hospital, did not pertain to matter of public concern).

[405]**[On page 15-92 of the Main Volume, in footnote 405, add the following at the end of the footnote.]**

See also Morin v. Tormey, 626 F.3d 40, 44, 31 IER Cases 705 (2d Cir. 2010) (court's chief clerk's refusal to engage in partisan spying was analyzed under "*Elrod/Branti/Rutan* trilogy" of cases rather than "*Garcetti/Connick/Pickering* trilogy" because abstention was not expression of views).

[406]**[On page 15-93 of the Main Volume, in footnote 406, add the following at the end of the footnote.]**

See also Foote v. Town of Bedford, 642 F.3d 80, 84, 86, 32 IER Cases 289 (1st Cir. 2011) (policymaker exception applies not only to political affiliation matters, but to free speech matters as well).

[407]**[On page 15-93 of the Main Volume, in footnote 407, add the following after "*Compare*".]**

Foote, 642 F.3d at 84, 86 (advisors can be policymakers, despite lacking ultimate decision-making authority), Faghri v. University of Conn., 621 F.3d 92, 97–98, 31 IER Cases 414 (2d Cir. 2010) (dean/professor stripped only of deanship role did not have First Amendment retaliation claim because he was policymaker, although conclusion may have differed if he were also stripped of professorship),

D. Federal Employees

[421][On page 15-95 of the Main Volume, in footnote 421, add the following at the end of the footnote.]

But see Jones v. United States, 625 F.3d 827, 829, 110 FEP 1139 (5th Cir. 2010) (per curiam) (retaliation claim challenging decision of FAA could not be raised in district court where employee's retaliation claim was inextricably linked with challenge to procedure utilized by FAA and merits of FAA order), *cert. denied*, 131 S. Ct. 3073, 112 FEP 960 (2011).

[432][On page 15-96 of the Main Volume, in footnote 432, add the following at the end of the footnote.]

See, e.g., Bonds v. Leavitt, 629 F.3d 369, 381–82, 111 FEP 171 (4th Cir. 2011) (employee who complained to supervisor three levels above made protected complaint, even if supervisor did not have actual authority to resolve concerns).

[434][On page 15-96 of the Main Volume, in footnote 434, add the following after "*See, e.g.,*".]

Whitmore v. Department of Labor, 680 F.3d 1353, 1371, 33 IER Cases 1527 (Fed. Cir. 2012) (agency official's merely being outside of whistleblower's chain of command and not directly involved in alleged retaliatory actions was insufficient to remove possibility of retaliatory motive or retaliatory influence on whistleblower's treatment);

CHAPTER 16

HIRING

I. GENERAL CONSIDERATIONS

[On page 16-1 of the Main Volume, replace the first paragraph and the first sentence of the second paragraph with the following.]

This chapter focuses on claims of discrimination arising out of the hiring process brought under either a disparate treatment or disparate impact theory. Key issues include the definition of an applicant, the formation of the applicant pool, selection from the applicant pool, and initial job placement.

Parties seeking to attack or defend a company's hiring procedures under a disparate impact theory normally engage in a three-step analysis.[1]

II. DEFINING THE APPLICANT POOL

D. Word-of-Mouth Recruitment

[21][On page 16-6 of the Main Volume, in footnote 21, add the following after "*E.g.*,".]

Barry v. Moran, 661 F.3d 696, 708 (1st Cir. 2011) (noting First Circuit's agreement with other circuits that employment decision motivated by cronyism rather than discrimination is perhaps "unsavory" but not unlawful);

[21][On page 16-7 of the Main Volume, in the carryover of footnote 21, add the following at the end of the footnote.]

See generally Chapter 3 (Disparate Impact).

E. Nepotism

[44][On page 16-11 of the Main Volume, in footnote 44, add the following after "*See*".]

Barry v. Moran, 661 F.3d 696, 708 (1st Cir. 2011) (employment decisions motivated by cronyism, although perhaps "unsavory," are not unlawful);

H. Job Opportunity Advertising

[67][On page 16-17 of the Main Volume, in footnote 67, add the following before "Banks v. Heun-Norwood".]

Culpepper v. Vilsack, 664 F.3d 252, 257 (8th Cir. 2011) (verdict for employer supported by evidence that hearing-impaired applicant failed to apply for opening due to recent death of her father, rather than because of announced job requirement that applicants have "listening" skills);

---

[1]*See* NAACP v. North Hudson Reg'l Fire & Rescue, 665 F.3d 464, 476–77, 113 FEP 1633 (3d Cir. 2011).

I. Deterred Applicants

[82]**[On page 16-20 of the Main Volume, in the carryover of footnote 82, add the following after "*But see*".]**

Stiefel v. Bechtel Corp., 624 F.3d 1240, 1246, 23 AD 1380 (9th Cir. 2010) (disabled applicant failed to attend required "roll call meetings" that were part of application process due to applicant's own scheduling conflicts rather than because he was deterred by fear of discrimination);

[88]**[On page 16-20 of the Main Volume, in footnote 88, add the following before "*See generally*".]**

See Meditz v. City of Newark, 658 F.3d 364, 374–75, 113 FEP 727 (3d Cir. 2011) (reversing grant of summary judgment because genuine issues of material fact existed as to whether residency requirement for non-uniformed jobs had impermissible disparate impact upon white, non-Hispanics).

III. Selecting From the Applicant Pool

A. Selection Criteria

[117]**[On page 16-26 of the Main Volume, in footnote 117, add the following at the end of the footnote, before the period.]**

, *available at* http//www.eeoc.gov/laws/guidance/ arrest_conviction.cfm. The EEOC's guidance on the applicability of disparate impact standards to criminal records screening practices has been published in several directives since at least 1987.

[118]**[On page 16-27 of the Main Volume, in footnote 118, add the following at the end of the footnote.]**

A provision of the Bankruptcy Code prohibits employers from terminating or otherwise discriminating against employees because they have filed for bankruptcy. At least two courts have held that this provision does not protect applicants, as distinguished from employees. *See* Myers v. TooJay's Mgmt. Corp., 640 F.3d 1278, 1283–87 (11th Cir. 2011) (Bankruptcy Code § 525(b) does not prohibit private employers from discriminating against job applicants who have filed for bankruptcy); Rea v. Federated Investors, 627 F.3d 937,

940–41, 31 IER 1209 (3d Cir. 2010) (job applicant who had filed for bankruptcy failed to state claim under Bankruptcy Code's antidiscrimination provisions because Code § 525(b) does not specifically reference job applicants).

B. Proof of Hiring Discrimination

[120][On page 16-27 of the Main Volume, in footnote 120, add the following after "*But see*".]

Webb v. IBM, 458 F. App'x 871, 877–78 (11th Cir. 2012) (applicant who did not follow employer's process for submitting formal application lacked prima facie case);

[121][On page 16-27 of the Main Volume, in footnote 121, add the following after "*See*".]

Torgerson v. City of Rochester, 643 F.3d 1031, 1047, 112 FEP 613 (8th Cir. 2011) (fact that minority and female firefighter applicants were included within eligibility list did not establish that they were objectively qualified where they ranked lower on list than successful applicants); Davis v. Dallas Indep. Sch. Dist., 448 F. App'x 485, 491 (5th Cir. 2011) (applicant who failed to achieve stated requirement of security clearance lacked prima facie case of discrimination);

[122][On page 16-27 of the Main Volume, in footnote 122, add the following after "*See, e.g.,*".]

Shelley v. Geren, 666 F.3d 599, 607, 114 FEP 303 (9th Cir. 2012) (*McDonnell Douglas* model of proof is to be applied at summary judgment stage in ADEA failure-to-hire or -promote case);

[125][On page 16-28 of the Main Volume, in footnote 125, add the following after "*See, e.g.,*".]

Keith v. County of Oakland, 703 F.3d 918, 923–24, 27 AD 551 (6th Cir. 2013) (genuine issue of material fact existed as to whether deaf lifeguard was qualified for position where he held required certification and passed training, but medical examiner concluded: "He's deaf; he can't be a life guard."); Henry v. Continental Airlines, 415 F. App'x 537, 540, 24 AD 805 (5th Cir. 2011) (plaintiff failed to establish prima facie case where his responses to screening questions disqualified him from consideration for position);

[128]**[On page 16-29 of the Main Volume, in footnote 128, add the following after "*See, e.g.*,".]**

Barber v. C1 Truck Driver Training, LLC, 656 F.3d 782, 793, 113 FEP 507 (8th Cir. 2011) (affirming summary judgment for employer in race discrimination case where, although plaintiff claimed comparable qualifications to selected applicant, "the mere existence of comparable qualifications between two applicants . . . alone does not raise an inference of racial discrimination"); Moss v. BMC Software, Inc., 610 F.3d 917, 924–26, 109 FEP 1173 (5th Cir. 2010) (affirming summary judgment for employer in age discrimination case where, although plaintiff showed that he had more total experience than successful applicant, plaintiff's experience was in area different from that relevant to open position);

[129]**[On page 16-30 of the Main Volume, in footnote 129, add the following after "*See, e.g.*,".]**

Manora v. Donahoe, 439 F. App'x 352, 356–57 (5th Cir. 2011) (employer's view that plaintiff had passive and confrontational management style constituted legitimate, nondiscriminatory reason for selection of another); Villalpando v. Salazar, 420 F. App'x 848, 852–53, 112 FEP 279 (10th Cir. 2011) (plaintiff failed to show that personal animosity directed toward him was basis for employer's decision, where supervisor had equally poor working relationships with others that were not related to race);

[136]**[On page 16-31 of the Main Volume, in footnote 136, add the following after "*See*".]**

Shelley v. Geren, 666 F.3d 599, 609–10 (9th Cir. 2012) (employer's stated reason that selection of younger applicant was preferable because it constituted lateral move, while selection of older applicant would constitute promotion, was evidence of pretext precluding summary judgment for employer); Powell v. Laborers Union Local 1271, 426 F. App'x 615, 619–22, 112 FEP 888 (10th Cir. 2011) (union established that plaintiff was not victim of race-based referral practices where it showed that it failed to refer plaintiff due to "no-rehire" letters received from previous employers);

[137]**[On page 16-32 of the Main Volume, in footnote 137, add the following after "*See*".]**

Shelley, 666 F.3d at 609–10 (reversing summary judgment in age discrimination case where employer questioned applicants about their projected retirement dates); Moss v. BMC Software, Inc., 610 F.3d 917, 929, 109 FEP 1173 (5th Cir. 2010) (employer's statement that it preferred to hire "junior level" lawyer was not direct evidence of age discrimination because employer also might have preferred applicant who had attended law school later in life);

[138]**[On page 16-33 of the Main Volume, in footnote 138, add the following after "*See*".]**

Ash v. Tyson Foods, Inc., 664 F.3d 883, 892–93, 114 FEP 102 (11th Cir. 2011) (vacating judgment as matter of law in favor of employer in race discrimination case where plaintiff had shown that he satisfied minimum qualifications but successful applicant had not, and that decision maker had referred to plaintiff and other African-Americans as "boy"); Colbert v. Tapella, 649 F.3d 756, 760, 112 FEP 884 (D.C. Cir. 2011) (reversing summary judgment for employer and holding that plaintiff did not need to prove both that employer's stated reason was pretextual and that discrimination was actual reason for failure to hire);

[139]**[On page 16-34 of the Main Volume, in footnote 139, add the following after "*See, e.g.,*".]**

Moss, 610 F.3d at 928 (employer's delay in interviewing plaintiff and subsequent brief interview were not evidence of pretext where plaintiff's qualifications were not clear from reading of his resume and where he had opportunity to present those qualifications at interview); Barrientos v. City of Eagle Pass, 444 F. App'x 756, 760 (5th Cir. 2011) (although plaintiff was required to pass physical agility test for hire into firefighter position and successful applicant for EMT position was not required to do so, two were not similarly situated and thus plaintiff raised no inference of discrimination);

[142]**[On page 16-34 of the Main Volume, in footnote 142, add the following after "*See*".]**

Luster v. Vilsack, 667 F.3d 1089, 1094, 115 FEP 922 (10th Cir. 2011) (Forest Service's exclusion of all applicants below GS-7 pay grade did not constitute gender discrimination despite plaintiffs' argument that women were underrepresented within pay grades that were permitted to apply); NAACP v. North Hudson Reg'l Fire & Rescue, 665 F.3d 464, 485, 113 FEP 1633 (3d Cir. 2011) (city residency requirement discriminated against qualified minority firefighter applicants); Brown v. Unified Sch. Dist., 459 F. App'x 705, 710 (10th Cir. 2012) (plaintiff's statistical evidence that school district hired far more Caucasian teachers than minorities did not show disparate impact where plaintiff did not offer evidence of races of applicants); Davis v. Dallas Indep. Sch. Dist., 448 F. App'x 485, 492, (5th Cir. 2011) (summary judgment for employer upheld where plaintiff failed to show sufficient statistical disparities demonstrating that employer's requirement that applicants have at least 20 years of experience and security clearance had disparate impact against minority applicants);

C. Preemployment Inquiries

[On page 16-37 of the Main Volume, after the sentence that ends with footnote 163, add the following new paragraph.]

The Eleventh and Third Circuits have held that a private employer does not violate Bankruptcy Code Section 525(b)—which prohibits employers from terminating or otherwise discriminating against employees because they have filed for bankruptcy—by rejecting applicants who have done so because Section 525(b), unlike Section 525(a), does not specifically reference job applicants.[2]

D. Issues of Standing

[On page 16-38 of the Main Volume, at the end of the first sentence of the second paragraph, add new footnote 165a.]

[165a]A plaintiff need not prove that he or she has a disability in order to contest an allegedly improper medical inquiry under the ADA. *See, e.g.*, Lee v. City of Columbus, Ohio, 636 F.3d 245, 252, 24 AD 257 (6th Cir. 2011); Harrison v. Benchmark Elecs. Huntsville, Inc., 593 F.3d 1206, 1214, 22 AD 1281 (11th Cir. 2010).

---

[2]Myers v. TooJay's Mgmt. Corp., 640 F.3d 1278, 1283–87 (11th Cir. 2011) (Bankruptcy Code § 525(b) does not prohibit private employers from discriminating against job applicants who have filed for bankruptcy); Rea v. Federated Investors, 627 F.3d 937, 940–41, 31 IER 1209 (3d Cir. 2010) (job applicant who had filed for bankruptcy failed to state claim under Bankruptcy Code's antidiscrimination provisions because Code § 525(b) does not specifically reference job applicants).

CHAPTER 17

PROMOTION, ADVANCEMENT, AND RECLASSIFICATION

I. INTRODUCTION

[1][On page 17-1 of the Main Volume, in footnote 1, add the following after "*See, e.g.,*".]

Shelley v. Geren, 666 F.3d 599, 608, 114 FEP 303 (9th Cir. 2012) (plaintiff may establish prima facie case of age discrimination in failure-to-promote action by showing that he or she was "(1) at least forty years old, (2) qualified for the position for which an application was submitted, (3) denied the position, and (4) the promotion was given to a substantially younger person"); Adams v. Trustees of Univ. of N.C.–Wilmington, 640 F.3d 550, 558, 111 FEP 1665 (4th Cir. 2011) (plaintiff establishes prima facie promotion discrimination case under *McDonnell Douglas* by showing that "(1) he belongs to a protected class; (2) he suffered an adverse employment action;

(3) at the time of the adverse action, he was performing his job at a level that met his employer's legitimate expectations and was qualified for the promotion; and (4) he was rejected under circumstances giving rise to an inference of unlawful discrimination");

II. PROMOTIONS VERSUS LATERAL TRANSFERS

[10][On page 17-4 of the Main Volume, in footnote 10, add the following after "*See, e.g.*,".]

Dass v. Chicago Bd. of Educ., 675 F.3d 1060, 1069–70, 114 FEP 1288 (7th Cir. 2012) (assignment of third-grade teacher to seventh-grade class was not shown to be adverse employment action merely because of plaintiff's subjective belief that she was denied position for which she was best suited and placed in more difficult position that impaired her ability to succeed);

[On page 17-4 of the Main Volume, replace the fourth sentence, which contains footnote 12, with the following.]

By contrast, pursuant to the Supreme Court's decisions in *Gross v. FBL Financial Services, Inc.*[1] and *Nassar v. University of Texas Southwestern Medical Center*,[2] ADEA plaintiffs and plaintiffs claiming Title VII retaliation cannot challenge a promotion or transfer under the mixed-motive theory.

[14][On page 17-5 of the Main Volume, in footnote 14, add the following after "*see also*".]

Holland v. Gee, 677 F.3d 1047, 1058, 114 FEP 1449 (11th Cir. 2012) (position transfer from telecommunications technician to help desk staffer was adverse employment action, because jury could have found transfer to be permanent "reassignment with significantly different duties" that included reduction in prestige and responsibility); *Dass*, 675 F.3d at 1069–70 (assignment of third-grade teacher to seventh-grade class was not shown to be adverse employment action merely because of plaintiff's subjective belief that she was denied position for which she was best suited and placed in more difficult position that impaired her ability to succeed);

---

[1] 129 S. Ct. 2343, 2351, 106 FEP 833 (2009).
[2] 133 S. Ct. 2517, 2527–30, 2533, 118 FEP 1504 (2013).

[20]**[On page 17-6 of the Main Volume, in footnote 20, add the following after "*see also*".]**

Geleta v. Gray, 645 F.3d 408, 412, 112 FEP 981 (D.C. Cir. 2011) (in Title VII retaliation case, genuine issue of material fact whether employee's transfer constituted adverse action, where jury could find that transfer resulted in plaintiff no longer having staff and otherwise being denied policymaking role);

III. Publicizing and Applying for the Opening

[30]**[On page 17-11 of the Main Volume, in footnote 30, add the following at the beginning of the footnote.]**

Culpepper v. Vilsack, 664 F.3d 252, 258, 25 AD 1072 (8th Cir. 2011) (plaintiff's claim for failure to receive accretion-of-duties promotion—which refers to noncompetitive promotion process by which employees performing work above their grade level can seek to be reclassified to level commensurate with their work—failed because she did not make every reasonable attempt to convey her interest in promotion, including, but not limited to, requesting desk audit of her position, asking her supervisors to request desk audit, or complaining to her supervisors that she was performing duties above her grade level without commensurate increase in her grade level);

IV. The Plaintiff's Burden to Demonstrate Qualifications

[42]**[On page 17-14 of the Main Volume, in footnote 42, add the following after "*see*".]**

Provenzano v. LCI Holdings, Inc., 663 F.3d 806, 814, 114 FEP 90 (6th Cir. 2011) (at prima facie stage, plaintiff need show only that she possessed "similar qualifications" to selectee, rather than identical qualifications);

[42]**[On page 17-14 of the Main Volume, in footnote 42, add the following at the end of the footnote.]**

See also Torgerson v. City of Rochester, 643 F.3d 1031, 1047, 112 FEP 613 (8th Cir.) (rejecting proposition that plaintiff must prove her relative qualifications at prima facie stage), *cert. denied*, 132 S. Ct. 513, 113 FEP 1152 (2011).

[On page 17-14 of the Main Volume, replace the sentence that ends with footnote 43 with the following.]

Rather, the plaintiff need show only, by a preponderance of the evidence, that he applied for and was qualified for the position, that he was rejected, and that the employer continued to seek applicants or filled the position with an employee of similar qualifications who was not a member of the protected class.

[43]**[On page 17-14 of the Main Volume, in footnote 43, add the following before "Lloyd v. Swifty Transp., Inc.".]**

Bennett v. Nucor Corp., 656 F.3d 802, 820, 113 FEP 616 (8th Cir. 2011) (plaintiffs could not survive summary judgment; conclusory assertions in their affidavits that they possessed qualifications necessary for promotion did not establish contested issue of fact); Jackson v. UPS, Inc., 643 F.3d 1081, 1086–87, 112 FEP 1094 (8th Cir. 2011) (plaintiff failed to establish prima facie case because she did not complete promotion application process and was not a viable candidate for job); Grigsby v. LaHood, 628 F.3d 354, 359, 110 FEP 1681 (7th Cir. 2010) (plaintiff's prima facie case failed because he lacked relevant certifications and, thus, was not qualified for vacant positions and because he was not more qualified than applicants selected);

[44]**[On page 17-15 of the Main Volume, in footnote 44, add the following after "*See*".]**

Goncalves v. Plymouth Cnty. Sheriff's Dep't, 659 F.3d 101, 105–06, 113 FEP 805 (1st Cir. 2011) (plaintiff not qualified for promotion where she failed to meet employer's job requirements of extensive information technology programming skills and relevant work experience);

[45]**[On page 17-15 of the Main Volume, in footnote 45, add the following after "*See*".]**

Lindsey v. Board of Sch. Comm'rs, 491 F. App'x 8, 10, 116 FEP 309 (11th Cir. 2012) (denial of transfer to African-American clerical employee because she failed to meet typing requirement, while waiving requirement for white employee, was suggestive of discrimination);

[46]**[On page 17-16 of the Main Volume, in footnote 46, add the following after "*See, e.g.*,".]**

Provenzano, 663 F.3d at 815 (employer presented evidence that selectee was more qualified and that plaintiff lacked good communication skills and ability to partner with supervisor); Barber v. CI Truck Driver Training, LLC, 656 F.3d 782, 792–93, 113 FEP 507 (8th Cir. 2011) (selectee had prior experience in position and understood business better than plaintiff and employer was concerned about plaintiff's abrasiveness and his willingness and ability to work with others);

[47]**[On page 17-17 of the Main Volume, in footnote 47, add the following at the beginning of the footnote.]**

See Provenzano, 663 F.3d at 814 ("Relative qualifications establish triable issues of fact as to pretext where the evidence shows that either: (1) the plaintiff was a plainly superior candidate such that no reasonable employer would have chosen the latter applicant over the former, or (2) plaintiff was as qualified, if not better qualified that the successful applicant, and the record contains 'other probative evidence of discrimination.'"); *see also* St. Martin v. City of St. Paul, 680 F.3d 1027, 1034, 26 AD 516 (8th Cir. 2012) (plaintiff failed to establish pretext where selectees were educationally superior and better understood fire department's vision, and where there was evidence that plaintiff came to job interview unprepared); Vega-Colon v. Wyeth Pharm., 625 F.3d 22, 28, 189 LRRM 2614 (1st Cir. 2010) (plaintiff's subjective belief that he was more qualified than selectee was insufficient to prove pretext);

[48]**[On page 17-18 of the Main Volume, in footnote 48, add the following after "*See, e.g.*,".]**

Barber, 656 F.3d at 793 (plaintiff failed to show pretext where applicants had different strengths, and absent showing of discrimination in weighing those strengths, employer was free to exercise its judgment in making personnel decisions);

[49]**[On page 17-19 of the Main Volume, in footnote 49, add the following after "*See, e.g.*,".]**

Shelley v. Geren, 666 F.3d 599, 609–10, 114 FEP 303 (9th Cir. 2012) (summary judgment reversed where evidence could create inference that employer considered age and projected retirement when making promotion decision); Ash v. Tyson Foods, Inc., 664 F.3d 883, 897–98, 114 FEP 102 (11th Cir. 2011) (new trial ordered based on evidence that employer's proffered race-neutral selection criterion was pretextual where plaintiff met job experience requirements and selectee did not and where, before challenged decision was made, decision maker used word "boy" in racially demeaning way to address plaintiff and another African-American employee); Clark v. Matthews Int'l Corp., 639 F.3d 391, 398, 112 FEP 249 (8th Cir. 2011) (genuine issue of material fact as to whether age was contributing factor in plaintiff's nonpromotion because plaintiff's skills were adequate, virtually every employee holding sought-after position was under age of 40, and employer directed American Association of Retired Persons (AARP) mailings and retirement-related jokes and comments to certain older employees); Talavera v. Shah, 638 F.3d 303, 313, 111 FEP 1574 (D.C. Cir. 2011) (reasonable jury could find that employer's reason for nonselection was pretext for sex discrimination based on supervisor's discriminatory attitude toward women, as illustrated by his stated preference for male colleagues in workplace, and his improper destruction of interview notes on which promotion selection was purportedly based);

[67]**[On page 17-23 of the Main Volume, in footnote 67, add the following after "*See, e.g.*,".]**

Gilbert v. Napolitano, 670 F.3d 258, 262, 114 FEP 923 (D.C. Cir. 2012) (reversing summary judgment because jury could believe supervisor's testimony that plaintiff's experience "dwarfed" selectee's experience); Hamilton v. Geithner, 666 F.3d 1344, 1352–55, 114 FEP 239 (D.C. Cir. 2012) (reversing summary judgment based on material issue as to whether discrimination motivated promotion at issue; employer's "nondiscriminatory explanation" questionable in light of significant disparity in candidates' qualifications, highly subjective nature of employer's explanation, and lack of documentation to support it);

[70]**[On page 17-23 of the Main Volume, in footnote 70, add the following at the beginning of the footnote.]**

Barry v. Moran, 661 F.3d 696, 708, 33 IER Cases 1 (1st Cir. 2011) (nepotism, rather than political affiliation discrimination, motivated selection);

[73]**[On page 17-24 of the Main Volume, in footnote 73, add the following at the beginning of the footnote.]**

Velazquez-Ortiz v. Vilsack, 657 F.3d 64, 75, 113 FEP 627 (1st Cir. 2011) (plaintiff could not prove age discrimination, although one decision maker described need to fill position at issue with "new blood," where that phrase was too ambiguous to demonstrate age bias and where selectee had more relevant experience and performed better than plaintiff in interview); Stinnett v. City of Chi., 630 F.3d 645, 647–48, 111 FEP 167 (7th Cir. 2011) (mere fact that City did not reach plaintiff's name on its eligibility list for field officer did not constitute race discrimination where City updated that list in order to ensure that newer employees were eligible for promotion within fire department and updating was done without regard to who was on list); Van Antwerp v. City of Peoria, 627 F.3d 295, 298, 110 FEP 1685 (7th Cir. 2010) (reasonable jury could not infer pretext where employer's reason for rescinding plaintiff's transfer was that position did not become available, as anticipated);

[76]**[On page 17-24 of the Main Volume, in footnote 76, add the following at the beginning of the footnote.]**

Hill v. Potter, 625 F.3d 998, 1004, 110 FEP 151 (7th Cir. 2010) (plaintiff did not provide credible evidence to show that Postal Service failed to hire him for reason other than Service's unofficial promotions policy);

[79]**[On page 17-25 of the Main Volume, in footnote 79, add the following after "*See, e.g.*,".]**

Shelley v. Geren, 666 F.3d 599, 611, 114 FEP 303 (9th Cir. 2012) (where rejection for temporary position was proved to be discriminatory, it could be inferred that decision makers for permanent position also were biased); Bennett v. Nucor Corp., 656 F.3d 802, 820–21, 113 FEP 616 (8th Cir. 2011) (although employer's policy and practice regarding minority employment may be relevant, general evidence of racially hostile work environment in one department does not mean that African-American employee in another department suffered such discrimination absent specific evidence to rebut employer's proffered nondiscriminatory reason);

[On page 17-25 of the Main Volume, add the following after footnote 79.]

- whether the plaintiff was "*significantly* better qualified" than the selectee;[3]

[81]**[On page 17-26 of the Main Volume, in footnote 81, add the following after "*See, e.g.*,".]**

Hanners v. Trent, 674 F.3d 683, 694–95, 114 FEP 965 (7th Cir. 2012) (affirming summary judgment where plaintiff's promotional rating was lowered for disciplinary reasons and deviation from established disciplinary procedures was explained and merely tangential and not shown to be pretextual);

[83]**[On page 17-27 of the Main Volume, in footnote 83, add the following after "*See, e.g.*,".]**

Tyler v. University of Ark. Bd. of Trs., 628 F.3d 980, 988, 111 FEP 161 (8th Cir. 2011) (although evidence of preselection and arbitrary manipulation of job requirements to benefit preselected applicant may act to discredit employer's proffered explanation, nondiscriminatory revision of job description is not indicative of pretext where it accurately represents job responsibilities; here, selection committee offered "a solid, qualifications-driven explanation for their decision to hire [the selectee] and pass over [the plaintiff]");

[87]**[On page 17-28 of the Main Volume, in footnote 87, add the following after "*See, e.g.*,".]**

Colbert v. Tapella, 649 F.3d 756, 760, 112 FEP 884 (D.C. Cir. 2011) (plaintiff need not show both that employer's articulated reason was pretext and that discrimination was actual reason for plaintiff's nonselection; evidence of employer's false explanation for its decision, apparent lack of knowledge of plaintiff's experience or training, and other evidence that its hiring and promotion practices were "generally inhospitable to minorities" were sufficient to survive summary judgment);

---

[3]*See* Ford v. Mabus, 629 F.3d 198, 203, 110 FEP 165 (D.C. Cir. 2010).

V. EXPERIENCE REQUIREMENTS AND SENIORITY

[99]**[On page 17-32 of the Main Volume, in footnote 99, add the following after "*See, e.g.*,".]**

Gilbert v. Napolitano, 670 F.3d 258, 262, 114 FEP 923 (D.C. Cir. 2012) (reversing grant of summary judgment because if jury believed supervisor's testimony that plaintiff's experience "dwarfed" that of selectee, jury could conclude that race or age motivated selection process);

VI. SUBJECTIVE SELECTION CRITERIA

[106]**[On page 17-33 of the Main Volume, in footnote 106, add the following after "*See, e.g.*,".]**

Torgerson v. City of Rochester, 643 F.3d 1031, 1049–50, 112 FEP 613 (8th Cir.) (subjectivity in promotions process is not itself grounds for challenging process as discriminatory and adds nothing to proof of pretext), *cert. denied*, 132 S. Ct. 513, 113 FEP 1152 (2011);

[107]**[On page 17-34 of the Main Volume, in footnote 107, add the following after "*See, e.g.*,".]**

Adams v. Trustees of Univ. of N.C.–Wilmington, 640 F.3d 550, 559–60, 111 FEP 1665 (4th Cir. 2011) (rejecting plaintiff's attempt to compare qualifications with other previously promoted professors, because of "inevitable element of subjectivity involved in promotion decisions in the university setting" and because "professors are individuals" who perform different roles within a department);

[109]**[On page 17-35 of the Main Volume, in footnote 109, add the following after "*See, e.g.*,".]**

Hamilton v. Geithner, 666 F.3d 1344, 1356–57, 114 FEP 239 (D.C. Cir. 2012) (secretary's subjective, nondiscriminatory explanation that selectee outperformed plaintiff in interview should be treated with caution where job description did not emphasize communication skills, employer failed to provide documentation related to interviews and provided only vague examples of poor answers, and plaintiff's performance evaluation rated him highly in category of communication skills);

VII. STATISTICAL PROOF: THE QUALIFIED ACTUAL OR POTENTIAL APPLICANT POOL

[118][On page 17-38 of the Main Volume, in footnote 118, add the following after "*see also*".]

Chin v. Port Auth. of N.Y. & N.J., 685 F.3d 135, 154–55, 115 FEP 720 (2d Cir. 2012) (rejecting employer's argument that plaintiffs' disparate impact claim should fail based on their failure to identify specific promotion practice resulting in disparate impact on Asian-Americans, or their failure to show that Port Authority's promotion process could not be separated into component parts, specifically, recommendation, approval, and selection; "[w]hether a particular decisionmaking process is capable of separation for analysis largely turns on the details of the specific process and its implementation in a given case");

[128][On page 17-42 of the Main Volume, in footnote 128, add the following after "*See*".]

Bennett v. Nucor Corp., 656 F.3d 802, 818, 113 FEP 616 (8th Cir. 2011) (rejecting plaintiffs' statistical evidence as inadequate to create genuine issue of fact precluding summary judgment where plaintiffs' expert failed to identify specific employment practices responsible for alleged disparate impact in promotions or to show that their statistical "applicant pools" contained only individuals who were at least minimally qualified for promotions in question);

[130][On page 17-43 of the Main Volume, in footnote 130, add the following after "*See, e.g.,*".]

Tyler v. University of Ark. Bd. of Trs., 628 F.3d 980, 990, 111 FEP 161 (8th Cir. 2011) (inference of discriminatory intent not supported where top two contenders for position happened to be female but sample consisted of only six applicants);

VIII. REMEDIES

[145][On page 17-46 of the Main Volume, in footnote 145, add the following after "*See, e.g.,*".]

Ash v. Tyson Foods, Inc., 664 F.3d 883, 899–900, 114 FEP 102 (11th Cir. 2011) (district court did not abuse its discretion in denying motion for remittitur of mental anguish component of plaintiff's compensatory damages award);

[146]**[On page 17-46 of the Main Volume, in footnote 146, add the following after "*But see*".]**

Ash, 664 F.3d at 901–07 (affirming district court's vacatur of punitive damages jury award where there was no proof that employer knew about or ratified discriminatory acts, or that discriminating official was sufficiently high in corporate hierarchy that his discriminatory acts should be imputed to employer, and where employer had implemented several policies to prevent discrimination in promotion decisions);

IX. AFFIRMATIVE ACTION

[168]**[On page 17-50 of the Main Volume, in footnote 168, add the following after "*See, e.g.,*".]**

Finch v. Peterson, 622 F.3d 725, 728–30, 110 FEP 260 (7th Cir. 2010) (racial classifications in promotion decisions undertaken by government officials were constitutionally suspect and subject to strict scrutiny; defendants' promotion decisions were not supported by consent decree designed to remedy unlawful racial discrimination and correct underrepresentation of African-Americans in police department because decree did not require use of race as factor in making promotion decisions);

CHAPTER 18

SENIORITY

II. SENIORITY AND TRANSFER RIGHTS

B. The Bona Fide Seniority System Defense

[On page 18-11 of the Main Volume, at the end of the second sentence of the full paragraph, add new footnote 53a.]

[53a]*See* Harrell v. Donahue, 638 F.3d 975, 982, 111 FEP 1559 (8th Cir.) (employers need not violate bona fide seniority system to accommodate employee's religious beliefs, even if bona fide seniority system is not created by collective bargaining agreement), *rehearing denied*, 2011 U.S. App. LEXIS 26373 (June 14, 2011).

[57]**[On page 18-12 of the Main Volume, in footnote 57, add the following at the end of the footnote.]**

See also Harrell, 638 F.3d at 980–82 (Title VII does not require employers to "transgress upon their seniority systems to make accommodations" for employee's religious beliefs even where those systems were not the product of collective bargaining).

III. SENIORITY AND THE REMEDIAL POWER OF COURTS

C. Seniority and Affirmative Action

[On page 18-29 of the Main Volume, after the sentence that ends with footnote 142, add the following new paragraphs.]

The Second Circuit further defined the limitations on the extent to which employers can modify seniority systems through voluntary settlements in *United States v. Brennan*,[1] where a group composed primarily of white male employees filed suit, alleging that the employer committed reverse discrimination in violation of Title VII by voluntarily entering into a settlement agreement with the United States to resolve a pending action charging it with disparate impact discrimination. The settlement provided, in pertinent part, that certain minority and female individuals who had failed or been deterred from taking certain pre-employment tests relied on by the employer would receive job offers with retroactive seniority.

---

[1]650 F.3d 65 (2d Cir. 2009).

The Second Circuit held that under *Ricci v. DeStefano*,[2] the employer could not avoid liability by asserting as to certain intervenors that the settlement agreement was a voluntary "affirmative action plan" because it was not a forward-looking grant of benefits to *all* members of the protective classes.[3] Rather, the settlement agreement was an award of individualized "make-whole" relief to specific employees who allegedly were the victims of discrimination.[4] Under such circumstances, the employer could defend its action by showing only a "strong basis in evidence" to believe that it would have been subjected to disparate impact liability if it failed to take the race- or gender-conscious action (i.e., granting the challenged retroactive seniority).[5]

---

[2]557 U.S. 557, 106 FEP 929 (2009).

[3]650 F.3d at 104.

[4]*Id.*

[5]*Id.* at 104, 113–14. In order to assert this defense, the employer must prove that it had a strong basis in evidence to believe that: (1) the minority plaintiffs could have established a prima facie case of disparate impact discrimination; and (2) either: (a) the employer's prior practices were not job-related or consistent with business necessity; or (b) there was an equally valid, less discriminatory alternative to the employer's prior practices that it refused to adopt, but would have served its needs. The court remanded the action to the district court to address whether the employer had satisfied this standard.

CHAPTER 19

COMPENSATION

II. THE EQUAL PAY ACT

A. Coverage

1. The Parties

[43][On page 19-11 of the Main Volume, in footnote 43, add the following before "*See generally*".]

But see Skrzypczak v. Roman Catholic Diocese of Tulsa, 611 F.3d 1238, 1243–44, 109 FEP 1293 (10th Cir. 2010) (church minister's Title VII and EPA claims barred by ministerial exception because minister's position was "important to the spiritual and pastoral mission of the church," involving supervising church's religious studies program, development and planning of theological and other religious education programs, and teaching multiple religious courses), *cert. denied*, 132 S. Ct. 1088, 114 FEP 224 (2012).

B. The Relevant Comparison

1. "Wages"

[46][On page 19-12 of the Main Volume, in footnote 46, add the following after "*See*".]

Goodman v. National Sec. Agency, Inc., 621 F.3d 651, 656–57, 110 FEP 134 (7th Cir. 2010) (female security guard formerly employed by National Security Agency (NSA) failed to show wage discrimination, where male co-worker was not paid more than she until after she resigned, co-worker and she received similar raises when they received similar promotions, and, although plaintiff alleged that male co-workers were hired same day and were paid more than she, she failed to identify those co-workers, their duties, where they worked, and their backgrounds);

C. Determining the Equality of Jobs

1. The Applicable Standard

[59][On page 19-15 of the Main Volume, in footnote 59, add the following after "*see, e.g.,*".]

Randall v. Rolls-Royce Corp., 637 F.3d 818, 822–23, 111 FEP 1565 (7th Cir. 2011) (element of showing substantial equality of jobs is "stringent statutory requirement," and where female employees in manufacturing plant failed to identify any male worker who was paid more for substantially same work, they failed to satisfy requirement);

[64][On page 19-17 of the Main Volume, in footnote 64, add the following after "*See, e.g.*,".]

Randall, 637 F.3d at 823–24 (job title of "Director of Operations," held both by female employees and by some male comparators who allegedly were paid more for same work, was irrelevant to EPA claim because title covered multitude of positions differing in authority and responsibility); Santiago v. United States, 107 Fed. Cl. 154, 163–65, 116 FEP 874 (Fed. Cl. 2012) (male employee who was temporarily promoted to supervisory position and was paid less than woman who was permanently assigned to position did not make out claim under EPA, where he did not perform same work as permanent incumbent; "relevant issue ... is not the name under which the position was classified but rather the work that was actually performed");

2. *Equal Skill, Effort, and Responsibility*

[93][On page 19-23 of the Main Volume, in footnote 93, add the following after "*See, e.g.*,".]

Randall v. Rolls-Royce Corp., 637 F.3d 818, 823, 111 FEP 1565 (7th Cir. 2011) (job title of "Director of Operations," held by both female employees and some of male comparators who allegedly were paid more for same work, was irrelevant to EPA claim because title covered multitude of positions differing in authority and responsibility); Santiago v. United States, 107 Fed. Cl. 154, 163–64, 116 FEP 874 (Fed. Cl. 2012) (male employee who was temporarily promoted to supervisory position and was paid less than woman who was permanently assigned to position did not make out claim under EPA where he did not perform same work as permanent incumbent; "relevant issue ... is not the name under which the position was classified but rather the work that was actually performed");

[103][On page 19-26 of the Main Volume, in footnote 103, add the following after "*See*".]

Santiago v. United States, 107 Fed. Cl. 154, 163–65, 116 FEP 874 (Fed. Cl. 2012) (work of EEO specialist who was temporarily promoted to position of EEO supervisor was not same as that of permanent incumbent because, unlike supervisor, specialist was never responsible for accepting and dismissing EEO complaints and for supervising subordinate staff);

[112]**[On page 19-27 of the Main Volume, in footnote 112, add the following after "*See, e.g.*,".]**

Santiago v. United States, 107 Fed. Cl. 154, 163–65, 116 FEP 874 (Fed. Cl. 2012) (work of EEO specialist who was temporarily promoted to position of EEO supervisor was not same as that of permanent incumbent because, unlike supervisor, specialist was never responsible for accepting and dismissing EEO complaints and for supervising subordinate staff);

D. Statutory Defenses

4. *"Differences ... Pursuant to ... a Differential Based on Any Factor Other Than Sex"*

a. *Factors Other Than Sex Generally*

[On page 19-38 of the Main Volume, add new footnote 158a at the end of the second sentence.]

[158a]*See, e.g.*, Yant v. United States, 588 F.3d 1369, 1372–73, 107 FEP 1793 (Fed. Cir. 2009) (female nurse practitioners (NPs) failed to raise fact issue as to whether pay differential between predominantly female NPs and predominantly male physician assistants (PAs) was either historically or presently based on sex, where NP pay scale was regionally based and separate from nationally based PA pay scale, both NPs and PAs were paid on same nationally based scale prior to 1991, salary of NPs exceeds that of PAs in some areas of country, and ratios of men to women were irrelevant because claimants had not met their burden of showing that sex-based discrimination exists or at one time existed).

[On page 19-39 of the Main Volume, in the first sentence, delete "Fourth,".]

[On page 19-39 of the Main Volume, in the first sentence, place brackets around footnote 161.]

[161]**[On page 19-39 of the Main Volume, replace footnote 161 with the following.]**

[161][Reserved.]

c. Market Rate

[184]**[On page 19-43 of the Main Volume, in footnote 184, add the following after "*See, e.g.,*".]**

Randall v. Rolls-Royce Corp., 637 F.3d 818, 823, 111 FEP 1565 (7th Cir. 2011) (where there are "more male than female employees in jobs that command a higher market wage, the average compensation of male employees would exceed that of female employees in the same job category for a reason unrelated to sex discrimination");

[184]**[On page 19-43 of the Main Volume, in footnote 184, add the following at the end of the footnote.]**

Cf. Price v. Northern States Power Co., 664 F.3d 1186, 1193–94, 114 FEP 70 (8th Cir. 2011) (three female field representatives failed to establish that employer violated EPA by hiring male field representatives at higher base pay, where they did not address employer's policy of red-circling new employees' wages at level paid by previous employer, which is factor other than sex).

d. Miscellaneous Other Factors

[203]**[On page 19-48 of the Main Volume, in footnote 203, add the following at the end of the footnote.]**

But see King v. University Healthcare Sys., 645 F.3d 713, 724, 112 FEP 973 (5th Cir. 2011) (hospital violated EPA by failing to pay female anesthesiologist bonus similar to that paid to male colleague, where their jobs required equal skill, effort, and responsibility, despite contention that he had different certifications and qualifications; relevant issue is "'actual job requirements and performance'") (quoting 29 C.F.R. § 1620.13(e)).

[On page 19-48 of the Main Volume, add new footnote 203a at the end of the second sentence in the full paragraph.]

[203a]*See* King v. Acosta Sales & Mktg., Inc., 678 F.3d 470, 474, 114 FEP 897 (7th Cir. 2012) (female employee alleging EPA violation was not required to show that education and experience alleged by employer as reason for paying men more was pretextual, even

though she would have this burden under Title VII, because "factor other than sex" is EPA affirmative defense on which employer has burdens of both production and persuasion).

[205]**[On page 19-48 of the Main Volume, in footnote 205, delete "*King*, 645 at 723–25".]**

[205]**[On page 19-48 of the Main Volume, in footnote 205, add the following after "*accord*".]**

King v. Acosta Sales & Mktg., Inc., 678 F.3d 470, 474–75, 114 FEP 897 (7th Cir. 2012) (although education and experience may explain differences in starting salaries, such factors do not explain why men received substantially greater increases during employment, salaries of men and women did not converge during their employment, and male employee was paid almost three times as much as plaintiff despite comparable performance); King v. University Healthcare Sys., 645 F.3d 713, 723–25, 112 FEP 973 (5th Cir. 2011);

III. TITLE VII COMPENSATION DISCRIMINATION CLAIMS

B. "Comparable Worth"

[289]**[On page 19-65 of the Main Volume, in footnote 289, add the following after "*See*".]**

Randall v. Rolls-Royce Corp., 637 F.3d 818, 823, 111 FEP 1565 (7th Cir. 2011) ("Maybe workers in different jobs that are in some sense of comparable value, though the market thinks otherwise, should be paid the same as a moral matter; but 'comparable worth' is not recognized as a theory on which to base a federal discrimination suit.");

C. The Prima Facie Case

1. Introduction

[291]**[On page 19-66 of the Main Volume, in footnote 291, add the following after "*See, e.g.*,".]**

Puffer v. Allstate Ins. Co., 675 F.3d 709, 720 n.7, 114 FEP 1025 (7th Cir. 2012) (disparate impact claim failed where record did not show that employer's compensation policies specified by plaintiffs—awarding merit increases as percentage of base pay, and comparing salaries to competitors—were "uniformly applied or caused gender-based earning disparities");

3. *Intentional Perpetuation of Past Discrimination*

[320]**[On page 19-72 of the Main Volume, in the carryover of footnote 320, add the following before "Auto Workers v. Michigan".]**

Wood v. City of San Diego, 678 F.3d 1075, 1086, 114 FEP 1552 (9th Cir. 2012) (plaintiff failed to state Title VII disparate impact claim regarding gender-neutral surviving spouse benefit, which plaintiff claimed had disproportionately heavy impact on female employees, because differential was "based on any other factor other than sex," as authorized under EPA) (citing Los Angeles Dep't of Water & Power v. Manhart, 435 U.S. 702, 712 (1978));

[339]**[On page 19-74 of the Main Volume, in footnote 339, add the following at the end of the footnote.]**

But see Santiago v. United States, 107 Fed. Cl. 154, 159, 116 FEP 874 (Fed. Cl. 2012) (male civilian employed by Army was time-barred from pursuing EPA claims as to paychecks issued more than two years before filing suit, as "'each deficient paycheck gives rise to a separate violation of the [Act], and each violation must have occurred within the limitations period in order to be actionable'") (quoting Lange v. United States, 79 Fed. Cl. 628, 629 (Fed. Cl. 2007)).

IV. THE INTERPLAY BETWEEN TITLE VII AND THE EQUAL PAY ACT

C. Prima Facie Case and Burden of Proof for EPA Cases

[357]**[On page 19-78 of the Main Volume, in footnote 357, add the following before "Brown v. Fred's, Inc.".]**

Goodman v. National Sec. Agency, Inc., 621 F.3d 651, 656–67, 110 FEP 134 (7th Cir. 2010) (female security guard failed to establish that employer paid her less than male employees, in violation of EPA, where she failed to show that lower pay resulted from discrimination, or that higher wages were paid to male employees for equal work, and failed to adduce details as to two alleged comparators, including what their duties were and when they started work);

[361][On page 19-80 of the Main Volume, in footnote 361, add the following after "*see also*".]

Bauer v. Curators of Univ. of Mo., 680 F.3d 1043, 1044, 115 FEP 161 (8th Cir. 2012) ("[B]usiness-judgment instruction should not be given in an EPA case" because '"[u]nder the EPA, a defendant cannot escape liability merely by articulating a legitimate non-discriminatory reason for the employment action. Rather, the defendant must prove that the pay differential was based on a factor other than sex.'") (citations omitted); King v. Acosta Sales & Mktg., Inc., 678 F.3d 470, 474, 114 FEP 897 (7th Cir. 2012) (under EPA, employer cannot merely assert that education and experience are "factor[s] other than sex" that account for pay disparities, employer must prove it; unlike under Title VII, "factor other than sex" is EPA affirmative defense on which employer has burdens of both production and persuasion);

D. Title VII Prima Facie Case and Burden of Proof

[367][On page 19-80 of the Main Volume, in footnote 367, add the following after "*See*".]

Goodman v. National Sec. Agency, Inc., 621 F.3d 651, 656–57, 110 FEP 134 (7th Cir. 2010) (female security guard failed to establish that employer paid her less than male employees in violation of Title VII, where she failed to show that lower pay resulted from discrimination, or that higher wages were paid to male employees for equal work, and she failed to adduce details as to two alleged comparators, including what their duties were and when they started work);

[369][On page 19-81 of the Main Volume, in footnote 369, add the following after "*See, e.g.,*".]

Martinez v. W.W. Grainger, Inc., 664 F.3d 225, 231, 114 FEP 98 (8th Cir. 2011) (plaintiff failed to prove pretext merely by showing that he was only branch manager paid below recommended salary range at branch level; evidence showed that employer determined plaintiff's salary by other considerations, including sales volume and business complexity, and that he was paid more than managers at other comparable branches at various points during his tenure);

E. Impact of the Bennett Amendment

[387][On page 19-85 of the Main Volume, in footnote 387, add the following after "*See, e.g.,*".]

King v. University Healthcare Sys., 645 F.3d 713, 723–25, 112 FEP 973 (5th Cir. 2011) (analyzing Title VII and EPA claims separately because of different burdens of proof; jury's finding that hospital did not discriminate in compensation against female anesthesiologist under Title VII did not preclude it from rejecting hospital's affirmative defense under EPA that pay disparity was based on factor other than sex);

CHAPTER 20

SEXUAL AND OTHER FORMS OF HARASSMENT

II. Sexual Harassment

A. Overview and Historical Perspective

4. *The 1998 Supreme Court Harassment Trilogy*

b. Faragher v. City of Boca Raton *and* Burlington Industries, Inc. v. Ellerth

[On page 20-16 of the Main Volume, after the sentence that ends with footnote 69, add the following new paragraph.]

In *Vance v. Ball State University*,[1] the Supreme Court revisited the issue of employer liability for harassment by persons who, although they may be in a position to exercise some degree of control over a plaintiff's terms and conditions of employment, lacked "supervisory" status. The Court held that the *Faragher* affirmative defense was applicable only to instances where the harasser was a true "supervisor"—one who is empowered to take "tangible employment actions against the victim."[2] Thus, where the harasser is not a supervisor, employer liability turns on a plaintiff's proof that the employer was negligent in its response to plaintiff's complaints.[3]

5. National Railroad Passenger Corp. v. Morgan—*Timeliness of Charge Filing*

[86][On page 20-19 of the Main Volume, in footnote 86, add the following after "*see*".]

Ayala-Sepúlveda v. Municipality of San Germán, 671 F.3d 24, 30–31, 114 FEP 234 (1st Cir. 2012) (where alleged discriminatory acts as whole did not rise to level of hostile working environment, otherwise time-barred acts could not be considered along with timely claims in order to support continuing violation theory); Baird v. Gotbaum, 662 F.3d 1246, 1252–53, 114 FEP 11 (D.C. Cir. 2011) (improper to dismiss plaintiff's time-barred claims without determination that allegedly unlawful but untimely actions are not sufficiently linked

---

[1] 133 S. Ct. 2434, 118 FEP 1481 (2013).

[2] *Id.* at 2441.

[3] *Id.* at 2454. For a further discussion of *Vance*, which arose within the racial harassment context, see Sections 20.II.E.2 and 20.II.E.6.a, *infra*.

to timely claims in order to amount to same actionable hostile work environment);

B. The First Element of a Sexual Harassment Case: The Conduct Is "Because of Sex"

1. *Introduction*

[94][On page 20-22 of the Main Volume, in footnote 94, add the following after "*see also*".]

EEOC v. Boh Bros. Constr. Co., 731 F.3d 444, 120 FEP 15 (5th Cir. 2013) (reinstating jury verdict in favor of charging party, Woods, based on "almost-daily verbal and physical harassment because Woods did not conform to [co-worker's] view of how a man should act"; homophobic epithets, lewd gestures, and teasing for use of "Wet Ones" tissues in restroom); McBride v. Peak Wellness Ctr., Inc., 688 F.3d 698, 712–13, 115 FEP 1185 (10th Cir. 2012) (abusive e-mails of which plaintiff was not aware until after her discharge were not based upon gender and plaintiff failed to establish elements of hostile environment based upon sex); Redd v. New York State Div. of Parole, 678 F.3d 166, 181–82, 115 FEP 399 (2d Cir. 2012) (summary judgment reversed because jury could infer that female harasser's actions—touching breasts of female employee—was because of sex); Hoyle v. Freightliner, LLC, 650 F.3d 321, 332–33, 111 FEP 1537 (4th Cir. 2011) (factual dispute existed as to whether placement in workplace of photos of nude women and women in sexually provocative attire constituted hostile environment based upon gender); Dawson v. Entek, Int'l, 630 F.3d 933, 937–38, 111 FEP 306 (9th Cir. 2011) (co-worker comments, including "homo," "fag," and "queer," directed at gay employee did not establish hostile environment based upon gender where plaintiff testified that he did not exhibit effeminate traits or otherwise fail to satisfy sexual stereotype);

2. *Common Types of Sexual Harassment*

a. *Sexual Advances*

[101][On page 20-26 of the Main Volume, in footnote 101, add the following after "*See*".]

Cordero v. Wal-Mart P.R., Inc., 656 F.3d 19, 28 (1st Cir. 2011) (where supervisor's harassing conduct is motivated by plaintiff's refusal to establish romantic relationship with supervisor, plaintiff's gender is inextricably linked to harassment and harassment is because of her sex);

b. Gender-Based Animosity

[106]**[On page 20-27 of the Main Volume, in footnote 106, add the following after "*See*".]**

Tuli v. Brigham & Women's Hosp., 656 F.3d 33, 39–40, 113 FEP 116 (1st Cir. 2011) (plaintiff established that her male colleagues created hostile work environment based upon gender where they openly questioned her surgical abilities and undermined her authority in presence of subordinates);

3. Same-Sex Harassment

[112]**[On page 20-30 of the Main Volume, in footnote 112, replace "," with "." at the end of the footnote.]**

[112]**[On page 20-30 of the Main Volume, in footnote 112, add the following at the end of the footnote.]**

But cf. Wasek v. Arrow Energy Servs., Inc., 682 F.3d 463, 468, 115 FEP 384 (6th Cir. 2012) (plaintiff's speculation that alleged harasser was bisexual was inadequate to support claim that harassing conduct was motivated by sex); Cherry v. Shaw Coastal, Inc., 668 F.3d 182, 188, 114 FEP 320 (5th Cir. 2012) (adequate evidence supported jury's verdict that harassment was sexual in nature rather than merely humiliating).

[115]**[On page 20-32 of the Main Volume, in the carryover of footnote 115, add the following at the end of the footnote.]**

But cf. Ayala-Sepúlveda v. Municipality of San Germán, 671 F.3d 24, 28–29, 114 FEP 234 (1st Cir. 2012) (harassment based upon sexual orientation is actionable under 42 U.S.C. § 1983, which incorporates Equal Protection Clause of Fourteenth Amendment; such claims are analyzed under similar standards to those of Title VII harassment claims).

4. *The Equal Opportunity Harasser*

[121][On page 20-33 of the Main Volume, in footnote 121, add the following at the end of the footnote.]

But see Sheriff v. Midwest Health Partners, PC, 619 F.3d 923, 930, 110 FEP 161 (8th Cir. 2010) (jury verdict upheld where doctor who repeatedly pulled female employees to his body and embraced them and touched their breasts created sexually hostile environment, even though harasser also frequently touched male employees, including slapping their buttocks, where nature of that touching was not sexual in nature).

C. Element Two: The Behavior Is "Severe or Pervasive"

3. *Assessing "Severe or Pervasive"*

[158][On page 20-43 of the Main Volume, in footnote 158, add the following after "*see*".]

Redd v. New York State Div. of Parole, 678 F.3d 166, 179–80, 115 FEP 299 (2d Cir. 2012) (conduct was sufficiently severe or pervasive where female supervisor touched plaintiff's breasts on three occasions, once in presence of others); Cherry v. Shaw Coastal, Inc., 668 F.3d 182, 189, 114 FEP 320 (5th Cir. 2012) (unwanted touching of intimate body parts coupled with suggestive text messages were sufficient to meet severe or pervasive standard);

[158][On page 20-43 of the Main Volume, in footnote 158, add the following after "*But see*".]

Morris v. Colorado Springs, 666 F.3d 654, 665–66, 114 FEP 225 (10th Cir. 2012) (evidence that male surgeon twice "flicked" plaintiff on her head with his thumb and forefinger not sufficient to show hostile environment, despite fact that surgeon was previously reprimanded for throwing human tissue at plaintiff that struck her on pants);

[159][On page 20-44 of the Main Volume, in footnote 159, add the following before "Ziskie v. Mineta".]

Alvarez v. Des Moines Bolt Supply, Inc., 626 F.3d 410, 420, 110 FEP 1353 (8th Cir. 2010) (suggestive jokes, sexual innuendo, and inappropriate touchings spanning period in excess of two years was sufficient to show hostile working environment);

[170]**[On page 20-45 of the Main Volume, in footnote 170, add the following after "*E.g.*,".]**

EEOC v. Management Hospitality of Racine, Inc., 666 F.3d 422, 432–33, 114 FEP 145 (7th Cir. 2012) (supervisor's degree of authority over plaintiffs was factor in assessing degree of severity of alleged harassment);

[171]**[On page 20-46 of the Main Volume, in footnote 171, add the following after "*see also*".]**

Kalich v. AT&T Mobility, LLC, 679 F.3d 464, 473–774, 114 FEP 1560 (6th Cir. 2012) (single comment referencing necrophilia was insufficient to rise to level of actionable harassment); Egan v. Freedom Bank, 659 F.3d 639, 643, 113 FEP 801 (7th Cir. 2011) (one-time sexual proposition by member of bank's board of directors insufficient to create hostile working environment); Wilkie v. Department of Health & Human Servs., 638 F.3d 944, 953, 112 FEP 100 (8th Cir. 2011) (supervisor's conduct in spreading rumor that plaintiff was having affair with subordinate not sufficient to constitute hostile work environment);

[172]**[On page 20-46 of the Main Volume, in footnote 172, add the following after "*Compare*".]**

Overly v. KeyBank, NA, 662 F.3d 856, 862–63, 113 FEP 1345 (7th Cir. 2011) (references to plaintiff as "cutie" on 5 to 10 occasions within two months not sufficiently severe or pervasive to constitute hostile environment),

[172]**[On page 20-47 of the Main Volume, in the carryover of footnote 172, add the following after "*with*".]**

EEOC v. Prospect Airport Servs., Inc., 621 F.3d 991, 999–1000, 110 FEP 271 (9th Cir. 2010) (frequent sexual propositions and romantic advances spanning several months were sufficient to create hostile working environment based upon gender),

[180]**[On page 20-48 of the Main Volume, in footnote 180, add the following after "*See, e.g.*,".]**

EEOC v. Management Hospitality of Racine, Inc., 666 F.3d 422, 432–33, 114 FEP 145 (7th Cir. 2012) (numerous instances of unwelcomed touching along with numerous sexually related statements sufficient to establish hostile working environment); Tuli v. Brigham

& Women's Hosp., 656 F.3d 33, 39–40, 113 FEP 116 (1st Cir. 2011) (cumulative effect of five years of offensive and humiliating conduct by harasser was sufficient to establish severe or pervasive gender harassment); Sheriff v. Midwest Health Partners, PC, 619 F.3d 923, 930, 110 FEP 161 (8th Cir. 2010) (consistent pattern of unwelcome touching was sufficient to show severe or pervasive harassment);

[180]**[On page 20-49 of the Main Volume, in the carryover of footnote 180, add the following at the end of the footnote.]**

But cf. EEOC v. CRST Van Expedited, Inc., 679 F.3d 657, 687–88, 114 FEP 1566 (8th Cir. 2012) (physical proximity of harassers to victims, coupled with other factors including touchings, was not sufficient to establish severe or pervasive harassment).

4. *The Standard for Evaluating Whether the Conduct Is "Severe or Pervasive"*

[189]**[On page 20-51 of the Main Volume, in footnote 189, add the following after "*accord*".]**

Pérez-Cordero v. Wal-Mart P.R., Inc., 656 F.3d 19, 30, 113 FEP 125 (1st Cir. 2011) (male employee demonstrated that harassing conduct on part of his female supervisor was subjectively offensive and that reasonable employee in his position would find conduct to be offensive); EEOC v. Prospect Airport Servs., Inc., 621 F.3d 991, 1000, 110 FEP 271 (9th Cir. 2010) (plaintiff, recently widowed Christian, established that he found married female co-worker's advances to be subjectively offensive and that "a reasonable victim in Plaintiff's position" would similarly find advances to be offensive);

[190]**[On page 20-52 of the Main Volume, in footnote 190, add the following after "*see*".]**

Pérez-Cordero, 656 F.3d at 28–29 (supervisor's months'-long campaign of retaliation against employee who rejected her earlier sexual advances was sufficient to constitute sexually hostile environment);

[193]**[On page 20-52 of the Main Volume, in footnote 193, add the following at the beginning of the footnote.]**

Overly v. KeyBank, NA, 662 F.3d 856, 862–63, 113 FEP 1345 (7th Cir. 2011) (isolated comment by alleged harasser that plaintiff and co-worker should attend company golf outing because "your pretty faces are much better than my ugly mug" failed objective test);

[195]**[On page 20-53 of the Main Volume, in footnote 195, add the following at the end of the footnote.]**

But see EEOC v. Management Hospitality of Racine, Inc., 666 F.3d 422, 433, 114 FEP 145 (7th Cir. 2012) (evidence that plaintiff had posted sexually explicit video to her "MySpace" page did not establish that plaintiff found sexually harassing conduct at work to be welcome; sharing such information with friends outside of workplace is dissimilar from sexually explicit remarks at work).

[206]**[On page 20-55 of the Main Volume, in footnote 206, add the following after "*See, e.g.,*".]**

EEOC v. CRST Van Expedited, Inc., 679 F.3d 657, 687, 114 FEP 1566 (8th Cir. 2012) (plaintiffs' evidence that co-workers exhibited poor personal hygiene, boasted about past sexual exploits, and sporadically made sexually vulgar remarks was insufficient to establish severe or pervasive gender harassment); King v. Acosta Sales & Mktg., Inc., 678 F.3d 470, 472, 114 FEP 897 (7th Cir. 2012) (minor incidents of harassment at rate of once every four to six months insufficient to be either severe or pervasive); Ayala-Sepúlveda v. Municipality of San Germán, 671 F.3d 24, 31, 114 FEP 234 (1st Cir. 2012) (plaintiff, in action under 42 U.S.C. § 1983, could not show that his work performance suffered due to statements ridiculing his sexual orientation); Overly v. Keybank, NA, 662 F.3d 856, 862–63, 113 FEP 1345 (7th Cir. 2011) (references by alleged harasser to plaintiff as "cutie" between 5 and 10 times over course of two months inadequate to establish severe or pervasive standard); Egan v. Freedom Bank, 659 F.3d 639, 643, 113 FEP 801 (7th Cir. 2011) (single sexual proposition by member of bank's board of directors insufficient to establish hostile working environment); Wilkie v. Department of Health & Human Servs., 638 F.3d 944, 953, 112 FEP 100 (8th Cir. 2011) (supervisor's spreading of rumor that plaintiff was having affair with co-worker insufficient, standing alone, to constitute severe or pervasive harassment);

[206]**[On page 20-57 of the Main Volume, in the carryover of footnote 206, add the following at the end of the footnote.]**

But see Passananti v. Cook Cnty., 689 F.3d 655, 667–68, 115 FEP 956 (7th Cir. 2012) (female employee established severe or pervasive standard as matter of law where she had evidence of being referred to as "bitch" for several years and was falsely accused of having had inappropriate sexual relationship).

[207]**[On page 20-57 of the Main Volume, in footnote 207, add the following after "*See, e.g.*,".]**

EEOC v. CRST Van Expedited, Inc., 679 F.3d 657, 687–88, 114 FEP 1566 (8th Cir. 2012) (plaintiffs raised genuine issues of material fact as to existence of hostile working environment where co-workers asked them to drive naked, urinate in public parking lot, and clean plastic bottles containing urine); EEOC v. Prospect Airport Servs., Inc., 621 F.3d 991, 1000–01, 110 FEP 271 (9th Cir. 2010) (several months of frequent sexual propositions and advances was sufficiently severe or pervasive to raise genuine issue of material fact to meet hostile environment standard);

D. Element Three: The Behavior Is "Unwelcome"

[210]**[On page 20-58 of the Main Volume, in footnote 210, add the following after "*See, e.g.*,".]**

Redd v. New York State Div. of Parole, 678 F.3d 166, 179, 115 FEP 399 (2d Cir. 2012) (evidence that plaintiff physically backed away from harasser and tried to avoid her in general established that harasser's conduct was unwelcome); EEOC v. Management Hospitality of Racine, Inc., 666 F.3d 422, 433, 114 FEP 145 (7th Cir. 2012) (repeatedly informing alleged harasser that his conduct was unwelcome and complaining to managers was sufficient to demonstrate that conduct was unwelcome); Pérez-Cordero v. Wal-Mart P.R., Inc., 656 F.3d 19, 21, 113 FEP 125 (1st Cir. 2011) (plaintiff established that advances were unwelcome through evidence that he repeatedly lied about his lunch location and twice clearly rejected advances); Mosby-Grant v. City of Hagerstown, 630 F.3d 326, 334, 111 FEP 51 (4th Cir. 2010) (numerous complaints were sufficient to demonstrate element that harassment was unwelcome);

E. Element Four: The Basis for Employer Liability

2. *Harasser Is a "Supervisor" or "Manager"*

[229]**[On page 20-64 of the Main Volume, in footnote 229, add the following after "*See*".]**

Townsend v. Benjamin Enters., Inc., 679 F.3d 41, 53–54, 114 FEP 1537 (2d Cir. 2012) (*Faragher/Ellerth* affirmative defense unavailable where harasser was employer's proxy or alter ego);

[229]**[On page 20-64 of the Main Volume, in footnote 229, add the following at the end of the footnote.]**

See also Helm v. Kansas, 656 F.3d 1277, 1287, 113 FEP 225 (10th Cir. 2011) (state district court judge was not proxy or alter ego of employer because he lacked exceptional authority or control over state's operations).

[230]**[On page 20-64 of the Main Volume, in footnote 230, add the following after "*See*".]**

Dawson v. Entek, Int'l, 630 F.3d 928, 940–41, 111 FEP 306 (9th Cir. 2011) (factual issue existed as to whether alleged harasser was supervisor of employee, based upon degree of control he was granted over employee); Rojas v. Roman Catholic Diocese of Rochester, 660 F.3d 98, 105–06, 113 FEP 708 (2d Cir. 2011) (summary judgment proper where plaintiff presented "sham evidence" that harasser was her supervisor);

[231]**[On page 20-64 of the Main Volume, in footnote 231, add the following after "*See*".]**

Dawson, 630 F.3d at 940 (summary judgment improper where factual issues existed as to whether alleged harasser was supervisor of plaintiff because actual degree of control is more significant than employer's description of alleged harasser's authority);

[On page 20-67 of the Main Volume, after the sentence that ends with footnote 244, add the following new paragraph.]

The Supreme Court resolved the division among the circuits in *Vance v. Ball State University*.[4] In *Vance*, the Court held that the *Faragher* affirmative defense is applicable only to situations in which the alleged harasser is truly a "supervisor"—one who has been "empowered by the employer to take tangible employment actions against the victim."[5] Where the alleged harasser lacks that status, employer liability for the harassment can attach only where the plaintiff proves that the employer was negligent in failing to take effective action to stop the harassment of which it knew or should have known.[6]

---

[4]133 S. Ct. 2434, 118 FEP 1481 (2013).
[5]*Id.* at 2454.
[6]*Id.* at 2451.

3. *What Is a Tangible Employment Action?*

[247][On page 20-68 of the Main Volume, in footnote 247, add the following at the end of the footnote.]

See also Dulaney v. Packaging Corp. of Am., 673 F.3d 323, 331–32, 114 FEP 980 (4th Cir. 2012) (genuine issue of material fact existed as to whether employer took tangible employment action when it presented employee with severance agreement in exchange for compensation and benefits after termination and escorted her from premises, but later sent plaintiff letter stating that she had not been terminated).

[249][On page 20-68 of the Main Volume, in footnote 249, add the following after "*See, e.g.,*".]

Tepperwien v. Energy Nuclear Operations, Inc., 663 F.3d 556, 562–63, 113 FEP 1153 (2d Cir. 2011) (judgment as matter of law in favor of employer proper where alleged adverse actions consisted of three well-grounded investigations of employee for misconduct, counseling letter that was later rescinded, two termination threats, and transfer from day to evening shift that plaintiff had requested);

4. *Constructive Discharge as a "Tangible Employment Action"*

[271][On page 20-77 of the Main Volume, in footnote 271, add the following after "*See also*".]

Benningfield v. City of Hous., 157 F.3d 369, 378, 78 FEP 173 (5th Cir. 1998) (proof of constructive discharge requires "greater severity of pervasiveness or harassment than the minimum required to prove a hostile work environment"; fear of future retaliation does not suffice);

5. *Lack of a Tangible Employment Action*

c. *Reasonable Care to Prevent Sexual Harassment*

[279][On page 20-79 of the Main Volume, in footnote 279, add the following after "*See, e.g.,*".]

EEOC v. Management Hospitality of Racine, Inc., 666 F.3d 422, 436, 114 FEP 145 (7th Cir. 2012) (investigation that did not commence until two months after plaintiff's complaint was not sufficiently prompt); Crawford v. BNSF Ry., 665 F.3d 978, 984, 114 FEP 249 (8th Cir. 2012) (plaintiff's preference for harsher response toward harasser and single failure by employer to follow its own policy does not establish that employer's investigation was inadequate); Sheriff v. Midwest Health Partners, PC, 619 F.3d 923, 931, 110 FEP 161 (8th Cir. 2010) (ignoring plaintiff's first complaint, waiting seven weeks to confront alleged harasser after plaintiff's second complaint, and failing to inform plaintiff of status of investigation was not sufficiently prompt);

[On page 20-83 of the Main Volume, in the carryover sentence that ends with footnote 287, replace "inadequate" with "adequate".]

[287]**[On page 20-83 of the Main Volume, in footnote 287, add the following after "*See, e.g.*,".]**

EEOC v. Management Hospitality of Racine, Inc., 666 F.3d 422, 435, 114 FEP 145 (7th Cir. 2012) (assistant manager's testimony that she never received sex harassment training, even though she was responsible for orientation and training of new employees, raised issue of fact as to whether employer's training practices were adequate);

[288]**[On page 20-83 of the Main Volume, in footnote 288, add the following before "*with*".]**

and EEOC v. KarenKim, Inc., 698 F.3d 92, 100–01, 116 FEP 385 (2d Cir. 2012) (employer's policy was inadequate because it directed employees to report harassment to owner, who had ignored their previous complaints, was written in overly technical language, and set 30-day time limit for filing any complaints),

d. Reasonable Care to Correct Sexual Harassment

[289]**[On page 20-83 of the Main Volume, in footnote 289, add the following after "*See, e.g.*,".]**

Aponte-Rivera v. DHL Solutions (USA), Inc., 650 F.3d 803, 809–10, 112 FEP 590 (1st Cir. 2011) (employer failed to promptly correct harassing behavior where it continued after employee's complaints, employee had made two written complaints, and employee ultimately resigned due to stress over harassment); Crawford v. BNSF Ry., 665 F.3d 978, 985, 114 FEP 249 (8th Cir. 2012) (termination of harasser within two weeks of plaintiff's complaint established reasonable care to correct harassment); EEOC v. Xerxes Corp., 639 F.3d 658, 671–72, 112 FEP 109 (4th Cir. 2011) (employer's suspension of workers who used racial slurs, re-training of said employees in company's harassment policies, and warnings of consequences of future harassment was adequate to establish prompt corrective action);

[294]**[On page 20-85 of the Main Volume, in footnote 294, add the following after "*See*".]**

Milligan v. Board of Trs. of S. Ill. Univ., 686 F.3d 378, 383–84, 115 FEP 750 (7th Cir. 2012) (summary judgment proper where university promptly investigated student employee's allegations that 79-year-old professor sexually harassed him, reprimanded professor, sent him to sexual harassment training, and barred him from contact with student employees; employee's contention that university discouraged him from pursuing complaint was immaterial given university's ultimate actions);

[294]**[On page 20-86 of the Main Volume, in the carryover of footnote 294, add the following at the end of the footnote.]**

But see EEOC v. KarenKim, Inc., 698 F.3d 92, 100–01, 116 FEP 385 (2d Cir. 2012) (district court improperly denied EEOC's request for injunctive relief beyond termination of harasser, where harasser remained in romantic relationship with owner and was permitted upon premises; injunctive relief in form of distribution to employees of wallet-sized photos of harasser was overbroad and properly denied).

e. Unreasonable Failure to Take Advantage of Preventative or Corrective Opportunities or to Avoid Harm Otherwise

[304]**[On page 20-88 of the Main Volume, in footnote 304, add the following after "*See*".]**

Bertsch v. Overstock.com, 684 F.3d 1023, 1028, 115 FEP 745 (10th Cir. 2012) (where employer promptly issued written warning to alleged harasser, plaintiff's failure to report later instances constituted failure to take advantage of preventative opportunities; it is plaintiff's burden to seek relief if harassing conduct continues); Crawford v. BNSF Ry., 665 F.3d 978, 985, 114 FEP 249 (8th Cir. 2012) (employee's delay of eight months in reporting harassment was not reasonable where employee was mid-level supervisor who had been trained in company harassment policy and told that company had "zero tolerance" policy for harassment); Helm v. Kansas, 656 F.3d 1277, 1291–92, 113 FEP 225 (10th Cir. 2011) (affirming summary judgment where plaintiff waited several years to report sexual harassment by judge for whom she served as administrative assistant and had acknowledged receipt of antiharassment policy); Wilson v. Moulison N. Corp., 639 F.3d 1, 8, 13–14, 111 FEP 1451 (1st Cir. 2011) (where employer promptly berated alleged harassers and warned them of potential termination, plaintiff's failure to "re-report" later harassment justified summary judgment for employer);

[304]**[On page 20-89 of the Main Volume, in the carryover of footnote 304, add the following after "*But see*".]**

Passananti v. Cook Cnty., 689 F.3d 655, 671–72 (7th Cir. 2012) (female employee established basis for employer liability even though she failed to fill out complaint form mandated by employer's policy, where policy was ineffective and she otherwise reported harassment);

[315]**[On page 20-92 of the Main Volume, in footnote 315, add the following after "*see also*".]**

Crawford v. BNSF Ry., 665 F.3d 978, 985, 114 FEP 249 (8th Cir. 2012) (employer's prompt response when notified of harassment complaints, coupled with its strong overall antiharassment policy, raised strong inference that plaintiff was unreasonable in not reporting harassment sooner);

6. Harasser Is a Co-Worker

a. The Negligence Standard

[317]**[On page 20-93 of the Main Volume, in footnote 317, add the following after "*See, e.g.,*".]**

Espinal v. National Grid NE Holdings 2, LLC, 693 F.3d 31, 36, 115 FEP 1418 (1st Cir. 2012) (standard for imposing liability upon employer is "heightened where the perpetrators of that harassment were plaintiff's coworkers, not his supervisors");

[On page 20-93 of the Main Volume, delete the last sentence of the first full paragraph and insert the following new paragraphs.]

In *Vance v. Ball State University*,[7] the Supreme Court settled the standard to be applied in analyzing claims of co-worker harassment by holding that the negligence standard was applicable to harassment claims where the person responsible was a co-worker who lacked true supervisory status. Even though the co-worker may have had some degree of control over the plaintiff's terms and conditions of employment, the co-worker lacked the power to take "tangible employment actions against the victim."[8]

The Court noted that a plaintiff could establish such negligence by evidence that the employer did not respond reasonably to incidents of which it was aware and negligently allowed the harassment to continue.[9] The Court added that "the jury should be instructed that the nature and degree of authority wielded by the harasser is an important factor to be considered in determining whether the employer was negligent."[10]

[318][On page 20-94 of the Main Volume, in footnote 318, add the following after "*See*".]

Cherry v. Shaw Coastal, Inc., 668 F.3d 182, 189, 114 FEP 320 (5th Cir. 2012) (employer was "on notice" of harassment where plaintiff's supervisor made 10 complaints within two months and reported having witnessed harassment);

III. HARASSMENT ON BASES OTHER THAN SEX

B. Race, Color, and National Origin

[356][On page 20-103 of the Main Volume, in footnote 356, add the following after "*See*".]

Rivera v. Regional Transp. Auth., 702 F.3d 685, 697–98, 116 FEP 1473 (2d Cir. 2012) (amended and superseded by 121 FEP 1083 (Feb. 10, 2014) (summary judgment improper where Puerto Rican bus driver showed that supervisor referred to him as "Spic," "n*****,"

---

[7] 133 S. Ct. 2434, 118 FEP 1481 (2013).
[8] *Id.* at 2451.
[9] *Id.* at 2454.
[10] *Id.* at 2451.

and "Taco Bell" on repeated occasions; despite plaintiff having told human resources representative that conflict may have been based on personality); Hernandez v. Valley View Hosp. Ass'n, 684 F.3d 950, 958–59, 115 FEP 592 (10th Cir. 2012) (Mexican food service employee showed severe or pervasive hostile environment where supervisors made repeated racially insensitive and offensive comments over period of 14 months, including accusing family member of employee of being murderer based upon similar surname); Jones v. UPS Ground Freight, 683 F.3d 1283, 1299, 115 FEP 278 (11th Cir. 2012) (African-American employee established severe or pervasive standard where he showed that co-worker stated that he had trained "your kind" before, employee found bananas on his truck on four occasions, and co-workers wore Confederate hats and shirts);

[358]**[On page 20-105 of the Main Volume, in footnote 358, add the following after "*But see*".]**

Brown v. Advocate S. Suburban Hosp., 700 F.3d 1101, 1105–06, 116 FEP 1059 (7th Cir. 2012) (summary judgment proper where evidence of racial harassment by African-American nurses consisted of race-neutral terms such as "crybabies" and "trouble makers"; "relatively mild epithets" were not materially adverse and would not have dissuaded individual from complaining); *Jones*, 683 F.3d at 1294–95 (plaintiff's inadmissible allegation that supervisor made "racial remarks all the time"—which contradicted his deposition testimony—was insufficient to defeat motion for summary judgment, where evidence contradicted plaintiff's deposition testimony); Hernandez v. Yellow Transp., Inc., 670 F.3d 644, 653–54, 114 FEP 545 (5th Cir. 2012) (four racially motivated statements over 10-year period insufficient to establish hostile environment; incidents of harassment directed toward African-American employees not probative of harassment against Hispanic employees); Berryman v. SuperValu Holdings, Inc., 669 F.3d 714, 718, 114 FEP 808 (6th Cir. 2012) (affirming summary judgment in favor of employer where plaintiffs failed to show sufficient instances of racially motivated harassment over 25-year period; only harassment of which plaintiffs were aware had relevance); Harris v. Warrick Cnty. Sheriff's Dep't, 666 F.3d 444, 448, 114 FEP 266 (7th Cir. 2012) (plaintiff failed to show severe or pervasive harassment based upon fact that co-workers referred to him with nicknames of African-American television characters and watched movie "Blazing Saddles" at work, inasmuch as that film depicts racism as offensive rather than acceptable); Bhatti v. Trustees of Bos. Univ., 659 F.3d 64, 73–74, 113 FEP 722 (1st Cir. 2011) (African-American employee's evidence of hostile environment was inadequate, reprimands that she received after complaining of racial bias were not related to her complaints and were not materially adverse, and her evidence that she sought psychological counseling established only that conduct was subjectively offensive); Ellis v. CCA of Tenn., LLC, 650 F.3d 640, 647–48, 112 FEP 791 (7th Cir. 2011) (although African-American nurses were subjectively offended by manager's use of book entitled "The One-Minute Manager Meets the Monkey"—management book that makes frequent references to employees as monkeys—plaintiffs failed to establish objectively hostile environment because "the metaphor employed by the book is unlikely to cause confusion"); Malone v. Ameren UE, 646 F.3d 512, 517, 112 FEP 1458 (8th Cir. 2011) (just four incidents of racial harassment over two-year period insufficient to meet severe or pervasive standard where some statements had been made outside of plaintiff's presence and one involved racial graffiti in washroom not directed specifically toward plaintiff); Williams v. CSX Transp. Co., 643 F.3d 502, 512–13, 112 FEP 961 (6th Cir. 2011) (comments, while viewing a political convention, that included references to African-American politicians as "monkeys," suggestions that plaintiff must be Democrat because of her race, and that African-Americans should "go back to where they came from," confined to two-day period, were insufficient to demonstrate racially hostile environment); Pye v. Nu Aire, Inc., 641 F.3d 1011, 1020–21, 112 FEP 865 (8th Cir. 2011) (statement to African-American employee by payroll department representative that plaintiff's application for housing assistance was "dumb," coupled with one racial slur that payroll employee thought plaintiff did not hear, were insufficient to meet severe or pervasive standard); Smith v. Fairview Ridges Hosp., 625 F.3d 1076, 1085, 110 FEP 1025 (8th Cir. 2010) (racial incidents over one-year period that included exhibiting photograph of fictional character Buckwheat, and statements concerning fried chicken and ghettos, were insufficient to establish hostile environment); Mosby-Grant v. City of Hagerstown, 630 F.3d 326, 335, 111 FEP 51 (4th Cir. 2010) (remarks disparaging Mexicans, made twice in five-month period and not directed specifically at plaintiff, insufficient to establish hostile environment);

[360]**[On page 20-106 of the Main Volume, in footnote 360, add the following after "*see also*".]**

May v. Chrysler Grp., LLC, 692 F.3d 734, 743, 115 FEP 1409 (7th Cir. 2012) (jury verdict upheld where plaintiff presented evidence that employer failed to respond to multiple racial and anti-Semitic death threats);

[361]**[On page 20-108 of the Main Volume, in footnote 361, add the following after "*See, e.g.*,".]**

Rivera v. Rochester Genesee Reg'l Transp. Auth., 702 F.3d 685, 697–98, 116 FEP 1473 (2d Cir. 2012) (amended and superseded by 121 FEP 1083 (2d Cir. 2014) (summary judgment improper on racial harassment claim where supervisor referred to plaintiff as "n*****"; "no single act can more quickly create an abusive working environment than use of unambiguously racial epithets such as "n*****");

[363]**[On page 20-108 of the Main Volume, in footnote 363, add the following after "*with*".]**

Yancick v. Hanna Steel Corp., 653 F.3d 532, 544–45, 112 FEP 1537 (7th Cir. 2011) (white employee failed to show hostile environment based upon evidence that African-American co-worker dropped 940-pound steel coil on him and made racial remarks and "Black power" fist gestures, where evidence showed that co-worker was "equal opportunity harasser"),

C. Religion

[367]**[On page 20-109 of the Main Volume, in footnote 367, add the following after "*See, e.g.*,".]**

Dediol v. Best Chevrolet, Inc., 655 F.3d 435, 443–44, 113 FEP 353 (5th Cir. 2011) ("born-again" Christian car salesman established hostile working environment based upon religion where supervisor forced him to work on July 4, refused to give him time off to attend church event, said "Your God did not buy me these shoes," and that employee should "Get outside and catch a customer");

[370]**[On page 20-110 of the Main Volume, in footnote 370, add the following after "*See*".]**

May v. Chrysler Grp., LLC, 692 F.3d 734, 743, 115 FEP 1409 (7th Cir. 2012) (upholding jury verdict for Cuban Jewish employee where he had presented evidence of multiple racial and anti-Semitic death threats);

[371]**[On page 20-111 of the Main Volume, in footnote 371, add the following after "*See*".]**

Jajeh v. County of Cook, 678 F.3d 560, 569, 114 FEP 1441 (7th Cir. 2012) (plaintiff's written statements to employer "did not even hint" that his complaints were related to religion, such that reasonable employer would not believe employee to have been complaining of religious harassment);

[372]**[On page 20-111 of the Main Volume, in footnote 372, add the following after "*See*".]**

May, 692 F.3d at 743 (upholding jury verdict for Cuban Jewish employee where he had presented evidence of multiple racial and anti-Semitic death threats);

E. Disability

[381]**[On page 20-113 of the Main Volume, in footnote 381, add the following after "*See*".]**

Ryan v. Capital Constr., Inc., 679 F.3d 772, 778, 26 AD 385 (8th Cir. 2012) (supervisor's derogatory remarks about plaintiff's limited mental functioning not sufficiently offensive to rise to level of hostile working environment);

IV. SPECIAL ISSUES IN HARASSMENT CASES

D. Relief

2. *Injunctive Relief*

[430]**[On page 20-130 of the Main Volume, in footnote 430, add the following after "*See, e.g.,*".]**

EEOC v. KarenKim, Inc., 698 F.3d 92, 100–01, 116 FEP 385 (2d Cir. 2012) (district court erred in denying EEOC's request for injunctive relief barring terminated harasser from premises; he had romantic relationship with company owner and had been permitted on premises; court properly denied request for injunction requiring employer to provide wallet-sized photos of harasser to all employees);

3. Compensatory Damages

[434]**[On page 20-130 of the Main Volume, in footnote 434, add the following after "*See*".]**

Aponte-Rivera v. DHL Solutions (USA), Inc., 650 F.3d 803, 811–12, 112 FEP 590 (1st Cir. 2011) (district court properly awarded plaintiff $200,000 as emotional distress damages, after remittitur of jury's award of $350,000, because evidence of plaintiff's distress was "at best, mixed");

4. Punitive Damages

[440]**[On page 20-132 of the Main Volume, in footnote 440, add the following after "*see also*".]**

Tepperwien v. Entergy Nuclear Operations, Inc., 663 F.3d 556, 572–73, 113 FEP 1153 (2d Cir. 2011) (jury improperly awarded punitive damages where there was no evidence of malice or reckless indifference inasmuch as employer made good faith effort to establish and follow antiharassment policy);

CHAPTER 21

DISCHARGE AND REDUCTION IN FORCE

I. INTRODUCTION

[1]**[On page 21-1 of the Main Volume, in footnote 1, add the following at the end of the footnote.]**

See also Brown v. City of Syracuse, 673 F.3d 141, 150, 114 FEP 992 (2d Cir. 2012) (in general, placing employee on administrative leave with pay during investigation of his conduct does not constitute discharge and is not tangible employment action). Of the approximately 100,000 charges that the Equal Employment Opportunity Commission (EEOC) received during fiscal year (FY) 2012 under all the statutes it enforces, nearly 78,000 listed discharge as at least one of the issues as to which the charging party was alleging discrimination. http://www.eeoc.gov/eeoc/statistics/enforcement/statutes_by_issue.cfm (last visited Nov. 1, 2013).

II. DISPARATE TREATMENT DISCHARGE CASES

A. The Allocation of Proof

[14][On page 21-4 of the Main Volume, in footnote 14, add the following before "Carter v. Pathfinder Energy Servs., Inc.".]

Ondricko v. MGM Grand Detroit, LLC, 689 F.3d 642, 650, 115 FEP 1300 (6th Cir. 2012) (employer's statement, "How could I keep the white girl?," made at time that plaintiff and African-American woman both were being discharged, reasonably may be viewed as direct evidence that plaintiff's discharge was racially motivated); Dixon v. Hallmark Cos., 627 F.3d 849, 855, 110 FEP 1675 (11th Cir. 2010) (supervisor's statement to Christian employee "You're fired, too. You're too religious," constituted direct evidence of discrimination; supervisor did not have to say "You're fired *because* you're too religious" for statement to be direct evidence, and statement was comparable to directive to "Fire employee—he is too old");

[15][On page 21-4 of the Main Volume, in footnote 15, add the following after "*E.g.*,".]

Ondricko, 689 F.3d at 649 (plaintiff who alleged that her discharge was result of race and sex discrimination was required to give employer notice of her intent to pursue mixed-motive claim);

[16][On page 21-5 of the Main Volume, in footnote 16, add the following at the end of the footnote.]

See also Texas Sw. Med. Ctr. v. Nassar, 133 S. Ct. 2517, 2528–29, 118 FEP 1504 (2013) (plaintiff claiming retaliatory discharge could not proceed on mixed-motive theory but instead had to show "but for" causation); Serwatka v. Rockwell Automation, Inc., 591 F.3d 957, 962, 22 AD 1379 (7th Cir. 2010) (extending ruling in *Gross* to claims under ADA).

[17]**[On page 21-5 of the Main Volume, in footnote 17, add the following after "*See*".]**

Dixon, 627 F.3d at 854–55, 110 FEP 1675 (11th Cir. 2010) (comment from supervisor, "You're fired, too. You're too religious," was direct evidence of religious discrimination);

[17]**[On page 21-5 of the Main Volume, in footnote 17, add the following immediately after the parenthetical for "Auguster v. Vermillion Parish Sch. Bd.".]**

; *see also* Guimaraes v. SuperValu, Inc., 674 F.3d 962, 973, 114 FEP 1032 (8th Cir. 2012) (hearsay report that supervisor was trying to fire plaintiff to stop her from obtaining green card insufficient to constitute direct evidence of discriminatory discharge); Moss v. BMC Software, Inc., 610 F.3d 917, 929, 109 FEP 1173 (5th Cir. 2010) (statement that employer was looking for employee on "more junior level" insufficient to constitute direct evidence of discrimination)

[18]**[On page 21-6 of the Main Volume, in footnote 18, add the following before "Hossack v. Floor Covering Assocs. of Joliet, Inc.".]**

Pye v. Nu Aire, Inc., 641 F.3d 1011, 1019, 112 FEP 865 (8th Cir. 2011) (setting out *McDonnell Douglas* proof formulation in context of discharge case);

[20]**[On page 21-7 of the Main Volume, in footnote 20, add the following before "Jackson v. Cal-Western Packaging Corp.".]**

Jones v. Oklahoma City Pub. Sch., 617 F.3d 1273, 1276, 110 FEP 4 (10th Cir. 2010) (application of *McDonnell Douglas* proof formulation in ADEA cases remains unaltered by Supreme Court's decision in *Gross v. FBL Financial Services, Inc.*) (citation omitted);

[21]**[On page 21-7 of the Main Volume, in footnote 21, add the following after "*See, e.g.*,".]**

Ramos-Echevarria v. Pichis, Inc., 659 F.3d 182, 186, 25 AD 545 (1st Cir. 2011) (employee claiming discrimination under ADA may prove his case indirectly "by using the *prima facie* case and burden shifting methods that originated in *McDonnell Douglas Corp. v. Green*") (citation omitted);

[22]**[On page 21-8 of the Main Volume, in footnote 22, add the following before "Mickelson v. New York Life Ins. Co.".]**

Bone v. G4S Youth Servs., 686 F.3d 948, 953, 115 FEP 1077 (8th Cir. 2012) (when plaintiff does not present direct evidence of discriminatory discharge, she must satisfy her burden under the *McDonnell Douglas* order of proof); Twiggs v. Selig, 679 F.3d 990, 993, 115 FEP 173 (8th Cir. 2012) (applying tripartite framework in § 1983 gender discrimination claim); Holland v. Gee, 677 F.3d 1047, 1055, 114 FEP 1449 (11th Cir. 2012) (applying shifting burden to pregnancy discharge claim); Martinez v. W.W. Grainger, Inc., 664 F.3d 225, 229–30, 114 FEP 98 (8th Cir. 2011) (Title VII race and national origin); Crowe v. ADT Sec. Servs., Inc., 649 F.3d 1189, 1194, 112 FEP 1 (10th Cir. 2011) (42 U.S.C. § 1981 claim); Alvarez v. Royal Atl. Developers, Inc., 610 F.3d 1253, 1264, 109 FEP 1162 (11th Cir. 2010) (Title VII claim);

B. The Plaintiff's Prima Facie Case

[23]**[On page 21-8 of the Main Volume, in footnote 23, add the following after the citation to "*Hicks*".]**

; Good v. University of Chi. Med. Ctr., 673 F.3d 670, 679, 114 FEP 903 (7th Cir. 2012) (even where plaintiff, a white employee who was terminated for poor performance, established that she was treated less favorably than poor performing African-American employees who were permitted to accept demotion in lieu of termination, she did not establish that her discharge was discriminatory where there was nothing to suggest that there was anything "fishy" about her termination and she was replaced by another Caucasian individual);

[24]**[On page 21-9 of the Main Volume, in the carryover of footnote 24, add the following after "*see also*".]**

Davis v. Jefferson Hosp. Ass'n, 685 F.3d 675, 681–82,115 FEP 705 (8th Cir. 2012) (African-American cardiologist, whose medical-staff privileges were revoked by hospital, allegedly because of his behavior toward hospital staff, poor record of patient care, and failure to maintain proper medical records, failed to establish that similarly situated nonminority employees were treated more favorably, despite contention that three white doctors who behaved inappropriately toward staff were not disciplined, where there was no evidence that they provided poor patient care or kept inadequate medical records); Abuelyaman v. Illinois State Univ., 667 F.3d 800, 810–11, 114 FEP 1 (7th Cir. 2011) (Arab Muslim associate professor failed to establish that decision not to renew his contract, allegedly for poor performance, was based on his race, national origin, or religion, where he failed to show that similarly situated professors outside his protected classes were treated more favorably; other nontenured professors with similarly poor records were also terminated and he could not compare himself to assistant and full professors); Rodgers v. White, 657 F.3d 511, 512–13, 113 FEP 241 (7th Cir. 2011) (African-American employee able to make out disparate treatment claim where he showed that he was disciplined more severely than supervisor for engaging in same alleged misconduct where supervisor was only demoted and he was discharged; formal job titles and rank are not dispositive when uneven discipline is basis for discrimination claim);

[25]**[On page 21-9 of the Main Volume, in footnote 25, add the following after "*E.g.*,".]**

Martinez, 664 F.3d at 229–30 (for fourth element of prima facie case, plaintiff must show that similarly situated employees outside protected class were treated differently); Smith v. Lockheed-Martin Corp., 644 F.3d 1321, 1325, 112 FEP 1119 (11th Cir. 2011) (fourth element of prima facie case is satisfied by showing that employer treated plaintiff less favorably than similarly situated individual outside of protected class);

[27]**[On page 21-10 of the Main Volume, in footnote 27, add the following after "*E.g.*,".]**

Serednyj v. Beverly Healthcare, LLC, 656 F.3d 540, 551–52, 113 FEP 104 (9th Cir. 2011) (no prima facie case where nonpregnant employees identified as comparators were not described specifically and there was evidence that some nonpregnant comparators were treated almost identically to plaintiff); *Twiggs*, 679 F.3d at 993 (plaintiff may establish prima facie case by "minimal evidentiary showing that she was treated less favorably than someone outside of the protected class"); *Holland*, 677 F.3d at 1055 (Title VII claim of discriminatory discharge because of pregnancy analyzed on same basis as any other Title VII discharge claim);

[29]**[On page 21-11 of the Main Volume, in footnote 29, add the following after "*see also*".]**

Rahlf v. Mo-Tech Corp., Inc., 642 F.3d 633, 637, 112 FEP 787 (8th Cir. 2011) (plaintiff may satisfy fourth prong in ADEA case by submitting some additional evidence that age was factor in termination decision); Melendez v. Autogermana, Inc., 622 F.3d 46, 50, 110 FEP 832 (1st Cir. 2010) (ADEA plaintiff can satisfy fourth prong of prima facie case by showing that employer filled position, showing continuing need for service that he had performed); Jones v. Oklahoma City Pub. Sch., 617 F.3d 1279, 1276, 110 FEP 4 (10th Cir. 2010) (ADEA plaintiff may satisfy fourth prong of prima facie case by showing that she was treated less favorably than others not in protected class);

[30]**[On page 21-11 of the Main Volume, in footnote 30, add the following after "*E.g.*,".]**

Carter v. Pathfinder Energy Servs., Inc., 662 F.3d 1134, 1142, 25 AD 679 (10th Cir. 2011 (prima facie case in ADA discharge case required showing of disability, qualification with or without reasonable accommodation, and termination because of disability); Ramos-Echevarria v. Pichis, Inc., 659 F.3d 182, 186, 25 AD 545 (1st Cir. 2011) (in ADA case, fourth element of prima facie case required replacement by nondisabled person or evidence that employee was treated less favorably than nondisabled employees);

[34]**[On page 21-12 of the Main Volume, in footnote 34, add the following after "*E.g.*,".]**

Naik v. Boehringer Ingelheim Pharms., 627 F.3d 596, 600, 110 FEP 1443 (7th Cir. 2010) (protected-age Indian salesman terminated allegedly for falsifying his call records failed to show that he was meeting employer's legitimate expectations at time of discharge and could not compare himself to other employees who failed to meet sales expectations but did not falsify records); *Melendez*, 622 F.3d at 51 (employer's asserted reason for discharge—failure to meet sales quotas—could not be considered in determining whether plaintiff had established prima facie case; if asserted reason is used in determining whether plaintiff was qualified, then there is no opportunity for him to show that asserted reason was pretext for discrimination); Lake v. Yellow Transp. Inc., 596 F.3d 571, 108 FEP 1029 (8th Cir. 2010) (in determining whether plaintiff claiming discriminatory discharge established that he was qualified, court could not consider employer's proffered reason for his discharge as evidence of qualification and determine whether he was otherwise meeting expectations);

[35]**[On page 21-13 of the Main Volume, in footnote 35, add the following after "*See*".]**

Alvarez v. Royal Atl. Developers, Inc., 610 F.3d 1253, 1266–67, 109 FEP 162 (11th Cir. 2010) (individual's own assessment of her performance was relevant but not dispositive);

[40]**[On page 21-15 of the Main Volume, in footnote 40, add the following after "*E.g.*,".]**

Rahlf v. Mo-Tech Corp., Inc., 642 F.3d 633, 637, 112 FEP 787 (8th Cir. 2011) (final prong of prima facie case under ADEA is that employee adduce "some additional evidence that age was a factor in the employer's termination decision");

[41]**[On page 21-16 of the Main Volume, in footnote 41, add the following after "*E.g.*,".]**

Makowski v. SmithAmundsen LLC, 662 F.3d 818, 824, 113 FEP 1351 (7th Cir. 2011) (evidence that employees outside protected group were treated more favorably in RIF contributed to finding of discrimination);

C. The Employer's Legitimate, Nondiscriminatory Reason and the Plaintiff's Burden to Show Pretext for Discrimination

[42]**[On page 21-17 of the Main Volume, in footnote 42, add the following after "*see also*".]**

Carter v. Pathfinder Energy Servs., Inc., 662 F.3d 1134, 1149, 25 AD 679 (10th Cir. 2011) (employer's testimony that it terminated plaintiff for two episodes of misbehavior in workplace, including argument where he hung up on his supervisor, satisfied its burden to articulate legitimate, nondiscriminatory reason for its action); Martinez v. W.W. Grainger, Inc., 664 F.3d 225, 230, 114 FEP 98 (8th Cir. 2011) (no showing that employer's explanation for discharging plaintiff—his management style and leadership deficiencies—were pretext for discrimination);

[43]**[On page 21-17 of the Main Volume, in footnote 43, add the following after "*See, e.g.,*".]**

Harper v. C.R. England, Inc., 687 F.3d 297, 311, 115 FEP 290 (7th Cir. 2012) (plaintiff's discharge related to excessive absenteeism); Gibson v. American Greetings Corp., 670 F.3d 844, 114 FEP 927 (8th Cir. 2012) (African-American employee's evidence was insufficient to show that employer's explanation for discharging him was pretext where, even though he had received good performance reviews, evidence showed that employer followed policy set out in its handbook concerning progressive discipline); Crowe v. ADT Sec. Servs., Inc., 649 F.3d 1189, 1196, 112 FEP 1 (10th Cir. 2011) (sexual harassment and insubordination); Sarkar v. McCallin, 636 F.3d 572, 576, 111 FEP 999 (10th Cir. 2011) (poor management performance); El Sayed v. Hilton Hotels Corp., 627 F.3d 931, 933, 110 FEP 1764 (2d Cir. 2010) (misrepresentation of prior employment history); Naik v. Boehringer Ingelheim Pharms., 627 F.3d 596, 601, 110 FEP 1443 (7th Cir. 2010) (falsifying records of sales calls); Gomez-Gonzalez v. Rural Opportunities, Inc., 626 F.3d 654, 662, 110 FEP 1542 (1st Cir. 2010) (opening island bank account despite instructions to contrary); Melendez v. Autogermana, Inc., 622 F.3d 46, 52, 110 FEP 832 (1st Cir. 2010) (failure to meet sales quota); Jackson v. Watkins, 619 F.3d 463, 466–67, 110 FEP 257 (5th Cir. 2010) (negative interaction with incoming district attorney); Fercello v. County of Ramsey, 612 F.3d 1069, 1080, 109 FEP 1516 (8th Cir. 2010) (being argumentative and difficult);

[43]**[On page 21-18 of the Main Volume, in the carryover of footnote 43, add the following at the end of the footnote.]**

But see Turner v. Kansas City So. Ry., 675 F.3d 887, 901–02, 114 FEP 1044 (5th Cir. 2012) (railroad cannot meet its burden of producing nondiscriminatory reason for discharge decisions where decision maker had no memory of reasons for discharge, made no effort to reevaluate evidence to determine what reason he had for discharging claimants, and claimants' discharge letters did not provide reasons).

[44]**[On page 21-18 of the Main Volume, in footnote 44, add the following after "*See also*".]**

Griffin v. Finkbeiner, 689 F.3d 584, 115 FEP 1422 (6th Cir. 2012) (plaintiff's circumstantial evidence in response to employer's claim that his discharge was part of RIF—including evidence that white employee took over his job duties at equivalent salary, that racially biased city mayor was in position to influence discharge decision even if he was not decision maker, and city's inconsistent explanations for his discharge, including budget cuts and poor performance—demonstrated pretext and satisfied plaintiff's rebuttal burden); *Martinez*, 664 F.3d at 231 (plaintiff failed to rebut employer's reason for termination—creating a fearful working environment—where he could not identify similarly situated individuals who behaved as he did but were retained); Zeinali v. Raytheon Co., 639 F.3d 544, 554–55, 111 FEP 1681 (9th Cir. 2011) (plaintiff, Iranian engineer, established that articulated reason for his discharge—that he had been denied security clearance—was pretext for discrimination where he demonstrated that two non-Iranian engineers whose security clearances were revoked were not discharged); *Crowe*, 649 F.3d at 1196 (plaintiff may demonstrate pretext by showing weaknesses, inconsistencies, and contradictions in proffered reason, as well as through direct evidence that proffered reason was false or that plaintiff was treated differently from similarly situated employees); Jackson v. Watkins, 619 F.3d 463, 466–67, 110 FEP 257 (5th Cir. 2010) (where employer offered four reasons for termination, plaintiff was required to rebut all proffered reasons in order to avoid summary judgment); Alvarez v. Royal Atl. Developers, Inc., 610 F.3d 1253, 1266–67, 109 FEP 162 (11th Cir. 2010) (plaintiff failed to rebut performance-based reasons for her termination merely by stating that she performed as well as she could under circumstances);

[44]**[On page 21-18 of the Main Volume, in footnote 44, add the following before "*Compare*".]**

Cf. Baltodano v. Merck, Sharp & Dohme (I.A.) Corp., 637 F.3d 38, 111 FEP 1099 (1st Cir. 2011) (court prematurely granted employer summary judgment on plaintiff's claim that he was terminated because he was not Puerto Rican, where employer repeatedly refused to respond to his discovery requests seeking information that he asserted would show that Puerto Rican employees who committed similar misconduct were treated more favorably).

[On page 21-18 of the Main Volume, after the carryover paragraph that ends with footnote 44, add the following]

The evidence presented to show pretext must squarely meet all elements of the employer's articulated reason.[1]

[45]**[On page 21-19 of the Main Volume, in footnote 45, add the following after "*see also*".]**

Alvarez, 610 F.3d at 1264 (showing only that employer's reason was false does not necessarily entitle plaintiff to overcome summary judgment; question is whether employer was dissatisfied with plaintiff's work performance for nondiscriminatory reasons; parties cannot litigate accuracy or wisdom of business decisions);

[48]**[On page 21-20 of the Main Volume, in footnote 48, add the following after "*see also*".]**

Chaney v. Plainfield Healthcare Ctr., 612 F.3d 908, 915–16, 109 FEP 1377 (7th Cir. 2010) (African-American nursing aide at long-term health care facility raised factual question as to whether employer's explanation for her discharge, which changed from her alleged use of profanity to ignoring patient call light, was pretextual, where justification shifted and there was evidence that she was treated differently than similarly situated white man);

[49]**[On page 21-20 of the Main Volume, in footnote 49, add the following before "Webber v. International Paper Co.".]**

Jackson, 619 F.3d at 467 (plaintiff must rebut each of four legitimate, nondiscriminatory reasons);

[50]**[On page 21-20 of the Main Volume, in footnote 50, add the following after "*See*".]**

Sarkar v. McCallin, 636 F.3d 572, 576–77, 111 FEP 999 (10th Cir. 2011) (Indian-born chief information officer, who had responsibility

---

[1]*See* Hernandez v. Yellow Transp., Inc., 670 F.3d 644, 114 FEP 545 (5th Cir. 2012) (evidence of Caucasian employees who violated same policy as plaintiff but were not discharged insufficient to establish that employer's articulated reason for plaintiff's discharge was pretextual, where claimant failed to show that comparators shared same job or responsibilities, reported to same supervisor, had comparable violation histories, or that their conduct was nearly identical to his; no evidence was presented to show that decision makers acted with discriminatory animus, or that biased co-workers exerted influence over discharge decision).

for managing company's contract with vendor of its new computer system, did not show that employer's explanation for his discharge—that he was not succeeding in his role—was pretextual, where he showed only that he disagreed with his employer's assessment of his performance and nothing suggested that company officials did not honestly believe that there were issues with his performance and that they acted in good faith);

[51]**[On page 21-21 of the Main Volume, in footnote 51, add the following after "*See*".]**

Jaramillo v. Adams Cnty. Sch. Dist. 14, 680 F.3d 1267, 1270, 115 FEP 274 (10th Cir. 2012) (Hispanic school principal, who was discharged for insubordination when she refused to disclose certain information requested by school board, failed to establish that board's proffered reason for her discharge was pretextual; court will not second-guess school board's business judgment concerning what constitutes insubordination, and whether its request was reasonable); Harris v. Warrick Cnty. Sheriff's Dep't, 666 F.3d 444, 449, 114 FEP 266 (7th Cir. 2012) (although plaintiff contended that his mistakes were less serious than those of comparators, court would "not sit as a super personnel department to determine which employment infractions deserve greater punishment"); Simmons v. Sykes Enters., Inc., 647 F.3d 943, 948, 112 FEP 596 (10th Cir. 2011) (evidence that employer should not have made termination decision or was mistaken or used poor business judgment is not evidence of pretext); Wierman v. Casey's Gen. Stores, 638 F.3d 984, 996–97, 111 FEP 1547 (8th Cir. 2011) (minor discrepancies between reasons for discharge and actual facts and minor shortcomings in investigation are not evidence of discrimination; differences did not negate consistent reason for termination—plaintiff's violation of employee discount policy); Silverman v. Board of Educ., 637 F.3d 729, 738–39, 111 FEP 1461 (7th Cir. 2011) (plaintiff's disagreement with principal's evaluations did not raise questions as to whether evaluations served as basis for decision and did not cast doubt on principal's credibility); *Sarkar*, 636 F.3d at 576–77 (mere disagreement with supervisor's assessment of work performance did not establish pretext; issue was whether employer honestly believed in evaluation of situation); Vatel v. Alliance of Auto. Mfrs., 627 F.3d 1245, 1246–47, 111 FEP 389 (D.C. Cir. 2011) (although highly subjective reasons, such as "incompatible working styles," should be viewed with caution, evidence overwhelmingly showed that supervisor honestly and reasonably believed that working styles were incompatible); Naik v. Boehringer Ingelheim Pharms., Inc., 627 F.3d 596, 601, 110 FEP 1443 (7th Cir. 2010) (question at pretext stage was not whether plaintiff actually falsified sales call reports; only relevant inquiry was whether employer reasonably believed that misconduct occurred); Melendez v. Autogermana, Inc., 622 F.3d 46, 52–53, 110 FEP 832 (1st Cir. 2010) (courts are not "super personnel departments" to second-guess failure to meet quota over past 18 months despite good sales record over prior 10 years); Alvarez v. Royal Atl. Developers, Inc., 610 F.3d 1253, 1266, 109 FEP 162 (11th Cir. 2010) ("it is not our role to second-guess the wisdom of an employer's business decisions—indeed the wisdom of them is irrelevant—as long as those decisions were not made with a discriminatory motive");

[53]**[On page 21-22 of the Main Volume, in footnote 53, add the following after "*E.g.*,".]**

Harper v. C.R. England, Inc., 687 F.3d 297, 308, 115 FEP 290 (7th Cir. 2012) (temporal proximity alone will rarely create inference of retaliatory discharge; three-month period between protected activity and termination was insufficient); Dass v. Chicago Bd. of Educ., 675 F.3d 1060, 1072, 114 FEP 1288 (7th Cir. 2012) (comment that plaintiff should look for job on North Side where most Indian kids went did not establish that subsequent discharge was discriminatory where it was made 10 months before decision not to renew plaintiff); Gibson v. American Greetings Corp., 670 F.3d 844, 857 (8th Cir. 2012) (no inference of discrimination where timing was only basis for retaliation claim, especially where adverse employment acts started occurring significantly before complaint); Makowski v. SmithAmundsen, LLC, 662 F.3d 818, 824, 113 FEP 1351 (7th Cir. 2011) (termination of employee while she was on maternity leave constituted suspicious timing that served as some evidence of pretext); Twigg v. Hawker Beechcraft Corp., 659 F.3d 987, 1001–02, 113 FEP 938 (10th Cir. 2011) (evidence of temporal proximity in retaliatory discharge case has minimal probative value where there are intervening events between protected activity and adverse employment action—employer pointed to plaintiff's unreported absences that occurred after complaint of discrimination as reason for discharge); Crowe v. ADT Sec. Servs., Inc., 649 F.3d 1189, 1196, 112 FEP 1 (10th Cir. 2011) (where employer provided some evidence that termination was based on plaintiff's entire disciplinary history, most of which pre-dated protected activity, timing did not establish pretext even though termination occurred two months after protected activity); Loudermilk v. Best Pallet Co., LLC, 636 F.3d 312, 314–15, 111 FEP 865 (7th Cir. 2011) (temporal proximity is usually not enough but, when termination occurred day after employee verbally complained of race discrimination, it was significant even though supervisor claimed that he was unaware of complaint; evidence showed that supervisor told plaintiff to "put it in writing" day before when he was complaining about race discrimination); El-Sayed v. Hilton Hotels Corp., 627 F.3d 921, 933, 110 FEP 64 (2d Cir. 2010) (evidence of temporal proximity—three weeks after complaint—may suffice for prima facie case of retaliatory discharge, but without more, such proximity was insufficient evidence of pretext);

[54]**[On page 21-23 of the Main Volume, in footnote 54, add the following after "*E.g.*,".]**

Crowe v. ADT Sec. Servs., Inc., 649 F.3d 1189, 1197, 112 FEP 1 (10th Cir. 2011) (company's prior leniency in disciplining individual for inappropriate conduct did not establish that its assertion that same conduct was basis for his discharge was pretext for discrimination where his extensive history of alleged harassment and continuing complaints to his employer about his "inappropriate behavior showed the futility of disciplinary actions short of termination");

[55]**[On page 21-23 of the Main Volume, in footnote 55, add the following after "*Compare*".]**

Harper, 687 F.3d at 308 (rejecting pretext argument that proper investigation was not conducted before plaintiff was discharged where supervisor cautioned employees that racial slurs would constitute terminable offense and human resources (HR) conducted investigation), Romans v. Michigan Dep't of Human Servs., 668 F.3d 826, 836–37, 114 FEP 1404 (6th Cir. 2012) (notwithstanding investigator's report falsely accusing him of racially motivated harassment-evinced racial animus, plaintiff did not establish that he was discriminatorily discharged where he did not show that investigator's intent to discriminate could be imputed to decision maker who conducted independent investigation and determined that plaintiff's termination for disrupting work environment was justified), Anderson v. Durham D&M, LLC, 606 F.3d 515, 522, 109 FEP 561 (8th Cir.

2010) (discharge of white plaintiff by African-American supervisor "on the spot" with no investigation does not imply pretext inasmuch as driver had two accidents just days before final incident, and ultimate decision was made by white upper level manager),

[55]**[On page 21-24 of the Main Volume, in the carryover of footnote 55, add the following after "*with*".]**

Hampton v. Vilsack, 685 F.3d 1096, 1101, 115 FEP 854 (D.C. Cir. 2012) (employer successfully demonstrated nondiscriminatory reason for African-American employee's discharge, despite contention that decision maker could have imposed less severe sanction but acted on recommendation of his racially biased supervisor, where deciding official conducted independent review of evidence, found that claimant had falsified reimbursement requests, and concluded that discharge was warranted because agency could no longer trust claimant to perform ethically), Bonds v. Leavitt, 629 F.3d 369, 386, 111 FEP 171 (4th Cir. 2011) (minor flaws in employer's investigation of plaintiff's misconduct insufficient to undercut its articulated nondiscriminatory reason where plaintiff conceded that misconduct had occurred),

[56]**[On page 21-24 of the Main Volume, in footnote 56, add the following after "*E.g.*,".]**

Carter v. Pathfinder Energy Servs., Inc., 662 F.3d 1134, 1150, 25 AD 679 (10th Cir. 2011) (pretext can take form of evidence that stated reason for employment action was false and that in discharging plaintiff, defendant acted contrary to company policy prescribing action to be taken in specific circumstances); Earl v. Nielsen Media Research, Inc., 658 F.3d 1108, 1117–18, 113 FEP 609 (9th Cir. 2011) (evidence of pretext included applying disciplinary policy and procedure more leniently to younger employees); Rahlf v. Mo-Tech Corp., Inc., 642 F.3d 633, 639–40, 112 FEP 787 (8th Cir. 2011) (plaintiff failed to show that employer violated its handbook in implementing RIF where handbook mentioned length of service; other factors that were listed were considered and given varying weight, and appropriate factors that were not listed were considered under the circumstances); Chism v. Curtner, 619 F.3d 979, 984 (8th Cir. 2010) (plaintiff failed to demonstrate that employer's assertion that he was terminated for multiple arrests, including felony charge, was pretextual where policy specifically referred to "conviction of a felony" but also stated that it was non-exhaustive and included good conduct requirement);

[57]**[On page 21-25 of the Main Volume, in footnote 57, add the following after "*E.g.*,".]**

Twiggs v. Selig, 679 F.3d 990, 994, 115 FEP 173 (8th Cir. 2012) (pretext can be established where employer gives two completely different explanations for terminations, but difference must be substantial; any shift in this case was not substantial); Holland v. Gee, 677 F.3d 1047, 1969, 114 FEP 1449 (11th Cir. 2012) (decision maker's testimony about plaintiff's performance problems was directly rebutted by defendant's own witnesses); Black v. Pan Am. Labs., LLC, 646 F.3d 254, 260, 112 FEP 1185 (5th Cir. 2011) (evidence that management, including plaintiff's immediate supervisors, made sexist comments sufficiently supported jury verdict that sex was motivating factor in decision to terminate her); *Rahlf*, 642 F.3d at 638 (irrelevant in RIF case that new employees were hired year later where those employees filled positions requiring less skill than positions designated for layoff); Gomez-Gonzalez v. Rural Opportunities, Inc., 626 F.3d 654, 664, 110 FEP 1542 (1st Cir. 2010) (evidence that plaintiff was performing capably and making progress was not inconsistent with terminating her for opening island bank account despite specific instructions not to do so); McFadden v. Ballard Spahr Andrews & Ingersoll, LLP, 611 F.3d 1, 4, 109 FEP 1057 (D.C. Cir. 2010) (African-American former legal secretary, with medical condition that prevented her from typing, failed to show that law firm's proffered reasons for discharging her were pretext where evidence demonstrated that position she sought as accommodation was available for only limited period and proposed comparators were not similarly situated);

[59]**[On page 21-26 of the Main Volume, in footnote 59, add the following before "Blair v. Henry Filters, Inc.".]**

Rahlf, 642 F.3d at 637–38 (plaintiffs established prima facie case where they were oldest employees in department and only 3 out of 11 in department terminated in RIF); Jackson v. Watkins, 619 F.3d 463, 467–68, 110 FEP 257 (5th Cir. 2010) (statistical evidence that district attorney replaced white division chiefs with African-Americans did not constitute statistically significant or meaningful information about employment decisions and was insufficient, without more, to rebut asserted reason for plaintiff's termination—negative personal interactions; statistical evidence usually cannot rebut stated nondiscriminatory reason);

[60][On page 21-26 of the Main Volume, in footnote 60, add the following after "*See, e.g.*,".]

Schechner v. KPIX-TV, 686 F.3d 1018, 1025, 115 FEP 307 (9th Cir. 2012) (statistical evidence of age disparities may establish prima facie case in RIF, but will not constitute evidence of pretext where it does not rebut employer's legitimate, nondiscriminatory reason; station laid off general assignment reporters based on date of contract expiration and two younger general assignment reporters who were retained did not have written contracts);

[63][On page 21-27 of the Main Volume, in footnote 63, add the following after "*See*".]

Ondricko v. MGM Grand Detroit, LLC, 689 F.3d 642, 652, 115 FEP 1300 (6th Cir. 2012) (idiosyncratic distinctions between "shuffling" offenses and fact that plaintiff had clean disciplinary record prior to offense, while comparator had prior disciplinary issues, supported her claim that employer's explanation for her termination was pretext for discrimination); Chapter 7 Trustee v. Gate Gourmet, Inc., 683 F.3d 1249, 1256, 115 FEP 391 (11th Cir. 2012) (plaintiff may use direct or circumstantial evidence other than treatment of comparators to raise inference of discrimination; testimony by HR manager that pregnancy was substantial or motivating factor in her termination supports plaintiff's claim of pretext); Hamilton v. Southland Christian Sch., Inc., 680 F.3d 1316, 1320–21, 114 FEP 1633 (11th Cir. 2012) (comparative evidence not required where there was enough other circumstantial evidence indicating pretext; comments about plaintiff's pregnancy such as "we feared something like this would happen" and statement that plaintiff would have to take off full year because of difficulty of replacing teacher after school year started, were evidence of pretext); Turner v. Kansas City S. Ry., 675 F.3d 887, 893–95, 114 FEP 1044 (5th Cir. 2012) (in work rule violation cases, plaintiff establishes prima facie case by showing either that he did not violate rule or that, even if he did, employees outside protected class who committed same violation were not punished similarly; plaintiffs and comparator both had roles in accident for which only plaintiffs were terminated, they had same supervisor and similar disciplinary histories, indicating that employer's articulated reason for discharging African-American employees while suspending white worker was pretext for discrimination); Coleman v. Donahoe, 667 F.3d 835, 851–52, 114 FEP 160 (7th Cir. 2012) (comparator evidence is particularly relevant at pretext stage and court must be flexible in evaluating whether plaintiff and comparators were similar in relevant respects); Serednyj v. Beverly Healthcare, LLC, 656 F.3d 540, 551–52, 113 FEP 104 (7th Cir. 2011) (evidence concerning comparators who were not specifically identified and were described through only hearsay does not constitute evidence of comparative discrimination); Smith v. Lockheed-Martin Corp., 644 F.3d 1321, 1341, 112 FEP 1119 (11th Cir. 2011) (rejecting defendant's argument that white plaintiff was not similarly situated to African-American nonsupervisors, all of whom violated company's zero-tolerance discrimination policy by circulating racist e-mails, where it terminated white nonsupervisors around this time for same violation); Zeinali v. Raytheon Co., 636 F.3d 544, 553–54, 111 FEP 1681 (9th Cir. 2011) (summary judgment was inappropriate where employer terminated Iranian engineer whose security clearance had been denied but retained two similarly situated non-Iranian engineers whose clearances were revoked), *rev'd on other grounds after remand,* 425 F. App'x 643 (9th Cir. 2011);

[64]**[On page 21-28 of the Main Volume, in footnote 64, add the following after "*See, e.g.,*".]**

Harper v. C.R. England, Inc., 687 F.3d 297, 310, 115 FEP 290 (7th Cir. 2012) (plaintiff did not identify appropriate attendance comparator where he did not include attendance records or indicate how much time comparator missed; appropriate comparison would have involved identifying employees who received favorable treatment while on probation); Onyiah v. St. Cloud State Univ., 684 F.3d 711, 717–18, 115 FEP 582 (8th Cir. 2012) (pay comparators not similarly situated to plaintiff where they were hired and offered salaries by different deans; two decisions are rarely similarly situated in all relevant respects when different decision makers are involved); *Twiggs v. Selig*, 679 F.3d at 994 (plaintiff was not similarly situated to employee who also lied to employer because that employee's admission of lie was mitigating circumstance); Abuelyaman v. Illinois State Univ., 667 F.3d 800, 810, 114 FEP 1 (7th Cir. 2011) (comparator must be directly comparable in all material respects;

analysis depends on whether employees had same job description; were subject to same standards; were subordinate to same supervisor; and had comparable experience, education, and other qualifications); Harris v. Warrick Cnty. Sheriff's Dep't, 666 F.3d 444, 449, 114 FEP 545 (7th Cir. 2012) (white employees with performance problems were not similarly situated to plaintiff because they did not violate standard operating procedures, disobey orders, or show lack of commitment to their jobs during their probationary periods); Martinez v. W.W. Grainger, Inc., 664 F.3d 225, 231, 114 FEP 98 (8th Cir. 2011) (employees not similarly situated where there were no concerns about volatile conduct, one had different supervisor than plaintiff, and one gave thoughtful responses to concerns about behavior, whereas plaintiff did not take responsibility for working environment); Weber v. Universities Research Ass'n, 621 F.3d 589, 594–95, 110 FEP 138 (7th Cir. 2010) (employee terminated for personal Internet use, including use for outside business, did not show that men who conducted other business at office had trouble getting their work done and did not show that employer treated similarly situated male employees more favorably where she did not show that men she identified as comparators spent as much time on Internet as she); Chism v. Curtner, 619 F.3d 979, 984 (8th Cir. 2010) (plaintiff failed to show comparative evidence after he was terminated for felony arrest—comparator arrested for drunk driving served under different fire chief and police officer terminated for drunk driving was not member of fire department—there were different decision makers in both comparisons, and employees will rarely be similarly situated in all relevant respects when that is case); Hawn v. Executive Jet Mgmt., Inc., 615 F.3d 1151, 1160, 109 FEP 1824 (9th Cir. 2010) (pilots terminated for sexual harassment could not demonstrate that other employees who engaged in similar activity were proper comparators where identified "comparators" participated in consensual behavior while plaintiffs' conduct was unwelcome and gave rise to complaint);

[64]**[On page 21-29 of the Main Volume, in the carryover of footnote 64, add the following immediately after the parenthetical for "Lee v. Kansas City S. Ry.".]**

; Bobo v. United Parcel Serv., Inc., 665 F.3d 741, 751, 114 FEP 254 (6th Cir. 2012) (discovery of comparator evidence by terminated African-American employee should not have been limited to sole white employee who had same supervisor; plaintiff was not required to demonstrate exact correlation between himself and white employees in order to show that similarly situated nonminorities were treated more favorably; he had to show only that they were similar in all relevant respects, and same supervisor criterion is not inflexible requirement); Coleman v. Donahoe, 667 F.3d 835, 849, 114 FEP 160 (7th Cir. 2012) (U.S. Postal Service employee, who was discharged for violating agency's policy against violence or threats, established prima facie disparate treatment claim, where white male proposed comparators were similar enough to enable "meaningful comparison," inasmuch as they worked at same job site, were subject to same standards of conduct, violated same rule and were disciplined by same manager even though they reported to different supervisors); Earl v. Nielsen Media Research, Inc., 658 F.3d 1108, 1115–16, 113 FEP 609 (9th Cir. 2011) (recording incorrect household address was similar to collecting incorrect demographic information because they were of comparable seriousness and covered in same policies; requiring exact match was inappropriate); Smith v. Lockheed-Martin Corp., 644 F.3d 1321, 112 FEP 1119 (11th Cir. 2011) (white supervisor who was terminated allegedly for forwarding e-mail entitled "Top Ten Reasons Why There Are No Black NASCAR Drivers" established reverse discrimination claim where African-American nonsupervisory employees who forwarded "How to Dance Like a White Guy" e-mail were not terminated; comparators need not be identical when there is extrinsic evidence that employer was more sensitive to white-on-black racism after workplace shooting spree by employee who was white supremacist, and recorded only white employees' race on spreadsheet used to impose discipline)

[65]**[On page 21-29 of the Main Volume, in footnote 65, add the following after "*See, e.g.*,".]**

Dass v. Chicago Bd. of Educ., 675 F.3d 1060, 1072 n.13, 114 FEP 1288 (7th Cir. 2012) (fact that four non-Indian teachers were nonrenewed was evidence that plaintiff's nonrenewal was not discriminatory); *Abuelyaman*, 667 F.3d at 811–12 (plaintiff's discharge case failed, in part, because other nontenured professors who were not in protected class also were terminated for poor recordkeeping); Alvarez v. Royal Atl. Developers, Inc., 610 F.3d 1253, 1267, 110 FEP 4 (11th Cir. 2010) (fact that plaintiff's non-Cuban predecessors were not fired under similar circumstances was strong evidence of pretext);

[66]**[On page 21-29 of the Main Volume, in footnote 66, add the following after "*See, e.g.*,".]**

Everett v. Cook Cnty., 655 F.3d 723, 730, 113 FEP 9 (7th Cir. 2011) (plaintiff failed to show pretext in employer's explanation that he was terminated for low productivity by relying on three-year-old productivity report that was not consulted in layoff decision, and did not dispute many other bases for decision, such as superior experience; when defendant offers multiple nondiscriminatory reasons, showing that one of reasons is false is not enough); Wierman v. Casey's Gen. Stores, 638 F.3d 984, 996 (8th Cir. 2011) (plaintiff did not raise issue of fact as to pretext where she did not identify similarly situated individuals whose rules violations were tolerated by current district manager; two decisions are rarely similarly situated when different decision makers are involved); Silverman v. Board of Educ. of City of Chi., 637 F.3d 729, 737, 111 FEP 1461 (7th Cir. 2011) (teacher's termination properly based on subjective evaluations from principal even though plaintiff thought that principal mischaracterized teaching skills compared to retained teacher);

[67]**[On page 21-29 of the Main Volume, in footnote 67, add the following after "*See, e.g.*,".]**

Good v. University of Chi. Med. Ctr., 673 F.3d 670, 676–77, 114 FEP 903 (7th Cir. 2012) (no demonstration of illicit motive even though comparators were offered demotion prior to placing them on performance improvement plan, but plaintiff received no such offer and ultimately was discharged for failure to improve sufficiently); Lefevers v. GAF Fiberglass Corp., 667 F.3d 721, 726 (6th Cir. 2012) (no pretext shown in RIF case where company retained employees near or above plaintiff's age in positions similar to one he held); Fercello v. County of Ramsey, 612 F.3d 1069, 1082, 109 FEP 1516 (8th Cir. 2010) (discharge due to being argumentative and difficult not pretextual even though plaintiff was productive and hard worker); Medlock v. United Parcel Serv., Inc., 608 F.3d 1185, 1192–93, 109 FEP 1010 (10th Cir. 2010) (although company had no policy of reinstating remorseful rules violators, court held that comparators were not similarly situated to plaintiff because they showed remorse, whereas plaintiff did not);

III. DISPARATE IMPACT DISCHARGE CASES

[76][On page 21-32 of the Main Volume, in footnote 76, add the following after "*E.g.*,".]

Clark v. Matthews Int'l Corp., 628 F.3d 462, 469 (8th Cir. 2010) (there is no rigid minimum disparity in ADEA case sufficient to indicate discrimination; 4.5% decrease in employment of workers older than age 40 after RIF did not establish disparate impact claim), *vacated in part on other grounds*, 639 F.3d 391 (8th Cir. 2011); Aliotta v. Bair, 614 F.3d 556, 569–70, 109 FEP 1701 (D.C. Cir. 2010) (plaintiff's statistical evidence in RIF case was faulty where plaintiff included employees involved in voluntary buyout with those who were involuntarily terminated; no statistical significance after voluntary buyout individuals were removed from analysis);

IV. CONSTRUCTIVE DISCHARGE

A. Introduction

[On page 21-34 of the Main Volume, at the end of the carryover paragraph, add new footnote 82a.]

[82a]*Compare* Sanders v. Lee Cnty. Sch. Dist. No. 1, 669 F.3d 888, 894, 114 FEP 705 (8th Cir. 2012) (claim of constructive discharge sustained where both white supervisors were transferred immediately following election of majority African-American school board and, in particular, plaintiff was transferred from position as school district's finance coordinator to that of food service assistant, change that was both demotion and demeaning reassignment), *with* Overly v. KeyBank Nat'l Ass'n, 662 F.3d 856, 862–63, 113 FEP 1345 (7th Cir. 2011) (plaintiff, who resigned after supervisor occasionally referred to her as "cute," suggested that she and other female employees should represent company at golf tournament because they looked better than men, and required her to leave her purse and planner outside room at meeting, did not establish situation so intolerable that it should be characterized as constructive discharge).

B. Establishing a Constructive Discharge Claim

[90][On page 21-37 of the Main Volume, in footnote 90, add the following after "*See*".]

Thompson v. Memorial Hosp. of Carbondale, 625 F.3d 394, 401–02, 110 FEP 1129 (7th Cir. 2010) (African-American paramedic failed to establish that he was constructively discharged where supervisor's comments, including that he could not do what other paramedics could do because he was African-American, and that she was afraid of what her neighbors would think if she invited him to party at her home, did not reflect severe or pervasive conduct sufficient to support constructive discharge claim);

[91][On page 21-38 of the Main Volume, in footnote 91, add the following after "*Sixth Circuit:*".]

Regan v. Faurecia Auto. Seating, Inc., 679 F.3d 475, 481 (6th Cir. 2012) (plaintiff is required to show that employer deliberately created intolerable working conditions, as seen by reasonable employee, with intention of forcing employee to resign); Savage v. Gee, 665 F.3d 732, 739 (6th Cir. 2012) (constructive discharge plaintiff must show that employer deliberately created intolerable working conditions, as perceived by reasonable person, and that employer did this with intention of forcing plaintiff to quit);

[91][On page 21-29 of the Main Volume, in footnote 91, add the following after "*Eighth Circuit:*".]

Sanders v. Lee Cnty. Sch. Dist. No. 1, 669 F.3d 888, 893 (8th Cir. 2012) (employee must show that employer deliberately created intolerable conditions with intention of forcing her to quit; intolerability is objective, not subjective, standard); Wilkie v. Department of Health & Human Servs., 638 F.3d 944, 954, 112 FEP 100 (8th Cir. 2011) (plaintiff must show that reasonable person in her situation would find working conditions intolerable and that employer must have intended to force her to quit); Alvarez v. Des Moines Bolt Supply, Inc., 626 F.3d 410, 418, 110 FEP 1353 (8th Cir. 2010) (employee must show that employer deliberately created intolerable working conditions with intention of forcing her to quit); Fercello v. County of Ramsey, 612 F.3d 1069, 1083, 109 FEP 1516 (8th Cir. 2010) (plaintiff must show that reasonable person would find working conditions intolerable and that employer intended to force her to quit);

[92]**[On page 21-40 of the Main Volume, in footnote 92, add the following after "*See, e.g.*,".]**

Smith v. Fairview Ridges Hosp., 625 F.3d 1076, 1087, 110 FEP 1025 (8th Cir. 2010) (plaintiff must show that she subjectively perceived environment to be abusive *and* that reasonable person would have found employment intolerable, as well as that employer either intended to force her to resign or could have reasonably foreseen that she would do so as result of its actions);

[97]**[On page 21-41 of the Main Volume, in footnote 97, add the following after "*E.g.*,".]**

Chapin v. Fort-Rohr Motors, Inc., 621 F.3d 673, 680, 110 FEP 129 (7th Cir. 2010) (litigation to determine what would have happened is no substitute for evidence of what really happened);

[99]**[On page 21-42 of the Main Volume, in footnote 99, add the following after "*See, e.g.*,".]**

Trierweiler v. Wells Fargo Bank, 639 F.3d 456, 461, 111 FEP 1768 (8th Cir. 2011) (employee has obligation to not assume worst and not to conclude too quickly that employer is trying to force him to quit); Alvarez v. Des Moines Bolt Supply, Inc., 626 F.3d 410, 419, 110 FEP 1353 (8th Cir. 2010) (part of employee's obligation is to be reasonable, and to not assume worst); Helton v. Southland Racing Corp., 600 F.3d 954, 108 FEP 1505 (8th Cir. 2010) (plaintiff who was told that another employee had accused her of being responsible for missing funds failed to establish constructive discharge claim, where she did not investigate rumor that she was being blamed for lost funds but instead resigned out of concern that she would be "set up" for future blame; accusation did not present imminent danger that would compel reasonable person to quit);

[100]**[On page 21-42 of the Main Volume, in footnote 100, add the following after "*See*".]**

Dediol v. Best Chevrolet, Inc., 655 F.3d 435, 441–42, 113 FEP 353 (5th Cir. 2011) (protected-age car salesman claiming constructive discharge adduced evidence sufficient that reasonable person would have resigned his position where manager called him names such as "old mother ******," "old man," and "pops" half-dozen times daily, threatened to "kick his ass," charged at him during meeting, and steered deals away from him and toward younger salespersons); Regan v. Faurecia Auto. Seating, 679 F.3d 475, 481–82, 114 FEP 1651 (6th Cir. 2012) (plaintiff's claim that she was denied adjustment in hours that was given to men did not demonstrate that she was constructively discharged where refusal to alter hours was "mere inconvenience," not adverse action taken with intention of forcing plaintiff to resign);

[102]**[On page 21-43 of the Main Volume, in footnote 103, add the following after "*See*".]**

Chapin, 621 F.3d at 680 (no constructive discharge where reasonable employee would not think that termination was "imminent and inevitable event"; court explained that there was no "handwriting on the wall" and plaintiff was asking court to speculate that constructive discharge would have occurred if he had returned to work);

[103]**[On page 21-44 of the Main Volume, in footnote 103, add the following after "*See*".]**

Sanders v. Lee Cnty. Sch. Dist. No. 1, 669 F.3d 888, 893, 114 FEP 705 (8th Cir. 2012) (plaintiff must give employer opportunity to resolve problem before quitting); *Trierweiler*, 639 F.3d at 460 (employee was not constructively discharge where she did not give employer reasonable opportunity to work out her problem—she never spoke with HR and never attempted to return to work after her first and only pregnancy absence); Wilkie v. Department of Health & Human Servs., 638 F.3d 944, 954, 112 FEP 100 (8th Cir. 2011) (in order to maintain constructive discharge claim, employee must grant her employer reasonable opportunity to remedy intolerable condition before resigning); Alvarez v. Des Moines Bolt Supply, Inc., 626 F.3d 410, 418–19, 110 FEP 1353 (8th Cir. 2010) (constructive discharge claim must fail where plaintiff did not complain about post-suspension harassment and give employer reasonable opportunity to remedy problem; plaintiff could not reasonably assume that complaint would be futile); Whitten v. Fred's, Inc., 601 F.3d 231, 249, 108 FEP 1510 (4th Cir. 2010) (where plaintiff, who had been physically assaulted, reported assault to harasser's superior and superior dismissed matter and failed to offer her protection from further harassment, her resignation could be viewed as reasonably foreseeable and constructive discharge), *abrogated on other grounds by* Vance v. Ball State Univ., 133 S. Ct. 2434 (2013);

[105]**[On page 21-45 of the Main Volume, in footnote 105, add the following after "*See*".]**

Hernandez v. Valley View Hosp. Ass'n, 684 F.3d 930, 961, 115 FEP 592 (10th Cir. 2012) (plaintiff demonstrated that her resignation constituted constructive discharge where, among other things, hospital officials denied her requests to be transferred away from supervision of two individuals who allegedly were subjecting her to hostile environment, confronted her with performance criticisms only after she complained of harassment, suspended her, and then prevented her from returning to work for 10 days after suspension); Trierweiler v. Wells Fargo Bank, 639 F.3d 456, 460, 111 FEP 1768 (8th Cir. 2011) (while plaintiff was on leave, her supervisors and HR explored possible accommodations for absences, which "shows an intent to maintain an employment relationship with Trierweiler, not to cause her to quit"); Chapin v. Fort-Rohr Motors, Inc., 621 F.3d 673, 680, 110 FEP 129 (8th Cir. 2010) (no constructive discharge where employer made efforts to have plaintiff return to work, told him that his employment was not terminated, and expressed desire to continue his employment); Fercello v. County of Ramsey, 612 F.3d 1069, 1083, 109 FEP 1516 (8th Cir. 2010) (no constructive discharge where employer accommodated plaintiff by giving her parking space to which she would not otherwise be entitled, gave her time off, suggested that she speak to HR, provided her with alternative work schedule, and tried to understand problems with her work load; such accommodations showed intent to maintain employment relationship, not force her to quit);

C. Necessity of Aggravating Factors

[113]**[On page 21-48 of the Main Volume, in footnote 113, add the language after "*E.g.*,".]**

Nassar v. University of Texas Sw. Med. Ctr., 674 F.3d 448, 453 (5th Cir. 2012) (constructive discharge requires aggravating factor such as demotion, pay cut, reduction in job responsibility, reassignment to menial work, reassignment to younger supervisor, badgering harassment, humiliation calculated to cause resignation, and offers of early retirement on terms less favorable than employee's former status), *reversed on other grounds*, 133 S. Ct. 2317 (2013); Dediol v. Best Chevrolet, Inc., 655 F.3d 435, 444, 113 FEP 353 (5th Cir. 2011) (constructive discharge claim requires greater severity or pervasiveness of harassment than minimum required to prove hostile work environment); Trierweiler v. Wells Fargo Bank, 639 F.3d 456, 460, 111 FEP 1768 (constructive discharge requires considerably more than unpleasant and unprofessional work environment that plaintiff experienced); Ahern v. Shinseki, 629 F.3d 49, 59 (1st Cir. 2010) (plaintiff's constructive discharge claim must fail because there was no evidence of gender-based discrimination that polluted workplace); Thompson v. Memorial Hosp. of Carbondale, 625 F.3d 394, 401 (7th Cir. 2010) (plaintiff must show work environment more egregious than that required for hostile work environment claim, so much so that he was forced to resign from standpoint of reasonable employee, because working conditions had become unbearable);

[113]**[On page 21-48 of the Main Volume, in footnote 113, add the following after "*But see*".]**

Sanders v. Lee Cnty. Sch. Dist. No. 1, 669 F.3d 888, 894, 114 FEP 705 (8th Cir. 2012) (Caucasian finance coordinator for county school district was constructively discharged where school board reassigned her to be food-service assistant—demotion that reasonable employee would find demeaning—she gave employer reasonable chance to solve problem before she quit, and board members attempted to abolish her new position after reassigning her to it);

[116]**[On page 21-49 of the Main Volume, in footnote 116, add the following after "*see also*".]**

Hernandez v. Valley View Hosp. Ass'n, 684 F.3d 950, 961, 115 FEP 592 (10th Cir. 2012) (former food-service employee of Mexican origin who stated actionable claim for racially hostile environment also established constructive-discharge claim where hospital officials repeatedly denied her requests to be transferred away from supervision of two individuals who subjected her to severe harassment, confronted her with after-the-fact performance criticisms once she complained about harassment, suspended her for a half day, and then prevented her from returning to work for 10 days "until they could meet with her");

[117]**[On page 21-49 of the Main Volume, in footnote 117, add the following after "*See*".]**

Nassar, 674 F.3d at 453 (plaintiff proved racial harassment but his proof was no more than minimum required to prove hostile work environment—no aggravating factors to show intolerable working conditions);

[118]**[On page 21-49 of the Main Volume, in footnote 118, add the following after "*See*".]**

Hernandez, 684 F.3d at 961 (constructive discharge claim dismissed because it was premised on hostile work environment claim, which was dismissed); Overly v. Keybank Nat'l Ass'n, 662 F.3d 856, 864–65 (7th Cir. 2011) (dismissal of sexually hostile work environment claim required dismissal of constructive discharge claim); Ellis v. CCA of Tenn., LLC, 650 F.3d 640, 650, 112 FEP 791 (7th Cir. 2011) (failure of harassment claim dooms constructive discharge claim); Wilkie v. Department of Health & Human Servs., 638 F.3d 944, 954, 112 FEP 100 (8th Cir. 2011) (constructive discharge claim failed because evidence of sexually hostile work environment was insufficient); Ahern v. Shinseki, 629 F.3d 49, 59, 110 FEP 1785 (1st Cir. 2010) (no constructive discharge where plaintiffs did not prevail on sex discrimination claim and abusive supervisor subjected both men and women to same treatment yet they chose to stay); Smith v. Fairview Ridges Hosp., 625 F.3d 1076, 1087, 110 FEP 1025 (8th Cir. 2010) (constructive discharge claim failed because race hostile work environment claim failed); Thompson v. Memorial Hosp. of Carbondale, 625 F.3d 394, 401–02, 110 FEP 1129 (7th Cir. 2010) (because race hostile work environment claim failed, plaintiff's constructive discharge claim failed as well);

[127]**[On page 21-52 of the Main Volume, in footnote 127, add the following after "*See, e.g.,*".]**

Fercello v. County of Ramsey, 612 F.3d 1069, 1083, 109 FEP 1516 (8th Cir. 2010) (no constructive discharge where county "sought to accommodate Fercello at nearly every turn"; no evidence showing that county intended to force her to quit);

[130]**[On page 21-53 of the Main Volume, in footnote 130, add the following after "*See*".]**

Hernandez v. Valley View Hosp. Ass'n, 684 F.3d 950, 961, 115 FEP 592 (10th Cir. 2012) (employer is strictly liable for constructive discharge that results from tangible employment action);

[132]**[On page 21-53 of the Main Volume, in footnote 132, add the following after "*See, e.g.*,".]**

Thompson v. Memorial Hosp. of Carbondale, 625 F.3d 394, 401, 110 FEP 1129 (7th Cir. 2010) (comments that plaintiff could not do what others could do because he was African-American, and statement by supervisor that she was not sure what her neighbors would think if she invited African-American person to her home, were not severe or pervasive);

[138]**[On page 21-56 of the Main Volume, in footnote 138, add the following after "*See*".]**

Sanders v. Lee Cnty. Sch. Dist. No. 1, 669 F.3d 888, 893–94, 114 FEP 705 (8th Cir. 2012) (demotion from finance director to food services assistant was of such magnitude that reasonable person in plaintiff's position would find it demeaning; failure to provide job description also supported constructive discharge claim);

[141]**[On page 21-56 of the Main Volume, in footnote 141, add the following after "*See, e.g.*,".]**

Savage v. Gee, 665 F.3d 732, 739–40, 33 IER Cases 193 (6th Cir. 2012) (no constructive discharge where many faculty members disliked plaintiff, were critical of him, did not want him helping them with research, and publicly challenged his professionalism—no evidence that university intended to force him to quit);

[142]**[On page 21-57 of the Main Volume, in footnote 142, add the following after "*See, e.g.*,".]**

Ahern v. Shinseki, 629 F.3d 49, 59, 110 FEP 1785 (1st Cir. 2010) (no constructive discharge despite supervisor who created "nerve-wracking environment" that caused employees to take stress leaves of absence);

[150]**[On page 21-59 of the Main Volume, in footnote 150, add the following after "*E.g.*,".]**

Trierweiler v. Wells Fargo Bank, 639 F.3d 456, 460, 111 FEP 1768 (8th Cir. 2011) (employee who was told that she could not miss one more day while on maternity leave was not constructively discharged);

[153]**[On page 21-59 of the Main Volume, in footnote 153, add the following after "*See, e.g.*,".]**

Dediol v. Best Chevrolet, Inc., 655 F.3d 435, 444–45, 113 FEP 353 (5th Cir. 2011) (religious harassment and ultimate physical altercation contributed to reversal of summary judgment on constructive discharge claim);

[154]**[On page 21-59 of the Main Volume, in footnote 154, add the following after "*See, e.g.*,".]**

Regan v. Faurecia Auto. Seating, Inc., 679 F.3d 475, 482, 114 FEP 1651 (6th Cir. 2012) (denial of modified work schedule to accommodate employee's narcolepsy not intolerable and not intended to force plaintiff to resign);

CHAPTER 22

EMPLOYERS

I. Private Sector Employers

A. Who Is an Employer?

1. Definition

a. Statutory Provisions

[5][On page 22-3 of the Main Volume, in footnote 5, add the following at the end of the footnote.]

Cf. Bryson v. Middlefield Volunteer Fire Dep't, Inc., 656 F.3d 348, 354, 113 FEP 97 (6th Cir. 2011) (volunteer fire department may constitute Title VII "employer," despite contention that it does not meet 15-employee threshold, because its firefighter-members receive only de minimis benefits for their services; remuneration is only one factor in determining whether employment relationship exists, not independent antecedent requirement).

[On page 22-3 of the Main Volume, at the end of the second sentence of the second full paragraph, add new footnote 6a.]

[6a]Courts are divided on the nature of "employer-like" functions that determine whether volunteers are included in counting the number of employees at a particular business. *Compare* Middlefield Volunteer Fire Dep't, Inc., 656 F.3d 348, 354, 113 FEP 97 (6th Cir. 2011) (including volunteer firefighters in determining whether fire department meets 15-employee threshold—remuneration is only one factor in determining whether employment relationship exists, rather than independent antecedent requirement; each volunteer firefighter-member is "hired party" with contractual relationship with department, providing firefighting services in exchange for benefits, including workers' compensation coverage, insurance coverage, gift cards, personal use of the Department's facilities and assets,

training, and access to an emergency fund), *with* Juino v. Livingston Parish Fire Dist., 717 F.3d 431, 437–39, 118 FEP 885 (5th Cir. 2013) (collecting cases; volunteer who received benefits but no pay was not employee for purposes of determining whether Fire District met 15-employee threshold; citing EEOC Compliance Manual, which provides that volunteers generally are not protected employees).

2. *Determining Who Is the "Employer"*

b. The "Single Employer" Theory

[24]**[On page 22-8 of the Main Volume, in footnote 24, add the following at the end of the footnote.]**

See also Wellman v. DuPont Dow Elastomers, LLC, 414 F. App'x 386, 389, 24 AD 659 (3d Cir.) (per curiam) (parent and subsidiary corporation were not integrated enterprises where they did not share common management, ownership, or financial controls; employee could not apply to certain positions within parent because she was considered nonparent employee; and parent was not consulted or informed about employee's termination), *cert. denied*, 132 S. Ct. 555 (2011).

c. The "Joint Employer" Theory

[29]**[On page 22-9 of the Main Volume, in footnote 29, add the following after "*See*".]**

Service Employees Int'l Union Local 32BJ v. NLRB, 647 F.3d 435, 442–43, 191 LRRM 2170 (2d Cir. 2011) ("an essential element" of any joint employer determination is "sufficient evidence of immediate control over the employees,"... "whether the alleged joint employer (1) did the hiring and firing; (2) directly administered any disciplinary procedures; (3) maintained records of hours, handled the payroll, or provided insurance; (4) directly supervised the employees; or (5) participated in the collective bargaining process");

d. The "Agent" Theory

[39]**[On page 22-13 of the Main Volume, in footnote 39, add the following after "*See*".]**

Whitten v. Fred's, Inc., 601 F.3d 231, 244, 108 FEP 1510 (4th Cir. 2010) (absence of ability to take tangible employment actions does not resolve whether person who committed discriminatory act at issue was plaintiff's supervisor and agent of employer for purposes of imposing vicarious liability; court must also consider "other features of the employment relations" including job titles and "rank" in "particular employment hierarchy");

[On page 22-14 of the Main Volume, replace the last sentence of the first full paragraph with the following.]

In *Burlington Industries, Inc. v. Ellerth*[1] and *Faragher v. City of Boca Raton*,[2] the Supreme Court held that an employer may be liable for conduct by a supervisor. Thereafter, courts of appeals disagreed on the characteristics that distinguished supervisors from rank-and-file workers for the purpose of assessing employer liability, an issue that was left open by the two decisions.[3] The Supreme Court addressed this question in *Vance v. Ball State University*.[4]

The plaintiff in *Vance*, an African-American "catering assistant," claimed that she had been racially harassed by Ms. Davis, a white employee whose job title was "catering specialist." Although Ms. Davis generally oversaw the plaintiff's work, there was no evidence that she had the authority to take any tangible action with regard to Ms. Vance's employment. The trial court granted summary judgment against Ms. Vance on the basis that only those with such authority could be considered "agents" for whose actions the employer was liable. The Seventh Circuit affirmed, as did the Supreme Court.

---

[1]524 U.S. 742, 77 FEP 1 (1998) (employers are liable for hostile work environment harassment by supervisory employees).

[2]524 U.S. 775, 77 FEP 14 (1998) (employers are liable for hostile work environment harassment by supervisory employees).

[3]Some courts, including the Seventh Circuit, held that an employee is not a supervisor unless he or she has the power to hire, fire, demote, promote, transfer, or discipline the victim. *See, e.g.*, Vance v. Ball State Univ., 646 F.3d. 461, 470, 112 FEP 582 (7th Cir. 2011), *aff'd*, 133 S. Ct. 2434, 118 FEP 1481 (2013); Noviello v. Boston, 398 F.3d 76, 96 (1st Cir. 2005); Weyers v. Lear Operations Corp., 359 F.3d 1049, 1057, 93 FEP 507 (8th Cir. 2004). Others followed a more open-ended approach, which tied supervisor status to the ability to exercise significant direction over another's daily work. *See, e.g.*, Mack v. Otis Elevator Co., 326 F.3d 116, 126–27 (2d Cir. 2003); Whitten v. Fred's, Inc., 601 F.3d 231, 245–47 (4th Cir. 2010). The EEOC adopted this open-ended view in its *Enforcement Guidance: Vicarious Employer Liability for Unlawful Harassment by Supervisors*, EEOC COMPL. MAN. § 615:530 (1999) ("The determination as to whether a harasser had such authority is based on his or her job function rather than job title (e.g., "team leader") and must be based on the specific facts.").

[4]133 S. Ct. 2434, 118 FEP 1481 (2013).

Writing for the majority, Justice Alito reviewed the history leading to the *Faragher* and *Ellerth* decisions, noting that the holdings in those two cases distinguished between true supervisors and those who were merely co-workers, even those who served as "straw bosses," "leadmen," or working foremen.[5] Rejecting "the nebulous definition of a 'supervisor' advocated in the EEOC Guidance and substantially adopted by several courts of appeals,"[6] the Court adopted as its holding what had been declared in *Ellerth* only in dictum:

> Only a supervisor has the power to cause "direct economic harm" by taking a tangible employment action. "Tangible employment actions fall within the special province of the supervisor. The supervisor has been empowered by the company *as a distinct class* of agent to make economic decisions affecting other employees under his or her control. . . . Tangible employment actions are the means by which the supervisor brings the official power of the enterprise to bear on subordinates."[7]

The Court stated further that linking agency and supervisory status to the authority to take tangible employment actions makes the question of whether a particular employee is a supervisor "one that can usually be readily determined, generally by written documentation," in contrast to the fact-specific inquiry suggested by the EEOC guidance.[8]

B. Certain Exemptions and Exclusions From Employer and Employee Status

1. Introduction

[50][On page 22-15 of the Main Volume, in footnote 50, add the following at the beginning of the footnote.]

See, e.g., Nanomantube v. Kickapoo Tribe, 631 F.3d 1150, 111 FEP 610 (10th Cir. 2011) (federal court lacked jurisdiction over tribal casino worker's discrimination claim against tribe, even though tribal

---

[5] *Id.* at 2446 (referring to legislative history of National Labor Relations Act, S. Rep. No. 105, 80th Cong., 1st Sess., at 4 (1947)).

[6] 133 S. Ct. at 2446.

[7] *Id.* at 2448 (quoting *Ellerth*, 524 U.S. at 762).

[8] 133 S. Ct. at 2443.

handbook included agreement to comply with Title VII; handbook does not trump statutory exemption).

3. Exemption of Elected Officials, Policymaking Appointees, and Their Advisors

[85]**[On page 22-21 of the Main Volume, in footnote 85, add the following after "*See, e.g.*,".]**

Opp v. Office of the State's Attorney of Cook Cnty., 630 F.3d 616, 619–20, 111 FEP 1 (7th Cir. 2010) (assistant state's attorneys excluded from ADEA protection as policymaking appointees, regardless whether their individual job duties include policy making, where policy making is inherent to position), *cert. denied*, 132 S. Ct. 92 (2011);

4. Aliens Employed Outside the United States

[93]**[On page 22-22 of the Main Volume, in footnote 93, add the following at the end of the footnote.]**

See also Rabé v. United Air Lines, Inc., 636 F.3d 866, 869, 111 FEP 1094 (7th Cir. 2011) (although foreign employee working outside United States generally is excluded from protection of Title VII and ADEA, issue is substantive and should be decided on merits rather than as question of subject matter jurisdiction; employment contract also had effect of applying substantive federal and state law).

II. PUBLIC SECTOR EMPLOYEES—SOVEREIGN IMMUNITY

A. Introduction

[127]**[On page 22-29 of the Main Volume, in footnote 127, add the following at the end of the footnote.]**

Cf. United States v. Alabama Dep't of Mental Health & Mental Retardation, 673 F.3d 1320, 1328, 192 LRRM 3242 (11th Cir. 2012) (Eleventh Amendment sovereign immunity does not bar action under Uniform Services Employment and Reemployment Rights Act (USERRA), 38 U.S.C. § 4301 et seq., because United States has clear and substantial interest in enforcing statute to achieve goal of encouraging service in armed forces).

B. Abrogation of Sovereign Immunity by Federal Statutes

2. *The Clear Statement Rule of Statutory Interpretation*

[146][On page 22-32 of the Main Volume, replace footnote 146 with the following.]

[146]473 U.S. 234, 38 FEP 96 (1985).

[On page 22-32 of the Main Volume, at the end of the first sentence of the first full paragraph, add new footnote 147a.]

[147a]*See* Lee-Thomas v. Prince George's Cnty. Pub. Schs., 666 F.3d 244, 251, 25 AD 1193 (4th Cir. 2012) (in assessing whether Eleventh Amendment immunity has been waived under particular statute, courts must apply "stringent test" enunciated by Supreme Court in *Atascadero*, and in absence of construction of relevant state statute by state's highest court, examine and decide state-law issue independently).

3. *The Validity of Federal Statutes Abrogating State Sovereign Immunity*

a. *Statutes Whose Validity the Supreme Court Has Resolved*

[164][On page 22-34 of the Main Volume, in footnote 164, add the following at the end of the footnote.]

See also Guttman v. Khalsa, 669 F.3d 1101, 1112, 25 AD 1316 (10th Cir. 2012) (Supreme Court has not arrived at concrete definition of congruence and proportionality, but it is clear that Congress enjoys greater power under § 5 of Fourteenth Amendment when it responds to clearly discernible pattern of state encroachment on fundamental or other important constitutional rights).

C. Governmental Entities Entitled to Sovereign Immunity

[218][On page 22-45 of the Main Volume, in footnote 218, add the following at the end of the footnote.]

See also Ross v. Jefferson Cnty. Dep't of Health, 701 F.3d 655, 659–60, 116 FEP 930 (county health department is state agency under Alabama law and therefore is entitled to sovereign immunity under

Eleventh Amendment from complaint of discrimination under ADA seeking monetary damages).

[On page 22-49 of the Main Volume, after the sentence that ends with footnote 239, add the following new paragraph.]

Tribally owned enterprises may also have sovereign immunity from Title VII, if organized under tribal (rather than state) law.[9]

D. Waivers of Sovereign Immunity

2. Waiver by Statute

[243]**[On page 22-51 of the Main Volume, in footnote 243, add the following at the end of the footnote.]**

But see Lee-Thomas v. Prince George's Cnty. Pub. Schs., 666 F.3d 244, 248, 253–55, 25 AD 1193 (4th Cir. 2012) (even where statute is not specific in waiving Eleventh Amendment immunity generally, federal court should defer to ruling of state's highest court interpreting statute to provide such waiver).

E. Limitations on Remedies Against Individuals

1. Introduction

[On page 22-56 of the Main Volume, at the end of the first full paragraph, add new footnote 275a.]

[275a]*See* B.A.B., Jr. v. Board of Educ. of the City of St. Louis, 698 F.3d 1037, 1042 (8th Cir. 2012) (where defendant Board of Education was entitled to sovereign immunity from § 1983 negligent supervision claim, that immunity applied with equal force to Board nurse who was sued only in her official capacity, because suit against nurse was equivalent to suit against Board).

---

[9]*See* Somerlott v. Cherokee Nation Distribs., Inc., 686 F.3d 1144, 1148–50, 115 FEP 1085 (10th Cir. 2012) ("Indian tribes are immune from suit absent congressional abrogation or clear waiver by the tribe," including commercial activities by tribe, though in this case Title VII applied to tribally owned casino that was organized under state, rather than tribal, law). *See generally* Chapter 8 (Native Americans).

3. Actions Against Individuals in Their Personal Capacities

[333][On page 22-67 of the Main Volume, in footnote 333, add the following after "*E.g.*,".]

Haybarger v. Lawrence Cnty. Adult Probation & Parole, 667 F.3d 408, 416, 18 WH Cases 2d 1467 (3d Cir. 2012) (FMLA permits individual supervisors at public agency to be sued in their personal capacity);

CHAPTER 23

UNIONS

I. A UNION'S LIABILITY FOR ITS OWN DISCRIMINATION

A. Liability of a Union in Its Role as an Employer

[4][On page 23-3 of the Main Volume, in footnote 4, add the following after "*see also*".]

Blue v. International Bhd. of Elec. Workers Local Union 159, 676 F.3d 579, 586, 114 FEP 1210 (7th Cir. 2012) (affirming denial of post-trial motions by union employer, which jury held had retaliated against administrative employee who participated in an equal employment opportunity (EEO) investigation arising out of charge filed by African-American electrician removed from union's referral list);

B. Liability of a Union in its Role as a Union

1. Discrimination With Respect to Membership

[On page 23-6 of the Main Volume, delete "trucking," from the second full paragraph.]

[On page 23-7 of the Main Volume, replace the first full paragraph with the following.]

Special rules apply to the discrimination claims of federal employees covered by collective bargaining agreements.[1]

5. Breach of the Duty of Fair Representation

a. Origins and Scope of the Duty

[73][On page 23-16 of the Main Volume, in footnote 73, add the following before "Arnold v. Mine Workers".]

Chapman v. United Auto Workers Local 1005, 670 F.3d 677, 685, 192 LRRM 3020 (6th Cir. 2012) (applying *Clayton* factors to affirm summary judgment in favor of union in DFR action based on union member's failure to exhaust internal union remedies);

---

[1]*See* Chapter 32, Section II.A.4.

b. Handling of Grievances

[82] **[On page 23-18 of the Main Volume, in footnote 82, in the citation to "Wesley v. General Drivers Warehousemen & Helpers Local 745," add the following before "(5th Cir. 2011)".]**

, 113 FEP 705

[92] **[On page 23-21 of the Main Volume, in footnote 92, add the following after "*See, e.g.,*".]**

Wesley v. General Drivers, Warehousemen & Helpers Local 745, 660 F.3d 211, 214–15, 113 FEP 705 (5th Cir. 2011) (modified *McDonnell Douglas* framework applied; summary judgment affirmed in favor of union where plaintiff failed to show adverse union action or that other union members were treated differently in grievance procedure);

d. Bargaining Obligations

[On page 23-27 in the Main Volume, after the sentence that ends with footnote 114, add the following new paragraph.]

Similarly, unions are accorded latitude in negotiating a settlement in the context of a bankruptcy claim distribution.[2]

II. JOINT UNION-EMPLOYER LIABILITY

A. Joint Liability for Discrimination Premised on the Provisions of a Collective Bargaining Agreement

[150] **[On page 23-36 of the Main Volume, in footnote 150, add the following after "*E.g.,*".]**

EEOC v. Minnesota Dep't of Corr., 648 F.3d 910, 913, 113 FEP 6 (8th Cir. 2011) (affirming summary judgment for EEOC under ADEA where employer and union negotiated early retirement

---

[2] *See* Bondurant v. Air Line Pilots Ass'n, Int'l, 679 F.3d 386, 394, 114 FEP 1645 (6th Cir. 2012) (summary judgment upheld in favor of union in DFR and Age Discrimination in Employment Act (ADEA) action where union negotiated cutoff date for distribution of bankruptcy claims in manner favoring pilots who retired under early retirement program over those who retired at mandatory retirement age prior to claim cutoff, where plaintiff failed to establish that union was motivated by discriminatory purpose).

incentive that required employees to retire by age 55 to receive employer contributions to health premiums);

IV. Union Challenges to Employer Actions Taken Pursuant to Conciliation Agreements and Court or Government Directives

B. Grievance Arbitration by Unions

[199]**[On page 23-45 of the Main Volume, in footnote 199, add the following at the end of the footnote.]**

Cf. Thompson v. Air Transport Int'l Ltd. Liability Co., 664 F.3d 723, 726–27, 192 LRRM 2454 (8th Cir. 2011) (where collective bargaining agreement mandates arbitration, there is clear waiver of judicial forum; Family and Medical Leave Act (FMLA) waiver of judicial forum held permissible).

[200]**[On page 23-45 of the Main Volume, in footnote 200, add the following at the end of the footnote.]**

Where the arbitration clause of a collective bargaining agreement does *not* clearly mandate the arbitration of statutory discrimination claims, however, there is neither waiver of the judicial forum nor claim preclusion. *See* Coleman v. Donahoe, 667 F.3d 835, 854, 114 FEP 160 (7th Cir. 2012) (rejecting argument that arbitration decision precluded court's consideration of pretext where arbitrator found just cause rather than pretext, and where union was not party to subsequent lawsuit; under *Alexander v. Gardner-Denver*, 415 U.S. 36, 7 FEP 81 (1974), arbitration decisions are without preclusive effect in Title VII actions, and no waiver of judicial forum occurs where collective bargaining agreement does not clearly and unmistakably require union members to arbitrate statutory discrimination claims).

CHAPTER 24

EMPLOYMENT AGENCIES

I. OVERVIEW

[4][On page 24-2 of the Main Volume, in footnote 4, add the following after "*See, e.g.*,".]

EEOC v. Kelly Servs., Inc., 598 F.3d 1022, 1030, 108 FEP 1409 (8th Cir. 2010) (discussing obligations of employment agencies under Title VII; Equal Employment Opportunity Commission (EEOC) failed to establish that agency discriminated on basis of religion when it did not refer Muslim woman who wore head scarf as part of practicing her religion to client printing company that had safety-related policy prohibiting employees from wearing any head covering around machinery in which it could become caught);

III. UNLAWFUL PRACTICES

E. EEOC Investigations of Alleged Unlawful Practices

[69][On page 24-16 of the Main Volume, in footnote 69, add the following at the end of the footnote.]

See also EEOC v. Randstad, 685 F.3d 433, 439, 450–52, 115 FEP 801 (4th Cir. 2012) (enforcing EEOC subpoena seeking information concerning literacy requirement that employment agency applied to those seeking placement as temporary employees, notwithstanding Randstad's claim that production would be both expensive and burdensome; both EEOC and Fourth Circuit characterized those seeking referrals through agency as "employees").

F. Agency Liability for Unlawful Practices of Clients

[72][On page 24-16 of the Main Volume, in footnote 72, add the following at the end of the footnote.]

Cf. Williamson v. Adventist Health Sys./Sunbelt. Inc., 372 F. App'x 936, 938–39, 108 FEP 1776 (11th Cir. 2010) (plaintiff, who was referred to temporary positions at defendant hospital by co-defendant medical staffing service, and who was removed from that assignment and no longer assigned to defendant hospital, did not show either direct evidence of discrimination by service that was responsible for his assignments or evidence of discriminatory conduct by hospital, which was displeased with his work and requested that he no longer be assigned to them).

G. Joint Employer–Employment Agency Liability

[85][On page 24-20 of the Main Volume, in footnote 85, add the following at the end of the footnote.]

See also Johnson v. Manpower Prof'l Servs., Inc., 442 F. App'x 977, 982, 113 FEP 809 (5th Cir. 2011) (unpublished) (applying hybrid test to determine that client company, rather than placement agency, was individual's employer responsible for denying him overtime work; even when "economic realities" factors suggest that Manpower was employer, "more important" right-to-control factors point to client company as employer and are dispositive).

Chapter 25

CHARGING PARTIES AND PLAINTIFFS

II. CHARGES FILED BY PERSONS WHO ARE MEMBERS OF THE PROTECTED GROUP IN QUESTION AND AFFECTED BY AN ADVERSE EMPLOYMENT DECISION OR PRACTICE

A. Is the Charging Party Personally Aggrieved?

[11][On page 25-4 of the Main Volume, in footnote 11, add the following after "*See*".]

McCollum v. California Dep't of Corr. & Rehab., 647 F.3d 870, 879–80 (9th Cir. 2011) ("to demonstrate third party standing, a plaintiff must show his own injury, a close relationship between himself and the parties whose rights he asserts, and the inability of the parties to assert their own rights"; volunteer prison chaplain of the Pagan-Revivalist religion known as "Wicca" lacked standing to state claim for religious discrimination on behalf of prison inmates based upon prison's refusal to designate chaplain position as paid position, where prisoners were able to file their own religious discrimination claims) (citations omitted);

[12][On page 25-4 of the Main Volume, in footnote 12, add the following at the end of the footnote.]

Cf. Wood v. City of San Diego, 678 F.3d 1075, 1082–84, 114 FEP 1552 (9th Cir. 2012) (although denying plaintiff's claim on other grounds, discussing whether retired single female employee had standing to challenge as disparate impact sex discrimination "surviving spouse" element of City's retirement plan, where plaintiff could not "predict the ultimate value of her pension or whether she and her hypothetical spouse would have received more money had she been married").

[15][On page 25-5 of the Main Volume, in footnote 15, add the following at the end of the footnote.]

Cf. Chapman v. Pier 1 Imports (U.S.) Inc., 631 F.3d 939, 946–47, 954, 24 AD 284 (9th Cir. 2011) (en banc) (customer alleging that physical barriers interfered with full access to store for individuals with disabilities lacked standing because he could not demonstrate "injury in fact" (i.e., that specific alleged physical barriers denied him "full and equal enjoyment" of premises)).

[21][On page 25-6 of the Main Volume, in footnote 21, add the following after "*See, e.g.*,".]

Breiner v. Nevada Dep't of Corr., 610 F.3d 1202, 1206, 109 FEP 1153 (9th Cir. 2010) (plaintiffs had standing to sue alleging sex discrimination in denial of promotion, despite never having applied for promotions, where they could show that they would have applied had it not been for alleged discriminatory practices of employer);

[25][On page 25-7 of the Main Volume, in the carryover of footnote 25, add the following before "*But see*".]

See also Chen v. Siemens Energy, Inc., 467 F. App'x 852, 853 (11th Cir. 2012) (per curiam) (plaintiff's bankruptcy trustee in Chapter 7 proceeding was only party with standing to prosecute plaintiff's Title VII claim).

[25][On page 25-7 of the Main Volume, in the carryover of footnote 25, add the following after "*But see*".]

Ponton v. AFSCME, AFL-CIO, 395 F. App'x 867, 872 n.1 (3d Cir. 2010) (plaintiff's Chapter 13 bankruptcy proceeding did not prevent adjudication of her Title VII claim because "Chapter 13 debtors have standing to bring claims in their own name on behalf of the bankruptcy estate") (quoting Smith v. Rockett, 522 F.3d 1080, 1081 (10th Cir. 2008));

B. Is the Charging Party Protected by Title VII?

2. Independent Contractors

[32][On page 25-8 of the Main Volume, in footnote 32, add the following new paragraph at the end of the footnote.]

Despite these limitations under Title VII, independent contractors may challenge under § 1981 discriminatory treatment occurring during the course of the contractual relationship. *See, e.g.*, Brown v. Kaz, Inc., 581 F.3d 175, 180–81, 107 FEP 229 (3d Cir. 2009) (sales trainee for company that exerted only minimum controls necessary "to maintain the quality of its product and services, and consistency in its business practices," was independent contractor rather than employee and, as such, did not have standing to pursue claim for discrimination under Title VII but could challenge under § 1981 allegedly discriminatory conduct "occurring within the scope of the independent contractor relationship"). *See generally* Chapter 36 (The Civil Rights Acts of 1866 and 1871).

[33][On page 25-8 of the Main Volume, in footnote 33, add the following after "*See, e.g.*,".]

Glascock v. Linn Cnty. Emergency Med., PC, 698 F.3d 695, 698, 116 FEP 628 (8th Cir. 2012) (Title VII does not protect independent contractors; where degree of control by hiring party was inconclusive, evidence that physician received no benefits, paid self-employment taxes and taxes for her professional licenses, and exercised independent control of method and timing of her work indicated that she was contractor rather than employee); Rabé v. United Air Lines, Inc., 636 F.3d 866, 868, 111 FEP 1094 (7th Cir. 2011) (where French flight attendant's employment contract provided that her employment would be governed "by applicable United States law," she could pursue claims of discrimination under Title VII or the ADEA even though she worked solely on flights outside of United States and otherwise would not be covered);

[36][On page 25-9 of the Main Volume, in footnote 36, add the following after "*see also*".]

Bryson v. Middlefield Volunteer Fire Dep't, Inc., 656 F.3d 348, 354, 113 FEP 97 (6th Cir. 2011) (although remuneration is factor in determining whether employment relationship exists, it is not independent antecedent requirement that plaintiff needs to establish in order to proceed);

[38][On page 25-10 of the Main Volume, in footnote 38, add the following at the end of the footnote.]

See also Glascock, 698 F.3d at 698–99 (court does not require that specific number of *Darden* factors favor independent contractor status but looks at relationship as whole).

4. Volunteers

[62][On page 25-17 of the Main Volume, in footnote 62, add the following after "*See, e.g.*,".]

Bryson v. Middlefield Volunteer Fire Dep't, Inc., 656 F.3d 348, 354, 113 FEP 97 (6th Cir. 2011) (remuneration is one significant but non-decisive factor in determining whether non-salaried fire department volunteers are proper party plaintiffs in discrimination suit); Waisgarber v. City of L.A., 406 F. App'x 150, 152 (9th Cir. 2010) (although salary is not only form of remuneration that may create employer–employee relationship, a non-salaried volunteer reserve police officer must receive "substantial benefits" in order to be considered employee eligible to bring discrimination suit);

6. Former Employees

[67][On page 25-18 of the Main Volume, in footnote 67, add the following after "*See*".]

Gerner v. County of Chesterfield, 674 F.3d 264, 268–69, 114 FEP 976 (4th Cir. 2012) (former county department head may pursue Title VII claim alleging gender discrimination in county's severance pay policies);

D. Other Politically Related Exemptions

[75][On page 25-19 of the Main Volume, in footnote 75, add the following at the end of the footnote.]

See Opp v. Office of State's Attorney of Cook Cnty., 630 F.3d 616, 621, 111 FEP 1 (7th Cir. 2010) (assistant state's attorneys are appointees on policy-making level and are, therefore, exempt from coverage under ADEA, 29 U.S.C. § 630(f)).

IV. CHARGES FILED BY PERSONS WHO ARE NOT MEMBERS OF THE PROTECTED GROUP BUT STILL CLAIM TO BE AGGRIEVED

[86][On page 25-23 of the Main Volume, in footnote 86, add the following after "*See*".]

Hernandez v. Yellow Transp., Inc., 641 F.3d 118, 128–29, 112 FEP 417 (5th Cir. 2011) (Caucasian male plaintiff's relationship with

African-American and Hispanic co-workers not sufficiently "personal" to sustain claim for harassment directed against co-workers; plaintiff failed to show that any harassment directed against him was because of his relationship with minority co-workers);

V. CHARGES "ON BEHALF OF" AN AGGRIEVED PERSON

[98]**[On page 25-26 of the Main Volume, in footnote 98, add the following at the end of the footnote.]**

But see Chin v. Port Auth. of N.J. & N.Y., 685 F.3d 135, 142–43, 115 FEP 720 (2d Cir. 2012) (right-to-sue letter was issued to Asian Jade Society on behalf of aggrieved individuals whom it represented).

[108]**[On page 25-28 of the Main Volume, in footnote 108, add the following at the end of the footnote.]**

Cf. Department of Fair Emp't & Hous. v. Lucent Techs., Inc., 642 F.3d 728, 737, 24 AD 915 (9th Cir. 2011) (mere presence of State as party in action on behalf of individual employee with disability will not defeat diversity jurisdiction of federal court where State has no real interest in controversy).

Chapter 26

EEOC ADMINISTRATIVE PROCESS[1]

[1]This chapter references extensively the EEOC Compliance Manual, which is available online at http://www.eeoc.gov/eeoc/foia/hb-3.cfm (last visited Nov. 21, 2013) and on Bloomberg BNA's Labor Resource Center. The present edition of the Manual is divided by Volume and Section number, but not by page number, so those numbers have been deleted in this Supplement.

I. STRUCTURE AND STATUTES ENFORCED

A. Structure of the EEOC

[On page 26-3 of the Main Volume, in the sentence that ends with footnote 5, replace "and authorize the filing of suits." with the following.]

and authorize the filing of some litigation.

[5][On page 26-3 of the Main Volume, replace footnote 5 with the following.]

[5]FY 2012 Performance and Accountability Report, *available at* http://www.eeoc.gov/eeoc/plan/2012par.cfm (last visited Nov. 20, 2013).

B. Statutes Enforced

2. *ADEA and EPA*

[20][On page 26-5 of the Main Volume, replace footnote 20 with the following.]

[20]EEOC COMPL. MAN. (BNA) § 633:1, *available at* http://www.eeoc.gov/policy/docs/compensation.html#A.%20Expeditious%20Investigation%20Required (last visited Nov. 20, 2013).

II. GENERAL ADMINISTRATIVE POWERS

A. Rulemaking Powers

1. *Regulations*

[On page 26-7 of the Main Volume, add a comma before the callout for footnote 31.]

[On page 26-7 of the Main Volume, after the callout for footnote 31, add the following.]

GINA,[2]

B. EEOC Posting Requirements

[On page 26-10 of the Main Volume, in the last sentence of the first full paragraph, after "GINA," add new footnote 49a.]

[49a]29 C.F.R. § 1635.10(c).

---

[2]42 U.S.C. § 2000ff-10 (requiring EEOC to issue regulations implementing Title II of GINA).

C. Records and Reports

3. Records to Be Made or Kept

[On page 26-13 of the Main Volume, in the last sentence of the first paragraph, add the following after "ADEA".]

, GINA,

III. The EEOC Enforcement Process

[85]**[On page 26-16 of the Main Volume, in footnote 85, in the first sentence, replace "four" with "five".]**

[85]**[On page 26-16 of the Main Volume, in footnote 85, replace ", at 60:0001 (same)." with the following.]**

(same); *see also* 42 U.S.C. §§ 12117(a), 2000ff-6(a)(1) (incorporating into ADA and GINA, respectively, powers, procedures, and remedies set forth in Title VII; throughout balance of this chapter, references to EEOC's powers, procedures, and remedies under Title VII should be read to apply as well to ADA and GINA).

A. Evolution of the Current System

[92]**[On page 26-17 of the Main Volume, in footnote 92, delete ", at 2:0006".]**

B. What Is a Charge?

[On page 26-17 of the Main Volume, in the first sentence of the carryover paragraph, add the following after "Title VII".]

, GINA,

[96]**[On page 26-18 of the Main Volume, in footnote 96, delete ", at 1:0001-02" and ", at 2:0001" .]**

[101]**[On page 26-19 of the Main Volume, in the carryover of footnote 101, add the following after "*see also*".]**

Williams v. CSX Transp. Co., 643 F.3d 502, 509–10, 112 FEP 961 (6th Cir. 2011) ("Charge Information Form" constituted charge for purpose of exhausting administrative remedies, because it was in writing and could be read as request for EEOC to act);

[103]**[On page 26-19 of the Main Volume, in footnote 103, add the following after "*see also*".]**

Williams, 643 F.3d at 509 (error to hold that unverified "Charge Information Form" did not constitute charge for purpose of exhausting administrative remedies, where subsequent filing of EEOC charge "amended—and verified" first filing; although Charge Information Form did not indicate that it must be signed under penalty of perjury, it otherwise satisfied requirements of valid charge);

[105]**[On page 26-20 of the Main Volume, in footnote 105, add the following at the beginning of the footnote.]**

Williams, 643 F.3d at 509 (district court erred in concluding that unverified "Charge Information Form" did not constitute charge for purpose of exhausting administrative remedies, where subsequent filing of EEOC charge "amended—and verified" first filing);

C. Place for Filing Charge and Venue

[110]**[On page 26-21 of the Main Volume, in footnote 110, add the following at the beginning of the footnote.]**

Where an employer (or other respondent) does not have a facility within the jurisdiction of the EEOC District Office where the charge is filed, that office will forward the charge to the appropriate District Office for filing and processing. *See*

[110]**[On page 26-21 of the Main Volume, in footnote 110, at the end of the first sentence, delete ", at 2:0006".]**

D. The Intake and Initial Investigation of a Charge

[111]**[On page 26-21 of the Main Volume, in footnote 111, replace the first sentence with the following.]**

EEOC COMPL. MAN. (BNA) § 200:151.

[111]**[On page 26-21 of the Main Volume, in footnote 111, replace the citation after "*Compare*" with the following.]**

Questions and Answers: Issuance of Revision to EEOC Compliance Manual Section on Threshold Issues, EEOC COMPL. MAN. (BNA) § 605:1,

[On page 26-22 of the Main Volume, replace the block quotation with the following.]

> Central to the new approach is a charge prioritization system, the subject of this memorandum, which provides for the classification of charges into three categories: Category A (charges that fall within the national or local enforcement plans as well as other charges in which it also appears "more likely than not" that discrimination has occurred); Category B (charges where further evidence is required to determine whether it is more likely than not that a violation has occurred); and, Category C (charges subject to immediate dismissal). Category A cases will receive priority treatment; Category B cases will be investigated as resources permit; and, Category C cases will be dismissed.

[112]**[On page 26-22 of the Main Volume, replace footnote 112 with the following.]**

[112]PCHP, EEOC COMPL. MAN. (BNA) § 200:152(II)(a). The PCHP was modified when the EEOC adopted its Five-Year Strategic Plan in December 2012. The Plan identified the Commission's enforcement priorities for the period 2012–2016 and provided that Category A priority was to be given to charges raising those priority issues. *See* EEOC COMPL. MAN. (BNA) § 200:422.

[118]**[On page 26-23 of the Main Volume, replace footnote 118 with the following.]**

[118]National Enforcement Plan (Feb. 8, 1996), EEOC COMPL. MAN. (BNA) § 200:221. The National Enforcement Plan was replaced by the Commission as part of its Five-Year Strategic Plan in December 2012. EEOC COMPL. MAN. (BNA) § 200:417.

[On page 26-23 of the Main Volume, after the sentence that ends with footnote 119, add the following.]

The priorities are discussed in the EEOC's Five-Year Strategic Plan, adopted by the Commission on December 17, 2012.[3]

[121]**[On page 26-23 of the Main Volume, in footnote 121, delete ", at 2:0001–09".]**

E. Deferral and Contracts With State and Local Agencies

[On page 26-23 of the Main Volume, in the first sentence of the first paragraph, add the following after "—the ADA".]

and GINA

[133]**[On page 26-25 of the Main Volume, in footnote 133, delete ", at 5:0001–08".]**

[136]**[On page 26-26 of the Main Volume, in footnote 136, delete ", at 5:0004–05".]**

F. Service of Notice of the Charge on the Respondent

[139]**[On page 26-27 of the Main Volume, in footnote 139, after "EEOC Form 5.", replace the citation to the EEOC Compliance Manual with the following.]**

EEOC COMPL. MAN. (BNA) § 6.

[141]**[On page 26-27 of the Main Volume, replace footnote 141 with the following.]**

[141]EEOC COMPL. MAN. (BNA) § 6.

---

[3]The Five-Year Strategic Plan is available online at http://www.eeoc.gov/eeoc/plan/strategic_plan_12to16.cfm (last visited Oct. 6, 2013) and at EEOC COMPL. MAN. (BNA) § 200:417.

G. Administrative Closures

1. Withdrawal

[147][On page 26-29 of the Main Volume, in footnote 147, replace the citation before "*see also*" with the following.]

EEOC COMPL. MAN. (BNA) §§ 7.1(a), 7.3(a), 7.5(b);

[148][On page 26-29 of the Main Volume, in footnote 148, delete ", at 7:0001".]

3. Other Administrative Closures

[153][On page 26-30 of the Main Volume, in footnote 153, delete ", at 4:0001–02".]

I. Settlement—Pre-Determination Settlements, Negotiated Settlements, and Settlement of Commissioner Charges

[On page 26-31 of the Main Volume, in the sentence that ends with footnote 167, add the following after "The Commission's Title VII".]

, GINA,

[167][On page 26-31 of the Main Volume, in footnote 167, replace "(2011)" with the following.]

(2012)

[168][On page 26-32 of the Main Volume, in footnote 168, delete ", at 15:0001–02".]

[172][On page 26-32 of the Main Volume, in footnote 172, delete ", at 2:0005".]

[173][On page 26-32 of the Main Volume, replace footnote 173 with the following.]

[173]*Flexible Investigation Procedures*, EEOC COMPL. MAN. (BNA) §§ 14.5 & 14.8.

[175]**[On page 26-32 of the Main Volume, in footnote 175, delete ", at 15:0002".]**

[176]**[On page 26-33 of the Main Volume, in footnote 176, replace the first sentence with the following.]**

Negotiated Settlement, EEOC COMPL. MAN. (BNA) § 15.8(b).

[177]**[On page 26-33 of the Main Volume, in footnote 177, delete ", at 15:0004–05".]**

[178]**[On page 26-33 of the Main Volume, replace footnote 178 with the following.]**

[178]EEOC COMPL. MAN. (BNA) § 80.13-14.

[180]**[On page 26-34 of the Main Volume, in footnote 180, delete ", at 80:0003".]**

[185]**[On page 26-34 of the Main Volume, in footnote 185, delete ", at 15:0001".]**

J. Investigations and Determinations

1. The Assignment Process and the Respondent's Position Statement

[188]**[On page 26-35 of the Main Volume, in footnote 188, replace the first sentence with the following.]**

Respondent Notification Procedures, EEOC COMPL. MAN. (BNA) § 3.4(b)(2) & exh. 3-A.

[189]**[On page 26-35 of the Main Volume, replace footnote 189 with the following.]**

[189]EEOC COMPL. MAN. (BNA) § 3.4(b)(2) & exh. 3-A.

[190]**[On page 26-35 of the Main Volume, in footnote 190, replace the sentence after "*See*" with the following.]**

Investigation Procedures, EEOC COMPL. MAN. (BNA) § 22.2; *see also Respondent Notification Procedures*, EEOC COMPL. MAN. (BNA) § 3.4(b)(2).

2. *Requests for Information (RFIs) and On-Site Reviews*

[191]**[On page 26-36 of the Main Volume, in footnote 191, replace the second sentence with the following.]**

Respondent Notification Procedures, EEOC COMPL. MAN. (BNA) § 3.4(b)(2); *Flexible Investigation Procedures*, *id.* § 14(3)(b); *Investigation Procedures*, *id.* § 22.3; *Selection and Analysis of Evidence*, *id.* § 26.3.

[192]**[On page 26-36 of the Main Volume, replace footnote 192 with the following.]**

[192]*Flexible Investigation Procedures*, EEOC COMPL. MAN. (BNA) § 14(3)(b); *Investigation Procedures*, *id.* § 22.2(b).

[193]**[On page 26-36 of the Main Volume, replace footnote 193 with the following.]**

[193]*Respondent Notification Procedures*, EEOC COMPL. MAN. (BNA) § 3.4(b)(2); *Flexible Investigation Procedures*, *id.* § 14(3); *Investigation Procedures*, *id.* § 22.3; *Selection and Analysis of Evidence*, *id.* § 26.3.

[197]**[On page 26-36 of the Main Volume, replace footnote 197 with the following.]**

[197]*Dismissals*, EEOC COMPL. MAN. (BNA) § 4.4(e).

3. *Fact-Finding Conference*

[On page 26-37 of the Main Volume, in the first paragraph, in item (4), add the following after "in ADA".]

or GINA

[199]**[On page 26-37 of the Main Volume, in footnote 199, delete ", at 14:0004–05".]**

[200]**[On page 26-37 of the Main Volume, in footnote 200, delete ", at 14:0004".]**

[201]**[On page 26-37 of the Main Volume, in footnote 201, delete ", at 14:0004".]**

[202]**[On page 26-37 of the Main Volume, in footnote 202, delete ", at 14:0005".]**

[203]**[On page 26-37 of the Main Volume, in footnote 203, delete ", at 14:0006".]**

4. Adverse Inference Rule

[204]**[On page 26-38 of the Main Volume, in footnote 204, in the first sentence, delete ", at 26.0001".]**

[205]**[On page 26-38 of the Main Volume, replace footnote 205 with the following.]**

[205]*Selection and Analysis of Evidence*, EEOC COMPL. MAN. (BNA) § 26:1.

5. Scope of the Investigation

[206]**[On page 26-38 of the Main Volume, in footnote 206, replace the last sentence with the following.]**

Flexible Investigative Procedures, EEOC COMPL. MAN. (BNA) § 14.3; *Investigation Procedures*, *id.* § 22.2.

[207]**[On page 26-38 of the Main Volume, in footnote 207, delete ", at 2:0009".]**

[208]**[On page 26-38 of the Main Volume, replace footnote 208 with the following.]**

[208]*Investigation Procedures*, EEOC COMPL. MAN. (BNA) § 22:1.

[209]**[On page 26-38 of the Main Volume, in footnote 209, in the first sentence, delete ", at 22:0001".]**

[210]**[On page 26-38 of the Main Volume, in footnote 210, replace the first sentence with the following.]**

On Site Investigation, EEOC COMPL. MAN. (BNA) § 5:2.

6. Determination Interview and the Investigative Memorandum

[211]**[On page 26-39 of the Main Volume, in footnote 211, replace the first sentence with the following.]**

Investigation Procedures, EEOC COMPL. MAN. (BNA) § 22:6.

[212]**[On page 26-39 of the Main Volume, replace footnote 212 with the following.]**

[212]*Pre-determination Interviews*, EEOC COMPL. MAN. (BNA) § 27:1; *Issuance of a Commissioner Charge Decision*, *id.* § 34.3; *Issuance of Cause Determinations*, *id.* § 40.3.

[213]**[On page 26-39 of the Main Volume, replace footnote 213 with the following.]**

[213]*Pre-determination Interviews*, EEOC COMPL. MAN. (BNA) §§ 27.2, 27.4.

[214]**[On page 26-39 of the Main Volume, replace footnote 214 with the following.]**

[214]*Id.* §§ 22.16, 22.17, 29.2.

[215]**[On page 26-39 of the Main Volume, replace footnote 215 with the following.]**

[215]EEOC COMPL. MAN. (BNA) § 28.

7. EEOC Letters of Determination and EEOC Decisions

[216]**[On page 26-40 of the Main Volume, in footnote 216, replace the last sentence with the following.]**

PCHP II-F, EEOC COMPL. MAN. (BNA) § 200:155.

[On page 26-40 of the Main Volume, in the second sentence of the second full paragraph, add the following after "Title VII".]

, GINA,

[217]**[On page 26-40 of the Main Volume, replace footnote 217 with the following.]**

[217]*Dismissals*, EEOC COMPL. MAN. (BNA) § 4:5 (a) & exh. 4-F.

[218]**[On page 26-40 of the Main Volume, in footnote 218, replace the first sentence with the following.]**

EEOC COMPL. MAN. (BNA) § 12.

[219]**[On page 26-40 of the Main Volume, in footnote 219, replace the first sentence with the following.]**

Issuance of Cause Determinations, EEOC COMPL. MAN. (BNA) § 40:1.

[220]**[On page 26-41 of the Main Volume, in footnote 220, replace the second sentence with the following.]**

Issuance of Cause Determinations, EEOC COMPL. MAN. (BNA) § 40:1.

[221]**[On page 26-41 of the Main Volume, in footnote 221, delete ", at 40:0002".]**

[222]**[On page 26-41 of the Main Volume, in footnote 222, in the first sentence, delete ", at 40:0001".]**

[222]**[On page 26-41 of the Main Volume, in footnote 222, at the end of the footnote, delete ", at 40:0001".]**

8. Reconsideration

[227]**[On page 26-42 of the Main Volume, replace footnote 227 with the following.]**

[227]PCHP II-F(3), EEOC COMPL. MAN. (BNA) at § 200:154.

K. The Conciliation Process

[230]**[On page 26-42 of the Main Volume, in footnote 230, replace the last sentence with the following.]**

Negotiated Settlement, EEOC COMPL. MAN. (BNA) § 15:3; *Conciliation Agreements and Provisions for Filing Lawsuits*, *id.* § 60:3.

[232]**[On page 26-43 of the Main Volume, replace footnote 232 with the following.]**

[232]*The Conciliation Conference*, EEOC COMPL. MAN. (BNA) §§ 62-64.

[233]**[On page 26-43 of the Main Volume, in footnote 233, in the first sentence, replace "*See id.* at O:3505;" with the following.]**

See EEOC COMPL. MAN. § 64 (discussing conciliation process);

[233]**[On page 26-43 of the Main Volume, in footnote 233, add the following at the end of the footnote.]**

See also EEOC v. CRST Van Expedited, Inc., 679 F.3d 657, 671–77, 114 FEP 1566 (8th Cir. 2012) (EEOC's claims as to 67 women properly dismissed for failure to investigate and conciliate, where EEOC did not attempt to ascertain size of class until after filing lawsuit and refused to identify individuals for whom it was seeking remedies; EEOC may not use discovery "as a fishing expedition to uncover more violations," and its conduct "demonstrate[d] that it did not reasonably investigate the class allegations of sexual harassment" during its pre-suit investigation of charge); EEOC v. Service Temps Inc., 679 F.3d 323, 331 n.11, 26 AD 129 (5th Cir. 2012) (emphasizing that, as it relates to EEOC's obligation to conciliate in good faith, "as a matter of best practice, the EEOC should be conscientious about sharing settlement offers with those it represents").

[237]**[On page 26-44 of the Main Volume, in footnote 237, replace the first citation with the following.]**

Conciliation Agreements Without Charging Party Approval and Signature, EEOC COMPL. MAN. (BNA) § 63:1.

[239]**[On page 26-44 of the Main Volume, replace footnote 239 with the following.]**

[239]*The Conciliation Agreement*, EEOC COMPL. MAN. (BNA) §§ 65.2(c)(1), (5) & (6), 65.6.

[240]**[On page 26-44 of the Main Volume, in footnote 240, replace the citation after "*see*" with the following.]**

Conciliation Failures, Litigation Review and Notice of Private Suit Rights, EEOC COMPL. MAN. (BNA) § 66.2.

[240]**[On page 26-44 of the Main Volume, in footnote 240, replace the citation at the end of the footnote with the following.]**

Id. § 66.2(b).

[241]**[On page 26-44 of the Main Volume, in footnote 241, replace the first citation with the following.]**

Id. § 66:1.

[241]**[On page 26-44 of the Main Volume, in footnote 241, replace the citation to the "EEOC Regional Attorneys' Manual" with the following.]**

Initiating Litigation, EEOC Regional Attorneys' Manual *Part 2, Section III, Delegated Litigation Authority*, EEOC COMPL. MAN. (BNA) § 8000:429.

[242]**[On page 26-45 of the Main Volume, in footnote 242, replace the last citation with the following.]**

Title VII/ADA Administrative Relief, EEOC COMPL. MAN. (BNA) § 66.6.

L. Issuance of Notice of Right to Sue under Title VII, the ADA, and GINA [Revised Heading]

[248]**[On page 26-46 of the Main Volume, in footnote 248, replace the citation to the "EEOC COMPL. MAN." with the following.]**

Dismissals, EEOC COMPL. MAN. (BNA) § 4:1;

[249]**[On page 26-46 of the Main Volume, in footnote 249, replace the citation after "*see also*" with the following.]**

Notice of Right to Sue (Issued on Request), EEOC COMPL. MAN. (BNA) § 6:1.

[On page 26-46 of the Main Volume, in the sentence that ends with footnote 253, add the following after "A Title VII, ADA,".]

GINA,

[259]**[On page 26-47 of the Main Volume, replace footnote 259 with the following.]**

[259]*Representation of Parties by Attorneys*, EEOC COMPL. MAN. (BNA) § 82:2.

[261]**[On page 26-47 of the Main Volume, in footnote 261, delete ", at 82.0001".]**

[271]**[On page 26-49 of the Main Volume, in footnote 271, replace the language after the citation to the regulations with the following.]**

Assistance to Complaining Parties in Obtaining Attorneys, EEOC COMPL. MAN. (BNA) § 81.

[272]**[On page 26-49 of the Main Volume, replace footnote 272 with the following.]**

[272]*Assistance to Complaining Parties in Obtaining Attorneys*, EEOC COMPL. MAN. (BNA) § 81.1.

[273]**[On page 26-49 of the Main Volume, replace footnote 273 with the following.]**

[273]*Id.* § 81.2.

N. The Systemic Program

[On page 26-50 of the Main Volume, after the sentence that ends with footnote 276, add the following .]

Although there is no mention of systemic or pattern-or-practice charges in GINA, the EEOC powers, remedies, and procedures set out in Title VII are incorporated by reference into that statute.[4]

O. Interagency Cooperation

[283]**[On page 26-51 of the Main Volume, in footnote 283, delete "; *see*" and replace the citation that follows with the following.]**

. The Memorandum of Understating was last revised on November 16, 2011, and is printed at 76 Fed. Reg. 71,029.

[286]**[On page 26-52 of the Main Volume, in footnote 286, add the following at the end of the footnote.]**

The Memorandum of Understating was last revised on November 16, 2011, and is printed at 76 Fed. Reg. 71,029.

[287]**[On page 26-52 of the Main Volume, in footnote 287, add the following at the end of the footnote.]**

The Memorandum of Understating was last revised on November 16, 2011, and is printed at 76 Fed. Reg. 71,029.

---

[4]42 U.S.C. § 2000ff-6.

[291]**[On page 26-52 of the Main Volume, in footnote 291, replace the last citation with the following.]**

Processing Complaints Transferred or Referred From Federal Fund Granting Agencies, EEOC COMPL. MAN. (BNA) § 90.

[295]**[On page 26-53 of the Main Volume, in footnote 295, replace "*reprinted in*" and the citation that follows with the following.]**

reprinted, in pertinent part, at *Administering the FCC/EEOC Memorandum of Understanding (MOU)*, EEOC COMPL. MAN. (BNA) exh. 91-A.

[296]**[On page 26-53 of the Main Volume, replace footnote 296 with the following.]**

[296]*Administering the FCC/EEOC Memorandum of Understanding (MOU)*, EEOC COMPL. MAN. (BNA) § 91:1.

[297]**[On page 26-53 of the Main Volume, in footnote 297, replace "*reprinted in*" and the citation that follows with the following.]**

reprinted, in pertinent part, at *Administering the EEOC/OSC Memorandum of Understanding (MOU)*, EEOC COMPL. MAN. (BNA) exh. 94-A.

[299]**[On page 26-53 of the Main Volume, in footnote 299, delete ", *reprinted in* 1 EEOC COMPL. MAN. (BNA) 94:0002".]**

IV. EEOC INVESTIGATION AND SUBPOENA POWERS

A. Statutory Authority[5]

1. Title VII, the ADA, and GINA [Revised Heading]

[On page 26-54 of the Main Volume, in the first sentence, add the following after "ADA".]

and by § 2000ff-6(a)(1) of GINA

---

[5]Both the ADA and GINA incorporate by reference the "powers, procedures, and remedies provided in sections 705, 706, 707, 709, 710, and 711 of the Civil Rights Act of 1964." *See* 42 U.S.C. §§ 12117(a), 2000ff-6(a)(1). References to EEOC's procedures and authority throughout this Section therefore apply as well to its procedures and authority under the ADA and GINA.

[304]**[On page 26-55 of the Main Volume, in the carryover of footnote 304, replace the citation after "*See generally*" with the following.]**

Subpoenas, EEOC COMPL. MAN. (BNA) § 24.

[314]**[On page 26-56 of the Main Volume, in footnote 314, replace the last citation with the following.]**

Subpoenas, EEOC COMPL. MAN. (BNA) § 24.5(b).

B. The "Valid Charge" Requirement Under Title VII, the ADA, and GINA [Revised Heading]

[319]**[On page 26-57 of the Main Volume, in footnote 319, add the following at the end of the footnote.]**

Cf. Williams v. CSX Transp. Co., 643 F.3d 502, 509, 112 FEP 961 (6th Cir. 2011) (district court erred in concluding that unverified "Charge Information Form" did not constitute charge for purpose of exhausting administrative remedies, where subsequent filing of EEOC charge "amended—and verified" first filing, Charge Information Form did not indicate that it must be signed under penalty of perjury, and it otherwise satisfied requirements of valid charge).

[322]**[On page 26-57 of the Main Volume, in footnote 322, replace the citation for "Federal Express Corp. v. Holowecki" with the following.]**

552 U.S. 389, 402, 102 FEP 1153 (2008); *see also Williams*, 643 F.3d at 510 (applying *Holowecki* to charge under Title VII).

[330]**[On page 26-59 of the Main Volume, in footnote 330, add the following after "*see also*".]**

EEOC v. Schwan's Home Serv., 644 F.3d 742, 747, 112 FEP 1227 (8th Cir. 2011) ("charge is valid regardless of the strength of its evidentiary foundation");

[332]**[On page 26-60 of the Main Volume, in footnote 332, add the following after "*See*".]**

Schwan's Home Serv., 644 F.3d at 746–47 (employer asserted that portion of amended charge alleging gender discrimination was invalid because alleged discrimination occurred more than 300 days before filing of amended charge; "the appropriate time to address the timeliness issue is if and when an actual lawsuit is filed, not during the subpoena enforcement stage");

C. Permissible Scope of Inquiry

[337][On page 26-61 of the Main Volume, in footnote 337, add the following after "*E.g.*,".]

EEOC v. Washington Suburban Sanitary Comm'n, 631 F.3d 174, 180, 111 FEP 481 (4th Cir. 2011) (in ADEA context, EEOC's investigatory powers, which include its authority to subpoena information, "do not turn on the particulars of a complainant's charge");

[340][On page 26-62 of the Main Volume, in footnote 340, add the following after "*See*".]

EEOC v. Konica Minolta Bus. Solutions U.S.A., Inc., 639 F.3d 366, 369, 112 FEP 97 (7th Cir. 2011) ("standard of relevance is broader than the standard embodied in the Federal Rule of Evidence 401"); EEOC v. Kronos, Inc., 620 F.3d 287, 296, 110 FEP 392 (3d Cir. 2010) (*Kronos I*) ("Courts have given broad construction to the term 'relevant' and have traditionally allowed the EEOC access to any material that 'might cast light on the allegations against the employer.'") (quoting EEOC v. Shell Oil Co., 466 U.S. 54, 68–69 (1984));

[341][On page 26-62 of the Main Volume, in footnote 341, add the following at the end of the footnote.]

See also EEOC v. Burlington N. Santa Fe R.R., 669 F.3d 1154, 1157, 25 AD 1572 (10th Cir. 2012) (although relevance requirement is "'not especially constraining,'" it should not be construed "'so broadly as to 'render[] that requirement a nullity'") (quoting *Shell Oil Co.*, 466 U.S. at 68–69); *Konica Minolta Bus. Solutions U.S.A., Inc.*, 639 F.3d at 369 ("generous standard of relevance" similar to discovery standard under FED. R. CIV. P. 26); *Kronos I*, 620 F.3d at 296 ("The relevance requirement is not particularly onerous.");

[342][On page 26-63 of the Main Volume, in footnote 342, add the following after "*But see*".]

EEOC v. Kronos, Inc., 694 F.3d 351, 364–65, 26 AD 1409 (3d Cir. 2012) (*Kronos II*) (where EEOC was investigating whether certain pre-employment tests disproportionately excluded individuals with disabilities, enforcing subpoena sought all validity studies documents regarding tests, not merely those related to impact of tests on those with disabilities; such documents were relevant to whether tests were "job related" and "consistent with business necessity"; moreover, "[i]f the documents produced by Kronos in response to the subpoena reveal that there was a racially related impact on hiring, then, as we noted in Kronos I, the EEOC need not ignore this new evidence," but could file Commissioner's charge raising that issue);

[346][On page 26-64 of the Main Volume, in footnote 346, add the following after "*See, e.g.,*".]

EEOC v. Kronos, Inc., 620 F.3d 287, 298, 110 FEP 392 (3d Cir. 2010) (*Kronos I*) (district court abused its discretion by limiting EEOC subpoena seeking information related to pre-employment use by employer of test that allegedly had disparate impact on disabled applicants to data pertaining to positions sought by charging party, where employer purportedly used assessment test in hiring for every retail position, and "[s]uch data, at the very least, provides comparative information on the Assessment");

[347][On page 26-64 of the Main Volume, in footnote 347, add the following after "*See*".]

EEOC v. Konica Minolta Bus. Solutions U.S.A., Inc., 639 F.3d 366, 369–70, 112 FEP 97 (7th Cir. 2011) (enforcing subpoena seeking records relating to hiring practices at four facilities even though charging party was alleging discrimination in discipline and terms and conditions of employment; "Commission is entitled generally to investigate employers within its jurisdiction to see if there is a prohibited pattern or practice of discrimination," and records would "cast light" on allegation that minority party was subjected to different terms and conditions of employment); *Kronos I*, 620 F.3d at 298–99 (district court erred in limiting EEOC subpoena related to customer service assessment test used by employer to facility at which individual alleging disability discrimination applied, where employer used assessment in hiring nationwide; "employer's nationwide use of a practice under investigation supports a subpoena for nationwide data on that practice");

[348]**[On page 26-64 of the Main Volume, in footnote 348, add the following after "*See*".]**

EEOC v. Kronos, Inc., 694 F.3d 351, 364, 26 AD 1409 (3d Cir. 2012) (*Kronos II*) (enforcing EEOC subpoena seeking information from third-party vendor that created customer service assessment test utilized by defendant employer); *Kronos I*, 620 F.3d at 292 (same);

[349]**[On page 26-64 of the Main Volume, in footnote 349, add the following after "*E.g.*,".]**

EEOC v. Burlington N. Santa Fe R.R., 669 F.3d 1154, 1158, 25 AD 1572 (10th Cir. 2012) (declining to enforce EEOC subpoena demanding nationwide recordkeeping data, where two charges of individual disability discrimination were filed by two men who applied for same type of job in same state; EEOC was not entitled to "plenary discovery where the information sought is not 'relevant to [a] charge under investigation'") (quoting 42 U.S.C. § 2000e–8(a));

[349]**[On page 26-64 of the Main Volume, in footnote 349, add the following at the end of the footnote.]**

But see Kronos II, 694 F.3d at 364 (subpoena enforced against third-party test developer; where EEOC was investigating whether pre-employment test disproportionately excluded individuals with disabilities, validity studies measuring racial impact of test were relevant to whether it was "job related" and "consistent with business necessity").

[358]**[On page 26-66 of the Main Volume, in footnote 358, add the following after "*see also*".]**

EEOC v. Burlington N. Santa Fe R.R., 669 F.3d 1154, 1156–57, 25 AD 1572 (10th Cir. 2012) (declining to enforce EEOC subpoena demanding nationwide recordkeeping data, where two charges of individual disability discrimination were filed by two men who applied for same type of job in same state; EEOC was not entitled to "plenary discovery that was not 'relevant to [a] charge under investigation'") (quoting 42 U.S.C. § 2000e–8(a));

[358]**[On page 26-66 of the Main Volume, in footnote 358, add the following at the end of the footnote.]**

But see EEOC v. Kronos, Inc., 694 F.3d 351, 364, 26 AD 1409 (3d Cir. 2012) (*Kronos II*) (where EEOC was investigating charge that pre-employment test disproportionately excluded individuals with disabilities, validity studies measuring racial impact of test were relevant to whether it was "job related" and "consistent with business necessity"; if those studies also indicated disparate racial impact, EEOC may then expand its investigation to issue of race discrimination).

[359][On page 26-66 of the Main Volume, in footnote 359, add the following after "*See*".]

EEOC v. Washington Suburban Sanitary Comm'n, 631 F.3d 174, 180, 182, 111 FEP 481 (4th Cir. 2011) (after being modified to avoid infringing on privilege, EEOC subpoena for records on restructuring of WSSC department enforced despite assertion that disclosure would encroach on legislative immunity and legislative privilege, where EEOC was investigating claim that restructuring was motivated by age discrimination; EEOC's proceedings were at "very preliminary stage," and it would be premature to refuse to enforce subpoena simply "because a legitimate claim of privilege might ripen at some point down the road"); EEOC v. Kronos, Inc., 620 F.3d 287, 302, 110 FEP 392 (3d Cir. 2010) (*Kronos I*) (party seeking confidentiality order has burden of demonstrating with specificity that "disclosure will work a clearly defined and serious injury to the moving party");

V. ACCESS TO EEOC FILES AND ADMISSIBILITY OF THE EEOC DETERMINATION

A. Access to EEOC Files

1. Statutory Framework

a. Title VII, the ADA, and GINA [Revised Heading]

[373][On page 26-69 of the Main Volume, in footnote 373, add the following at the end of the footnote.]

The Commission has amended EEOC COMPL. MAN. (BNA) § 83 to make it clear that it applies to requests under the ADEA, GINA, and the EPA, as well as Title VII and the ADA. The section also is available online at http://www.eeoc.gov/eeoc/foia/section83.cfm (last visited Nov. 21, 2013).

B. Admissibility of EEOC Findings

[416][On page 26-76 of the Main Volume, in footnote 416, add the following after "*see also*".]

Ponce v. Billington, 679 F.3d 840, 847, 115 FEP 1 (D.C. Cir. 2012) (agreeing with "at least seven of our sister circuits" and determining that it was "best to leave the admissibility of" recommended finding of discrimination included in report of investigation by Personnel Appeals Board of Government Accountability Office "to the discretion of the trial court"); Silverman v. Board of Educ. of Chi., 637 F.3d 729, 732–33, 111 FEP 1461 (7th Cir. 2011) (district court "acted well within its discretion, and pursuant to its obligation to make a de novo decision on the plaintiff's claims," when it chose not to consider EEOC's reasonable cause determination in granting Board's motion for summary judgment); Hawn v. Executive Jet Mgmt., Inc., 615 F.3d 1151, 1161–62, 109 FEP 1824 (9th Cir. 2010) (per se rule regarding plaintiff's right to introduce EEOC reasonable cause determination in Title VII lawsuit is not applicable to all EEOC documents; district court properly exercised its discretion in denying motion to strike references to EEOC's determination in charge filed by third party);

[417][On page 26-77 of the Main Volume, in footnote 417, add the following at the end of the footnote.]

Cf. Hawn, 615 F.3d at 1161–62 (district court properly exercised its discretion in denying motion to strike references to EEOC's determination in charge filed by third party).

[419][On page 26-77 of the Main Volume, in footnote 419, add the following after "*See, e.g.*,".]

Xodus v. Wackenhut Corp., 619 F.3d 683, 687, 110 FEP 1 (7th Cir. 2010) (although EEOC intake questionnaire cannot be used to expand legal scope of EEOC charge, it may be used for evidentiary purposes, such as to show prior consistent statement where plaintiff's credibility is disputed);

CHAPTER 27

TIMELINESS

II. TIMELINESS OF FILING THE EEOC CHARGE

A. The 180/300-Day Limitations Periods

1. General Charge-Filing Requirements

[24][On page 27-8 of the Main Volume, in footnote 24, add the following at the end of the footnote.]

See, e.g., Johnson v. Lucent Tech., Inc., 653 F.3d 1000, 1008–09 & n.7, 112 FEP 1549 (9th Cir. 2011) (filing period is extended to 300 days "if proceedings are initially instituted with a state or local government agency having the authority to grant or seek the requested relief").

[25][On page 27-8 of the Main Volume, in footnote 25, add the following after "*See*".]

Tuli v. Brigham & Women's Hosp., 656 F.3d 33, 40, 113 FEP 116 (1st Cir. 2011) (charge-filing deadline is 300 days in deferral state); Brooks v. Midwest Heart Grp., 655 F.3d 796, 800, 113 FEP 382 (8th Cir. 2011) (Missouri is deferral state in which 300-day charge filing deadline applies);

[27]**[On page 27-9 of the Main Volume, in footnote 27, add the following after "*See*".]**

Puryear v. City of Roanoke, 214 F.3d 514, 518, 84 FEP 155 (4th Cir. 2000) (former employee effectively filed timely charge with state agency by filing with EEOC under work-sharing agreement between two agencies);

[27]**[On page 27-9 of the Main Volume, in footnote 27, add the following at the end of the footnote.]**

Compare Surrell v. California Water Serv. Co., 518 F.3d 1097, 1104–05, 102 FEP 1345 (9th Cir. 2008) (charge that is timely filed with state agency satisfies requirement under Title VII that charge be filed with EEOC and failure to obtain right-to-sue letter from EEOC does not preclude federal jurisdiction over Title VII claim), *with* Montes v. Vail Clinic, 497 F.3d 1160, 1164–65, 101 FEP 492 (10th Cir. 2007) (employees who filed charges with EEOC after 300-day time limit expired cannot revive their claims by asserting that they filed to state agency earlier by letter complaining of discrimination where they did not provide letter or evidence that it was adequate to satisfy state agency's filing requirements).

5. Availability of the 300-Day Filing Period

[75]**[On page 27-17 of the Main Volume, in footnote 75, add the following after "*see also*".]**

Stiefel v. Bechtel Corp., 624 F.3d 1240, 1244–45, 23 AD 1380 (9th Cir. 2010) (plaintiff not required to file charge with EEOC where he had filed timely charge with state agency with which EEOC had work sharing agreement; charge considered to be dual-filed);

[75]**[On page 27-17 of the Main Volume, in footnote 75, add the following at the end of the footnote.]**

Compare Surrell v. California Water Serv. Co., 518 F.3d 1097, 1104–05, 102 FEP 1345 (9th Cir. 2008) (charge that is timely filed with state agency satisfies requirement under Title VII that charge be filed with EEOC and failure to obtain right-to-sue letter from EEOC does not preclude federal jurisdiction over Title VII claim), *with* Montes v. Vail Clinic, 497 F.3d 1160, 1164–65, 101 FEP 492 (10th Cir. 2007) (employees who filed charges with EEOC after 300-day time limit expired cannot revive their claims by asserting that they filed to state agency earlier by letter complaining of discrimination where they did not provide letter or evidence that was adequate to satisfy state agency's filing requirements).

6. *Effect of State Action or Inaction on Title VII Rights*

b. State Action

[91]**[On page 27-20 of the Main Volume, in footnote 91, add the following at the end of the footnote.]**

See also Herrera v. Churchill McGee, LLC, 680 F.3d 539, 548 n.7, 114 FEP 1636 (6th Cir. 2012) (agency decisions that have been reviewed by state courts have preclusive effect based upon Full Faith and Credit Clause of Constitution, whereas unreviewed agency decisions are subject to "common law preclusion principles"); Hayes v. City of Chi., 670 F.3d 810, 813–16, 114 FEP 801 (7th Cir. 2012) (plaintiff's Title VII claims were barred by res judicata not due to unreviewed ruling of Illinois Human Rights Commission but due to ruling by Police Board that had been reviewed by state circuit and appellate courts).

[93]**[On page 27-20 of the Main Volume, in footnote 93, add the following after "*see also*".]**

Herrera, 680 F.3d at 547–49 (plaintiff's race discrimination claims were precluded because plaintiff had "opportunity to present, on the record, though informally, his charges against his employer" before state agency; no preclusion, however, of plaintiff's retaliation claims because he had not raised retaliation claims before state agency); Morales-Cruz v. University of P.R., 676 F.3d 220, 223–24, 114 FEP 1185 (1st Cir. 2012) (EEOC charge-filing requirement is mandatory but not jurisdictional); Abner v. Illinois Dep't of Transp., 674 F.3d 716, 719–22, 114 FEP 961 (7th Cir. 2012) (plaintiff was barred by res judicata from filing retaliatory discharge action where he could have raised said claim before administrative board during his dismissal hearing; fact that plaintiff was not actually discharged until administrative board upheld discharge insufficient grounds to overcome res judicata); White v. City of Pasadena, 671 F.3d 918, 926–28, 25 AD 1185 (9th Cir. 2012) (federal courts must apply same preclusive effect to administrative proceedings that have been reviewed by state court as would state court, so long as administrative proceedings afforded minimum standards of due process); Coleman v. Donahoe,

667 F.3d 835, 853, 114 FEP 160 (7th Cir. 2012) (state administrative adjudications may have preclusive effect if test of *University of Tennessee v. Elliott*, 478 U.S. 742, 748 (2001), is met); Eckerman v. Tennessee Dep't of Safety, 636 F.3d 202, 210, 31 IER Cases 1110 (6th Cir. 2010) (factual findings of administrative law judge (ALJ) in state administrative hearing that plaintiff was not guilty of wrongdoing at work were res judicata in plaintiff's subsequent § 1983 suit); Brooks v. Arthur, 626 F.3d 194, 200, 110 FEP 1446 (4th Cir. 2010) (state agency determination can have same preclusive effect as prior state court judgment where party had been provided "adequate opportunity to litigate" his claims); Artis v. Bernanke, 630 F.3d 1031, 1034 n.4, 111 FEP 300 (D.C. Cir. 2011) (exhaustion of administrative remedies, like timely filing, is not jurisdictional requirement);

7. *Effect of Complainant's Failure to Verify Charge*

[101]**[On page 27-23 of the Main Volume, in the carryover of footnote 101, add the following after "*See*".]**

Brooks v. Midwest Heart Grp., 655 F.3d 796, 800–01, 113 FEP 382 (8th Cir. 2011) (district court erred in granting motion to dismiss claims on timeliness grounds where questions of fact existed as to whether complainant's late "Charge of Discrimination Information Form" perfected intake questionnaire that had been filed within 300-day period); Williams v. CSX Transp. Co., 643 F.3d 502, 507–09, 112 FEP 961 (6th Cir. 2011) (plaintiff's "Charge Information Form" delivered to EEOC, although not under oath, stating that she felt that employer owed her money because of hostile work environment, coupled with her later untimely charge, was sufficient to meet administrative prerequisite);

B. When Did the Discrimination Occur?

1. *Individual Acts*

[111]**[On page 27-24 of the Main Volume, in footnote 111, delete the "." after "*Ricks*)" and add the following before "*But cf.*".]**

; Draper v. Martin, 664 F.3d 1110, 1113 n.6, 33 IER Cases 330 (7th Cir. 2011) (in discriminatory discharge cases, period for filing charge begins when decision to terminate is made, not at point termination actually occurs); Coppinger-Martin v. Solis, 627 F.3d 745,

749 n.1, 31 IER Cases 801 (9th Cir. 2010) (applying principle that charge-filing time limit begins at point that plaintiff is informed of termination to charges filed under Sarbanes-Oxley Act of 2002, 18 U.S.C. § 1514(a)).

[115]**[On page 27-25 of the Main Volume, in footnote 115, add the following after "*See*".]**

Draper, 664 F.3d at 1113–14 (date of alleged unlawful employment practice is date that "final, ultimate, and non-tentative decision" was made and was unequivocally communicated to employee, not when decision was implemented); Phillips v. Leggett & Platt, Inc., 658 F.3d 452, 458, 113 FEP 490 (5th Cir. 2011) (reversing jury verdict in favor of plaintiff on basis that charge-filing period began to run on date that plaintiff was notified of layoff even though plaintiff had been re-hired for temporary position four days after her layoff; court was sympathetic to, but not influenced by, plaintiff's argument that she feared that filing charge would harm her chances to remain employed);

[116]**[On page 27-26 of the Main Volume, in footnote 116, add the following after "*See*".]**

Begolli v. Home Depot USA, 701 F.3d 1158, 1160, 116 FEP 1057 (7th Cir. 2012) (because filing deadline is merely defense to Title VII suit that is indistinguishable from other defenses, court may permit jury to determine which event triggered charge-filing period);

[117]**[On page 27-27 of the Main Volume, in footnote 117, add the following after "*See, e.g.,*".]**

Daniels v. United Parcel Serv., Inc., 701 F.3d 620, 628–29, 116 FEP 1281 (10th Cir. 2012) (time period for filing charge of discrimination related to promotion denial began when employee learned that she had not been promoted rather than when she learned subsequently that selection process had been discriminatory); Draper v. Martin, 664 F.3d 1110, 1114–15, 33 IER Cases 330 (7th Cir. 2011) (plaintiffs' receipt of letters informing them of impending layoff was sufficient to trigger charge-filing period, despite fact that employer subsequently re-hired some employees who had been notified that they would be laid off);

3. Continuing Violations

a. National Railroad Passenger Corp. v. Morgan

[158]**[On page 27-35 of the Main Volume, in footnote 158, add the following after "*see also*".]**

Benuzzi v. Board of Educ. of City of Chi., 647 F.3d 652, 663, 112 FEP 1444 (7th Cir. 2011) (plaintiff may not challenge "entire course of conduct" that included events outside of charge-filing period where plaintiff's charge alleged discrimination but not hostile environment);

[164]**[On page 27-36 of the Main Volume, in footnote 164, add the following at the end of the footnote.]**

But see Rodriguez v. Municipality of San Juan, 659 F.3d 168, 174, 32 IER Cases 1770 (1st Cir. 2011) (continuing violations doctrine allows plaintiff to wait to file charges until series of acts "blossoms" into injury for which suit can be brought).

[168]**[On page 27-37 of the Main Volume, in footnote 168, add the following at the end of the footnote.]**

See also Daniels v. United Parcel Serv., Inc., 701 F.3d 620, 628–29, 116 FEP 1281 (10th Cir. 2012) (time period for filing charge of discrimination in promotion began when employee learned that she had not been promoted rather than when she discovered subsequently that selection process had been discriminatory).

b. Discrete Acts

[172]**[On page 27-37 of the Main Volume, in footnote 172, add the following after "*See*".]**

Keohane v. United States, 669 F.3d 325, 329–30, (D.C. Cir. 2012) (continuing violation doctrine applies to violation that "could not reasonably have been expected to be made the subject of a lawsuit when it first occurred because its character as a violation did not become clear until it was repeated during the limitations period"); Bowerman v. UAW Local 12, 646 F.3d 360, 366, 190 LRRM 3287 (6th Cir. 2011) (continuing violations doctrine as utilized in Title VII, ADEA, and § 1983 cases applied to plaintiff's fair representation claim); Jackson v. United Parcel Serv., Inc., 643 F.3d 1081, 1087, 112 FEP 1094 (8th Cir. 2011) (continuing violation doctrine is not applicable to series of discrete promotion denials; plaintiff could raise only promotion denial for which she filed timely charge);

[172]**[On page 27-39 of the Main Volume, in the carryover of footnote 172, add the following at the end of the footnote.]**

Cf. McDonald-Cuba v. Santa Fe Protective Servs., 644 F.3d 1096, 1100–01, 112 FEP 327 (10th Cir. 2011) (discrete retaliatory act that occurs after individual files EEOC charge, e.g., defendant's filing of counterclaim once employee filed discrimination action, must be subject of separate, timely EEOC charge).

[174]**[On page 27-39 of the Main Volume, in footnote 174, add the following after "*See*".]**

Chin v. Port Authority of N.Y. & N.J., 685 F.3d 135, 150, 115 FEP 720 (7th Cir. 2012) (events that occurred prior to 300 days before charge was filed were admissible as background evidence to support plaintiff's timely allegations); Rodriguez v. Municipality of San Juan, 659 F.3d 168, 177, 32 IER Cases 1770 (1st Cir. 2011) (permissible to consider claims of discrimination that fell outside limitations period as "background evidence" to support timely claims); Davis v. Time Warner Cable of Se. Wis., 651 F.3d 664, 667, 112 FEP 1099 (7th Cir. 2011) (time-barred events admissible evidence to support timely claims);

[175]**[On page 27-39 of the Main Volume, in footnote 175, add the following at the beginning of the footnote.]**

See, e.g., Gowski v. Peake, 682 F.3d 1299, 1313, 115 FEP 163 (11th Cir. 2012) (discrete acts alone cannot form basis for hostile environment claim on continuing violations theory); Ayala-Sepúlveda v. Municipality of San Germán, 671 F.3d 24, 30–31, 114 FEP 234 (1st Cir. 2012) (declining to apply continuing violations theory in Equal Protection case where plaintiff failed to show sufficient evidence of hostile environment claim within statute of limitations period);

[176]**[On page 27-39 of the Main Volume, in footnote 176, add the following after "*See*".]**

Diaz v. Jiten Hotel Mgmt., Inc., 671 F.3d 78, 85–86, 114 FEP 449 (1st Cir. 2012) (applying Massachusetts law regarding statute of limitations for age claims, jury could reasonably have concluded that at least one discriminatory act occurred within limitations period, even where jury did not specify how its award of damages was allocated among plaintiff's claims); Johnson v. Lucent Techs., Inc., 653 F.3d 1000, 1008–09, 112 FEP 1549 (9th Cir. 2011) (employee alleging intentional infliction of emotional distress may include in his claim actions that occurred within two-year state limitations period);

c. *Hostile Work Environment Claims in the Post-*Morgan *Era*

[178]**[On page 27-40 of the Main Volume, in footnote 178, add the following at the end of the footnote.]**

See also Baird v. Gotbaum, 662 F.3d 1246, 1251, 114 FEP 11 (D.C. Cir. 2011) (although discrete acts, even if related to timely charges, are not actionable when they arose outside of limitations period, hostile environment claims are different because they are considered as one illegal employment practice composed of series of acts over time).

[181]**[On page 27-40 of the Main Volume, in footnote 181, add the following after "*See*".]**

King v. Acosta Sales & Mktg., Inc., 678 F.3d 470, 472, 114 FEP 897 (7th Cir. 2012) (district court erred in failing to allow plaintiff to allege all acts comprising hostile work environment because hostile environment extended into 300-day filing period; error to disallow claims preceding charge-filing period where plaintiff had adequately linked acts into coherent hostile environment claim); Tuli v. Brigham & Women's Hosp., 656 F.3d 33, 40–41, 113 FEP 116 (1st Cir. 2011) (district court properly considered claims that occurred outside of charge-filing period because plaintiff showed timely act within period); Jenkins v. Mabus, 646 F.3d 1023, 1027, 112 FEP 1454 (8th Cir. 2011) (no continuing violation where only contact within limitations period consisted of insults, slights, and affronts); Wilkie v. Department of Health & Human Servs., 638 F.3d 944, 950–52, 112 FEP 100 (8th Cir. 2011) (plaintiff's untimely claims of "sexual advances" were closely enough related to her timely claims, which were of "markedly different" character); *Baird*, 662 F.3d at 1251–52 (district court erred by categorically excluding time-barred complaints in considering hostile work environment claim, thereby failing to determine "which acts exhibit the relationship necessary to be considered 'part of the same actionable hostile environment claim'"); Moore v. Vital Prods., Inc., 641 F.3d 253, 256, 112 FEP

513 (7th Cir. 2011) (plaintiff's claim time-barred because of failure to show any evidence of act that occurred within charge filing period);

[183]**[On page 27-41 of the Main Volume, in footnote 183, add the following after "*See*".]**

King, 678 F.3d at 472 (female employee did not establish hostile work environment where she did not connect harassment by supervisor that occurred outside charge-filing period with hostile acts within filing period but in which supervisor had no role); *Baird*, 662 F.3d at 1252–53 (district court improperly granted § 12(b)(6) motion to dismiss on fact that, within complaint, plaintiff had not sufficiently segregated events that contributed to alleged hostile environment from discrete acts of discrimination);

[186]**[On page 27-43 of the Main Volume, in footnote 186, add the following after "*See*".]**

King, 678 F.3d at 472–73 (plaintiff's hostile environment claim failed where hostile acts by supervisor occurred outside of limitations period and supervisor was not involved in harassment that occurred within charge-filing period);

4. Claims for Compensation Discrimination

[195]**[On page 27-44 of the Main Volume, in footnote 195, add the following at the end of the footnote.]**

See Puffer v. Allstate Ins. Co., 675 F.3d 709, 713–15, 114 FEP 1025 (7th Cir. 2012) (noting that Lilly Ledbetter Fair Pay Act overruled *Ledbetter* decision and reinstated paycheck accrual rule); Figueroa v. District of Columbia Div. of Police, 633 F.3d 1129, 1134 (D.C. Cir. 2011) (each paycheck created new filing period, in accordance with Lilly Ledbetter Fair Pay Act).

[204]**[On page 27-46 of the Main Volume, in footnote 204, add the following at the end of the footnote.]**

Reduction in Pension Benefits: *See* Aubrey v. City of Bethlehem Fire Dep't, 466 F. App'x 88, 93–94 (3d Cir. 2012) (Lilly Ledbetter Fair Pay Act did not apply where plaintiff had not claimed wage discrimination but rather complained of reduction in pension benefits resulting from time-barred act).

Attack on Arbitration Decision: *See* Schwartz v. Merrill Lynch & Co., 665 F.3d 444, 453–54, 113 FEP 1479 (2d Cir. 2011) (upholding arbitration panel's decision to exclude evidence of discrimination that had occurred prior to plaintiff having executed release of claims and noting that issue was governed by Federal Arbitration Act rather than Lilly Ledbetter Fair Pay Act).
Demotions: *See* Almond v. Unified Sch. Dist. #501, 665 F.3d 1174, 1180–81, 113 FEP 1473 (10th Cir. 2011) (Lilly Ledbetter Fair Pay Act not applicable to demotions).

b. Failure to Promote

[209][On page 27-47 of the Main Volume, in footnote 209, add the following after "*with*".]

Daniels v. United Parcel Serv., Inc., 701 F.3d 620, 628–29, 116 FEP 1281 (10th Cir. 2012) (promotion denial not compensation decision subject to Lilly Ledbetter Fair Pay Act),

C. Tolling of the Charge-Filing Period

1. A Jurisdictional Prerequisite, or a Statute of Limitations That May Be Tolled for Equitable Reasons?

[217][On page 27-49 of the Main Volume, in footnote 217, add the following at the end of the footnote.]

See also Farris v. Shinseki, 660 F.3d 557, 563, 25 AD 955 (1st Cir. 2011) (only in exceptional circumstances should equitable doctrines of tolling and estoppel be applied); Vera v. McHugh, 622 F.3d 17, 30, 110 FEP 705 (1st Cir. 2010) (equitable doctrines are to be "applied sparingly").

[219][On page 27-49 of the Main Volume, in footnote 219, add the following after "*See, e.g.,*".]

Louisiana Environmental Action v. Baton Rouge, 667 F.3d 737, 748 (5th Cir. 2012) (charge-filing requirement not jurisdictional in Title VII cases); Shelley v. Geren, 666 F.3d 599, 605, 114 FEP 303 (9th Cir. 2012) (although administrative exhaustion requirement is not jurisdictional, plaintiff's failure to show waiver, estoppel, or equitable tolling is fatal to claim); *Farris*, 660 F.3d at 563 (1st Cir. 2011) (Title VII charge-filing time limits are not jurisdictional); Brooks v. Midwest Heart Grp., 655 F.3d 796, 801, 113 FEP 382 (8th Cir. 2011) (court erred in not permitting plaintiff to try to develop grounds to support equitable tolling); Johnson v. Lucent Tech., Inc., 653 F.3d 1000, 1008–09, 112 FEP 1549 (9th Cir. 2011) (requirement of timely EEOC charge is subject to waiver, estoppel, and equitable tolling); Granger v. Aaron's Inc., 636 F.3d 708, 711, 111 FEP 1448 (5th Cir. 2011) (timely filing with EEOC not jurisdictional prerequisite to suit because it is subject to doctrines of waiver, tolling, and estoppel);

[220]**[On page 27-49 of the Main Volume, in footnote 220, add the following at the beginning of the footnote.]**

See, e.g., Draper v. Martin, 664 F.3d 1110, 1113, 33 IER Cases 330 (7th Cir. 2011) (plaintiff waived claim of equitable tolling by failing to offer any supporting evidence); *Farris*, 660 F.3d at 563 (burden of proof is upon plaintiff to prove entitlement to equitable tolling);

[221]**[On page 27-49 of the Main Volume, in footnote 221, add the following after "*See, e.g.*,".]**

Farris, 660 F.3d at 565 (plaintiff not entitled to equitable tolling where her attorney failed to file timely EEOC charge because parties are bound by acts of lawyer-agent); Harris v. Tunica, 628 F.3d 237, 239–40, 111 FEP 60 (5th Cir. 2010) (equitable tolling not allowed where plaintiff's counsel's paralegal made clerical error that led to missing of deadline; "garden variety" negligence by attorney or attorney's staff not grounds for tolling);

[221]**[On page 27-49 of the Main Volume, in footnote 221, add the following at the end of the footnote.]**

But see Granger v. Aaron's, Inc., 636 F.3d 708, 712–13, 111 FEP 1448 (5th Cir. 2011) (tolling applied where plaintiff's attorney filed complaint with OFCCP rather than EEOC; "the fact that a complainant is represented does not automatically bar the application of equitable tolling").

[222]**[On page 27-50 of the Main Volume, in footnote 222, add the following after "*E.g.*,".]**

Gilbert v. Napolitano, 670 F.3d 258, 260–61, 114 FEP 923 (D.C. Cir. 2012) (employer not entitled to dismissal of failure-to-promote claim that had not been subject of timely charge where it did not raise defense in its answer, but raised it later in motion to dismiss); McClain v. Lufkin Indus., Inc., 649 F.3d 374, 386–87, 112 FEP 1665

(5th Cir. 2011) (refusing to vacate damages award that was based upon untimely claims where employer did not raise defense before trial court or in appellate court); Artis v. Bernanke, 630 F.3d 1031, 1038, 111 FEP 300 (D.C. Cir. 2011) (defendant waived claim that plaintiff had failed to complete counseling within 45 days of alleged discriminatory act by failing to raise it);

[222][On page 27-50 of the Main Volume, in footnote 222, add the following at the end of the footnote.]

Cf. EEOC v. Schwan's Home Serv., 644 F.3d 742, 746–47, 112 FEP 1227 (8th Cir. 2011) (employer's challenge of EEOC subpoena on grounds of failure to exhaust administrative procedures denied as premature; employer could raise issue later at trial).

2. *The Effect of Equitable Tolling or Estoppel*

[223][On page 27-50 of the Main Volume, in footnote 223, add the following after "*See, e.g.,*".]

Granger, 636 F.3d at 712 (equitable tolling is to be applied sparingly and burden of proof to justify tolling is upon plaintiff); Jones v. Res-Care, Inc., 613 F.3d 665, 670, 109 FEP 1383 (7th Cir. 2010) (equitable tolling applies only where despite due diligence, plaintiff cannot obtain information necessary to realize that he has a claim);

3. *Tolling Because of Resort to Another Forum*

[225][On page 27-50 of the Main Volume, in footnote 225, add the following at the end of the footnote.]

See also Cintron-Lorenzo v. Estado, 634 F.3d 1, 2, 111 FEP 609 (1st Cir. 2011) (declining to decide issue of whether plaintiff's filing of EEOC charge tolled statute of limitations for her § 1983 claim because statute of limitations would have been violated even if date of EEOC charge controlled).

[230][On page 27-51 of the Main Volume, in footnote 230, add the following after "*See, e.g.,*".]

United States v. Brennan, 650 F.3d 65, 122–23, 112 FEP 93 (2d Cir. 2011) (collective bargaining remedies and remedies under Title VII are "separate and independent" of one another; filing union grievance therefore does not toll EEOC filing period);

[233][On page 27-51 of the Main Volume, in footnote 233, add the following at the end of the footnote.]

Cf. Granger v. Aaron's, Inc., 636 F.3d 708, 712–13, 111 FEP 1448 (5th Cir. 2011) (tolling applied where plaintiff's attorney filed complaint with OFCCP rather than EEOC; "the fact that a complainant is represented does not automatically bar the application of equitable tolling").

4. Other Grounds for Estoppel and Tolling

a. Employer Misconduct

[238][On page 27-52 of the Main Volume, in footnote 238, add the following after "*See*".]

Vera v. McHugh, 622 F.3d 17, 30–32, 110 FEP 705 (1st Cir. 2010) (equitable tolling applies where employee is aware of her Title VII rights but does not make timely filing due to reasonable reliance upon employer's misleading or confusing representations or conduct);

[250][On page 27-55 of the Main Volume, in footnote 250, add the following after "*see also*".]

Johnson v. Lucent Tech., Inc., 653 F.3d 1000, 1009, 112 FEP 1549 (9th Cir. 2011) (plaintiff not entitled to estoppel based upon employer's allegedly fraudulent concealment of form that plaintiff needed to file because plaintiff actually possessed form); Coppinger-Martin v. Solis, 627 F.3d 745, 751–52, 31 IER Cases 801 (9th Cir. 2010) (plaintiff lacked any evidence of employer misconduct to support estoppel theory beyond evidence that plaintiff alleged in her underlying discrimination claim);

b. Plaintiff's Exercise of Due Diligence

[266][On page 27-58 of the Main Volume, in footnote 266, add the following after "*See*".]

Johnson v. Lucent Tech., Inc., 653 F.3d 1000, 1010, 112 FEP 1549 (9th Cir. 2011) (mental incompetence can toll charge-filing period where plaintiff meets two-part test that he or she: (1) was either unable to rationally or factually understand need to timely file, or his or her mental state prevented preparation of charge; and (2) diligent in pursuing claim to extent that he or she could understand the matter); Wilkie v. Deparment of Health & Human Servs., 638 F.3d 944, 949–50, 112 FEP 100 (8th Cir. 2011) (plaintiff must show that mental state prevented him from understanding and managing his affairs generally and from complying with charge-filing deadline in particular);

5. "Piggybacking" or the "Single-Filing" Rule

[282][On page 27-61 of the Main Volume, in footnote 282, add the following after "*See*".]

Harris v. County of Orange, 682 F.3d 1126, 1136–37, 33 IER Cases 1676 (9th Cir. 2012) (applying Title VII and ADEA "piggybacking" principle to claim under California Fair Employment and Housing Act);

III. TIMELINESS OF FILING SUIT

A. Introduction

[284][On page 27-61 of the Main Volume, in footnote 284, add the following after "*See*".]

Lee v. Cook Cnty., 635 F.3d 969, 973, 111 FEP 1457 (7th Cir. 2011) (employer can raise limitations defense as late as at trial);

C. Time of Issuing Notice of Right to Sue

3. Premature Issuance of Right-to-Sue Notices and Premature Filing of Suit

[320][On page 27-69 of the Main Volume, in footnote 320, add the following after "*see also*".]

Stiefel v. Bechtel Corp., 624 F.3d 1240, 1244–45, 23 AD 1380 (9th Cir. 2010) (plaintiff not barred from filing prior to receipt of right-to-sue letter where plaintiff had been entitled to receive letter due to issuance of right-to-sue letter from state agency);

D. Timely Court Filing

2. What Triggers Commencement of the 90-Day Period

[330][On page 27-72 of the Main Volume, in footnote 330, add the following after "*E.g.*,".]

DeTata v. Rollprint Packaging Prods., Inc., 632 F.3d 962, 969–70, 111 FEP 295 (7th Cir. 2011) (actual receipt of right-to-sue letter starts 90-day clock; fact that EEOC had sent letter to person it erroneously believed to be plaintiff's attorney did not control);

[332][On page 27-72 of the Main Volume, in footnote 332, add the following at the end of the footnote.]

See also Loubriel v. Fondo del Seguro del Estado, 694 F.3d 139, 144, 26 AD 1537 (1st Cir. 2012) (plaintiff's attorney is presumed to have received right-to-sue letter within reasonable time of its issuance); Tiberio v. Allergy Asthma Immunology of Rochester, 664 F.3d 35, 37, 25 AD 929 (2d Cir. 2011) (where plaintiff filed suit 92 days after right-to-sue letter reached her but 90 days after letter reached her attorney, she filed too late).

3. What Constitutes a "Filing"

[368][On page 27-80 of the Main Volume, in footnote 368, add the following after "*See, e.g.*,".]

Hernandez v. Valley View Hosp. Ass'n, 684 F.3d 950, 961–62, 115 FEP 592 (10th Cir. 2012) (retaliation claim untimely where it was included in Amended Complaint after 90-day limitations period had run and claim did not "relate back" to plaintiff's underlying discrimination claim);

4. Tolling

[379][On page 27-81 of the Main Volume, in footnote 379, add the following after "*See*".]

Slater v. Energy Serv. Grp. Int'l, 634 F.3d 1326, 1331, 111 FEP 1185 (11th Cir. 2011) (rejecting, as speculation, plaintiff's challenge to forum-selection clause that it would be too late to re-file her Title VII claim in appropriate forum because 90-day period had expired);

[380]**[On page 27-82 of the Main Volume, in footnote 380, add the following after "*see also*".]**

Lee v. Cook Cnty., 635 F.3d 969, 972–73, 111 FEP 1457 (7th Cir. 2011) (equitable tolling not applicable where attorney was not diligent in filing; "a lawyer's ineptitude does not support equitable tolling");

[381]**[On page 27-82 of the Main Volume, in footnote 381, add the following after "*E.g.*,".]**

Lee, 635 F.3d at 971–72 (where district court erroneously dismissed without prejudice Title VII suit for improper joinder and gave plaintiff 40 days to re-plead but plaintiff re-filed action more than 40 days but fewer than 90 days later, suit was untimely; for statute of limitations purposes, suits dismissed without prejudice are treated as though they were never filed);

CHAPTER 28

JURISPRUDENTIAL BARS TO ACTION

I. PRECLUSION

A. Preclusion Issues Resulting From Prior Resort to Another Forum

1. Introduction

[1][On page 28-2 of the Main Volume, in footnote 1, add the following at the end of the footnote.]

Cf. Brooks v. Arthur, 626 F.3d 194, 201–03, 110 FEP 1446 (4th Cir. 2010) (plaintiffs may proceed with § 1983 discrimination claims against certain prison officials in their individual capacities even though corrections department had prevailed in state court action on claims arising out of same facts; individuals sued are in privity with corrections department only when sued in their official capacities).

[5][On page 28-3 of the Main Volume, in footnote 5, add the following after "*see also*".]

EEOC v. CRST Van Expedited, Inc., 679 F.3d 657, 681, 114 FEP 1566 (8th Cir. 2012) (EEOC not estopped from litigating sexual harassment claim, even though individual claimants had been unsuccessful in litigating same claim, where EEOC sued in public interest rather than for individual relief; claimants, not EEOC, had taken inconsistent position in prior case);

2. Preclusive Effect of Prior State Court Judgments and Reviewed State Administrative Decisions

[10][On page 28-3 of the Main Volume, in footnote 10, add the following after "*accord*".]

Bragg v. Flint Bd. of Educ., 570 F.3d 775, 777, 106 FEP 311 (6th Cir. 2009) (federal action raising Title VII and state employment discrimination claims barred by state court action dismissing identical claims for failure to prosecute; FED. R. CIV. P. 41(b) plainly states that involuntary dismissal pursuant to its terms constitutes judgment on merits);

[On page 28-4 of the Main Volume, replace the second sentence of the first full paragraph with the following.]

Subsequent to certification of the class in the federal court case, the named representatives brought a discrimination action in state court in their individual capacities, challenging the same allegedly discriminatory policy under state law.

[On page 28-5 of the Main Volume, in the first sentence of the first full paragraph, replace "*Sondel v. Smith*" with "*Sondel. Smith*".]

[On page 28-6 of the Main Volume, in the first sentence of the first full paragraph, delete ", however".]

3. *Preclusive Effect of State Court Judgments on Claims Not Raised*

[49]**[On page 28-10 of the Main Volume, in footnote 49, add the following after "*See, e.g.*,".]**

Hayes v. City of Chi., 670 F.3d 810, 815–16, 114 FEP 801 (7th Cir.) (plaintiff barred from bringing Title VII claim challenging his discharge where he had already brought claims under §§ 1981 and 1983 and action before state human rights commission; all of these bases for suit involved same employment decision and could have been raised conveniently in single case), *cert. denied*, 133 S. Ct. 353 (2012); Groesch v. City of Springfield, 635 F.3d 1020, 1026–28, 111 FEP 1441 (7th Cir. 2011) (dismissal of prior state court discrimination and state constitutional claims on statute of limitation grounds was res judicata as to claims that arose prior to date of state court dismissal; plaintiffs could, however, pursue Title VII and § 1983 claims that arose after date of state court dismissal);

[54]**[On page 28-13 of the Main Volume, in the carryover of footnote 54, add the following after "*But see*".]**

Bragg v. Flint Bd. of Educ., 570 F.3d 775, 777, 106 FEP 311 (6th Cir. 2009) (federal action raising Title VII and state employment discrimination claims barred by state court action dismissing identical claims for failure to prosecute);

[59]**[On page 28-14 of the Main Volume, in footnote 59, add the following after "*Compare*".]**

Cox v. DeSoto Cnty., 564 F.3d 745, 748, 105 FEP 1571 (5th Cir. 2009) (collateral estoppel does not apply to ADEA claim of retaliation, even though plaintiff had been denied unemployment compensation in final administrative proceeding; estoppel does not preclude claim "where Congress has provided for a detailed administrative remedy" such as that found in ADEA), *cert. denied*, 131 S. Ct. 3075 (2011),

4. *Preclusive Effect of Prior Unreviewed State Administrative Decisions*

[70]**[On page 28-16 of the Main Volume, in footnote 70, add the following at the end of the footnote.]**

But see Abner v. Illinois Dep't of Transp., 674 F.3d 716, 719, 114 FEP 961 (7th Cir. 2012) (plaintiff's Title VII action precluded when state employee failed to raise retaliation claim during earlier administrative proceeding in which he challenged discharge).

5. *Preclusive Effect of Prior Federal Proceedings*

[82]**[On page 28-19 of the Main Volume, in footnote 82, add the following after "*E.g.,*".]**

M.O.C.H.A. Soc'y, Inc. v. City of Buffalo, 689 F.3d 263, 283, 115 FEP 929 (2d Cir. 2012) (where plaintiffs' disparate impact challenge to 1988 promotional examination failed because City proved that exam was job-related, they were estopped from challenging 2002 version of exam; even though questions on 2002 test were not identical to those on 1998 test, two tests were based upon same job analysis, tested same content, and were scored in same manner); Czarniecki v. City of Chi., 633 F.3d 545, 550, 111 FEP 490 (7th Cir.) (plaintiff barred by res judicata from pursuing Title VII claim of discharge based on national origin discrimination where City was granted summary judgment in earlier § 1983 claim challenging same discharge, even though plaintiff arguably could not have raised Title VII claim in first proceeding because he was not entitled to right-to-sue (RTS) letter at time of filing; plaintiff could have sought stay in first proceeding until he was entitled to RTS letter and then amended his complaint), *cert. denied*, 132 S. Ct. 241 (2011);

[84]**[On page 28-21 of the Main Volume, in the carryover of footnote 84, add the following at the end of the footnote.]**

Cf. M.O.C.H.A. Soc'y, Inc., 689 F.3d at 284 (where plaintiffs had agreed to bench trial on issue of job-relatedness in connection with their disparate impact challenge to promotional examination used by City, plaintiffs were estopped from presenting same issue to jury as part of disparate treatment claim).

7. Preclusion Based on Prior Federal Agency Determination

[112]**[On page 28-26 of the Main Volume, in footnote 112, add the following at the end of the footnote.]**

See also Plummer v. Western Int'l Hotels Co., 656 F.2d 502, 505, 26 FEP 1292 (9th Cir. 1981) (EEOC probable cause determination is per se admissible in Title VII action and excluding same is reversible error).

9. Preclusive Effect of Prior Arbitration Decisions

[130]**[On page 28-29 of the Main Volume, in footnote 130, add the following before "Ciambriello v. County of Nassau".]**

Coleman v. Donahoe, 667 F.3d 835, 853–55, 114 FEP 160 (7th Cir. 2012) (no issue preclusion resulted from arbitration award because (1) arbitrator did not decide issue of pretext, and (2) general rule is that arbitration decisions do not bind either side regarding statutory discrimination claims); Mathews v. Denver Newspaper Agency, LLP, 649 F.3d 1199, 1206–07, 112 FEP 432 (10th Cir. 2011) (arbitration clause did not provide for waiver of judicial forum, and lawsuit subsequent to arbitration could proceed because arbitration clause authorized arbitrator to resolve only dispute submitted by union and employer, which did not specifically include statutory claims under Title VII and § 1981);

[131]**[On page 28-31 of the Main Volume, in footnote 131, add the following at the end of the footnote.]**

See also Thompson v. Air Transport Int'l, LLC, 664 F.3d 723, 727, 18 WH Cases 2d 872 (8th Cir. 2011) (applying *14 Penn Plaza* to dismiss FMLA lawsuit because collective bargaining agreement covering plaintiff's employment required arbitration of alleged "violations of state or federal law," and clearly and unmistakably waived right to judicial forum; although labor contract included provision waiving "each and every cause of action and remedies provided under these statutes and common law frameworks," court interpreted provision to waive only right to judicial forum for such claims, not substantive rights).

[140]**[On page 28-32 of the Main Volume, in footnote 140, add the following at the end of the footnote.]**

Cf. Manganella v. Evanston Ins. Co., 700 F.3d 585, 591, 116 FEP 1161 (1st Cir. 2012) (even though issues were not identical, where arbitrators ruled that company's ex-president violated company policy by engaging in sexual harassment, he was estopped from litigating whether his conduct was covered by company's insurance policy; issue was previously determined as necessary to arbitrators' decision).

B. Judicial Estoppel and Preclusive Effect of Prior Sworn Statements

[149]**[On page 28-34 of the Main Volume, in footnote 149, add the following after "*see also*".]**

Solomon v. Vilsack, 628 F.3d 555, 557, 563, 23 AD 1697 (D.C. Cir. 2010) (receipt of disability benefits under Federal Employees' Retirement System Act, which are available only to an employee who cannot fulfill duties of his or her position even with reasonable accommodation, did not judicially estop federal employee from asserting claims for disability discrimination under Rehabilitation Act; application for disability benefits did not directly inquire whether employee could work with reasonable accommodations; applying de novo review, rather than abuse-of-discretion standard, to district court's application of judicial estoppel);

[151]**[On page 28-35 of the Main Volume, in footnote 151, add the following after "*see also*".]**

Matthews v. Denver Newspaper Agency LLP, 649 F.3d 1199, 1206–07, 111 FEP 1313 (10th Cir. 2011) (individual who filed for SSDI benefits claiming that he was totally disabled from performing his job was not necessarily judicially estopped from asserting qualification for job in subsequent Title VII proceeding; however, he must explain inconsistency between that statement and necessary elements of his discrimination claim);

[155]**[On page 28-36 of the Main Volume, in footnote 155, add the following after "*see also*".]**

EEOC v. CRST Van Expedited, Inc., 679 F.3d 657, 680–81, 114 FEP 1566 (8th Cir. 2012) (judicial estoppel barred individual claimant from litigating sexual harassment claim that was not listed in her bankruptcy proceeding; failure to list is equivalent to representation that claim does not exist); Love v. Tyson Foods, Inc., 677 F.3d 258, 262, 114 FEP 1189 (5th Cir. 2012) (applying judicial estoppel to bar employment discrimination action when it was not initially disclosed to bankruptcy court, despite later disclosure; relevant inquiry is intent at time of non-disclosure);

C. Issue Preclusion

[158]**[On page 28-37 of the Main Volume, in footnote 158, add the following at the end of the footnote.]**

See also White v. City of Pasadena, 671 F.3d 918, 926–27, 25 AD 1185 (9th Cir. 2012) (setting out framework for analyzing when state court decision is preclusive of subsequent federal proceeding and providing overview of claim preclusion, issue preclusion, and res judicata).

[159]**[On page 28-37 of the Main Volume, in footnote 159, add the following after "*see also*".]**

M.O.C.H.A. Soc'y, Inc. v. City of Buffalo, 689 F.3d 263, 283, 115 FEP 929 (2d Cir. 2012) (where plaintiffs' disparate impact challenge to 1988 promotional examination failed because City proved that exam was job-related, they were estopped from challenging 2002 version of exam; even though questions on 2002 test were not identical to those on 1998 test, two tests were based upon same job analysis, tested same content, and were scored in same manner);

III. JUSTICIABILITY DOCTRINES AS BARS TO ACTION

A. Introduction

1. The Justiciability Doctrine of Standing

[202]**[On page 28-44 of the Main Volume, in footnote 202, delete the semicolon following the parenthetical for "Price v. Choctaw Glove & Safety Co." and add the following.]**

. *But see* Brooks v. District Hosp. Partners, LP, 606 F.3d 800, 807 109 FEP 648 (D.C. Cir. 2010) (single-filing rule satisfied charge-filing requirement for intervenor job applicant's discrimination claim; intervenor permitted to "piggyback" on EEOC charge previously filed by incumbent employee challenging same screening test administered by employer);

IV. PREEMPTION AS A BAR TO ACTION

[On page 28-50 of the Main Volume, after the sentence that ends with footnote 237, add the following new section.]

V. FORUM-SELECTION CLAUSE AS A BAR TO ACTION [NEW TOPIC]

In some instances, federal claims properly may be dismissed due to a forum-selection clause. The Eleventh Circuit has upheld the dismissal without prejudice of Title VII claims filed in Florida where the plaintiff's employment agreement included a forum-selection clause requiring all claims to be brought in Richmond, Virginia.[1]

---

[1]Slater v. Energy Servs. Grp. Int'l, Inc., 634 F.3d 1326, 1333, 111 FEP 1185 (11th Cir. 2011) (affirming dismissal without prejudice of one defendant pursuant to FED. R. CIV. P. 12(b)(3), rather than transfer pursuant to 28 U.S.C. § 1404(a), where other defendants had answered and conceded proper venue).

CHAPTER 29

TITLE VII LITIGATION PROCEDURE

II. Effect of Deficiencies in the EEOC Administrative Process on Charging Party's Right to Sue

A. Introduction

[On page 29-3 of the Main Volume, at the end of the third sentence of the first paragraph, add new footnote 1a after ": of the alleged discriminatory act.".]

[1a]*See, e.g.*, Lore v. City of Syracuse, 670 F.3d 127, 169, 114 FEP 466 (2d Cir. 2012) (claim for discrimination is time-barred if administrative complaint is not filed within 300 days of alleged discriminatory employment practice); Noel v. Boeing Co., 622 F.3d 266, 270, 110 FEP 609 (3d Cir. 2010) (plaintiff must file charge of discrimination with EEOC within 300 days of alleged unlawful employment practice).

[2]**[On page 29-3 of the Main Volume, in footnote 2, add the following at the end of the footnote.]**

See also Phillips v. Leggett & Platt, Inc., 658 F.3d 452, 455–56, 113 FEP 490 (5th Cir. 2011) (when discriminatory act is termination, 180-day limitation begins to run when charging party receives notice of termination and not on actual termination date; "[t]he existence of notice is based upon an objective standard, focusing upon when the employee knew, or reasonably should have known, that the adverse employment decision had been made") (internal quotation marks and citations omitted); Johnson v. Lucent Techs. Inc., 653 F.3d 1000, 1009–10, 112 FEP 1549, 25 AD 7 (9th Cir. 2011) (although 180-day period may be subject to equitable tolling, allegations of mental incompetence cannot form basis for equitable tolling where, as here, plaintiff's conduct demonstrated that he was competent to actively participate in prior litigation).

[3]**[On page 29-3 of the Main Volume, in footnote 3, add the following at the end of the footnote.]**

See also Begolli v. Home Depot U.S.A., Inc., 701 F.3d 1158, 1160, 116 FEP 1057 (7th Cir. 2012) ("Title VII ... does not require exhaustion. It states that 'a charge ... shall be filed ... within three hundred days after the alleged unlawful employment practice occurred,' 42 U.S.C. § 2000e-5(e)(1), but not that an administrative proceeding shall have been conducted before the employee can file suit.") (citations omitted).

C. EEOC Failure to Investigate and/or Conciliate

[23][On page 29-7 of the Main Volume, in footnote 23, add the following before "*Asplundh Tree Expert Co.*".]

EEOC v. Philip Servs. Corp., 635 F.3d 164, 165, 111 FEP 1189 (5th Cir. 2011) ("The [EEOC] may file a civil action only if it has first been unable to secure a conciliation agreement from the employer."); EEOC v. CRST Van Expedited, Inc., 679 F.3d 657, 672–75, 114 FEP 1566 (8th Cir. 2012) (Title VII permits suits by EEOC upon only unsuccessful attempts to conciliate; where EEOC brings claim on behalf of class of individuals, EEOC's obligations to investigate and attempt conciliation are not abandoned, and dismissal is proper as to those claims to extent wrongdoing was not discovered during investigation);

D. Charge Not Under Oath

[26][On page 29-8 of the Main Volume, in footnote 26, add the following at the end of the footnote.]

See also Williams v. CSX Transp. Co., 643 F.3d 502, 507–10, 112 FEP 961 (6th Cir. 2011) (plaintiff's EEOC filing constituted "charge" necessary to exhaust administrative remedies under Title VII because: (1) it was verified; (2) it contained information sufficiently precise to identify parties and described alleged discriminatory actions or practices; and (3) objective observer would believe plaintiff's filing—taken as whole—requested EEOC to activate its remedial processes).

[27][On page 29-8 of the Main Volume, in footnote 27, add the following at the end of the footnote.]

But cf. EEOC v. Summer Classics, Inc., 471 F. App'x 868, 872, 26 AD 1177 (11th Cir. 2012) (intake questionnaire was not "Charge of Discrimination" because nothing in questionnaire indicated desire to activate machinery and remedial processes of EEOC).

E. EEOC Failure to Issue Notice of Right to Sue When Charging Party Is Entitled to It

[39][On page 29-11 of the Main Volume, in footnote 39, add the following after "*See, e.g.*,".]

Farris v. Shinseki, 660 F.3d 557, 563, 25 AD 955 (1st Cir. 2011) (plaintiff not entitled to equitable tolling of Title VII time limits absent showing that her failure to timely file was due to circumstances beyond her control; "equitable tolling will not rescue a party from his or her lack of diligence");

[39][On page 29-11 of the Main Volume, in footnote 39, add the following before "*But see*".]

Cf. Tiberio v. Allergy Asthma Immunology of Rochester, 664 F.3d 35, 37, 25 AD 929 (2d Cir. 2011) (90-day period in which to file suit begins to run on date right-to-sue letter is received by either claimant or her counsel, whichever is earlier).

III. SUIT AGAINST PARTY NOT NAMED IN EEOC CHARGE

[42][On page 29-11 of the Main Volume, in footnote 42, add the following after "*See, e.g.*,".]

Rĭos-Colón v. Toledo-Dávila, 641 F.3d 1, 4, 111 FEP 1571 (1st Cir. 2011) (dismissal of complaint that named supervisory officers in their official capacities, instead of police department, was error where officers were acting as agents of department and department had knowledge of EEOC charge underlying action); EEOC v. National Educ. Ass'n, Alaska, 422 F.3d 840, 847–48 (9th Cir. 2005) (failure to name national organization in EEOC charge is not dispositive of whether it can be named as party to ensuing litigation; "where the EEOC or defendants themselves 'should have anticipated' that the claimant would name those defendants in a Title VII suit, the court has jurisdiction over those defendants") (citation omitted);

[43][On page 29-12 of the Main Volume, in footnote 43, add the following after "*See*".]

Olsen v. Marshall & Ilsely Corp., 267 F.3d 597, 604, 86 FEP 1404 (7th Cir. 2001) (employee of subsidiary company could not sue parent corporation that was not named in charge even though parent had notice of charge and participated in administrative process);

[48][On page 29-13 of the Main Volume, in footnote 48, replace citation for "Olsen v. Marshall & Ilsely Corp." with the following.]

Olsen, 267 F.3d at 604

IV. SCOPE OF EEOC CHARGE AS LIMITING THE SCOPE OF A TITLE VII LAWSUIT

B. Application of Rationale

1. Issues and Bases of Discrimination Not Asserted in the Charge

[113][On page 29-29 of the Main Volume, in footnote 113, add the following after "*See*".]

Richter v. Advance Auto Parts, Inc., 686 F.3d 847, 851, 115 FEP 1067 (8th Cir. 2012) (barring plaintiff's claim of retaliatory termination because it was not reasonably related to her charge of race and sex discrimination and she did not file separate charge of retaliation); Sydnor v. Fairfax Cnty., Va., 681 F.3d 591, 593–94, 26 AD 648 (4th Cir. 2012) (claims in judicial complaint must be reasonably related to contents of EEOC charge); Morales-Cruz v. University of P.R., 676 F.3d 220, 223, 114 FEP 1185 (1st Cir. 2012) (Title VII action confined by allegations averred in administrative charge; "the judicial complaint must bear some close relation to the allegations presented to the agency") (quoting Jorge v. Rumsfeld, 404 F.3d 556, 565, 95 FEP 964 (1st Cir. 2005)); Velazquez-Ortiz v. Vilsack, 657 F.3d 64, 71, 113 FEP 627 (1st Cir. 2011) (allegations in charge must "bear some close relation" to claims in subsequent judicial complaint); Tyler v. University of Ark. Bd. of Trs., 628 F.3d 980, 989, 111 FEP 161 (8th Cir. 2011) (plaintiff did not exhaust administrative remedies on claim of gender discrimination where his charge did not mention gender and was based solely on retaliation, because claims of gender discrimination and retaliation are not reasonably related); Spengler v. Worthington Cylinders, 615 F.3d 481, 109 FEP 1526 (6th Cir. 2010) (plaintiff adequately exhausted administrative remedies with regard to retaliation claim; plaintiff alleged sufficient facts to put EEOC on notice of his retaliation claim even though he failed to check appropriate box on form); Jones v. Res-Care, Inc., 613 F.3d 665, 670, 109 FEP 1383 (7th Cir. 2010) (plaintiff alleged only discrete acts of discrimination in her EEOC charge, which was filed more than 300 days after their occurrence, and discrete acts are not sufficient to establish continuing violation);

[115]**[On page 29-30 of the Main Volume, in footnote 115, add the following at the end of the footnote.]**

Cf. Bissada v. Arkansas Children's Hosp., 639 F.3d 825, 830, 112 FEP 321 (8th Cir. 2011) (plaintiff satisfies exhaustion requirement where "the civil claim grows out of or is like or reasonably related to the substance of the allegations in the administrative charge"; however, "the civil suit can be only as broad as the scope of any investigation that reasonably could have been expected to result from the initial charge of discrimination") (quoting Fanning v. Potter, 614 F.3d 845, 851–52, 109 FEP 1727 (8th Cir. 2010)).

[116]**[On page 29-30 of the Main Volume, in footnote 116, add the following at the end of the footnote.]**

But see Morris v. Cabela's Wholesale, Inc., 486 F. App'x 701, 704 (10th Cir. 2012) (claim of retaliatory failure-to-rehire must be exhausted in addition to wrongful termination claim).

[118]**[On page 29-31 of the Main Volume, in footnote 118, add the following after "*But see*".]**

Richter, 686 F.3d at 851 (plaintiff failed to exhaust retaliation claim because it was not reasonably related to her charge of race and sex discrimination and she did not file separate charge alleging retaliatory termination);

[123]**[On page 29-33 of the Main Volume, in footnote 123, add the following after "*See*".]**

Moore v. Vital Prods., Inc., 641 F.3d 253, 256–57, 112 FEP 513 (7th Cir. 2011) (individual who filed charge of race and sex discrimination with respect to hostile work environment and retaliation did not exhaust claim of discriminatory discharge which, as matter of law, is outside scope of his charge);

2. *Incidents Occurring Subsequent to the Filing of the EEOC Charge*

[128][On page 29-35 of the Main Volume, in footnote 128, add the following after "*Compare*".]

McDonald-Cuba v. Santa Fe Protective Servs., Inc., 644 F.3d 1096, 1101, 112 FEP 327 (10th Cir. 2011) (employee's retaliation claim based on counterclaim filed by employer in pending lawsuit was barred because of failure to exhaust; employee required to exhaust discrete acts of retaliation occurring after filing of suit),

[129][On page 29-36 of the Main Volume, in the carryover of footnote 129, add the following at the end of the footnote.]

Even where retaliation allegations are the subject matter of a timely charge, they may be barred in a subsequent federal action if not made a part of the judicial complaint within the 90-day period for filing a lawsuit. *See* Hernandez v. Valley View Hosp. Ass'n, 684 F.3d 950, 961–62, 115 FEP 592 (10th Cir. 2012) (administratively exhausted retaliation claim was time-barred by Title VII's 90-day statute of limitations where not asserted until five months after original complaint was filed; retaliation claim did not relate back under FED. R. CIV. P. 15 because based on new and discrete facts not pled in original complaint).

4. *Pleading Requirements of the Complaint*

[138][On page 29-39 of the Main Volume, in footnote 138, add the following after "*cf.*".]

Jajeh v. County of Cook, 678 F.3d 560, 566–67, 114 FEP 1441 (7th Cir. 2012) (plaintiff properly raised hostile work environment claim although words "hostile work environment" never appear in complaint and were first used in response to defendant's motion for summary judgment; Federal Rules require only that complaint be "sufficient to provide the defendant with fair notice of the plaintiff's claim and its basis," which plaintiff did by alleging facts sufficient to notify employer of hostile work environment);

[143][On page 29-39 of the Main Volume, in footnote 143, add the following at the end of the footnote.]

See also Keys v. Humana, Inc., 684 F.3d 605, 610, 115 FEP 588 (6th Cir. 2012) (complaint need not allege prima facie case, which is evidentiary standard; rather, complaint must meet plausibility standard, which was satisfied here because it alleged sufficient facts from which court, informed by its judicial experience and common sense, could draw reasonable inference that plaintiff was subjected to discrimination); Khalik v. United Air Lines, 671 F.3d 1188, 1193, 114 FEP 500 (10th Cir. 2012) (conclusory allegations that plaintiff was (1) targeted because of her race, religion, and national and ethnic heritage; (2) subjected to false investigation and false criticism; and that (3) defendant's stated reasons for terminating plaintiff were exaggerated and false, and were not entitled to assumption of truth at pleading stage; "*Twombly/Iqbal* standard recognizes plaintiff should have at least some relevant information to make the claims plausible on their face").

VI. SUMMARY JUDGMENT

B. General Principles

[160][On page 29-42 of the Main Volume, in footnote 160, add the following at the end of the footnote.]

See, e.g., Martinez-Burgos v. Guayama Corp., 656 F.3d 7, 11, 113 FEP 253 (1st Cir. 2011) (summary judgment record is viewed in light most favorable to nonmoving party, drawing all reasonable inferences in that party's favor).

[163][On page 29-43 of the Main Volume, in footnote 163, add the following at the end of the footnote.]

See also Torgerson v. City of Rochester, 643 F.3d 1031, 1043–44, 112 FEP 613 (8th Cir. 2011) ("[s]ummary judgment procedure is properly regarded not as a disfavored procedural shortcut, but rather as an integral part of the Federal Rules as a whole, which are designed to secure the just, speedy and inexpensive determination of every action"; moreover, "[t]here is 'no discrimination case' exception to the application of summary judgment, which is a useful pretrial tool to determine whether any case, including one alleging discrimination, merits a trial.").

C. The Impact of *Reeves*

[168][On page 29-45 of the Main Volume, in the carryover of footnote 168, add the following after "*See*".]

Redd v. New York Div. of Parole, 678 F.3d 166, 174, 115 FEP 399 (2d Cir. 2012) ("[c]redibility determinations, the weighing of the evidence, and the drawing of legitimate inferences from the facts are jury functions, not those of a judge"; on motion for summary judgment, court "must disregard all evidence favorable to the moving party that the jury is not required to believe") (quoting *Reeves*, 530 U.S. at 151); Muñoz v. Sociedad Española de Auxilio Mutuo y Beneficiencia de P.R., 671 F.3d 49, 55, 114 FEP 412 (1st Cir. 2012) (review of motion for judgment as matter of law "encompasses all of the evidence in the record, but not 'evidence favorable to the moving party that the jury is not required to believe'"); Valle-Arce v. Puerto Rico Ports Auth., 651 F.3d 190, 199, 24 AD 1537 (1st Cir. 2011) (court must not "consider the credibility of witnesses, resolve conflicts in testimony, or evaluate the weight of the evidence" on motion for judgment as matter of law); Williams v. CSX Transp. Co., 643 F.3d 502, 511, 112 FEP 961 (6th Cir. 2011) (when reviewing request for judgment as matter of law, "court should review the record as a whole" but "disregard all evidence favorable to the moving party that the jury is not required to believe");

[171][On page 29-46 of the Main Volume, in the carryover of footnote 171, add the following before "Defreitas v. Horizon Inv. Mgmt.".]

Ryan v. Capital Contractors, Inc., 679 F.3d 772, 777–78, 26 AD 385 (8th Cir. 2012) (plaintiff unable to show pretext in absence of evidence that employer treated plaintiff differently than his comparator because of discriminatory animus where two employees engaged in different conduct; although other employee instigated altercation, plaintiff escalated incident and actually hit other employee); Adams v. Trustees of the Univ. of N.C.-Wilmington, 640 F.3d 550, 559–60,

111 FEP 1665 (4th Cir. 2011) (plaintiff cannot rely on own assertions of discrimination to prove pretext when there is substantial evidence of legitimate, nondiscriminatory reasons for adverse employment action); Jackson v. Watkins, 619 F.3d 463, 467, 110 FEP 257 (5th Cir. 2010) ("a plaintiff asserting a Title VII claim must rebut each of the defendant's nondiscriminatory reasons in order to survive summary judgment"; plaintiff in this case was able to rebut only some of employer's nondiscriminatory reasons for his termination, and therefore summary judgment for employer affirmed); Spengler v. Worthington Cylinders, 615 F.3d 481, 493, 109 FEP 1526 (6th Cir. 2010) ("a plaintiff's prima facie case, combined with sufficient evidence to find that the employer's asserted justification is false, may permit the trier of fact to conclude that the employer unlawfully discriminated") (quoting *Reeves*, 530 U.S. at 147–48); *cf.* Tepperwien v. Entergy Nuclear Operations, Inc., 663 F.3d 556, 567, 113 FEP 1153 (2d Cir. 2011) (FED. R. CIV. P. 50 motion "may only be granted if there exists such a complete absence of evidence supporting the verdict that the jury's findings could only have been the result of sheer surmise and conjecture, or the evidence in favor of the movant is so overwhelming that reasonable and fair minded [persons] could not arrive at a verdict against [it]") (internal quotation marks omitted) (quoting Brady v. Wal-Mart Stores, Inc., 531 F.3d 127, 133 (2d Cir. 2008));

[On page 29-47 of the Main Volume, add new footnote 171a at the end of the first sentence of the paragraph.]

[171a]Nevertheless, facts presented for consideration, although supported, may be stricken for failure to comply with local rules. *See* Martinez-Burgos v. Guayama Corp., 656 F.3d 7, 11, 113 FEP 253 (1st Cir. 2011) (it was not error for lower court to refuse to consider Spanish-language exhibits attached to plaintiff's opposition to summary judgment where she failed for 11 months to comply with local rule requiring that English translation of such documents be provided); Benuzzi v. Board of Educ. of City of Chi., 647 F.3d 652, 655–56, 112 FEP 1444 (7th Cir. 2011) (plaintiff submitted statement of additional facts, consisting of 40 numbered paragraphs; district court properly struck those paragraphs that were deemed unreasonable in length for failure to comply with local rule requiring that paragraphs be short).

[172]**[On page 29-47 of the Main Volume, in footnote 172, add the following after "*See*".]**

Jones v. Walgreen Co., 679 F.3d 9, 21–22, 26 AD 261 (1st Cir. 2012) (plaintiff may demonstrate pretext by showing that reasonable fact-finder could conclude defendant acted based on retaliatory motives instead of legitimate reasons it proffered; plaintiff did not show that employer's decision to terminate employee for inability to perform functions of job—based on information provided by employee's orthopedist—was pretextual); Yeschick v. Mineta, 675 F.3d 622, 632, 114 FEP 1202 (6th Cir. 2012) (plaintiff unable to rebut proffered legitimate, nondiscriminatory reason for adverse employment decision when other applicants possessed knowledge and experience that plaintiff lacked); Hernandez v. Yellow Transp., Inc., 670 F.3d 644, 660–61, 114 FEP 545 (5th Cir.) (plaintiff unable to establish pretext despite allegations that he was treated less favorably than similarly situated employees and that employer's investigation had procedural irregularities and its grievance procedures were unfair where, in each case, plaintiff's claims were based on mere speculation, not raised in district court, or were controverted by plaintiff's admission that he committed acts for which he was terminated), *cert. denied sub nom.* Kitterer v. Yellow Transp., Inc., 133 S. Ct. 136, 116 FEP 224 (2012); Vaughn v. Woodforest Bank, 665 F.3d 632, 637–40, 114 FEP 118 (5th Cir. 2011) (under *McDonnell Douglas*, once employer produces legitimate, nondiscriminatory explanation for adverse employment action, plaintiff must show that proffered explanation is false; evidence of disparate treatment could not establish pretext where comparators had different job responsibilities than those held by plaintiff; plaintiff survived summary judgment, however, based on rebuttal evidence regarding alleged unsatisfactory conduct, which cast doubt on whether stated nondiscriminatory reasons for firing were real); Romans v. Michigan Dep't of Human Servs., 668 F.3d 826, 839, 114 FEP 1404 (6th Cir. 2012) (employer's well-founded belief, based on particularized facts from investigation, that plaintiff was harassing co-employee and that this behavior justified termination was sufficient to rebut plaintiff's pretext claim); Lefevers v. GAF Fiberglass Corp., 667 F.3d 721, 725–26, 114 FEP 385 (6th Cir. 2012) (where employer proffered evidence of plaintiff's poor work performance and retained employees near or above plaintiff's age, plaintiff unable to prove justification for termination was pretext for age discrimination); Provenzano v. LCI Holdings, Inc., 663 F.3d

806, 815–18, 114 FEP 90 (6th Cir. 2011) (employer's decision not to promote plaintiff based on poor work performance and to promote more qualified candidate not pretextual where record contained no evidence of discrimination and plaintiff was unable to demonstrate that (1) she was superior candidate such that no reasonable employer would have chosen other applicant for position, or (2) she was as qualified if not more qualified than employee promoted); *Martinez-Burgos*, 656 F.3d at 14 ("rebutting proffered legitimate reason for the adverse [employment] action is more demanding than the relatively low bar at the prima facie stage of the burden-shifting framework"); Stansberry v. Air Wis. Airlines Corp., 651 F.3d 482, 488, 24 AD 1544 (6th Cir. 2011) (fact that employer knew of plaintiff's wife's disability for number of years undercut plaintiff's inference that he was terminated due to her disability); Hoyle v. Freightliner, LLC, 650 F.3d 321, 337–38, 111 FEP 1537 (4th Cir. 2011) (closeness in time between discriminatory conduct and adverse employment action is insufficient, without more, to prove pretext); Amini v. City of Minneapolis, 643 F.3d 1068, 1075, 112 FEP 1089 (8th Cir. 2011) (city's explanation that it failed to hire plaintiff because he became defensive and agitated during interview was not pretextual where corroborated by audio recording), *cert. denied*, 132 S. Ct. 1144, 114 FEP 288 (2012); Rahlf v. Mo-Tech Corp., Inc., 642 F.3d 633, 638–39, 112 FEP 787 (8th Cir. 2011) (plaintiffs' argument that reduction in force (RIF) was pretext for age discrimination failed, in part, because although employer hired five additional employees after plaintiffs' termination, newly hired employees were for different, lower-level positions and "when a company exercises its business judgment in deciding to reduce its work force, it need not provide evidence of financial distress to make it a legitimate RIF") (internal quotation marks and citations omitted); Bonds v. Leavitt, 629 F.3d 369, 386, 111 FEP 171 (4th Cir.) (plaintiff cannot prove pretext by focusing on minor discrepancies that do not cast doubt on validity of employer's explanation for action or by raising points irrelevant to that explanation), *cert. denied*, Bonds v. Sebelius, 132 S. Ct. 398, 113 FEP 800 (2011); El Sayed v. Hilton Hotels Corp., 627 F.3d 931, 933, 110 FEP 1764 (2d Cir. 2010) (temporal proximity between protected activity and adverse employment action, without more, is insufficient to demonstrate pretext in retaliation case); Gómez-González v. Rural Opportunities, Inc., 626 F.3d 654, 662–64, 110 FEP 1542, 23 AD 1569 (1st Cir. 2010) (party may prove pretext by demonstrating that employer has offered differing or shifting justifications for its adverse employment action); Meléndez v. Autogermana, Inc., 622 F.3d 46, 52–53, 110 FEP 832 (1st Cir. 2010) (plaintiff unable to prove pretext in age discrimination termination case where employer dismissed four other salespersons of various ages); Collazo v. Bristol-Myers Squibb Mfg., Inc., 617 F.3d 39, 50, 109 FEP 1601 (1st Cir. 2010) (reasonable jury could find that employer's stated reasons for terminating plaintiff were pretext for unlawful retaliation when there was close temporal connection between plaintiff's protected conduct and his termination and employer's proffered reasons were inconsistent with evidence); *Spengler*, 615 F.3d at 493–95 (jury could reasonably conclude that employer's proffered reason for terminating plaintiff was pretext; plaintiff proffered evidence that rules were selectively enforced, supervisor's attitude toward him changed after complaint of ageist comments, he was valued employee at time of discharge, and he earned referral to prestigious division of company prior to termination);

[173]**[On page 29-47 of the Main Volume, in footnote 173, add the following after "*See*".]**

St. Martin v. City of St. Paul, 680 F.3d 1027, 1033–34, 26 AD 516 (8th Cir. 2012) (no pretext where city articulated nondiscriminatory reasons for failing to promote plaintiff to fire chief despite his high test scores and experience; other high-ranking candidates were not offered position over lower-ranked candidates that had come to interview prepared and shared department's vision); Guimaraes v. SuperValu, Inc., 674 F.3d 962, 973, 114 FEP 1032 (8th Cir. 2012) (although "[p]roof of pretext coupled with a strong prima facie case, may suffice to create a triable question of fact," plaintiff "retains, at all times, the ultimate burden of proof and persuasion that [defendant] discriminated against her") (internal quotation marks and citations omitted); Gibson v. American Greetings Corp., 670 F.3d 844, 854–55, 114 FEP 927 (8th Cir.) (plaintiff unable to show intentional discrimination where she received multiple warnings for violating company policy and alleged that nonprotected employees did not; plaintiff did not specifically identify any favorably treated employee by name, and further did not present any evidence to suggest that warnings were for discriminatory reasons), *cert. denied*, 133 S. Ct. 313, 116 FEP 224 (2012); Othman v. City of Country Club Hills, 671 F.3d 672, 677, 114 FEP 804 (8th Cir. 2012) (in pretext cases, "[a]lthough intermediate evidentiary burdens shift back and forth under [the *McDonnell Douglas*] framework, the ultimate burden of persuading the trier of fact that the defendant intentionally discriminated against the plaintiff remains at all times with the plaintiff") (internal quotation marks and citations omitted); Bonefont-Igaravidez v. International Shipping Corp., 659 F.3d 120, 124, 113 FEP 934 (1st Cir. 2011) ("pretext can be established by such weaknesses, implausibilities, inconsistencies, incoherencies, or contradictions in the employer's offered reasons for the termination that a reasonable factfinder could rationally find them unworthy of credence and hence infer that the employer did not act for the asserted non-discriminatory reasons") (internal quotation marks omitted) (citing *Gómez-González*, 626 F.3d at 662–63); Serednyj v. Beverly Healthcare, LLC, 656 F.3d 540, 548, 113 FEP 104, 25 AD 103 (7th Cir. 2011) (absent direct evidence, plaintiff must show through indirect evidence "convincing mosaic of circumstantial evidence from which a reasonable juror could infer intentional discrimination"); Okoli v. City of Baltimore, 648 F.3d 216, 223, 112 FEP 1675 (4th Cir. 2011) (trier of fact can infer pretext from falsity of explanation that employer is attempting to cover up discriminatory purpose; employer's justification suspicious when plaintiff terminated hours after she rejected her supervisor's sexual advancements by filing complaint); Haigh v. Gelitia USA, Inc., 632 F.3d 464, 470, 111 FEP 614 (8th Cir. 2011) (to defeat summary judgment motion, showing of pretext "requires more than merely discrediting an employer's asserted reasons for terminating an employee. A plaintiff must also demonstrate that the circumstances permit a reasonable inference of discriminatory animus."); *Meléndez*, 622 F.3d at 52–53 ("[i]t is not enough for a plaintiff merely to impugn the veracity of the employer's justification; he must elucidate specific facts which would enable a jury to find that the reason given is not only a sham, but a sham intended to cover up the employer's real motive: age discrimination") (internal citations and quotation marks omitted); *Spengler*, 615 F.3d at 493 ("plaintiff can rebut an employer's legitimate, nondiscriminatory reason and show pretext by demonstrating that: (1) the employer's stated reason for terminating the employee had no basis in fact, (2) the reason offered for terminating the employee was not the actual reason for the termination, or (3) the reason offered was insufficient to explain the employer's action");

[175]**[On page 29-49 of the Main Volume, in footnote 175, add the following after "*See, e.g.*,".]**

Holland v. Gee, 677 F.3d 1047, 1056, 114 FEP 1449 (11th Cir. 2012) (issue at pretext stage is whether there is "a convincing mosaic of circumstantial evidence that would allow jury to infer intentional discrimination"); *Gibson*, 670 F.3d at 854 (plaintiff may show pretext in one of two ways: "[f]irst, a plaintiff may succeed indirectly by showing the proffered explanation has no basis in fact. Second, a plaintiff can directly persuade the court that a prohibited reason more likely motivated the employer"); Shelley v. Geren, 666 F.3d 599, 609–12, 114 FEP 303 (9th Cir. 2012) (plaintiff's direct evidence—that persons involved in decision-making process inquired about projected retirement dates of applicants—and circumstantial evidence—of plaintiff's greater years of experience, superior educational qualifications, and current employment within hiring department—supported reasonable inference of age discrimination when viewed on whole); Hamilton v. Geithner, 666 F.3d 1344, 1357, 114 FEP 239 (D.C. Cir. 2012) (viewing record as whole, "the evidence of a significant disparity in the candidates' qualifications, the highly subjective nature of the [decision maker's] proffered nondiscriminatory explanation, and the absence of any contemporaneous documentation supporting [the employer's] explanation" could support reasonable inference of pretext); Earl v. Nielsen Media Research, Inc., 658 F.3d 1108, 1114–18, 113 FEP 609 (9th Cir. 2011) (plaintiff's evidence that younger employees with similar histories of policy violations created question of fact regarding pretext; violations need not be identical to be similarly situated and, in contrast to Title VII, comparators under ADEA may be within protected class); Talavera v. Shah, 638 F.3d 303, 312–13, 111 FEP 1574 (D.C. Cir. 2011) (plaintiff established question of fact on pretext through decision maker's statements that constituted admissions of party opponent and his destruction of interview notes, which supported more than "weak adverse inference" of spoliation); Zeinali v. Raytheon Co., 636 F.3d 544, 554, 111 FEP 1681 (9th Cir. 2011) (plaintiff presented sufficient evidence to defeat summary judgment; plaintiff controverted employer's claim that he was terminated after his application for security clearance was denied by evidence that other non-Iranian employees were retained after revocation of their security clearances, where there was no material distinction between security clearances that were "denied" or "revoked"); Calhoun v. Johnson, 632 F.3d 1259, 1264, 111 FEP 499 (D.C. Cir. 2011) (qualifications gap alone does not support inference of pretext that employer failed to hire based on merit, as claimed, unless gap is "great enough to be inherently indicative of discrimination"); Dixon v. Hallmark Cos., 627 F.3d 849, 854–55, 110 FEP 1675 (11th Cir. 2010) (plaintiffs created issue of fact on pretext based on supervisor's comment at time of termination—"You're fired, too. You're too religious."—which took place on heels of dispute as to whether plaintiffs' religious beliefs violated company policy); Mogenhan v. Napolitano, 613 F.3d 1162, 1166–67, 23 AD 705 (D.C. Cir. 2010) (plaintiff established material factual dispute through unrebutted testimony that—20 days after she internally complained of discrimination—her supervisor posted complaint on agency's intranet and allegedly increased plaintiff's caseload five or six times to keep her "too busy to file complaints"); Alvarez v. Royal Atl. Developers, Inc. 610 F.3d 1253, 1267, 109 FEP 1162 (11th Cir. 2010) (employer did not act unlawfully by insisting that person in plaintiff's position be "miracle worker;" plaintiff did not create fact issue of pretext by showing that her performance was satisfactory where she simply failed to meet her supervisor's unreasonable expectations);

D. Common Procedural Issues

1. *Inadmissible Evidence and Motions to Strike*

[177][On page 29-50 of the Main Volume, in footnote 177, add the following after "*see also*".]

Wilson v. Moulison N. Corp., 639 F.3d 1, 6, 111 FEP 1451 (1st Cir. 2011) ("A properly supported summary judgment motion cannot be defeated with conclusory allegations, improbable inferences, periphrastic circumlocutions, or rank speculation.");

[On page 29-52 of the Main Volume, after the sentence that ends with footnote 185, add the following.]

Moreover, a court may decline to consider an affidavit from a witness who has not been identified pursuant to Federal Rule of Civil Procedure 26(a) or (e).[1]

---

[1] *See* Malone v. Ameren UE, 646 F.3d 512, 515–16, 112 FEP 1458 (8th Cir. 2011) (in deciding motion for summary judgment, district court did not abuse discretion in failing to consider affidavits from three witnesses who had not been identified previously as required by Rule 26(a) or (e)).

[190]**[On page 29-53 of the Main Volume, in footnote 190, add the following after "*See, e.g.*,".]**

Jones v. UPS Ground Freight, 683 F.3d 1283, 1294–96, 115 FEP 278 (11th Cir. 2012) (because supervisor's e-mail statement that plaintiff reported racially derogatory remarks to him was inadmissible and contrary to supervisor's deposition testimony, it could not be considered at summary judgment); Bhatti v. Trustees of Boston Univ., 659 F.3d 64, 71, 113 FEP 722 (1st Cir. 2011) (court will not consider hearsay in deciding motion for summary judgment; only admissible evidence can be considered); Luster v. Illinois Dep't of Corr., 652 F.3d 726, 731 n.2, 112 FEP 1321 (7th Cir. 2011) (party's own answers to interrogatories, lacking proper foundation, are inadmissible);

2. *Affidavit in Conflict With Deposition*

[193]**[On page 29-54 of the Main Volume, in the carryover of footnote 193, add the following after "*see also*".]**

Faulk v. Volunteers of Am., 444 F. App'x 316, 318 (11th Cir. 2011) (plaintiff's affidavit properly stricken where she gave clear answers to unambiguous questions in her deposition, which she contradicted in her affidavit);

[193]**[On page 29-54 of the Main Volume, in the carryover of footnote 193, add the following after "*But cf.*".]**

Hernandez v. Valley View Hosp. Ass'n, 684 F.3d 950, 956 n.3 (10th Cir. 2012) (affidavit did not contradict prior sworn testimony where deposition testimony provided only "examples" of racial jokes of which plaintiff testified there were "so many;" affidavit simply provided additional examples of racial jokes);

[194]**[On page 29-54 of the Main Volume, in footnote 194, add the following after "*See*".]**

Valley View, 684 F.3d at 956 n.3 (affidavit did not contradict prior deposition testimony, which provided only "examples" of racial jokes of which there were "so many," and affidavit submitted on summary judgment simply provided additional examples of racial jokes); *Faulk*, 444 F. App'x at 318 (affidavits properly stricken where employee failed to list affiants as potential witnesses in her initial disclosures and did not supplement her disclosures or otherwise explain this omission);

[197]**[On page 29-55 of the Main Volume, in footnote 197, add the following after "*See*".]**

Valley View, 684 F.3d at 956 n.3 (affidavit did not contradict prior sworn testimony but merely provided additional examples of racial jokes exemplified in plaintiff's deposition);

3. Federal Rule of Civil Procedure 56(f)

[198]**[On page 29-56 of the Main Volume, in footnote 198, add the following after "*See, e.g.,*".]**

Sánchez-Rodríguez v. AT&T Mobility P.R., Inc., 673 F.3d 1, 10, 114 FEP 912 (1st Cir. 2012) (party's request for additional discovery pursuant to FED. R. CIV. P. 56(f) will be denied absent explanation why she could not obtain information needed to contest motion for summary judgment prior to close of discovery);

VII. JURY TRIAL

A. Issues Tried to Jury and Bench

[208]**[On page 29-59 of the Main Volume, in footnote 208, add the following after "*see also*".]**

McInerney v. United Air Lines, Inc., 463 F. App'x 709, 724–26, 112 FEP 7 (10th Cir. 2011) (district court's denial of front-pay award was not abuse of discretion);

[209]**[On page 29-60 of the Main Volume, in footnote 209, add the following after "*See, e.g.,*".]**

Bergerson v. New York State Office of Mental Health, Cent. N.Y. Psychiatric Ctr., 652 F.3d 277, 287–88, 112 FEP 1313 (2d Cir. 2011) (award of front pay is within discretion of court; front pay is awarded when reinstatement is inappropriate—either because of animosity between employer and employee or because position is no longer available—and party has been unable to find job since his or her termination);

[212]**[On page 29-61 of the Main Volume, in footnote 212, add the following after "*see*".]**

Thomas v. iStar Fin., Inc., 652 F.3d 141, 152 (2d Cir.) (per curiam) (because back pay is equitable remedy, it is to be decided by court, not jury; however, parties may consent to have jury decide questions of economic damages), *cert. denied*, 132 S. Ct. 856 (2011);

B. Jury Instructions and Verdict Forms

[213]**[On page 29-61 of the Main Volume, in footnote 213, add the following after "*see also*".]**

Schandelmeier-Bartels v. Chicago Park Dist., 634 F.3d 372, 386–87, 111 FEP 739 (7th Cir. 2011) (objection to jury instructions is timely only if made prior to giving of instructions and closing arguments);

[217]**[On page 29-62 of the Main Volume, in footnote 217, add the following after "*E.g.*,".]**

Hicks v. Forest Pres. Dist. of Cook Cnty., Ill., 677 F.3d 781, 790, 114 FEP 1281 (7th Cir. 2012) ("[e]ven if we believe that the jury was confused or misled [by deficiencies in the jury instructions], we must find that the [objecting party] was prejudiced before ordering a new trial") (citation omitted);

[217]**[On page 29-62 of the Main Volume, in footnote 217, add the following after "*But see*".]**

Sanders v. City of Newport, 657 F.3d 772, 781–83, 17 WH Cases 2d 588 (9th Cir. 2011) (erroneous jury instruction misplacing burden of proof was not harmless error and warranted new trial);

[218]**[On page 29-62 of the Main Volume, in footnote 218, add the following after "*See, e.g.*,".]**

EEOC v. Service Temps, Inc., 679 F.3d 323, 335, 26 AD 129 (5th Cir. 2012) (defendant failed to object to jury instruction at trial, raising standard of review to plain error and requiring defendant to show "(1) that an error occurred; (2) that the error was plain, which means clear or obvious; (3) [that] the plain error must affect substantial rights; and (4) [that] not correcting the error would seriously affect the fairness, integrity, or public reputation of judicial proceedings") (internal quotation marks and citation omitted);

[221]**[On page 29-64 of the Main Volume, in footnote 221, add the following after "*See, e.g.,*".]**

Ponce v. Billington, 679 F.3d 840, 845–46, 115 FEP 1 (D.C. Cir. 2012) (district court did not abuse its discretion in instructing jury on but-for theory of liability when it stated that plaintiff must prove prohibited reason was "sole reason" for termination, and then later defined "sole reason" as "but-for" causation); Jones v. UPS, Inc., 674 F.3d 1187, 1198 (10th Cir.) (decision to give particular instruction is reviewed for abuse of discretion, and instructions are reviewed de novo, on the whole, to determine whether they accurately state law), *cert. denied*, 133 S. Ct. 413 (2012);

[222]**[On page 29-64 of the Main Volume, in footnote 222, add the following after "*See*".]**

Hicks, 677 F.3d at 790 (jury instructions are reviewed de novo to "determine whether, taken as a whole, they correctly and completely informed the jury of the applicable law") (citations omitted); Lore v. City of Syracuse, 670 F.3d 127, 156 (2d Cir. 2012) (jury instruction is erroneous if it fails to proffer correct legal standard or does not adequately apprise jury of law);

[223]**[On page 29-65 of the Main Volume, in footnote 223, add the following after "*See, e.g.,*".]**

Booker v. Massachusetts Dep't of Pub. Health, 612 F.3d 34, 43 (1st Cir. 2010) (court has wide discretion over particular words used to describe legal standards at issue);

[224]**[On page 29-66 of the Main Volume, in footnote 224, add the following after "*See, e.g.,*".]**

Henry v. Wyeth Pharm., Inc., 616 F.3d 134, 154, 109 FEP 1618 (2d Cir. 2010) (to prevent confusion, courts should exercise extreme caution when importing *McDonnell Douglas* formulation into jury charges);

[228]**[On page 29-67 of the Main Volume, in footnote 228, add the following after "*see also*".]**

Henry, 616 F.3d at 157 (although finding that plaintiff could not object to "pretext" charge that he requested, concluding that "pretext" can be misinterpreted as including intent to deceive, and therefore stating that "for the future we caution district courts to avoid charging juries to the effect that a plaintiff must show that the employer's stated reason for an adverse action was a 'pretext'");

[On page 29-71 of the Main Volume, after the sentence that ends with footnote 248, add the following.]

However, a special interrogatory or verdict form need not address an affirmative defense where the defense is incorporated in the jury instructions.[2]

---

[2]EEOC v. Management Hospitality of Racine, Inc., 666 F.3d 422, 440, 114 FEP 145 (7th Cir. 2012) (failure of special verdict form to include reference to *Faragher/ Ellerth* affirmative defense did not take issue away from jury where jury instructions were proper; finding of liability as to sexual harassment was implicit rejection of affirmative defense).

Chapter 30

EEOC LITIGATION

II. ADMINISTRATIVE PREREQUISITES TO SUIT

A. Administrative Prerequisites to Suit Under § 706 and the ADEA

1. A Timely Charge

[On page 30-7 of the Main Volume, after the first sentence of the first paragraph, add new footnote 22a.]

[22a]EEOC v. Schwan's Home Serv., 644 F.3d 742, 746–47 112 FEP 1227 (8th Cir. 2011) (district court correctly refused to consider timeliness of amended charge at subpoena enforcement stage).

3. Investigation

[43][On page 30-11 of the Main Volume, in footnote 43, add the following after "*See*".]

EEOC v. Konica Minolta Bus. Solutions USA, Inc., 639 F.3d 366, 369–70, 112 FEP 97 (7th Cir. 2011) (enforcing subpoena seeking records relating to hiring practices even though charging party was alleging discrimination in discipline and terms and conditions of employment, on basis that records might cast light on charging party's allegations of differential treatment);

[43][On page 30-11 of the Main Volume, in footnote 43, add the following at the end of the footnote.]

But see EEOC v. Burlington N. Santa Fe R.R., 669 F.3d 1154, 1157–59, 25 AD 1572 (10th Cir. 2012) (affirming district court's refusal to enforce subpoena seeking companywide information where investigation was based on two charges that did not contain allegations of systemic discrimination and EEOC had provided no basis for expanding investigation).

[45]**[On page 30-11 of the Main Volume, in footnote 45, add the following after "*Compare*".]**

Konica Minolta Bus. Solutions USA, Inc., 639 F.3d at 369–70 (EEOC is entitled to subpoena employer's records concerning its hiring activity; although charge alleged only race discrimination in terms and conditions of employment, hiring information might "cast light" on those claims), EEOC v. Kronos, Inc., 620 F.3d 287, 298, 23 AD 1105 (3d Cir. 2010) (*Kronos I*) (district court abused its discretion when it limited EEOC subpoena seeking information related to customer service assessment test used by employer that allegedly had disparate impact on disabled applicants to data pertaining to positions sought by charging party, where employer purportedly used assessment test in hiring for every retail position, and "[s]uch data, at the very least, provides comparative information on the Assessment"),

[46]**[On page 30-12 of the Main Volume, in footnote 46, add the following at the end of the footnote.]**

But see EEOC v. Burlington N. Santa Fe R.R., 669 F.3d 1154, 1157–59, 25 AD 1572 (10th Cir. 2012) (affirming district court's refusal to enforce subpoena seeking companywide information where EEOC provided no basis for its intention to expand investigation beyond parameters of charges).

[47]**[On page 30-12 of the Main Volume, in footnote 47, add the following after "*with*".]**

EEOC v. Randstad, 685 F.3d 433, 451–52, 115 FEP 801 (4th Cir. 2012) (subpoena enforced where EEOC sought to investigate possible national origin discrimination based upon charge that initially raised that issue but was subsequently amended to limit allegations to only disability discrimination), *Kronos I*, 620 F.3d at 300–02 (denying enforcement of subpoena relating to alleged race discrimination as unjustified "fishing expedition" where underlying charge was limited to allegation of disability discrimination),

[50][On page 30-12 of the Main Volume, in footnote 50, add the following after "*See*".]

Randstad, 685 F.3d at 451–52 (employer's affidavit attesting that it would require three employees at 40 hours each, and labor costs of up to $19,000, in order to assemble documents subpoenaed by EEOC was insufficient to establish that compliance would be unduly burdensome);

[51][On page 30-13 of the Main Volume, in footnote 51, add the following after "*See, e.g.*,".]

EEOC v. Schwan's Home Serv., 644 F.3d 742, 746–47, 112 FEP 1227 (8th Cir. 2011) (employer's argument that charge raised time-barred allegations was to be addressed after lawsuit was filed, not at subpoena enforcement stage of investigation); EEOC v. Konica Minolta Bus. Solutions USA, Inc., 639 F.3d 366, 369, 112 FEP 97 (7th Cir. 2011) (standard of relevance to be applied to enforcement of EEOC subpoena is broader than relevance standard of Fed. R. Evid. 401; better analogy would be relevance standard of Fed. R. Civ. P. 26);

[53][On page 30-13 of the Main Volume, in footnote 53, add the following at the end of the footnote.]

See also EEOC v. CRST Van Expedited, Inc., 679 F.3d 657, 680–82, 114 FEP 1566 (8th Cir. 2012) (doctrine of judicial estoppel may not be invoked against EEOC when it brings suit in its own name to remedy discrimination against employee who failed to disclose her discrimination claims in bankruptcy proceeding).

4. Reasonable Cause Determination

[70][On page 30-17 of the Main Volume, in footnote 70, add the following at the end of the footnote.]

See also Silverman v. Board of Educ. of Chi., 637 F.3d 729, 732–33, 111 FEP 1461 (7th Cir. 2011) (because Congress provided de novo trial in district court rather than more limited APA review and because "the fact-finder is a judge rather than an administrative hearing officer... H.R. Rep. No. 92-238 at 58-63," district court did not abuse its discretion in determining that EEOC reasonable cause finding was not probative evidence of discrimination and was not dispositive of liability under Title VII).

5. Conciliation

[79]**[On page 30-18 of the Main Volume, in footnote 79, add the following before "EEOC v. Sears, Roebuck & Co.".]**

EEOC v. CRST Van Expedited, Inc., 679 F.3d 657, 672–77, 114 FEP 1566 (8th Cir. 2012) (affirming dismissal of § 706 claims where EEOC failed to investigate underlying class allegations of sexual harassment, did not issue reasonable cause determination apprising employer of charges lodged against it, and thus provided employer no meaningful opportunity to conciliate);

[90]**[On page 30-20 of the Main Volume, in footnote 90, add the following after "*See*".]**

EEOC v. CRST Van Expedited, Inc., 679 F.3d 657, 677, 114 FEP 1566 (8th Cir. 2012) (affirming dismissal where district court determined that EEOC had "wholly abdicated its role in the administrative process" by failing to investigate, issue reasonable cause determination, and attempt to conciliate class claims that it was attempting to assert in court);

[On page 30-20 of the Main Volume, after the first full sentence, add the following new paragraph.]

Where a defendant wishes to assert the EEOC's failure to conciliate as a defense in litigation, it must plead such failure with particularity under FED. R. CIV. P. 9(c).[1]

[On page 30-20 of the Main Volume, after the sentence that ends with footnote 94, add the following new paragraph.]

However, the EEOC may not attempt to enforce an alleged oral settlement agreement reached during conciliation because the plain language of Title VII prohibits the use of anything said or done as part of conciliation in a subsequent proceeding without the other party's written consent.[2]

---

[1]EEOC v. Service Temps, Inc., 679 F.3d 323, 333, 26 AD 129 (5th Cir. 2011).

[2]EEOC v. Philip Servs. Corp., 635 F.3d 164, 166, 111 FEP 1189 (5th Cir. 2011).

B. Administrative Prerequisites to Pattern-or-Practice Suits under § 707

[98][On page 30-21 of the Main Volume, in footnote 98, add the following at the end of the footnote.]

See also Serrano v. Cintas Corp., 699 F.3d 884, 894–95, 116 FEP 801 (6th Cir. 2012) (allowing EEOC to bring pattern-or-practice case under § 706, inasmuch as § 707 is not sole source of EEOC's pattern-or-practice authority); *cf.* Reynolds v. Barrett, 685 F.3d 193, 202–03, 115 FEP 738 (2d Cir. 2012) (private class action alleging disparate treatment under § 1983 may not be analyzed under pattern-or-practice proof model); Chin v. Port Authority of N.Y. & N.J., 685 F.3d 135, 150, 115 FEP 720 (2d Cir. 2012) (pattern-or-practice method of proof not available to private, nonclass plaintiffs).

VI. Scope of the Litigation

B. Expansion of Basis and Issues

[On page 30-32 of the Main Volume, in the last sentence of the carryover paragraph, replace "When" with the following.]

Under the Sixth Circuit rule, when

XII. EEOC Liability for Attorney's Fees and Costs

[260][On page 30-56 of the Main Volume, in footnote 260, add the following after "*cf.*".]

EEOC v. Great Steaks, Inc., 667 F.3d 510, 522, 114 FEP 289 (4th Cir. 2012) (because Title VII has its own fee-shifting provision, EAJA's mandatory fee provision is unavailable to defendants who prevail against EEOC under Title VII);

CHAPTER 31

JUSTICE DEPARTMENT LITIGATION

I. OVERVIEW

[On pages 31-1 to 31-2, replace the carryover paragraph with the following.]

There are two primary means by which the Attorney General of the United States and the Department of Justice (Justice Department or DOJ) become involved in Title VII litigation. In the case of a Title VII charge against a state or local governmental agency, if the Equal Employment Opportunity Commission (EEOC) finds reasonable cause to believe that a violation has occurred but is unsuccessful at conciliation, it will refer the case to the DOJ, which may file a civil action under Section 706 of Title VII.[1] Under Section 707 of Title VII, the Justice Department may—without any referral—initiate pattern-or-practice suits against state or local government employers[2] or intervene in private actions of "general public importance" brought by public employees.[3] Where the EEOC determines that prompt judicial action is necessary to carry out the purposes of Title VII, the Attorney General also may bring an action against a governmental body for "appropriate temporary or preliminary relief pending final disposition of such charge."[4]

---

[1]*See* 42 U.S.C. § 2000e-5(f)(1) (2013) ("In the case of a respondent which is a government, governmental agency, or political subdivision, if the Commission has been unable to secure from the respondent a conciliation agreement acceptable to the Commission, the Commission shall take no further action and shall refer the case to the Attorney General who may bring a civil action against such respondent in the appropriate United States district court.").

[2]Section 707 of Title VII, 42 U.S.C. § 2000e-6(a) (2006), provides that "whenever the Attorney General has reasonable cause to believe that any person or group of persons is engaged in a pattern or practice of resistance to the full enjoyment of any of the rights secured by this subchapter, and that the pattern or practice is of such a nature and is intended to deny the full exercise of the rights herein described, the Attorney General may bring a civil action." Statutory references to the terms "Department of Justice (DOJ)," "United States," and "Attorney General" can be confusing and are somewhat interchangeable. The party plaintiff in such cases is the United States. Specifically, the Attorney General (who heads the DOJ) is the United States representative authorized by statute to conduct such litigation, and the DOJ is the governmental entity that exercises these responsibilities. To some extent, these terms are interchangeable in this context.

[3]*See* 42 U.S.C. § 2000e-5(f)(1) (2013).

[4]42 U.S.C. § 2000e-5(f)(2) (2013).

The DOJ also enforces Title I of the Americans with Disabilities Act (ADA) against governmental employers.[5] This authority is coextensive with the DOJ's authority under Title VII.[6]

II. JURISDICTION AND PROCEDURE FOR JUSTICE DEPARTMENT LITIGATION

A. Enforcement Upon Referral by the EEOC: Individual Charges

[On page 31-4 of the Main Volume, delete the sentence that ends with footnote 16 and also delete footnote 16.]

---

[5]*See* 42 U.S.C. § 12117 (2013).

[6]*See* Board of Trs. v. Garrett, 531 U.S. 356, 374 n.9, 11 AD 737 (2001) (affirming Justice Department's authority to pursue relief on behalf of individuals under ADA).

CHAPTER 32

FEDERAL EMPLOYEE LITIGATION

I. INTRODUCTION AND HISTORICAL OVERVIEW

A. Statutory Background

[5][On page 32-4 of the Main Volume, in footnote 5, add the following before "Baqir v. Principi".]

Diggs v. Department of Hous. & Urban Dev., 670 F.3d 1353, 1357, 113 FEP 1120 (Fed. Cir. 2011) (rejecting agency's argument that plaintiff could not pursue retaliation claim under Title VII and therefore Federal Circuit could accept jurisdiction over plaintiff's remaining Civil Service Reform Act (CSRA) claims); Velazquez-Ortiz v. Vilsack, 657 F.3d 64, 71, 113 FEP 627 (1st Cir. 2011) (federal employee denied promotion may allege that denial was in retaliation for earlier equal employment opportunity (EEO) complaint; even though § 717 contains no express retaliation prohibition applicable to federal sector, various provisions of Title VII operate, either alone or in concert with more general federal sector prohibition, to ensure that those employees are protected from same types of conduct as those in private sector);

[5][On page 32-4 of the Main Volume, in footnote 5, replace ";" with "." before "*see also*".]

[5][On page 32-4 of the Main Volume, in footnote 5, add the following before "*see also*".]

One limitation on the issues that federal employees may raise arises from agency removal procedures. The Equal Employment Opportunity Commission's (EEOC's) 2012 regulations provide that a complaint alleging that a proposal or preliminary steps to take a personnel action is discriminatory can be dismissed unless the complaint alleges that the proposal is retaliatory. 29 C.F.R. § 1614.107(a)(5);

[On page 32-5 of the Main Volume, at the end of the first sentence of the full paragraph, add new footnote 10a.]

[10a]*Cf.* Velazquez-Ortiz v. Vilsack, 657 F.3d 64, 71, 113 FEP 627 (1st Cir. 2011) (court of appeals declined to decide whether Supreme Court's "but for" standard of proof under ADEA also applies to claims brought by federal employees).

[18]**[On page 32-6 of the Main Volume, in footnote 18, add the following after "*See, e.g.,*".]**

Youssef v. FBI, 687 F.3d 397, 402, 115 FEP 974 (D.C. Cir. 2012) (in determining whether post–9/11 reassignment of plaintiff, counterterrorism expert of Egyptian national origin, to position in document room was discriminatory, proof must be examined under *Burdine/McDonnell Douglas* framework applied in actions against private employer); Shelley v. Geren, 666 F.3d 599, 606, 114 FEP 303 (9th Cir. 2012) (district court erred when it failed to apply *McDonnell Douglas* criteria in determining whether plaintiff demonstrated that reasons advanced for failure to promote him to supervisory position were pretext for impermissible age discrimination);

C. The Equal Employment Opportunity Act of 1972 Amended Title VII to Cover Certain Federal Employees

[On page 32-10 of the Main Volume, after the sentence that ends with footnote 39, add the following new paragraph.]

In contrast to the specific enumeration in § 701 of employment actions in which discrimination is prohibited, the language of § 717's prohibition is general in nature.[1] Most courts have read into that language the more specific substantive terms of § 701.[2] Although the law protecting private employees and that which is applied to federal workers are substantively very similar, there are significant procedural differences in both administrative and judicial enforcement.[3]

---

[1]"All personnel actions affecting employees or applicants for employment... shall be made free from any discrimination based on race, color, religion, sex, or national origin." 42 U.S.C. § 2000(e)-16.

[2]*See, e.g.*, Diggs v. Department of Hous. & Urban Dev., 670 F.3d 1353, 1357, 113 FEP 1120 (Fed. Cir. 2011) (rejecting agency's argument that plaintiff could not pursue retaliation claim under Title VII and therefore Federal Circuit could accept jurisdiction over plaintiff's remaining CSRA claims, court found that Supreme Court's interpretation of ADEA § 633a in *Gomez-Perez v. Potter* dictated that "when Congress broadly drafts provisions prohibiting 'any discrimination' by the federal government, it intends to bar the government from engaging in, among other practices applicable to private employers, retaliation against an employee who complains of illegal discrimination"; because § 633a was modeled on Title VII's federal sector provision, Title VII also must prohibit retaliation by federal agencies).

[3]*See, e.g.*, Bullock v. Napolitano, 666 F.3d 281, 284, 114 FEP 297 (4th Cir. 2012) (even though Supreme Court has held that Title VII actions could be brought in either state or federal court, cases brought under § 717 must be brought in federal court;

D. The Civil Service Reform Act of 1978 Restructured the Administrative Enforcement of § 717

[58][On page 32-14 of the Main Volume, in footnote 58, add the following at the end of the second sentence, after "(1976)".]

, and has specified that, even in the case of a "mixed" case decided by the MSPB, the complainant has the option of seeking de novo review in district court, rather than before the Federal Circuit. Kloeckner v. Solis, 133 S. Ct. 596, 606–07, 116 FEP 1153 (2012)

II. ADMINISTRATIVE ENFORCEMENT

A. Employees Covered by § 717

1. General Overview of Procedures and Timeliness

[90][On page 32-20 of the Main Volume, in footnote 90, add the following after "*see also*".]

Vera v. McHugh, 622 F.3d 17, 29, 110 FEP 705 (1st Cir. 2010) ("EEOC regulations provide a highly structured set of steps which must be taken by the agency and the aggrieved party as the complaint process proceeds");

[96][On page 32-21 of the Main Volume, in footnote 96, add the following at the end of the footnote.]

See Santiago v. United States, 107 Fed. Cl. 154, 158, 116 FEP 874 (Ct. Cl. 2012) (civilian Army employee was time-barred from pursuing EPA claims with respect to paychecks issued more than two years before action was filed, absent any evidence of willfulness sufficient to extend statute of limitations to three years).

[101][On page 32-22 of the Main Volume, in footnote 101, add the following after "*But see*".]

Wilkie v. Department of Health & Human Servs., 638 F.3d 944, 951, 112 FEP 100 (8th Cir. 2011) (although continuing violation doctrine from *National R.R. Passenger Corp. v. Morgan* applies to 45-day timeframe for contacting EEO counselor, it is inapplicable where

---

federal court cannot acquire jurisdiction of § 717 case that is removed from state court because state court never had jurisdiction over matter).

untimely harassing acts, concerning sexual advances, were different in nature from alleged harassment occurring within 45 days of counselor contact, which involved performance/work issues);

[104][On page 32-23 of the Main Volume, in footnote 104, replace the sentence before "*See*" with the following.]

The EEOC's new regulations regarding federal employees' complaints of discrimination require an agency that does not complete its investigation within 180 (or 360) days to provide the complainant with written notice of his or her right to request a hearing as well as an estimate of the date on which it expects to complete its investigation.

2. Individual Complaints

[On page 32-24 of the Main Volume, following "jurisdiction over "mixed" cases", add new footnote 113a.]

[113a]*See, e.g.*, Carver v. Holder, 606 F.3d 690, 696, 109 FEP 556 (5th Cir. 2010) (where federal agency has failed to comply with EEOC's decision awarding relief, employee may file petition for enforcement of relief order with EEOC Office of Federal Operations).

[114][On page 32-24 of the Main Volume, replace footnote 114 with the following.]

[114]Adverse actions that can be appealed to the MSPB are set out at 5 U.S.C. § 7512. A mixed case arises where the employee claims, among other things, that the agency discriminated against him or her in violation of a federal statute. Kloeckner v. Solis, 133 S. Ct. 596, 601, 116 FEP 1153 (2012).

a. Individual Discrimination Complaints Not Appealable to the MSPB ("Pure EEO Cases")

(i.) Pre-complaint and counseling stage

[117][On page 32-26 of the Main Volume, in the carryover of footnote 117, add the following at the end of the footnote.]

The EEOC's 2012 amendments to its regulations concerning federal employees provide that agency EEO programs must comply with part 1614 and EEOC Management Directives and Management Bulletins. The EEOC may review agency programs for compliance and issue notices to agencies when noncompliance is found. 29 C.F.R. § 1614.102(e) (2012). The EEOC Chair has discretion to determine whether a notice of noncompliance will be made public. *Id.*

[120]**[On page 32-27 of the Main Volume, in footnote 120, add the following at the end of the footnote.]**

But see Vera v. McHugh, 622 F.3d 17, 31, 110 FEP 705 (1st Cir. 2010) (even though agency did not give employee required notice of time period for filing formal complaint at conclusion of pre-complaint counseling stage, her failure to file in timely fashion was not excused where her conduct demonstrated that she was aware of time periods involved and was not prejudiced by lack of notice).

(iii.) Investigation

[On page 32-29 of the Main Volume, after the sentence that ends with footnote 132, add the following new section.]

(a) Settlement during the administrative process [New Topic]

At any point during the administrative process, the complainant and the agency may reach a voluntary settlement of the complaint. The EEOC's regulations provide that any such settlement shall be final and binding.[4] Settlements reached in the administrative process must be in writing, signed by the parties, and identify the claims being settled.[5] Where a complainant believes that the agency has failed to comply with the terms of the agreement, he or she may file a new complaint with the agency's EEO Director. The agency has a brief period in which to investigate the alleged noncompliance and issue a written decision. At any time beyond 35 days after alleging noncompliance, but no later than 30 days after the agency issues a decision on the complainant's noncompliance allegations, the complainant may present the allegations to the Office of Federal Operations (OFO) at the EEOC.[6] The OFO reviews the record and may supplement it as it deems appropriate. The Office then issues a written decision applying a "preponderance of the evidence"

[4]29 C.F.R. § 1614.504 (2012).
[5]29 C.F.R. § 1614.603.
[6]29 C.F.R. § 1614.402.

standard. Within 90 days following the issuance of the decision (or if 180 days have passed without a decision), the complainant may seek de novo review in federal district court.[7]

In *Munoz v. Mabus*,[8] an employee and her federal employer agreed to settle administrative claims early in the complaint process, before any determinations had been made. Thereafter, the employee filed an administrative claim with the EEOC alleging that the settlement had been breached. After the EEOC found no evidence of breach, the plaintiff appealed to federal district court. The Ninth Circuit held that there was no subject matter jurisdiction, agreeing with the Fourth, Tenth, and D.C. Circuits that "Congress' waiver of sovereign immunity under Title VII does not extend to suits to enforce settlement agreements entered into without genuine investigation, reasonable cause determination, and conciliation efforts by the EEOC."[9] The court found no explicit waiver of sovereign immunity for breach allegations,[10] especially because the complainant withdrew her original EEOC charge once the settlement agreement was reached.[11]

---

[7]29 C.F.R. §§ 1614.405–407. Questions have been raised concerning the appropriate court to review a claim that a settlement agreement has been breached. *See, e.g.*, Van Desande v. United States, 673 F.3d 1342, 1351–52, 114 FEP 1061 (Fed. Cir. 2012) (EEOC-approved "stipulation agreement" in administrative process may be treated as both "consent decree" and "contract" subject to jurisdiction of Court of Federal Claims).

[8]630 F.3d 856, 111 FEP 40 (9th Cir. 2010).

[9]*Id.* at 1346–47 (rejecting lower court's finding that jurisdiction is obtained by implication because EEOC regulations allow breach claims to be raised with Commission and provide appeal rights to district courts from final EEOC determinations; only "complaints" are appealable to federal district courts, and "complaint" is term of art in EEOC's regulations referring to substantive claims, not allegations of breach).

[10]29 C.F.R. § 1614.504.

[11]Following the decision in Munoz, the EEOC amended its regulations to provide:

> 1614.504***
>
> (c) * * * If the Commission determines that the agency is not in compliance with a decision or settlement agreement, and the noncompliance is not attributable to acts or conduct of the complainant, it may order such compliance with the decision or settlement agreement, or, alternatively, for a settlement agreement, it may order that the complaint be reinstated for further processing from the point processing ceased. * * *

(v.) Final written agency decision

[147]**[On page 32-32 of the Main Volume, in footnote 147, add the following at the end of the footnote.]**

Agencies must submit appeals and complaint files to the EEOC in a digital format, unless they can establish good cause for not doing so. Complainants are encouraged to submit their documentation electronically. 29 C.F.R. § 1614.403(g) (2012).

b. Individual Discrimination Complaints Appealable to the MSPB ("Mixed Cases")

(i.) Overview of mixed cases

[157]**[On page 32-33 of the Main Volume, in footnote 157, add the following at the end of the footnote.]**

See Bonds v. Leavitt, 629 F.3d 369, 379, 111 FEP 171 (4th Cir. 2011) (complainant adequately exhausted her administrative remedies where she filed suit after her complaint had been pending with her agency for more than 120 days with no decision or appeal to MSPB).

(ii.) Covered employees and personnel actions

[161]**[On page 32-34 of the Main Volume, in footnote 161, add the following at the end of the footnote.]**

See Shelley v. Geren, 666 F.3d 599, 605 & n.1, 114 FEP 303 (9th Cir. 2012) (employee had option of pursuing administrative remedies for his ADEA failure-to-promote claim through EEO process or through MSPB).

(iv.) Judicial review in mixed cases

[194]**[On page 32-39 of the Main Volume, in footnote 194, add the following before "Chappell v. Chao".]**

Diggs v. Department of Hous. & Urban Dev., 670 F.3d 1353, 1357–58, 113 FEP 1170 (Fed. Cir. 2011) (in "mixed case" raising both issues of discrimination and other substantive or procedural issues, Federal Circuit has jurisdiction to hear appeal from MSPB decision only where employee has abandoned her discrimination (or in this case, retaliation) claim);

3. *Class Complaints*

[On page 32-42 of the Main Volume, at the end of the first sentence of the first full paragraph, add new footnote 205a.]

[205a]*See* Artis v. Bernanke, 630 F.3d 1031, 1038–39, 111 FEP 300 (D.C. Cir. 2011) (class of secretaries who participated in pre-charge conciliation had sufficiently exhausted their administrative remedies to permit them to file discrimination claims in federal district court).

[On page 32-43 of the Main Volume, replace the third full paragraph with the following.]

Because the agency does not investigate the class complaint, the EEOC administrative judge must develop a record through discovery and a hearing. The administrative judge issues a written decision, which constitutes a final decision rather than a recommended decision, that an agency can implement or appeal.[12]

5. *Retaliation*

[230]**[On page 32-47 of the Main Volume, in footnote 230, add the following before "*cf.*".]**

see Payne v. Salazar, 619 F.3d 56, 63, 110 FEP 264 (D.C. Cir. 2010) (employee who prevailed on discrimination claim before EEOC administrative judge may pursue her retaliation claim in federal court even though she did not seek judicial review of underlying discrimination claim);

[230]**[On page 32-47 of the Main Volume, in footnote 230, add the following after "*cf.*".]**

Bonds v. Leavitt, 629 F.3d 369, 384, 111 FEP 171 (4th Cir. 2011) (review of statutory provisions "leaves us with little doubt that [in 42 U.S.C. § 2000e-16] Congress 'incorporated the protections against retaliation' afforded to private employees by 2000e-3(a)");

---

[12]29 C.F.R. §§ 1614.204(i) & (j) (2012).

[On page 32-47 of the Main Volume, replace the first full paragraph with the following.]

A complainant also may file a retaliation charge with the Office of the Special Counsel (OSC).[13] The OSC is an independent investigative and prosecutorial agency with authority to receive and investigate complaints of prohibited personnel practices, including discrimination.[14] Although, in order to avoid duplication of effort, the OSC typically refers complaints of discrimination to either the employing agency or the EEOC,[15] it does on occasion retain jurisdiction to investigate on its own and to file enforcement actions before the MSPB.[16] Filing a complaint with the OSC does not toll the 15-day time limit for filing a formal complaint.[17]

III. LITIGATION PROCEDURE

A. Administrative Exhaustion

[286][On page 32-56 of the Main Volume, in the carryover of footnote 286, add the following at the end of the footnote.]

But cf. Ramirez v. Department of Transp., 686 F.3d 1239, 1250–52, 115 FEP 711 (11th Cir. 2012) (agency waived its right to raise failure of employee to consult EEO counselor within 45 days of adverse action where it failed to raise timeliness defense when it appealed EEOC's adverse ruling on issue to district court).

[288][On page 32-56 of the Main Volume, in footnote 288, add the following at the end of the footnote, after "(2006))".]

; Vera v. McHugh, 622 F.3d 17, 29–30, 110 FEP 705 (1st Cir. 2010) (typically, failure to exhaust administrative remedies will bar suit in federal court, but exhaustion requirement under Title VII is not jurisdictional prerequisite to filing action in federal court)

---

[13]5 U.S.C. §1212(e); 5 C.F.R. §1801.1.

[14]A detailed description of the OSC, its authority and processes is found at www.osc.gov (last visited Feb. 15, 2014), and 5 C.F.R. Parts 1800–1850 (2012). *See also* Reorganization Plan No. 2 of 1978, § 204, 45 Fed. Reg. 36,037.

[15]5 C.F.R. § 1810.1

[16]*Id.*

[17]Farris v. Shinseki, 660 F.3d 557, 565, 25 AD 955 (1st Cir. 2011).

[291]**[On page 32-57 of the Main Volume, in footnote 291, add the following after "*See*".]**

Vera, 622 F.3d at 32 ("We have recognized two related doctrines whereby a plaintiff may modify or avoid the Title VII filing period: equitable estoppel and equitable tolling.");

[292]**[On page 32-57 of the Main Volume, in footnote 292, add the following after "*See*".]**

Gilbert v. Napolitano, 670 F.3d 258, 260–61 (D.C. Cir. 2012) (agency waived its defense that plaintiff failed to exhaust administrative remedies where it failed to raise issue in its responsive pleadings);

[298]**[On page 32-59 of the Main Volume, in footnote 298, add the following before "*cf.*".]**

see Jenkins v. Mabus, 646 F.3d 1023, 1038–39, 112 FEP 1454 (8th Cir. 2011) (employee seeking equitable estoppel due to failure to meet administrative deadlines must show that delay was caused either by employer's "deliberate design," or as result of employer acts that it should have understood would cause employee to delay; merely telling employee that agency generally preferred to handle complaints internally was not such act);

[300]**[On page 32-59 of the Main Volume, in footnote 300, add the following at the end of the footnote.]**

See also Wilkie v. Department of Health & Human Servs., 638 F.3d 944, 950, 112 FEP 100 (8th Cir. 2011) (former clinical director is not entitled to equitable tolling of 45-day period for making EEO complaint, despite her claim that she suffered mental incapacity, where neither testimony of psychiatrist that she personally witnessed CEO's intrusions at clinical director's home and that clinical director "seemed pretty stressed and depressed," nor testimony by one of her friends, provided information regarding whether her depression affected her ability to understand her legal rights and act on them).

[301]**[On page 32-59 of the Main Volume, in footnote 301, add the following after "*See, e.g.*".]**

Velazquez-Ortiz v. Vilsack, 657 F.3d 64, 71, 113 FEP 627 (1st Cir. 2011) (plaintiff may not pursue in litigation claim of sex discrimination that was not specifically raised in her formal complaint; fact that sex discrimination was generally referenced in formal complaint was insufficient to alert agency to nature of her allegations); Bonds v. Leavitt, 629 F.3d 369, 379, 111 FEP 171 (4th Cir. 2011) (applying "like or related" standard of Title VII to CSRA claims; such claims must be raised in plaintiff's mixed-case complaint, along with discrimination claims, in order to raise them in court);

[302][On page 32-60 of the Main Volume, in footnote 302, add the following after "*see also*".]

Hamilton v. Geithner, 666 F.3d 1344, 1350, 114 FEP 239 (D.C. Cir. 2012) (employee cannot exhaust administrative remedies where he does not include in his formal agency complaint issues on which his litigation is based; merely raising issue during pre-complaint counseling does not satisfy exhaustion requirement); Shelley v. Geren, 666 F.3d 599, 605–06, 114 FEP 303 (9th Cir. 2012) (employee who claimed that he was discriminatorily denied both 120-day temporary detail to particular position and subsequent permanent promotion to that position, but raised only denial of permanent promotion in his formal agency complaint, may raise both claims in litigation where temporary detail claim was like or reasonably related to promotion claim such that adequate investigation into promotion claim would include "investigation of the hiring process for the temporary position"; decisions "were part of a single, two-step, hiring process");

[302][On page 32-60 of the Main Volume, in footnote 302, add the following at the end of the footnote.]

A complainant who has prevailed on some, but not all, the issues raised before the EEOC may seek a trial de novo in federal court limited to those issues on which he or she did not prevail in the administrative process. *See* Payne v. Salazar, 619 F.3d 56, 63, 110 FEP 264 (D.C. Cir. 2010).

B. Timeliness

[326][On page 32-65 of the Main Volume, in footnote 326, add the following after "*See, e.g.,*".]

Wilkie v. Department of Health & Human Servs., 638 F.3d 944, 952, 112 FEP 100 (8th Cir. 2011) (dismissal of plaintiff's case is appropriate where she failed to comply with 45-day requirement for contacting EEO counselor, and neither equitable tolling nor continuing violation doctrine apply); Vera v. McHugh, 622 F.3d 17, 31, 110

FEP 705 (1st Cir. 2010) (despite "procedural irregularities," including agency EEO counselor's failure to provide plaintiff with notice that her claim remained unresolved at conclusion of counseling, equitable tolling did not apply because plaintiff had been made aware of time limit for filing formal complaint and she failed to diligently pursue it);

[326]**[On page 32-65 of the Main Volume, in footnote 326, add the following at the end of the footnote.]**

But cf. Baird v. Gotbaum, 662 F.3d 1246, 1252, 114 FEP 11 (D.C. Cir. 2011) (employee may allege that discrete acts, untimely as independent claims of discrimination, comprise part of hostile work environment claim, when combined with timely filed allegations).

[328]**[On page 32-66 of the Main Volume, in footnote 328, add the following at the end of the footnote.]**

But see Vera, 622 F.3d at 31 (despite "procedural irregularities," including agency EEO counselor's failure to provide plaintiff with notice that her claim remained unresolved at conclusion of counseling, equitable tolling did not apply because plaintiff had been made aware of time limit for filing formal complaint and she failed to diligently pursue it).

[330]**[On page 32-66 of the Main Volume, in footnote 330, add the following after "*with*".]**

Farris v. Shinseki, 660 F.3d 557, 565, 25 AD 955 (1st Cir. 2011) (although plaintiff's attorney was responsible for timely filing complaint, neither his failure to do so nor fact that 15-day time period fell during holidays operated to toll time limit),

[331]**[On page 32-66 of the Main Volume, in footnote 331, add the following after "*See, e.g.,*".]**

Jenkins v. Mabus, 646 F.3d 1023, 1028, 112 FEP 1454 (8th Cir. 2011) (although there was "some confusion" about whether civilian-contract employee's claim should be handled in administrative process, equitable tolling did not apply where agency did not "lull or trick" employee into letting 45-day period in which to contact EEO counselor pass);

[334][On page 32-67 of the Main Volume, in footnote 334, add the following at the beginning of the footnote.]

See Wilkie v. Department of Health & Human Servs., 638 F.3d 944, 949–50, 112 FEP 100 (8th Cir. 2011) (tolling due to mental incapacity occurs in only "exceptional circumstances, such as when the complainant is institutionalized or adjudged mentally incompetent," and psychologist's testimony that plaintiff "seemed pretty stressed and depressed" did not meet this high standard) (quoting Jessie v. Potter, 516 F.3d 709, 714 (8th Cir. 2008));

[335][On page 32-67 of the Main Volume, in footnote 335, add the following at the end of the footnote.]

But see Jenkins, 646 F.3d at 1028–29 (although equitable tolling is available where plaintiff lacks "general knowledge" of right not to be discriminated against, it is not appropriate where, as here, plaintiff received training on agency's EEO procedures, was provided with pamphlet that informed readers of 45-day counselor contact requirement, and repeatedly was encouraged by co-worker to bring her concerns to agency's EEO office).

C. Trial de Novo

[On page 32-72 of the Main Volume, replace the first full paragraph with the following.]

The Supreme Court has held unanimously that where the MSPB dismisses or decides a mixed-case complaint adversely to the employee, judicial review of both the CSRA and the discrimination claims lies in the district court and the employee is entitled to trial de novo on both the CSRA and EEO claims.[18]

E. Exclusivity of Remedy

[364][On page 32-74 of the Main Volume, in footnote 364, add the following after "*cf.*".]

Harrell v. Donahue, 638 F.3d 975, 983–84, 111 FEP 1559 (8th Cir. 2011) (legislative history of Religious Freedom Restoration Act

---

[18]Kloeckner v. Solis, 133 S. Ct. 596, 603–04, 116 FEP 1153 (2012).

(RFRA) reveals clear intent not to affect religious accommodation under Title VII; purpose of RFRA was to restore status quo of requiring government to show compelling interest for any law that substantially burdens free exercise of religion, as it existed prior to Supreme Court's decision in *Employment Division v. Smith*, 494 U.S. 872 (1990));

[367]**[On page 32-74 of the Main Volume, in footnote 367, add the following before "*See generally*".]**

Brown, 425 U.S. at 834. The District of Columbia Circuit has reached the same conclusion regarding the CSRA. *See* Davis v. Billington, 681 F.3d 377, 381–82, 33 IER Cases 1684 (D.C. Cir. 2012) (court lacks jurisdiction over *Bivens* claim alleging violation of First Amendment Rights, because CSRA provides "comprehensive remedial scheme for administering public rights" that is exclusive remedy for federal employees even though it does not protect probationary employees such as plaintiff; "as a member of the civil service, as defined by the CSRA, the plaintiff is covered by its statutory scheme, even though Congress deliberately excluded employees in his situation from participating in its remedies").

[368]**[On page 32-74 of the Main Volume, in footnote 368, add the following after "*See*".]**

Walden v. Centers for Disease Control & Prevention, 669 F.3d 1277, 1284–85, 114 FEP 454 (11th Cir. 2012) (federal government contractor may sue government officials in their individual capacities for violating her constitutional rights; professional Employee Assistance Program (EAP) counselor was terminated at agency's request for refusing to counsel employee in same-sex relationship; although "[w]hen the government acts as an employer, it has far broader powers than the government acting as sovereign," First Amendment claims by employees or contractors must be analyzed under Supreme Court's balancing test from *Pickering v. Board of Educ.*, 391 U.S. 563 (1968));

F. Scope of Relief

[381][On page 32-77 of the Main Volume, in footnote 381, add the following at the end of the footnote.]

There may be a difference between remedies available under Title VII and those that federal employees may obtain under other statutes. *See, e.g.*, Ford v. Mabus, 629 F.3d 198, 207, 110 FEP 1665 (D.C. Cir. 2010) (although federal sector employee may establish ADEA liability by proving that age was motivating factor in agency's decision, thus entitling him to declaratory or injunctive relief, "but for" standard of causation is necessary in order to obtain instatement or recover back pay).

[383][On page 32-77 of the Main Volume, in footnote 383, add the following after "*see also*".]

Adam v. Norton, 636 F.3d 1190, 1193, 111 FEP 1089 (9th Cir. 2011) ("Back Pay Act's waiver of immunity from interest awards applies to a federal employee's termination or reduction in pay in violation of substantive anti-discrimination statutes," even though ADEA itself does not mention interest on back-pay awards);

G. Attorney's Fees

[395][On page 32-79 of the Main Volume, in footnote 395, add the following after "*with*".]

Porter v. Winter, 603 F.3d 1113, 1116–17, 109 FEP 225 (9th Cir. 2010) (federal court has jurisdiction to award attorney's fees for legal work done in administrative proceedings related to federal employee's Title VII complaint, even if plaintiff raised no substantive claims in federal court; allowing such suits is consistent with "integrated system . . . of administrative and judicial remedies . . . to provide complete relief to victims of employment discrimination") (citing Jones v. American State Bank, 857 F.2d 494 (8th Cir. 1988)), *and*

CHAPTER 33

CLASS ACTIONS

I. INTRODUCTION—THE APPLICATION OF RULE 23 TO TITLE VII CLASS ACTIONS

[On page 33-4 of the Main Volume, after the sentence that ends with footnote 5, add the following new paragraph.]

Courts have held that where plaintiffs seek monetary relief, certification under Rule 23(b)(2) is improper unless the monetary relief sought is merely incidental to the injunctive or declaratory relief.[1] As the Supreme Court explained in *Wal-Mart Stores, Inc. v. Dukes*,[2] "Rule 23(b)(2) applies only when a single injunction or declaratory judgment would provide relief to each member of the class."[3] Rule 23(b)(3) "allows class certification in a much wider set of circumstances but with greater procedural protections [in terms of the notice requirement]."[4]

[On page 33-5 of the Main Volume, after the sentence that ends with footnote 9, add the following.]

In contrast to disparate impact cases, pattern-or-practice suits require proof of intentional discrimination.[5]

---

[1]Wal-Mart Stores, Inc. v. Dukes, 131 S. Ct. 2541, 2557, 112 FEP 769 (2011) (*Dukes*). Before the 1991 amendments to Title VII allowing for compensatory and punitive damages, most employment discrimination class actions were certified under Rule 23(b)(2). *See* discussion at Section V., *infra*.

[2]131 S. Ct. 2541, 112 FEP 769 (2011).

[3]*Id.* at 2557.

[4]*Id.*

[5]*See, e.g.*, Puffer v. Allstate Ins. Co., 675 F.3d 709, 720, 114 FEP 1025 (7th Cir. 2012).

[On page 33-8 of the Main Volume, after the sentence that ends with footnote 22, add the following.]

Notably, the *Dukes* Court held that certification is improper under Rule 23(b)(2) where monetary relief is claimed that is not merely incidental to equitable remedies sought.[6] More recently, in *Comcast Corp. v. Behrend*,[7] the Court reversed class certification based on the plaintiffs' failure to demonstrate that individual injuries arising out of an alleged antitrust violation were capable of proof common to the class, and that the resulting damages could be determined based on a common methodology.[8]

III. THE REQUIREMENTS OF RULE 23(a)

A. Numerosity

[60]**[On page 33-14 of the Main Volume, in footnote 60, add the following at the beginning of the footnote.]**

See, e.g., Bolden v. Walsh Constr. Co., 688 F.3d 893, 895, 115 FEP 1153 (7th Cir. 2012) ("Using a future decision on the merits to specify the scope of the class makes it impossible to determine who is in the class until the case ends, and it creates the prospect that, if the employer should prevail on the merits, this would deprive the judgment of preclusive effect. . . ."); Turnage v. Norfolk S. Corp., 307 F. App'x 918, 921 (6th Cir. 2009) (requirement described as "numerosity" is really requirement to demonstrate impracticably of joinder; although numerosity may demonstrate impracticability of joinder, court should also consider ease of service and geographic dispersion);

[62]**[On page 33-15 of the Main Volume, in footnote 62, add the following after "*See, e.g.*,".]**

Marcus v. BMW of N. Am., LLC, 687 F.3d 583, 593 (3d Cir. 2012) (reversing class certification as insufficiently precise and noting that to achieve certification plaintiff must show by preponderance of

---

[6]*Dukes*, 131 S. Ct. at 2557.
[7]133 S. Ct. 1426 (2013).
[8]*Id.* at 1433–34.

evidence that is "currently and readily ascertainable based on objective criteria");

[63]**[On page 33-15 of the Main Volume, in footnote 63, add the following at the beginning of the footnote.]**

See, e.g., *Turnage*, 307 F. App'x at 921;

B. Commonality and Typicality

1. General Principles

[67]**[On page 33-16 of the Main Volume, in footnote 67, add the following at the beginning of the footnote.]**

See Amgen, Inc. v. Connecticut Retirement Plans & Trust Funds, 133 S. Ct. 1184, 1195–96 (2013) (plaintiff need not prove that each element of claim can be established by classwide proof; what Rule 23(a) requires is that "common questions *predominate* over any questions affecting only individual [class] members"); Ellis v. Costco Wholesale Corp., 285 F.R.D. 492, 506, 116 FEP 118 (2012) ("Plaintiffs need not demonstrate that all questions are common to the class; rather, it is sufficient if either 'shared legal issues with divergent factual predicates' or 'a common core of salient facts coupled with disparate legal remedies within the class' are present."), *on remand from* 657 F.3d 970, 983, 113 FEP 496 (9th Cir. 2011).

[69]**[On page 33-16 of the Main Volume, in footnote 69, add the following at the end of the footnote.]**

See, e.g., Bolden v. Walsh Constr. Co., 688 F.3d 893, 898, 115 FEP 1153 (7th Cir. 2012) (reversing certification of multi-site classes in reliance on *Dukes*; "when multiple managers exercise independent discretion, conditions at different stores (or sites) do not present a common question"—"*Wal-Mart* tells us that local discretion cannot support a company-wide class no matter how cleverly lawyers may try to repackage local variability as uniformity"); *Ellis*, 657 F.3d at 981 (remanding question of nationwide class certification where district court failed to conduct "rigorous analysis" required by *Dukes* with respect to commonality; "[W]hat matters is not the raising of common questions' ... but, rather the capacity of a classwide proceeding to generate common *answers* apt to drive the resolution of the litigation.") (quoting Wal-Mart Stores, Inc. v. Dukes, 131 S. Ct. 2541, 2551, 112 FEP 769 (2011)); Bennett v. Nucor Corp., 656 F.3d 802, 813–16, 113 FEP 616 (8th Cir. 2011) (affirming denial of class certification in disparate treatment and impact case based on finding that plaintiffs failed to establish commonality, because defendant's "departments varied widely in their employment practices, working environments, and functions"), *cert. denied*, 132 S. Ct. 1861, 114 FEP 1088 (2012). *But cf.* McReynolds v. Merrill Lynch, Pierce Fenner & Smith, Inc., 672 F.3d 482, 490–91, 114 FEP 710 (7th Cir.) (post-*Dukes* decision finding class treatment to be appropriate in disparate impact case challenging "company-wide policies authorizing broker-initiated teaming, and basing account distributions on past success"; class certified only on disparate impact claim and only as to injunctive and back-pay relief), *cert. denied*, 133 S. Ct. 338, 116 FEP 288 (2012).

[71]**[On page 33-16 of the Main Volume, in footnote 71, add the following at the end of the footnote.]**

Typicality is not destroyed by differing factual scenarios where the plaintiff's claim is of the same nature as that of other class members. *Ellis*, 657 F.3d at 984 & n.9 (remanding class certification to apply proper analysis of commonality and typicality requirements and to resolve numerous disputed issues of fact and law critical to such analysis).

2. *A Historical Perspective—Rejection of the Across-the-Board Approach and the General Policy of Discrimination Exception*

[On page 33-19 of the Main Volume, in the second sentence of the first full paragraph, replace "The plaintiff must identify the questions of law and fact common to the class" with the following.]

The plaintiff must identify the questions of law and/or fact common to the class

C. Adequacy of Representation

[102][On page 33-21 of the Main Volume, in footnote 102, add the following at the end of the footnote.]

See also Ellis v. Costco Wholesale Corp., 657 F.3d 970, 986, 113 FEP 496 (9th Cir. 2011) (former employees do not have standing to pursue injunctive relief but could represent current and former employees to pursue monetary relief). Hypothetical conflicts, however, will not defeat class certification. *See* Johnson v. Meriter Health Servs. Emp. Ret. Plan, 702 F.3d 364, 368–69, 54 EB Cases 1865 (7th Cir. 2012).

2. *Potential Conflicts of Interest Between the Named Plaintiff and Absent Class Members*

[120][On page 33-24 of the Main Volume, in footnote 120, add the following at the beginning of the footnote.]

See, e.g., Ellis v. Costco Wholesale Corp., 657 F.3d 970, 985–86, 113 FEP 496 (9th Cir. 2011) (former employees could represent current employees to pursue monetary, but not injunctive, relief); Glass v. UBS Fin. Servs., Inc., 331 F. App'x 452, 455 (9th Cir. 2009) (former employees could represent class of current and former employees where they were "equally interested in obtaining compensation for the assertedly unlawful practices set forth in the complaint");

[121][On page 33-24 of the Main Volume, in footnote 121, add the following after "*See, e.g.*,".]

Randall v. Rolls-Royce Corp., 637 F.3d 818, 824, 111 FEP 1565 (7th Cir. 2011) (plaintiffs, who were high-level employees with authority over compensation of male and female employees, could not serve as class representatives in sex discrimination pay and promotion case);

3. *Organizations as Named Plaintiffs*

[130][On page 33-26 of the Main Volume, in footnote 130, add the following at the end of the footnote.]

Courts in Title VII cases have certified unions as adequate to represent a subset of their members even though the appropriate remedy might disadvantage their members who are outside the class, such as in representing a plaintiff class in a race or sex discrimination action even though the remedy achieved for class members may disadvantage members of the union who are not minorities or are of the opposite gender. *See, e.g.*, Social Serv. Union Local 535 v. County of Santa Clara, 609 F.2d 944, 948, 21 FEP 684 (9th Cir. 1979) (no basis in record to assume that union would be unable to conduct litigation vigorously; possibility that remedy for its female members might adversely affect pecuniary interests of its male members is "purely speculative"); International Woodworkers of Am. v. Georgia-Pacific Corp., 568 F.2d 64, 67–68, 16 FEP 258 (8th Cir. 1977) (no showing that union that has both male and female members would not adequately represent its female members in class action alleging sex discrimination).

D. Frequently Contested Rule 23(a) Issues

1. Subjective Decision-Making Processes

[On page 33-31 of the Main Volume, at the end of the carryover sentence at the top of the page, add new footnote 159a after "supervisors violates Title VII.".]

[159a]*See, e.g.*, Bolden v. Walsh Constr. Co., 688 F.3d 893, 897–98, 115 FEP 1153 (7th Cir. 2012) (*Dukes* recognized that discretion might facilitate discrimination but does not establish that all managers with discretionary authority will discriminate; "*Wal-Mart* tells us that local discretion cannot support a company-wide class no matter how cleverly lawyers may try to repackage local variability as uniformity").

[166]**[On page 33-32 of the Main Volume, in footnote 166, add the following at the end of the footnote.]**

At least one court has stated that a seemingly neutral corporate policy that is implemented by local managers in a manner that disparately impacts minorities may be challenged companywide. *See* McReynolds v. Merrill, Lynch, Pierce, Fenner & Smith, Inc., 672 F.3d 482, 489–92, 114 FEP 710 (7th Cir.) (allowing African-American brokers to challenge on disparate impact grounds company's "teaming policy," which authorized employees—rather than managers—to form staff teams, and its "account distribution policy," which based account distributions on success of past account transfers), *cert. denied*, 133 S. Ct. 138 (2012). The *McReynolds* court distinguished *Dukes* on the facts, stating that "permitting brokers to form their own teams and prescribing criteria for account distributions that favor the already successful... are practices of Merrill Lynch, rather than practices that local managers can choose or not at their whim."

2. *Different Types of Claims Asserted*

[168][On page 33-32 of the Main Volume, in footnote 168, add the following after "*accord*".]

Puffer v. Allstate Ins. Co., 675 F.3d 709, 720, 114 FEP 1025 (7th Cir. 2012) (members of putative class, who intervened to appeal denial of class certification, waived their sex discrimination disparate impact claim because plaintiff did not meaningfully develop it before district court where she argued only pattern-or-practice discrimination; intervenors stood in plaintiff's shoes and could present arguments only that plaintiff could have appealed);

[175][On page 33-33 of the Main Volume, in footnote 175, add the following after "*Compare*".]

Ellis v. Costco Wholesale Corp., 657 F.3d 970, 985–86, 113 FEP 496 (9th Cir. 2011) (former employees could represent current employees to pursue monetary, but not injunctive, relief), *and*

[175][On page 33-33 of the Main Volume, in footnote 175, add the following at the end of the footnote.]

The answer to this question may hinge on the extent to which the former employees' interests differ from those of the current employees whom they seek to represent. *See* Glass v. UBS Fin. Servs., Inc., 331 F. App'x 452, 455 (9th Cir. 2009) (former employees could represent class of current and former employees where they were "equally interested in obtaining compensation for the assertedly unlawful practices set forth in the complaint").

4. *Multiple Organizational Units or Geographical Facilities*

[182][On page 33-35 of the Main Volume, in footnote 182, add the following before "*Bacon*".]

Bennett v. Nucor Corp., 656 F.3d 802, 813–16, 113 FEP 616 (8th Cir. 2011) (certification denied where plaintiffs worked among plants and various production departments and "departments varied widely in their employment practices, working environments, and functions"), *cert. denied*, 132 S. Ct. 1861 (2012);

IV. THE REQUIREMENTS OF RULE 23(b)

[184][On page 33-35 of the Main Volume, in footnote 184, add the following after "*See, e.g.*,".]

Johnson v. Meriter Health Servs. Emp. Ret. Plan, 702 F.3d 364, 372, 54 EB Cases 1865 (7th Cir. 2012) (certifying Rule 23(b)(2) class of more than 4,000 defined benefit plan participants seeking reformation of plan and declaration of their rights under plan, as well as injunction ordering company to conform text of plan to declaration); McReynolds v. Merrill, Lynch, Pierce, Fenner & Smith, Inc., 672 F.3d 482, 492, 114 FEP 710 (7th Cir.) (reversing district court's denial of certification of nationwide class under Rules 23(b)(2) and 23(c)(4)), *cert. denied*, 133 S. Ct. 338 (2012);

E. Partial Certification of Liability and Injunctive Relief Only

[221][On page 33-43 of the Main Volume, in footnote 221, add the following after "*see also*".]

McReynolds v. Merrill, Lynch, Pierce, Fenner & Smith, Inc., 672 F.3d 482, 492, 114 FEP 710 (7th Cir.) (noting that, should plaintiffs prevail on liability, certification under Rule 23(b)(2) may be reconsidered and even individual remedy trials may be required; "we have trouble seeing the downside of the limited class action"), *cert. denied*, 133 S. Ct. 338 (2012);

V. JURISDICTIONAL AND PROCEDURAL REQUIREMENTS

[On page 33-48 of the Main Volume, after the carryover sentence that ends with footnote 248, add the following new sections V.B. and V.C.]

B. Class Action Fairness Act [New Topic]

The Class Action Fairness Act (CAFA)[9] provides federal district courts with original jurisdiction to hear a class action if the class has more than 100 members, the parties are minimally diverse, and the matter in controversy exceeds $5 million in sum or value.[10] To determine whether a matter exceeds CAFA's $5 million jurisdictional threshold, courts aggregate the claims of individual class members (both named and unnamed) who fall within the proposed class definition.[11]

A putative class action named plaintiff cannot avoid removal to federal court under CAFA by stipulating—prior to class certification—that he or she and the putative class will not seek damages in excess of $5 million.[12] Although that stipulation may bind the individual named plaintiff, it cannot bind putative class members before the class is certified.[13]

C. Class Action Arbitration Waivers [New Topic]

In *American Express Co. v. Italian Colors Restaurant*,[14] the Supreme Court held that the Federal Arbitration Act does not permit courts to invalidate a contractual waiver of class arbitration because the cost of individually arbitrating a federal statutory claim is prohibitive.[15] The Court expressly rejected the notion that cost factors alone could prevent the effective vindication of federal statutory rights and thereby eliminate the viability of class action waivers in arbitration agreements. In the Court's view, the terms of an arbitration agreement govern except in rare cases, where a contrary congressional intent is evident or where the arbitration agreement forbids a federal statutory claim.[16]

---

[9]28 U.S.C. § 1332.

[10]28 U.S.C. § 1332(d)(2), (d)(5)(B).

[11]28 U.S.C. § 1332(d)(1)(D), (d)(6).

[12]Standard Fire Ins. Co. v. Knowles, 133 S. Ct. 1345, 1349 (2013).

[13]*Id.* at 1350. A named plaintiff and his or her attorneys conceivably may avoid CAFA by structuring classes so that they have fewer than 100 members. 28 U.S.C. § 1332(d)(2), (d)(5)(B).

[14]133 S. Ct. 2304 (2013).

[15]*Id.* at 2309–10.

[16]*Id.* at 2310. Where the agreement allows for class arbitration, the terms of the agreement govern. *See* Jock v. Sterling Jewelers, Inc., 646 F.3d 113, 123–24, 112 FEP 1137 (2d Cir. 2011) (broad agreement to arbitrate made it permissible for arbitrator to

[On page 33-48 in the Main Volume, renumber Section V.B. as follows.]

D. Intervention [Renumbered Topic (Formerly B.)]

[On page 33-50 in the Main Volume, renumber Section V.C. as follows.]

E. Tolling the Limitations Period [Renumbered Topic (Formerly C.)]

[On page 33-53 in the Main Volume, renumber Section V.D. as follows.]

F. The Employer in Bankruptcy [Renumbered Topic (Formerly D.)]

[On page 33-53 in the Main Volume, renumber Section V.E. as follows.]

G. Article III Standing [Renumbered Topic (Formerly E.)]

[282]**[On page 33-54 of the Main Volume, in footnote 282, add the following at the end of the footnote.]**

But cf. Genesis Healthcare Corp. v. Symczyk, 133 S. Ct. 1523, 20 WH Cases 2d 801 (2013) (collective Fair Labor Standards Act (FLSA) action brought by single employee no longer justiciable where Rule 68 offer of judgment that made her whole admittedly mooted her individual claim and thereby mooted collective action). Notably, *Symczyk* originated in the Third Circuit, which adheres to the principle that an individual claim could be mooted with a full-relief Rule 68 offer of judgment; because the parties did not appropriately seek review of this determination, the Supreme Court did not resolve the issue. *Id.* at 1528–29. Therefore, in jurisdictions not adopting this principle, such as the Second Circuit, the Court's ruling may be of limited significance, at least until the circuit split is resolved. Moreover, the language in *Symczyk* may limit its applicability to

---

conclude that parties intended to include right to proceed as class, without exceeding authority), *cert. denied*, 132 S. Ct. 1742, 114 FEP 960 (2012). *See generally* Chapter 43 (Alternative Dispute Resolution), Section III.C.5.

other statutes, such as the EPA and ADEA, which share the FLSA's procedural framework for collective actions, as distinguished from the Rule 23 construct that governs Title VII class actions.

[On page 33-54 in the Main Volume, renumber Section V.F. as follows.]

H. Effect of Denial of Class Certification [Renumbered Topic (Formerly F.)]

VI. THE CLASS CERTIFICATION HEARING

B. Discovery Before the Class Determination

[On page 33-57 of the Main Volume, after the sentence that ends with footnote 300, add the following new paragraph.]

In *Comcast Corp. v. Behrend*,[17] the Supreme Court once again addressed the rigorous analysis district courts must undertake to determine whether Rule 23's requirements are met at the class certification stage.[18] The *Comcast* Court underscored that "[s]uch an analysis will frequently entail 'overlap with the merits of the plaintiff's underlying claim,'"[19] because "'class determinations generally involve considerations that are enmeshed in the factual and legal issues comprising the plaintiff's cause of action.'"[20] Nevertheless, as the Supreme Court explained in *Amgen, Inc. v. Connecticut Retirement Plans & Trust Funds*,[21] a court's inquiry into merits evidence is not without limitations:

> Rule 23 grants courts no license to engage in free-ranging merits inquiries at the class certification stage. Merits questions may be considered to the extent—but only to the extent—that they are relevant to determining whether the Rule 23 prerequisites for class certification are satisfied.[22]

---

[17] 133 S. Ct. 1426 (2013).

[18] *Id.* at 1432.

[19] *Id.* (quoting Wal-Mart Stores, Inc. v. Dukes, 131 S. Ct. 2541, 2551, 112 FEP 769 (2011)).

[20] *Id.*, 131 S. Ct. at 1432 (quoting General Tel. Co. of Sw. v. Falcon, 457 U.S. 147, 160, 102 S. Ct. 2364 (1982)).

[21] 133 S. Ct. 1184 (2013).

[22] *Id.* at 1194–95.

Applying these principles to the facts in *Comcast*, the Court reversed a grant of class certification in a putative antitrust class action. The Court rejected a damages regression model developed by the plaintiff's expert as insufficient to satisfy Rule 23 standards, because the model could not measure damages across the entire class in a manner that was consistent with the plaintiff's only viable theory of liability.[23] Subsequent to *Comcast*, the Sixth Circuit has held that the Supreme Court's holding is of limited application where determinations on liability and damages are bifurcated pursuant to Rule 23(c)(4).[24]

[304][On page 33-59 of the Main Volume, in footnote 304, add the following at the end of the footnote.]

As courts undertake more expansive analysis of merits-related issues at the class certification stage, the scope of permitted pre-certification discovery also is likely to expand. The touchstone presumably will be whether the facts as to which discovery is sought "are relevant to determining whether the Rule 23 prerequisites for class certification are satisfied." *Amgen, Inc.*, 133 S. Ct. at 1194–95.

C. Inquiry Into the Merits

[307][On page 33-59 of the Main Volume, in footnote 307, add the following at the end of the footnote.]

See also Comcast Corp. v. Behrend, 133 S. Ct. 1426, 1432 (2013).

D. Types of Evidence in Support of and in Opposition to Class Certification

[On page 33-60 of the Main Volume, replace the second sentence in the first full paragraph with the following.]

Prior to *Dukes* and *Comcast*, courts held that an evidentiary hearing is not required under Rule 23.

---

[23] 133 S. Ct. at 1432–33.

[24] *See In re* Whirlpool Corp. Front-Loading Washer Prods. Liab. Litig., 722 F.3d 838, 860–61 (6th Cir. 2013) (noting that district court certified only liability class, and reserved all issues concerning damages for individual determination).

[On page 33-60 of the Main Volume, after the first full paragraph, add the following new paragraph.]

The Supreme Court's decision in *Comcast Corp. v. Behrend*[25] suggests that in reviewing statistical evidence proffered at the class certification stage, courts may scrutinize damages models to determine whether the model can establish that damages are capable of measurement on a classwide basis.[26]

---

[25] 133 S. Ct. 1426 (2013).

[26] *Id.* at 1432–33. *But see In re* Whirlpool Corp. Front-Loading Washer Prods. Liab. Litig., 722 F.3d 838, 860 (6th Cir. 2013) (class may be certified under Rule 23(b)(3) "when liability questions common to the class predominate over damages questions unique to class members"; class certified as to liability only).

CHAPTER 34

DISCOVERY

I. INTRODUCTION

[2]**[On page 34-2 of the Main Volume, in footnote 2, add the following at the end of the footnote.]**

See also Serrano v. Cintas Corp., 699 F.3d 884, 901, 116 FEP 801 (6th Cir. 2012) (denying order protecting chief executive officer from being deposed pursuant to "apex rule" where company presented no evidence of any harm other than executive's "bald assertion," and his prior statements suggested that he had knowledge of company's allegedly discriminatory hiring practices).

[4][On page 34-2 of the Main Volume, in footnote 4, replace the parenthetical for "Schwab v. Wyndham Int'l, Inc." with the following.]

(request for premises inspection made by claimant bringing Title VII claim overly broad because most of the departments the plaintiff wanted to inspect and photograph had nothing to do with the case and maintained confidential and sensitive information)

[6][On page 34-2 of the Main Volume, in footnote 6, add the following after "*See, e.g.*,".]

Bull v. United Parcel Serv., Inc., 665 F.3d 68, 80–83, 25 AD 1204 (3d Cir. 2012) (district court abused its discretion in concluding that plaintiff–employee spoliated evidence and dismissing case as sanction, where plaintiff did not disclose original documents to defendant–employer until third day of trial but there was insufficient evidence that original documents were intentionally withheld or properly requested);

[6][On page 34-3 of the Main Volume, in the carryover of footnote 6, add the following at the end of the footnote.]

But see Everett v. Cook Cnty., 655 F.3d 723, 727, 113 FEP 9 (7th Cir. 2011) (defendant's destruction of documents does not create inference of spoliation in Title VII action absent showing that documents were intentionally destroyed in bad faith); Norman-Nunnery v. Madison Area Tech. Coll., 625 F.3d 422, 428–30, 110 FEP 1121 (7th Cir. 2010) (rejected applicant for college administrator position not entitled to inference of spoliation where college lost her application and other hiring documents as result of office moves before she filed any claims, and where there was no evidence that documents were destroyed to hide adverse information).

[7][On page 34-3 of the Main Volume, in footnote 7, add the following after "*E.g.*,".]

Brown v. Oil States Skagit Smatco, 664 F.3d 71, 77, 113 FEP 1537 (5th Cir. 2011) (per curiam) (Title VII case properly dismissed for perjured deposition testimony where plaintiff testified that he quit for only one reason—racial harassment—but testified in his personal injury lawsuit that he left his job "solely" because of back pain caused by accident; "dismissal with prejudice [is] a more appropriate sanction when the objectionable conduct is that of the client, not the attorney"); Norelus v. Denny's, Inc., 628 F.3d 1270, 1280–81, 111 FEP 4 (11th Cir. 2010) (attorney submitted errata sheet making 868 changes to client's deposition testimony, many of which were contradictory and not merely corrective; in assessing costs against her, court stated that an attorney "who so multiplies the proceedings in any case unreasonably and vexatiously ... [can be required] to satisfy personally the excess costs, expenses and attorney's fees"), *cert. denied sub nom.* Amlong & Amlong v. Denny's, Inc.,133 S. Ct. 104 (2012);

[11]**[On page 34-5 of the Main Volume, in footnote 11, add the following after "*See*".]**

Yong Quan-Sun v. Board of Trs. of Univ. of Ill., 473 F.3d 799, 99 FEP 897 (7th Cir. 2007) (reversing grant of default judgment as unduly harsh sanction for failure of defendant's counsel to answer interrogatories even after two orders compelling answers);

II. STRATEGY CONSIDERATIONS

A. Discovery by Plaintiffs

[14]**[On page 34-6 of the Main Volume, in footnote 14, add the following before "Sempier v. Johnson & Higgins".]**

Baltodano v. Merck, Sharp & Dohme Corp., 637 F.3d 38, 44, 111 FEP 1099 (1st Cir. 2011) (reversing summary judgment where employee was deprived of discovery as to whether decision maker ever disciplined other managers under similar circumstances to plaintiff; "where a plaintiff's case depends on his ability to secure evidence within the possession of the defendants, courts should not render summary judgment because of gaps in plaintiff's proofs without first determining that plaintiff has had a fair chance to obtain necessary and available evidence from the other party") (internal quotations omitted);

[16]**[On page 34-6 of the Main Volume, in footnote 16, add the following before "Guthrey v. California Dep't of Corr. & Rehab.".]**

Sallis v. University of Minn., 408 F.3d 470, 478, 95 FEP 1281 (8th Cir. 2005) (although courts have permitted liberal discovery in Title VII cases, that discovery must be tailored to plaintiff's case in terms of time period covered by request, facility, and practices at issue in case);

[18]**[On page 34-7 of the Main Volume, in footnote 18, add the following after "*See, e.g.*,".]**

EEOC v. Burlington N. Santa Fe R.R., 669 F.3d 1154, 1157–59, 25 AD 1572 (10th Cir. 2012) (EEOC not entitled to nationwide database where information was not "'relevant to the charge[s] under investigation'"; "nationwide recordkeeping data is not 'relevant to' charges of individual disability discrimination filed by two men who applied for the same type of job in the same state");

[31]**[On page 34-9 of the Main Volume, replace footnote 31 with the following.]**

[31]Generally, the duty to preserve evidence is triggered when it is known or should be known that the evidence may be relevant to pending or anticipated litigation. *See, e.g.*, Rimkus Consulting Grp., Inc. v. Cammarata, 688 F. Supp. 2d 598, 612 (S.D. Tex. 2010) ("Generally the duty to preserve arises when a party 'has notice that the evidence is relevant to litigation or . . . should have known that the evidence may be relevant to future litigation'") (quoting John B. v. Goetz, 531 F.3d 448, 459 (6th Cir. 2008)); Scalera v. Electrograph Sys., Inc., 262 F.R.D. 162, 171 (E.D.N.Y. 2009) ("The obligation to preserve evidence arises when the party has notice that the evidence is relevant to litigation or when a party should have known that the evidence may be relevant to future litigation."). The filing of an EEOC charge or an internal complaint, or receipt of a "litigation hold" letter from counsel, generally will suffice to trigger the preservation duty. *See Scalera*, 262 F.R.D. at 171 (EEOC charge triggered duty to preserve evidence related to charge); Port Auth. Police Asian Jade Soc'y of N.Y. & N.J., Inc. v. Port Auth. of N.Y. & N.J., 601 F. Supp. 2d 566, 570–71 (S.D.N.Y. 2009) (failure to preserve documents and to issue "litigation hold" did not warrant adverse inference instruction as sanction where failure to preserve was partly attributable to 9/11/01 attack on Port Authority offices and where plaintiffs

had other information and documents in their possession to support their allegations at trial), *aff'd sub nom.* Chin v. Port Auth. of N.Y. & N.J., 685 F.3d 135, 162, 115 FEP 720 (2d Cir. 2012) (failure to institute "litigation hold" was not gross negligence per se); Goodman v. Praxair Servs., Inc., 632 F. Supp. 2d 494, 511 (D. Md. 2009) (letter openly threatening litigation triggers duty to preserve evidence relevant to dispute); Zubulake v. UBS Warburg, LLC, 220 F.R.D. 212, 216–17, 92 FEP 1539 (S.D.N.Y. 2003) ("the duty to preserve may have arisen even before the EEOC complaint was filed" because "almost everyone associated with [plaintiff] recognized the possibility that she might sue" following her internal complaint). Courts have held that the "preservation obligation first runs to counsel, who has a duty to advise his client of the type of information potentially relevant to the lawsuit and of the necessity of preventing its destruction." Richard Green (Fine Paintings) v. McClendon, 262 F.R.D. 284, 290 (S.D.N.Y. 2009) (internal quotations omitted); *see also Scalera,* 262 F.R.D. at 177–78 (attorney's communication of duty to preserve held to be insufficient where she did not clearly inform key players of their need to produce electronic copies of active files rather than merely relying on electronically stored information (ESI) system for back-up, and where attorney failed to timely communicate need to preserve ESI files to information technology (IT) manager and others in IT department). *See generally* Section IV, *infra.*

[32]**[On page 34-9 of the Main Volume, in footnote 32, add the following after "*See*".]**

Chin, 685 F.3d at 162 (failure to preserve documents and to issue "litigation hold" did not warrant adverse inference instruction as sanction where failure to preserve was partly attributable to 9/11/01 attack on Port Authority offices and where plaintiffs had other information and documents in their possession to support their allegations at trial); Talavera v. Shah, 638 F.3d 303, 311, 111 FEP 1574 (D.C. Cir. 2011) (defendant's destruction of relevant documents supported inference that information documents contained would have supported plaintiff's claim);

[32]**[On page 34-9 of the Main Volume, in footnote 32, add the following at the end of the footnote.]**

But see Everett v. Cook Cnty., 655 F.3d 723, 727, 113 FEP 9 (7th Cir. 2011) (no adverse inference based on destruction of records where there was no evidence that documents were intentionally destroyed in bad faith).

[33][On page 34-9 of the Main Volume, in footnote 33, add the following at the beginning of the footnote.]

Chin, 685 F.3d at 162 (failure to preserve documents and to issue "litigation hold" did not warrant adverse inference instruction as sanction where failure to preserve was partly attributable to 9/11/01 attack on Port Authority offices and where plaintiffs had other information and documents in their possession to support their allegations at trial); *Talavera*, 638 F.3d at 311–13 (presumption that destroyed documents contained information favorable to opposing party is sanction most commonly imposed for such destruction; more drastic measure such as entry of default judgment is warranted only when lesser sanction would be futile);

[34][On page 34-10 of the Main Volume, in footnote 34, add the following after "*See*".]

Hoyle v. Freightliner, LLC, 650 F.3d 321, 330, 111 FEP 1537 (4th Cir. 2011) (employer's motion to strike declaration of belatedly disclosed witness granted because failure to disclose was neither substantially justified nor harmless);

D. Motions for Protective Order or to Compel

[41][On page 34-11 of the Main Volume, in footnote 41, add the following after "*See*".]

Arnold v. ADT Sec. Servs., 627 F.3d 716, 722–23, 110 FEP 1781 (8th Cir. 2010) (employer's motion to compel properly granted where employer attempted to confer with plaintiffs in good faith without court intervention and also repeatedly attempted to confer with their counsel regarding incomplete discovery responses);

[42][On page 34-12 of the Main Volume, in footnote 42, in the parenthetical for "Finzie v. Shineski," add the following after "Rule 56(f)".]

(now Rule 56(d))

[42]**[On page 34-12 of the Main Volume, in footnote 42, add the following before "*See generally*".]**

Cf. Sánchez-Rodríquez v. AT&T Mobility P.R., Inc., 673 F.3d 1, 10, 114 FEP 912 (1st Cir. 2012) (plaintiff's Rule 56(f) (now Rule 56(d)) request for additional discovery properly denied where he failed to demonstrate why he could not have obtained information prior to close of discovery).

III. LIMITATIONS ON DISCOVERY

A. Discovery Sought by Plaintiffs

1. Privileged Materials

[52]**[On page 34-14 of the Main Volume, in footnote 52, add the following at the beginning of the footnote.]**

EEOC v. Philip Servs. Corp., 635 F.3d 164, 167, 111 FEP 1189 (5th Cir. 2011) (Title VII prohibits use of conciliation material in subsequent litigation, even by parties to proceeding);

[On page 34-19 of the Main Volume, after the sentence that ends with footnote 72, add the following new paragraph.]

Legislative immunity is not limited to actual office-holders, but also covers those properly acting in a legislative capacity.[1] The legislative acts subject to immunity typically involve the adoption of prospective legislative-type rules that establish a general policy affecting the larger population.[2] Legislative privilege against compulsory evidentiary process exists to safeguard legislative immunity and "to further encourage the republican issues it promotes."[3]

---

[1]*See* Supreme Court of Va. v. Consumers Union of the U.S., 446 U.S. 719, 731–34 (1980) (state's supreme court acted in legislative capacity in declining to amend rule regulating state bar, and hence enjoyed absolute legislative immunity from attorney's fee award with respect to that determination).

[2]*See* EEOC v. Washington Suburban Sanitary Comm'n, 631 F.3d 174, 180–81, 111 FEP 481 (4th Cir. 2011) (utility's assertion of legislative immunity and privilege was premature and, thus, did not provide basis for court to decline to enforce EEOC subpoena).

[3]*Id.* at 181 (citing Burtnick v. McLean, 76 F.3d 611, 613, 70 FEP 173 (4th Cir. 1996)).

[85][On page 34-21 of the Main Volume, in footnote 85, add the following at the end of the footnote.]

But c.f. Fuller v. Fiber Glass Sys., L.P., 618 F.3d 858, 866, 110 FEP 176 (8th Cir. 2010) (employer's motion for new trial properly denied, despite plaintiff's counsel's improper ex parte communication with former company supervisor and co-worker, where their testimony was only relevant to establish first prong of *Ellerth-Faragher* defense in sex harassment case and district court held that employer had established that prong).

2. *Burdensome or Irrelevant Discovery*

[94][On page 34-25 of the Main Volume, in footnote 94, add the following after "*Compare*".]

Bobo v. United Parcel Serv., Inc., 665 F.3d 741, 751–53, 114 FEP 254 (6th Cir. 2012) (African-American employee terminated for violating employer's integrity policy entitled to discover information about similarly situated employees outside protected group; in relying on employer's designation of comparators, district court unduly limited plaintiff's discovery to only white employee who had same supervisor),

B. Discovery Sought by Defendants

2. *Burdensome or Irrelevant Discovery*

[113][On page 34-30 of the Main Volume, in the carryover of footnote 113, add the following at the end of the footnote.]

See also EEOC v. Simply Storage Mgmt., 270 F.R.D. 430, 436–37, 110 FEP 49 (S.D. Ind. 2010) (EEOC ordered to produce online communications on social networking sites, notwithstanding privacy issues, to extent they "reveal, refer, or relate to any emotion, feeling or mental state," or to "events that reasonably could be expected to produce" such emotions, where plaintiff claimed severe emotional or mental injury from alleged sexual harassment; content from social networking sites is not shielded from discovery simply because it is "locked" so that only certain designated individuals may obtain access to it).

IV. ELECTRONIC DISCOVERY

[On page 34-37 of the Main Volume, at end of first full paragraph, add new footnote 142a.]

[142a]For a detailed treatment of electronic discovery issues in employment cases, see the AMERICAN BAR ASSOCIATION, SECTION OF LABOR & EMPLOYMENT LAW, WORKPLACE DATA: LAW AND LITIGATION (Robert L. Sprague, ed., Bloomberg BNA 2013).

[On page 34-38 of the Main Volume, in the second full paragraph, add the following after "(4) e-mail".]

and social networking information,

[On page 34-38 of the Main Volume, after the second full paragraph, add the following new paragraph.]

Increasingly, courts are being called upon to resolve disputes between the parties regarding the appropriate search methodologies for conducting electronically stored information (ESI) discovery. This often involves determining the search terms that will be used[4] and the circumstances under which predictive coding is permissible in a case that features extensive electronic documentation.[5]

[148]**[On pages 34-38 to 34-39 of the Main Volume, replace footnote 148 with the following.]**

[148]Generally, the duty to preserve evidence is triggered when it is known or should be known that the evidence may be relevant to pending or anticipated litigation. *See, e.g.*, Philips Elecs. N. Am. Corp. v. BC Technical, 773 F. Supp. 2d 1149, 1195 (D. Utah 2011) (duty to preserve documents, including electronic documents, triggered once

---

[4]*See* Cannata v. Wyndham Worldwide Corp., 2012 U.S. Dist. LEXIS 20625, at *9–11 (D. Nev. Feb. 17, 2012) (ESI containing sexual terms is discoverable and such key words should be included in ESI search in sex discrimination and sexual harassment case, where such terms are relevant to plaintiff's claims and to the subject matter of the lawsuit); Linnebur v. United Tel. Ass'n, 2011 U.S. Dist. LEXIS 124473, at *14–15, *20–21 (D. Kan. Oct. 27, 2011) (approving use of term "discrimination" in keyword e-mails and approving production of e-mails in native format).

[5]DaSilva Moore v. Publicas Groupe SA, 287 F.R.D. 182, 189, 18 WH Cases 2d 1479 (S.D.N.Y. 2012) (ordering predictive coding of ESI in class action discrimination case, where there were over 3,000,000 documents to be retrieved and computer-assisted review was superior to available alternatives; parties' proposed protocol dealing with predictive coding search methodology made a part of decision).

"party has notice that future litigation is likely"); Rimkus Consulting Grp., Inc. v. Cammarata, 688 F. Supp. 2d 598, 612 (S.D. Tex. 2010) ("Generally the duty to preserve arises when a party 'has notice that the evidence is relevant to litigation or ... should have known that the evidence may be relevant to future litigation'") (quoting John B. v. Goetz, 531 F.3d 448, 459 (6th Cir. 2008)); Scalera v. Electrograph Sys., Inc., 262 F.R.D. 162, 171 (E.D.N.Y. 2009) ("The obligation to preserve evidence arises when the party has notice that the evidence is relevant to litigation or when a party should have known that the evidence may be relevant to future litigation."); Benton v. Dlorah, Inc., 2007 WL 3231431 (D. Kan. Oct. 30, 2007) ("Once a party reasonably anticipates litigation, it must suspend its routine document retention/destruction policy and put in place a litigation hold to ensure the preservation of relevant documents."); *cf.* Kronisch v. United States, 150 F.3d 112, 126 (2d Cir. 1998) (once party learns it has or may have information relevant to case, it is under duty to protect that information from spoliation). The filing of an EEOC charge or an internal complaint, or receipt of a "litigation hold" letter from counsel, generally will suffice to trigger the preservation duty. *See Scalera*, 262 F.R.D. at 171 (EEOC charge triggered duty to preserve evidence related to charge); Port Auth. Police Asian Jade Soc'y of N.Y. & N.J., Inc. v. Port Auth. of N.Y. & N.J., 601 F. Supp. 2d 566, 570–71 (S.D.N.Y. 2009) (failure to preserve documents and to issue "litigation hold" did not warrant adverse inference instruction as sanction where failure to preserve was partly attributable to 9/11/01 attack on Port Authority offices and where plaintiffs had other information and documents in their possession to support their allegations at trial), *aff'd sub nom.* Chin v. Port Auth. of N.Y. & N.J., 685 F.3d 135, 162, 115 FEP 720 (2d Cir. 2012) (failure to institute "litigation hold" was not gross negligence per se); Goodman v. Praxair Servs., Inc., 632 F. Supp. 2d 494, 511 (D. Md. 2009) (letter openly threatening litigation triggers duty to preserve evidence relevant to dispute); Zubulake v. UBS Warburg, LLC, 220 F.R.D. 212, 216–17, 92 FEP 1539 (S.D.N.Y. 2003) ("the duty to preserve may have arisen even before the EEOC complaint was filed" because "almost everyone associated with [plaintiff] recognized the possibility that she might sue" following her internal complaint).

[On page 34-39 of the Main Volume, after the first sentence of the first full paragraph, add the following.]

Courts have held that the "preservation obligation first runs to counsel, who has a duty to advise his client of the type of information potentially relevant to the lawsuit and of the necessity of preventing its destruction."[6] As a result, counsel cannot rely exclusively on clients to gather, review, and produce discoverable information, and to determine which forms of information must be preserved, and should carefully document the steps that he or she has taken to ensure the preservation of relevant evidence.[7]

[On page 34-39, before the sentence that ends with footnote 150, add the following.]

When evidence alleged to exist cannot be found or has been destroyed, courts determine whether the evidence has been "spoliated" and, if so, whether sanctions are warranted.[8]

---

[6]Richard Green (Fine Paintings) v. McClendon, 262 F.R.D. 284, 290 (S.D.N.Y. 2009) (internal quotations omitted).

[7]*See, e.g.*, *Scalera*, 262 F.R.D. at 177–78 (attorney's communication of duty to preserve evidence held to be insufficient where she did not clearly inform key players of their need to produce electronic copies of active files rather than merely relying on the ESI system for back-up, and where attorney failed to timely communicate need to preserve ESI files to IT manager and others in IT department).

[8]*See* Chura v. Delmar Gardens of Lenexa, Inc., 2012 U.S. Dist. LEXIS 36893, *5–8 (D. Kan. Mar. 20, 2012) (where defendant failed to produce plaintiff's written complaints and related e-mails, phone logs, and investigative documents under circumstances that were "questionable," court ordered "an evidentiary hearing regarding Defendant's efforts to preserve and search for ESI responsive to Plaintiff's interrogatories and requests for production"). "Spoliation" refers to the destruction or material alteration of evidence or to the failure to preserve property for another's use as evidence in pending or reasonably foreseeable litigation." *See* Pension Comm. of Univ. of Montreal Pension Plan v. Banc of Am. Sec., 685 F. Supp. 2d 456, 465 (S.D.N.Y. 2010), *abrogated on other grounds by* Chin v. Port Auth. of N.Y. & N.J., 685 F.3d 135, 162, 115 FEP 720 (2d Cir. 2012). For an extensive discussion of the sanctions available in spoliation cases, *see* D'Onofrio v. SFX Sports Grp., Inc., 2010 U.S. Dist. LEXIS 86711, *13–36 (D.D.C. Aug. 24, 2010) (describing series of decisions regarding search protocols, privilege log testing, spoliation determination, and sanctions).

[On page 34-39, replace the sentence that ends with footnote 150 with the following.]

Courts have broad discretion in imposing an appropriate sanction against a party that has failed to preserve relevant evidence, including electronic materials.

[150]**[On page 34-39 of the Main Volume, in footnote 150, add the following after the parenthetical for "Leon v. IDX Sys. Corp.".]**

; EEOC v. Fry's Elecs., Inc., 874 F. Supp. 2d 1042, 1047, 115 FEP 432 (W.D. Wash. 2012) (adverse inference against defendant regarding validity of its sales justification for plaintiff's termination warranted as sanction where hard drives were destroyed that contained information about employee productivity); Hudson v. AIH Receivable Mgmt. Servs., 2012 U.S. Dist. LEXIS 49189, *10–16 (D. Kan. Mar. 14, 2012) (adverse inference allowed based on evidence that one of defendant's employees continued to erase potentially relevant e-mails months after litigation-hold letter was received; court nevertheless refused to strike answer and affirmative defenses as sanction for destruction), *report and recommendation adopted, as modified*, 2012 U.S. Dist. LEXIS 49187 (D. Kan. Apr. 9, 2012). *See generally* Silvestri v. General Motors Corp., 271 F.3d 583, 590 (4th Cir. 2001) (discussing spoliation principles in context of products liability action).

CHAPTER 35

STATISTICAL AND OTHER EXPERT PROOF

I. USE OF EXPERTS IN LITIGATION

D. Considerations in Selection and Use of Experts

2. *Pretrial Use of the Expert*

[34][On page 35-7 of the Main Volume, in footnote 34, add the following at the end of the footnote.]

In *Comcast Corp. v. Behrend*, 133 S. Ct. 1426 (2013), the Supreme Court underscored that courts must consider the merits and related expert testimony, if necessary, to decide whether the requirements of Rule 23 have been met. Although it rejected the damages model proposed by the plaintiff's expert, the *Comcast* Court declined to define the standard for analyzing expert evidence at the class certification stage. *Id.* at 1432–34.

[35]**[On page 35-7 of the Main Volume, in footnote 35, delete "*and*" before "Ellis v. Costco Wholesale Co.".]**

[35]**[On page 35-7 of the Main Volume, in footnote 35, add the following before "*with*".]**

and American Honda Motor Co. v. Allen, 600 F.3d 813, 815–16 (7th Cir. 2010) (where expert testimony is critically necessary to determine class certification, court must resolve all *Daubert* challenges prior to ruling on class certification),

[35]**[On page 35-7 of the Main Volume, in footnote 35, delete ", *and*" and the citation and parenthetical for "Behrend v. Comcast Corp." at the end of the footnote.]**

[38]**[On page 35-8 of the Main Volume, in footnote 38, add the following after "*See, e.g.*,".]**

Comcast Corp. v. Behrend, 133 S. Ct. 1426, 1434–35 (2013) (trial court must examine merits of case, to extent necessary, to determine whether class certification is proper, even if that means assessing parties' expert evidence);

II. STATISTICAL PROOF

[41]**[On page 35-9 of the Main Volume, in footnote 41, add the following before "Garner v. Cuyahoga Cnty. Juvenile Court".]**

NAACP v. North Hudson Reg'l Fire & Rescue, 665 F.3d 464, 477, 113 FEP 1633 (3d Cir. 2011) (statistical disparities alone can suffice to establish prima facie case of discrimination so long as they are substantial and reliable), *cert. denied*, 132 S. Ct. 2749 (2012);

[43]**[On page 35-10 of the Main Volume, in footnote 43, add the following after "*See, e.g.*,".]**

Acevedo-Parrilla v. Novartis Ex-Lax, 696 F.3d 128, 147, 116 FEP 289 (1st Cir. 2012) (reversing grant of summary judgment to defendant where jury could find that plaintiff's statistical evidence, in conjunction with evidence regarding employer's retirement plan and circumstantial proof, was sufficient to show that defendant's stated reason for discharging plaintiff was pretextual);

[43]**[On page 35-10 of the Main Volume, in footnote 43, add the following at the end of the footnote.]**

But cf. Luster v. Vilsack, 667 F.3d 1089, 1094, 115 FEP 922 (10th Cir. 2011) (statistics rarely suffice to show pretext; to be probative, statistics must "eliminate nondiscriminatory explanations for the [claimed] disparity"); Jackson v. Watkins, 619 F.3d 463, 467–68, 110 FEP 257 (5th Cir. 2010) (in rejecting plaintiff's statistics as not "assembled or compiled to present any . . . meaningful information" about plaintiff's termination, court noted that statistics alone are insufficient to demonstrate pretext).

[44]**[On page 35-11 of the Main Volume, in footnote 44, add the following after "*See*".]**

Schechner v. KPIX-TV & CBS Broad., Inc., 686 F.3d 1018, 1024–26, 115 FEP 307 (9th Cir. 2012) (statistics may "give rise to an inference of discrimination" to satisfy plaintiff's prima facie burden under *McDonnell Douglas*, but play limited role in proving pretext);

[49]**[On page 35-12 of the Main Volume, in footnote 49, add the following at the end of the footnote.]**

See also Bennett v. Nucor Corp., 656 F.3d 802, 817–18, 113 FEP 616 (8th Cir. 2011) (statistical evidence of "bottom line" disparity not probative of disparate impact in hiring where underlying analysis failed to show that applicant pools contained only individuals at least minimally qualified for positions at issue), *cert. denied*, 132 S. Ct. 1807 (2012) and 132 S. Ct. 1861 (2012).

III. TYPES OF STATISTICAL PROOF

A. Statistical Comparisons

[On page 35-17 of the Main Volume, in the carryover paragraph, delete the sentence that ends with footnote 68, and add the following new paragraph.]

In *Wal-Mart Stores, Inc. v. Dukes*,[1] the Supreme Court reversed certification of a nationwide class, finding that the plaintiffs had not satisfied the commonality requirement of Federal Rule 23, where

---

[1]131 S. Ct. 2541, 112 FEP 769 (2011).

the manner in which the challenged policies were implemented varied and was a matter of local managerial discretion.[2] By contrast, the Seventh Circuit certified a companywide injunctive-relief class where the plaintiffs established that nationwide policies and practices, rather than local managerial discretion, were at issue.[3]

B. Selection Rate Comparisons

[On page 35-20 of the Main Volume, in the first sentence of the second paragraph, add new footnote 83a after "Procedures,"].

[83a]*See* 29 C.F.R. § 1607.1 et seq. (2011). The Uniform Guidelines were jointly adopted in 1978 by the EEOC, the Civil Service Commission, the Department of Labor, and the Department of Justice.

[84]**[On page 35-20 of the Main Volume, in footnote 84, add the following at the beginning of the footnote.]**

Ricci v. DeStefano, 557 U.S. 557, 586–87, 106 FEP 929 (2009) (characterizing Uniform Guidelines' 80% standard as "rule of thumb for the courts" and stating that "[t]he pass rates of minorities, which were approximately one-half of the pass rates for white candidates, fall well below the 80-percent standard set by the EEOC to implement the disparate-impact provision of Title VII");

C. Potential Selection Rate Comparisons

[107]**[On page 35-24 of the Main Volume, in footnote 107, add the following at the end of the footnote.]**

Note, however, that RIF analyses in age discrimination cases should not include as part of the negatively impacted group older workers who accepted voluntary buyouts. *See* Aliotta v. Bair, 614 F.3d 556,

---

[2]*Id.* at 2555.

[3]*See* McReynolds v. Merrill Lynch, Pierce, Fenner & Smith, 672 F.3d 482, 488–91, 114 FEP 710 (7th Cir.) (allowing companywide class seeking injunctive relief where issue was whether company's "teaming" policy, which authorized employees rather than managers to form teams, and its "account distribution" policy, which based account distributions on past success of employees competing for transfers, had disparate impact on African-American employees; unlike *Dukes*, policies or practices challenged were those of company "rather than practices that local managers can choose or not at their whim"), *cert. denied*, 133 S. Ct. 338 (2012).

567–69, 109 FEP 1701 (D.C. Cir. 2010) (voluntary buyouts are not adverse employment action; thus, any RIF analysis should include only involuntary layoffs as part of negatively impacted group).

D. Population/Workforce Comparisons

[122][On page 35-27 of the Main Volume, in footnote 122, add the following at the beginning of the footnote.]

NAACP v. North Hudson Reg'l Fire & Rescue, 665 F.3d 464, 479–80, 113 FEP 1633 (3d Cir. 2011) (pool of full-time protective service employees "fairly, and as nearly as possible," approximated pool of qualified firefighters and, thus, supported finding of disparate impact), *cert. denied*, 132 S. Ct. 2749, 183 L. Ed. 2d 616 (2012); Bennett v. Nucor Corp., 656 F.3d 802, 818, 113 FEP 616 (8th Cir. 2011) (statistics should be based on applicant pool of individuals with minimum qualifications for job; analysis that assumed all workers would be eligible for promotion to supervisor was over-inclusive and of little probative value), *cert. denied*, 132 S. Ct. 1807 (2012) and 132 S. Ct. 1861 (2012);

[122][On page 35-27 of the Main Volume, in footnote 122, add the following at the end of the footnote.]

Cf. Meditz v. City of Newark, 658 F.3d 364, 374, 113 FEP 727 (3d Cir. 2011) (remanding to district court to determine relevant labor market, to conduct statistical analysis comparing makeup of city's non-uniformed labor force with similarly skilled labor force in relevant labor market, and to properly analyze business necessity defense).

E. Regression Analyses

[126][On page 35-28 of the Main Volume, in footnote 126, add the following after "*see also*".]

Randall v. Rolls-Royce Corp., 637 F.3d 818, 822–23, 111 FEP 1565 (7th Cir. 2011) (regression analysis in pay discrimination action must control for differences in jobs performed by male and female employees in each compensation category; recognizing importance of employer's use of market wage rates to differentiate jobs within category);

[141]**[On page 35-32 of the Main Volume, in footnote 141, add the following at the beginning of the footnote.]**

Anderson v. Westinghouse Savannah River Co., 406 F.3d 248, 262–63, 266, 95 FEP 1121 (4th Cir. 2005) (affirming exclusion of plaintiff's expert's testimony regarding ranking system used to set pay rates when expert used EEO job groupings instead of job titles to control for job and failed to control for education and experience);

[On page 35-33 of the Main Volume, after the sentence that ends with footnote 145, add the following.]

Given the possible combination of variables, it is not surprising that courts often struggle to determine the statistical significance and probative value of regression equations that omit variables, particularly where an expert fails to control for a variable because data for that variable are not available.[4]

[On page 35-33 of the Main Volume, replace the sentence that ends with footnote 148 with the following.]

Statistical tests, such as the Chow test and tests of multicollinearity and statistical significance, may be used to determine which interaction terms should be included in a pooled regression.

[148]**[On page 35-33 of the Main Volume, in footnote 148, add the following at the end of the footnote.]**

See also Coates v. Johnson & Johnson, 756 F.2d 524, 536–42, 37 FEP 467 (7th Cir. 1985) (discussing use of Chow and log linear tests to assess "whether two or more sets of data may be grouped as a single sample in a statistical model").

G. The Bottom-Line Concept and the Inexorable Zero

[170]**[On page 35-36 of the Main Volume, replace footnote 170 with the following.]**

---

[4]*See* McClain v. Lufkin Indus., Inc., 519 F.3d 264, 280, 102 FEP 1362 (5th Cir. 2008) (affirming district court decision that gave more credence to plaintiff's promotion analysis based on potential pools than defendant's analysis based on bid sheets, where "the bid data were incomplete and unreliable, [with] more than half of the promotions . . . missing from the bid database which Lufkin prepared in anticipation of this litigation"); Pottenger v. Potlatch Corp., 329 F.3d 740, 748, 91 FEP 1530 (9th Cir. 2003) (court rejected plaintiff's analyses for certain variables but stated that it would have ruled differently if such information was not available).

[170]*Id.* at 1275–76. In a subsequent decision in the case, the court reviewed individual disparate treatment claims and said that it would consider the claims of nonapplicants who could show that they refrained from applying due to a justifiable belief that the employer's discriminatory practices "made application a futile gesture." 296 F.3d 1265, 1274, 89 FEP 522 (11th Cir. 2002), *cert. denied*, 539 U.S. 941 (2003).

IV. SOURCES OF STATISTICS

B. Applicant Flow Data

[199][On page 35-42 of the Main Volume, in footnote 199, add the following after "*See*".]

Tyler v. University of Ark. Bd. of Trs., 628 F.3d 980, 990, 111 FEP 161 (8th Cir. 2011) (sample size of six applicants too small for meaningful statistical analysis of sex discrimination);

C. Population/Labor Market Data

4. Employer's Workforce Data

[256][On page 35-55 of the Main Volume, in footnote 256, add the following at the end of the footnote.]

Note, however, that any qualifications that create a statistically significant disparate impact must be "job related for the position in question and consistent with business necessity." *See generally* 42 U.S.C. § 2000e-2(k)(1)(A)(i).

V. PROPER GEOGRAPHIC SCOPE OF STATISTICS

[274][On page 35-59 of the Main Volume, in footnote 274, add the following after "*See, e.g.,*".]

NAACP v. North Hudson Reg'l Fire & Rescue, 665 F.3d 464, 479, 113 FEP 1633 (3d Cir. 2011) (commute times and tendency of public safety professionals to search for jobs statewide were persuasive factors in defining tri-county area and entire State of New Jersey as appropriate geographic scopes for relevant labor market), *cert. denied*, 132 S. Ct. 2749 (2012); Meditz v. City of Newark, 658 F.3d

364, 373, 113 FEP 727 (3d Cir. 2011) (in order to determine parameters of relevant labor market, court should consider "geographical location, flow of transportation facilities, locations from which private employers draw their workforce, and commuting patterns");

VII. PROPER WEIGHT TO BE GIVEN STATISTICAL PROOF

A. Reliability Standards

[312][On page 35-67 of the Main Volume, in footnote 312, add the following after "*E.g.*,".]

Luster v. Vilsack, 667 F.3d 1089, 1094, 115 FEP 922 (10th Cir. 2011) (raw statistics, without analysis, are "nearly meaningless");

B. Degree of the Disparity

[315][On page 35-69 of the Main Volume, in footnote 315, add the following at the end of the footnote.]

Cf. Apsley v. Boeing Co., 691 F.3d 1184, 1199–1200, 115 FEP 1573 (10th Cir. 2012) (affirming summary judgment for employer; selection rates would not permit jury to conclude that age discrimination in hiring by successor was company's standard operating procedure; plaintiffs' "statistics suggest, at most, isolated or sporadic instances of age discrimination").

[On page 35-70 of the Main Volume, in the carryover paragraph, delete the semicolon before footnote 320.]

[320][On page 35-70 of the Main Volume, in footnote 320, replace "; *cf.* EEOC v. Federal Reserve Bank" citation and parenthetical with the following.]

. *But see* D. BALDUS & J. COLE, STATISTICAL PROOF OF DISCRIMINATION 129–30 (1986 Cumulative Supp.) (footnote omitted) (stating preference for legal rule that would allow one-tailed test "if the possibility of intentional discrimination favoring the protected group represented by the plaintiff can be ruled out as defying logic, *i.e.*, the available evidence excluding the statistic in question gives strong support to the conclusion that the system is either nondiscriminatory or disadvantageous to the plaintiff's group").

[On page 35-70 of the Main Volume, in the carryover paragraph, replace the phrase "the former decreases the likelihood that a statistically significant disparity will be found." with the following.]

in any disparate treatment claim where the hypothesis to be tested is whether the challenged selection process "treated men and women equally, not that the selection process treated women at least as well or better than men."

[On page 35-70 of the Main Volume, in the carryover paragraph, after the sentence that ends with footnote 321, add the following.]

Another appellate court explained that the approach should depend on the hypothesis, specifically, that "one-tailed analysis tests whether a group is disfavored in hiring decisions while two-tailed analysis tests whether the group is preferred *or* disfavored."[5]

[328][On page 35-71 of the Main Volume, in footnote 328, add the following at the beginning of the footnote.]

See, e.g., Meditz v. City of Newark, 658 F.3d 364, 372, 113 FEP 727 (3d Cir. 2011) (vacating summary judgment for employer and remanding; disparity of slightly over six standard deviations between racial groups goes far beyond *Hazelwood*'s "two or three standard deviations" standard and establishes prima facie case of discrimination);

C. Size of the Statistical Sample

[338][On page 35-75 of the Main Volume, in footnote 338, add the following after "*See, e.g.*,".]

Tyler v. University of Ark. Bd. of Trs., 628 F.3d 980, 990, 111 FEP 161 (8th Cir. 2011) (sample of six applicants too small for meaningful statistical analysis in sex discrimination action);

---

[5]Hartman v. Duffy, 88 F.3d 1232, 1238 (D.C. Cir. 1996) (affirming judgment where defendant did not introduce alternative two-tailed statistical analysis at trial, and never objected to plaintiff's expert's use of one-tailed analysis) (emphasis in original).

D. Conflicting Statistical Conclusions

[345][On page 35-77 of the Main Volume, in the second full paragraph, delete both the callout in text and footnote 345.]

VIII. OTHER CATEGORIES OF EXPERTS IN EMPLOYMENT CASES

B. Mental Health Experts

[368][On page 35-81 of the Main Volume, in footnote 368, add the following after "*See*".]

Aponte-Rivera v. DHL Solutions (USA), Inc., 650 F.3d 803, 811–12, 112 FEP 590 (1st Cir. 2011) (expert testimony is not required to prove emotional distress damages in hostile environment case, but absence of such testimony is relevant to maximum award that court should allow);

C. Economic Damages Experts

[374][On page 35-82 of the Main Volume, in footnote 374, add the following after "*See, e.g.,*".]

Kapche v. Holder, 677 F.3d 454, 469–70, 26 AD 1 (D.C. Cir. 2012) (competing experts testified to value of plaintiff's current salary and benefits as compared to what he would have earned as FBI special agent, position that he allegedly was discriminatorily denied);

CHAPTER 36

THE CIVIL RIGHTS ACTS OF 1866 AND 1871

II. Scope and Coverage of the Civil Rights Act of 1866, 42 U.S.C. § 1981

A. Statutory Authority

[13][On page 36-4 of the Main Volume, in footnote 13, add the following at the end of the footnote.]

See also Jimenez v. Wellstar Health Sys., 596 F.3d 1304, 1309–10, 108 FEP 790 (11th Cir. 2010) (looking to state contract law to determine whether plaintiff, African-American physician whose staff privileges were suspended, failed to state claim under § 1981 because granting and suspension of those privileges is covered by hospital bylaws, rather than by contract).

B. Cognizable Defendants Under § 1981

1. Private Entities

[On page 36-5 of the Main Volume, in the first paragraph, at the end of the fourth sentence, add new footnote 18a after "prerequisites, procedures, and available relief.".]

[18a]*Id.*; *cf.* Grutter v. Bollinger, 539 U.S. 306, 343, 91 FEP 1761 (2003) ("Title VI . . . proscribes only those racial classifications that would violate the Equal Protection Clause or the Fifth Amendment"); General Bldg. Contractors Ass'n, Inc. v. Pennsylvania, 458 U.S. 375, 389–91(1982) (prohibition against discrimination in § 1981 is co-extensive with Equal Protection Clause).

3. State and Local Governments

[On page 36-7 of the Main Volume, replace the sentence that ends with footnote 32 with the following.]

The Ninth Circuit has interpreted subsection 1981(c), created by the 1991 amendments, to permit direct causes of action against governmental actors for violations of § 1981, thus finding that the 1991 amendments overruled this aspect of *Jett*.

[32]**[On page 36-7 of the Main Volume, in footnote 32, add the following at the end of the footnote.]**

But see McGovern v. City of Phila., 554 F.3d 114, 120, 105 FEP 481 (3d Cir. 2009) (nothing in 1991 Civil Rights Act implies that it creates private right of action under § 1981; § 1981 describes substantive rights only, § 1983 provides procedure for enforcing those rights).

[33]**[On page 36-8 of the Main Volume, in footnote 33, add the following after "*See*".]**

McCormick v. Miami Univ., 693 F.3d 654, 660–61, 116 FEP 24 (6th Cir. 2012) (under § 1981, individual cannot sue state actor in his or her individual capacity).

[37]**[On page 36-9 of the Main Volume, in footnote 37, add the following at the end of the footnote.]**

But see McCormick, 693 F.3d at 661 (in accordance with *Jett*, more specific and express cause of action contained in § 1983 provides exclusive mechanism to address violation of § 1981 against officials sued in their individual capacities, as well as against agencies themselves).

C. Types of Discrimination Prohibited by § 1981

1. Race Discrimination

[53]**[On page 36-12 of the Main Volume, in footnote 53, add the following after "*See*".]**

Good v. University of Chi. Med. Ctr., 673 F.3d 670, 677–79, 114 FEP 903 (7th Cir. 2012) (applying higher proof standard to claim of Caucasian employee terminated for poor performance who identified three similarly situated minority employees with similar performance problems who were allowed to accept demotion in lieu of discharge, where she was replaced by white person and failed to demonstrate that UCMC was unusual employer who had reason or inclination to discriminate invidiously against whites);

[53]**[On page 36-12 of the Main Volume, in footnote 53, add the following after the parenthetical for "Bass v. Board of Cnty. Comm'rs".]**

Parker v. Baltimore & Ohio R.R., 652 F.2d 1012, 1027, 25 FEP 889 (D.C. Cir. 1981) ("Whites are also a protected group under Title VII, but it defies common sense to suggest that the promotion of a black employee justifies an inference of prejudice against white coworkers in our present society.... This court has allowed majority plaintiffs to rely on the *McDonnell Douglas* criteria to prove a prima facie case of intentionally disparate treatment when background circumstances support the suspicion that the defendant is that unusual employer who discriminates against the majority...."). *See generally* Chapter 38 ("Reverse" Discrimination and Affirmative Action).

2. *Retaliation*

[On page 36-16 of the Main Volume, in the first paragraph, after the sentence that ends with footnote 70, add the following.]

One court has determined that individual liability may exist under § 1981 for causing the employer to retaliate against another employee.[1]

III. SCOPE AND COVERAGE OF THE CIVIL RIGHTS ACT OF 1871, 42 U.S.C. § 1983

B. Cognizable Defendants Under § 1983

1. *The State Action Requirement and Private Discrimination*

[86]**[On page 36-20 of the Main Volume, in footnote 86, add the following after "*See, e.g.*,".]**

Karl v. City of Mountlake Terrace, 678 F.3d 1062, 1066, 33 IER Cases 1415 (9th Cir. 2012) (evaluating § 1983 claims of "free speech retaliation" brought by administrative assistant against city police department and individual officer);

[92]**[On page 36-21 of the Main Volume, in footnote 92, add the following at the end of the footnote.]**

See also Paige v. Coyner, 614 F.3d 273, 280, 30 IER Cases 1789 (6th Cir. 2010) (when state action is not discriminatory but induces private act of discrimination, § 1983's state action requirement is satisfied and court will ask whether discrimination itself was reasonably foreseeable).

[On page 36-23 of the Main Volume, in the carryover paragraph, after the sentence that ends with footnote 106, add the following.]

State action is also implicated where it induces a reasonably foreseeable private act of discrimination.[2]

---

[1]Smith v. Bray, 681 F.3d 888, 889, 115 FEP 81 (7th Cir. 2012) (also recognizing that cat's paw theory may support entity liability for retaliation under Title VII, § 1981, and § 1983).

[2]*See* Paige v. Coyner, 614 F.3d 273, 280, 30 IER 1789 (6th Cir. 2010) (when state action is not itself discriminatory, but induces private act of discrimination, § 1983's state action requirement is satisfied if private act of discrimination itself was reasonably foreseeable).

[106]**[On page 36-23 of the Main Volume, in footnote 106, add the following at the end of the footnote.]**

But see Faragalla v. Douglas Cnty. Sch. Dist., 411 F. App'x 140, 159, 111 FEP 523 (10th Cir. 2011) (union that refused to arbitrate dispute on behalf of employee did not act "in concert" with state to satisfy § 1983's state action requirement).

[108]**[On page 36-23 of the Main Volume, in footnote 108, add the following at the beginning of the footnote.]**

See Dodds v. Richardson, 614 F.3d 1185, 1195, 1198–99 (10th Cir. 2010) (rejecting respondeat superior liability in accordance with *Monell*, but creating theory of supervisory liability that requires plaintiff to link supervisor's actions to specific constitutional violation and to demonstrate supervisor's "personal involvement" and intent);

[112]**[On page 36-24 of the Main Volume, in footnote 112, add the following at the beginning of the footnote.]**

See Faragalla v. Douglas Cnty. Sch. Dist., 411 F. App'x 140, 159, 111 FEP 523 (10th Cir. 2011) (union that refused to arbitrate dispute on behalf of employee did not act "in concert" with state to satisfy § 1983's state action requirement);

3. State and Local Governments

a. Local Governments

[126]**[On page 36-26 of the Main Volume, in footnote 126, add the following after "*see also*".]**

Lee v. City of Syracuse, 446 F. App'x 319, 322 (2d Cir. 2011) (*Monell* liability attached, despite jury's finding that sole individual defendant did not personally violate plaintiff's rights, where other individuals retaliated against plaintiff due to city's custom or practice); Dodds v. Richardson, 614 F.3d 1185, 1203–04 (10th Cir. 2010) (sheriff liable for enforcing discriminatory policies that he did not establish, "where the policies' enforcement caused the constitutional [due process] violation" at issue);

[128]**[On page 36-27 of the Main Volume, in footnote 128, add the following after "*see also*".]**

Palka v. City of Chi., 662 F.3d 428, 435 (7th Cir. 2011) (police academy supervisor lacked final policy-making authority where other department personnel reviewed supervisor's decision);

[On page 36-27 of the Main Volume, in the carryover paragraph, replace "The Court explained that:" with the following.]

A plurality of the Court explained that:

[130]**[On page 36-27 of the Main Volume, in footnote 130, add the following after "*see also*".]**

Palka, 662 F.3d at 435 (city not liable under § 1983 ratification theory where plaintiff failed to show that municipal official with final policy-making authority shared subordinate's discriminatory animus);

[136]**[On page 36-29 of the Main Volume, in footnote 136, add the following at the end of the footnote.]**

But see Palka v. City of Chi., 662 F.3d 428, 434–35 (7th Cir. 2011) (declining to endorse "new 'inaction' theory of municipal liability" where plaintiff's allegation that city failed to stop supervisor's discrimination was "more like a fact-specific application of ordinary *Monell* policy or custom doctrine").

[145]**[On page 36-30 of the Main Volume, in footnote 145, add the following at the end of the footnote.]**

See also Bagley v. Blagojevich, 646 F.3d 378, 391–93,190 LRRM 2983 (7th Cir. 2011) (determining whether act is legislative in form requires court to ask whether defendant acted pursuant to constitutional procedures, whether his actions were "integral steps in the legislative process," and whether action substantially "bore all of the hallmarks of traditional legislation").

[146]**[On page 36-30 of the Main Volume, replace footnote 146 with the following.]**

In re *Montgomery Cnty.*, 215 F.3d at 376; *see also* Community House, Inc. v. City of Boise, 623 F.3d 945, 960 (9th Cir. 2010) (using four-factor test to determine whether act is legislative in its character and effect for immunity purposes: (1) whether act involves ad hoc decision making or formulation of policy; (2) whether act applies to few individuals or public at large; (3) whether act is formally legislative in character; and (4) whether act bears all hallmarks of traditional legislation).

[148][On page 36-31 of the Main Volume, in footnote 148, add the following after "*See*".]

Bendix v. Village of Hanover Park, 677 F.3d 317, 318–19, 33 IER Cases 1192 (7th Cir. 2012) (upholding legislative immunity for village president and board members for supporting ordinance that eliminated plaintiff's job, but determining that village could not claim immunity for ordinance as its own policy);

b. State Governments

[164][On page 36-33 of the Main Volume, in footnote 164, add the following at the end of the footnote.]

See also Pucci v. Nineteenth Dist. Ct., 628 F.3d 752, 764, 110 FEP 1766 (6th Cir. 2010) (Michigan's district courts were sufficiently integrated into state judicial system to be "arm of the state," qualifying for sovereign immunity under Eleventh Amendment); Talbert v. Judiciary of N.J., 420 F. App'x 140, 141, 111 FEP 1701 (3d Cir. 2011) ("The New Jersey court system is a non-consenting entity entitled to immunity under the Eleventh Amendment.").

[175][On page 36-34 of the Main Volume, in footnote 175, add the following at the end of the footnote.]

See also Guttman v. Khalsa, 669 F.3d 1101, 1125, 25 AD 1316 (10th Cir. 2012) (Title II of ADA did not validly abrogate states' Eleventh Amendment immunity).

4. State and Local Governmental Officials in Their Individual Capacities

[208][On page 36-40 of the Main Volume, in footnote 208, add the following after "*See*".]

Sherrod v. Johnson, 667 F.3d 1359, 1364, 33 IER Cases 453 (11th Cir. 2012) (school administrators entitled to qualified immunity for firing teacher who engaged in protected speech; immunity turned on whether decision was objectively reasonable in light of facts known at time and not on whether administrators knew that law generally forbade retaliation for protected speech);

[208]**[On page 36-40 of the Main Volume, in the second paragraph of footnote 208, add the following before "Robinson v. York".]**

Karl v. City of Mountlake Terrace, 678 F.3d 1062, 1072–74, 33 IER Cases 1415 (9th Cir. 2012) (assistant police chief not entitled to qualified immunity because he was subordinate officer and not the final decision maker in plaintiff's termination; § 1983 liability attaches if subordinate officer "sets in motion" actions that he should have known would cause constitutional injury); Juarez v. Aguilar, 666 F.3d 325, 336, 33 IER Cases 336 (5th Cir. 2011) (school board members not entitled to qualified immunity where established law made it unreasonable for board members to believe that employment decision was not "adverse action" if made without formal vote); Wagner v. Jones, 664 F.3d 259, 273–75, 33 IER Cases 199 (8th Cir. 2011) (law school dean not entitled to qualified immunity where she was on notice that plaintiff's political beliefs and associations may have impermissibly affected faculty's recommendation not to hire her and dean still refused to hire plaintiff for any position);

[212]**[On page 36-41 of the Main Volume, in footnote 212, add the following at the end of the footnote.]**

Fact questions related to qualified immunity may be submitted to a jury, but the court must ultimately decide whether immunity attaches. *See* Lore v. City of Syracuse, 670 F.3d 127, 162, 114 FEP 466 (2d Cir. 2012) (trial court erred in having jury decide ultimate legal question of immunity).

[214]**[On page 36-42 of the Main Volume, in the carryover of footnote 214, replace the parenthetical for "Nanda v. Moss" with the following.]**

(university dean did not have qualified immunity from terminated female professor's § 1983 action that alleged violation of her clearly established right under Equal Protection Clause to be free from gender and ethnic discrimination).

[215][On page 36-42 of the Main Volume, in footnote 215, add the following after "*See*".]

Levin v. Madigan, 692 F.3d 607, 622, 115 FEP 1281 (7th Cir. 2012) (availability of immunity defense turned on whether plaintiff's constitutional right to be free from age discrimination was clearly established right at time of alleged violation; court held that it was so established); Hunt v. County of Orange, 672 F.3d 606, 615–16, 33 IER Cases 586 (9th Cir. 2012) (sheriff-coroner entitled to immunity for wrongful demotion of subordinate for political disloyalty where he reasonably but mistakenly could have believed at time that political loyalty was required of someone in plaintiff's position); Bardzik v. County of Orange, 635 F.3d 1138, 1152, 32 IER Cases 13 (9th Cir. 2011) (sheriff entitled to qualified immunity from plaintiff's claim regarding demotion from policy-making position that required political loyalty but not for claims regarding later retaliatory acts taken against plaintiff in non–policy-making position);

C. Bases of Discrimination Prohibited by § 1983

1. *Introduction*

[224][On page 36-44 of the Main Volume, in footnote 224, add the following at the end of the footnote.]

See also Reynolds v. Barrett, 685 F.3d 193, 201–02, 115 FEP 738 (2d Cir. 2012) ("pattern-or-practice" framework used in Title VII cases cannot be used in § 1983 suit brought against state officials for intentional discrimination). *But see* Groesch v. City of Springfield, Ill., 635 F.3d 1020, 1025, 111 FEP 1441 (7th Cir. 2011) (some standards, such as Lilly Ledbetter Act "paycheck accrual rule," apply equally to Title VII and § 1983 claims).

[On page 36-45 of the Main Volume, after the carryover sentence that ends with footnote 228, add the following new paragraph.]

In *Levin v. Madigan*,[3] the Seventh Circuit adopted the *Fitzgerald* analysis and held that the ADEA neither provides the exclusive mechanism for addressing age discrimination in employment nor

---

[3] 692 F.3d 607, 115 FEP 1281 (7th Cir. 2012), *cert. granted*, 133 S. Ct. 1600 (2013).

precludes a § 1983 claim based on age discrimination.[4] All of the other circuits considering the issue prior to the Supreme Court's decision in *Fitzgerald* had reached the opposite conclusion.[5]

2. *Equal Protection*

[On page 36-45 of the Main Volume, replace the first sentence of the first full paragraph in the section with the following.]

The section that follows reviews the Equal Protection Clause, which is one of the principal constitutional provisions invoked in support of § 1983 employment discrimination claims.

[229]**[On page 36-45 of the Main Volume, in footnote 229, move the citation and parenthetical for "Thigpen v. Bibb Cnty., Ga., Sheriff's Dep't" after parenthetical for "English v. Colorado Dep't of Corr.".]**

[On page 36-47 of the Main Volume, after the sentence that ends with footnote 234, add the following new paragraph.]

The Eleventh Circuit has held that the § 1983 prohibition against sex-based discrimination extends to transgendered and transsexual employees based on their gender nonconformity.[6] Other courts have considered sex-based equal protection claims under § 1983 by employees claiming discrimination or retaliation based on sexual orientation.[7]

---

[4]*Id.* at 619–22.

[5]*See, e.g.*, Ahlmeyer v. Nevada Sys. of Higher Educ., 535 F.3d 1051, 1057, 105 FEP 865 (9th Cir. 2009); Tapia-Tapia v. Potter, 322 F.3d 742, 745, 91 FEP 547 (1st Cir. 2003); Migneault v. Peck, 158 F.3d 1131, 1140, 78 FEP 600 (10th Cir. 1998), *vacated on other grounds*, 425 U.S. 1131, 1140, 81 FEP 1088 (2000); Lafleur v. Texas Dep't of Health, 126 F.3d 758, 760, 75 FEP 225 (5th Cir. 1997); Chennareddy v. Bowsher, 935 F.2d 315, 318, 56 FEP 127 (D.C. Cir. 1991); Zombro v. Baltimore City Police Dep't, 868 F.2d 1364, 1368, 49 FEP 297 (4th Cir. 1989).

[6]Glenn v. Brumby, 663 F.3d 1312, 1320, 113 FEP 1542 (11th Cir. 2011) ("a government agent violates the Equal Protection Clause's prohibition of sex-based discrimination when he or she fires a transgender or transsexual employee because of his or her gender non-conformity").

[7]*See* Ayala-Sepúlveda v. Municipality of San Germán, 671 F.3d 24, 30–33, 114 FEP 234 (1st Cir. 2012) (examining under Equal Protection Clause claims of retaliatory transfer and failing to stop co-worker harassment based on sexual orientation, but finding no evidence of disparate treatment); *see also* Flaherty v. Massapequa Pub. Sch., 462 F. App'x 38, 39 (2d Cir. 2012) (expressing no opinion "whether a person *perceived* as homosexual is in a protected class for equal protection purposes," but affirming determination that she had failed to demonstrate intentional discrimination).

[On page 36-47 of the Main Volume, begin a new paragraph with the sentence that ends with footnote 235, which begins "The right to be free from racial and gender discrimination, . . .".]

[241]**[On page 36-48 of the Main Volume, in footnote 241, add the following after "*See*".]**

Levin v. Madigan, 692 F.3d 607, 622, 115 FEP 1281 (7th Cir. 2012);

[On page 36-48 of the Main Volume, in the first full paragraph, after the sentence that ends with footnote 242, add the following.]

Although *Levin* involved a state employee, the Seventh Circuit opinion generally considers whether the ADEA precludes § 1983 constitutional claims based on age,[8] and thus may have implications for all public-sector employees. Similarly, the Ninth Circuit has held that although § 1983 disability claims may not be based on whether there is a statutory violation of the ADA, they may be asserted based on equal protection grounds, pursuant to the rational-basis test.[9]

[253]**[On page 36-50 of the Main Volume, in footnote 253, add the following before "Whitney v. City of Milan".]**

McDonald v. City of St. Paul, 679 F.3d 698, 705–06 (8th Cir. 2012) (§ 1983 equal protection claim based on retaliation for filing prior civil rights suit);

---

[8]692 F.3d at 622 (ADEA does not preclude age-based equal protection claims).

[9]*See* Okwu v. McKim, 682 F.3d 841, 846, 26 AD 513 (9th Cir. 2012) (Title I of ADA precludes § 1983 claims for alleged violations of that statute but does not preclude examining disability claims on equal protection grounds; state's decision to reinstate employee was rationally based on former employee's inability to fulfill her job duties).

IV. SCOPE AND COVERAGE OF THE CIVIL RIGHTS ACT OF 1871, 42 U.S.C. §§ 1985 AND 1986

B. Cognizable Defendants

1. The Applicability of § 1985 to Private Discrimination

[271]**[On page 36-55 of the Main Volume, in footnote 271, add the following after "*see, e.g.*,".]**

Henley v. Brown, 686 F.3d 634, 641, 115 FEP 949 (8th Cir. 2012) (plaintiff may not invoke purely remedial statute, such as § 1985(3), to redress violation of right conferred by only Title VII; when employer's conduct violates not only rights created by Title VII, but also rights conferred by independent source, Title VII supplements, rather than supplants, existing remedies for employment discrimination);

V. LITIGATION, PROOF, PROCEDURE, AND REMEDIES

B. Timeliness

[336]**[On page 36-67 of the Main Volume, in footnote 336, add the following at the end of the footnote.]**

See also Cintron-Lorenzo v. Fondo Del Securo Del Estado, 634 F.3d 1, 1, 111 FEP 609 (1st Cir. 2011) (EEOC charge does not toll limitations period for filing § 1983 claim).

[338]**[On page 36-68 of the Main Volume, in footnote 338, add the following before the last sentence.]**

Cf. Groesch v. City of Springfield, Ill., 635 F.3d 1020, 1026, 111 FEP 1441 (7th Cir. 2011) (Title VII's paycheck accrual rule, where each paycheck constitutes new cause of action to challenge discriminatory pay practices, applies to § 1983 claims);

D. Proof

[357]**[On page 36-70 of the Main Volume, in footnote 357, add the following after "*See*".]**

Smith v. Wilson, 705 F.3d 674, 681–82, 117 FEP 1438 (7th 2013) ("Smith's Equal Protection claim under § 1983 requires separate consideration. Well before *Price Waterhouse* approved of burden-shifting in the Title VII context, federal courts used an identical framework to assess constitutional claims. . . . In race discrimination cases, for example, once plaintiff discharges her burden of establishing that decision 'was motivated in part by a racially discriminatory purpose,' burden shifts to defendant to 'establish[] that the same decision would have resulted even had the impermissible purpose not been considered.'") (citations omitted); Hanners v. Trent, 674 F.3d 683, 691–96, 114 FEP 965 (7th Cir. 2012) (applying Title VII direct method of proof in § 1981 and § 1983 actions); Tademy v. Union Pac. Corp., 520 F.3d 1149, 1170, 102 FEP 1798 (10th Cir. 2008) (hostile environment case; standards and burdens under § 1981 are same as those under Title VII, but § 1981 has longer statute of limitations);

[357]**[On page 36-70 of the Main Volume, in footnote 357, add the following before "Patterson v. Oneida".]**

Metoyer v. Chessman, 504 F.3d 919, 930, 101 FEP 993 (9th Cir. 2007) (under § 1981, "the same legal principles as those applicable in a Title VII disparate treatment case" are applied), *cert. dismissed*, 553 U.S. 1039 (2008);

[358]**[On page 36-71 of the Main Volume, in footnote 358, add the following after "*See*".]**

Radentz v. Marion Cnty., 640 F.3d 754, 756–61, 111 FEP 1676 (7th Cir. 2011) (applying *McDonnell Douglas* framework to white plaintiffs' § 1983 race discrimination claims);

[359]**[On page 36-71 of the Main Volume, in footnote 359, add the following after the parenthetical for "Brown v. J. Kaz, Inc.".]**

; *Metoyer*, 504 F.3d at 934 (case law precedent applying same burdens of proof under Title VII and § 1981 remains valid; thus, even though Congress did not expressly amend § 1981 to establish mixed-motive proof formulation under that statute, standard for mixed motive prescribed under Title VII applies equally to claims under § 1981)

G. Res Judicata

[401][On page 36-79 of the Main Volume, in footnote 401, add the following after "*Compare*".]

Groesch v. City of Springfield, Ill., 635 F.3d 1020, 1029–30, 111 FEP 1441 (7th Cir. 2011) (res judicata barred police officers' pay discrimination claims arising before date of final judgment in prior state court suit, but did not bar claims based on paychecks issued after such judgment was entered),

[402][On page 36-79 of the Main Volume, in footnote 402, add the following after "*But see*".]

Palka v. City of Chi., 662 F.3d 428, 437–38 (7th Cir. 2011) (dismissal of plaintiff's § 1983 suit barred subsequent Title VII action based on same set of facts);

[412][On page 36-81 of the Main Volume, in footnote 412, add the following after "*See, e.g.,*".]

White v. City of Pasadena, 671 F.3d 918, 929–30, 25 AD 1185 (9th Cir. 2012) (giving res judicata effect to state agency's decision that city had just cause to terminate plaintiff and that plaintiff's termination was not retaliatory, where that decision was upheld on review by state trial and appellate courts);

CHAPTER 37

THE NATIONAL LABOR RELATIONS ACT

I. INTRODUCTION

[2][On page 37-2 of the Main Volume, in footnote 2, add the following at the end of the footnote.]

> It is hereby declared to be the policy of the United States to eliminate the causes of certain substantial obstructions to the free flow of commerce and to mitigate and eliminate these obstructions when they have occurred by encouraging the practice and procedure of collective bargaining and by protecting the exercise by workers of full freedom of association, self-organization, and designation of representatives of their own choosing, for the purpose of negotiating the terms and conditions of their employment or other mutual aid or protection.

29 U.S.C. § 151(d).

[On page 37-3 of the Main Volume, at the beginning of the paragraph, add the following.]

Section 8(a)(3) of the NLRA makes it unlawful for an employer to discriminate against an employee (interpreted to include a job applicant) who has engaged in conduct protected by the Act.

[13][On page 37-3 of the Main Volume, in footnote 13, delete the first sentence.]

II. REMEDIES AGAINST UNIONS

C. Challenges to Certification

[52][On page 37-11 of the Main Volume, in footnote 52, add the following after "*See*".]

Ashland Facility Operations v. NLRB, 701 F.3d 983, 991–92, 116 FEP 1412 (4th Cir. 2012) (NLRB properly certified union over employer's objection to National Association for the Advancement of Colored People (NAACP) official's remarks about employees being treated like "chattel enslaved captives," where remarks were made in context of raising legitimate concerns about working conditions and remarks by third-party are not subject to same scrutiny as those of union itself);

D. Remedies for Breach of the Duty of Fair Representation

[On page 37-14 of the Main Volume, after the carryover sentence, add the following.]

As does retaliation.[1]

E. Union Opposition to Employer Efforts to Remedy Discrimination

[70][On page 37-15 of the Main Volume, in footnote 70, add the following after "illegal contractual provision" in the parenthetical for "Graphic Arts v. NLRB".]

; "[B]oth the Supreme Court and the Board have held that the elimination of discrimination and its vestiges is an appropriate subject of bargaining. ... And the Board has found that an employer's failure to bargain in good faith about eliminating discrimination can constitute an unfair labor practice." (citations omitted)

IV. The Railway Labor Act

[149][On page 37-28 of the Main Volume, in footnote 149, add the following after "*See, e.g.*,".]

Thompson v. Air Transport Int'l Ltd. Liab. Co., 664 F.3d 723, 726, 18 WH Cases 2d 872 (8th Cir 2011) (affirming dismissal of claims under Family and Medical Leave Act (FMLA) where collective bargaining agreement contained mandatory arbitration clause; although determining whether particular claim is covered by mandatory arbitration clause typically requires interpretation of clause and generally is preempted under RLA where party does not dispute meaning provision, its application to given set of facts involves only reference to

---

[1]Gilbert v. Country Music Ass'n, Inc., 432 F. A'ppx 516, 520–21, 112 FEP 1711 (6th Cir. 2011) (duty of fair representation extends to all aspects of union activity; complaint alleging that union had manipulated hiring hall to avoid giving referrals to member who was homosexual and who had complained of harassment by other union members in workplace stated claim of breach of duty of fair representation).

provision rather than interpretation and therefore is not preempted); Rabé v. United Airlines, Inc., 636 F. 3d 866, 873, 111 FEP 1094 (7th Cir. 2011) (even though state-law claim of discrimination concerns employment dispute or tangentially involves provision of collective bargaining agreement it is not generally preempted by RLA; principal issue presented by such claim is not likely to require court to interpret collective bargaining agreement);

V. ARBITRATION OF STATUTORY CLAIMS UNDER COLLECTIVE BARGAINING AGREEMENTS

[153]**[On page 37-30 of the Main Volume, in footnote 153, add the following at the end of the footnote.]**

See also Coleman v. Donahoe, 667 F.3d 835, 853, 114 FEP 160 (7th Cir. 2012) (where collective bargaining agreement did not mandate arbitration of discrimination claims, employee is not precluded from litigating discrimination case; decision by arbitrator that postal service had "lied about" its reasons for discharging African-American postal service employee was not identical to finding of pretext under Title VII; nevertheless, employee demonstrated sufficient proof of pretext to survive summary judgment); Matthews v. Denver Newspaper Agency, 649 F.3d 1199, 1207, 112 FEP 432, 24 AD 1156 (10th Cir. 2011) (former employee may maintain action asserting discrimination claims in action challenging his discharge despite previous, adverse arbitration decision where collective bargaining agreement arbitration clause did not permit or require statutory claims to be submitted to arbitrator).

[157]**[On page 37-31 of the Main Volume, in footnote 157, add the following after "*See*".]**

Ibarra v. United Parcel Serv., 695 F.3d 354, 116 FEP 20 (5th Cir. 2012) (employee was not foreclosed from pursuing her claim of sex discrimination in federal court by collective bargaining agreement provision that established grievance procedure as exclusive remedy for employee complaints where nondiscrimination provision of agreement did not mention grievance process and did not expressly waive right to pursue Title VII claims in judicial forum); Gove v. Career Sys. Dev. Corp., 689 F.3d 1, 7–8, 115 FEP 828 (1st Cir. 2012) (rejected applicant was not required to arbitrate her pregnancy discrimination claim despite language in collective bargaining agreement stating that arbitration clause applied to "any issue prior to your employment which arises out of the employment process" where she reasonably believed that clause would apply to her only if she ultimately was hired, clause was ambiguous, and under Maine law ambiguities in such clause are construed against drafter of contract); Nino v. Jewelry Exch., Inc., 609 F.3d 191, 201–04, 109 FEP 769 (3d Cir. 2010) (pervasive one-sidedness of agreement barred employer from invoking its right to arbitrate employee's discrimination claims where agreement was presented on take-it-or-leave-it basis, disparity in bargaining power made it procedurally unconscionable, and provisions requiring parties to bear their own attorneys' fees and permitting employer to strike more arbitrators are substantively unconscionable);

[160]**[On page 37-31 of the Main Volume, in footnote 160, add the following at the end of the footnote.]**

But see Matthews v. Denver Newspaper Agency, 649 F.3d 1199, 1204–05, 112 FEP 432, 24 AD 1156 (10th Cir. 2011) (employee who was unsuccessful in arbitration of his discrimination claims under collective bargaining agreement did not waive right to litigate his statutory discrimination claims where agreement authorized arbitrator "only to resolve the dispute submitted," amended grievance asserted violation of agreement but no statutory claims, and agreement did not require such claims to be arbitrated).

CHAPTER 38

"REVERSE" DISCRIMINATION AND AFFIRMATIVE ACTION

I. INTRODUCTION

[10]**[On page 38-4 of the Main Volume, in footnote 10, add the following at the end of the footnote.]**

In the aftermath of *Ricci*, the lower courts have been required to deal with the disparate impact claim that the City of New Haven feared would be asserted. *See* Briscoe v. City of New Haven, 654 F.3d 200, 112 FEP 1793 (2d Cir. 2011), *cert. denied*, 132 S. Ct. 2741 (2012). The Second Circuit reversed the district court's dismissal of the lawsuit, concluding that the plaintiff's disparate impact lawsuit, "alleging that the weighting of the written and oral sections of the test—60% and 40%, respectively, as dictated by the collective bargaining agreement between the city and the firefighter's union—was arbitrary and unrelated to job requirements," was not foreclosed by the Supreme Court's decision in *Ricci*. 654 F.3d at 205. The appellate court acknowledged the Supreme Court's statement that if the City subsequently faces a disparate impact suit, "then in light of our holding today it should be clear that the City would avoid disparate-impact liability based on the strong basis in evidence that, had it not certified the results, it would have been subject to disparate-treatment liability." *Id.* at 205 (quoting *Ricci*, 129 S. Ct. at 2681). The Second Circuit further noted that the City had not taken the steps necessary to make the plaintiff, and others like him, a party to the prior litigation, and therefore *Ricci* did not have preclusive effect over his claim. 654 F.3d at 209. "To rule for the City, we would have to conclude that the Supreme Court intended to effect a substantial change in Title VII disparate-impact litigation in a single sentence of dicta." *Id.*; *see also* National Ass'n for the Advancement of Colored People v. North Hudson Reg'l Fire & Rescue, 665 F.3d 464, 484–85, 11 FEP 1633 (3d Cir. 2011) (refusing to extend *Ricci*'s "strong basis in evidence" defense to City in disparate impact suit challenging residency requirement for firefighters that had racially discriminatory impact).

II. "Reverse" Discrimination Outside the Context of Affirmative Action Programs

A. Prohibited Bases for Discrimination

[14][On page 38-5 of the Main Volume, in footnote 14, add the following after "*See, e.g.*,".]

Meditz v. City of Newark, 658 F.3d 364, 372–73, 113 FEP 727 (3d Cir. 2011) (reversing grant of summary judgment to city on job applicant's claim that city's residency requirement for non-uniformed employees had disparate impact on white, non-Hispanics, where, among other things, county seat was located in Newark and did not impose the same residency rule, and representation of white, non-Hispanics among city employees was substantially lower than their representation among county's public employees); Vivenzio v. City of Syracuse, 611 F.3d 91, 105–06, 109 FEP 1181 (2d Cir. 2010) (reversing grant of summary judgment to City in reverse discrimination action brought by white applicants for firefighter positions; absence of evidence in record as to racial composition of City's hiring pool at time of challenged decisions created genuine issues of material fact as to whether City's reliance upon 1980 consent decree requiring City to hire black applicants from separate hiring list constituted non-discriminatory reason for failing to hire white applicants in 2004 and 2005);

[15]**[On page 38-5 of the Main Volume, in footnote 15, add the following after "*See, e.g.*,".]**

Hanners v. Trent, 674 F.3d 683, 692–94, 114 FEP 965 (7th Cir. 2012) (same analytical model that applies to other discrimination cases is used in white police officer's claim of discrimination in disciplining him for rules violation); Good v. University of Chi. Med. Ctr., 673 F.3d 670, 677–79, 114 FEP 903 (7th Cir. 2012) (affirming summary judgment for employer even though Caucasian plaintiff identified three minority employees with similar performance problems who were permitted to accept demotions in lieu of termination; demotions were insufficient circumstantial evidence to infer race-based animus against Caucasian employees where record contained no other evidence that employer had history of discrimination against Caucasians); Sanders v. Lee Cnty. Sch. Dist. No. 1, 669 F.3d 888, 893–94, 114 FEP 705 (8th Cir. 2012) (Caucasian finance coordinator was constructively discharged when school board reassigned her to position of food-service assistant, where new assignment was demotion and reasonable employee would have found reassignment to be demeaning, where both Caucasian employees in district's administration were removed within months after African-Americans became majority on school board, and where board did not respond to efforts to repeated requests for job description); Romans v. Michigan Dep't of Human Servs., 668 F.3d 826, 836-88, 114 FEP 1404 (6th Cir. 2012) (evidence of employer's affirmative action policy in hiring and that employee who investigated complaints about Caucasian plaintiff displayed racial animus against Caucasians generally was insufficient to show that his termination for using foul language and racial slurs was result of reverse discrimination); Vaughn v. Woodforest Bank, 665 F.3d 632, 638–39, 114 FEP 118 (5th Cir. 2011) (although Caucasian employee terminated for making racial remarks failed to establish pretext through her evidence that she was allegedly treated more harshly than three African-American employees, summary judgment reversed based upon other evidence suggesting that employer's stated reason may have been untrue); Radentz v. Marion Cnty., 640 F.3d 754, 111 FEP 1676 (7th Cir. 2011) (applying Title VII proof standards in § 1983 case and holding that Caucasian forensic pathologists established that county discriminated when it terminated company's contract in order to replace Caucasian employees with African-American employees, despite contention that contract was too costly, where contract gave county authority to modify scope of contract and county did not show why that option was not exercised); Smith v. Lockheed-Martin Corp., 644 F.3d 1321, 1329, 112 FEP 1119 (11th Cir. 2011) (district court erred in dismissing race discrimination claim of Caucasian employee terminated after sending racially offensive e-mail where evidence showed that African-American employees who did so received lesser discipline); Schandelmeier-Bartels v. Chicago Park Dist., 634 F.3d 372, 375, 11 FEP 739 (7th Cir. 2011) (reversing district court's entry of judgment for defendant as matter of law after jury verdict for Caucasian plaintiff who showed that her termination was caused by disagreements with African-American supervisor over issue of corporal punishment of children, where supervisor indicated that such disagreements were cultural in nature; although supervisor was not ultimate decision maker, evidence showed that supervisor had decisive input into termination decision); Jackson v. Watkins, 619 F.3d 463, 466, 110 FEP 257 (5th Cir. 2010) (affirming summary judgment in race discrimination discharge claim where plaintiff lacked evidence to rebut employer's contention that decision maker had had negative interactions with plaintiff); Marion Cnty. Coroner's Office v. EEOC, 612 F.3d 924, 925, 109 FEP 1510 (7th Cir. 2010) (upholding Equal Employment Opportunity Commission (EEOC) ruling in favor of discharged Caucasian employee whose termination resulted from disagreements with African-American supervisor over variety of race-related issues, including employer's racial hiring preferences);

[16]**[On page 38-6 of the Main Volume, in footnote 16, add the following after "*See, e.g.,*".]**

Finch v. Peterson, 622 F.3d 725, 728, 110 FEP 260 (7th Cir. 2010) (city officials not entitled to qualified immunity from suit by three Caucasian police lieutenants who were denied promotions to captain despite ranking higher on eligibility list than three African-American lieutenants who were promoted; earlier consent decree that had "long-term goal . . . of promoting blacks," was not controlling where decree explicitly prohibited use of race as criterion for promotion); Stockwell v. City of Harvey, 597 F.3d 895, 108 FEP 1153 (7th Cir. 2010) (applying *McDonnell Douglas Corp. v. Green*, 411 U.S. 792, 5 FEP 965 (1973), analysis to reverse discrimination claim, four Caucasian firefighters who signed up to be interviewed for promotion but were rejected failed to show that City's explanation that applicants were rejected because of their "negative" attitudes was pretextual);

[On page 38-6 of the Main Volume, add a comma between "demotion" and footnote 17.]

[On page 38-6 of the Main Volume, after the bullet item that ends with footnote 17, add the following.]

- discipline,[1]
- layoff,[2]

[20]**[On page 38-7 of the Main Volume, in footnote 20, add the following after "*See, e.g.*,".]**

Yancick v. Hanna Steel Corp., 653 F.3d 532, 545, 112 FEP 1537 (7th Cir. 2011) (Caucasian employee failed to present evidence that harassment was sufficiently severe or pervasive where employee lacked evidence that African-American co-worker intentionally dropped steel coil onto him due to his race and where racial remarks allegedly made by African-American co-worker were made outside of his presence);

[22]**[On page 38-8 of the Main Volume, in footnote 22, add the following after "*But see*".]**

Hernandez v. Yellow Transp., Inc., 670 F.3d 644, 654–55, 114 FEP 545 (5th Cir.) (summary judgment upheld where Caucasian employee failed to establish that he was harassed for reasons related to

---

[1]*See, e.g.*, Hanners v. Trent, 674 F.3d 683, 692, 114 FEP 965 (7th Cir. 2012) (Caucasian police sergeant disciplined for sending racially and sexually offensive e-mails failed to present evidence of similarly situated non-Caucasian employees who had received lesser discipline for similar conduct).

[2]Everett v. Cook Cnty., 655 F.3d 723, 729, 113 FEP 9 (7th Cir. 2011) ("Title VII of the Civil Rights Act prohibits an employer from firing an employee based on race, a prohibition that includes so-called 'reverse discrimination' against white employees"; however, Caucasian dentist who was selected for layoff while minority dentist was retained failed to show that employer's articulated explanation—that minority dentist was better qualified—was pretext for discrimination); Taxman v. Board of Educ., 91 F.3d 1547, 1563, 71 FEP 848 (3d Cir. 1996) (employer's affirmative action plan and interest in maintaining diverse faculty insufficient to support its consideration of race when deciding which of two teachers to lay off).

his association with minority employees), *cert. denied*, 2012 U.S. LEXIS 7538 (Oct. 1, 2012);

[28]**[On page 38-10 of the Main Volume, in footnote 28, add the following after the citation to "*Parker*".]**

("Whites are also a protected group under Title VII, but it defies common sense to suggest that the promotion of a black employee justifies an inference of prejudice against white co-workers in our present society. . . . This court has allowed majority plaintiffs to rely on the *McDonnell Douglas* criteria to prove a prima facie case of intentionally disparate treatment when background circumstances support the suspicion that the defendant is that unusual employer who discriminates against the majority. . . .")

[29]**[On page 38-10 of the Main Volume, in footnote 29, add the following after "*Background evidence found*:".]**

Romans v. Michigan Dep't of Human Servs., 668 F.3d 826, 837–38, 114 FEP 1404 (6th Cir. 2012) (plaintiff established background circumstances based upon his evidence that employer had considered race in previous hiring decisions, but failed to establish element of prima facie case that he was treated differently than similarly situated minority employees);

[29]**[On page 38-11 of the Main Volume, in the carryover of footnote 29, add the following after "*No background evidence found*:", before "Briggs v. Potter".]**

Everett v. Cook Cnty., 655 F.3d 723, 730, 113 FEP 9 (7th Cir. 2011) (Caucasian dentist's evidence of positive productivity reports reflecting good performance was not sufficient to establish background evidence of discriminatory conduct that would support inference of reverse discrimination);

[33]**[On page 38-11 of the Main Volume, in footnote 33, add the following after "*See*".]**

Smith v. Lockheed-Martin Corp., 644 F.3d 1321, 1325 n.15, 112 FEP 1119 (11th Cir. 2011) (background circumstances are not necessarily required in race discrimination action brought by Caucasian employee);

III. REVERSE" DISCRIMINATION PURSUANT TO AFFIRMATIVE ACTION PROGRAMS

B. Affirmative Action Under the Equal Protection Clause

[On page 38-13 of the Main Volume, in the last sentence of the carryover paragraph, add new footnote 40a after "strict scrutiny".]

[40a]In *Kimel v. Florida*, 528 U.S. 62, 84, 81 FEP 970 (2000), the Court reiterated that a strict scrutiny standard was to be applied to race-based preferences, whereas gender-based preferences must be "substantially related" to achievement of "important governmental objectives," while age-based preferences are subject to only "rational basis" review and "will be overturned only if the varying treatment of different groups or persons is so unrelated to the achievement of any combination of legitimate purposes that we can only conclude that the [government's] actions were irrational."

[On page 38-13 of the Main Volume, in the last sentence of the carryover paragraph, add the following after "a pair of 2003 decisions,".]

and the 2013 decision in *Fisher v. University of Texas at Austin*,[3]

[On page 38-13 of the Main Volume, in the last sentence of the carryover paragraph, replace "25 years earlier in *Bakke*" with the following.]

in the 1978 decision in *Bakke*.

1. Voluntary State and Local Government Plans

a. Race-Based Plans

[On page 38-21 of the Main Volume, after the carryover paragraph, add the following new paragraphs.]

The Supreme Court revisited the issue of race-conscious admissions policies in *Fisher v. University of Texas at Austin*.[4] In 2004, after determining that it lacked a "critical mass" of minority students, the University adopted a race-conscious admissions plan under which a minority applicant's race added points to his or her

[3]133 S. Ct. 2411, 118 FEP 1459 (2013).
[4]133 S. Ct. 2411, 118 FEP 1459 (2013).

"Personal Achievement Index" score. The result was that more minority students achieved an overall score that placed them "above a certain score" on a grid, which would not have occurred if race was not used as a factor in the scoring.[5]

The *Fisher* Court ruled that the Fifth Circuit had erred in considering whether the University acted in good faith in its belief that its plan was preferable to workable race-neutral alternatives. Noting that a defendant's good faith is not a factor to be considered, the Court reiterated its holdings in *Grutter* and *Gratz* that any race-conscious school admissions plan must withstand the strict scrutiny standard.[6] The Court then focused on the distinction between whether a defendant has established a compelling state interest to justify its race-conscious plan and whether the plan is narrowly tailored to achieve its stated purpose. With respect to demonstrating a compelling state interest, the Court held that lower courts should grant some deference to a university's determination that a racially diverse student body carries sufficiently significant educational value to meet that standard. With respect to whether a particular plan is narrowly tailored to achieve that objective, however, the Court stated that universities are entitled to no such deference; the focus by courts should be on "serious, good faith consideration of workable race-neutral alternatives."[7] Thus, the Court remanded the case to allow the lower court to determine whether the University had offered sufficient evidence to prove that its admission program was sufficiently narrowly tailored to achieve its objective.[8]

A year later, in *Schuette v. Coalition to Defend Affirmative Action, Integration, Immigration Rights and Fight for Equality by Any Means Necessary*,[9] the Supreme Court reviewed its history of decisions related to the legality of affirmative action in admissions policies and held that—those decisions notwithstanding—no authority within the U.S. Constitution allowed the judiciary to set aside an amendment to the Michigan Constitution that prohibited affirmative action in university admissions policies.

---

[5] *Id.* at 2416.
[6] *Id.* at 2419–20.
[7] *Id.* at 2420.
[8] *Id.*
[9] 134 S. Ct. 1623, 1637–38 (2014).

[137]**[On page 38-32 of the Main Volume, in footnote 137, add the following at the end of the footnote.]**

See Cleveland Firefighters for Fair Hiring Practices v. City of Cleveland, 669 F.3d 737, 741, 743, 114 FEP 398 (6th Cir. 2012) (court erred in terminating 31-year-old consent decree without making "careful" and "specific" finding as to whether "the classifications continue to remedy the Fire Department's past discrimination in firefighter hiring"; applying strict scrutiny analysis—"the Supreme Court has laid down 'particular standards as to when and to what extent race may be used by government as a factor to disadvantage some Americans at the expense of others.' Those standards must be met here if the decree's racial classifications are to apply longer than they already have.") (citations omitted).

C. Voluntary Affirmative Action Plans Under Title VII

2. *Requirements for a Valid Plan*

a. *The Supreme Court's Evolving View–From* Weber *to* Johnson

[On page 38-43 of the Main Volume, at the end of the carryover paragraph, add the following.]

The Supreme Court addressed the nature of the factual predicate necessary to support a voluntary affirmative action plan eight years later in *Johnson v. Transportation Agency*,[10] which is discussed in greater detail in Section III.C.2.b.

b. *The Necessary Factual Predicate*

[On page 38-48 of the Main Volume, after the first sentence in the second paragraph, add the following.]

As a threshold matter, however, the Second Circuit, in *United States v. Brennan*,[11] has cautioned that before automatically applying the

---

[10]480 U.S. 616, 631, 43 FEP 411 (1987) (making clear that in cases that lack constitutional dimension, employers need neither admit nor demonstrate prior discrimination in order to support voluntary affirmative action plan, but instead may justify plan by pointing to manifest imbalance between representation of protected group in employer's workforce and group's representation in relevant portion of area's labor market).

[11]650 F.3d 65, 112 FEP 193 (2d Cir. 2011).

Johnson/Weber analysis, a court must determine whether the plan under consideration is truly an affirmative action plan at all. The Second Circuit determined in *Brennan* that unless the employer's plan is a race- or gender-conscious plan designed to benefit all members of a protected category "in a forward-looking manner," rather than an effort to provide individualized race- or gender-conscious "make-whole" benefits to particular employees, the "'affirmative action' defense of *Johnson* and *Weber*" does not apply; thus, there is no need to determine whether a manifest imbalance exists within the workforce or whether the plan unnecessarily trammels upon the rights of the majority group.[12] In *Brennan*, the court deemed the employer's plan to not be a true affirmative action plan at all because it merely provided benefits to employees whom the employer believed to be victims of a previous selection process that had a disparate impact upon the protected group to which the benefitted employees belonged.[13] The court concluded that an employer defending such individualized race- or gender-conscious employment decisions in this context must meet the *Ricci v. DeStefano* standard,[14] rather than the *Johnson* or *Weber* tests, of demonstrating a strong basis in evidence to believe that its prior practices created the disparate impact that it seeks to remedy.[15]

[On page 38-48 of the Main Volume, in the second sentence of the second paragraph, create a new paragraph that begins with "In *Higgins v. City of Vallejo*,".]

---

[12]*Id.* at 104 ("We therefore hold that § 703(a), like § 706(g) draws a distinction between *affirmative action* plans, which are intended to provide *ex ante* benefits to all members of a racial or gender class, and *make-whole relief*, which is intended to provide *ex post* benefits to specified individuals who have suffered discrimination. And where this latter form of benefits is at issue, the employer may not invoke the 'affirmative action' defense of *Johnson* and *Weber*.") (emphasis in original).

[13]*Id.* at 109.

[14] 557 U.S. 557 (2009). *See* the Main Volume, Section I.

[15]*Brennan*, 650 F.3d at 110; *see also Ricci*, 557 U.S. at 586 (before employer can engage in disparate treatment against one group in order to avoid or remedy disparate impact against another group, employer must have strong basis in evidence to believe that it will be subject to disparate impact liability if it fails to engage in such race-conscious decision making).

c. Permissible Scope of a Voluntary Plan

(ii.) Attaining, not maintaining, balanced workforces

[On page 38-58 of the Main Volume, in the first sentence of the first full paragraph, delete "most recent".]

CHAPTER 39

FEDERAL CONTRACTOR AFFIRMATIVE ACTION COMPLIANCE

[On page 39-7 of the Main Volume, replace the "Authors' Note" with the following.]

[**Authors' Note**: On August 23, 2013, the Office of Federal Contract Compliance Programs (OFCCP) issued a new Federal Contract Compliance Manual (FCCM), which is available at http://www.dol.gov/ofccp/regs/compliance/fccm/fccmanul.htm (last visited Mar. 11, 2014). The revised manual will be integrated fully into the next Supplement. Readers should consult the new manual when preparing affirmative action plans or interacting with the OFCCP in the course of a compliance review. In this Supplement, the new manual is referred to as "2013 FCCM."

Because Federal Contractor Affirmative Action Compliance is an area in which key issues seldom reach the appellate, or even the district court, level, this summary extends to all substantive cases decided by the Department of Labor's Administrative Review Board (ARB), which issues final agency decisions in OFCCP matters.]

I. INTRODUCTION

[**Editors' Note:** Executive Order 11246 does not cover claims of discrimination on the basis of sexual orientation or gender identity. On June 16, 2014, the White House announced President Obama's intention to sign an executive order prohibiting discrimination by federal contractors on the basis of sexual orientation or gender identity. The statement indicated that the order "would build upon existing protections, which generally prohibit federal contractors and subcontractors from discriminating in employment decisions on the basis of race, color, religion, sex, or national origin." *White House to Issue Executive Order Banning LGBT Bias by Federal Contractors*, 115 DAILY LAB. REP. A-1 (June 16, 2014)]

[7]**[On page 39-8 of the Main Volume, in footnote 7, delete the citations to 41 C.F.R. pt. 60-250 (Part 60-250 was rescinded by OFCCP's 2013 regulations).]**

[On page 39-8, replace the last sentence of the carryover paragraph with the following.]

According to OFCCP, as of fiscal year 2011, these requirements cover an estimated 200,000 businesses and approximately $700 billion in federal contracts, pursuant to which nearly one in four American workers are employed.[1]

[9]**[On page 39-8 of the Main Volume, in footnote 9, delete the citations to 41 C.F.R. pt. 60-250 (Part 60-250 was rescinded by OFCCP's 2013 regulations).]**

[11]**[On page 39-8 of the Main Volume, in footnote 11, delete the reference to 41 C.F.R. pt. 60-250 (Part 60-250 was rescinded by OFCCP's 2013 regulations).]**

[13]**[On page 39-9 of the Main Volume, in footnote 13, delete the citations to 41 C.F.R. pt. 60-250 (Part 60-250 was rescinded by OFCCP's 2013 regulations).]**

[14]**[On page 39-9 of the Main Volume, replace footnote 14 with the following.]**

[14]The 2013 FCCM does not have the same force and effect as regulations that have been issued pursuant to the requirements of the Administrative Procedure Act (APA).

---

[1]2013 FCCM, A-00 (Introduction).

II. COVERAGE AND EXEMPTIONS

A. Contracts and Covered Subcontracts

1. Prime Contracts

[17] [On page 39-10 of the Main Volume, in footnote 17, delete the reference to 41 C.F.R. pt. 60-250 (Part 60-250 was rescinded by OFCCP's 2013 regulations).]

[18][On page 39-10 of the Main Volume, in footnote 18, delete the reference to 41 C.F.R. pt. 60-250 (Part 60-250 was rescinded by OFCCP's 2013 regulations).]

[19][On page 39-10 of the Main Volume, in footnote 19, delete the reference to 41 C.F.R. pt. 60-250 (Part 60-250 was rescinded by OFCCP's 2013 regulations).]

[21][On page 39-11 of the Main Volume, in footnote 21, delete the reference to 41 C.F.R. pt. 60-250 (Part 60-250 was rescinded by OFCCP's 2013 regulations).]

[22][On page 39-11 of the Main Volume, in footnote 22, delete the reference to 41 C.F.R. pt. 60-250 (Part 60-250 was rescinded by OFCCP's 2013 regulations).]

[On page 39-11 of the Main Volume, after the carryover sentence that ends with footnote 22, add the following new paragraph.]

In determining whether a particular contract is one for personal services which are not covered by the OFCCP programs or for non-personal services which are, the ARB has looked to the Federal Acquisition Regulations (FAR).[2] In *Office of Federal Contract Compliance Programs v. O'Melveny & Meyers LLP*,[3] the ARB considered whether an agreement pursuant to which the law firm provided nearly a decade of legal advice to the Department of Energy relating to its divestiture of the Elk Hills Naval Petroleum Reserve was one for personal or non-personal services. The Board found that the FAR identified six factors that it described as determinative of the

[2]The FAR are the regulations that describe all aspects of government procurement and are set out in 48 C.F.R. pts. 1-9005 (2011.) The definitional section referenced by the ARB appears at 48 C.F.R. § 37.104(d)(6) (2011).

[3]Case No. 2011-OFC-00007, 2011 WL 5668757, at *6 (U.S. Dep't of Labor, Aug. 31, 2011).

issue. It vacated a Recommended Decision of an administrative law judge (ALJ), holding that the contract was covered, and remanded the matter for further consideration of two of the six factors: whether agency personnel were or could be performing the same services, and the nature and degree of agency supervision of the firm's personnel. The more that a firm's personnel resemble those of an employee of the agency, the greater the likelihood that the contract will be viewed as one for personal services and will not be covered by OFFCP programs.[4]

[24][On page 39-11 of the Main Volume, in footnote 24, delete the reference to 41 C.F.R. pt. 60-250 (Part 60-250 was rescinded by OFCCP's 2013 regulations).]

[26][On page 39-12 of the Main Volume, in footnote 26, delete the reference to 41 C.F.R. pt. 60-250 (Part 60-250 was rescinded by OFCCP's 2013 regulations).]

2. *Subcontracts*

[On pages 39-14 to 39-15 of the Main Volume, replace the carryover paragraph with the following.]

Subsequent to the *UPMC* ruling, the OFCCP issued compliance review letters to several hospitals, asserting that the hospitals were federal contractors because of agreements under which they provided services to beneficiaries of TRICARE.[5] One of these hospitals challenged OFCCP's jurisdiction, asserting that the provision of TRICARE services did not make it a federal subcontractor. In *OFCCP v. Florida Hospital of Orlando*,[6] an ALJ granted summary judgment against the hospital, concluding that it had subcontracted to perform a portion of the prime contractor's obligations by providing certain medical services to TRICARE beneficiaries.[7] TRICARE had contracted with Humana Military Healthcare Services, Inc. (HMHS) to provide its beneficiaries with a "network or networks of

[4]*Id.* at *11–12.

[5]TRICARE is the Department of Defense health care program for active and retired members of the military and their families.

[6]Case No. 2009-OFC-00002, Recommended Decision of the ALJ, at *1 (Oct. 18, 2010).

[7]*Id.* at *2.

individual and institutional health care providers" to be established through "contractual arrangements." HMHS in turn contracted with Florida Hospital of Orlando and other institutions to provide services to those eligible to receive TRICARE benefits. The ALJ reasoned that Florida Hospital of Orlando had contractually agreed to assume a portion of HMHS's obligations under its prime contract with TRICARE.[8] The ALJ's recommendation, however, was rejected by the ARB in its final decision.[9]

The ARB decision did not turn on the nature of a federal subcontract generally, but held instead that OFCCP was prohibited from reviewing the hospital by § 715 of the National Defense Authorization Act (NDAA), a law that was enacted while the recommended decision was pending on appeal. That section provides that:

> For the purpose of determining whether network providers under [TRICARE] provider network agreements are subcontractors for purposes of the Federal Acquisition Regulations or any other law, a TRICARE managed care support contract that includes the requirement to establish, manage, or maintain a network of providers may not be considered to be a contract for the performance of health care services or supplies on the basis of such requirement.[10]

The Board concluded that application of § 715 to the Florida Hospital of Orlando was proper even though it was enacted after the compliance review in this case and was not retroactive, because the question of OFCCP's jurisdiction was still undecided at the time the law became effective. It noted that OFCCP itself had withdrawn a 2010 policy directive concerning its authority to review health care providers and insurers shortly after the NDAA was enacted.[11]

---

[8] *Id.* at *4.

[9] OFCCP v. Florida Hosp. of Orlando, ARB 11-011 (Oct. 19, 2012) (en banc).

[10] 10 U.S.C. § 1097b.

[11] On May 7, 2014, OFCCP issued a directive concerning "TRICARE subcontractor enforcement activities" in which it declared that as a matter of prosecutorial discretion it was imposing a five-year enforcement moratorium on entities whose only federal contracts were as subcontractors to TRICARE and would administratively close any such compliance reviews that were open as of the date of issue. OFCCP Directive 2014-01, *available at* http://www.dol.gov/ofccp/regs/compliance/directives/Dir2014_01_508c.pdf.

3. *Extension of Coverage to Related Entities*

[42][On page 39-15 of the Main Volume, in footnote 42, add the following after "*See*".]

OFCCP v. Manheim Auctions, Inc., Case No. 2011-OFC-00005 (Recommended Decision, June 14, 2011) (where one business controlled at least 1/3 of board of directors and at least 3/5 of officer positions, managed funding, and set personnel practices of second business, two could be treated as single entity for purpose of determining whether second business (which held government contracts) had 50 or more employees and was therefore covered by OFCCP programs);

B. Coverage Thresholds

1. *Basic Threshold*

[On page 39-18 of the Main Volume, at the end of the first sentence of the first paragraph, add new footnote 48a.]

[48a]Federally assisted construction contractors are covered by only the Executive Order, not by § 503 or the Jobs for Veterans Act.

[58][On page 39-19 of the Main Volume, in footnote 58, delete the reference to 41 C.F.R. pt. 60-250 (Part 60-250 was rescinded by OFCCP's 2013 regulations).]

[59][On page 39-19 of the Main Volume, in footnote 59, delete the reference to 41 C.F.R. pt. 60-250 (Part 60-250 was rescinded by OFCCP's 2013 regulations).]

[60][On page 39-19 of the Main Volume, in footnote 60, delete the reference to 41 C.F.R. pt. 60-250 (Part 60-250 was rescinded by OFCCP's 2013 regulations).]

[61][On page 39-19 of the Main Volume, in footnote 61, delete the reference to 41 C.F.R. pt. 60-250 (Part 60-250 was rescinded by OFCCP's 2013 regulations).]

[62][On page 39-20 of the Main Volume, in footnote 62, delete the reference to 41 C.F.R. pt. 60-250 (Part 60-250 was rescinded by OFCCP's 2013 regulations).]

[64]**[On page 39-20 of the Main Volume, in footnote 64, delete the reference to 41 C.F.R. pt. 60-250 (Part 60-250 was rescinded by OFCCP's 2013 regulations).]**

[77]**[On page 39-22 of the Main Volume, in footnote 77, delete the reference to 41 C.F.R. pt. 60-250 (Part 60-250 was rescinded by OFCCP's 2013 regulations).]**

[78]**[On page 39-22 of the Main Volume, in footnote 78, delete the reference to 41 C.F.R. pt. 60-250 (Part 60-250 was rescinded by OFCCP's 2013 regulations).]**

III. EXECUTIVE ORDER 11246

A. Mandates of the Order

[82]**[On page 39-23 of the Main Volume, in footnote 82, delete the reference to 41 C.F.R. pt. 60-250 (Part 60-250 was rescinded by OFCCP's 2013 regulations).]**

B. Components of the Executive Order 11246 Affirmative Action Program for Supply and Service Contractors

2. *Narrative Sections*

a. Background Issues

(iii) Maintaining the confidentiality of AAPs

[104]**[On page 39-29 of the Main Volume, in footnote 104, delete the reference to 41 C.F.R. pt. 60-250 (Part 60-250 was rescinded by OFCCP's 2013 regulations).]**

C. Construction Contractors

[220]**[On page 39-54 of the Main Volume, in footnote 220, add the following at the end of the footnote.]**

As noted earlier, federally assisted construction contractors are subject to the requirements of Executive Order 11246, but not those of § 503 or the Jobs for Veterans Act.

IV. SECTION 503 OF THE REHABILITATION ACT OF 1973

[On page 39-56 of the Main Volume, after the sentence that ends with footnote 239, add the following new paragraph.]

OFCCP regulations state that compliance with the requirements of § 503 and its implementing regulations does not necessarily determine compliance with other statutes.[12] However, where a contractor is subject to the provisions of both § 503 and § 504 of the Rehabilitation Act, compliance with the requirements of § 503 will satisfy its obligations under § 504.

V. THE VETERANS ACT

[249][On page 39-59 of the Main Volume, replace footnote 249 with the following.]

[249]On September 24, 2013, OFCCP revised its regulations pertaining to the Veterans Act. These regulations became effective on March 24, 2014, and will be discussed in detail in the next Supplement. Contractors that have affirmative action plans on the effective date will have additional time to comply with the new regulations. Although major changes in the regulations are included here, readers should consult the regulations themselves at 78 Fed. Reg. 58,613.

VI. AFFIRMATIVE ACTION PROGRAMS FOR VETERANS AND INDIVIDUALS WITH DISABILITIES

[On page 39-60 of the Main Volume, delete the callout to footnote 255 at the end of the heading.]

---

[12]41 C.F.R. § 60-741.1(c) (2013). On September 24, 2013, OFCCP revised its regulations pertaining to § 503. These regulations became effective on March 24, 2014, and will be discussed in detail in the next Supplement. Contractors that have affirmative action plans in place on the effective date will have additional time to comply with the new regulations. Although major changes in the regulations are included here, the editors caution that readers should consult the regulations themselves at 78 Fed. Reg. 58,861.

[255]**[On page 39-60 of the Main Volume, replace footnote 255 with the following.]**

[255][Reserved].

[256]**[On page 39-60 of the Main Volume, in footnote 256, delete the citations to 41 C.F.R. pt. 60-250 (Part 60-250 was rescinded by OFCCP's 2013 regulations).]**

[257]**[On page 39-61 of the Main Volume, in footnote 257, delete the citation to 41 C.F.R. pt. 60-250 (Part 60-250 was rescinded by OFCCP's 2013 regulations).]**

[260]**[On page 39-61 of the Main Volume, in footnote 260, delete the citations to 41 C.F.R. pt. 60-250 (Part 60-250 was rescinded by OFCCP's 2013 regulations).]**

[262]**[On page 39-61 of the Main Volume, in footnote 262, delete the citations to 41 C.F.R. pt. 60-250 (Part 60-250 was rescinded by OFCCP's 2013 regulations).]**

[On pages 39-61 to 39-62 of the Main Volume, replace the carryover paragraph with the following.]

The 2013 regulations require that contractors invite applicants to self-identify as protected veterans at both the pre- and post-offer phases of the application process.[13] The new regulations include sample invitations to self-identify that contractors may use.[14] Similarly, contractors must invite applicants to self-identify as individuals with disabilities at both the pre- and post-offer phases of the application process, using language prescribed by OFCCP.[15] The new regulations also require that every five years, contractors invite their employees to self-identify as individuals with disabilities, using the language prescribed in a Self-Identification Form appended to the regulations.

[263]**[On page 39-61 of the Main Volume, in footnote 263, delete the citations to 41 C.F.R. pt. 60-250 (Part 60-250 was rescinded by OFCCP's 2013 regulations).]**

---

[13]41 C.F.R. § 60-300.42(b). . The information that must be contained in the application is prescribed at 41 C.F.R. § 60-300.42(c).

[14]*Id.* at Appendix B.

[15]41 C.F.R. § 60-741.42, 78 Fed. Reg. at 58,743.

[264]**[On page 39-61 of the Main Volume, in footnote 264, delete the citations to 41 C.F.R. pt. 60-250 (Part 60-250 was rescinded by OFCCP's 2013 regulations).]**

[266]**[On page 39-62 of the Main Volume, in footnote 266, delete the citations to 41 C.F.R. pt. 60-250 (Part 60-250 was rescinded by OFCCP's 2013 regulations).]**

[267] **[On page 39-62 of the Main Volume, in footnote 267, delete the citations to 41 C.F.R. pt. 60-250 (Part 60-250 was rescinded by OFCCP's 2013 regulations).]**

[268]**[On page 39-62 of the Main Volume, in footnote 268, delete the citations to 41 C.F.R. pt. 60-250 (Part 60-250 was rescinded by OFCCP's 2013 regulations).]**

[269]**[On page 39-62 of the Main Volume, in footnote 269, delete the citations to 41 C.F.R. pt. 60-250 (Part 60-250 was rescinded by OFCCP's 2013 regulations).]**

[270]**[On page 39-62 of the Main Volume, in footnote 270, delete the citations to 41 C.F.R. pt. 60-250 (Part 60-250 was rescinded by OFCCP's 2013 regulations).]**

[271]**[On page 39-62 of the Main Volume, in footnote 271, delete the citations to 41 C.F.R. pt. 60-250 (Part 60-250 was rescinded by OFCCP's 2013 regulations).]**

[272]**[On page 39-62 of the Main Volume, in footnote 272, delete the citations to 41 C.F.R. pt. 60-250 (Part 60-250 was rescinded by OFCCP's 2013 regulations).]**

[273]**[On page 39-62 of the Main Volume, in footnote 273, delete the citations to 41 C.F.R. pt. 60-250 (Part 60-250 was rescinded by OFCCP's 2013 regulations).]**

[274]**[On page 39-62 of the Main Volume, in footnote 274, delete the citations to 41 C.F.R. pt. 60-250 (Part 60-250 was rescinded by OFCCP's 2013 regulations).]**

[275]**[On page 39-62 of the Main Volume, in footnote 275, delete the citations to 41 C.F.R. pt. 60-250 (Part 60-250 was rescinded by OFCCP's 2013 regulations).]**

[276]**[On page 39-62 of the Main Volume, in footnote 276, delete the citations to 41 C.F.R. pt. 60-250 (Part 60-250 was rescinded by OFCCP's 2013 regulations).]**

[On page 39-62 of the Main Volume, in the carryover paragraph at the bottom of the page, replace the first sentence, ending with footnote 277, with the following.]

Both the AAP for veterans and that for individuals with disabilities must contain some statistical analysis, albeit far less than what is required under the Executive Order. Contractors must establish annual hiring benchmarks for protected veterans, and they must use one of two methods to establish their benchmarks. Contractors may choose to establish a benchmark equal to the national percentage of veterans in the civilian labor force, which is published in the Benchmark Database and will be updated annually by OFCCP. Alternatively, contractors may establish their own benchmarks using certain data from the Bureau of Labor Statistics (BLS) and the Veterans' Employment and Training Service/Employment and Training Administration (VETS/ETA) that is also published by OFCCP, as well other factors that reflect a contractor's unique hiring circumstances.[16] The new regulations establish a nationwide 7 percent utilization goal for qualified individuals with disabilities (IWDs). Contractors apply the goal to each of their job groups, or to the entire workforce if a contractor has 100 or fewer employees. Contractors must conduct an annual utilization analysis and assessment of problem areas, and establish specific action-oriented programs to address any identified problems.[17]

[278]**[On page 39-63 of the Main Volume, in footnote 278, delete the citations to 41 C.F.R. pt. 60-250 (Part 60-250 was rescinded by OFCCP's 2013 regulations).]**

[279]**[On page 39-63 of the Main Volume, in footnote 279, delete the citations to 41 C.F.R. pt. 60-250 (Part 60-250 was rescinded by OFCCP's 2013 regulations).]**

---

[16]41 C.F.R. § 60-300.45 (2014).
[17]41 C.F.R. § 60-741.45(2014).

[280]**[On pages 39-63 to 39-64 of the Main Volume, in footnote 280, delete the citations to 41 C.F.R. pt. 60-250 (Part 60-250 was rescinded by OFCCP's 2013 regulations).]**

[281]**[On page 39-64 of the Main Volume, in footnote 281, delete the citations to 41 C.F.R. pt. 60-250 (Part 60-250 was rescinded by OFCCP's 2013 regulations).]**

[282]**[On page 39-64 of the Main Volume, in footnote 282, delete the citations to 41 C.F.R. pt. 60-250 (Part 60-250 was rescinded by OFCCP's 2013 regulations).]**

[283]**[On page 39-64 of the Main Volume, in footnote 283, delete the citations to 41 C.F.R. pt. 60-250 (Part 60-250 was rescinded by OFCCP's 2013 regulations).]**

[284]**[On page 39-65 of the Main Volume, in footnote 284, delete the citations to 41 C.F.R. pt. 60-250 (Part 60-250 was rescinded by OFCCP's 2013 regulations).]**

[285]**[On page 39-65 of the Main Volume, in footnote 285, delete the citations to 41 C.F.R. pt. 60-250 (Part 60-250 was rescinded by OFCCP's 2013 regulations).]**

[286]**[On page 39-65 of the Main Volume, in footnote 286, delete the citations to 41 C.F.R. pt. 60-250 (Part 60-250 was rescinded by OFCCP's 2013 regulations).]**

[287]**[On page 39-65 of the Main Volume, in footnote 287, delete the citations to 41 C.F.R. pt. 60-250 (Part 60-250 was rescinded by OFCCP's 2013 regulations).]**

[290]**[On page 39-66 of the Main Volume, in footnote 290, delete the citations to 41 C.F.R. pt. 60-250 (Part 60-250 was rescinded by OFCCP's 2013 regulations).]**

[291]**[On page 39-66 of the Main Volume, in footnote 291, delete the citations to 41 C.F.R. pt. 60-250 (Part 60-250 was rescinded by OFCCP's 2013 regulations).]**

[292]**[On page 39-66 of the Main Volume, in footnote 292, delete the citations to 41 C.F.R. pt. 60-250 (Part 60-250 was rescinded by OFCCP's 2013 regulations).]**

[296][On page 39-67 of the Main Volume, in footnote 296, delete the citations to 41 C.F.R. pt. 60-250 (Part 60-250 was rescinded by OFCCP's 2013 regulations).]

VII. Compliance Evaluation and Complaint Investigation Process: Desk Audit Letter Through Exit Conference

A. Compliance Evaluation

1. Compliance Review

[On page 39-67 of the Main Volume, after the sentence that ends with footnote 297, add the following.]

A compliance evaluation is initiated by OFCCP through a written scheduling letter informing the contractor that the audit will take place and requesting that the contractor submit the facility's affirmative action plan and supporting documents for review by a certain date.[18]

[On page 39-69 of the Main Volume, after the carryover sentence that ends with footnote 303, add the following new paragraph.]

The regulations do not require OFCCP to complete each of these phases. Depending upon the results of its analysis, OFCCP may end its evaluation at the conclusion of the desk audit or the on-site analysis, or proceed with its off-site review.[19] OFCCP conducts certain compliance reviews that are not entirely facility based, such as corporate management compliance evaluations (CMEs) and reviews of functional affirmative action plans (FAAPs).[20] The 2013 FCCM states that the same procedures apply to these reviews as well.[21]

---

[18] 2013 FCCM § 1B03.

[19] 2013 FCCM § 1A00.

[20] FAAPs are discussed in Section III.B.1, and CMEs are discussed in Section III.B.6 in the Main Volume.

[21] 2013 FCCM §§ 1A08 & 1A09.

2. *Off-Site Review*

[304]**[On page 39-69 of the Main Volume, in footnote 304, delete the citations to 41 C.F.R. pt. 60-250 (Part 60-250 was rescinded by OFCCP's 2013 regulations).]**

3. *Compliance Check*

[On page 39-69 of the Main Volume, in the first sentence of the carryover paragraph, add the following after "§ 60-1.12".]

and those that pertain to the statutes that OFCCP enforces

[306]**[On page 39-69 of the Main Volume, in footnote 306, delete the citations to 41 C.F.R. pt. 60-250 (Part 60-250 was rescinded by OFCCP's 2013 regulations).]**

4. *Focused Review*

[307]**[On page 39-70 of the Main Volume, in footnote 307, delete the citations to 41 C.F.R. pt. 60-250 (Part 60-250 was rescinded by OFCCP's 2013 regulations).]**

[308]**[On page 39-70 of the Main Volume, in footnote 308, delete the citations to 41 C.F.R. pt. 60-250 (Part 60-250 was rescinded by OFCCP's 2013 regulations).]**

B. Selection for Evaluation

1. *Federal Contractor Selection System*

[Add the following paragraph at the bottom of page 39-71.]

Questions concerning the neutrality of OFCCP's selection procedures remain a subject of litigation. In *Bank of America v. Solis*,[22] the district court agreed with the Bank's contentions that: (1) OFCCP's selection system is not entitled to a presumption of regularity; (2) that, while a request for the production of documents at the outset of a compliance review is not an entry on the contractor's premises, information from those documents may be used as a reasonable cause for an on-site visit where the scheduling of the

[22]2011 U.S. Dist. LEXIS 152576, at *55–59 (D.D.C. 2011).

review was conducted under a neutral scheme that was neutrally implemented; and (3) that a contractor's production of documents in compliance with an OFCCP scheduling letter did not constitute consent to an on-site review. In the court's view, Bank of America was not required to permit OFCCP to conduct an on-site review unless the agency demonstrated by a preponderance of the evidence that its selection system was neutral *and* that it had been applied in a neutral manner.[23]

3. *Discrimination Complaint*

[324]**[On page 39-73 of the Main Volume, in footnote 324, delete the citations to 41 C.F.R. pt. 60-250 (Part 60-250 was rescinded by OFCCP's 2013 regulations).]**

[326]**[On page 39-73 of the Main Volume, in footnote 326, delete the citations to 41 C.F.R. pt. 60-250 (Part 60-250 was rescinded by OFCCP's 2013 regulations).]**

[327]**[On page 39-73 of the Main Volume, in footnote 327, delete the citations to 41 C.F.R. pt. 60-250 (Part 60-250 was rescinded by OFCCP's 2013 regulations).]**

[328]**[On page 39-73 of the Main Volume, in footnote 328, delete the citations to 41 C.F.R. pt. 60-250 (Part 60-250 was rescinded by OFCCP's 2013 regulations).]**

[330]**[On page 39-74 of the Main Volume, in footnote 330, delete the citations to 41 C.F.R. pt. 60-250 (Part 60-250 was rescinded by OFCCP's 2013 regulations).]**

[331]**[On page 39-74 of the Main Volume, in footnote 331, delete the citations to 41 C.F.R. pt. 60-250 (Part 60-250 was rescinded by OFCCP's 2013 regulations).]**

[333]**[On page 39-74 of the Main Volume, in footnote 333, delete the citations to 41 C.F.R. pt. 60-250 (Part 60-250 was rescinded by OFCCP's 2013 regulations).]**

---

[23]*But see* OFCCP v. United Space Alliance, LLC, 824 F. Supp. 2d 68, 93–94, 2011 U.S. Dist. LEXIS 130938 (D.D.C. 2011), in which another judge in the same court held that in responding to the OFCCP's scheduling letter and providing the data requested therein, the contractor effectively consented to the on-site portion of the review.

[336]**[On page 39-75 of the Main Volume, in footnote 336, delete the citations to 41 C.F.R. pt. 60-250 (Part 60-250 was rescinded by OFCCP's 2013 regulations).]**

[337]**[On page 39-75 of the Main Volume, in footnote 337, delete the citations to 41 C.F.R. pt. 60-250 (Part 60-250 was rescinded by OFCCP's 2013 regulations).]**

[338]**[On page 39-75 of the Main Volume, in footnote 338, delete the citations to 41 C.F.R. pt. 60-250 (Part 60-250 was rescinded by OFCCP's 2013 regulations).]**

C. Preparation for an OFCCP Compliance Evaluation

9. Analysis of Compensation by Race and Gender for Each Pay Grade and for Persons of Comparable Performance, Skill, and Seniority

[On pages 39-83 to 39-85 of the Main Volume, replace all text and footnotes from the carryover paragraph through the numbered list with the following.]

The 2006 guidance committed OFCCP to the use of regression analysis in reviewing compensation practices and identified the factors that would be included in the agency's compensation regression model as well as others that might be included.[24] Guidance was also provided on the methodology that contractors should adopt in evaluating their compensation practices in the course of updating their AAPs.[25] Although contractors and OFCCP both experienced difficulty in implementing the standards (particularly in forming the required job groups), the 2006 guidance provided a set of standards and a uniform process for assessing compliance.[26]

In 2013, however, OFCCP rescinded its guidance on compensation.[27] Rather than providing a specific formula that the agency will follow in all of its reviews, the new guidance emphasizes flexibility and that consideration of various types of evidence "is critical because discrimination [in compensation] may be difficult to spot. . . .[28]

[24] 71 Fed. Reg. 35,138–35 to 35,140 (June 16, 2006).
[25] 41 C.F.R. § 60-22.17(b)(3) (2011); 71 Fed. Reg. 38,120 (June 16, 2006).
[26] 71 Fed. Reg. 38,114 (June 16, 2006).
[27] 78 Fed. Reg. 13,508 (Feb. 28, 2013).
[28] *Id.*

The preamble to the new guidance gives some examples of what OFCCP views as possible discrimination that may not be disclosed by statistical analysis alone. Principal among these is in the assignment of work to employees in a single job category, particularly those who work on commission (e.g., assigning route salespeople to routes near their residence or where they will service customers of the same race or ethnicity, a practice that may result in lower pay for minorities because they have less lucrative routes).[29]

D. The Desk Audit

1. Purpose of the Desk Audit

[401][On page 39-89 of the Main Volume, in footnote 401, replace the citation following "*See*" with the following.]

2013 FCCM, § 1A02, *available at* http://www.dol.gov/ofccp/regs/compliance/fccm/FCCM_FINAL_508c.pdf.

[On page 39-89 of the Main Volume, at the end of the second sentence of the carryover paragraph, add new footnote 401a.]

[401a]Under the regulations at 41 C.F.R. § 60-1.20(g), Public Access to Information, OFCCP must treat information obtained during the compliance evaluation as confidential to the maximum extent the information is exempt from public disclosure under the FOIA, 5 U.S.C. § 552. 2013 FCCM, § 1A06.

2. OFCCP's Activities Preceding the Desk Audit

b. The Scheduling Letter

[406][On page 39-91 of the Main Volume, replace footnote 406 with the following language.]

[406]OFCCP's data request may go beyond the items set out in its sample letter. *See, e.g.*, Bank of Am., N.A. v. Solis, No. 09-2009, 2011 U.S. Dist. LEXIS 152576, at *46–50 (D.D.C. Dec. 13, 2011) (OFCCP complied with Fourth Amendment requirements in requesting records during desk audit where agency's request was "authorized by law, the materials sought were relevant, and the information sought was particularly described").

---

[29]*Id.*

[On page 39-91, at the end of the first full sentence of the carry-over paragraph, add new footnote 406a.]

[406a]*See* Bank of Am., N.A. v. Solis, 2011 U.S. Dist. LEXIS 152576, at *46–50 (D.D.C. Dec. 13, 2011) (OFCCP complied with Fourth Amendment requirements in requesting records during desk audit where agency's request was "authorized by law, the materials sought were relevant, and the information sought was particularly described").

3. The Contractor's Response to the Scheduling Letter

[On page 39-92 of the Main Volume, after the sentence that ends with footnote 411, add the following new paragraph.]

The contractor should keep in mind that the date of the scheduling letter does not represent a cut off for the compliance review. OFCCP's position that it is entitled to review post-scheduling letter data was upheld in *Office of Federal Contract Compliance Programs v. Frito-Lay, Inc.*[30] In *Frito-Lay*, the ARB held that because the contractor had an ongoing duty to comply with Executive Order 11246, it was required to respond to a request for affirmative action plan data covering activity occurring *after* the date of the scheduling letter where further inquiries were about statistically significant disparities identified in its initial data analysis and were relevant to proper disparate impact analysis.

[412]**[On page 39-92 of the Main Volume, in footnote 412, delete the citations to 41 C.F.R. pt. 60-250 (Part 60-250 was rescinded by OFCCP's 2013 regulations).]**

4. OFCCP's Initial Review of the AAP and Supporting Data

d. Review, for Acceptability, of AAPs for Individuals With Disabilities and Veterans

[431]**[On page 39-96 of the Main Volume, in footnote 431, delete the citations to 41 C.F.R. pt. 60-250 (Part 60-250 was rescinded by OFCCP's 2013 regulations).]**

---

[30]2012 OFCCP LEXIS *2, at *7–11 (Final Decision of ARB, May 8, 2012).

[432][On page 39-96 of the Main Volume, in footnote 432, delete the citations to 41 C.F.R. pt. 60-250 (Part 60-250 was rescinded by OFCCP's 2013 regulations).]

6. Preliminary Discrimination Analyses

d. Compensation Analyses

[On page 39-101 of the Main Volume, at the end of the heading, "*d. Compensation Analyses*", add new footnote 456a.]

[456a]On February 28, 2013, OFCCP rescinded its 2006 Guidance with Respect to Compensation Discrimination Standards and its Voluntary Guidelines for Self-Evaluation of Compensation Practices under Executive Order 11246, 78 Fed. Reg. 13508.

[460][On page 39-102 of the Main Volume, in footnote 460, replace the first paragraph of the footnote with the following.]

At the same time that it rescinded its 2006 guidance on February 28, 2013, OFCCP issued new Procedures for Reviewing Contractor Compensation Systems and Practices, Directive 2013-03, 78 Fed. Reg. 13,508. The new directive emphasizes that OFCCP will engage in a case-by-case analysis of compensation practices rather than applying a formulaic approach across all of its compliance reviews. 78 Fed. Reg. 13,508 at 13,518. It notes that contractors have a duty to evaluate their compensation systems and records to determine whether there are sex-, race-, or disability-based disparities or disparities on the basis of veterans' status, and must maintain records "including but not limited to rates of pay or other terms of compensation."

E. The On-Site Review

2. Notice of the On-Site Review

[467][On page 39-104 of the Main Volume, replace footnote 467 with the following.]

[467]OFCCP's analysis in compensation matters may go beyond a preliminary screen. United Space Alliance, LLC v. Solis, 824 F. Supp. 2d 68, 88–89 (D.D.C. 2011) (OFCCP's reliance on analyses beyond preliminary analysis was not arbitrary or capricious in

relation to its evaluation of federal contractor compliance with nondiscrimination obligations, where, even if OFCCP was bound by its own directive, that document required only that OFCCP conduct threshold analysis, but did not forbid OFCCP from also performing other analyses).

[On page 39-104 of the Main Volume, at the end of the first sentence of the second full paragraph, add new footnote 467a.]

[467a]*See* Bank of Am., N.A. v. Solis, 2011 U.S. Dist. LEXIS 152576, at *53 (D.D.C. Dec. 13, 2011) (record contained sufficient evidence of contractor's voluntary consent to desk audit where contractor responded to standard scheduling letter, which was not coercive in nature and did not include any threatening language or mention any penalties for failure to allow inspection).

VIII. Enforcement Procedures and Sanctions for Noncompliance

[541]**[On page 39-122 of the Main Volume, in footnote 541, delete the citations to 41 C.F.R. pt. 60-250 (Part 60-250 was rescinded by OFCCP's 2013 regulations).]**

[542]**[On page 39-122 of the Main Volume, in footnote 542, delete the citations to 41 C.F.R. pt. 60-250 (Part 60-250 was rescinded by OFCCP's 2013 regulations).]**

A. Administrative Enforcement

[545]**[On page 39-123 of the Main Volume, in footnote 545, delete the citations to 41 C.F.R. pt. 60-250 (Part 60-250 was rescinded by OFCCP's 2013 regulations).]**

[546]**[On page 39-123 of the Main Volume, in footnote 546, delete the citations to 41 C.F.R. pt. 60-250 (Part 60-250 was rescinded by OFCCP's 2013 regulations).]**

[547]**[On page 39-124 of the Main Volume, in footnote 547, delete the citations to 41 C.F.R. pt. 60-250 (Part 60-250 was rescinded by OFCCP's 2013 regulations).]**

B. Cancellation, Debarment, and Other Sanctions Following Administrative Hearing

[560][On page 39-126 of the Main Volume, in footnote 560, delete the citations to 41 C.F.R. pt. 60-250 (Part 60-250 was rescinded by OFCCP's 2013 regulations).]

[561][On page 39-126 of the Main Volume, in footnote 561, delete the citations to 41 C.F.R. pt. 60-250 (Part 60-250 was rescinded by OFCCP's 2013 regulations).]

[562][On page 39-127 of the Main Volume, in footnote 562, delete the citations to 41 C.F.R. pt. 60-250 (Part 60-250 was rescinded by OFCCP's 2013 regulations).]

[563][On page 39-127 of the Main Volume, in footnote 563, delete the citations to 41 C.F.R. pt. 60-250 (Part 60-250 was rescinded by OFCCP's 2013 regulations).]

[565][On page 39-127 of the Main Volume, in footnote 565, delete the citations to 41 C.F.R. pt. 60-250 (Part 60-250 was rescinded by OFCCP's 2013 regulations).]

[567][On page 39-127 of the Main Volume, in footnote 567, delete the citations to 41 C.F.R. pt. 60-250 (Part 60-250 was rescinded by OFCCP's 2013 regulations.)]

[569][On page 39-127 of the Main Volume, in footnote 569, delete the citations to 41 C.F.R. pt. 60-250 (Part 60-250 was rescinded by OFCCP's 2013 regulations).]

CHAPTER 40

INJUNCTIVE AND AFFIRMATIVE RELIEF

I. STATUTORY AUTHORITY AND OBJECTIVES

[3]**[On page 40-2 of the Main Volume, in footnote 3, add the following at the end of the footnote.]**

Similarly, Title VII retaliation claims require a showing of "but-for" causation. University of Tex. Sw. Med. Ctr. v. Nassar, 133 S. Ct. 2517, 118 FEP 1504 (2013); *see also* Lewis v. Humboldt Acquisition Corp., 681 F.3d 312, 321, 26 AD 389 (6th Cir. 2011) (extending *Gross* analysis to bar mixed-motive claims under ADA). More comprehensive discussions of *Gross* and *Nassar* appear in Chapters 12 (Age), and 15 (Retaliation), respectively. Following *Gross*, several courts of appeals have discussed the standards of proof and availability of relief in mixed-motive cases. *Compare* Ford v. Mabus, 629 F.3d 198, 208, 110 FEP 1665 (D.C. Cir. 2010) (federal sector employees can prove ADEA violation even if age played only "some role" in decision, but reinstatement and back pay are available only if plaintiffs show "but-for" causation), *with* Harley v. Potter, 416 F. App'x 748, 751–52, 111 FEP 1780 (10th Cir. 2011) (trial court correctly applied "but for" standard of *Gross* in federal employee case, noting that age need not be sole motivating factor so long as age was factor that made difference), *and* Velazquez-Ortiz v. Vilsack, 657 F.3d 64, 74, 113 FEP 627 (1st Cir. 2011) (acknowledging decision in *Ford*, but declining to rule on issue raised for first time on appeal).

[5][On page 40-3 of the Main Volume, in the carryover of footnote 5, replace the second paragraph with the following.]

Prior to *Nassar*, courts were divided over the applicability of the mixed-motive provisions of the 1991 Civil Rights Act to retaliation cases. *See, e.g.*, Gowski v. Peake, 682 F.3d 1299, 1314, 115 FEP 163 (11th Cir. 2012) (injunctive relief unavailable where defendant prevailed in Title VII mixed-motive retaliation case; district court abused its discretion in ordering injunctive relief for individual plaintiffs under such circumstances). *See generally* Chapter 15 (Retaliation), Section IV.E.

II. ENJOINING PRACTICES FOUND TO BE UNLAWFUL

[29][On page 40-7 of the Main Volume, in footnote 29, add the following after "*See, e.g.*,".]

Gowski v. Peake, 682 F.3d 1299, 1314, 115 FEP 163 (11th Cir. 2012) (affirming order requiring employer to publicly post jury verdict finding that employer had created hostile work environment and requiring managers to participate in antidiscrimination workshops); EEOC v. Service Temps, Inc., 679 F.3d 323, 338–39, 26 AD 129 (5th Cir. 2012) (upholding order requiring employer to post and provide employees with notice of ADA protections, to provide ADA training to manager, and to notify EEOC of any future disability discrimination complaints);

[30]**[On page 40-8 of the Main Volume, in footnote 30, add the following after "*See*".]**

Gowski, 682 F.3d at 1314 (requiring prior independent review of any planned disciplinary action for three-year period);

[31]**[On page 40-8 of the Main Volume, in footnote 31, add the following after "*See, e.g.,*".]**

Gowski, 682 F.3d at 1314 (affirming order preventing employer from engaging in "any retaliatory practices" to remedy employer's "scheme" of retaliating against employees who had filed discrimination charges);

III. RELIEF FOR IDENTIFIABLE VICTIMS OF UNLAWFUL EMPLOYMENT PRACTICES

[47]**[On page 40-13 of the Main Volume, in footnote 47, add the following after "*accord*".]**

Gowski v. Peake, 682 F.3d 1299, 1314, 115 FEP 163 (11th Cir. 2012) (affirming order requiring prior independent review of any planned disciplinary action for three-year period);

[69]**[On page 40-17 of the Main Volume, in footnote 69, add the following at the end of the footnote.]**

See also Kapche v. Holder, 677 F.3d 454, 466, 26 AD 1 (D.C. Cir. 2012) (upholding denial of front pay and instatement due to candidate's demonstrated lack of candor during background investigation).

[72]**[On page 40-18 of the Main Volume, in footnote 72, add the following after "*See, e.g.,*".]**

Hicks v. Forest Preserve Dist. of Cook Cnty., 677 F.3d 781, 792, 114 FEP 1281 (7th Cir. 2012) (mutual dislike between employer and employee is not sufficient grounds upon which to deny reinstatement);

[82]**[On page 40-21 of the Main Volume, in footnote 82, add the following at the end of the paragraph.]**

Cf. Bergerson v. New York State Office of Mental Health, 652 F.3d 277, 286, 112 FEP 1313 (2d Cir. 2011) (lower court erred in failing to consider reinstatement, front pay, or back pay due to its assumption that plaintiff's compensatory damages award was sufficient to make plaintiff whole).

IV. AFFIRMATIVE RELIEF BENEFITING PERSONS OTHER THAN IDENTIFIED VICTIMS OF DISCRIMINATION

[92]**[On page 40-23 of the Main Volume, in footnote 92, add the following at the end of the footnote.]**

See generally United States v. Brennan, 650 F.3d 65, 99–104, 112 FEP 193 (2d Cir. 2011) (in suit challenging employer's voluntary efforts to remedy previous disparate impact discrimination, court examined at length distinction between affirmative action—"when an employer, acting *ex ante*, although in the light of past discrimination, establishes hiring or promotion procedures designed to promote equal opportunity and eradicate future discrimination"—and ex post modifications of established procedures because of racial or gender composition associated with those results).

B. Race- or Gender-Conscious Affirmative Relief

[125]**[On page 40-30 of the Main Volume, in the carryover of footnote 125, add the following before "*But see*".]**

See also Cleveland Firefighters for Fair Hiring Practices v. City of Cleveland, 669 F.3d 737, 741, 114 FEP 398 (6th Cir. 2012) (vacating and remanding district court's order that refused to extend 31-year-old consent decree that required city to hire fixed percentages of minorities as firefighters).

[135]**[On page 40-31 of the Main Volume, in footnote 135, add the following after "*See, e.g.,*".]**

Cleveland Firefighters for Fair Hiring Practices v. City of Cleveland, 669 F.3d 737, 741, 114 FEP 398 (6th Cir. 2012) (racial classifications within consent decrees are as subject to strict scrutiny standard just as are any racial classifications);

V. MONITORING THE COURT DECREE

[140][On page 40-33 of the Main Volume, in footnote 140, add the following after "*See*".]

Cleveland Firefighters for Fair Hiring Practices v. City of Cleveland, 669 F.3d 737, 742, 114 FEP 398 (6th Cir. 2012) (remanding case to district court for further proceedings to determine whether additional extension of 31-year-old consent decree was warranted); EEOC v. Product Fabricators, Inc., 666 F.3d 1170, 1171–72, 25 AD 1314 (8th Cir. 2012) (district court abused its discretion in rejecting two-year continuing jurisdiction provision in proposed consent decree in case where employer had longstanding policy of requiring employees to disclose their medications);

[141][On page 40-33 of the Main Volume, in footnote 141, add the following before "EEOC v. Plumbers & Pipefitters Local 120".]

EEOC v. Service Temps Inc., 679 F.3d 323, 338–39 & n.53, 26 AD 129 (5th Cir. 2012) (rejecting employer's argument that compliance with court's order was too difficult due to alleged lack of specificity as to method of reporting future disability discrimination complaints by employees to EEOC);

[145][On page 40-33 of the Main Volume, in footnote 145, add the following after "*See*".]

Cleveland Firefighters for Fair Hiring Practices, 669 F.3d at 741 (vacating and remanding district court's refusal to extend 31-year-old consent decree because court failed to make specific factual findings as to whether decree remained effective in remedying past discrimination);

[On page 40-33 of the Main Volume, after the sentence that ends with footnote 145, add the following.]

Further, a court has discretion to extend or terminate a decree even if the decree's terms state otherwise or if the parties oppose the extension or termination.[1]

---

[1]*See* Cleveland Firefighters for Fair Hiring Practices v. City of Cleveland, 669 F.3d 737, 741, 114 FEP 398 (6th Cir. 2012) (this discretion is subject to limitations, including "'first making explicit findings concerning Defendants' compliance with the decree's goals and specific terms'") (quoting Gonzales v. Galvin, 151 F.3d 526, 77 FEP 1573 (6th Cir. 1998)).

[154][On page 40-35 of the Main Volume, in footnote 154, add the following after "*see, e.g.*,".]

Briscoe v. City of New Haven, 654 F.3d 200, 204–05, 112 FEP 1793 (2d Cir. 2011) (nonparty to prior proceedings not bound by judgment because he did not have "reasonable opportunity" to object to judgment due to lack of pre-judgment fairness hearing);

VI. PRELIMINARY INJUNCTIONS

A. Rule 65 Preliminary Relief

[166][On page 40-39 of the Main Volume, in the carryover of footnote 166, add the following at the end of the footnote.]

But see Johnson v. City of Memphis, 444 F. App'x 856, 860 (6th Cir. 2011) (potential lost work experience and opportunity to compete for promotions constituted irreparable harm supporting injunction requiring promotion of 28 African-American police officers).

CHAPTER 41

MONETARY RELIEF

II. BACK PAY

A. The Right to Back Pay in General

[24][On page 41-7 of the Main Volume, in footnote 24, add the following after "*See*".]

Bergerson v. New York State Office of Mental Health, Cent. N.Y. Psychiatric Ctr., 652 F.3d 277, 287, 112 FEP 1313 (2d Cir. 2011) (district court erred in not awarding back pay based on its mistaken belief that compensatory damages were sufficient to make plaintiff whole; back pay is rule not exception in Title VII cases and requires separate inquiry; compensatory damages are to be awarded in addition to economic damages, including back pay, in usual case);

[24][On page 41-8 of the Main Volume, in the carryover of footnote 24, add the following before "EEOC v. Ilona of Hungary, Inc.".]

Gowski v. Peake, 682 F.3d 1299, 1310 n.10, 115 FEP 163 (11th Cir. 2012) (affirming district court's vacatur of lost wages award in hostile work environment case because plaintiffs were not constructively discharged);

[29][On page 41-8 of the Main Volume, in footnote 29, add the following at the end of the footnote.]

On June 27, 2002, however, following the decision in *Hoffman*, the EEOC rescinded its earlier policy guidance on the subject, which stated that undocumented aliens who were the victims of illegal discrimination were entitled to back pay. *See* EEOC Enforcement Guidance No. 915.002.

B. Calculation of the Back-Pay Award

1. Elements of a Back-Pay Award

[33][On page 41-9 of the Main Volume, in footnote 33, add the following before "Hartley v. Dillard's, Inc.".]

Wai v. Federal Express Corp., 461 F. App'x 876, 885, 18 WH Cases 2d 1451 (11th Cir. 2012) (recognizing two constituent parts to back-pay award; "[t]he first is determined by the difference between the actual wages earned and the wages the individual would have earned but for the defendant's violation," and "[t]he second is the recovery of health-insurance coverage and other fringe benefits");

a. Wages and Salary

[34][On page 41-9 of the Main Volume, in footnote 34, add the following before "Durham Life Ins. Co. v. Evans".]

Hemmings v. Tidyman's, Inc., 285 F.3d 1174, 1192, 88 FEP 945 (9th Cir. 2002) (testimony of expert witness, certified public accountant, concerning methodology he employed in calculating plaintiffs' earnings losses, was sufficient to support jury back-pay award);

[35][On page 41-9 of the Main Volume, in footnote 35, add the following after "*See*".]

Bruso v. United Airlines, Inc., 239 F.3d 848, 856, 84 FEP 1780 (7th Cir. 2001) (denying plaintiff's motion for new trial on issue of damages; jury's back-pay award included losses plaintiff occurred following retaliatory demotion, including lower wages, union dues plaintiff had to pay upon returning to bargaining unit, and uniforms he was required to purchase, but did not include plaintiff's request for time lost during voluntary leave of absence he took to appeal employer's action, alleged lost overtime that plaintiff did not prove was unavailable, lost wages due to surgery for medical condition whose onset preceded demotion, or emotional suffering and mental anguish; credibility determinations related to these damages were within jury's province); United States v. City of Warren, 138 F.3d 1083, 1097, 79 FEP 1603 (6th Cir. 1998) (remanding for determination of back pay, using either "attrition factor" or actual date plaintiff stopped working, but not both; district court should keep "in mind that ambiguity in what the claimant would have received but for the discrimination should be resolved against the discriminating employer") (internal quotations omitted);

b. Fringe Benefits

[46][On page 41-11 of the Main Volume, in footnote 46, add the following at the end of the footnote.]

As with other elements of back pay, the plaintiff must prove the value of any retirement benefits sought. *See* Wai v. Federal Express Corp., 461 F. App'x 876, 886, 18 WH Cases 2d 1451 (11th Cir. 2012) (rejecting portion of jury award attributable to retirement and 401(k) benefits as speculative, because plaintiff failed to prove value of those benefits).

[48][On page 41-11 of the Main Volume, in footnote 48, add the following after "*See*".]

Partington v. Broyhill Furniture Indus., Inc., 999 F.2d 269, 273, 62 FEP 534 (5th Cir. 1993) (inclusion of profit sharing in back-pay award of wrongfully terminated employee affirmed as not too speculative; plaintiff could proceed with mechanical estimation assuming that profit sharing would remain constant, particularly given employer's failure to introduce evidence about its profit-sharing arrangements);

[58][On page 41-13 of the Main Volume, in footnote 58, add the following at the end of the footnote.]

Cf. Metz v. Merrill Lynch, Pierce, Fenner & Smith, Inc., 39 F.3d 1482, 1493, 66 FEP 439 (10th Cir. 1994) ("lost fringe benefits are available under the remedial provisions of Title VII," and it was error for district court to deny them, even though only evidence regarding benefits was plaintiff's testimony of amount at which she calculated them based on information provided by employer).

c. Interest

[73][On page 41-16 of the Main Volume, in footnote 73, add the following after "*see*".]

Adam v. Norton, 636 F.3d 1190, 1192–93, 111 FEP 1089 (9th Cir. 2011) (extending Back Pay Act's waiver of immunity from interest against government to ADEA case);

[75][On page 41-17 of the Main Volume, in footnote 75, add the following after "*See*".]

Thomas v. iStar Fin., Inc., 629 F.3d 276, 279–80, 110 FEP 1761 (2d Cir. 2010) (federal interest rate, rather than higher state-law rate, applied in Title VII action with supplemental state-law claims);

2. The Period of Recovery

b. Termination of the Back-Pay Period

(ii.) Failure to mitigate

[126][On page 41-30 of the Main Volume, in footnote 126, add the following after "*See*".]

Thom v. American Standard, Inc., 666 F.3d 968, 975, 18 WH Cases 2d 1132 (6th Cir. 2012) (given skill and location limitations, plaintiff satisfied duty to mitigate by passing the General Educational Development (GED) test and then accepting best employment opportunity offered to him, even though it paid $8 per hour less than what he was paid by defendant);

[127][On page 41-30 of the Main Volume, in footnote 127, move the citation and parenthetical for "Dailey v. Societe Generale" to the beginning of the footnote.]

[127][On page 41-30 of the Main Volume, in footnote 127, add the following after "*see also*".]

Thom, 666 F.3d at 975 (no reduction in back-pay award for five months plaintiff spent getting his GED in light of his limited skill set and rural nature of community in which he worked);

(iv.) After-acquired evidence of employee misconduct or fraud

[168]**[On page 41-38 of the Main Volume, in footnote 168, add the following at the end of the footnote.]**

Cf. Holland v. Gee, 677 F.3d 1047, 1064–65, 114 FEP 1449 (11th Cir. 2012) (district court erred in vacating back-pay award based on after-acquired evidence doctrine; that doctrine applies only to cases involving employee wrongdoing and employer agreed that there was no evidence that employee engaged in wrongdoing).

[174]**[On page 41-39 of the Main Volume, in footnote 174, add the following at the beginning of the footnote.]**

Kapche v. Holder, 677 F.3d 454, 466–68, 26 AD 1 (D.C. Cir. 2012) (plaintiff not entitled to front pay or reinstatement because defendant would have revoked conditional offer of employment, regardless of plaintiff's diabetes, due to his lack of candor revealed during background investigation);

(v.) Other events terminating the back-pay period

[177]**[On page 41-39 of the Main Volume, in footnote 177, add the following after "*See, e.g.*,".]**

Tyler v. Union Oil, 304 F.3d 379, 401–02, 89 FEP 1226 (5th Cir. 2002) (back-pay award properly terminated on date on which business unit ceased operation, even though that date preceded date of judgment, because surviving business was found not be alter ego or agent of original employer);

[178]**[On page 41-39 of the Main Volume, in footnote 178, add the following after "*E.g.*,".]**

Thom v. American Standard, Inc., 666 F.3d 968, 975, 18 WH Cases 2d 1132 (6th Cir. 2012) (Family and Medical Leave Act (FMLA) plaintiff's back pay would not be cut off because his employer sold plant and terminated all union employees, where new owners rehired all employees similarly situated to plaintiff);

[179]**[On page 41-40 of the Main Volume, in footnote 179, add the following after "*See*".]**

Blackburn v. Martin, 982 F.2d 125, 129 (4th Cir. 1992) (rejecting plaintiff's contention that he was entitled to back pay after project on which he had worked was terminated where "[a]mple evidence indicate[d] [the defendant] would not have retained [the plaintiff] beyond the end of project");

III. FRONT PAY

[183][On page 41-41 of the Main Volume, in footnote 183, add the following after "*See*".]

Barton v. Zimmer, Inc., 662 F.3d 448, 455, 113 FEP 929 (7th Cir. 2011) ("To recover front pay as an equitable remedy in lieu of reinstatement [in an ADEA case], [the plaintiff] would have to establish causation—that is, that . . . the discriminatory removal of his job duties caused the disability that prevents his reinstatement"); Bergerson v. New York State Office of Mental Health, 652 F.3d 277, 287–88, 112 FEP 1313 (2d Cir. 2011) (award of front pay is alternative to make plaintiff whole where reinstatement is inappropriate (e.g., because of animosity between plaintiff and former employer); on remand, court must determine whether plaintiff is entitled to one or the other);

[190][On page 41-43 of the Main Volume, in footnote 190, add the following after "*See*".]

Serricchio v. Wachovia Sec., LLC, 658 F.3d 169, 191–94, 191 LRRM 2617 (2d Cir. 2011) (affirming order requiring Uniformed Services Employment and Reemployment Rights Act (USERRA) plaintiff's reinstatement to his prior financial advisor position with fixed salary, even though his pre-service compensation was wholly commission-based, because plaintiff needed time to reinstate his expired license and would not earn commissions during this time period);

[194][On page 41-44 of the Main Volume, in footnote 194, add the following after "*E.g.*,".]

Bergerson v. New York State Office of Mental Health, 652 F.3d 277, 287–88, 112 FEP 1313 (2d Cir. 2011) (award of front pay is alternative to make plaintiff whole where reinstatement is inappropriate (e.g., because of animosity between plaintiff and former employer));

[196]**[On page 41-45 of the Main Volume, in footnote 196, add the following after "*But see*".]**

Banks v. Travelers Cos., 180 F.3d 358, 80 FEP 30 (2d Cir. 1999) (district court erred in instructing jury that it could not award back pay to plaintiff terminated in 1994 for period between 1996 reduction in force (RIF) and date of verdict; given her seniority, jury could have found that plaintiff would have survived 1996 RIF but for her termination; on remand, court should consider how this question affects plaintiff's entitlement to reinstatement or front pay as appropriate remedies);

[201]**[On page 41-46 of the Main Volume, in footnote 201, add the following before "*see also*".]**

Kapche v. Holder, 677 F.3d 454, 466–68, 26 AD 1 (D.C. Cir. 2012) (ADA plaintiff not entitled to front pay or reinstatement because defendant would have revoked its conditional offer of employment based on lack of candor discovered during investigation of plaintiff's background, regardless of plaintiff's diabetes);

[205]**[On page 41-46 of the Main Volume, in footnote 205, add the following after "*E.g.*,".]**

McInerney v. United Air Lines, Inc., 463 F. App'x 709, 725–26, 112 FEP 7 (10th Cir. 2011) (despite lack of appropriate calculation, district court could have properly denied front pay based on plaintiff's inadequate attempts to secure other employment; plaintiff documented only two attempts to find employment with other airlines and accepted position that paid less than previous position);

[214]**[On page 41-49 of the Main Volume, in footnote 214, add the following after "*E.g.*,".]**

Muñoz v. Sociedad Española de Auxilo Mutuo y Beneficiencia de P.R., 671 F.3d 49, 62, 114 FEP 412 (1st Cir. 2012) ("relatively modest" award of $250,000 in front pay to cardiologist prevailing on age discrimination claim was appropriate given his age and nature of his practice);

IV. DEFENSES TO EQUITABLE FORMS OF MONETARY RELIEF

A. The Mixed-Motive Defense

[229][On page 41-52 of the Main Volume, in footnote 229, add the following at the beginning of the footnote.]

Lewis v. Humboldt Acquisition Corp., 681 F.3d 312, 321 (6th Cir. 2012);

[229][On page 41-52 of the Main Volume, in footnote 229, add the following at the end of the footnote.]

See also Palmquist v. Shinseki, 689 F.3d 66, 73–74 (1st Cir. 2012) (Rehabilitation Act, which borrows causation standard from ADA, requires retaliation to be "but for" cause of adverse action).

[On page 41-53 of the Main Volume, replace the last two sentences of the carryover paragraph with the following.]

The reasoning of *Gross* was extended to Title VII retaliation cases in *University of Texas Southwest Medical Center v. Nassar,*[1] and to ADA cases in *Serwatka v. Rockwell Automation, Inc.*[2] Accordingly, a plaintiff seeking to establish a Title VII retaliation claim, or a disparate treatment claim of age or disability discrimination, must prove that a prohibited factor was the "but-for" cause of the employer's adverse action.[3]

C. Equitable Defenses to Monetary Relief

4. Deductions and Offsets

a. Interim Earnings

[284][On page 41-63 of the Main Volume, in footnote 284, add the following after "*See*".]

Kapche v. Holder, 677 F.3d 454, 469–70, 26 AD 1 (D.C. Cir. 2012) (district court did not abuse its discretion in denying back pay where

[1]133 S. Ct. 2517 (2013).

[2]591 F.3d 957, 959–63, 22 AD 1379 (7th Cir. 2010).

[3]*Gross*, 557 U.S. at 177–78; *Nassar*, 133 S. Ct. at 2533. *But cf.* Metoyer v. Chassman, 504 F.3d 919, 934, 101 FEP 993 (9th Cir. 2007) (finding, prior to *Gross*, that mixed-motive standard applies to claims of discrimination and retaliation under 42 U.S.C. § 1981).

ADA plaintiff earned more in his current job than he would have earned during period between defendant's revocations of first and second conditional offers of employment);

V. COMPENSATORY AND PUNITIVE DAMAGES

B. The Entitlement to, and Calculation of, Compensatory Damages

[352][On page 41-77 of the Main Volume, in footnote 352, add the following after "*E.g.*,".]

McInerney v. United Air Lines, Inc., 463 F. App'x 709, 723–24, 12 FEP 7 (10th Cir. 2011) (affirming award of $300,000 in compensatory damages based on plaintiff's testimony that she was "devastated" and "humiliated" by her termination, that she "couldn't stop crying, and for weeks on end, [ ] didn't really sleep," that her career with defendant was "part of her identity" and that her termination and thought of having to tell potential employers about it "put [her] over the edge"; plaintiff also testified that termination affected her confidence and home life and that she had prematurely born son in critical condition at time of her termination);

[353][On page 41-78 of the Main Volume, in footnote 353, add the following after "*See*".]

Ash v. Tyson Foods, Inc., 664 F.3d 883, 899–900, 114 FEP 102 (11th Cir. 2011) (testimony of plaintiff, his wife, and human resources manager held sufficient to support compensatory damages award of $300,000 for emotional distress);

[359][On page 41-80 of the Main Volume, in footnote 359, add the following after "*See, e.g.*,".]

Trainor v. HEI Hospitality, LLC, 699 F.3d 19, 32–33, 116 FEP 615 (1st Cir. 2012) (jury award of $1 million in emotional distress damages, although reduced to $500,000 by trial court, was "grossly excessive" and was further reduced to $200,000; reduced amount was consistent with awards in similar cases with no evidence of medical treatment, counseling, or other attention for despondency);

[361][On page 41-81 of the Main Volume, in footnote 361, add the following after "*See*".]

Trainor, 699 F.3d at 32–33 (plaintiff awarded $500,000 in emotional distress damages by trial court required to remit amount to $200,000 or submit to new trial, where there was no evidence that he received medical treatment or counseling "or suffered any physical infirmity as a result of his ouster"); Aponte-Rivera v. DHL Solutions (USA), Inc., 650 F.3d 803, 811–12, 112 FEP 590 (1st Cir. 2011) (affirming district court's remittitur from $350,000 to $200,000 in compensatory damages in hostile environment case where plaintiff's evidence of emotional distress was "at best, mixed"; plaintiff's testimony about her physical and mental issues and work stress was corroborated by e-mails to human resources and by other documentation and testimony, but no medical expert testimony was proffered);

C. The Entitlement to, and Calculation of, Punitive Damages

1. Willfulness

[389][On page 41-87 of the Main Volume, in footnote 389, add the following after "*see also*".]

EEOC v. Service Temps., Inc., 679 F.3d 323, 336–37, 26 AD 129 (5th Cir. 2012) (affirming punitive damages award remitted to $68,800; evidence that supervisor was aware of ADA through discussions in semi-annual managers' meetings controverted defendant's argument that supervisor could not have acted with malice or reckless indifference because he was unaware of ADA's prohibitions);

2. Vicarious Liability and Good Faith as a Defense

[401][On page 41-90 of the Main Volume, in footnote 401, add the following after "*See, e.g.,*".]

Ash v. Tyson Foods, Inc., 664 F.3d 883, 901–07, 114 FEP 102 (11th Cir. 2011) (punitive damages award properly set aside by district court where, inter alia, discriminating employee was not far enough up corporate ladder to impute actions to employer); *see also*

[404]**[On page 41-91 of the Main Volume, in footnote 404, add the following after "*see also*".]**

Ash, 664 F.3d at 901–07 (district court properly set aside punitive damages award based, in part, on employer's anti-discrimination policies relating to hiring and promotion decisions);

3. Due Process Concerns

[420]**[On page 41-95 of the Main Volume, in footnote 420, add the following after "*See*".]**

Thomas v. iStar Fin., Inc., 652 F.3d 141, 148–50, 112 FEP 1556 (2d Cir. 2011) (jury's award of $1.6 million in punitive damages was unconstitutionally excessive where ratio to compensatory damages was 3.6:1—5.7:1 following remittitur of compensatory damages award—and where plaintiff was awarded substantial compensatory damages and defendant's conduct was only moderately reprehensible);

D. Statutory Caps

[438]**[On page 41-99 of the Main Volume, in footnote 438, add the following after "*see*".]**

Hernandez-Miranda v. Empresas Diaz Masso, Inc., 651 F.3d 167, 173, 112 FEP 1113 (5th Cir. 2011) (statutory cap on compensatory and punitive damages under Title VII is determined by reference to year in which discrimination occurred, not year in which damages are awarded);

VII. LIQUIDATED DAMAGES

[On page 41-105 of the Main Volume, after the sentence that ends with footnote 471, add the following new paragraph.]

Liquidated damages are also available for willful violations of the Uniformed Services Employment and Reemployment Rights Act (USERRA).[4] The same standard of willfulness developed under the EPA and ADEA applies in USERRA cases: An employer's conduct

---

[4]Frye v. A.S.A.P. Fire & Safety Corp., 658 F.3d 85, 91, 191 LRRM 2635 (1st Cir. 2011) (referencing 38 U.S.C. § 4323(d)(1)(C) and Supreme Court precedent under Fair Labor Standards Act (FLSA)).

is "willful" if the employer knew or showed reckless disregard for whether its conduct violated USERRA.[5] Willfulness has been found where the employer failed to rehire an employee after his military service ended, despite Department of Labor instructions that it do so,[6] and where management failed to respond to a request for reinstatement despite knowledge that USERRA requires "prompt" reinstatement and the employer ultimately placed the employee in a lower-paying position that was tantamount to a constructive discharge.[7]

VIII. BACK-PAY CLAIMS IN CLASS AND COLLECTIVE PROCEEDINGS

A. Determining Back-Pay Damages

1. Introduction

[On page 41-109 of the Main Volume, after the sentence that ends with footnote 484, add the following new paragraph.]

More recently, in reversing a decision certifying an antitrust class action in *Comcast Corp. v. Behrend*,[8] the Supreme Court held that any damages model must measure "damages resulting from the particular ... injury" alleged, and must be able to quantify damages on a classwide basis.[9] The Court reversed class certification upon finding that the econometric model on which the plaintiffs' expert relied failed to meet this standard.[10]

---

[5] *Id.*

[6] *Id.* at 92. In addition to refusing to reinstate the employee, the employer told him to "shut his mouth" about reinstatement because another employee was in his job. *Id.* at 91–92.

[7] *See* Serricchio v. Wachovia Sec., LLC, 658 F.3d 169, 191–92, 191 LRRM 2617 (2d Cir. 2011) (jury's award of liquidated damages was supported by delay in reinstatement of several months and placement of plaintiff in position that paid much less than his previous position, knowing that salary was insufficient to allow him to support his family).

[8] 133 S. Ct. 1426 (2013).

[9] *Id.* at 1433–34.

[10] *Id.*

CHAPTER 42

ATTORNEY'S FEES

I. Introduction

[5]**[On page 42-3 of the Main Volume, in footnote 5, add the following after "*See, e.g.*,".]**

Arnold v. ADT Sec. Servs., 627 F.3d 716, 720–21, 110 FEP 1781 (8th Cir. 2010) (upholding district court's award of attorney's fees against one of several plaintiffs and plaintiffs' attorney where employer had attempted several times to obtain answers to discovery and plaintiff had failed to comply with court's order to provide complete responses); Collins v. Illinois, 554 F.3d 693, 696–97, 105 FEP 760 (7th Cir. 2009) (refusing to vacate lower court's order requiring pro-se plaintiff who walked out during her deposition to pay defendants' costs and attorney's fees incurred in preparing for deposition);

II. THE PREVAILING PLAINTIFF'S RIGHT TO ATTORNEY'S FEES

B. The General Fee Rule for Prevailing Plaintiffs

1. Who Is a Prevailing Plaintiff?

a. The Relevance of Minimal Success

[42]**[On page 42-11 of the Main Volume, in footnote 42, add the following at the end of the footnote.]**

Cf. Myers v. Central Fla. Invs., Inc., 592 F.3d 1201, 1226, 108 FEP 111 (11th Cir. 2010) (despite award of damages on state-law battery claim, for which fee award is not available, jury determination that defendants subjected plaintiff to sexual harassment, but that her Title VII claim was time-barred, provided no basis for award of fees to plaintiff; outcome did nothing to advance plaintiff's legal rights under Title VII because defendants needed not curtail their behavior nor pay plaintiff money, and legal relationship between them was unaltered).

[43]**[On page 42-11 of the Main Volume, in footnote 43, add the following after "*See, e.g.*,".]**

Trainor v. HEI Hospitality, LLC, 699 F.3d 19, 35–36, 116 FEP 615 (1st Cir. 2012) (court properly denied employer's request to reduce prevailing retaliation claimant's attorney's fees by time spent on unsuccessful age discrimination claim; claims were interrelated based upon plaintiff's need to show reasonable and good faith belief that employer engaged in age discrimination in order to prevail on retaliation claim); Flitton v. Primary Residential Mortg., Inc., 614 F.3d 1173, 1178–79, 109 FEP 1610 (10th Cir. 2010) (where plaintiff lost summary judgment on two claims but prevailed at trial on third, appellate court reversed summary judgment ruling and remanded case for retrial, and plaintiff was unsuccessful on those two claims at retrial but was awarded more than $350,000 on her successful claim, lower court properly viewed her as prevailing party who achieved substantial relief and awarded her attorney's fees for time spent on both trials);

[44]**[On page 42-11 of the Main Volume, in footnote 44, add the following after "*See, e.g.*,".]**

Fuller v. Fiber Glass Sys. LP, 618 F.3d 858, 868–69, 110 FEP 176 (8th Cir. 2010) (plaintiff who secured monetary judgment of $65,000 as remedy for claim of racial harassment but did not prevail on claims of discriminatory selection and retaliation was prevailing party, but court acted within its discretion in considering degree of success in determining amount of fee award); Heaton v. Weitz Co., 534 F.3d 882, 892, 103 FEP 1570 (8th Cir. 2008) (10% reduction in requested fee award upheld where plaintiff obtained award of more than $150,000 despite abandoning three of his five claims at summary judgment; lower court properly considered interrelated nature of claims and substantiality of judgment in determining overall level of success);

[47]**[On page 42-13 of the Main Volume, in footnote 47, add the following at the end of the footnote.]**

Cf. Myers, 592 F.3d at 1226 (despite award of damages on state-law battery claim, for which fee award is not available, determination that defendants subjected plaintiff to sexual harassment, but that her Title VII claim was time-barred, provided no basis for award of fees to plaintiff; outcome did nothing to advance plaintiff's legal rights under Title VII because defendants needed not curtail their behavior nor pay plaintiff money, and legal relationship between them was unaltered).

b. The Relevance of Judicial Involvement

[52]**[On page 42-14 of the Main Volume, in footnote 52, add the following after "*see also*".]**

Breneisen v. Motorola, Inc., 656 F.3d 701, 706 (7th Cir. 2011) (defendant's voluntary tender of sums owed for alleged violations of FMLA did not entitle plaintiff to attorney's fee award), *cert. denied*, 132 S. Ct. 2382 (2012);

D. Awards to Prevailing Plaintiffs in Suits Against the Federal Government

[165][On page 42-31 of the Main Volume, in footnote 165, add the following after "*See, e.g.*,".]

Porter v. Winter, 603 F.3d 1113, 1115–16, 109 FEP 225 (9th Cir. 2010) (Title VII permits award of attorney's fees to prevailing federal employee plaintiff for legal work performed in administrative process, and courts have jurisdiction over actions where sole issue is request for fees incurred during that process) (citing New York Gaslight Club, Inc. v. Carey, 447 U.S. 54, 58 (1980));

H. Awards for Interim Success

[202][On page 42-38 of the Main Volume, in footnote 202, add the following after "*with*".]

Kansas Judicial Watch v. Stout, 653 F.3d 1230, 1239–40 (10th Cir. 2011) (fees awarded where plaintiffs secured preliminary injunction providing some of their requested relief and where attainment of injunction indicated probable success on merits), *cert. denied*, 132 S. Ct. 1715 (2012), *and*

I. Awards to Prevailing Plaintiffs for Services on Appeal

[213][On page 42-40 of the Main Volume, in footnote 213, add the following at the end of the footnote.]

But cf. Flitton v. Primary Residential Mortg., Inc., 614 F.3d 1173, 1179–80, 109 FEP 1610 (10th Cir. 2010) (following retrial, plaintiff who appealed successfully from summary judgment ruling on two counts of her claim is not entitled to attorney's fees for time spent on appeal where she failed to request fees from appellate court).

J. Awards to Prevailing Plaintiffs for Time Spent on the Fee Claim

[219][On page 42-41 of the Main Volume, in footnote 219, add the following at the end of the footnote.]

See also Pickett v. Sheridan Health Care Ctr., 664 F.3d 632, 654, 114 FEP 76 (7th Cir. 2011) (no question that prevailing plaintiff's entitlement to fees includes compensation for time spent pursuing fees).

III. Computation of Attorney's Fees for Prevailing Plaintiffs

B. Applying the General Criteria

1. *Lodestar Components*

a. Rates

[283]**[On page 42-60 of the Main Volume, in footnote 283, add the following after "*E.g.*,".]**

Townsend v. Benjamin Enters., Inc., 679 F.3d 41, 59, 114 FEP 1537 (2d Cir. 2012) (affirming district court's award of fees at rate higher than rate specified in plaintiff's retainer agreement with counsel);

[288]**[On page 42-61 of the Main Volume, in footnote 288, add the following after "*E.g.*,".]**

McClain v. Lufkin Indus., Inc., 649 F.3d 374, 383, 112 FEP 1665 (5th Cir. 2011) (out-of-state plaintiffs' attorneys were entitled to prevailing rates in their home market where there were no qualified or willing local counsel to bring case), *cert. denied*, 132 S. Ct. 589 (2011);

c. The Partially Prevailing Plaintiff

[311]**[On page 42-69 of the Main Volume, in footnote 311, add the following after "*E.g.*,".]**

Diaz v. Jiten Hotel Mgmt., Inc., 704 F.3d 150, 153, 116 FEP 411 (1st Cir. 2012) (proper to reduce lodestar figure where plaintiff prevailed on only one claim of multi-claim cause of action, but trial court erred when it further reduced attorney's fees based on plaintiff's rejection of larger pre-trial settlement offer);

2. *Adjustments to the Lodestar*

a. Contingency

[321]**[On page 42-71 of the Main Volume, in footnote 321, add the following after "*See*".]**

Pickett v. Sheridan Health Care Ctr., 664 F.3d 632, 640–41, 114 FEP 76 (7th Cir. 2011) (district court erred in reducing plaintiff counsel's hourly rate where retainer agreement entitled him to contingency fee and flat fee in addition to statutory fees; fees from client and fees from statutory award are distinct entitlements);

b. Results Achieved

[328]**[On page 42-73 of the Main Volume, in footnote 328, add the following after "*see also*".]**

Millea v. Metro-North R.R., 658 F.3d 154, 169, 17 WH Cases 2d 1825 (2d Cir. 2011) (court erred in limiting fees to proportion of plaintiff's FMLA monetary damages award; "Especially for claims where the financial recovery is likely to be small, calculating attorneys' fees as a proportion of damages runs directly contrary to the purpose of fee-shifting statutes: assuring that civil rights claims of modest cash value can attract competent counsel.");

[342]**[On page 42-77 of the Main Volume, in footnote 342, add the following after "*see also*".]**

Diaz v. Jiten Hotel Mgmt., Inc., 704 F.3d 150, 154, 116 FEP 411 (1st Cir. 2012) (district court erred in reducing lodestar figure where plaintiff had rejected reasonable settlement offer; settlement offer pursuant to Fed. R. Civ. P. 68 is only vehicle by which defendant can limit fee exposure through rejected proposal);

C. Procedure

2. Documentation

[363]**[On page 42-81 of the Main Volume, in footnote 363, add the following after "*See*".]**

McDole v. City of Saginaw, 471 F. App'x 464, 483, 114 FEP 1220 (6th Cir. 2012) (trial court's decision to deny attorney's fees to prevailing plaintiff, whose attorney failed despite repeated requests by court to provide documentation supporting requested award, was not abuse of discretion);

IV. The Prevailing Defendant's Right to Attorney's Fees

[382]**[On page 42-85 of the Main Volume, in footnote 382, add the following after "*see, e.g.*,".]**

Lamboy-Ortiz v. Ortiz-Velez, 630 F.3d 228, 240–43 (1st Cir. 2010) (district court abused its discretion in awarding attorney's fees to defendant where there were reasonable grounds for plaintiffs to file suit and where there was no evidence that plaintiffs were clearly unreasonable in continuing to prosecute their claims to trial);

[390]**[On page 42-88 of the Main Volume, in footnote 390, add the following at the end of the footnote.]**

Cf. Braunstein v. Arizona Dep't of Transp., 683 F.3d 1177, 1189, 115 FEP 481 (9th Cir. 2012) (defendant not entitled to fees where plaintiff's frivolous § 1981 and § 1983 claims were intertwined with other non-frivolous claims); Harris v. Maricopa Cnty. Superior Ct., 631 F.3d 963, 973, 111 FEP 503 (9th Cir. 2011) (defendant's fee entitlement is limited to time expended upon frivolous claims only; error to prorate fee award between claims deemed frivolous vis-à-vis claims deemed non-frivolous).

[394]**[On page 42-89 of the Main Volume, in footnote 394, add the following at the end of the footnote.]**

See also EEOC v. Great Steaks, Inc., 667 F.3d 510, 519–20, 114 FEP 289 (4th Cir. 2012) (to gain fees against EEOC in Title VII case, defendant must show that action was frivolous; Equal Access to Justice Act standard of "substantially justified" is inapplicable to Title VII cases).

[397]**[On page 42-89 of the Main Volume, in footnote 397, add the following at the beginning of the footnote.]**

See EEOC v. CRST Van Expedited, Inc., 679 F.3d 657, 694–95, 114 FEP 1566 (8th Cir. 2012) (vacating award of attorney's fees to "prevailing" defendant where appellate court reversed district court's summary judgment orders; defendant cannot be considered prevailing party in Title VII case where number of pending EEOC claims against employer remained);

V. INTERVENORS AND ATTORNEY'S FEES

A. Prevailing Intervenors

[413]**[On page 42-93 of the Main Volume, in footnote 413, add the following after "*Compare*".]**

NAACP v. North Hudson Reg'l Fire & Rescue, 665 F.3d 464, 486 n.12, 113 FEP 1633 (3d Cir. 2011) (Title VII intervenors not entitled to fees for successfully influencing court to vacate preliminary injunction; temporary victory was not material alteration of parties' legal relationship), *cert. denied*, 132 S. Ct. 2749 (2012),

CHAPTER 43

ALTERNATIVE DISPUTE RESOLUTION

II. AUTHORITY FOR ARBITRATION

A. The Federal Arbitration Act

[On page 43-3 of the Main Volume, at the end of the carryover sentence, add new footnote 4a.]

[4a]*See* Soto-Fonalledes v. Ritz-Carlton San Juan Hotel Spa & Casino, 640 F.3d 471, 475, 112 FEP 275 (1st Cir. 2011) (FAA establishes that arbitration clause is contractual agreement between employer and employee and is to be interpreted in accordance with state law); *cf.* Hergenreder v. Bickford Senior Living, 656 F.3d 411, 416–17, 25 AD 97 (6th Cir. 2011) (refusing to enforce arbitration clause contained in employee handbook but not in papers employee signed at any time during course of her employment; handbook was not a contract and it was not apparent that employee had notice of or agreed to the arbitration provision).

[9]**[On page 43-4 of the Main Volume, in footnote 9, add the following at the end of the footnote.]**

Cf. Wheeling Hosp., Inc. v. Health Plan of the Upper Ohio Valley, Inc., 683 F.3d 577, 584 (4th Cir. 2012) (under federal rules, order favoring litigation over arbitration is immediately appealable) (citing Stedor Enters., Ltd. v. Armtex, Inc., 947 F.2d 727, 730 (4th Cir. 1991)); Quilloin v. Tenet HealthSystem Phila., Inc., 673 F.3d 221, 227–28, 18 WH Cases 2d 1563 (3d Cir. 2012) (denial of motion to compel arbitration, even without prejudice, is immediately appealable "regardless of whether the appeal is from a final decision").

B. The Supreme Court Decisions Concerning Private Employment Arbitration

[33][On page 43-6 of the Main Volume, in footnote 33, add the following after "*See*".]

Soto v. State Indus. Prods., Inc., 642 F.3d 67, 72, 24 AD 774 (1st Cir. 2011) ("employers and employees may contractually agree to submit federal claims, including claims under the ADA, to arbitration");

[On page 43-7 of the Main Volume, at the end of the carryover sentence, add the following block quote.]

> In deciding a motion to compel arbitration, a court must ascertain whether: "(i) there exists a written agreement to arbitrate, (ii) the dispute falls within the scope of that arbitration agreement, and (iii) the party seeking an arbitral forum has not waived its right to arbitration." As the Supreme Court has explained, it is a "fundamental principle that arbitration is a matter of contract." Accordingly, "principles of state contract law control the determination of whether a valid agreement to arbitrate exists."[1]

[On page 43-8 of the Main Volume, after the sentence that ends with footnote 43, add new footnote 43a after "railroad employees,".]

[43a]*See* Emswiler v. CSX Transp. Inc., 691 F.3d 782, 788, 26 AD 1160 (6th Cir. 2012) (court properly dismissed disability bias claim

---

[1]Gove v. Career Sys. Dev. Corp., 689 F.3d 1, 5–6, 115 FEP 828 (1st Cir. 2012) (quoting Rent-A-Center, West, Inc., v. Jackson, 130 S. Ct. 2772, 2776 (2010); Combined Energies v. CCI, Inc., 514 F.3d 168, 171 (1st Cir. 2008), and Soto-Fonalledas v. Ritz Carlton San Juan Hotel Spa & Casino, 640 F.3d 471, 475, 24 AD 1165, 112 FEP 275 (1st Cir. 2011)) (individual who claimed that employer refused to hire her because she was pregnant was not required to arbitrate claim where dispute resolution provision in employment application was ambiguous as to whether it applied to job applicants); *cf.* Mathews v. Denver Newspaper Agency LLC, 2011 U.S. App. LEXIS 11454, at *18, 24 AD 1156, 112 FEP 432 (10th Cir. 2011) (employee who submits allegations to arbitrator pursuant to employment agreement does not waive hearing by judicial forum where agreement does not expressly provide for such waiver).

of diabetic train engineer who alleged that his seniority was adjusted in violation of Ohio employment discrimination statute, where Railway Labor Act (RLA) preempted his discrimination and breach of contract claims and required that he exhaust RLA-mandated arbitration procedures before filing suit).

[48]**[On page 43-9 of the Main Volume, in footnote 48, add the following at the end of the footnote.]**

Some courts have created an exception to the obligation to submit a claim to arbitration where an individual alleges conduct by the employer that is potentially tortious, notwithstanding a mandatory arbitration clause contained in the underlying agreement. *See, e.g.*, Doe v. Princess Cruise Lines, 657 F.3d 1204, 1213–14, 113 FEP 734 (11th Cir. 2011) (claim of bar server on cruise ship that company imprisoned her on ship and destroyed evidence after she was drugged and raped by other crew members did not fall within scope of arbitration clause contained in crew's employment agreement; to be arbitrable, parties' dispute had to relate to, arise from, or be connected with employee's crew agreement or with employment services she performed for cruise line); Jones v. Halliburton, 583 F.3d 228, 238–39, 107 FEP 353 (5th Cir. 2009) (where employee working overseas alleged she was gang-raped by co-workers in employer-provided housing, claims of assault and battery; intentional infliction of emotional distress; negligent hiring, retention, and supervision; and false imprisonment are not subject to arbitration).

[61]**[On page 43-11 of the Main Volume, in footnote 61, add the following at the end of the footnote.]**

See Momot v. Mastro, 652 F.3d 982, 988 (9th Cir. 2011) (clear language in arbitration provision delegated "gateway" or threshold issues to arbitrator).

[62]**[On page 43-11 of the Main Volume, in footnote 62, replace "*Id.* at 2778–79" with the following.]**

Rent-A-Center, 130 S. Ct. at 2778–79.

[68]**[On page 43-12 of the Main Volume, in footnote 68, add the following at the end of the footnote.]**

See also Jock v. Sterling Jewelers, Inc., 646 F.3d 113, 123–24, 112 FEP 1137 (2d Cir. 2011) (reversing district court order vacating arbitration award; parties committed to arbitrator determination of whether agreement to arbitrate permitted plaintiff to proceed as class, and decision that class arbitration was permitted therefore was within arbitrator's authority under law as it then existed), *cert. denied*, 132 S. Ct. 1742, 114 FEP 960 (2012).

[69][On page 43-12 of the Main Volume, in footnote 69, add the following at the end of the footnote.]

Cf. Jock, 646 F.3d at 123 ("*Stolt-Nielsen* does not foreclose the possibility that parties may reach an 'implicit'—rather than express—'agreement to authorize class action arbitration'") (citation omitted).

[On page 43-12 of the Main Volume, after the sentence that ends with footnote 69, add the following new paragraph.]

More recently, in *Oxford Health Plans, LLC v. Sutter*,[2] the Supreme Court reiterated that class arbitration is a matter of consent. An arbitrator may employ class procedures only if the parties have authorized them.[3]

[On page 43-12 of the Main Volume, in the first sentence of the first full paragraph, replace "Most recently," with the following.]

In

[72][On page 43-12 of the Main Volume, in footnote 72, add the following at the end of the footnote.]

See also Cruz v. Cingular Wireless, LLC, 648 F.3d 1205, 1212–13 (11th Cir. 2011) (applying *Concepcion*, FAA preempts Florida state law to enforce class action waiver and compel arbitration of claims on individual basis).

[On page 43-12 of the Main Volume, after the sentence that ends with footnote 73, add the following new paragraph.]

Similarly, in *American Express Co. v. Italian Colors Restaurant*,[4] the Supreme Court held that merchants who accept American Express cards were bound by an arbitration agreement that prohibited them from bringing a class action against American Express even though the cost of successfully arbitrating the federal

---

[2]133 S. Ct. 2064 (2013).
[3]*Id.* at 2069.
[4]133 S. Ct. 2304 (2013).

claims on an individual basis exceeded the potential recovery. This holds true, the Court explained, for federal statutory claims "unless the FAA's mandate has been 'overridden by a contrary congressional command.'"[5] The Court also rejected what it described as "a judge-made exception to the FAA" that allows courts to invalidate agreements that "prevent the 'effective vindication' of a federal statutory right."[6] The Court clarified that this judge-made exception is a very narrow one, which "certainly cover[s] a provision in an arbitration agreement forbidding the assertion of certain statutory rights" and "perhaps cover[s] filing and administrative fees attached to arbitration that are so high as to make access to the forum impracticable."[7]

C. Other Federal and State Sources of Arbitration Law

[77]**[On page 43-13 of the Main Volume, in footnote 77, add the following at the end of the footnote.]**

See also Nitro-Lift Techs., LLC v. Howard, 133 S. Ct. 500, 503 (2012) (reversing Oklahoma Supreme Court decision that invalidated on state-law grounds noncompetition agreement without addressing enforceability of pre-dispute arbitration agreement; FAA compelled enforcement of arbitration clause and, therefore, arbitrator should have determined validity of noncompetition agreement); Marmet Health Care Ctr., Inc. v. Brown, 132 S. Ct. 1201, 1203–04, 182 L. Ed. 2d 42 (2012) (West Virginia's prohibition against pre-dispute arbitration agreements for personal-injury or wrongful-death claims against nursing homes is categorical rule prohibiting arbitration of particular type of claim and conflicts with terms of coverage of FAA so as to be preempted by FAA).

---

[5]*Id.* at 2310 (quoting CompuCredit Corp. v. Greenwood, 132 S. Ct. 665, 667 (2012)).

[6]133 S. Ct. at 2310.

[7]*Id.* at 2309–10. This was a point of contention for the dissenting justices, who opined that the majority opinion "prevents effective vindication of federal statutory rights." *Id.* at 2319–20 (Kagan, J., dissenting, joined by Ginsburg, J., and Breyer, J.).

III. PROCEDURES AND ENFORCEMENT OF ARBITRATION AGREEMENTS

A. Introduction

[94][On page 43-15 of the Main Volume, in footnote 94, add the following after "*See, e.g.,*".]

Bagdasarian Prods., LLC v. Twentieth Century Fox Film Corp., 673 F.3d 1267, 1273 (9th Cir. 2012) (if arbitration is erroneously compelled, appellate court may later vacate award and remand to district court for proceedings on merits, but if motion to compel arbitration is denied, that ruling is immediately appealable);

B. Formation of Arbitration Agreements

1. Arbitration Required as a Condition of Employment

[102][On page 43-16 of the Main Volume, in footnote 102, add the following after "*see also*".]

Soto v. State Indus. Prods., Inc., 642 F.3d 67, 73–74, 24 AD 774 (1st Cir. 2011) (continued employment is sufficient consideration under Puerto Rico law);

[102][On page 43-16 of the Main Volume, in footnote 102, add the following after the citation to "Ragone v. Atlantic Video at Manhattan Ctr.".]

(New York law requires a showing of both procedural and substantive unconscionability in order to find contract unconscionable)

[104][On page 43-17 of the Main Volume, in footnote 104, add the following after "*See*".]

Hergrenreder v. Bickford Senior Living Grp., LLC, 656 F.3d 411, 421, 25 AD 97 (6th Cir. 2011) (where there was no evidence that employee knew that employer's dispute resolution process contained arbitration agreement, employee did not "accept" arbitration provisions by accepting or continuing employment, and arbitration was not compelled);

[106]**[On page 43-18 of the Main Volume, in footnote 106, add the following at the end of the footnote.]**

Cf. Soto, 642 F.3d at 78 (Spanish-speaking employee's consent to arbitration was not in error or void due to her lack of fluency in English; in absence of fraud, fact that employee could not read, write, speak, or understand English did not mean that she was not bound by contract that she signed).

[108]**[On page 43-18 of the Main Volume, in footnote 108, add the following after "*See*".]**

Kawasaki Heavy Indus., Ltd. v. Bombardier Recreational Prods., Inc., 660 F.3d 988, 994 (7th Cir. 2011) (for waiver of right to arbitrate to be inferred, court must determine—based on totality of circumstances—whether party has acted inconsistently with right to arbitrate; party's diligence or lack thereof in pursuing arbitration is factor that "weighs heavily" in this analysis); Wheeling Hosp., Inc. v. Health Plan of the Upper Ohio Valley, Inc., 683 F.3d 577, 587 (4th Cir. 2012) (party loses right to stay court proceedings in order to arbitrate if it is "in default in proceeding with such arbitration"; delay and participation in litigation will not constitute default unless party "so substantially utilize[s] the litigation machinery that to subsequently permit arbitration would prejudice the party opposing the stay"); Gray Holdco, Inc. v. Cassady, 654 F.3d 444, 451, 32 IER Cases 1182 (3d Cir. 2011) (refusal to compel arbitration was upheld based on prejudice to party opposing arbitration that would result from delay of party seeking arbitration);

2. Contract Law: Unconscionability and Mutuality

[112]**[On page 43-19 of the Main Volume, in footnote 112, add the following after "*accord*".]**

Gore v. Alltel Commc'ns, LLC, 666 F.3d 1027, 1036 (7th Cir. 2012) (determination of whether arbitration provision is procedurally unconscionable is to be resolved by arbitrator where entire agreement, and not just arbitration clause, is attacked as unconscionable);

[113]**[On page 43-19 of the Main Volume, in footnote 113, add the following at the beginning of the footnote.]**

In re Checking Account Overdraft Litig. v. M&T Bank Corp., 674 F.3d 1252, 1257 (11th Cir. 2012) (on remand, district court must consider whether agreement is unconscionable);

[115][On page 43-19 of the Main Volume, in footnote 115, add the following after "*see also*".]

Cappuccitti v. DirecTV, Inc., 623 F.3d 1118, 1123–24 (11th Cir. 2010) (arbitration agreements may be unenforceable where requiring arbitration would be unconscionable under state contract law); *Gore*, 666 F.3d at 1032 (federal courts apply state-law contract formation principles to determine whether contract's arbitration clause applies to given dispute);

[125][On page 43-21 of the Main Volume, in footnote 125, add the following at the end of the footnote.]

See also Soto-Fonalledas v. Ritz-Carlton San Juan Hotel Spa & Casino, 640 F.3d 471, 478–79, 112 FEP 275, 24 AD 1165 (1st Cir. 2011) (evidence did not support plaintiff's assertion that she received inadequate notice that agreement she signed covered statutory discrimination claims).

[On page 43-21 of the Main Volume, after the first sentence in the first full paragraph, add the following.]

Unconscionability analysis focuses on the bargaining process leading up to the agreement to arbitrate (sometimes called "procedural unconscionability") and the fairness of the agreement's terms ("substantive unconscionability"). Most jurisdictions require a showing of both procedural and substantive unconscionability as a predicate to striking an agreement as unconscionable.[8] The clear trend, following Supreme Court precedent,[9] is to enforce the arbitration contract as written, even if it evinces an inequality in bargaining power.[10]

---

[8]*See, e.g.*, Kilgore v. KeyBank Nat'l Ass'n, 673 F.3d 947, 963 (9th Cir. 2012) (California law); Quilloin v. Tenet HealthSystem Phila., Inc., 673 F.3d 221, 230, 18 WH Cases 2d 1563 (3d Cir. 2012) (Pennsylvania law); Adler v. Fred Lind Manor, 153 Wash. 2d 331, 344–45, 103 P.3d 773, 781 (Wash. 2004) (Washington law). *But see* Razor v. Hyundai Motor Am., 222 Ill.2d 75, 99, 854 N.E.2d 607, 622 (2006) (under Illinois law, finding of unconscionability may be based on either procedural or substantive unconscionability or a combination of both).

[9]*See, e.g.*, American Express Co. v. Italian Colors Rest., 133 S. Ct. 2304, 2309–10 (2013) (noting "over-arching principle" that arbitration is matter of contract, so that courts must enforce arbitration agreements according to their terms except, in rare cases, where contrary congressional intent is evident or where arbitration agreement forbids federal statutory claim).

[10]*See* Oblix, Inc. v. Winiecki, 374 F.3d 488, 491 (7th Cir. 2004) (courts should enforce contract as written); Harris v. Green Tree Fin. Corp., 183 F.3d 173, 183–84 (3d Cir. 1999) (finding arbitration clause not unconscionable where it gave drafter unilateral control over whether dispute was arbitrated or litigated).

[On page 43-21 of the Main Volume, start a new paragraph with the second sentence of the first full paragraph, beginning with "Under California law,". In the same sentence, delete "for example,".]

[127]**[On page 43-21 of the Main Volume, in footnote 127, add the following after "*see also*".]**

Quilloin v. Tenet HealthSystem Phila., Inc., 673 F.3d 221, 230, 18 WH Cases 2d 1563 (3d Cir. 2012) (in order for contract to be deemed unconscionable under Pennsylvania law, it must be both substantively and procedurally unconscionable);

[142]**[On page 43-23 of the Main Volume, in footnote 142, add the following at the end of the footnote.]**

See also Quilloin v. Tenet HealthSystem Phila., Inc., 673 F.3d 221, 230–31, 18 WH Cases 2d 1563 (3d Cir. 2012) (in Fair Labor Standards Act (FLSA) action, substantive unconscionability includes terms that are unreasonably or grossly favorable to one side and to which disfavored party does not assent, including preclusion of attorney's fees otherwise available under applicable law).

[On page 43-23 of the Main Volume, after the sentence that ends with footnote 143, add the following.]

In a later case,[11] applying the Supreme Court's ruling in *AT&T Mobility LLC v. Concepcion*,[12] the Ninth Circuit held that the FAA preempts state law on the substantive unconscionability of class action waivers,[13] but that analyzing potential procedural unconscionability entails a review of applicable state law.[14]

[146]**[On page 43-23 of the Main Volume, in footnote 146, add the following at the beginning of the footnote.]**

Soto v. State Indus. Prods., Inc., 642 F.3d 67, 76, 24 AD 774 (1st Cir. 2011) ("the equal obligation of an employee and employer to arbitrate disputes falling in the coverage of an ADR plan 'is enough to ensure mutuality of obligation and thus constitute consideration'");

---

[11]Coneff v. AT&T Corp., 673 F.3d 1155 (9th Cir. 2012).
[12]131 S. Ct. 1740 (2011).
[13]*Coneff*, 673 F.3d at 1158–61.
[14]*Id.* at 1161–62.

[147]**[On page 43-24 of the Main Volume, in footnote 147, add the following after "*Compare*".]**

Nino v. Jewelry Exch., 609 F.3d 191, 204, 109 FEP 769 (3d Cir. 2010) (court refused to enforce arbitration clause based on its one-sided or "take-it-or-leave-it" nature—which was found to be unconscionable per se—and fact that arbitration clause was not severable from balance of contract),

[148]**[On page 43-24 of the Main Volume, in footnote 148, add the following after "*See*".]**

Carey v. 24 Hour Fitness, USA, Inc., 669 F.3d 202, 206–07, 18 WH Cases 2d 1127 (5th Cir. 2012) (arbitration clause was illusory because it allowed employer to make unilateral changes with no guarantee that changes would be only prospective);

C. Procedural Issues

3. Forum Selection

[161]**[On page 43-26 of the Main Volume, in footnote 161, add the following before "; *accord*".]**

see also Kawasaki Heavy Indus., Ltd. v. Bombardier Recreational Prods., 660 F.3d 988, 997 (7th Cir. 2011) (courts cannot grant Section 4 order to compel arbitration unless they are in same district as arbitration venue; no similar requirement applies to Section 3 order to stay pending arbitration but court must have jurisdiction to stay matter);

4. Allocation of Fees and Costs

[168]**[On page 43-27 of the Main Volume, in footnote 168, add the following after "*See*".]**

Nino v. Jewelry Exch., 609 F.3d 191, 203, 109 FEP 769 (3d Cir. 2010) (arbitration agreement's restriction on arbitrator's ability to award attorney's fees, costs, and expenses is substantively unconscionable and was not severable from balance of agreement);

5. *Class Arbitrations*

[174][On page 43-30 of the Main Volume, in footnote 174, add the following at the end of the footnote.]

In *D.R. Horton, Inc.*, 357 NLRB No. 184 (2012), the National Labor Relations Board (NLRB) held that the class-action waiver violates the employees' substantive right to engage in concerted activity under Section 7 of the NLRA; that decision is on appeal to the Fifth Circuit. *See* D.R. Horton, Inc. v. NLRB, No. 12-60031. However, the overwhelming number of federal courts considering the issue have refused to follow the NLRB, including the Eighth Circuit. *See* Owen v. Bristol Care, 702 F.3d 1050, 1053, 20 WH Cases 2d 24 (8th Cir. 2013) (rejecting NLRB's reasoning in *D.R. Horton* and enforcing class-action waiver in FLSA case).

[On page 43-31 of the Main Volume, after the carryover paragraph, add the following new paragraph.]

In *Oxford Health Plans LLC v. Sutter*,[15] the Supreme Court refused to vacate an arbitrator's decision that the parties' contract permitted class arbitration. The parties "agreed that the arbitrator should decide whether their contract authorized class arbitration."[16] Given that agreement, the Court explained that "[t]he sole question for the Court is whether the arbitrator (even arguably) interpreted the parties' contract, not whether he got its meaning right or wrong."[17] The *Oxford Health Plans* Court did not resolve the issue, left open by *Stolt-Nielsen*, of whether the availability of class arbitration is a gateway question presumptively for the court to decide, when the parties have not expressly committed its determination to the arbitrator.

---

[15] 133 S. Ct. 2064, 2069, 2071 (2013).
[16] *Id.* at 2067.
[17] *Id.* at 2068.

D. Contractual Limitations of Claims or Procedures

1. Damages

[179][On page 43-32 of the Main Volume, in footnote 179, correct the spelling of the case name in "Soto-Fonelladas" to the following.]

Soto-Fonalledas

2. Limitations Periods

[184][On page 43-33 of the Main Volume, in footnote 184, add the following after "*See*".]

Escobar-Noble v. Luxury Hotels Int'l of P.R., Inc., 680 F.3d 118, 115 FEP 301 (1st Cir. 2012) (arbitrator should decide whether Puerto Rico law permits or prohibits contractually abbreviated limitation periods);

[186][On page 43-33 of the Main Volume, in footnote 186, add the following at the end of the footnote.]

See also Nino v. Jewelry Exch., 609 F.3d 191, 202–03, 109 FEP 769 (3d Cir. 2010) (arbitration clause that allows employee only five days within which to grieve allegedly discriminatory action is per se unreasonable).

F. Collective Bargaining Issues Related to Discrimination Claims

[220][On page 43-38 of the Main Volume, in footnote 220, add the following at the end of the footnote.]

See also Ibarra v. United Parcel Service, 695 F.3d 354, 360, 116 FEP 20 (5th Cir. 2012) (general arbitration clause in CBA does not require arbitration of employment discrimination claims where clause contains no express waiver of judicial forum and states that employer will comply with applicable state and federal laws).

[235][On page 43-40 of the Main Volume, in footnote 235, add the following at the end of the footnote.]

See also Thompson v. Air Transport Int'l Ltd. Liab. Co., 664 F.3d 723, 727, 18 WH Cases 2d 872, 192 LRRM 2454 (8th Cir. 2011) (employment-related civil rights claims (e.g., Family and Medical Leave Act (FMLA) and Arkansas Civil Rights Act claims) can be subject to mandatory arbitration provision); Teamsters Local Union No. 783 v. Anheuser-Busch, Inc., 626 F.3d 256, 263, 189 LRRM 2609 (6th Cir. 2010) (collective bargaining agreement's exclusion of pension claims from arbitration enforced).

[On page 43-40 of the Main Volume, after the sentence that ends with footnote 235, add the following new paragraph.]

Unless the collective bargaining agreement's arbitration provision expressly extends to statutory claims, an arbitration ruling on issues common to a discrimination claim may not have any preclusive effect.[18]

G. Judicial Enforcement

1. Statutory Standards Under the FAA

[236][On page 43-41 of the Main Volume, in footnote 236, add the following after "*See*".]

Johnson v. Wells Fargo Home Mortg., Inc., 635 F.3d 401, 412 (9th Cir. 2011) (under FAA, district court must review proper and timely motions to vacate, modify, or confirm arbitral award filed in response to motion to confirm);

[245][On page 43-42 of the Main Volume, in footnote 245, add the following at the end of the footnote.]

Cf. Biller v. Toyota Motor Corp., 668 F.3d 655, 662–63, 33 IER Cases 600 (9th Cir. 2012) (although California contract law generally applied to contract terms, where parties chose FAA as vehicle for judicial review, they could not expand scope of judicial review beyond that which FAA authorizes).

[18]*See* Coleman v. Donahoe, 667 F.3d 835, 853–54, 114 FEP 160 (7th Cir. 2012) (issue preclusion could not apply to pretext issue in Title VII disparate treatment action based on arbitrator's prior ruling that employer lacked just cause to discharge, because arbitrator did not examine whether employer honestly believed that employee posed threat to supervisor); *cf.* Matthews v. Denver Newspaper Agency, 649 F.3d 1199, 1206, 112 FEP 432, 24 AD 1156 (10th Cir. 2011) (applying *Pyett*, arbitration decision had no preclusive effect on subsequent lawsuit absent arbitrator's express authority to address statutory claims as well as contractual ones).

[246][On page 43-42 of the Main Volume, in footnote 246, add the following after "*See*".]

MCI Constructors, LLC v. City of Greensboro, 610 F.3d 849, 858 (4th Cir. 2010) (enumerating three-pronged test for determining whether arbitration award was procured by improper means, fraud, or corruption);

[260][On page 43-45 of the Main Volume, in footnote 260, add the following at the end of the footnote.]

Cf. Wachovia Sec., LLC v. Brand, 671 F.3d 472, 479, 33 IER Cases 679 (4th Cir. 2012) (arbitrator not bound by state procedural requirements, such as whether to adjourn hearing or allow 30 days for briefing).

[On page 43-45 of the Main Volume, replace the sentence that ends with footnote 264 with the following.]

Review under § 10(a)(4) is limited to circumstances in which "the arbitrator act[s] outside the scope of his contractually delegated authority—issuing an award that 'simply reflect[s] [his] own notions of [economic] justice' rather than 'draw[ing] its essence from the contract.'"

[264][On page 43-45 of the Main Volume, in footnote 264, add the following at the beginning of the footnote.]

Oxford Health Plans LLC v. Sutter, 133 S. Ct. 2068 (2013); *see*

[On page 43-45 of the Main Volume, after the sentence that ends with footnote 264, add the following.]

Section 10(a)(4) "permits courts to vacate an arbitral decision only when the arbitrator strayed from his delegated task of interpreting a contract, not when he performed that task poorly."[19]

[19] *Oxford Health Plans LLC*, 133 S. Ct. at 2070; *see also* Jock v. Sterling Jewelers, Inc., 646 F.3d 113, 122, 112 FEP 1137 (2d Cir. 2011) ("Section 10(a)(4) does not permit vacatur for legal errors"), *cert. denied*, 132 S. Ct. 1742, 114 FEP 960 (2012).

[267][On page 43-46 of the Main Volume, in footnote 267, add the following after "*See*".]

Reed v. Florida Metro. Univ., 681 F.3d 630, 646 (5th Cir. 2012) (arbitrator exceeded his powers by ordering parties to submit to class arbitration without contractual or legal basis);

2. *Judicial Exceptions: Manifest Disregard of the Law and Public Policy*

[284][On page 43-48 of the Main Volume, in the carryover of footnote 284, add the following after "*see also*".]

Schwartz v. Merrill Lynch & Co., 665 F.3d 444, 453, 113 FEP 1479 (2d Cir. 2011) (not addressing *Ledbetter* or Fair Pay Act issues is not manifest disregard of law when another basis for arbitrator's ruling exists); Biller v. Toyota Motor Corp., 668 F.3d 655, 666, 33 IER Cases 600 (9th Cir. 2012) (denying vacatur because record at least implicitly established that vacatur standard was not met under California's test for manifest disregard of law); Wachovia Sec., LLC v. Brand, 671 F.3d 472, 483, 33 IER Cases 679 (4th Cir. 2012) (manifest disregard standard survived *Hall Street* as either independent ground for review or judicial gloss); STMicroelectronics N.V. v. Credit Suisse Sec. (USA) LLC, 648 F.3d 68, 78 (2d Cir. 2011) (arbitration award may be vacated on grounds enumerated in § 10 of FAA as well as for manifest disregard of law);

H. Scope of the Arbitration

[303][On page 43-51 of the Main Volume, in footnote 303, add the following after "*See*".]

Oxford Health Plans LLC v. Sutter, 133 S. Ct. 2068, 2069–70 (2013) (class arbitration is matter of consent; arbitrator may employ class procedures only if parties agreed to them);

[303][On page 43-51 of the Main Volume, in footnote 303, add the following at the end of the footnote.]

Cf. In re Checking Account Overdraft Litig. MDL No. 2036 v. M&T Bank Corp., 674 F.3d 1252, 1255–56 (11th Cir. 2012) (determination of whether arbitration agreement encompassed claims for injunctive relief lies first with arbitrator); Quilloin v. Tenet HealthSystem

Phila., Inc., 673 F.3d 221, 231–32, 18 WH Cases 2d 1563 (3d Cir. 2012) (ambiguity as to whether agreement allowed for arbitrator to award attorney's fees or whether agreement constituted class waiver should be first resolved by arbitrator); Green v. SuperShuttle Int'l, Inc. 653 F.3d 766, 769, 18 WH Cases 2d 109 (8th Cir. 2011) (arbitrator, not court, first determines whether transportation exemption in § 1 of FAA applies to plaintiffs in wage and hour action).

IV. MEDIATION

[315][On page 43-53 of the Main Volume, in footnote 315, add the following at the end of the footnote.]

See also In re Teligent, Inc. v. K&L Gates LLP, 640 F.3d 53, 58 (2d Cir. 2011) (confidentiality is critical to mediation process and only "extraordinary circumstances" warrant disclosure).

CHAPTER 44

SETTLEMENT

I. Validity of Waivers of Discrimination Claims

A. Knowing and Voluntary Waivers of Past Claims Are Valid

1. An Employee May Waive Past Claims

[8][On page 44-4 of the Main Volume, in footnote 8, add the following at the end of the footnote.]

See also Schwartz v. Merrill Lynch & Co., 665 F.3d 444, 454, 113 FEP 1479 (2d Cir. 2011) (refusing to disturb arbitration panel's decision where panel excluded testimony concerning employer's conduct occurring prior to signing of release and finding no merit in plaintiff's post-relief claim; nothing in Lilly Ledbetter Fair Pay Act or its legislative history suggests that Congress intended to alter legal principles set forth in *Alexander v. Gardner-Denver Co.* or to revive claims that had been previously released).

2. The Waiver Must Be Knowing and Voluntary

[11][On page 44-5 of the Main Volume, in footnote 11, add the following at the end of the footnote.]

The Sixth Circuit has been inconsistent in its analysis. *See* Gascho v. Scheurer Hosp., 400 F. App'x 978, 981–82 (6th Cir. 2010) (unpublished) (applying totality of circumstances test, including examination of plaintiff's background, education, and experience, access to counsel, and length of time she had to consider whether to sign release; waiver enforced).

[12][On page 44-5 of the Main Volume, in footnote 12, add the following after "*See*".]

Galera v. Johanns, 612 F.3d 8, 13, 109 FEP 1289 (1st Cir. 2010) (release must be knowing and voluntary as evidenced by totality of circumstances and, if it is, terms of release will ordinarily be given legal effect); *Gascho*, 400 F. App'x at 981–82 (enforcing waiver after applying totality of circumstances test, including examination of plaintiff's background, education, and experience; access to counsel; and length of time she had to consider whether to sign release);

[13]**[On page 44-6 of the Main Volume, in footnote 13, add the following after the sentence that discusses "*Adams v. Philip Morris, Inc.*".]**

Subsequently, in *Gascho*, 400 F. App'x at 981, the Sixth Circuit expressly applied a "totality of the circumstances" test that considered "(1) plaintiff's experience, background and education; (2) the amount of time the plaintiff had to consider whether to sign the waiver, including whether the employee had the opportunity to consult with a lawyer; (3) the clarity of the waiver; (4) consideration for the waiver; as well as (5) the totality of the circumstances."

[15]**[On page 44-7 of the Main Volume, in footnote 15, after the parenthetical for "Geraghty v. Insurance Servs. Office, Inc.,", replace the semi-colon with a period and add the following.]**

The agreement need not be signed or even in writing to be valid and enforceable. *See* Quesada v. Napolitano, 701 F.3d 1080, 116 FEP 1158 (5th Cir. 2012) (plaintiff bound by counsel's settlement offer made during court-ordered mediation and accepted by employer; even though employee e-mailed his objections to counsel immediately upon learning of agreement, he did not object at time offer was made and offer was binding because counsel of record is presumed to have authority to settle); *see also* Gregory v. Derry Twp. Sch. Dist., 418 F. App'x 148, 151, 111 FEP 1784 (3d Cir. 2011) (unpublished) (citing same factors as *Geraghty* and rejecting contention that either 15-minute period in which to review and sign agreement negotiated by her representative or presence of employer's representative during review session rendered agreement unenforceable, where settlement included elements of relief that were most important to plaintiff); *Gascho*, 400 F. App'x at 981 ("The test calls on us to examine '(1) plaintiff's experience, background and education; (2) the amount of time the plaintiff had to consider whether to sign the waiver, including whether the employee had the opportunity to consult with a lawyer; (3) the clarity of the waiver; (4) consideration for the waiver; as well as (5) the totality of the circumstances.'");

[16]**[On page 44-8 of the Main Volume, in footnote 16, add the following after "*First Circuit:*".]**

Galera, 612 F.3d at 13–14 (affirming summary judgment for employer based on unambiguous terms of agreement; release waived all claims for alleged conduct prior to effective date of settlement agreement, not just claims expressly referenced in settlement agreement);

[16]**[On page 44-8 of the Main Volume, in footnote 16, add the following after "*Second Circuit*:".]**

Aylaian v. Town of Huntington, 459 F. App'x 25, 27 (2d Cir. 2012) (nearly illiterate employee had duty to take action to have agreement read to him before he signed it and his failure to do so was negligence that binds him to agreement);

[16]**[On page 44-9 of the Main Volume, in the carryover of footnote 16, add the following after "*Sixth Circuit*:".]**

Gascho, 400 F. App'x at 983 (upholding release as matter of law after analysis of totality of circumstances and rejecting plaintiff's attempt to rescind on grounds of duress; plaintiff's belief that she had no choice in signing agreement in view of economic benefits offered and risk of economic hardship if she declined the offer does not, by itself, state claim "because this kind of threat is 'an accepted part of the bargaining process,'" and although physical and verbal threats during bargaining process may rise to level of coercion, conduct of hospital chief executive office did not operate to invalidate release against hospital because hospital played no role in conduct and took reasonable measures once it learned of unacceptable conduct on company premises);

[16]**[On page 44-9 of the Main Volume, in the carryover of footnote 16, add the following after "*Eighth Circuit*:".]**

Bissada v. Arkansas Children's Hosp., 639 F.3d 825, 831, 112 FEP 321 (8th Cir. 2011) (binding settlement agreement was reached where employer verbally indicated its acceptance of settlement offer e-mailed to it by plaintiff's counsel; employer's subsequent action evinced reliance on agreed settlement, even though plaintiff subsequently e-mailed employer stating that offer transmitted by his counsel was not acceptable to him; refusal to sign settlement agreement does not preclude its binding effect);

[19]**[On page 44-10 of the Main Volume, in footnote 19, add the following after "*See, e.g.*,".]**

Harmon v. Journal Publ'g Co., 476 F. App'x 756, 757–58 (5th Cir. 2012) (unpublished) (under federal law, party that challenges settlement has burden of proving invalidity and is entitled to evidentiary hearing on disputed issues of validity and scope) (citing Mid-South Towing Co. v. Har-Win, Inc., 733 F.2d 386, 392 (5th Cir. 1984); Galera v. Johanns, 612 F.3d 8, 13 n.9, 109 FEP 1289 (1st Cir. 2010) (finding terms of release unambiguous and rejecting plaintiff's contention that court should consider post-contract conduct to determine scope of release); Gascho v. Scheurer Hosp., 400 F. App'x 978, 981 (6th Cir. 2010) (unpublished) (affirming summary judgment for employer; effort to rescind settlement agreement is matter for jury to determine if there was material factual dispute);

B. Waivers of Future Claims Are Invalid

[33][On page 44-13 of the Main Volume, in footnote 33, add the following at the end of the footnote.]

See also Schwartz v. Merrill Lynch & Co., 665 F.3d 444, 451, 454 n.4, 113 FEP 1479 (2d Cir. 2011) (no provision in Lilly Ledbetter Fair Pay Act nor its legislative history suggests that Congress intended to alter legal principles set forth in *Alexander v. Gardner-Denver Co.*, 415 U.S. 36, 7 FEP 81 (1974), or to revive claims that had been previously released; affirming arbitration panel's denial of claim for alleged discriminatory compensation-related conduct after settlement date to extent that alleged conduct relied on or was related to acts occurring before settlement date).

D. Choice of Law

[43][On page 44-15 of the Main Volume, in footnote 43, add the following after "*with*".]

Bissada v. Arkansas Children's Hosp., 639 F.3d 825, 112 FEP 321, 325 (8th Cir. 2011) (applying state law to determine whether binding settlement had been reached),

[44][On page 44-15 of the Main Volume, in footnote 44, add the following at the beginning of the footnote.]

Kaczmarcyzk v. Dutton, 414 F. App'x 354, 355 (2d Cir. 2011) (declining to decide whether, in Second Circuit, state or federal common law determines whether parties have reached settlement where there is no material difference in standards);

II. WAIVER OF AGE DISCRIMINATION CLAIMS AFTER THE OLDER WORKERS BENEFIT PROTECTION ACT[1]

A. Requirements Applicable to All OWBPA Waivers

2. *Written in a Manner to Be Understood*

[58][On page 44-17 of the Main Volume, in footnote 58, add the following at the end of the footnote.]

See also Aylaian v. Town of Huntington, 459 F. App'x 25, 27 (2d Cir. 2012) (unpublished) (OWBPA does not require that agreement be explained orally; nearly illiterate plaintiff "has a duty, knowing of his limitation, to have the document read to him so that he may understand its contents").

[On page 44-19 of the Main Volume, after the block quote that ends with footnote 65, add the following new paragraph.]

Courts have upheld agreements containing release and covenant-not-to-sue provisions where these provisions are not used or combined in a manner found to be confusing.[2]

6. *Consultation With an Attorney*

[80][On page 44-21 of the Main Volume, in footnote 80, add the following at the end of the footnote.]

But see Ridinger v. Dow Jones & Co., 651 F.3d 309, 316, 112 FEP 1221 (2d Cir. 2011) (although it may be significant that OWBPA waiver signed by plaintiff did not set forth in so many words that he should consult with attorney before signing, he may not raise issue for first time on appeal; disallowing this argument does not result in "manifest injustice").

---

[1]Additional discussion of OWBPA waivers may be found in Chapter 12 (Age).

[2]*See, e.g.*, Ridinger v. Dow Jones & Co., 651 F.3d 309, 315–16, 112 FEP 1221 (2d Cir. 2011) (distinguishing provisions from those at issue in *Thomforde* and *Syverson*).

9. Burden of Proof

[95][On page 44-22 of the Main Volume, in footnote 95, add the following at the end of the footnote.]

See also Ridinger v. Dow Jones & Co., 651 F.3d 309, 314–15, 112 FEP 1221 (2d Cir. 2011) (§ 626(f)(1)(A)'s focus on both "individual participating employee" and "average individual" may warrant both particularized and generalized assessment; however, where individual has not presented evidence from which to infer that his own comprehension level was below that of average eligible employee, employer carries its burden with respect to this requirement if language is calculated to be understood by average eligible employee; whereas individual's comprehension level may present issue of fact, whether language is calculated to be understood by average eligible employee essentially is issue of law).

IV. TAX CONSIDERATIONS

B. Allocation Isssues

[199][On page 44-41 of the Main Volume, in footnote 199, add the following after "26 U.S.C. § 104(a) (2006).".]

See Espinoza v. Commissioner, 636 F.3d 747, 749–50, 111 FEP 1662 (5th Cir. 2011) (affirming tax court ruling that entire settlement payment made to plaintiff was includable as income; failure to allocate settlement payment to medical expenses for treatment of emotional distress precluded finding that payment was excludable).

V. RULE 68 OFFERS OF JUDGMENT

[On page 44-45 of the Main Volume, after the sentence that ends with footnote 210, add the following.]

Additional questions arise where the Rule 68 offer is made to the named plaintiff in a proposed class or collective action. In such cases the timing of the offer may be critical.[3]

---

[3]*See, e.g.*, Symczyk v. Genesis Healthcare Corp., 656 F.3d 189, 18 WH Cases 2d 1 (3d Cir. 2011) (Fair Labor Standards Act (FLSA) collective action did not become moot upon putative representative receiving Rule 68 offer that would fully satisfy claim prior

[On page 44-47 of the Main Volume, after the carryover paragraph, add the following new paragraph.]

In awarding attorney's fees in cases resolved by Rule 68 offers, courts may alter the standards applied in determining the rate of compensation. In *Townsend v. Benjamin Enterprises, Inc.*,[4] for example, the Second Circuit held that the district court was not required to use a retainer rate when determining the amount of attorney's fees incurred by the plaintiff as of the time of the offer of judgment. Rather, the court could use prevailing market rates for counsel of similar experience and skill, multiplied by the number of hours that were reasonably expended.

VI. "BUSTED" SETTLEMENTS

[233]**[On page 44-48 of the Main Volume, in footnote 233, add the following after "*accord*".]**

Harmon v. Journal Publ'g Co., 476 F. App'x 756, 757 (5th Cir. 2012) (unpublished) (attorney of record is presumed to have authority to compromise and settle litigation of his or her client; therefore, burden lies with party opposing enforcement to establish that there is some basis for holding that such authority was not present);

[On page 44-49 of the Main Volume, after the sentence that ends with footnote 237, add the following new paragraph.]

Suits alleging the failure to comply with the terms of a settlement agreement between an employer and the EEOC generally are enforced by the Commission in an action brought under the statute under which the charge of discrimination arose.[5] The issue in such a case is not whether discrimination occurred, or whether the EEOC

---

to moving for conditional certification; where there is no undue delay in seeking certification, motion will relate back to date of filing complaint), *rev'd on other grounds*, 133 S. Ct. 1523 (2013).

[4]679 F.3d 41, 58–59, 114 FEP 1537 (2d Cir. 2012) (affirming district court's use of prevailing market rate to find that amount of pre-offer fees and costs, in combination with plaintiff's ultimate recovery, exceeded Rule 68 offer; district court therefore properly awarded plaintiff fees and costs incurred both before and after Rule 68 offer).

[5]*See, e.g.*, *Safeway Stores, Inc.*, 714 F.2d at 574 ("the same rationale which convinced us that the federal courts have jurisdiction to consider conciliation agreements between employers, employees, and the EEOC compels us to hold that these courts have the power to enforce such agreements").

correctly found reasonable cause to believe that it had, but whether a valid conciliation agreement was entered into, and whether the employer complied with its terms.[6] In contrast, where a matter is settled by the parties through mediation rather than through formal conciliation with the EEOC, an action to enforce the settlement terms proceeds under state contract law.[7]

[246][On page 44-52 of the Main Volume, in footnote 246, add the following at the end of the footnote.]

See also Holmes v. United States, 657 F.3d 1303, 1307, 113 FEP 395 (Fed. Cir. 2011) (Title VII settlement agreements can be interpreted as mandating payment of money damages for breach by federal government and thus "are not per se beyond the Tucker Act jurisdiction of the Court of Federal Claims"); Munoz v. Mabus, 630 F.3d 856, 861, 864, 111 FEP 40 (9th Cir. 2010) (district court lacked jurisdiction to enforce Title VII predetermination settlement agreement because plaintiff failed to exhaust administrative remedies and Tucker Act provides exclusive remedy for contract claims against government).

---

[6]The proof in an action to enforce a conciliation agreement is circumscribed by Title VII's statutory limitation on disclosure of the substance of conciliation. 42 U.S.C. § 2000e-5(b); *see also* EEOC v. Philip Servs. Corp., 635 F.3d 164, 169, 111 FEP 1189 (5th Cir. 2011) (noting that statute does not carve out any exceptions to prohibition; distinguishing civil action to determine whether oral agreement was entered into, which is barred from enforcement, from action to enforce written agreement, which is permissible).

[7]*See, e.g.*, Smith v. Tillman, 958 So. 2d 333, 337 (Ala. 2006) (action to enforce settlement agreement that was not negotiated by EEOC does not arise under Title VII).

TABLE OF CASES

References are to chapter and footnote number (e.g., ***33:*** 14; ***43:*** 4 *refers to footnote 14 in Supplement Chapter 33 and to footnote 4 in Supplement Chapter 43). MV indicates an update in this Supplement to a footnote in the Main Volume (e.g.,* ***MV12:*** 370 *refers to footnote 370 in Main Volume Chapter 12). For the updates to the Main Volume, only new cases are included in the table. Cases that appear in the Appendix to Chapter 11 appear as* ***11App.*** *with the footnote number within the Appendix following. Alphabetization is letter-by-letter (e.g., "Vance" precedes "Van Desande").*

A

B

G

I

J

N

S

U

V

X

Y

Z